CASEBOOK ON RESTITUTION

CASEBOOK ON
RESTITUTION

Gerard McMeel B.C.L., M.A. (Oxon)

of the Inner Temple, Barrister, Lecturer in Law,
University of Bristol

BLACKSTONE
PRESS LIMITED

First published in Great Britain 1996 by Blackstone Press Limited,
9-15 Aldine Street, London W12 8AW. Telephone 0181-740 1173

ISBN: 1 85431 517 X

British Library Cataloguing in Publication Data
A CIP catalogue record for this book is available from the British Library

Typeset by Style Photosetting Ltd, Mayfield, East Sussex
Printed by Ashford Colour Press, Gosport, Hampshire

Contents

Preface vii

Acknowledgments ix

Abbreviations of Principal Works Cited x

A Note on Currency xi

Table of Cases xiii

Table of Statutes xxviii

1 Introduction 1

Section 1: the principle of unjust enrichment 1
Section 2: restitutionary techniques 27
Section 3: tests of enrichment 36

2 Mistake 47

Section 1: money paid under a mistake of fact 47
Section 2: money paid under a mistake of law 66
Section 3: services rendered under a mistake 84
Section 4: rescission for misrepresentation and mistake 95
Section 5: is 'ignorance' a restitutionary cause of action? 111

3 Compulsion 113

Section 1: benefits conferred under duress 113
Section 2: benefits obtained as a result of undue influence 143

Section 3: inequality 155
Section 4: legal compulsion 158
Section 5: necessity or moral compulsion 178

4 Failure of Consideration 200

Section 1: contracts discharged by breach 210
Section 2: contracts discharged by frustration 247
Section 3: restitution and pre-contractual liability 271
Section 4: void and unenforceable contracts 289
Section 5: free aceptance 296

5 Restitution and Public Law 298

Section 1: the *Woolwich* case 298
Section 2: the 'swaps' cases 310

6 Restitution and the Law of Wrongs 319

Section 1: restitution and torts 320
Section 2: restitutionary damages for breach of contract? 347
Section 3: breach of fiduciary duty 359
Section 4: breach of confidence 378
Section 5: accessory liability in equity 389

7 Tracing and Proprietary Remedies 398

Section 1: tracing at common law 400
Section 2: tracing in equity 419
Section 3: proprietary remedies 467

8 Defences 491

Section 1: bona fide purchase 491
Section 2: change of position and estoppel 497
Section 3: counter-restitution impossible? 527
Section 4: public policy 540

Index 548

Preface

Restitution has emerged over the last fifty years as an essential component in the modern law of obligations. Its central concerns are the reversal of unjust enrichments and the unscrambling of defective transactions. Until recently these difficult topics have been neglected in traditional legal education, with quasi-contract and constructive trusts hived off as appendices to more familiar 'core' subjects. Increasingly restitution is taught as a subject in its own right, at both undergraduate and postgraduate level. It is well-served with textbooks by Birks (*An Introduction to the Law of Restitution*, 1989), Burrows (*The Law of Restitution*, 1993) and Tettenborn (*The Law of Restitution*, 1993). However, as Professor Birks has observed: 'There is, at a time when such books have proliferated, no English collection of cases and materials relevant to restitution. The contrast with the state of affairs in tort and contract hardly needs to be further underlined.' (*Introduction*, 3)

This is a first attempt at plugging the gap. A major difficulty for first-time students of the subject is language. The cases utilise techniques such as the *action for money had and received* and the *equitable lien*, whereas modern juristic writings speak of *unjust factors* and *incontrovertible benefit*. Chapter 1 attempts to prepare students for this terminological minefield. Another characteristic of restitution scholarship is the creative re-interpretation of authorities. More commonly than in other fields of law, commentators classify cases by reference to grounds for restitution which are insufficiently articulated, or not articulated at all by the judges. The annotations and suggestions for further reading aim to provide some help here.

The structure of the chapters is intended to be lightweight, and not to be a grand theory of categorisation. Some topics do not yield much (or much worthwhile) judicial discussion: for example, enrichment. Similarly on the margins of the subject, emerging and controversial grounds for restitution, such as 'ignorance' and 'free acceptance', are discussed in outline only. Some of the materials on the emerging and much criticised judicial synthesis of 'no consideration' are to be found under the heading of convenience: 'Restitution and Public Law'. Inevitably there are omissions: subrogation, contribution and resulting trusts receive only superficial treatment.

Restitution has been blessed in the last couple of decades by a wealth of excellent academic writing. The sophistication of modern analysis is now being transplanted to the case law. Whilst I have provided references to academic writings, this is ultimately a case book, utilising traditional case method techniques. As Paul Matthews, a self-confessed restitution-sceptic recently wrote: '. . . there are now a number of judicial pronouncements on the central principle(s) of restitution as a discrete subject. But they are not altogether consistent, and in any event they run well ahead of the collective *results* of the cases in which they appear. The mosaic is yet tiny.' (in Birks (ed), *Laundering and Tracing*, 1995, 66). That may overstate the sceptical view somewhat, but contains a grain of truth. The basic aim of a casebook, especially in this area of the law, should be to identify the established grounds of recovery, and the limitations upon such recovery. Criticism and categorisation come later.

I have referred throughout to Professor Burrows's excellent student textbook, and where appropriate to the accounts of Goff and Jones and Professor Birks. I have attempted to trace developments, as known to me, up to March 1996.

Thank yous remain: to my friends; to my colleagues at the University of Bristol, in particular David Cowan, Michael Furmston, Laura Hoyano, Helen Norman and Joan Wadsley who all offered valuable comments on the draft; to Rachel Nee of the Departmental Office who was invaluable; to Peter Birks and Andrew Burrows who patiently introduced me to this subject; and finally, to Judith Laws.

Gerard McMeel
May 1996

Acknowledgments

The publishers and the author would like to thank the following for their kind permission to reproduce extracts from the publications listed below:

The Incorporated Council for Law Reporting for England and Wales – The Law Reports, The Weekly Law Reports and the Industrial Cases Reports;
Butterworths Law Publishers Ltd – The All England Law Reports and the Law Times;
The Estates Gazette Ltd – The Estates Gazette Law Reports;
The Law Book Company Ltd – The Commonwealth Law Reports;
Butterworths Legal Publishing, Australia – The Australian Law Reports;
Lloyd's of London Press Ltd – The Lloyd's List Reports and the Lloyd's Reports;
Lloyd's of London Press Ltd and author – extracts from Kit Barker, 'Restitution of Passenger Fare' [1993] *Lloyd's Maritime and Commercial Law Quarterly 291*;
The Federation Press and author – extract from Peter Birks, '*Restitution – The Future*' (1991);
Sweet and Maxwell Ltd and author – extract from Andrew Burrows, 'Free Acceptance and the Law of Restitution' (1988) 104 *Law Quarterly Review* 576;
Oxford University Press and author – extract from Jack Beatson, '*The Use and Abuse of Unjust Enrichment*' (1991).

Abbreviations of Principal Works Cited

Beatson, *Unjust Enrichment*	Beatson, J., *The Use and Abuse of Unjust Enrichment*, Oxford: Clarendon Press, 1991.
Birks, *Introduction*	Birks, Peter, *An Introduction to the Law of Restitution*, revised paperback edition, Oxford: Clarendon Press, 1989.
Birks, *Laundering and Tracing*	Birks, Peter (ed), *Laundering and Tracing*, Oxford: Clarendon Press, 1995.
Birks, *The Future*	Birks, Peter, *Restitution – The Future*, Sydney: The Federation Press, 1992.
Burrows, *Essays*	Burrows, Andrew (ed), *Essays on the Law of Restitution*, Oxford: Clarendon Press, 1991.
Burrows, *Restitution*	Burrows, Andrew, *The Law of Restitution*, London: Butterworths, 1993.
Finn, *Essays*	Finn, P. D. (ed), *Essays on Restitution*, Sydney: The Law Book Company, 1989.
Goff and Jones	Goff of Chieveley, Baron, and Jones, Gareth, *The Law of Restitution*, 4th edn., London: Sweet & Maxwell, 1993.
Treitel, *Contract*	Treitel, G. H., *The Law of Contract*, 9th edn., London: Sweet & Maxwell, 1995.

A Note on Currency

Restitution cases are primarily about money. Many of the cases in this book pre-date decimalisation of the pound sterling in 1970. Before then the pound was divided into 20 shillings (each now the equivalent of five new pence). Shillings were further sub-divided into twelve old pennies. Therefore there were 240 old pence in the pound. Amounts were expressed in '*lsd*': an '*l*' after a figure meaning pounds, an '*s*' denoting shillings and a '*d*' standing for pennies. For example, 157 *l.* 12 *s.* 6 *d.* or £157 12/6 is the equivalent of £157.62½ in today's terms. Similarly 12 *l.* 10 *s.* or £12 10/- is now £12.50. A guinea is a pound and a shilling, now £1.05. I have occasionally rounded up figures to the nearest pound in summaries of the facts. Soon perhaps books may have to explain what the pound sterling was.

Table of Cases

Cases from which extracts are given in the text, appear in bold type. The page at which the case is printed is shown in bold type.

Aas v Benham [1891] 2 Ch 244 371
Acatos v Burns (1878) 3 Ex D 282 182
Adam v Newbigging (1888) 13 App Cas 308, 59 LT Rep 267 (HL); (1886) 34 ChD 582 (CA)] 103, 105, 108, 109
Addie v The Western Bank Law Rep 1 HL Sc 165 100
Agip (Africa) Ltd v Jackson [1990] Ch 265 (Ch D); affd [1991] Ch 547 (CA) 25, 35, 112, **390**, 395, 400, **410**, 420, 423, 429, 511
Aiken v Short (1856) 1 H & N 210; 156 ER 1180; 25 LJ (Ex) 321 (Exchequer Chamber) 26, **49**, 55, 57, 58, 59, 61, 493
Air Canada v British Columbia (1989) 59 DLR (4th) 161 81, 83, 307
Allcard v Skinner (1887) 36 Ch D 145 (CA) 143, **144**, 155
Allcard v Walker [1896] 2 Ch 369 64
Allison, Johnson & Foster, Ld.; ex parte Birkenshaw, In re [1904] 2 KB 327 290, 291
Aluminium Industrie Vaassen BV v Romalpa Aluminium Ltd [1976] 1 WLR 676 (CA) 436
Amalgamated Investment & Property Co. Ltd v Texas Commerce International Bank Ltd [1982] QB 84 (QBD and CA) **93**, 502
Amministrazione delle Finanze dello Stato v SpA San Giorgio (Case 199/82) [1983] ECR 3595 307
Anglo-Austrian Printing and Publishing Union, In re [1895] 2 Ch 891 192
Appleby v Myers (1867) LR 2 CP 651 (Exchequer Chamber) **249**, 252, 270
Archer v Cutler [1980] 1 NZLR 386 157
Armory v Delamirie (1722) 1 Stra 505 452
Armstrong v Jackson [1917] 2 KB 822 (KBD) **107**, 529
Arris & Arris v Stukely (1677) 2 Mod 260 329
Ashpitel v Sercombe (1850) 5 Ex 147 255
Associated Japanese Bank (International) v Credit du Nord SA [1989] 1 WLR 255 (QBD) 111
Astley v Reynolds (1731) 2 Str 915; 93 ER 939 (KB) **118**, 125, 129, 155
Atchison, Topeka & Santa Fe Railway Co. v O'Connor, 223 US 280 305
Atlantic Mutual Insurance Co. v Huth (1880) 16 Ch D 474 182
Atlas Express Ltd v Kafco (Importers and Distributors) Ltd [1989] QB 833 (QBD) **137**

Atlee v Backhouse 3 M & W 633 120
Attorney-General for Hong Kong v Reid [1994] 1 AC 324 (PC) 34, 378, 465, 468, 470, **479**, 483, 489
Attorney-General v Goddard (1929) 98 LJKB 743 481
Attorney-General v Guardian Newspapers Ltd (No. 2) [1990] 1 AC 109 (HL) **384**
Attorney-General v Horner (No. 2) [1913] 2 Ch 140 120
Auckland Harbour Board v The King [1924] AC 318 307
Australia and New Zealand Banking Group Ltd v Westpac Banking Corporation (1988) 78 ALR 157; (1988) 164 CLR 662 83, 518, 520
Australian Steam Navigation Co. v Morse (1872) LR 4 PC 222 182
Avon County Council v Howlett [1983] 1 WLR 605; [1983] 1 All ER 1073 (CA) **62**, **501**, 515, 517, 521
Avon Finance Co. Ltd v Bridger [1985] 2 All ER 281 152
Ayres v Hazelgrove (unreported, 9 February 1984) 157

B & S Contracts and Design Ltd v Victor Green Publications Ltd [1984] ICR 419 (CA) **133**
Baden, Delvaux and Lecuit v Société Général pour Favoriser le Développement du Commerce et de l'Industrie en France SA [1983] BCLC 325; [1993] 1 WLR 509; [1992] 4 All ER 161 390, 391, 392, 395, 396, 419, 422, 423, 424, 427
Baily's Case Sir T. Raym 71 325
Baltic Shipping Co. v Dillon, The 'Mikhail Lermontov' (1993) 111 ALR 289 (High Court of Australia) **209**
Banco Exterior Internacional v Mann [1995] 1 All ER 936 155
Bank Belge pour l'Etranger v Hambrouck [1921] 1 KB 321 412
Bank of Credit and Commerce International SA v Aboody [1990] 1 QB 923 (CA) 144, **147**, 149, 153
Bank of Montreal v Stuart [1911] AC 120 150
Bank of New South Wales v Murphett [1983] 1 VR 489 518, 521
Bank Tejerat v Hong Kong and Shanghai Banking Corporation (CI) Ltd [1995] 1 Lloyd's Rep 239 416
Banque Belge pour l'Etranger v Hambrouck [1921] 1 KB 321 32, 400, **403**, 411, 444, 493
Barber v NWS Bank plc, [1996] 1 All ER 906 (CA) 207
Barclays Bank Ltd v W.J. Simms, Son & Cooke (Southern) Ltd [1980] QB 677 (QBD) 26, **57**, 66, 83, 313, 492, 493, 512, 514
Barclays Bank plc v O'Brien [1994] 1 AC 180 (HL) 26, 31, 144, **148**, 153
Barlow Clowes International Ltd v Vaughan [1992] 4 All ER 22 (CA) 429, 432, **455**, 464
Barnes v Addy (1874) LR 9 Ch App 244 372, 390, 392, 394
Barrell, ex parte Law Rep 10 Ch 512 221
Barton v Armstrong (1973) [1976] AC 104 (PC) **115**, 127, 128, 132, 139
Barton v Capewell (1893) 68 LT 857 234
Baylis v Bishop of London [1913] 1 Ch 127 (CA) 6, 9, 10, 12, 21, 72, 500, **508**, 515, 516, 517, 521
Bell v Lever Bros Ltd [1932] AC 161 53, 67, 111
Belmont Finance Corporation Ltd v Williams Furniture Ltd [1979] Ch 250 391, 395
Berkeley Applegate (Investment Consultants) Ltd (in liquidation), In re [1989] Ch 32 (Ch D) **189**
Bernstein v Pamson Motors (Golders Green) Ltd [1987] 2 All ER 220 208
Bilbie v Lumley (1802) 2 East 469; 102 ER 448 (KB) 48, 49, 65, **66**, 68, 69, 72, 80, 81, 302
Binstead v Buck (1777) 2 W Bl 1117, 96 ER 660 183, 194
Bishopsgate Investment Management Ltd (in liquidation) v Homan [1994] 3 WLR 1270 (CA) 443, **464**
Bisset v Wilkinson [1927] AC 177 (PC) 97
Bize v Dickason 1 Term Rep 285 72
Blaauwpot v Da Costa, 1 Ed 130 476

Blackburn and District Benefit Building Society v Cuncliffe Brooks & Co. 22 Ch D 61; 9 App Cas 857 438
Blackburn v Smith (1848) 2 Ex 783 530
Blackpool and Fleetwood Tramroad Co. v Bispham with Norbreck Urban District Council [1910] 1 KB 592 75
Blakeley v Muller & Co. [1903] 2 KB 760n 252
Boardman v Phipps [1967] 2 AC 46 (HL) **367**, 372, 528, 529, 538, 539
Bolton Partners v Lambert (1889) 41 Ch D 295 418
Bolton v Mahadeva [1972] 1 WLR 1009 242
Bond Worth Ltd, In re [1980] Ch 228 436
Bonner v Tottenham and Edmonton Permanent Investment Building Society [1899] 1 QB 161 (CA) **161**, 168
Boomer v Muir 24 P 2d 570 (1933) (District Court of Appeal of California) **219**
Borden (UK) Ltd v Scottish Timber Products Ltd [1981] Ch 25 466
Boscawen v Bajwa [1995] 4 All ER 769 33, 36, 399, 421, 513
Boston Deep Sea Fishing & Ice Co. v Ansell 39 Ch D 339 377
Boyd & Forrest v Glasgow & South-Western Railway Company [1915] SC (HL) 20 **105**, 528, 529
BP Exploration Co. (Libya) Ltd v Hunt (No. 2) [1979] 1 WLR 783 (QBD (Commercial Court)); [1981] 1 WLR 232 (CA); [1983] 2 AC 352 (HL) **36**, 40, 91, 105, 259, **260**, 512
Bracewell v Appleby [1975] 1 All ER 993, [1975] Ch 408 355
Brewer Street Investments Ltd v Barclays Woollen Co. Ltd [1954] 1 QB 428 (CA) **274**
Brinks Ltd v Abu-Sakh (No. 3), The Times, 23 October 1995 397
Brisbane v Dacres (1813) 5 Taunt 143; 128 ER 641 (Common Pleas) **67**, 72, 80, 81, 120, 510
British Red Cross Balkan Fund, British Red Cross Society v Johnson, Re [1914] 2 Ch 419, [1914–15] All ER Rep 459 457, 461
British Steel Corp. v Cleveland Bridge & Engineering Co. (1981) [1984] 1 All ER 504 (QBD (Commercial Court)) 29, **280**, 286, 287
Brook's Wharf and Bull Wharf Ltd v Goodman Brothers [1937] 1 KB 534 (CA) **168**
Brooks v Beirnstein [1909] 1 KB 98 226
Brooks v MacDonnell (1835) 1 Y & C 500 476
Brown v Adams LR 4 Ch 764 437
Browning v Morris (1778) 2 Cowp 790 73
Buckley v Gross (1863) 3 B & S 566 440
Buller v Harrison (1777) 2 Cowp 565; 98 ER 1234 (KB) **504**, 505, 507, 510
Bunge Corp. New York v Tradax Export SA, Panama [1981] 1 WLR 711 202
Burnand v Rodocanachi Sons & Co., 7 App Cas 333 477
Bush v Canfield 2 Conn 495 (1818) 209
Butterworth v Kingsway Motors [1954] 1 WLR 1286 (Liverpool Assizes) **207**

C & P Haulage v Middleton [1983] 1 WLR 1461 (CA) 209
C. A. Stewart & Co. v Phs. Van Ommeren (London) Ltd [1918] 2 KB 560 215, 216
C.H.T. Ltd v Ward [1965] 2 QB 63 495
Campbell v Hall (1774) 1 Cowp 204 300, 308, 312, 505
Cannon v Meaburn (1823) 1 Bing 243 182
Cargo ex Argos (1873) LR 5 PC 134 180, 185
Cartwright v Rowley (1799) 2 Esp 723 80
Castellain v Preston (1883) 11 QBD 380 175, 477
CCC Films (London) Ltd v Impact Quadrant Films Ltd [1985] QB 16 209
Central London Property Trust Ltd v High Trees House Ltd [1947] KB 130 88, 93
Chandler v Webster [1904] 1 KB 493 225, 251, 253, 255
Chase Manhattan Bank NA v Israel-British Bank (London) Ltd (1979) [1981] Ch 105 (Ch D) 34, 423, 429, **470**, 488
Chatterton v Maclean [1951] 1 All ER 761 227

Cheese v Thomas [1994] 1 All ER 35, [1994] 1 WLR 129 513, 523, 532
Chesworth v Farrar [1967] 1 QB 407 (QBD) 321, 332
Chillingworth v Esche [1924] 1 Ch 97 200
China Pacific SA v Food Corporation of India, The 'Winson' [1982] AC 939 (HL) 43, 183
Christy v Row 1 Taunt 300 180
CIBC Mortgages plc v Pitt [1994] 1 AC 200 (HL) 26, 144, 147, 148, 153, 157
Clarke v Dixon EB & E 148 100
Clarke v Shee and Johnson (1774) 1 Cowp 197; 98 ER 1041 (KB) 9, 32, 401, 416, 493, 495, 520
Clayton's Case, Devaynes v Noble (1816) 1 Mer 572, [1814–23] All ER Rep 1; 15 RR 161 431, 435, 437, 441, 455, 456, 458, 460, 461, 463, 464
Cleadon Trust Ltd, In re [1939] 1 Ch 286 (CA) 13, 291
Clifton Securities Ltd v Huntley [1948] 2 All ER 283 343
Cocks v Masterman 9 B & C 902 59, 500
Collins v Stimson 11 QBD 142 220
Colonial Bank v Exchange Bank of Yarmouth, Nova Scotia (1885) 11 App Cas 84 (PC) 58
Commercial Banking Co. of Sydney Ltd v Mann [1961] AC 1 417
Commissioner of Public Works v Hills [1906] AC 368 234, 240
Commonwealth Trust v Akotey [1926] AC 72 501
Compania Colombiana de Seguros v Pacific Steam Navigation Co. [1965] 1 QB 101 175
Consul Development Pty Ltd v D. P. C. Estates Pty Ltd (1975) 132 CLR 373 395
Continental C & G Rubber Co. Pty Ltd, Re (1919) 27 CLR 194 212
Continental Caoutchouc Co. v Kleinwort 9 Com Cas 240 500
Cooden Engineering Co. v Stanford [1953] 1 QB 86; [1952] 2 TLR 822; [1952] 2 All ER 915 234
Cook v Addison (1869) LR 7 Eq. 466 452
Cooke, Ex parte (1876) 4 ChD 123 406
Cooper v Phibbs (1867) LR 2 HL 149 30, 53, 64, 79, 111
Cory Bros & Co Ltd v Turkish Steamship Mecca (owners), The Mecca [1897] AC 286 457
Couturier v Hastie (1856) 5 HL Cas 673; 10 ER 1065 111
Cowan de Groot Properties Ltd v Eagle Trust plc [1992] 4 All ER 700 33, 427, 429
Cox v Prentice (1815) 3 M & S 344 507, 510
Crabb v Arun District Council [1976] Ch 179, 95
Cranleigh Precision Engineering Ltd. v Bryant [1965] 1 WLR 1293 382
Craven-Ellis v Canons Ltd [1936] 2 KB 403 (CA) 29, 30, 43, 256, 279, **289**, 537, 538
Crescendo Management Pty. Ltd v Westpac Banking Corporation (1988) 19 NSWLR 40, 46 140
Cresswell v Potter (1968) [1978] 1 WLR 255 158
Crockford v Winter (1807) 1 Camp 124 9
CTN Cash and Carry Ltd v Gallaher Ltd [1994] 4 All ER 714 (CA) 2, 140
Cundy v Lindsay (1878) LR 3 App Cas 459 (HL) 110
Cutter v Powell (1795) 6 Term Rep 320; 101 ER 573 (KB); 2 Smith's LC1 241, **248**, 250

D & C Builders Ltd v Rees [1966] 2 QB 617 (CA) **121**, 123, 125, 155
D. P. C. Estates Pty Ltd v Grey and Consul Development Pty Ltd [1974] 1 NSWLR 443 390, 395
Dale & Co. (1879) 11 Ch D 772 434
David Securities Pty Ltd v Commonwealth Bank of Australia (1992) 175 CLR 353 (High Court of Australia) 79, 520
David v Frowd 1 My & K 200 71
Davis Contractors Ltd v Fareham Urban District Council [1956] AC 696 (HL) 107, 138
Dawson v Linton (1822) 5 B & Ald 521 169
De Bernardy v Harding (1853) 8 Ex 822; 155 ER 1586 (Exchequer Chamber) **218**
De Bussche v Alt (1878) 8 Ch D 286 181
Deacon v Transport Regulation Board [1958] VR 458 127

Deglman v Guaranty Trust Co. of Canada and Constantineau [1954] 3 DLR 785 19, 294
Depree v Bedborough 4 Giff 479 221
Dering v Earl of Winchelsea (1787)1 Cox 318; 29 ER 1184 (Exchequer) 176
Derry v Peek (1889) 14 App Cas 337, 58 LJ Ch 864 96, 105, 106
Deutsche Bank v Beriro 1 Com Cas 255; 73 LT 669 499, 500, 501
Devaux v Conolly 8 CB 640 255
Dew v Parsons, 2 B & Ald 562 308
Dick Bentley Productions Ltd v Harold Smith (Motors) Ltd [1965] 1 WLR 623 96
Dies v British and International Mining and Finance Corporation Ltd [1939] 1 KB 724 (KBD) 223, 227, 228, 231, 232, 233, 234
Dimskal Shipping Co. SA v International Transport Workers' Federation, The 'Evia Luck' (No. 2) [1992] 2 AC 152 (HL) 23, 139, 492, 542
Diplock, In re, Diplock v Wintle [1948] Ch 465 (CA); affd sub nom. Ministry of Health v Simpson [1951] AC 251 (HL)
25, 34, **69**, 79, 112, 315, 333, 411, 423, 429, **443**, 459, 461, 464, 466, 471, 489, 493, 512
Donoghue v Stevenson [1932] AC 562 306
Downshire Settled Estates, In re [1953] Ch 218 192
Duke de Cadaval v Collins (1836) 4 Ad & E 858; 111 ER 1006 (KB) 115, 158
Duke of Norfolk's Settlement Trusts, In re [1982] Ch 61 (CA) 190, 192
Duomatic Ltd, In re [1969] 2 Ch 365 537, 538
Durrant v Ecclesiastical Commissioners for England and Wales (1880) 6 QBD 234 500, 501, 517

Eadie v Township of Brantford (1967) 63 DLR (2d) 561 305
Eagle Trust plc v SBC Securities Ltd [1992] 4 All ER 363, [1993] 1 WLR 484; [1995] BCC 231 395, 420, 427, 428, 429, 494
Eastgate; Ex parte Ward, In re [1905] 1 KB 465 488
Edgington v Fitzmaurice (1885) 29 Ch D 459 (CA) 30, 97, 118
Edmunds v Wallingford (1885) 14 QBD 811 (CA) 164, 170
El Ajou v Dollar Land Holdings plc (No. 1) [1993] 3 All ER 717; [1994] 2 All ER 688 (CA) 35, 429
El Ajou v Dollar Land Holdings plc (No. 2) [1995] 2 All ER 213 429
England v Marsden LR 1 CP 529 165, 170
English and Colonial Produce Co. Ltd, In re [1906] 2 Ch 435 89
Equiticorp Industries Group Ltd v Hawkins [1991] 3 NZLR 700 395
Erlanger v New Sombrero Phosphate Company (1878) 3 App Cas 1218 (HL) 97, 99, 527, 529, 530
Esso Petroleum Co. v Hall, Russell & Co. Ltd, The 'Esso Bernicia' [1989] AC 643 (HL (Scotland)) 36, 174
Esso Petroleum Co. v Mardon [1975] QB 819 (CA) 96
Evanson v Crooks (1911) 28 TLR 123 73
Ewbank v Nutting (1849) 7 CB 797 182
Exall v Partridge (1799) 8 TR 308; 101 ER 1405 (KB) 29, 159, 164, 170

Fairbanks v Snow (1887) 13 NE 596 116, 117
Falcke v Scottish Imperial Insurance Company (1886) 34 Ch D 234 (CA)
40, 42, 89, 178, 191, **196**
Farmer v Arundel (1772) 2 W Bl 824 68, 72, 80
Farquharson & Co. v King & Co. [1902] AC 325 499, 501
Faure Electric Accumulator Co., In re (1888) 40 Ch D 141 365
Fibrosa Spolka Akcyjna v Fairbairn Lawson Combe Barbour Ltd [1943] AC 32; 58 TLR 308; [1942] 2 All ER 122, HL
16, 22, 60, 74, 190, 225, **251**, 293, 294, 299, 308, 312, 333, 531
Fitzpatrick v M'Glone [1897] 2 IR 542 509
Foakes v Beer (1884) 9 App Cas 605 (HL) 121
Forest of Dean Coal Mining Co., In re (1878) 10 Ch D 450 364

Foster v Stewart 3 M & S 191 326
French Marine v Compagnie Napolitaine d'Eclairage et de Chauffage par le Gaz [1921] 2 AC 494 215
Frith v Cartland (1865) 2 Hem & M 417 466
Fry v Lane (1888) 40 Ch D 312 155, 158

G. Percy Trentham Ltd v Archital Luxfer Ltd [1993] 1 Lloyd's Rep 25 282
Gamerco SA v I.C.M./Fair Warning (Agency) Ltd [1995] 1 WLR 1226 (QBD) 258
Garriock v Walker (1873) 1 R 100 185
Gebhardt v Saunders [1892] 2 QB 452 (QBD) 29, **166**
General and Finance Facilities Ltd v Cooks Cars (Romford) Ltd [1963] 1 WLR 644 85
Gibbon v Mitchell [1990] 3 All ER 338 79
Giles v Edwards (1797) 7 Term Rep 181; 101 ER 920 (KB) 203, 204, 255
Gillet v Peppercorne 3 Beav 78 108
Gluckstein v Barnes [1900] AC 240 (HL) 101, **359**
Glyn v Weston Feature Film Co. [1916] 1 Ch 261 385
Goldcorp Exchange Ltd, Re (in receivership) [1994] 3 WLR 199; [1994] 2 All ER 806; [1995] 1 AC 74 (PC) 34, 443, 464, 465, 467, 468, 483, 490
Goldsworthy v Brickell [1987] Ch 378 147
Golightly versus Reynolds (1772) Lofft 88 401
Grand Lodge, A.O.U.W. of Minnesota v Towne (1917), 161 NW 403 521
Gray v Haig (1855) 20 Beav 219 452
Great Northern Railway Co. v Swaffield (1874) LR 9 Ex 132 (Exchequer) 178, 181, 185
Great Western Railway Co. v Sutton, LR 4 HL 226 120, 303
Greenwood v Bennett [1973] QB 195 (CA) 43, **85**, 88, 493
Grist v Bailey [1967] Ch 532 111
Guinness plc v Saunders [1990] 2 AC 663 (HL) 22, 291, 373, 528, **536**
Gwilliam v Twist [1895] 2 QB 84 181, 183

Hadley v Baxendale (1854) 9 Exch 341 353
Hain Steamship Company Ltd v Tate & Lyle Ltd [1936] 2 All ER 597 (HL) 242, 256
Hain v Tate & Lyle [1936] 2 All ER 597 247
Halifax Building Society v Thomas [1995] 4 All ER 673 319, 321, 483
Hallett's Estate, Knatchbull, In re v Hallett (1880) 13 ChD 696; [1874–80] All ER Rep 793 (CA) 7, 34, 405, 406, 407, 408, **432**, 437, 439, 440, 441, 442, 443, 447, 448, 453, 459, 461, 463, 465, 466, 473
Hambly v Trott (1776) 1 Cowp 371; 98 ER 1136 (KB) 321, 324, 325, 326, 327, 333, 378
Harse v Pearl Life Assurance Co. [1904] 1 KB 558 73, 74
Hart v O'Connor [1985] AC 1000 157
Hartog v Colin & Shields [1939] 3 All ER 566 110
Haviland v Long [1952] 2 QB 80 335
Hawtayne v Bourne (1841) 7 M & W 595 181, 183
Hazell v Hammersmith and Fulham London BC [1990] 3 All ER 33, [1990] 2 QB 697; [1991] 1 All ER 545; [1992] 2 AC 1 310, 522, 524, 526
Healing Research Trustee Co. Ltd, Re [1992] 2 All ER 481 161
Hedley Byrne & Co. Ltd v Heller & Partners Ltd [1964] AC 465 (HL) 96
Henderson v Folkestone Waterworks Co. (1885) 1 TLR 329 303
Hennessy v Craigmyle & Co. Ltd [1986] ICR 461 (CA) 136
Herbert v Champion, 1 Campb 134 68
Heywood v Wellers [1976] QB 446 211, 214
Hichens v Congreve (1828) 4 Russ 562; (1829) 1 R & M 150; (1831) 4 Sim 420 101, 361
Hicks v Hicks (1802) 3 East 16 314
Hillas & Co. Ltd v Arcos Ltd [(1932) 147 LT 503] 272
Hinton v Sparkes Law Rep 3 CP 161 220
Hobourn Aero Components Ltd's Air-Raid Distress Fund, Ryan v Forrest, Re [1945] 2 All ER 711, [1946] Ch 86 457, 458, 462

Hoenig v Isaacs [1952] 2 All ER 176 242
Holbrook v Sharpey (1812) 19 VesJun 131 314
Holland v Russell (1861) 1 B & S 424, 121 ER 773 (QB); affd (1863) 4 B & S 514, 122 ER 365 (Exchequer Chamber) 506, 510
Holmes v Hall (1704) Holt 36 16
Holt v Markham [1923] 1 KB 504 (CA) 10, 12, 21, 63, 64, **69, 498,** 500, 501, 503, 514
Hong Kong Fir Shipping Ltd v Kawasaki Kishen Kaisha [1962] 2 QB 26 202
Hooper & Grass' Contract, (1949) VLR 269 123
Horton v Jones [No. 1] (1934) 34 SR (NSW) 295
Howard v Wood (1679) 2 Levinz 245 329
Howe v Smith (1884) 27 Ch D 89 (CA) 220, 238
Howes v Bishop [1909] 2 KB 390 150
Hudson v Robinson (1816) 4 M & S 475 315
Hughes v Metropolitan Railway Co., 2 App Cas 439 93
Huguenin v Baseley 14 Ves 273 145
Hunt v Silk (1804) 5 East 449; 102 ER 1142 (KB) 204, 530
Hunter v Prinsep, 10 East 378 331
Huntington Copper Co. v Henderson 1877 4 R 294 366
Hydro Electric Commission of Nepean v Ontario Hydro 81
Hyundai Heavy Industries Co. Ltd v Papadopoulos [1980] 1 WLR 1129 (HL) 212, **225,** 230, 232
Hyundai Shipbuilding & Heavy Industries Co. Ltd v Pournaras [1978] 2 Lloyds's Rep 502 212, 227

Imperial Bank of Canada v Bank of Hamilton [1903] AC 49 500
Imperial Hydropathic Hotel Co., Blackpool v Hampson 20 Ch D 1 365
Imperial Mercantile Credit Association (Liquidators) v Coleman (1873) LR 6 HL 189 366
Industrial Development Consultants Ltd v Cooley [1972] 1 WLR 443 (Birmingham Assize) 373
Ingram v Little [1961] 1 QB 31 (CA) 110
Inland v Bushell (1836) 5 Dowl PC 147 510
Inn Leisure v D. F. McCloy (1991) 28 FCR 151 82
Inverugie Investments Ltd v Hackett [1995] 1 WLR 713 (PC) 345
Islamic Republic of Iran Shipping Lines v Denby [1987] 1 Lloyd's Rep 367 482
Island Export Finance Ltd v Umunna [1986] BCLC 460 376

Jacob v Allen (1703) 1 Salk 27 508
Jaggard v Sawyer [1995] 2 All ER 189 357
James, ex parte (1874) LR 9 Ch App 609 75
James, ex parte 8 Ves 337 364, 367
James Roscoe (Bolton) Ltd v Winder [1915] 1 Ch 62 (Ch D) 440, 465, **467**
James v Thomas H. Kent & Co. Ltd [1951] 1 KB 551 294
Jebara v Ottoman Bank [1927] 2 KB 254 (CA); reversed [1928] AC 269 (HL) 182
Jegon v Vivian (1871) LR 6 Ch App 742 338, 353
Jenkins v Tucker (1788) 1 H Bl 90; 126 ER 55 (Common Pleas) 186
Jennings & Chapman Ld. v Woodman, Matthews & Co. [1952] 2 TLR 409 275, 276, 277, 284
Jesse v Roy 1 CM & R 316 250
Johnson v Agnew [1980] AC 367 32, 220, 226
Johnson v Goslett 3 CB (NS) 569 255
Johnson v Johnson (1802) 3 Bos & P 162, at p. 169 9
Johnson v Royal Mail Steam Packet Co. (1867) LR 3 CP 38 160, 165
Johnson v Youden [1950] 1 KB 544 74
Johnsons Tyne Foundry Pty. Ltd v Maffra Corporation (1948) 77 CLR 544 546
Jones (R. E.) Ld. v Waring and Gillow Ld [1926] AC 670 18, **50, 499,** 514
Joseph Thorley v Orchis [1907] 1 KB 660 245

Karak Rubber Co. Ltd v Burden (No. 2) [1972] 1 WLR 602 395
Kaufman v Gerson (1904) 1 KB 591 123
Kayford Ltd (In Liquidation), In re [1975] 1 WLR 279 486
Keech v Sandford (1726) Sel Cas t King (Macnaghten) 175; Sel Cas Ch 61 364, 367, 373, 482
Kelly v Solari (1841) 9 M & W 54; 152 ER 24 (Exchequer) 7, 10, 16, **48**, 51, 52, 58, 63, 66, 79, 81, 89, 93
Kennedy v Panama, New Zealand, and Australian Royal Mail Company Law Rep 2 QB 580 102
Kerrison v Glyn, Mills, Currie & Co. 15 Com Cas 1; 17 Com Cas 41; (1911) 81 LJ KB 465 (HL) 55, 56, 58, 59, 61, 500
King v Leith (1787) 2 Term Rep 141, 145 15
King v Victoria Insurance Co. Ltd [1896] AC 250 477
Kiriri Cotton Co. Ltd v Dewani [1960] AC 192 (PC) **73**, 294
Kleinwort, Sons & Co. v Dunlop Rubber Co. (1907) 97 LT 263 (HL) 58, 59, 499, 500, 509, 510, 514
Kleinwort Benson Ltd v Glasgow District Council [1994] 4 All ER 865; [1996] QB 57 (ECJ); [1996] 2 All ER 257 (CA) 311
Kleinwort Benson Ltd v South Tyneside Metropolitan Borough Council [1994] 4 All ER 972 311
Krell v Henry [1903] 2 KB 740 253

Lac Minerals Ltd v International Corona Resources Ltd (1989) 61 DLR (4th) 14 483
Lagunas Nitrate Co. v Lagunas Syndicate [1899] 2 Ch 392 109, 529, 530
Lamb v Bunce (1815) 4 M & S 275, 105 ER 836 297
Lamb v Cranfield (1874) 43 LJ (Ch) 408 7
Lamine v Dorrell 2 Ld Raym 1216 326, 329, 330
Lampleigh v Brathwait 1 Sm LC 9th ed. 151, p. 160 162, 164
Lancashire and Yorkshire Ry. Co. v Gidlow LR 7 HL 517 120
Larner v London County Council [1949] 2 KB 683 (CA) **56**, 512, 513
Laurence v Lexcourt Holdings Ltd [1978] 1 WLR 1128 111
Lazard Bros & Co. v Midland Bank Ltd [1933] AC 289 79
Leeds Industrial Co-operative Society Ltd v Slack [1924] AC 851 351
Leslie, In re 23 Ch D 552 198
Leslie Shipping Co. v Welstead [1921] 3 KB 420 227
Letang v Cooper [1965] 1 QB 232 21
Lever v Goodwin (1887) 36 ChD 1; 3 TLR 650, CA 353, 379
Lickbarrow v Mason 2 TR 63 499, 501
Liesbosch Dredger (Owners) v Edison S.S. (Owners) [1933] AC 449 334
Liggett v Kensington [1993] 1 NZLR 257 467
Lightly v Clouston (1808) 1 Taunt 112; 127 ER 774 (Common Pleas) **323**, 326, 330
Lindsay Petroleum Company v Hurd Law Rep 5 PC 239 100
Linggi Plantations Ltd v Jagatheesan [1972] 1 MLJ 89 239
Linz v Electric Wire Company of Palestine Ltd [1948] AC 371 (PC) **209**
Lipkin Gorman v Karpnale Ltd [1991] 2 AC 548 2, 20, 22, 25, 28, 32, 112, 298, 315, 400, **416**, 491, 493, **494**, 511, 512, 513, **516**, 521, 522, 524, 525
Liquidators of Imperial Mercantile Credit Association v Coleman (1873) LR 6 HL 189 374
Lister & Co. v Stubbs (1890) 45 Ch D 1 (CA) 378, **468**, 479, 480, 481, 482
Livingstone v Rawyards Coal Co. (1880) 5 App Cas 25 86, 343
Lloyds Bank Ltd v Brooks, 6 Legal Decisions Affecting Bankers 161 501, 503
Lloyds Bank Ltd v Bundy [1975] QB 326 **155**
Lloyds Bank v Cooke [1907] 1 KB 794 501
Lobb v Vasey Housing Auxiliary (War Widows Guild) [1963] VR 239 258
Lodder v Slowey [1904] AC 442 220
Lodge v National Union Investment Company [1907] 1 Ch 300 10
Logicrose Ltd v Southend United Football Club Ltd [1988] 1 WLR 1256 378

London and North Western Ry. v Duerden (1916) 32 Times LR 315 181
London and River Plate Bank Ltd v Bank of Liverpool [1896] 1 QB 7 500, 517
London Joint Stock Bank v Macmillan [1918] AC 777 501
London Wine case [1986] PCC 121 485, 490
Longchamp v Kenny (1779) 1 Doug 137 6, 9
Lord Napier and Ettrick v Hunter [1993] AC 713 (HL) 19, 34, 36, 465, 468, **473**, 489
Lowrie v Bourdieu, Dougl 467 67, 80
Lupton v White (1808) 15 Ves 432 437, 452
Luxor (Eastbourne) Ld. v Cooper [1941] AC 108 276
Lyell v Kennedy 14 App Cas 437 371
Lysaght v Pearson, The Times, 3 March 1879 241

Macadam, In re [1946] Ch 73 190, 539
Macmillan Inc. v Bishopsgate Investment Trust plc (No. 3) [1995] 3 All ER 747 (reversed [1996] 1 All ER 585 (CA)) 319, 399
Magee v Pennine Insurance Co. Ltd [1969] 2 QB 507 111
Mahesan v Malaysian Government Officers' Co-operative Housing Society [1979] AC 374 (PC) 378
Manby v Scott 1 Sid 112 189
Manchester Trust v Furness [1985] 2 QB 539 428, 494
Mareva Compañia Naviera SA v International Bulkcarriers SA (1975) [1980] 1 All ER 213 (CA) 470
Marine Mansions Co., In re LR 4 Eq 601 190, 192
Marr v Arabco Traders Ltd (1987) 1 NZBLC 102 395
Marriot v Hampton (1797) 7 TR 269; 2 Sm LC (11th ed.) 421; 101 ER 969 6, 9
Marsh v Keating (1834) 1 Bing (NC) 198 15, 418
Marshall Futures Ltd v Marshall [1992] 1 NZLR 316 395
Marston Construction Co. Ltd v Kigass Ltd (1989) 15 Con LR 116 285
Martin v Morgan (1819) 1 Brod & B 289 9
Martin v Porter (1839) 5 M & W 351 338
Maskell v Horner [1915] 3 KB 106 **119**, 124, 129, 132, 300, 302, 303
Mason v New South Wales, 102 CLR 108 302, 305
Massey v Midland Bank plc [1995] 1 All ER 929 (CA) 155
Maynard v Moseley (1676) 3 Swanst 651 236
Mayson v Clouet [1924] AC 980; 40 TLR 678 231, 234
McDonald v Dennys Lascelles Ltd (1933) 48 CLR 457 226, 230, 231, 232, 233
McRae v Commonwealth Disposals Commission 212
Mecca, The [1897] AC 286 458, 459
Mediana (Owners of Steamship) v Comet (Owners of Lightship) (The Mediana) [1900] AC 113 334, 346
Menetone v Athawes 3 Burr 1592 250
Metropolitan Bank v Heiron 5 Ex D 319 468, 481
Millar's Machinery Co. Ltd v David Way & Son (1935) 40 Com Cas 204 211, 214
Miller, Gibb & Co. Ltd, In re [1957] 1 WLR 703 477, 478
Miller v Atlee (1849) 3 Ex 799; 13 Jur 431 9
Miller v Race (1758) 1 Burr 452, 97 ER 398 32, 401, 404, 493
Milnes v Duncan 68 & C 761 49
Ministry of Agriculture and Fisheries v Matthews [1949] 2 All ER 724, [1950] 1 KB 148 524
Ministry of Defence v Ashman [1993] 2 EGLR 102 (CA) 340, 345, 347
Ministry of Defence v Thompson [1993] 2 EGLR 107 (CA) 344
Ministry of Health v Simpson [1951] AC 251 25, 64, 69, 443, 493, 512, 515, 516, 518
Moffatt v Kazana [1969] 2 QB 152 112
Montagu's Settlement Trusts, Dukeof Manchester, In re v National Westminster Bank Ltd [1987] Ch 264; [1992] 4 All ER 308 (Ch D) 391, 395, 420, 422, 424, 428
Montagu v Janverin (1811) 3 Taunt 442, 128 ER 175 67
Morgan case [1985] AC 686 535

Morgan Grenfell & Co. Ltd v Welwyn Hatfield District Council [1995] 1 All ER 1 311
Morgan Guaranty Trust Co. of New York v Lothian Regional Council [1995] SLT 299 83
Morgan v Ashcroft [1938] 1 KB 49 (CA) **11**, **53**, 57, 60
Morgan v Palmer, 2 B & C 729 302, 309
Morison v London County and Westminster Bank [1914] 3 KB 356 500
Moritz v Horsman (1943), 9 NW 2d 868 521
Morley v Attenborough (1849) 3 Ex 500 510
Morley v Moore [1936] 2 KB 359 478
Morris v Tarrant (1971) 2 QB 143 342
Morrison's case [1916] 2 KB 783 244, 245
Moses v Macferlan (1760) 2 Burr 1005; 97 ER 676 **4**, 6, 8, 9, 12,16, 20, 74, 158, 509, 517
Moss v Handcock [1899] 2 QB 111 404
Moule v Garrett (1872) LR 7 Ex 101 **160**, 162, 163, 168, 170
Munro v Butt 8 E & B 738 241, 242, 250
Munro v Willmott [1949] 1 KB 295 85, 87
Muschinski v Dodds (1985) 160 CLR 583 19, 295
Mussen v Van Dieman's Land Co. [1938] Ch 253 234, 235, 236, 237
Mutual Finance Ltd v John Wetton & Sons Ltd [1937] 2 KB 389 143
My Kinda Town Ltd v Soll [1983] RPC 15 (Ch D) (reversed on another ground [1983] RPC 407 (CA)) 35, 389

N.W.L. Ltd v Woods [1979] 1 WLR 1294 541, 542
National Association of Local Government Officers v Bolton Corporation [1943] AC 166 57
National Bolivian Navigation Co. v Wilson 5 App Cas 176 255
National Mutual Life Association of Australasia Ltd v Walsh (1987) 8 NSWLR 598 521
National Pari-Mutuel Association Ltd v The King, 47 TLR 110 303
National Westminster Bank plc v Morgan [1985] AC 686 141, 147, 153, 156
Neate v Harding (1851) 6 Ex 349, 155 ER 577 112
Neesom v Clarkson (1845) 4 Hare 97 191
Nelson v Larholt [1948] 1 KB 339 25, 400, **408**, 494
Nepean Hydro Electric Commission v Ontario Hydro [1982] 1 SCR 347 523
Neste Oy v Lloyds Bank Plc. [1983] 2 Lloyd's Rep 658 488
Newall v Tomlinson LR 6 CP 405 510
Newbigging v Adam, 34 Ch D 582; (1888) 13 App Cas 308 (CA) 97, **101**, 529, 533, 534
Newdigate v Davy (1936) 1 Ld Raym 742 300
Nicholson v Chapman (1793) 2 H Bl 254; 126 ER 536 (Common Pleas) 181, 183, **192**
Nimmo v Westpac Banking Corporation [1993] 3 NZLR 218 395
Nixon v Furphy (1925) 25 NSW 151 123
Nockels v Crosby (1825) 3 B & C 814 255
Noel v Robinson (1682) 1 Vern 90, 23 ER 334 71
North Central Wagon Finance Co. Ltd v Brailsford [1962] 1 WLR 1288 316
North Ocean Shipping Co. Ltd v Hyundai Construction Co. Ltd The 'Atlantic Baron' [1979] QB 705 **125**, 129, 130, 134, 135, 139
Norton Warburg Investment Management Ltd v Gibbons (31 July 1981, unreported) 458
Norwich Union Fire Insurance Society Ltd v W. H. Price Ltd [1934] AC 455 (PC) **52**, 58
Notara v Henderson (1872) LR 7 QB 225 180, 185
Notley v Buck (1828) 8 B & C 160 510

O'Rorke v Bolingbroke (1877) 2 App Cas 814 157
O'Sullivan v Management Agency and Music Ltd [1985] QB 428 (CA) 30, 107, 146, **528**, 535
Oatway 453
Oatway, Hertslet v Oatway, Re [1903] 2 Ch 356 **436**, 442, 453, 462, 463
Occidental Worldwide Investment Corporation v Skibs A/S Avanti, The 'Siboen' and the 'Sibotre' [1976] 1 Lloyd's Rep 293 (QBD (Commercial Court)) **121**, 128, 129, 130, 139, **348**

Ocean Tramp Tankers Corporation v V/O Sovfracht, The 'Eugenia' [1964] 2 QB 226 256
Oelkers v Ellis [1914] 2 KB 139 108
Old & Campbell Ltd v Liverpool Victoria Friendly Society (1979) [1982] QB 133 (Note) 94
Oliver v Court 8 Price 127 108
Ontario Hydro case [1982] SCR 367; (1982) 132 DLR (3d) 209 82
Ontario Securities Commission and Greymac Credit Corp, Re (1986) 55 OR (2d) 673 456
Orakpo v Manson Investments Ltd [1978] AC 95 (HL) **18, 22, 36**
Ormes v Beadel (1980) 2 Gif 166; 2 De GF & J 333 126, 154
Orton v Butler (1822) 5 B & Ald 652 9
Oscar Chess Ltd v Williams [1957] 1 WLR 370 96
OTM Ltd v Hydranautics [1981] 2 Lloyd's Rep 211 281
Owen v Challis (1848) 17 LJ (CP) 266 9
Owen v Tate [1976] QB 402 (CA) 29, **170,** 174

Paal Wilson & Co. A/S v Partenreederei Hannah Blumenthal, The 'Hannah Blumenthal' [1983] 1 AC 854 19, 110
Palmer v Temple (1839) 9 A & E 508 220, 228, 231, 233, 234
Palsgraf v Long Island Railroad 248 NY 339, 162 NE 99 (1928) 178
Pan Ocean Shipping Co. Ltd v Creditcorp Ltd, The 'Trident Beauty' [1994] 1 WLR 161 (HL) 26, **214**
Panton v Panton (undated) (cited in 15 Ves 432, 435, 440 452
Pao On v Lau Yiu Long [1980] AC 614 (PC) **128,** 130, 132, 134, 139, 140
Parker v Great Western Ry. Co. 7 Man & G 253 120
Parker v McKenna (1874) 10 Ch App 96 365, 374
Pattinson v Luckley (1875) LR 10 Ex 330 241
Pavey & Matthews Proprietary Ltd v Paul (1987) 162 CLR 221 (High Court of Australia) 19, 82, **294, 543**
Peek v Gurney Law Rep 13 Eq 79; 6 HL 377 102, 326
Penarth Dock Engineering Co. Ltd v Pounds [1963] 1 Lloyd's Rep 359 336, 337, **338,** 343, 346, **351, 355**
Penley v Watts 7 M & W 601 163
Pennell v Deffell 4 DM & G 372 435, 436
Perrott v Perrott (1811) 14 East 423 82
Peruvian Guano Co. v Dreyfus Brothers & Co. [1892] AC 166 86, 87
Peter Pan Manufacturing Corporation v Corsets Silhouette Ltd [1964] 1 WLR 96 (Ch D) **379,** 384
Peto v Blades 5 Taunt 657 509, 510
Phillips v Ellinson Bros. Pty Ltd (1941) 65 CLR 294
Phillips v Homfray, Fothergill v Phillips (1871) LR 6 Ch App 770; (1883) 24 Ch D 439 (CA) 43, **323,** 333, 338, 342, 346, 353
Phillips v London School Board [1898] 2 QB 447 10
Phipps v Boardman [1964] 1 WLR 993; [1967] 2 AC 46 190, 192, 374, 375, 482, 529, 531, 532, 538, 539
Photo Production Ltd v Securicor Transport Ltd [1980] AC 827 202, 220, 247
Planché v Colburn (1831) 8 Bing 14; 131 ER 305 (Common Pleas) **217**
Polly Peck International plc v Nadir (No. 2) [1992] 4 All ER 769 (CA) 33, 35, 395, 420, **425,** 429
Pond v Underwood 2 Ld Raym 1210 505, 508
Port Caledonia, The and The Anna [1903] P 184 155
Porter v Latec Finance (Qld) Pty Ltd (1964) 111 CLR 177 59
Powell & Thomas v Evans Jones & Co. [1905] 1 KB 11 481
Powell v Thompson [1991] 1 NZLR 597 395
Pownal v Ferrand 6 B & C 439 169
Prager v Blatspiel, Stamp and Heacock Ltd [1924] 1 KB 566 **180,** 183
Prenn v Simmonds [1971] 1 WLR 1381 226
Price v Neal (1762) 3 Burr 1355 517

Prince v Oriental Bank Corporation (1878) 3 App Cas 325 8
Proctor & Gamble Philippine Manufacturing Corp. v Peter Cremer GmbH & Co., The 'Manila' [1988] 3 All ER 834 (QBD (Commercial Court)) 43, 44
Pulbrook v Lawes (1876) 1 QBD 290 294

Queens of the River Steamship Co. Ltd v Conservators of the River Thames, 15 TLR 474 308
Quistclose Investments Ltd v Rolls Razor Ltd [1970] AC 567 486

R. E. Jones Ltd v Waring and Gillow Ltd [1926] AC 670 (HL) 16, **50**, 52, 58, 63, **499**, 501, 512, 517
R v Tower Hamlets London Borough Council, ex parte Chetnik Developments Ltd [1988] AC 858 (HL) **74**, 301, 512
Ramsden v Dyson (1866) LR 1 HL 129 (HL) **91**, 93, 94, 297
Randal v Cockran (1748) 1 Ves Sen 98 476
Reading v Attorney General [1951] AC 507 (HL) 335, **376**, 384, 385, 482
Reckitt v Barnett [1929] AC 176 409
Redgrave v Hurd (1881) 20 Ch D 1 (CA) 30, **97**, 103
Regal (Hastings) Ltd v Gulliver [1942] 1 All ER 378; [1967] 2 AC 134 (note) HL **363**, 368, 369, 371, 372, 374, 375, 481, 529
Regalian Properties plc v London Dockland Development Corp [1995] 1 WLR 212 (Ch D) **282**
Rex v Electricity Commissioners (1923) 39 Times LR 715, 718; [1924] 1 KB 171 181
Reynell v Sprye (1852) 1 De GM & G 660 116
Rhodes, In re (1890) 44 Ch D 94 (CA) 21, **187**, 294
Rhyl UDC v Rhyl Amusements Ltd [1959] 1 All ER 257, [1959] 1 WLR 465 524
Roberts v Crowe (1872) LR 7 CP 629 162
Roberts v Havelock 3 B & Ad 404 250
Rogers v Ingham (1876) 3 ChD 351, 355 7
Rogers v Ingham (1876) 3 ChD 351 10, 73
Rogers v Parish (Scarborough) Ltd [1987] 2 All ER 232 208, 214
Rogers v Price (1829) 3 Y & J 28; 148 ER 1080 (Exchequer) 30, **187**
Rolfe v Gregory (1865) 4 DJ & S 576, 108
Rookes v Barnard [1964] AC 1129 (HL) 121, 320
Rosenthal v Alderton & Sons Ltd [1946] KB 374 85
Rothschild v Brookman 5 Bli (NS) 165 108
Rover International Limited v Cannon Film Sales Ltd [1989] 1 WLR 912 (CA) 30, **65**, **89**, 90, 91, **230**, **292**, 317, **514**, 521
Rowland v Divall [1923] 2 KB 500 (CA) **204**, 207, 208, 293, 317, 493
Royal Brunei Airlines Sdn Bhd v Philip Tan Kok Ming [1995] 2 AC 378 (PC) 35, **393**, 420
Rugg v Minett (1809) 11 East 210 235, 255, 313
Rural Municipality of Storthoaks v Mobil Oil Canada Ltd. (1975), 55 DLR (3d) 1 518, 521
Russell v Thornton 4 H & N 788; affirmed on error, 6 Id 140 506, 508
Ruxley Electronics and Constructions Ltd v Forsyth [1995] 3 WLR 118 (HL) 358

S. S. Valeria, Re [1922] 2 AC 242 334
S.E.C. v Chenery Corporation (1943) 318 US 80 484
Sabemo Pty. Ltd v North Sydney Municipal Council [1977] 2 NSWLR 880 283, 285, 288, 297
Sadler v Evans (1766) 4 Burr 1984; 98 ER 34 6, 9, 10, 505, 508, 510
Saltman Engineering Co. v Campbell Engineering Co. (1948) 65 RPC 203; [1963] 3 All ER 413n 382
Sanders & Forster Ltd v A. Monk & Co. Ltd [1980] CA Transcript 35 281
Sargood Brothers v The Commonwealth, 11 CLR 258 303
Sawyer & Vincent v Window Brace Ltd, [1943] KB 32 82
Scarisbrick v Parkinson [(1869) 20 LT 175] 272

Schwarstein v Watson (1985) 3 NSWLR 134 544
Scott v Nesbitt, 14 Ves Jun 438 191, 192
Scott v Pattison [1923] 2 KB 723 295
Scott v Surman, Willes, 400 402
Seager v Copydex Ltd [1967] 1 WLR 923 (CA) 381
Seager v Copydex Ltd (No. 2) [1969] 1 WLR 809 (CA) 383
Sebel Products Ltd v Customs and Excise Commissioners [1949] Ch 409 303
Selangor United Rubber Estates Ltd v Cradock (No. 3) [1968] 1 WLR 1555 392, 395
Sharp Brothers & Knight v Chant [1917] 1 KB 771 73
Siddell v Vickers (1892) 9 RPC 152 381
Simmonds, ex parte (1885) 16 QBD 308 75
Simpson & Co. v Thomson, 3 App Cas 279 478
Sims & Co. v Midland Ry. Co. [1913] 1 KB 103 181, 182
Sinclair v Bowles 9 B & C 92 250
Sinclair v Brougham [1914] AC 398; [1914–15] All ER Rep 622
10, 11, 12, 13, 14, 17, 18, 21, 34, 36, 60, 223, 252, 315, 317, 400, 404, 405, 406, 407, 408, 429, **438**, 443, 444, 445, 447, 448, 449, 453, 456, 459, 461, 471, 488, 540
Sir Henry Sherrington's Estate, Savile, 40 325
Sir William Harbert's case, 3 Co. 11 b 176
Skeate v Beale (1841) 11 Ad & E 983; 113 ER 688 (KB) **119**, 123, 127, 129, 139
Skyring v Greenwood and Cox 4 B & C 281 498, 499, 503, 513
Slade's case (1602) 4 Coke 92(b) 14
Slater v Burnley Corporation, 59 LT 636 303
Slater v Hoyle & Smith Ld. [1920] 2 KB 11 335
Smiley v Townshend [1950] 2 KB 311 335
Smith v Baker (1873) LR 8 CP 350 330, 331
Smith v Bromley (1760) 2 Doug 696 74
Smith v Hodson (1791) 4 Term Rep 211; 100 ER 979 323
Smith v Jones (1842) 1 Dowl PC (NS) 526 7, 10
Snowdon v Davies (1808) 1 Taunt 359; 127 ER 872 (Common Pleas) 505
Société Franco Tunisienne d'Armement v Sidermar SPA, The 'Massalia' [1961] 2 QB 278 256
Solle v Butcher [1950] 1 KB 671 79, 111
South of Scotland Electricity Board v British Oxygen Co. Ltd [1959] 1 WLR 587 300, 303
South Tyneside Metropolitan Borough Council v Svenska International plc [1995] 1 All ER 545 (QBD (Commercial Court)) 311, 522
Space Investments Ltd v Canadian Imperial Bank of Commerce Trust Co. (Bahamas) Ltd [1986] 1 WLR 1072 (PC) 34, 464, 466, 467, **472**, 489
Spence v Crawford [1939] 3 All ER 271 (HL (Scotland)) 97, **108**, 527, 529, 530, 535
Spence v Union Marine Insurance Co. (1868) LR 3 CP 427 440
Springer v Great Western Ry. [1921] 1 KB 257 181, 182
Springfield Acres Ltd v Abacus (Hong Kong) Ltd [1994] 3 NZLR 502 395
St. Paul Fire & Marine Ins. Co. v Pure Oil Co. (1933), 63 F (2d) 771 82
Staffordshire Gas and Coke Co., In re [1893] 3 Ch 523 192
Standish v Ross (1849) 3 Ex 527 7, 10, 500
Stapylton Fletcher Ltd, Re [1995] 1 All ER 192 490
Stearns v Village Main Reef Gold Mining Co. Ltd, 10 Com Cas 89 477
Steedman v Drinkle [1916] 1 AC 275 234, 235
Steele v Williams (1853) 8 Exch 625, 155 ER 1502 155, 303, 308
Stenning, In re [1895] 2 Ch 433 443
Stilk v Myrick (1809) 2 Camp 317, 170 ER 1168 124, 138
Stockloser v Johnson [1954] 1 QB 476 (CA) 233, 239, 240
Stoke-on-Trent City Council v W & J Wass Ltd [1988] 1 WLR 1406 (CA) 337, 346, 354
Storthoaks case [1976] 2 SCR 147 523
Strand Electric and Engineering Co. Ltd v Brisford Entertainments Ltd [1952] 2 QB 246 (CA) 333, 336, 337, 338, 339, 350, 353

Stratford (J.T.) & Son Ltd v Lindley [1964] 2 WLR 1002 121
Straton v Rastall (1788) 2 TR 366 7, 9
Studdy v Sanders (1826) 5 B & C 628 545
Sumitomo Bank Ltd v Kartika Ratna Thahir [1993] 1 SLR 735 482
Sumpter v Hedges [1898] 1 QB 673 (CA) 30, **240**
Surrey County Council v Bredero Homes Ltd [1993] 3 All ER 705 (CA) **348**, 352, 357
Susquehanna, The [1926] AC 655 335
Swain v Wall 1 Cha Rep 149 176
Swordheath Properties Ltd v Tabet [1979] 1 WLR 285 338, 341, 343, 346

T. A. Sundell & Sons Pty. Ltd v Emm Yannoulatos (Overseas) Pty. Ltd [1956] SR (NSW) 323 123
T. and J. Brocklebank Ltd v The King [1925] 1 KB 52 303
Taylor v Caldwell 3 B & S 826; 32 LJ (QB) 164 250, 251, 254
Taylor v Laird (1856) 25 LJ Ex 329 40, 42, 86
Taylor v Metropolitan Ry. Co. [1906] 2 KB 55 510
Taylor v Plumer (1815) 3 M & S 562; 105 ER 721 (KB) 32, 400, **401**, 404, 407, 411, 417
Taylors Fashions Ltd v Liverpool Victoria Trustees Co. Ltd (1979) [1982] QB 133 94
Terrapin Ltd v Builders' Supply Co. (Hayes) Ltd [1960] RPC 128 382
Thomas v Brown (1876) 1 QBD 714 296
Thomas v Houston Corbett & Co. [1969] NZLR 151 58
Thorne v Motor Trade Association [1937] AC 797 133, 142
Tilley's Will Trusts, Burgin, In re v Croad [1967] Ch 1179 (Ch D) **451**
Tito v Waddell (No. 2) [1977] Ch 106; [1977] 3 All ER 129 348, 354, 355
Tonnelier v Smith (1897) 2 Com Cas 258 215
Towers v Barrett (1786) 1 TR 133 9
Tregoning v Attenborough (1830) 7 Bing 97 10
TSB Bank of Scotland plc v Hatfield & Welwyn District Council (1993) 2 Bank LR 267 311
TSB Bank plc v Camfield [1995] 1 All ER 951 155
Twyford v Manchester Corporation [1946] Ch 236 303

Union Bank of Australia Ltd v McClintock [1922] 1 AC 240 417
Union Pacific Railway Company v Public Service Commission of Missouri (1918) 248 US 67 143
United Australia Ltd v Barclays Bank Ltd [1941] AC 1 (HL) 14, 17, 22, 60, 321, **328**
United States Shipping Board v Bunge y Born (1925) 31 Com Cas 118 244, 245
Universe Tankships Inc. of Monrovia v International Transport Workers' Federation, The 'Universe Sentinel' [1983] 1 AC 366 35, 130, 134, 135, 142, **541**, 543
Upton-on-Severn Rural District Council v Powell [1942] 1 All ER 220 (CA) 84, **279**

Valpy v Manley 1 CB 594 120
Vantage Navigation Corporation v Suhail and Saud Bahwan Building Materials LLC, The 'Alev' [1989] 1 Lloyd's Rep 138 (QBD (Commercial Court)) **136**

Wait, In re [1927] 1 Ch 606 484
Wakefield v Newton, (1844) 6 QB 276 123
Walford v Miles [1992] 2 AC 128 354
Wallis, Son, & Wells v Pratt & Haynes [1910] 2 KB 1003 106
Walstab v Spottiswoode (1846) 15 M & W 501 211, 212
Walter J. Schmidt & Co., ex parte Feuerbach, In re (1923) 298 F 314 460
Ward & Co. v Wallis [1900] 1 QB 675 59
Warman v Southern Counties Car Finance Corporation Ltd [1949] 2 KB 576 207, 293
Watson, Laidlaw & Co. Ltd v Pott, Cassels and Williamson (1914) 31 RPC 104 349, 353
Way v Latilla [1937] 3 All ER 759 (HL) 267, **271**
Weatherby v Banham (1832) 5 C & P 228, 172 ER 950 297
Weaver, In re 21 Ch D 615 188

Weld-Blundell v Synott [1940] 2 KB 107 58, 59
Wenlock v River Dee Co. 10 App Cas 354 438
Westdeusche Landesbank Girozentrale v Islington London Borough Council [1994] 4 All ER 890, [1994] 1 WLR 138 35, 201, 289, **311**, 429, 472, 524
Weston v Downes (1778) 1 Doug 23 6, 9
Westpac Banking Corporation v Savin [1985] 2 NZLR 41 395, 523
Whincup v Hughes (1871) LR 6 CP 78 (Common Pleas) **250**, 256
Whitaker v Dunn 3 Times LR 602 241, 242
Whitcomb v Jacob, Salk 160 402
White v Dobinson, 14 Sim 273; 116 LTOS 233 476, 477, 478
Whitmore v Greene (1844) 13 M & W 104 510
Whittaker v Campbell [1983] 3 All ER 582 31
Whittington v Seale-Hayne (1900) 82 LT 49 (Ch D) **104**
Whitwham v Westminster Brymbo Coal & Coke Co. [1896] 2 Ch 538 335, 336, 338, 339, 343, 346, 349, 350, 353, 354
William Lacey (Hounslow) Ltd v Davis [1957] 2 All ER 712, [1957] 1 WLR 932 277, 281, 282, 284, 285, 287, 297
William Sindall plc v Cambridgeshire County Council [1994] 1 WLR 1016 99, 111
William Whiteley Ltd v The King (1909) 26 TLR 19; 101 LT 741 73, 303
Williams v Bayley (1866) LR 1 HL 200 143, 155
Williams v Roffey Bros & Nicholls (Contractors) Ltd [1991] 1 QB 1 (CA) 136, **137**
Willmott v Barber (1880) 15 Ch D 96 **92, 93, 94**, 297
Wilson v Church 13 Ch D 1 255
Wood v Morewood (1841) 3 QB 440 86
Woolwich Equitable Building Society v Inland Revenue Commissioners (No. 2) [1989] 1 WLR 137 (CA); [1992] 3 All ER 737; [1993] 1 AC 70 (HL) 20, 22, 83, 114, 298, **299**, 312, 316, 523
Workers Trust & Merchant Bank Ltd v Dojap Investments Ltd [1993] AC 573 (PC) **238**
Wrexham, Mold and Connah's Quay Ry. Co. [1898] 2 Ch 663; [1899] 1 Ch 440 438
Wright v Vanderplank 8 DM & G 137 145
Wrotham Park Estate Co. v Parkside Homes Ltd [1974] 2 All ER 321, [1974] 1 WLR 798 338, 339, **348**, 353, 355, 357

Yeoman Credit Ltd v Apps [1962] 2 QB 508 (CA) **207**
York Buildings Co. v Mackenzie 3 Pat App Cas 378 108
Yorkshire Insurance Co. Ltd v Nisbet Shipping Co. Ltd [1962] 2 QB 330 19, 477
Young v Queensland Trustees Ltd (1956) 99 CLR 545

Zuhal K and Selin, The [1987] 1 Lloyd's Rep 151 **173**

Table of Statutes

Statutes from which extracts are given in the text, appear in bold type. The page at which the statute is printed is shown in bold type.

Annuities Act 1777 (17 Geo.3, c.26) 314

Bankruptcy Act 1883
s.52 509
Bill of Rights 1688 304
Art.4 301
Bill of Rights 1689
Art.4 298
Bills of Exchange Act 1882 409
s.2 408
Building Societies Act 1836 7

Capital Transfer Tax 1984
s.241 301
Chancery Amendment Act *see* Lord Cairns' Act
Civil Liability (Contribution) Act 1978 158, 177
s.1(1) **177**
s.2(1) **178**
s.6(1) **178**
Common Law Procedure Act 1852 17, 18, 20
s.3 17
s.49 17
Companies Act 1862 361, 362
Consumer Credit Act 1974 156
Consumer Safety Act 1978 156
Copyright, Designs and Patents Act 1988
s.96-s.97 389
s.229 389
Criminal Justice Act 1988
Part VI 321

Customs Consolidation Act 1876 169
s.85 168, 169

Ecclesiastical Dilapidations Act 1871
s.13-s.20 509
Employment Act 1980 542
s.17 542

Finance Act 1984
s.40 299
Finance Act 1989
s.24 301
s.29 301

Gaming Act 1845 59
s.18 53, 493, 495, 496
Gaming Acts 495
General Rate Act 1967
s.9 76, 77, 78, 301
s.9(1) 74
s.12 76
s.14 77

Hire Purchase Act 1964
Part III 207

Insurance Companies Act 1982 156

Judicature Acts 1873–1875 13, 21, 100, 222

Law Reform (Frustrated Contracts) Act 1943 37, 90, 215, 247, **257**, 259, **260**, 261, 262, 263, 264, 265, 266, 267, 268, 269, 528

Law Reform (Frustrated Contracts) Act 1943 – *continued*
s.1 268
s.1(1) **257**
s.1(2) **257**, 258, 259, 261, 262, 265, 266, 268, 269
s.1(3) 259, **260**, 261, 262, 263, 264, 265, 266, 267, 268, 269
s.1(3)(a) **260**, 263, 265, 266
s.1(3)(b) **260**, 263, 265
s.2(3) **257**, 267, 268, 269
Law Reform (Miscellaneous Provisions) Act 1934 328, 333
s.1(3) 332, 333
Limitation Act 1939 332
s.2(1)(a) 333
Lord Cairns' Act 349, 353, 354, 357
Lottery Act 1772 (stat 12 Geo.3, c.63) 401

Misrepresentation Act 1967 110
s.1 107
s.2(1) 96
s.2(2) 97, 99, **110**
s.2(3) **110**

Partnership Act 1890
s.40 253, 256
Patents Act 1977
s.61-s.62 389
Proceedings Against Estates Act 1970 333
Public Health (London) Act 1891
s.4(1) 166, 167
s.4(3) 167
s.4(4) 166, 167
s.11 167, 168

Rent Restriction (Amendment) Ordinance 1954
s.3 74
Rent Restriction Ordinance 74
s.3(2) 74

Sale of Goods Act 1893 202, 205, 206
s.11(1)(c) 206
Sale of Goods Act 1979
s.8 30
s.11(4) 206
s.14 208
s.16 484, 490
s.35 208
Sale of Goods (Amendment) Act 1995 490
Sale and Supply of Goods Act 1994 208
Sequestration Act 1871 509
Stamp Act 1891
s.13(4) 301
Statute of Frauds 272, 545
Statute of Limitations 6, 70, 108
Supply of Goods (Implied Terms) Act 1973 156
Supply of Goods and Services Act 1982 156
s.15 29
Supreme Court Act 1981
s.35A 299
s.37(3) 470
s.50 357

Taxes Management Act 1970
s.33 301
Torts (Interference with Goods) Act 1977 88, 334
s.3(7) **88**
s.6 **88**
s.6(1)-(4) **88**
Trade Union and Labour Relations Act 1974 130, 131, 541, 542
s.13 131, 541, 542
s.13(1) 541, 542
s.14 131, 541
s.29 131, 541

Australian legislation
Builders Licensing Act 1971 (New South Wales)
s.45 294, 543, 544, 545, 546, 547
Income Tax Assessment Act 1936
s.261 79
Law Reform (Property, Perpetuities and Succession) Act 1962 (Western Australia)
s.24 518, 523
Property Law Act 1969 (Western Australia)
s.124 83
s.125 83
s.125(1) 521
Trustee Act 1962 (Western Australia)
s.65(8) 518, 523
Canadian legislation
Frustrated Contracts Act 1974 (British Columbia) 270
s.5(1) **270**
s.5(3)-(4) **270**
New Zealand legislation
Judicature Act 1908 523
s.94a 83
s.94b 83, 518, 521, 523
Sale of Goods Act 1908
s.18 484
US legislation
Restatement of the Law of Restitution 11, 14, 34, 331
para.69(1) 521
para.142(1)-(3) 513

1 INTRODUCTION

Section 1: the principle of unjust enrichment

What happens if an employer discovers that due to computer error one of its employees has been overpaid for a number of months? What if the employee, unaware of the problem, spends his increased disposable income on an expensive foreign holiday? Can the purchaser get her money back when she buys a brand new motor car which due to some hidden defect proves to be wholly unsatisfactory and unsafe after six months' driving? Are the people who clean another's windscreen uninvited at traffic lights entitled to some payment, even though the motorist neither requested the service, nor made any attempt to ask them to desist? These common occurrences provide some of the concerns of the law of restitution.

Restitution is a significant feature of a mature civil law. Property law establishes the interests that persons can have in things. It defines and constitutes what counts as wealth in an advanced society. The law of wrongs provides remedies for interference with and wrongfully caused harm to a person's interests, most significantly bodily integrity and proprietary rights, but also to some extent economic interests. Contracts, and the law of transactions generally, provide the dynamic component. Persons contract out their labour, by hand or by brain, in order to buy things – both necessaries, like food and shelter, and the non-essential essentials such as compact discs, dinner for two, a night at the cinema. All this exchanging is done via the medium of that strange repository of universal value: money. Not all transfers of wealth, however, are intended; and not all transactions turn out as planned. This is where restitution comes into the picture. Just as a mature legal system needs rules which give effect to and recognise voluntary transfers of wealth, so it needs rules which govern transactions that go wrong. Some shifts in wealth require reversal. Some transactions need to be unwound. The law of restitution 'mops-up' in these situations. It is the necessary corollary of the law of contract and the rules governing other voluntary dispositions of wealth.

The law of restitution is founded upon the principle of unjust enrichment (Goff and Jones, *The Law of Restitution*, 4th edn., 12–16). This is not an abstract principle, aspiring to effect natural justice or dependent upon the moral convictions of the particular judge; rather, the law of restitution is a body of positive law, derived from judicial responses to concrete fact situations in the decided cases.

> The recovery of money in restitution is not, as a general rule, a matter of discretion for the court. A claim to recover money at common law is made as a matter of right; and even though the underlying principle of recovery is the principle of unjust enrichment, nevertheless, where recovery is denied, it is denied on the basis of legal principle. (*per* Lord Goff of Chieveley in *Lipkin Gorman* v *Karpnale Ltd* [1991] 2 AC 548, at 578).

This is not to say that restitution is incapable of developing and adapting to meet new situations and new modes of transacting: 'The categories of unjust enrichment are not closed' (*per* Sir Donald Nicholls V-C in *CTN Cash and Carry Ltd* v *Gallaher Ltd* [1994] 4 All ER 714, at 720). Indeed the second half of the twentieth century has seen significant development and refinement of the principles of restitution both in the case law and in juristic writings. Established restrictions on recovery are being tested to see whether they are consistent with principle or can be justified for reasons of policy: see, for example, discussion of the mistake of law bar (Chapter 2, Section 2); the requirement that a failure of consideration should be *total* (Chapter 4, Section 1) and the insistence on *restitutio in integrum* or precise counter-restitution as a pre-condition to rescission (Chapter 2, Section 4 and Chapter 8, Section 3). Such development and refinement is proceeding in accordance with the common law tradition on a case-by-case basis.

A: *The components of a restitution claim*

There is now increasing consensus on the structure of the restitutionary inquiry. This sequence of questions informs all modern academic writing on the subject and increasingly is found in judicial utterance. It is derived from the path-breaking work of Goff and Jones and Professor Birks and depends upon the conception of restitution as aimed at reversing the unjust enrichment of the defendant at the expense of the plaintiff:

(a) Was the defendant *enriched*?
(b) If so, was the enrichment *at the expense of the plaintiff*?
(c) If so, is it *unjust* for the defendant to retain the benefit?
(d) Has the defendant any *defence* which extinguishes or reduces his prima facie liability to make restitution?

Enrichment
The defendant may have benefited either by receipt of money, property or services, or by profiting from wrongdoing. This is essential to the inquiry, although it is often simply assumed without explicit analysis in much discussion of restitutionary issues. The issues are analysed in Section 3 of this chapter.

At the expense of the plaintiff
This is essentially a causal question: Is the plaintiff a proper person to sue? To use a word more common in public law, does the plaintiff have *standing*? The question may be satisfied in two ways. First, the plaintiff can show a corresponding plus and minus: the defendant has benefited to a degree that precisely matches the diminution in the plaintiff's wealth, and that benefit can be identified as passing from the plaintiff to the defendant. Secondly, the plaintiff can assert that the defendant benefited by committing a wrong and thereby as a result of a breach of a legal duty owed to the plaintiff. For Professor Birks this question leads to the most signficant bifurcation in the law of restitution. The former category of case constitutes *autonomous* or *subtractive* unjust enrichment, and the latter *restitution for wrongs*. The former is the substantive part of the subject, whereas the latter is only one of a number of possible remedial responses to a cause of action arising in the law of wrongs (Birks, *Introduction*, 99).

Most of this book is concerned with subtractive unjust enrichment. Restitution for wrongs is considered in Chapter 6.

Unjust
Most of the law of restitution is concerned with whether or not the defendant should be made to disgorge the benefit received. English law has generally taken a concrete fact-based approach to this issue and asks questions which are readily intelligible to lawyer and lay-person alike: Was the plaintiff mistaken or compelled? Did the basis of the transfer collapse? Did the defendant benefit by reason of a wrong done to the plaintiff? Therefore mistake, compulsion, failure of consideration and wrongdoing are the main reasons for restitution in English law. These are commonly termed *unjust factors* or *grounds for restitution*. Both terms are used in this book. The former is inelegant but may be slightly preferable to the latter which is not sufficiently precise, being ambiguous between *unjust* enrichment and unjust enrichment. That is, it fails adequately to distinguish the inquiry into the injustice of receipt from the enrichment inquiry.

Defences
The defendant may still be able to defeat or diminish the plaintiff's prima facie entitlement to restitution by establishing the facts which entitle reliance on one of the restitutionary defences, such as good faith purchase or change of position. Alternatively, public policy may preclude a restitutionary claim. These matters are the concern of Chapter 8.

B: *Implied contract or unjust enrichment?*

Moses v *Macferlan*
(1760) 2 Burr 1005; 97 ER 676 (KB)

Action for money had and received

Moses endorsed to Macferlan four promissory notes, made by Jacob in favour of Moses, in order that Macferlan should recover the sums in his name against Jacob. It was agreed in writing that the endorsements should not prejudice Moses. However, when Jacob did not pay Macferlan sued Moses in the Court of Conscience, which decided that it could not look into the defence based on the agreement and therefore awarded Macferlan the sums owing on the promissory notes. Moses's agent paid the money into court. Then Moses sued Macferlan in the Court of King's Bench where at trial the jury found for Moses, and the court unanimously held that he was entitled to restitution.

LORD MANSFIELD: There was no doubt at the trial, but that upon the merits the plaintiff was entitled to the money; and the jury accordingly found a verdict for the 6l subject to the opinion of the Court upon this question, 'whether the money might be recovered by this form of action,' or 'must be by an action upon the special agreement only.'

Many other objections, besides that which arose at the trial, have since been made to the propriety of this action in the present case.

The 1st objection is, 'that an action of debt would not lie here; and no assumpsit will lie, where an action of debt may not be brought:' some sayings at Nisi Prius, reported by note takers who did not understand the force of what was said, are quoted in support of that proposition. But there is no foundation for it.

It is much more plausible to say, 'that where debt lies, an action upon the case ought not to be brought.' And that was the point relied upon in *Slade's case*: but the rule then settled and followed ever since is, 'that an action of assumpsit will lie in many cases where debt lies, and in many where it does not lie.'

A main inducement, originally, for encouraging actions of assumpsit was, 'to take away the wager of law:' and that might give rise to loose expressions, as if the action was confined to cases only where that reason held.

2d objection.—'That no assumpsit lies, except upon an express or implied contract: but here it is impossible to presume any contract to refund money, which the defendant recovered by an adverse suit.'

Answer. If the defendant be under an obligation, from the ties of natural justice, to refund; the law implies a debt, and gives this action, founded in the equity of the plaintiff's case, as it were upon a contract ('quasi ex contractu', as the Roman law expresses it).

This species of assumpsit, ('for money had and received to the plaintiff's use,') lies in numberless instances, for money the defendant has received from a third person; which he claims title to, in opposition to the plaintiff's right; and which he had, by law, authority to receive from such third person.

3d objection. Where money has been recovered by the judgment of a Court having competent jurisdiction, the matter can never be brought over again by a new action.

Answer. It is most clear, 'that the merits of a judgment can never be over-haled by an original suit, either at law or in equity.' Till the judgment is set aside, or reversed, it is conclusive, as to the subject matter of it, to all intents and purposes.

But the ground of this action is consistent with the judgment of the Court of Conscience: it admits the commissioners did right. They decreed upon the indorsement of the notes by the plaintiff: which indorsement is not now disputed. The ground upon which this action proceeds, was no defence against that sentence.

It is enough for us, that the commissioners adjudged 'they had no cognizance of such collateral matter.' We can not correct an error in their proceedings; and ought to suppose what is done by a final jurisdiction, to be right. But we think, 'the commissioners did right, in refusing to go into such collateral matter.' Otherwise, by way of defence against a promissory note for 30s. they might go into agreements and transactions of a great value: and if they decreed payment of the note, their judgment might indirectly conclude the balance of a large account.

The ground of this action is not, 'that the judgment was wrong:' but, 'that, (for a reason which the now plaintiff could not avail himself of against that judgment,) the defendant ought not in justice to keep the money.' And at Guildhall, I declared very particularly, 'that the merits of a question, determined by the commissioners, where they had jurisdiction, never could be brought over again, in any shape whatsoever.'

Money may be recovered by a right and legal judgment; and yet the iniquity of keeping that money may be manifest, upon grounds which could not be used by way of defence against the judgment.

Suppose an indorsee of a promissory note, having received payment from the drawer (or maker) of it, sues and recovers the same money from the indorser who knew nothing of such payment.

Suppose a man recovers upon a policy for a ship presumed to be lost, which afterwards comes home;—or upon the life of a man presumed to be dead, who afterwards appears;—or upon a representation of a risque deemed to be fair, which comes out afterwards to be grossly fraudulent.

But there is no occasion to go further: for the admission 'that unquestionably, an action might be brought upon the agreement,' is a decisive answer to any objection from the judgment. For it is the same thing, as to the force and validity of the judgment, and it is just equally affected by the action, whether the plaintiff brings it upon the equity of his case arising out of the agreement, that the defendant may refund the money he received; or upon the agreement itself, that besides refunding the money, he may pay the costs and expenses the plaintiff was put to.

This brings the whole to the question saved at Nisi Prius, 'viz. whether the plaintiff may elect to sue by this form of action, for the money only; or must be turned round, to bring an action upon the agreement.'

One great benefit, which arises to suitors from the nature of this action, is that the plaintiff needs not state the special circumstances from which he concludes 'that, ex æquo et bono, the money received by the defendant, ought to be deemed as belonging to him:' he may declare generally, 'that the money was received to his use;' and make out his case, at the trial.

This is equally beneficial to the defendant. It is the most favourable way in which he can be sued: he can be liable no further than the money he has received; and against that, may go into every equitable defence, upon the general issue; he may claim every equitable allowance; he may prove a release without pleading it; in short, he may defend himself by every thing which shews that the plaintiff, ex æquo et bono, is not entitled to the whole of his demand, or to any part of it.

If the plaintiff elects to proceed in this favourable way, it is a bar to his bringing another action upon the agreement; though he might recover more upon the agreement, than he can by this form of action. And therefore, if the question was open to be argued upon principles at large, there seems to be no reason or utility in confining the plaintiff to an action upon the special agreement only. . . .

This kind of equitable action, to recover back money, which ought not in justice to be kept, is very beneficial, and therefore much encouraged. It lies only for money which, ex æquo et bono, the defendant ought to refund: it does not lie for money paid by the plaintiff, which is claimed of him as payable in point of honor and honesty, although it could not have been recovered from him by any course of law; as in payment of a debt barred by the Statute of Limitations, or contracted during his infancy, or to the extent of principal and legal interest upon an usurious contract, or, for money fairly lost at play: because in all these cases, the defendant may retain it with a safe conscience, though by positive law he was barred from recovering. But it lies for money paid by mistake; or upon a consideration which happens to fail; or for money got through imposition, (express, or implied;) or extortion; or oppression; or an undue advantage taken of the plaintiff's situation, contrary to laws made for the protection of persons under those circumstances.

In one word, the gist of this kind of action is, that the defendant, upon the circumstances of the case, is obliged by the ties of natural justice and equity to refund the money. . . .

Notes

1. This powerful statement of restitutionary principle is weakened by the actual decision in the case. The Court of Conscience was a court of competent jurisdiction (a small claims court in effect) and under the general rule of *res judicata* the parties to an action already adjudicated are estopped from relitigating the question. There must be an end to litigation (see Goff and Jones, 763–4; *Marriott* v *Hampton* (1797) 7 Term Rep 269, 101 ER 969).

2. See Birks, 'English and Roman Learning in *Moses* v *Macferlan*' [1984] CLP 1, for a fascinating account of the case's importance in relation to the English forms of action and in relation to its reception of Roman law ideas. Birks makes the point that Lord Mansfield's references to 'equity' are a reference to natural justice (the Roman '*aequitas*') not to that body of law which was administered originally by the English Lord Chancellor.

Baylis* v *Bishop of London
[1913] 1 Ch 127 (CA)

Action for money had and received

Hamilton LJ cited Lord Mansfield in *Sadler* v *Evans* (1766) 4 Burr 1984 at 1986; 98 ER 34 at 35, where he said the action for money had and received 'is a liberal action, founded upon large principles of equity, where the defendant cannot conscientiously hold the money. The defence is any equity which will rebut the action'. Hamilton LJ continued:

HAMILTON LJ: . . . The truth is that the language of Lord Mansfield's judgment upon the action for money had and received must be applied to other cases with great caution. He described himself as being 'a great friend' to the action, and he was therefore 'not for stretching, lest I should endanger it': *Weston* v *Downes* (1778) 1 Doug 23. From his language in *Moses* v *Macferlan* 2 Burr 1005 and *Longchamp* v *Kenny* (1779) 1 Doug 137 he would seem to have favoured it quite as much because of the extreme informality of the pleadings, as because it was 'governed by the true equity and conscience of the case.' It is true that he says of it that the defendant may go into every equitable defence and claim every equitable allowance. So, too, Buller J (of whose knowledge of equity Lord Thurlow spoke disrespectfully) says in *Straton* v *Rastall* (1788) 2 TR 366, 370 that the action was extended by the Court of King's Bench 'on the principle of its being considered like a bill in equity,' and that 'to recover money in this form of action, the party must shew that he has equity and conscience on his side, and that he could recover it in a Court of Equity.' As late as 1842 the Court of Common Pleas spoke of the principle 'which has been held since the time of Lord Mansfield, that where money is due ex æquo et bono, it may be recovered in an action for money had and received': *Smith* v *Jones* (1842) 1 Dowl PC (NS) 526. But the appellant can derive little aid from such generalities. Since then a bill for money had and received, (being money paid under a mistake of fact) has been successfully demurred to for want of equity: *Lamb* v *Cranfield* (1874) 43 LJ (Ch) 408; and in *Rogers* v *Ingham* (1876) 3 ChD 351, 355 James LJ says: 'The law on the subject was exactly the same in the old Court of Chancery as in the old Courts of Common Law. There were no more equities affecting the conscience of the person receiving the money in the one Court than in the other Court, for the action for money had and received proceeded upon equitable considerations.' In effect, therefore, both the equitable and the legal considerations applicable to the recovery of money paid under a mistake of fact have been crystallized in the reported common law cases. The question is whether it is conscientious for the defendant to keep the money, not whether it is fair for the plaintiff to ask to have it back. To ask what course would be ex æquo et bono to both sides never was a very precise guide, and as a working rule it has long since been buried in *Standish* v *Ross* 3 Ex 527 and *Kelly* v *Solari* 9 M & W 54. Whatever may have been the case 146 years ago, we are not now free in the twentieth century to administer that vague jurisprudence which is sometimes attractively styled 'justice as between man and man.' . . .

Note
For the facts and further extracts from this case see Chapter 8, Section 2.

Sinclair v *Brougham*
[1914] AC 398 (HL)

Action for money had and received; tracing in equity
The Birkbeck Building Society was formed in 1851 under the Building Societies Act 1836. It developed a very considerable banking business and was popularly known as the Birkbeck bank. In 1911 the society was wound up. The assets were sufficient to pay outside creditors, but were insufficient to meet the claims of shareholders and depositors. The action was brought to determine the respective rights of shareholders and depositors. *Held*: first, the carrying on of the banking business by the society was *ultra vires*. Secondly, the depositors were not entitled to claim the money deposited *in personam* in an *action for money had and received*. Thirdly, the depositors were however entitled to trace their money and succeed in an *in rem* claim on the authority of *In re Hallett's Estate* (1880) 13 Ch D 696. Fourthly, the remaining assets ought to be distributed *pari passu* between the shareholders and depositors.

LORD SUMNER: The depositors' case has been put, first of all, as consisting in a right enforceable in a common law action. It is said that they paid their money under a mistake of fact, or for a consideration that has wholly failed, or that it has been had and received by the society to their use. My Lords, in my opinion no such actions could succeed. To hold otherwise would be indirectly to sanction an ultra vires borrowing. All these causes of action are common species of the genus assumpsit. All now rest, and long have rested, upon a notional or imputed promise to repay. The law cannot de jure impute promises to repay, whether for money had and received or otherwise, which, if made de facto, it would inexorably avoid.

To the other difficulties of such claims I will allude shortly. There was no mistake of fact. The facts were fully known so far as was material. The rules and objects of the society were accessible to all. The only mistake made was a mistake as to the law, or that mistake of conduct to which all of us are prone, of doing as others do and chancing the law.

There was no failure of consideration. As Bowen LJ says in the *Guardian Case* [*In re Guardian Permanent Benefit Building Society* (1882) 23 ChD 440], 'Those who deal with a society which professes to have power to borrow have equal means of knowledge with the society itself of the statutory powers of the company; they are put, so to speak, upon inquiry whether the company really can borrow validly or not, and if they choose to lend their money to a company which cannot properly borrow it cannot be said there is a failure of consideration. The company has got their money, it is true, but they must be taken to have known what they bought, and to have been willing to pay their money on the chance.'

Further, the depositors' money was not had and received by the society, but by its officers, and receipt is an essential: *Prince* v *Oriental Bank Corporation* (1878) 3 App Cas 325. If it was ultra vires for the society to take customers' accounts, that is, in the eye of the law, to borrow the money on its promise to repay, it was ultra vires for it to authorise its officers to do so on its behalf. The money—cheques, bills, and so forth—has no doubt reached the society's coffers, and thereafter has been dealt with as the depositors were willing and intended that it should be dealt with, and, so far as has appeared in this case, the officers of the society are not now chargeable. The society has the proceeds, or rather the liquidator has them, in that sense of possession which is necessary to found 'tracing orders' and otherwise for the purpose of the winding-up, but it has not got them and there is no receipt of them in the sense which is necessary to raise the implication of a promise to repay that would bind the society.

In these straits, Lord Mansfield's celebrated account of the action of money had and received in *Moses* v *Macferlan* 2 Burr 1005 was of course relied upon. It was said that for any one to keep the depositors' money as against them would be unconscientious, while that they should get it back would be eminently ex æquo et bono, though it appeared also that conscience had nothing to say against payment of the depositors in full at the expense of the shareholders, though all alike must be deemed cognizant of the invalidity of the society's banking business. . . . The action for money had and received cannot now be extended beyond the principles illustrated in the decided cases, and although it is hard to reduce to one common formula the conditions under which the law will imply a promise to repay money received to the plaintiff's use, I think it is clear that no authority extends them far enough to help the appellants now.

Resort was then had to equity, and, as I understand it, the argument was that the action for money had and received was founded on equity and good conscience, and imported a head of equity (apart altogether from its possibly too limited application at law), namely, that whenever it is ex æquo et bono for A to repay money which he has received from B, and would be against conscience for A to keep it, then B has an equity to have A decreed to repay it. For this again Lord Mansfield's authority in the same case was invoked.

My Lords, I cannot but think that Lord Mansfield's language has been completely misunderstood. Historically, the action for money had and received was not devised by the Court of Chancery, nor was it applied there either in form or in substance. It was a form of assumpsit, already old in Lord Mansfield's time, and his own citation of earlier actions of this sort should be enough to shew, if that were necessary, that he never thought otherwise. It was said to be a 'liberal' action in that it was attended by a minimum of formality, and was elastic and readily capable of being adapted to new circumstances. The action has been decsribed as 'liberal' because 'the party waives all torts, trespasses, and damages.' In and after Lord Mansfield's time its liberality in point of practice is shewn by the fact that the plaintiff declared with a minimum of particulars and the defendant pleaded the general issue, under which he could prove almost anything (see 2 Williams' Saunders, 120, Notes to *Chandler* v *Vilett*; *Orton* v *Butler* (1822) 5 B & Ald 652; *Owen* v *Challis* (1848) 17 LJ (CP) 266. No doubt it gave scope (at least in days when reported cases were less multitudinous than now) for decisions to meet what is called the 'justice of the case.' These features attracted Lord Mansfield, chafing already at the rigidity of the older forms of action, and emulous no doubt of the adaptability and growth which characterised the doctrines of equity in his name. He, and Buller J, spoke of the action in somewhat varying terms from time to time (see *Weston* v *Downes* (1778) 1 Doug 23; *Longchamp* v *Kenny* (1779) 1 Doug 137; *Sadler* v *Evans* (1766) 4 Burr 1984; *Straton* v *Rastall* (1788) 2 TR 366). Lord Mansfield, who in *Clarke* v *Shee* (1774) Cowp 197 merely described the action as 'a liberal action in the nature of a bill in equity,' in *Towers* v *Barrett* (1786) 1 TR 133 says it is 'founded on principles of eternal justice.' In *Straton* v *Rastall* (1788) 2 TR 366 Buller J says that 'Of late years this Court has very properly extended the action for money had and received; it is founded on principles of justice, and I do not wish to restrain it in any respect. But it must be remembered that it was extended on the principle of its being considered like a bill in equity. And, therefore, in order to recover money in this form of action, the party must show that he has equity and conscience on his side, and that he could recover it in a Court of Equity.' But the reported cases do not shew how, if at all, this obligation was enforced. I think it is evident that Lord Mansfield did not conceive himself to be deciding that this action was one in which the Courts of common law administered 'an equity' in the sense in which it was understood in the Court of Chancery (see observations of Farwell LJ in *Baylis* v *Bishop of London* [1913] 1 Ch 127, and the cases actually decided shew that the description of the action as being founded in the æquum et bonum is very far from being precise. Even the decision in *Moses* v *Macferlan* 2 Burr 1005, which has since been dissented from, for some time unsettled the law (see Smith's Leading Cases, Notes to *Marriot* v *Hampton* (1797) 7 TR 269; 2 Sm LC (11th ed.) 421, and this last-mentioned case is one which illustrates the proposition that money is not thus recoverable in all cases where it is unconscientious for the defendant to retain it, for no one could doubt that Hampton's retention of the money in that case was very like sharp practice. *Crockford* v *Winter* (1807) 1 Camp 124 and *Martin* v *Morgan* (1819) 1 Brod & B 289 are instances, on the other hand, which shew that Lord Ellenborough and Dallas CJ respectively understood that in that form of action the Court strove to do what was just and not to administer equity. With whatever complacency the Court of King's Bench might regard the views expressed in *Moses* v *Macferlan* 2 Burr 1005, protests were very early made against it in the Common Pleas (*Johnson* v *Johnson* (1802) 3 Bos & P 162, at p. 169), and in *Miller* v *Atlee* (1849) 3 Ex 799; 13 Jur 431 Pollock CB bluntly declared the notion that the action for money had and received was an equitable action to be 'exploded,' and Parke B, sitting by him, did not say him nay. This episode is reported only in 13 Jurist, but it smacks of truth. Since, then, allusions have been made from time to time to the connection between this cause of action and equity or the æquum et bonum (though they are not precisely the same things), for example, in *Smith* v *Jones* (1842) 1 Dowl PC (NS) 526, *Tregoning* v *Attenborough* (1830) 7 Bing 97, *Rogers* v *Ingham* (1876) 3 ChD 351, *Phillips* v *London School Board* [1898] 2 QB 447, at p. 453, and *Lodge* v *National Union Investment Company* [1907] 1 Ch 300, at p. 312, but I take them all to be merely descriptive of the undoubtedly wide scope of this essentially common law action. There is now no ground left for suggesting as a recognisable 'equity' the right to recover money in personam merely because it would be the right and fair thing that it should be refunded to the payer. . . .

Notes

1. Lord Sumner went on to hold that the depositors could in any event follow their money in equity.

2. For equitable tracing and further discussion of this case see Chapter 7, Section 2.

3. The question here, in plain language, was whether the building society's legal incapacity should operate as a defence to the depositors' restitutionary claim. Or in other words, did the public policy (*ultra vires*) which barred the claim on the invalid contract of loan, also preclude a restitutionary action? The 'implied contract' reasoning obscures that question. The resulting judgment, that the public policy matters to the claim at law but does not matter to the claim in equity, appears to be inconsistent. (See Burrows, *The Law of Restitution*, 457–9.) For discussion of public policy as a bar to restitution see Chapter 8, Section 4.

Holt v *Markham*
[1923] 1 KB 504 (CA)

Action for money had and received

SCRUTTON LJ: This is a troublesome instance of a particularly troublesome class of action. It is an action for money had and received to the plaintiffs' use, and is based upon the ground that the payment was made under a mistake of fact. Now ever since the time when that great judge, Lord Mansfield, with no doubt a praiseworthy desire to free the Court from the fetters of legal rules and enable them to do what they thought to be right in each case, obscured, in my respectful view, the nature of the action for money had and received, by saying in *Sadler* v *Evans* (1766) 4 Burr 1984, 1986: 'It is a liberal action, founded upon large principles of equity, where the defendant cannot conscientiously hold the money. The defence is any equity that will rebut the action,' the whole history of this particular form of action has been what I may call a history of well-meaning sloppiness of thought. I do not propose to repeat the very pungent criticisms which Lord Sumner has made upon that now discarded doctrine of Lord Mansfield in *Baylis* v *Bishop of London* [1913] 1 Ch 127 or in *Sinclair* v *Brougham* [1914] AC 398, but I respectfully entirely agree with what he says in the former case: 'To ask what course would be ex æquo et bono to both sides never was a very precise guide, and as a working rule it has long since been buried in *Standish* v *Ross* (1849) 3 Ex 527 and *Kelly* v *Solari* 9 M & W 54. Whatever may have been the case 146 years ago, we are not now free in the twentieth century to administer that vague jurisprudence which is sometimes attractively styled "justice as between man and man"'; and with the similar passage in *Sinclair* v *Brougham* [1914] AC 456: 'There is now no ground left for suggesting as a recognisable "equity" the right to recover money in personam merely because it would be the right and fair thing that it should be refunded to the payer.' I also agree with Lord Sumner's view that it is very hard to reduce to one common formula the conditions under which the law will imply a promise to repay money received to the plaintiff's use. I do not think the time has come in this case to do it. There is something to be said for the view that payment under a mistake of fact is not payment at all, and is therefore capable of rectification in cases in which the defendant receives the money under a mistake of fact or has done something to contribute to the plaintiff's mistake of fact, but that the position is otherwise where the defendant is under no mistake of fact and has done nothing to contribute to the plaintiff's mistake, and does not appreciate that the payer is making the payment under a mistake of fact. However, the time has not yet come to attempt to settle conclusively what is the one formula which will embrace all the cases in which the common law would have allowed an action for money had and received in consequence of a payment under a mistake of fact. . . .

Note

For further discussion of this case see Chapter 2, Section 1 and Chapter 8, Section 2.

Restatement of the Law of Restitution: Quasi Contracts and Constructive Trusts

(St. Paul, American Law Institute, 1937)

§ 1 Unjust enrichment

A person who has been unjustly enriched at the expense of another is required to make restitution to the other. . . .

§ 2 Officious conferring of a benefit

A person who officiously confers a benefit upon another is not entitled to restitution therefor. . . .

§ 3 Tortious acquisition of a benefit

A person is not permitted to profit by his own wrong at the expense of another. . . .

§ 160 Constructive trust

Where a person holding title to property is subject to an equitable duty to convey it to another on the ground that he would be unjustly enriched if he were permitted to retain it, a constructive trust arises.

Morgan v *Ashcroft*

[1938] 1 KB 49 (CA)

Action for money had and received

SCOTT LJ: . . . This whole group of common law actions known as 'implied assumpsit' or 'implied contract' permits the redress of so many widely different types of grievance, and thus is so useful in our jurisprudence, that it seems to me just as important not to cut them down as it is not to enlarge them beyond their true legal boundaries. And of them all the action for money had and received has the greatest variety of application and is perhaps the most useful. The name 'implied contracts' is ambiguous, as it is often used of true consensual contracts, which are not wholly expressed in writing or orally and have to be inferred in greater or lesser degree from the conduct of the parties. The implied contract for money had and received has no element of agreement about it; it is implied in law, the name being a misnomer. The history of implied contracts in the non-consensual sense has passed through two stages—the first during the 17th and 18th centuries, when it was being invented by the Courts and its range was ever expanding; the second from the middle of the 19th century, since when the pendulum has swung the other way and our common law Courts have tended to restrict it. It is not relevant to the present case to consider that history in detail, but the 14th Lecture by the late Professor Ames upon Implied Assumpsit printed in his Lectures on Legal History (Harvard 1913, p. 149) is full of illumination. He brings out clearly the complete absence of any consensual element. There is no doubt that the moral principle of 'unjust enrichment,' to which he refers and which is recognised in some systems of law as a definite legal principle, and indeed underlay Lord Mansfield's famous dictum in *Moses* v *Macferlan* 2 Burr 1005 in the year 1760, has now been rejected by English Courts as a universal or complete legal touchstone whereby to test this cause of action. But Professor Ames was as late as the early years of the present century still treating that principle as the underlying source of obligation upon the basis of which the action had been developed in our common law: see pp. 160 and 166. Leake devoted a long sub-division of the First Edition of his book on Contracts (published in 1867) to the title of 'Contracts Implied in Law' (pp. 38 to 75) and commenced it with these two paragraphs:

> Simple contracts arising independently of agreement, or contracts implied in law, include those transactions affecting the two parties, other than agreement between them, upon which the law operates by imposing a contract, that is, a liability on the one side and correlative right on the other.
>
> The transactions between two parties, other than agreement, which give rise to contracts, may be described generally as importing that some undue pecuniary inequality exists in the one party relatively to the other, which justice and equity require should be compensated, and upon which the law operates by creating a debt to the amount of the required compensation.

The Third Edition of Bullen & Leake (1868) at p. 44 under the title of the 'indebitatus count for money had and received,' repeated the effect of the second of the above sentences; so did Professor Dicey in his book on Parties to an Action, published in 1870, at p. 91.

So wide a statement of the principle upon which the action for money had and received is founded, however eminent the jurists who supported it, does not at the present time afford an authoritative criterion by which the Court can decide whether a given claim discloses a cause of action for money had and received. The test is too vague; and even if it was ever a test, it has certainly been modified by recent decisions which have restricted the field of this action: see *Baylis* v *Bishop of London* [1913] 1 Ch 127, 140, *per* Hamilton LJ; *Sinclair* v *Brougham* [1914] AC 398, 453, *per* the same learned judge as Lord Sumner; and *Holt* v *Markham* [1923] 1 KB 504, 513, *per* Scrutton LJ. But my citations from jurists of such high standing as writers on the common law do emphasize the importance of trying to find some common positive principles upon which these causes of action called 'implied contracts' can be said to rest, and which will not altogether exclude that of unjust enrichment embodied in those citations.

An additional reason for keeping the door open is the very heterogeneous list of causes of action which unquestionably fall within this field of implied contracts. They are so various in kind as almost irresistibly to invite the inference that there may be one or more unifying principles upon which they rest. If one takes the action for money had and received by way of illustration of this point, one finds assembled under that heading the following wholly different types of causes: (1) money paid in mistake of fact; (2) money paid for a consideration which has failed; (3) money paid because it was extorted colore officii, or by duress, etc.; (4) cases where the plaintiff has had an actionable wrong done him by the defendant, and 'waiving the tort' sues in assumpsit—whether any of his money has actually passed from himself to the defendant or not. In this context I venture humbly and respectfully to doubt whether the criterion suggested by Viscount Haldane LC in *Sinclair* v *Brougham* [1914] AC 398, 415 that 'the fiction' (i.e., the common law fiction of an implied contract) 'can only be set up with effect if such a contract would be valid if it really existed' is consistent with the common law history of these implied contracts; for some of them are quite incapable of formulation as real—i.e., consensual—contracts. . . .

In re Cleadon Trust Ltd
[1939] 1 Ch 286 (CA)

Action for money paid

SCOTT LJ: . . . As the law stands to-day, it is no doubt difficult to formulate any one principle which will unify all the recognised types of common law actions upon contracts implied in law, or even upon the actions for money paid. It may even be the right view, as Lord Sumner rather suggested in *Sinclair* v *Brougham* [1914] AC 398, 452 that all these old common law causes of action are to be regarded as just curious survivals of past legal history, stereotyped within the rigid boundaries of the particular facts of the decided cases, but resting on no general principle capable of wider application. There has, however, been a good deal of discussion recently on the subject by jurists; for example, Professor Winfield's 'The Province of the Law of Tort' (1931), pp. 167 to 176, and his 'Law of Tort' (1937), pp. 697 to 700; Mr Jackson on 'the History of Quasi-contract' (1936); and in the pages of the Law Quarterly Review, by Mr Jackson, vol. 53, p. 525, and by Dr C. K. Allen, vol. 54, p. 201; and I for one should be sorry to think that the common law is condemned out of hand to no further growth in this field. The fact that little development has occurred since the sixties of last century may well be an indirect result of the amalgamation of common law and equity under the Judicature Acts. As the common law judges had so often spoken of 'equitable principles' in cases of 'contracts implied in law,' it was only natural that when they became entitled to apply equity they should resort to it for the solution of new cases not directly covered by existing decisions at law. But whatever the explanation, it is clearly impossible to-day to accept Mr Evershed's submission that the common law recognises any rule of justice and fairness prima facie applicable to the present case. . . .

Note
For discussion of this case see Chapter 4, Section 4.

United Australia Ltd v *Barclays Bank Ltd*
[1941] AC 1 (HL)

Action for money had and received

LORD ATKIN: . . . I do not propose to discuss at any length the history of the claim in indebitatus assumpsit, and the cases through which that history has been traced. Very much learning has been devoted to this subject, and lawyers are indebted to Professor Ames, Sir William Holdsworth, and Professor Winfield for the light they have thrown upon the subject in well known works: and I should not like to omit the work of Mr R. M. Jackson on 'The History of Quasi-Contract in English Law,' published in 1936 in the Cambridge Studies in English Legal History, from which I have derived assistance. There is also what I hope I may respectfully call a valuable contribution to the discussion in the articles recently published by my noble and learned friend Lord Wright on *Sinclair* v *Brougham* [1914] AC 398, and a review of the American Restatement of the Law of Restitution at pp. 1 to 65 of Legal Essays and Addresses published in 1939. I have myself consulted most of the cases referred to in these works with the exception of the cases from the Year Books which I have accepted from the authors.

The story starts with the action of debt which was not necessarily based upon the existence of a contract, for it covered claims to recover sums due for customary dues, penalties for breaches of by-laws, and the like. The action of debt had its drawbacks, the chief being that the defendant could wage his law. There followed the application of the action on the case of assumpsit to debt. 'The defendant being indebted then promised.' At first there must be an express promise; then the Courts implied a promise from an executory contract: *Slade's* case (1602) 4 Coke 92(b). *Slade's* case was not a claim in indebitatus assumpsit, but the principle was applied, and it became unnecessary to prove an express promise in those cases. Then the action was allowed in respect of cases where there was no contract, executory or otherwise, as in the cases where debt would have lain for customary fees and the like; and by a final and somewhat forced application to cases where the defendant had received money of the plaintiff to which he was not entitled. These included cases where the plaintiff had intentionally paid money to the defendant, e.g., claims for money paid on a consideration that wholly failed and money paid under a mistake: cases where the plaintiff had been deceived into paying money, cases where money had been extorted from the plaintiff by threats or duress of goods. They also included cases where money had not been paid by the plaintiff at all but had been received from third persons, as where the defendant had received fees under colour of holding an office which in fact was held by the plaintiff: and finally cases like the present where the defendant had been wrongfully in possession of the plaintiff's goods, had sold them and was in possession of the proceeds. Now to find a basis for the actions in any actual contract whether express or to be implied from the conduct of the parties was in many of the instances given obviously impossible. The cheat or the blackmailer does not promise to repay to the person he has wronged the money which he has unlawfully taken: nor does the thief promise to repay the owner of the goods stolen the money which he has gained from selling the goods. Nevertheless, if a man so wronged was to recover the money in the hands of the wrongdoer, and it was obviously just that he should be able to do so, it was necessary to create a fictitious contract: for there was no action possible other than debt or assumpsit on the one side and action for damages for tort on the other. The action of indebitatus assumpsit for money had and received to the use of the plaintiff in the cases I have enumerated was therefore supported by the imputation by the Court to the defendant of a promise to repay. The fiction was so obvious that in some cases the judge created a fanciful relation between the plaintiff and the defendant. Thus in cases where the defendant had wrongly sold the plaintiff's goods and received the proceeds it was suggested in some cases, not in all, that the plaintiff chose to treat the wrongdoer as having sold the goods as his agent and so being under an implied contract to his principal to repay. Even here in the relatively more recent cases where this explanation is given by Grose J in *King* v *Leith* (1787) 2 Term Rep 141, 145 and *Marsh* v *Keating* (1834) 1 Bing NC 198, 215 by Park J in delivering the opinion of the judges in the House of Lords the wrongdoer had in fact in both cases purported to sell the goods as the agent of his principal. But the fiction is too transparent. The alleged contract by the blackmailer and the robber never was made and never could be made. The law, in order to do justice, imputed to the wrongdoer a promise which alone as forms of action then existed could give the injured person a reasonable remedy. But while it was just that the plaintiff in such cases should be able to recover the money in the possession of the other party, he was not bound to exercise this remedy: in cases where the money had been received as the result of a wrong he still had the remedy of claiming damages for tort in action for trespass, deceit, trover, and the like. But he obviously could not compel the wrongdoer to recoup him his losses twice over. Hence he was restricted to one of the two remedies: and herein as I think arose the doctrine of 'waiver of the tort.' Having recovered in contract it is plain that the plaintiff cannot go on to recover in tort. Transit in rem judicatam. The doctrine has thus alternatively been said to be based on election: i.e., election between two remedies and the stage at which this election takes place was the subject of discussion in the argument in the present case. I will treat of election later. But at present I wish to deal with the waiver of the tort which is said to arise whenever the injured person sues in contract for money received. If the plaintiff in truth treats the wrongdoer as having acted as his agent, overlooks the wrong, and by consent of both parties is content to receive the proceeds this will be a true waiver. It will arise necessarily where the plaintiff ratifies in the true sense an unauthorised act of an agent: in that case the lack of authority disappears, and the correct view is not that the tort is waived, but by retroaction of the ratification has never existed. But in the ordinary case the plaintiff has never the slightest intention of waiving, excusing or in any kind of way palliating the tort. If I find that a thief has stolen my securities and is in possession of the proceeds, when I sue him for them I am not excusing him. I am protesting violently that he is a thief and because of his theft I am suing him: indeed he may be in prison upon my prosecution. Similarly with the blackmailer: in such a case I do not understand what can be said to be waived. The man has my money which I have not delivered to him with any real intention of passing to him the property. I sue him because he has the actual property taken: and I suggest that it can make no difference if he extorted a chattel which he afterwards sold. I protest that a man cannot waive a wrong unless he either has a real intention to waive it, or can fairly have imputed to him such an intention, and in the cases which we have been considering there can be no such intention either actual or imputed. These fantastic resemblances of contracts invented in order to meet requirements of the law as to forms of action which have now disappeared should not in these days be allowed to affect actual rights. When these ghosts of the past stand in the path of justice clanking their mediæval chains the proper course for the judge is to pass through them undeterred. . . .

Note

For the facts and further extracts from this case see Chapter 6, Section 1.

Fibrosa Spolka Akcyjna v *Fairbairn Lawson Combe Barbour Ltd* [1943] AC 32 (HL)

Action for money had and received

LORD WRIGHT: My Lords, the claim in the action was to recover a prepayment of 1000*l*. made on account of the price under a contract which had been frustrated. The claim was for money paid for a consideration which had failed. It is clear that any civilized system of law is bound to provide remedies for cases of what has been called unjust enrichment or unjust benefit, that is to prevent a man from retaining the money of or some benefit derived from another which it is against conscience that he should keep. Such remedies in English law are generically different from remedies in contract or in tort, and are now recognised to fall within a third category of the common law which has been called quasi-contract or restitution. The root idea was stated by three Lords of Appeal, Lord Shaw, Lord Sumner and Lord Carson, in *R. E. Jones Ld.* v *Waring & Gillow Ld.* [1926] AC 670, 696, which dealt with a particular species of the category, namely, money paid under a mistake of fact. Lord Sumner referring to *Kelly* v *Solari* (1841) 9 M & W 54, where money had been paid by an insurance company under the mistaken impression that it was due to an executrix under a policy which had in fact been cancelled, said: 'There was no real intention on the company's part to enrich her.' Payment under a mistake of fact is only one head of this category of the law. Another class is where, as in this case, there is prepayment on account of money to be paid as consideration for the performance of a contract which in the event becomes abortive and is not performed, so that the money never becomes due. There was in such circumstances no intention to enrich the payee. This is the class of claims for the recovery of money paid for a consideration which has failed. Such causes of action have long been familiar and were assumed to be common-place by Holt CJ in *Holmes* v *Hall* (1704) Holt 36 in 1704. Holt CJ was there concerned only about the proper form of action and took the cause of the action as beyond question. He said:

> If A give money to B to pay to C upon C's giving writings, etc., and C will not do it, indebit will lie for A against B for so much money received to his use. And many such actions have been maintained for earnests in bargains, when the bargainor would not perform, and for premiums for insurance, when the ship, etc., did not go the voyage.

The Chief Justice is there using earnest as meaning a prepayment on account of the price, not in the modern sense of an irrevocable payment to bind the bargain, and he is recognising that the indebitatus assumpsit had by that time been accepted as the appropriate form of action in place of the procedure which had been used in earlier times to enforce these claims such as debt, account or case.

By 1760 actions for money had and received had increased in number and variety. Lord Mansfield CJ, in a familiar passage in *Moses* v *Macferlan* (1760) 2 Burr 1005, 1012, sought to rationalise the action for money had and received, and illustrated it by some typical instances. 'It lies,' he said, 'for money paid by mistake; or upon a consideration which happens to fail; or for money got through imposition (express, or implied;) or extortion; or oppression; or an undue advantage taken of the plaintiff's situation, contrary to laws for the protection of persons under those circumstances. In one word, the gist of this kind of action is, that the defendant, upon the circumstances of the case, is obliged by the ties of natural justice and equity to refund the money.' Lord Mansfield prefaced this pronouncement by observations which are to be noted.

'If the defendant be under an obligation from the ties of natural justice, to refund; the law implies a debt and gives this action [sc. indebitatus assumpsit] founded in the equity of the plaintiff's case, as it were, upon a contract ("quasi ex contractu" as the Roman law expresses it).' Lord Mansfield does not say that the law implies a promise. The law implies a debt or obligation which is a different thing. In fact, he denies that there is a contract; the obligation is as efficacious as if it were upon a contract. The obligation is a creation of the law, just as much as an obligation in tort. The obligation belongs to a third class, distinct from either contract or tort, though it resembles contract rather than tort. This statement of Lord Mansfield has been the basis of the modern law of quasi-contract, notwithstanding the criticisms which have been launched against it. Like all large generalisations, it has needed and received qualifications in practice. There is, for instance, the qualification that an action for money had and received does not lie for money paid under an erroneous judgment or for moneys paid under an illegal or excessive distress. The law has provided other remedies as being more convenient. The standard of what is against conscience in this context has become more or less canalised or defined, but in substance the juristic concept remains as Lord Mansfield left it.

The gist of the action is a debt or obligation implied, or, more accurately, imposed, by law in much the same way as the law enforces as a debt the obligation to pay a statutory or customary impost. This is important because some confusion seems to have arisen though perhaps only in recent times when the true nature of the forms of action have become obscured by want of user. If I may borrow from another context the elegant phrase of Viscount Simon LC in *United Australia, Ld.* v *Barclays Bank, Ld.* [1941] AC 1, 21, there has sometimes been, as it seems to me, 'a misreading of technical rules, now happily swept away.' The writ of indebitatus assumpsit involved at least two averments, the debt or obligation and the assumpsit. The former was the basis of the claim and was the real cause of action. The latter was merely fictitious and could not be traversed, but was necessary to enable the convenient and liberal form of action to be used in such cases. This fictitious assumpsit or promise was wiped out by the Common Law Procedure Act, 1852. As Bullen and Leake (Precedents of Pleading, 3rd ed., p. 36) points out, this Act, by s. 3, provided that the plaintiff was no longer required to specify the particular form of action in which he sued, and by s. 49 that (inter alia) the statement of promises in indebitatus counts which there was no need to prove were to be omitted; 'the action of indebitatus assumpsit,' the authors add, 'is [that is by 1868] virtually become obsolete.' Lord Atkin in the *United Australia* case, after instancing the case of the blackmailer, says: 'The man has my money which I have not delivered to him with any real intention of passing to him the property. I sue him because he has the actual property taken.' He adds: 'These fantastic resemblances of contracts invented in order to meet requirements of the law as to forms of action which have now disappeared should not in these days be allowed to affect actual rights.' Yet the ghosts of the forms of action have been allowed at times to intrude in the ways of the living and impede vital functions of the law. Thus in *Sinclair* v *Brougham* [1914] AC 398, 452, Lord Sumner stated that 'all these causes of action [sc. for money had and received] are common species of the genus assumpsit. All now rest, and long have rested, upon a notional or imputed promise to repay.' This observation, which was not necessary for the decision of the case, obviously does not mean that there is an actual promise of the party. The phrase 'notional or implied promise' is only a way of describing a debt or obligation arising by construction of law. The claim for money had and received always rested on a debt or obligation which the law implied or more accurately imposed, whether the procedure actually in vogue at any time was debt or account or case or indebitatus assumpsit. Even the fictitious assumpsit disappeared after the Act of 1852. I prefer Lord Sumner's explanation of the cause of action in *Jones's* case [1926] AC 670, 696. This agrees with the words of Lord Atkin which I have just quoted, yet serious legal writers have seemed to say that these words of the great judge in *Sinclair* v *Brougham* [1914] AC 398 closed the door to any theory of unjust enrichment in English law. I do not understand why or how. It would indeed be a reductio ad absurdum of the doctrine of precedents. In fact, the common law still employs the action for money had and received as a practical and useful, if not complete or ideally perfect, instrument to prevent unjust enrichment, aided by the various methods of technical equity which are also available, as they were found to be in *Sinclair* v *Brougham* [1914] AC 398. . . .

Note

For the facts and further extracts from this case see Chapter 4, Section 2.

Orakpo v *Manson Investments Ltd*
[1978] AC 95 (HL)

Subrogation

LORD DIPLOCK: . . . My Lords, there is no general doctrine of unjust enrichment recognised in English law. What it does is to provide specific remedies in particular cases of what might be classified as unjust enrichment in a legal system that is based upon the civil law. There are some circumstances in which the remedy takes the form of 'subrogation,' but this expression embraces more than a single concept in English law. It is a convenient way of describing a transfer of rights from one person to another, without assignment or assent of the person from whom the rights are transferred and which takes place by operation of law in a whole variety of widely different circumstances. Some rights by subrogation are contractual in their origin, as in the case of contracts of insurance. Others, such as the right of an innocent lender to recover from a company moneys borrowed ultra vires to the extent that these have been expended on discharging the company's lawful debts, are in no way based on contract and appear to defeat classification except as an empirical remedy to prevent a particular kind of unjust enrichment.

This makes particularly perilous any attempt to rely upon analogy to justify applying to one set of circumstances which would otherwise result in unjust enrichment a remedy of subrogation which has been held to be available for that purpose in another and different set of circumstances. . . .

Notes

1. Compare the view of Lord Edmund-Davies in the same case, who said 'Apart from specific agreement and certain well-established cases, it is conjectural how far the right of subrogation will be granted, though in principle there is no reason why it should be confined to the hitherto-recognised categories', and cited pp. 376–7 of the first edition of Goff and Jones. (See now for general discussion in the 4th edition, Goff and Jones, 589–600.)

2. Lord Diplock's theory about the contractual nature of the right to subrogation in insurance contracts, which he first advanced as Diplock J in

Yorkshire Insurance Co. Ltd v *Nisbet Shipping Co. Ltd* [1962] 2 QB 330 at 339–42, is based on the thesis that it is an implied term of every contract of indemnity insurance that the assured shall be fully indemnified but never more than fully indemnified. This theory of a peculiarly common law origin of subrogation has now been firmly rejected by the House of Lords in *Lord Napier and Ettrick* v *Hunter* [1993] AC 713 (see Chapter 7, Section 3 and especially the extract from the speech of Lord Goff of Chieveley).
3. Contrast also Lord Diplock's discussion of the objective rule of construction in contract law in *Paal Wilson & Co. A/S* v *Partenreederei Hannah Blumenthal, The 'Hannah Blumenthal'* [1983] 1 AC 854, 916. Together with estoppel he opined that the rule was 'an example of a general principle of English law that injurious reliance on what another person did may be a source of legal rights against him'. Lord Diplock therefore appears to be more sympathetic to a generalised right with respect to reliance-based liabilities, than to benefit-based liabilities.

Pavey & Matthews Proprietary Ltd* v *Paul
(1987) 162 CLR 221 (High Court of Australia)

Quantum meruit

DEANE J: . . . To identify the basis of such actions as restitution and not genuine agreement is not to assert a judicial discretion to do whatever idiosyncratic notions of what is fair and just might dictate. The circumstances in which the common law imposes an enforceable obligation to pay compensation for a benefit accepted under an unenforceable agreement have been explored in the reported cases and in learned writings and are unlikely to be greatly affected by the perception that the basis of such an obligation, when the common law imposes it, is preferably seen as lying in restitution rather than in the implication of a genuine agreement where in fact the unenforceable agreement left no room for one. That is not to deny the importance of the concept of unjust enrichment in the law of this country. It constitutes a unifying legal concept which explains why the law recognises, in a variety of distinct categories of case, an obligation on the part of a defendant to make fair and just restitution for a benefit derived at the expense of a plaintiff and which assists in the determination, by the ordinary processes of legal reasoning, of the question whether the law should, in justice, recognise such an obligation in a new or developing category of case: see *Muschinski* v *Dodds* (1985) 160 CLR 583, at pp. 619–620; Goff and Jones, *The Law of Restitution*, 2nd ed. (1978), p. 11ff [see now 4th ed., pp. 12–16].

Notes
1. For discussion of the cause of action in this case see Chapter 4, Section 4, and for extracts on the issue of public policy see Chapter 8, Section 4.
2. In this landmark case the majority of High Court of Australia, following the example of the Supreme Court of Canada in *Deglman* v *Guaranty Trust Co. of Canada and Constantineau* [1954] 3 DLR 785, at 788, 794–5, recognised unjust enrichment as the organising principle underlying causes of action in restitution.

3. The House of Lords eventually followed suit, affirming univocally in *Lipkin Gorman* v *Karpnale Ltd* [1991] 2 AC 548 (see Chapter 7, Section 1) and in *Woolwich Equitable Building Society* v *Inland Revenue Commissioners* [1993] 1 AC 70 (see Chapter 5, Section 1) that the basic principle was the prevention of unjust enrichment at the expense of the plaintiff.

4. For a discussion of the philosophical foundations of restitution see: Hedley, 'Unjust enrichment as the basis of Restitution — an overworked concept' (1985) 5 Legal Studies 56; Stoljar, 'Unjust Enrichment and Unjust Sacrifice' (1987) 50 MLR 603; McBride and McGrath, 'The Nature of Restitution' (1995) 15 OJLS 33, and Barker, 'Unjust Enrichment: Containing the Beast' (1995) 15 OJLS 457.

C. *A short history of restitution*

For the earlier history see Baker, *An Introduction to English Legal History* (London: Butterworths, 3rd ed., 1990), 409–26; Simpson, *A History of the Common Law of Contract* (Oxford: Oxford University Press, 1987), 489–505.

A convenient starting-point is the latter half of the eighteenth century when, in the celebrated (and controversial) case of *Moses* v *Macferlan* (1760) 2 Burr 1005; 97 ER 676, Lord Mansfield, the Chief Justice of the King's Bench, enumerated a list of instances where the court would award restitution in an *action for money had and received*. This taxonomy is substantially similar to any modern-day list of grounds for restitution. Lord Mansfield further stated that the reason why the court intervened was 'natural justice and equity'. This theoretical underpinning was what proved most controversial, and has proved controversial until recently.

Jumping ahead, the nineteenth century was not a period of significant development of the law of quasi-contract, but was the era of two significant Victorian reforms. First, the Common Law Procedure Act 1852 abolished the *forms of action*. The forms of action were the nominate sequence of writs which entitled a plaintiff to a remedy, if he could bring his case within the terms of a particular form. Modern law students often hear the echoes of these old forms: trespass, case, trover, assumpsit, covenant, and so on. The thing to appreciate is that what we now regard as the distinct categories of substantive law and procedure in fact developed hand-in-hand. As Professor Baker writes, 'There was a law of writs before there was a law of property, or of contract, or of tort' (see generally Baker, *An Introduction to English Legal History*, 63–83). A plaintiff had to bring his claim within the boundaries of one of these writs in order to succeed, and had to select the proper form. Development occurred as various necessary pleas were treated as fictional (that is, it became unnecessary to prove any factual basis for a routine allegation). Selecting the wrong form meant no remedy. After the reforms litigants would no longer fail because they elected to proceed by invoking an inappropriate writ. All that was necessary was to plead the facts constituting the *cause of action*, entitling the litigant to a remedy. It also became possible to join different causes of action in the same writ. ('A cause of action is simply a factual situation the existence of which entitles one person to obtain from the court a remedy against another person', *per* Diplock LJ in *Letang* v *Cooper* [1965] 1 QB 232, at 242–3.) Secondly, the Judicature Acts 1873–1875 introduced a new, unified Supreme Court (consisting of the High Court and the Court of Appeal), a new, unified set of procedural rules, and effected the *fusion* of the administration of law and equity. These reforms would eventually engender the modern law of restitution, but their immediate effect was paralysis.

The forms of action had constituted a familiar categorisation of legal ideas. A new intellectual framework for organising the body of legal material was needed. Some subjects fared better than others. For example, it was contemporaneous with these reforms that the first modern treatises on the law of contract began to be written and the subject was taught in the emerging university law schools. It was at this stage that quasi-contract, with its common procedural heritage and fictional promises and requests, was hived off as an appendix to the law of genuinely consensual contracts. This led to a hardening of the orthodoxy that the theoretical underpinning of quasi-contract was 'implied contract or promise'. But such a promise was clearly fictional and stigmatised as such by Cotton LJ in *In re Rhodes* (1890) 44 Ch D 94 (extracted in Chapter 3, Section 5). However, the 'implied contract fallacy' had an apparently distinguished pedigree. Some have attempted to trace it back to Roman law. (For discussion see Birks and Macleod, 'The Implied Contract Theory of Quasi Contract: Civilian Opinion Current in the Century before Blackstone' (1986) 6 OJLS 46.) It had commended itself to Sir William Blackstone in the first great modern treatment of English law: *Commentaries on the Laws of England* (Chicago University Press facsimile edition 1979/London, 1765–1769), III, 162). Even into the twentieth century this fictional device, useful for uniting a disparate set of precedents well understood by common lawyers before the abandonment of the forms of action, commended itself to positivist judges like Hamilton LJ, who later became Lord Sumner (*Baylis* v *Bishop of London* [1913] 1 Ch 127; *Sinclair* v *Brougham* [1914] AC 398), and Scrutton LJ (*Holt* v *Markham* [1923] 1 KB 504). It appealed to them more than what they perceived as abstract appeals to justice (especially in the rhetoric of Lord Mansfield) which they feared would introduce great uncertainty and indeterminacy into this area of the law. Those fears were not groundless and should not be ignored today, even if one rejects the adoption of the 'implied contract' theory as an inscrutable control device to ensure there is not too much restitution. (A clear parallel can be drawn with 'floodgates' fears in the tort of negligence, where similarly a control device of 'proximity' is constantly invoked by judges to deny liability, in a sense which has little to do with its true meaning of nearness in space and time.) For discussion and rejection of the 'implied contract' fallacy see Goff and Jones, 5–11.

English law still had a sequence of instances of recovery in search of a principle. The beginning of the end of the 'implied contract' theory was in the 1930s: 1931 saw the publication of Professor Winfield's very influential *The Province of the Law of Tort* with its excellent discussion of quasi-contract (at 116–89) organised around a concept of 'unjust benefit'. Even then, as Winfield remarked in his Preface (at vi), 'There is need of a good English law textbook on it and, given that, it ought to be taught as a post-graduate subject in the English law schools'. The next development was across the Atlantic with the publication by the American Law Institute of the *Restatement of the Law of Restitution* (1937). This sought to bring together for the first time the common law and equitable components of the subject as demonstrated by its sub-title: *Quasi Contracts and Constructive Trusts*. It was introduced to English lawyers in the pages of the *Law Quarterly Review* by its authors, Professors Seavey and Scott ((1938) 54 LQR 29: still an excellent introduction to this subject) and was immediately welcomed by Lord Wright ((1937) 51 Harv LR 383) and Professor Winfield ((1938) 54 LQR 529). Section 1 of the *Restatement* firmly established the theoretical underpinnings of the modern subject: restitution is awarded where one person 'has been unjustly enriched at the expense of another'. It was soon relied upon in the English appellate courts: see *United Australia Ltd* v *Barclays Bank Ltd* [1941] AC 1, where counsel (Denning KC, as he then was) relied on sections 144 and 147 (at 3), and this was adopted by Viscount Simon LC (at 18). Unjust enrichment reasoning underpins the landmark speech of Lord Wright in *Fibrosa Spolka Akcyjna* v *Fairbairn Lawson Combe Barbour Ltd* [1943] AC 32, which is today the most quoted *dictum* in restitution cases. The next landmark was the publication in 1966 of the first edition of Goff and Jones's account of *The Law of Restitution*, a truly magisterial account of English precedent. No other single event has had the same impact on the understanding and organisation of domestic law, except perhaps the publication in 1985 of Peter Birks's *An Introduction to the Law of Restitution*. These are two of the finest English law books of the century. For academic doubts about the utility of a distinct category of restitution see Atiyah, *The Rise and Fall of Freedom of Contract* (Oxford: Clarendon Press, 1979), 764–70. Meanwhile, on the judicial front, Lord Diplock remained sceptical about any general doctrine of unjust enrichment in 1978 (in *Orakpo* v *Manson Investments Ltd* [1978] AC 95), and in 1990 Lord Templeman was still resorting to the language of 'implied contract' (*Guinness plc* v *Saunders* [1990] 2 AC 663, at 689). However, in *Lipkin Gorman* v *Karpnale Ltd* [1991] 2 AC 548 and *Woolwich Equitable Building Society* v *Inland Revenue Commissioners* [1993] AC 70 the House of Lords univocally insisted that the basis of recovery in restitution was 'unjust enrichment at the expense of the plaintiff'. See Goff and Jones, 12–16 and Burrows, *Restitution*, 1–6.

D: *Contract and restitution*

Restitution has only recently emerged from the shadow of contract law, its previous subordination owing much to the 'implied contract' heresy. However, even with unjust enrichment established as the concept unifying all restitutionary claims, the relationship between these two components of the law of obligations will remain a necessarily close one. This is because, to put it broadly, restitution is concerned with defective transactions, and the majority of transactions are contracts. Contract is a massive subject, especially if one has regard to the special principles governing particular types of exchange: sale, employment, carriage and so on. The main concern of contract law is how to give effect to the parties' intentions, hence the rules governing the formation of contract, the content of the parties' obligations (express and implied terms, the construction of the contract) and the remedies for default in the event of one of the parties being in breach. All these doctrines are indubitably the province of the law of contract.

In contrast the concerns of contract and restitution intersect where for some reason the contract proves defective. The main vitiating factors in contract law clearly resemble some of the causes of action in unjust enrichment: duress, misrepresentation, mistake. Restitutionary principles may also apply where contracts are discharged following either termination for breach, or frustration. This intersection necessitates one of the most important ground rules of the law of restitution, a rule which is of structural significance for the law of obligations as a whole: *the law of restitution is not applicable where there is a subsisting contract between the parties, unless and until the contract is avoided or discharged in accordance with the rules of contract law*. This rule was elegantly stated by Lord Goff of Chieveley, in the context of a duress claim, in *Dimskal Shipping Co. SA* v *International Transport Workers' Federation, The 'Evia Luck' (No. 2)* [1992] 2 AC 152 at 165:

> . . . before the owners could establish any right to recover the money, they had first to avoid the relevant contract. Until this was done, the money in question was paid under a binding contract and so was irrecoverable in restitution. But once the contract was avoided, the money paid under it was recoverable in restitution, on the ground either of duress or possibly of failure of consideration.

So, for example, where a contract is tainted by a misrepresentation, the false statement of fact is a legal ground both for wiping out the parties' obligations and for the restoration of any benefits conferred under the defective contract. The process is compendiously known as *rescission*. Such cases may profitably be studied from the perspective either of contract, or of restitution.

Contractual and restitutionary principles also have overlapping concerns where a contract is held to be void or unenforceable. Contract is the source of the rules establishing the invalidity of the bargain. Restitution has often borne the burden of mopping-up where there has been part performance of the supposed obligations. However, judges must be sensitive to ensure that by utilising unjust enrichment ideas, they are not contradicting the policy of the law which made the deal void or unenforceable in the first place. Restitution lawyers therefore need to be acutely aware of the policies of the law of contract, and not just its cardinal principle: *pacta sunt servanda* (or, 'bargains must be upheld').

Some terminological caution is also necessary. Much has already been said about implied contracts and implied promises. These phrases should be approached warily and it should be remembered that for the old common lawyers the invocation of a fictional promise or request was simply a jurisdictional trigger which propelled a plaintiff into an appropriate form of action. Equally important, it is necessary not to confuse the *contractual doctrine of consideration* (which establishes bargain as a necessary, though not always sufficient, condition for the enforcement of promises not incorporated in deeds) with the restitutionary cause of action, *failure of consideration*. In the latter, *consideration* refers to the basis of the transaction. It is concerned with transfers of wealth which are conditional upon certain events coming to pass, or upon some stipulated counter-performance. In this sense it is wider than the contractual sphere (although the majority of cases in which the concept has been explicitly relied upon have been in the contractual context). Note also what is said about privity under the next heading.

Further reading
Birks, *Introduction*, 44–8.

E: *Direct and indirect recipients/two party and three party configurations*

Most cases in restitution concern direct recipients. A pays £100 to B by mistake. B's enrichment correlates exactly to the diminution of A's wealth. B is a direct recipient, and this is a simple two party configuration. But what if B in turn gives that £100 to C. Can A elect to sue C instead of B? There seems to be no reason in principle why A cannot pursue a remedy against either party who has been enriched at his expense, subject of course to rules ensuring that A cannot achieve double recovery. Both B and C have been incontrovertibly enriched at A's expense. It is unjust for either to retain the money as against A, because A's initial decision to transfer wealth was vitiated by mistake.

Is there any good reason of legal principle or policy why restitutionary claims should be confined to direct recipients? Some old cases contain a hint that restitution has such a restrictive rule, and christened it a 'privity' principle. The idea has been resuscitated in the work of Professor Burrows, who argues that in restitution there is a general privity restriction, confining plaintiffs to causes of action against direct recipients (Burrows, *Restitution*, 45–54). The rule as stated is subject to exceptions, but these are very closely tied to the cases where claims against indirect recipients have previously succeeded and have no obvious analytical consistency. They therefore provide little useful guidance as to when a restitutionary claim against an indirect recipient will succeed in future.

Another view is that advocated by Professor Birks: there is in principle no difference between direct and indirect recipients (Birks, *Introduction*, 138–9, 445–7; Birks, 'Misdirected Funds - Restitution from the Recipient' [1989] LMCLQ 296, at 306–8). The interests of direct and indirect recipients in the sanctity of any contracts they enter into, and their general interest in security of receipt, are adequately protected by the general defences in restitution, respectively bona fide purchase for value without notice and bona fide change of position. Bona fide purchase will be a total defence to a restitutionary claim for money brought against an indirect recipient where he exchanged some wealth for the enrichment and did so without notice of any defect in the transferor's intention. So, varying the facts of our original example, where A had paid B £100 by mistake, if B had paid the same £100 to C in exchange for a bicycle, A has no restitutionary claim against C. This is not due to a privity principle, but is a straightforward application of bona fide purchase. As was said in the previous section, a valid and subsisting contract between the parties ousts restitution in a simple two party case (where, for example, A pays B by mistake, if the payment was under the terms of binding contract A can have no recourse for restitution). In this three party configuration it is the contract between B and C which ousts restitutionary relief. The flipside of this is, unsurprisingly, that the cases where restitutionary claims have been successful against indirect recipients are, first, cases where the recipient is a volunteer (see *In re Diplock, Diplock* v *Wintle* [1948] Ch 465 (CA); affd *sub nom Ministry of Health* v *Simpson* [1951] AC 251 (HL)); secondly, cases where the recipient gave value, but that value was worthless in the eyes of the law (*Lipkin Gorman* v *Karpnale Ltd* [1991] 2 AC 548); thirdly, cases where the recipient was acting in bad faith or had notice of the circumstances giving rise to the right to restitution (*Nelson* v *Larholt* [1948] 1 KB 339).

Claims against indirect recipients often arise where B has misappropriated or misdirected A's funds, and they are then received by C. At common law and in some equity cases (e.g., *In re Diplock*) the liability of the recipient C is strict, but subject to the defence of bona fide purchase. In contrast some equity cases reach similar results, but seem to suggest that *notice* of a defect in B's entitlement to the fund is an *ingredient in the cause of action*, not a *factor negativing the defence of bona fide purchase*. These apparently fault-based restitution claims are termed '*knowing receipt*'. For discussion see Burrows, *Restitution*, 150–6 and Birks 'Misdirected Funds' [1989] LMCLQ 296.

The cases of indirect recipients or misdirected funds are often discussed in terms of *tracing* techniques, both at law and in equity. This is because to establish the indirect recipient's enrichment it is necessary to identify or follow the value which represents the plaintiff's missing wealth into the hands of the recipient. Tracing here is performing its characteristic function of identifying wealth in the hands of the defendant. Such an identification process is also necessary in straightforward two party cases, but is usually uncomplicated and rarely explicitly addressed. For tracing consider cases such as *In re Diplock*, *Lipkin Gorman* v *Karpnale Ltd* and *Agip (Africa) Ltd* v *Jackson* [1990] Ch 265, affd [1991] Ch 547, and see Chapter 7, Sections 1 and 2.

Professor Birks has also developed the concept of '*interceptive subtraction*' to cover cases where a defendant received wealth from the hands of a third party: 'If the wealth in question would certainly have arrived in the plaintiff if it had not been intercepted by the defendant *en route* from the third party, it is true to say that the plaintiff has lost by the defendant's gain' (Birks, *Introduction*, 133–4). This concept is used to explain a miscellany of cases such as *In re Diplock* (where it was the executors' misapplication of estate moneys to the charities which gave a cause of action to the next-of-kin), the cases on attornment and the old cases on usurpation of office, amongst others (Birks, *Introduction*, 133–8). For a thorough rejection of the concept as largely superfluous see Lionel Smith, 'Three-Party Restitution: A Critique of Birks's Theory of Interceptive Subtraction' (1991) 11 OJLS 481.

The case of misdirected or misappropriated funds and indirect recipients is one example of three party fact configuration (loosely described as such because it may involve more than three parties). Other multi-party configurations need to be distinguished. As will be explained below, the restitutionary techniques of the *action for money paid* and *subrogation* operate in a context where three players are relevant. Similar cases occur where a payer pays money to a defendant under an operative mistake, and that payment validly discharges an obligation owed by a third party to the defendant. The payer has no right of recourse against the defendant who received in good faith, on a principle which seems to be analogous to bona fide purchase: see *Aiken* v *Short* (1856) 1 H & N 210; 156 ER 1180 and compare *Barclays Bank Ltd* v *W. J. Simms, Son & Cooke (Southern) Ltd* [1980] QB 677 (see Chapter 2, Section 1).

Also to be distinguished are cases where B enters into a transaction with C (often a guarantee or a mortgage of property), but B's apparent consent has been procured by some legal wrong or vitiating factor committed by A. Whether the B–C transaction is tainted by A's conduct appears to turn on whether C has *notice* of the wrong or vitiating factor (usually undue influence or misrepresentation). Again there seems to be a powerful analogy with bona fide purchase, although recent discussions (again in terms of equitable jurisdiction) seem to locate *notice* as an ingredient in A's cause of action against C. For recent discussion compare *Barclays Bank plc* v *O'Brien* [1994] 1 AC 180 with *CIBC Mortgages plc* v *Pitt* [1994] 1 AC 200 (see Chapter 3, Section 2).

Three party problems have not been prominent in claims grounded upon failure of consideration, but for a recent example see *Pan Ocean Shipping Co. Ltd* v *Creditcorp Ltd, The 'Trident Beauty'* [1994] 1 WLR 161, where restitution was denied against an assignee of benefits on the basis of what was recognised to be a principle akin to bona fide purchase.

Therefore it can be seen that third parties cause problems in the law of restitution as well as in other branches of the law, such as contract. The view taken here is that the application of bona fide purchase as a defence, or principles analogous to it, will ensure that restitution reaches only those indirect recipients and third parties who ought to disgorge any benefits received. Together with the fundamental rule, discussed above, which ousts restitution from the two party context where there is a valid and effective contract, bona fide purchase protects the sanctity of contracts and facilitates commercial activity.

For a more sophisticated analysis of three party problems and bona fide purchase see Barker, 'After Change of Position: Good Faith Exchange in the

Modern Law of Restitution', in Birks, *Laundering and Tracing*, 191–215. See Chapter 8, Section 1.

Section 2: restitutionary techniques

A: *In rem and in personam*

Most restitutionary claims are *in personam*, whether having a common law or an equitable origin. Restitution is a component of the law of obligations, alongside contract and tort. Some restitutionary claims, however, amount to a claim to a right *in rem*, i.e. a claim to an interest in an asset, usually by way of trust or charge. This requires a moment's reflection on the difference between *in personam* and *in rem*, between *obligation* and *ownership*. For Professor Birks the question is one of 'exigibility'. An obligation or right *in personam* is a claim against a person. It may concern an asset, it may not. For example, a contract with a hairdresser gives rise to an obligation on the one part to cut hair, and on the other part to transfer an asset in return, normally money. In contrast a claim to ownership or a right *in rem* is a claim to an interest in a thing, which depends upon the continued existence of that thing (Birks, *Introduction*, 49–50). A claim *in personam* is a claim against a definite person, or a definite and finite number of persons in the case for example of multiple tortfeasors or a multilateral contract. In contrast a right *in rem* is a claim to an interest in an asset normally good against all the world. There may be exceptions. A finder's title to a Rolex watch, or the squatter's interest in a house may be good against all persons except the true owner, but it is still a species of right *in rem*.

Most restitutionary claims are ones which, if successful, result in a money judgment correlating to the value by which the defendant has been unjustly enriched. *In rem* claims, by contrast, result in judgment recognising or granting an interest in an asset usually by way of trust or charge. What are the motives for pursuing this sort of claim? The main one is to be a secured creditor in the event of the defendant's insolvency, to remove the asset from the (usually insufficient) pool available to general (unsecured) creditors. The other main motive is where the asset in question has increased in value, and an *in rem* claim clearly has added attractions in such circumstances.

B: *Terminology*

An unnecessary difficulty in studying restitution is terminological inexactitude. Words do not always mean what they ought to mean. The first lesson the student of this area of law must learn is to mistrust some of the labels used in the cases. Just as the canny supermarket shopper knows that 'I Can't Believe It's Not Butter' is really *margarine*, so the student must appreciate that quasi-contract has nothing to do with upholding bargains and constructive trusts bear little relation to the law regulating the administration of funds beneficially belonging to another. A further difficulty is learning to handle both the language of the old cases (*quantum meruit*, waiver of tort, etc.) and the language of the modern law (enrichment, unjust factors, and so on).

What follows is an attempt to explain in plain language some of the difficult terminology which will be encountered. These are a mixture of basic restitutionary techniques, some of them old common law forms of action, some of them devices used in the Court of Chancery. The full scope and function of these techniques will become clear only as the subject is studied. In this book, where a case has been pleaded or argued by reference to one or more of these techniques, that has been indicated before discussion of the facts. In this way the student will begin to appreciate the extent to which these techniques still dominate legal thinking, or the degree to which they are being quietly jettisoned. Obviously legal history can clarify the historical role and importance of these techniques, and for this the reader is referred to the historical material suggested earlier in the 'Short history of restitution' (above, Section 1). See, for a clear introduction, Goff and Jones, 3–5.

Action for money had and received

This form of action was the core of the old law of quasi-contract. It had a common law origin and was *personal* action which lay to recover *money* (*Nightingal* v *Devisme* (1770) 5 Burr 2589, 98 ER 361) paid by the plaintiff to the defendant in four principal situations: where the payment was made by reason of a *mistake*, or under *compulsion* or where there was a *total failure of consideration*; where the defendant was a tortfeasor, it was sometimes possible at common law by the device of *waiver of tort* for the injured plaintiff to sue for the benefits received by the defendant, rather than seek compensation for his loss in an action for damages. In addition to these two party configurations, the action also lay in some three party cases, of which the most significant was where the plaintiff could recover money which had been stolen from him or lost, which he could follow as his property in the hands of the defendant (even though the defendant was not necessarily the thief or original finder of the money). This somewhat anomalous cause of action, dependent on the arcane *common law tracing* rules, was recently revived in the leading case of *Lipkin Gorman* v *Karpnale Ltd* [1991] 2 AC 548.

The action for money had and received was derived from the versatile *indebitatus assumpsit* writ (literally 'having become indebted he promised to pay'), which originally was confined to causes of action which we would recognise today as genuinely contractual. At some point (probably during the eighteenth century) it came to be used regularly in situations which we would now recognise as restitutionary. As a pleading device it was still necessary to allege a (fictional) promise. This was a source of the 'implied contract' explanation of quasi-contract which plagued the development of a rational law of restitution long after the forms of action were buried. See Birks, *Introduction*, 29–39 and Goff and Jones, 5–11.

See in relation to *mistake*, Chapter 2, Sections 1 and 2; in relation to *compulsion*, Chapter 3, Section 1; in relation to *failure of consideration*, see Chapter 4, Sections 1 and 2; for *waiver of tort* see Chapter 6, Section 1 and for *common law tracing* see Chapter 7, Section 1.

Action for money paid
This is also a common law *personal* form of action constituting part of what was once called quasi-contract. It had a narrower scope than the action for money had and received. It lay in the following three party configuration. A plaintiff pays money to a third party and the defendant benefits from that payment. It is a prerequisite of recovery that the plaintiff's payment must discharge (extinguish) the defendant's debt. Historically it was necessary to plead that the defendant had *requested* the plaintiff's payment. Soon the form of action was used in situations where the request was implied and was clearly fictional. A clear example is *Exall* v *Partridge* (1799) 8 TR 308; 101 ER 1045. In modern restitutionary analysis the enrichment is constituted by the valid discharge of the defendant's debt, which is incontrovertibly beneficial. The ground for restitution is usually *legal compulsion*, as for example, where a plaintiff pays a defendant's debt in order to secure the release of his own goods which have been lawfully seized by the defendant's landlord as distress for rent arrears (as in *Exall* v *Partridge*), or which are subject to valid lien. The ground for restitution may also be *necessity* (see *Owen* v *Tate* [1976] QB 402). Other grounds for restitution will not be relevant while English law maintains a restrictive rule about when an unrequested payment of another's debt validly discharges the obligation. The old form of action was concerned with money, but in the modern law of restitution there is no reason why, for example, the conferment of services under legal compulsion which discharges another's obligations should not, by analogy with the action for money paid, give rise to a right to restitution (see *Gebhardt* v *Saunders* [1892] 2 QB 452).
For further discussion see Chapter 3, Sections 4 and 5.

Further reading
Birks, *Introduction*, 111–13.

Quantum meruit
This literally means 'as much as he deserved' and is now legal shorthand for 'reasonable remuneration'. It is a claim in respect of *services* rendered. There are both contractual and quasi-contractual (or restitutionary) claims on a *quantum meruit* basis. For example, if there is an otherwise complete express contract for services but no price is specified, a reasonable charge is payable (this is now statutory: s. 15, Supply of Goods and Services Act 1982). Therefore, in *British Steel Corporation* v *Cleveland Bridge & Engineering Co.* [1984] 1 All ER 504, Robert Goff J said (at 509) 'a *quantum meruit* claim (like the old actions for money had and received and for money paid) straddles the boundaries of what we now call contract and restitution, so the mere framing of a claim as a *quantum meruit* claim, or a claim for a reasonable sum, does not assist in classifying the claim as contractual or quasi-contractual'. Again history requires that a *request* is pleaded. In quasi-contractual claims this requirement is clearly satisfied where there has been a *request* for, or an *acceptance* of benefits. However, it also lies where there is no body capable of requesting or accepting services: *Craven-Ellis* v *Canons Ltd* [1936] 2 KB 403.

The courts have not been as explicit in relation to claims for services as they were in respect to claims for money, as to the ground for restitution, whether mistake, or compulsion or some other unjust factor. There are examples, however, of *quantum meruit* lying in cases of mistake (*Craven-Ellis* v *Canons Ltd*); necessity (*Rogers* v *Price* (1829) 3 Y & J 28, 148 ER 1080); and failure of consideration (*Rover International Ltd* v *Cannon Film Sales Ltd* [1989] 1 WLR 912). *Quantum meruit* cases produce further difficulties because the question of when services are enriching (if ever) is one of the most controversial in this area of the law. This question will be further discussed in relation to 'tests of enrichment' below in Section 3.

Further reading
Birks, *The Future*, 87–91.

Quantum valebat
This literally means 'as much as it was worth', and is used today to mean 'a reasonable price'. There is also the plural form: *quantum valebant*. It is a claim in respect of *goods*. It is less commonly encountered as *quantum meruit* is often used compendiously in respect of claims for both work and materials. Together they are often described as the common counts for work and materials. Again the form of action straddles contract and restitution: in an express contract for the sale of goods, if the price is not determined by the parties, a reasonable price is payable (this is now embodied in statute: s. 8, Sale of Goods Act 1979). Similarly as a matter of history a *request* is central to the pleadings, but there have been examples of quasi-contractual recovery, although again the courts have not been explicit about the ground for restitution. See, for example, the successful claim for chattels seized in *Sumpter* v *Hedges* [1898] 1 QB 673, discussed in Chapter 4, Section 1.

Rescission
This is a remedy familiar from contract law. It is often used interchangeably with the expression 'setting aside' the contract. Rescission effects the unwinding or unscrambling of a contract which is prima facie binding (because there has been offer, acceptance, consideration and/or compliance with any relevant formalities), but which in some other way has been defectively formed. It effects restitution and counter-restitution of all species of benefits: money, goods, land, intangibles. Unlike most other techniques, it was available both at common law and in equity before fusion. However, the common law remedy was restricted to fraudulent misrepresentation, so it is the more liberal rules of the Court of Chancery which are applied today. Contracts will be unwound for fraudulent misrepresentation (*Edgington* v *Fitzmaurice* (1885) 29 Ch D 459); negligent or innocent misrepresentation (*Redgrave* v *Hurd* (1881) 20 Ch D 1); mistake (*Cooper* v *Phibbs* (1867) LR 2 HL 149) and undue influence (*O'Sullivan* v *Management Agency & Music Ltd* [1985] QB 428). The language of rescission is also sometimes used in relation to the recently expanded common law doctrine of duress. Rescission is usually

concerned with two party cases, but it can also operate in three party configurations as a remedy against a person A, who benefits from a transaction with B, but does so with notice that the other party (B) has been subjected to some vitiating factor, for example misrepresentation or undue influence, by another person C: *Barclays Bank plc* v *O'Brien* [1994] 1 AC 180.

What is the role of rescission within the law of restitution? Where a contract has been defectively formed it effects mutual restitution of benefits conferred thereunder. Therefore, sometimes, rescission looks like a purely contractual remedy. For example, if a wholly executory (or unperformed) contract is rescinded because of misrepresentation, what role does restitution have? One argument is that when there is a *prima facie* binding contract each party has a legal right enforceable against the other to performance of their side of the bargain. This is recognised as a *chose in action*, a species of property right. What rescission achieves is the giving back and taking back of benefits on both sides, including each party's legal claim upon the other, whether the contract is wholly executory, or partly or fully executed. There is no reason in principle to treat the *chose in action* any differently from money or other property which passes under the contract. Therefore rescission is a characteristically restitutionary remedy. This view receives some support from a *dictum* of Robert Goff J in *Whittaker* v *Campbell* [1983] 3 All ER 582 (a criminal case) where he said (at 586):

> Looked at realistically, a misrepresentation, whether fraudulent or innocent, induces a party to enter into a contract in circumstances where it may be unjust that the representor should be permitted to retain the benefit (the chose in action) so acquired by him. The remedy of rescission, by which the unjust enrichment of the representor is prevented, though for historical and practical reasons treated in books on the law of contract, is a straightforward remedy in restitution subject to limits which are characteristic of that branch of the law.

This view is not necessarily the universally held one. For example, Professor Burrows prefers to regard rescission as a mixture of contractual and restitutionary techniques: Burrows, *Restitution*, 31–5. A different way of putting it is to say that it is a clear concern of contract law to determine when contracts are to be avoided or discharged. Rescission is one of a number of techniques for dealing with the consequences of voidability. As a technique it is clearly restitutionary in effect.

Rescission is often described as rescission *ab initio*, and it is true that it is a backward-looking remedy seeking broadly to put the parties back in the position as if the defective contract had never been made. However, it does not necessarily put the parties back precisely in the position they were before (the *status quo ante*); it operates by reversing still subsisting enrichments, and therefore aims simply to do practical justice between the parties. It can be clearly distinguished from the purely contractual remedy of *termination for*

breach (once often described as rescission for breach) which allows the victim of a breach to put an end to a contract because of a fundamental failure of performance or breach of a fundamental term by the other party. This remedy is prospective only and is combined with a right to damages (*Johnson* v *Agnew* [1980] AC 367). Termination is concerned with defective *performance*, not defective *formation*.
See further: Chapter 2, Section 4; Chapter 3, Section 2 and Chapter 8, Section 3.

Further reading
Birks, *Introduction*, 171–3.

Tracing at common law
Tracing is a technique which establishes that the defendant has been enriched and that the enrichment was at the plaintiff's expense. Of course, proof of enrichment is essential to all restitutionary claims. In claims against direct recipients (two party cases) in subtractive unjust enrichment it is usually relatively straightforward to identify a corresponding plus and minus. The language of tracing is consequently more usually found in claims against indirect recipients. The common law of tracing is underdeveloped, largely due to the flexibility of equity in this regard. Certain propositions can be advanced, though. Where money can be traced to the hands of either a direct or an indirect recipient who is not a bona fide purchaser for value without notice, the owner of the money can maintain an *action for money had and received* to recover it. Tracing in this sense is a *personal* cause of action at common law which is complete when it is shown that the money reached the hands of the recipient. It does not have to be shown that the money remains in the hands of the recipient.

In addition to the defence of *bona fide* purchase (which means that money passes into currency: *Miller* v *Race* (1758) 1 Burr 452, 97 ER 398) and other defences such as change of position, the main obstacle to claims based on tracing at common law is the dogma that money cannot be traced into a mixed fund. For examples see: *Clarke* v *Shee and Johnson* (1774) 1 Cowp 197, 98 ER 1041; *Banque Belge pour l'Etranger* v *Hambrouck* [1921] 1 KB 321 and the leading case of *Lipkin Gorman* v *Karpnale Ltd* [1991] 2 AC 548. Sometimes the common law is concerned with events after the receipt by the defendant. It seems the common law can trace value through substitution of money into other assets: *Taylor* v *Plumer* (1815) 3 M & S 562, 105 ER 721 (at least in that case against a wrongdoer). More generally the common law can trace through bank accounts, which involves the substitution of money for a claim against the bank, as long as it does not become mixed with other funds: *Banque Belge* v *Hambrouck*. For these cases and further discussion see Chapter 7, Section 1.

Further reading
Burrows, *Restitution*, 60–9; Goff and Jones, 75–83.

Tracing in equity

The equitable technique has the same object as the common law version, namely identifying the defendant's enrichment, and the same name. Apart from those two matters, the two techniques have very little in common. First, equity has no inhibitions about tracing assets into a mixed fund. Indeed it has developed sophisticated (and perhaps over-technical) rules and presumptions governing how the interests of competing claimants to commingled assets should be adjudicated. Secondly, it has its own restrictive dogma (albeit one often easily circumvented in practice) that a breach of trust or other fiduciary duty by the party misapplying assets is an essential precondition to success. Lastly, the consequences of a successful tracing exercise in equity are different. Sometimes tracing results in a personal claim termed *knowing receipt*. More usually a tracing claim in equity seeks to establish a *proprietary* entitlement to assets still identifiable in the hands of a recipient. This requires the identification exercise to proceed beyond the moment of receipt and actually to demonstrate that the enrichment survives, despite passage through mixed funds or numerous substitutions. Therefore equitable tracing is often concerned to show that the defendant was enriched and *remains enriched*. Such a claim results in one of the equitable proprietary remedies, usually either a beneficial entitlement to the property so identified generally in the shape of a *constructive trust*, or a charge over the asset in question to secure the plaintiff's claim in the shape of an *equitable lien* (as to which see below). As an equitable interest, the plaintiff's claim in tracing is always liable to be defeated by a *bona fide* purchaser.

Beyond these propositions the juridical nature of tracing in equity is controversial. In *Cowan de Groot Properties Ltd* v *Eagle Trust plc* [1992] 4 All ER 700 Knox J said (at 767) 'tracing is not an independent cause of action'. But in the very next case in the reports the Court of Appeal seemed to take a different view: *Polly Peck International plc* v *Nadir (No. 2)* [1992] 4 All ER 769. Scott LJ stated (at 776): 'Equitable tracing leads to a claim of a proprietary character. A fund is identified that, in equity, is regarded as a fund belonging to the claimant.' The view that tracing is simply a means of identification and not a remedy in itself (a view associated with the writings of Professor Birks) now has the influential support of Millett LJ in *Boscawen* v *Bajwa* [1995] 4 All ER 769, at 776.

For discussion and the cases see Chapter 7, Section 2.

Further reading

Burrows, *Restitution*, 69–76; Goff and Jones, 83–93; Birks, *Introduction*, 83–5, 91–3.

Constructive trust

An express trust divorces the legal (or paper) ownership of property from its beneficial or equitable ownership. A constructive trust is a trust imposed by law, meaning that the legal owner holds a particular asset on behalf of another. As such it is potentially a very potent restitutionary device. There is a tension between a conception of the constructive trust as a substantive institution which arises as a matter of law once certain facts are proved, and a conception of the constructive trust as a *proprietary* restitutionary remedy imposed by the court in its discretion to reverse unjust enrichment. The latter view is codified in the US *Restatement of Restitution* and is increasingly appearing in the pages of the English law reports. However, the former is supposed to be the traditional English view. This debate is often rightly castigated as an arid one. A better starting-point is not to assume that all manifestations of constructive trust are restitutionary. Within restitution the importance of the constructive trust is its *proprietary* character, which will guarantee a restitutionary claimant priority over unsecured creditors in the event of the defendant's insolvency. A constructive trust may follow a successful *tracing* exercise in subtractive unjust enrichment: compare *Chase Manhattan Bank NA* v *Israel-British Bank (London) Ltd* [1981] Ch 105 with *Re Goldcorp Exchange Ltd* [1994] 2 All ER 806. Constructive trusts are also used to force wrongdoers to disgorge their ill-gotten gains: *Attorney-General for Hong Kong* v *Reid* [1994] 1 AC 324.

See further Chapter 7, Sections 2 and 3.

Further reading
Burrows, *Restitution*, 35–45; Birks, *Introduction*, 87–90. Compare Hanbury and Martin, *Modern Equity*, 14th edn. (London: Sweet & Maxwell, 1993), 294–5. For more detail see Elias, *Explaining Constructive Trusts* (Oxford: Oxford University Press, 1990).

Equitable lien
An equitable lien or charge is a restitutionary *proprietary* remedy. It is often the result of a successful equitable *tracing* exercise. It is particularly appropriate where the plaintiff can identify an enrichment in the hands of the defendant in the form of an asset to which value belonging to the plaintiff has contributed, that is the plaintiff is entitled to a quantified interest or a part share in the asset. The lien or charge takes the form of a judicially imposed secured interest in the asset so identified. Equitable liens were discussed in *Re Hallett's Estate* (1879) 13 Ch D 696; *Sinclair* v *Brougham* [1914] AC 398; *Re Diplock* [1948] Ch 465, affd [1951] AC 251; *Space Investments Ltd* v *Canadian Imperial Bank of Commerce Trust Co. (Bahamas) Ltd* [1987] 1 WLR 1072 and *Lord Napier and Ettrick* v *Hunter* [1993] AC 713. See Chapter 7, Sections 2 and 3.

Further reading
Burrows, *Restitution*, 366–9; Birks, *Introduction*, 90–91.

Account
When the defendant is made liable to account he is subjected to a *personal* liability in equity. For example, a wrongdoer may be liable to account for profits derived from the tort of passing off:

> The purpose of ordering an account of profits in favour of a successful plaintiff in a passing off case is not to inflict punishment on the defendant. It is to prevent an unjust enrichment of the defendant by compelling him to surrender those profits, or those parts of the profit, actually made by him which were improperly made and nothing beyond this. (*per* Slade J in *My Kinda Town Ltd* v *Soll* [1983] RPC 15, at 55; reversed on another ground [1983] RPC 407 (CA).)

Account normally involves an inquiry into the gains made by a wrongdoer, and is therefore particularly appropriate for restitution for wrongs.

To add to the terminological confusion a hybrid liability has developed labelled *accountability as a constructive trustee*. This is most commonly used in the context of equitable liability for knowing receipt and knowing assistance. The words 'as a constructive trustee' do not appear to add anything and the claim appears to be a *personal* one: *Agip (Africa) Ltd* v *Jackson* [1990] Ch 265, affd [1991] Ch 547 and *Polly Peck International plc* v *Nadir (No. 2)* [1992] 4 All ER 769. The phrase is ambiguous (as well as convoluted) because in a case of knowing receipt the measure of recovery is based on the gain received by the defendant (and is properly characterised as restitutionary), whereas in knowing assistance (now better termed 'dishonest accessory liability') the liability is to make good the loss to the plaintiff, that is, it is a compensatory measure: *Royal Brunei Airlines Sdn Bhd* v *Tan* [1995] 2 AC 378.

For restitution for wrongs generally see Chapter 6 and on 'knowing assistance' or 'accessory liability' see Chapter 6, Section 5.

Resulting trust

This is included in order to ensure completeness. A resulting trust is another species of judicially imposed trust, most typically arising where a transferor's intentions have been frustrated. There is a well-known terminological and factual overlap between the operation of resulting trusts and constructive trusts. Recently, in *El Ajou* v *Dollar Land Holdings plc (No. 1)* [1993] 3 All ER 717, at 734, reversed on another ground [1994] 2 All ER 688 (CA), Millett J further muddied the waters by stating that in a tracing claim 'the trust which is operating in these cases is not some new model constructive trust, but an old-fashioned institutional resulting trust'. See also Sir Peter Millett, 'Tracing the Proceeds of Fraud' (1991) 107 LQR 71, at 76. For argument that the resulting trust is a restitutionary remedy see Birks, *Introduction*, 57–64 and Birks, 'Restitution and Resulting Trusts' in Goldstein (ed.), *Equity and Contemporary Legal Developments* (Jerusalem, 1992, 335–73). For another view see Swadling, 'A new role for resulting trusts' (1996) 16 *Legal Studies* 110. Consider also the fate of the argument based on resulting trust in *Universe Tankships Inc. of Monrovia* v *International Transport Workers' Federation, The 'Universe Sentinel'* [1983] 1 AC 366 and most recently *Westdeutsche Landesbank Girozentrale* v *Islington London Borough Council* [1994] 4 All ER 890 (see Chapter 5, Section 2).

Subrogation
Subrogation means substitution, or, using the favoured metaphor, stepping into the shoes of another. This can be a restitutionary remedy and can be *proprietary* in effect. The two main (familiar) examples of subrogation are contracts of guarantee and contracts of indemnity insurance. In the former the guarantor (or surety) undertakes an accessory liability for the debt of another (the debtor). If the creditor proceeds against the guarantor rather than against the debtor in the first instance and recovers the sum from him, the guarantor is entitled to be substituted for the *creditor* as against the debtor, and therefore has a claim for reimbursement from the debtor. It may even extend to rights in any other security given by the debtor to the creditor. In the latter, where an insurer pays the insured under an indemnity policy following the occurrence of an insured event, the insurer is entitled to be subrogated to the position of the *insured* with respect to any claims the insured has against any wrongdoer in respect of the event. For example, if my car is damaged by the negligent driving of another, and my insurance company reinstates the car, it is entitled to bring proceedings (albeit in my name) against the other motorist. In this context the technique works in tandem with the *principle of indemnity*: that is that the insured must be indemnified, but never more than fully indemnified. Therefore in both situations subrogation operates to ensure that neither the debtor nor the insured is unjustly enriched.

The technique is potentially one of more general application. However, the subject is not dealt with in detail in this text. See, for further discussion, the cases of *Sinclair* v *Brougham* [1914] AC 398, *Orakpo* v *Manson Investments Ltd* [1978] AC 95, *Esso Petroleum Co.* v *Hall, Russell & Co. Ltd, The 'Esso Bernicia'* [1989] AC 643 (Chapter 3, Section 4) and *Lord Napier and Ettrick* v *Hunter* [1993] AC 713 (Chapter 7, Section 3). See also, for clarification of the relationship between *tracing* and *subrogation*, *Boscawen* v *Bajwa* [1995] 4 All ER 769.

Further reading
Burrows, *Restitution*, 76–93; Birks, *Introduction*, 93–8, 191–2, 389–93; Mitchell, 'The Law of Subrogation' [1992] LMCLQ 483 or Mitchell, *The Law of Subrogation* (Oxford: Clarendon Press, 1994).

Section 3: tests of enrichment

BP Exploration Co. (Libya) Ltd v *Hunt (No. 2)*
[1979] 1 WLR 783 (QBD (Commercial Court)); [1981] 1 WLR 232 (CA); [1983] 2 AC 352 (HL)

ROBERT GOFF J: . . . it is always necessary to bear in mind the difference between awards of restitution in respect of money payments and awards where the benefit conferred by the plaintiff does not consist of a payment of money. Money has the peculiar character of a universal medium of exchange. By its receipt, the recipient is inevitably benefited; and (subject to problems arising from such matters as inflation, change of position and the time value of money) the loss suffered by the plaintiff is generally equal to the defendant's gain, so that no difficulty arises concerning the amount to be repaid. The same cannot be said of other benefits, such as goods or services. By their nature, services cannot be restored; nor in many cases can goods be restored, for example where they have been consumed or transferred to another. Furthermore the identity and value of the resulting benefit to the recipient may be debatable. From the very nature of things, therefore, the problem of restitution in respect of such benefits is more complex than in cases where the benefit takes the form of a money payment. . . .

Note

These general observations on the difficult question of enrichment were made in the context of claims under the Law Reform (Frustrated Contracts) Act 1943. For further discussion of the Act and this case see Chapter 4, Section 2.

J. Beatson, 'Benefit, Reliance and the Structure of Unjust Enrichment' in *The Use and Abuse of Unjust Enrichment* (Oxford: Clarendon Press, 1991), 21–5 (originally published as (1987) 40 *Current Legal Problems* 71)

I. Introduction

There is a danger that we tend to overuse our favourite concepts, particularly once we have left the familiar territory of contract and tort. For restitution lawyers the temptation is artificially to enlarge the category of obligations which are based on the defendant's unjust enrichment at the expense of the plaintiff by an overinclusive concept of enrichment. Restitution scholars have encouraged a broad approach to 'enrichment' and argued that the subject's boundaries should be limited by the grounds of relief (the question of 'unjustness') and the meaning of 'at the expense of'.[1] One consequence of a broad approach to enrichment may be to marginalise the concept of 'reliance'.[2] It is perhaps no accident that neither of the English books on Restitution[3] refers to 'reliance' in the index. In so far as reliance is considered in the text it is treated as a factor in the determination of whether something is enriching and, if so, whether it is 'at the expense of' the intervener/plaintiff. In effect reliance is treated as a sub-category of enrichment.

There is, however, an equal tendency on the part of others less enthusiastic about restitution to marginalise the role of 'unjust enrichment' as a source of obligations. This is either done by reintegrating part of quasi-contract into a new broad conception of contract[4] or by emphasising reliance as a source of obligation. Where reliance is emphasised, the fact that a plaintiff has relied on a defendant's words or conduct (especially where the reliance is detrimental) justifies imposing an obligation whether or not the defendant has gained a benefit or an enichment. The restitution interest, where such a benefit or enrichment is gained, is, on this approach, treated as a sub-category of the reliance interest. The classic example of such reasoning is Fuller and Purdue's seminal article on the reliance interest where it is said that: '. . . all of the cases coming under the restitution interest will be covered by the reliance interest'.[5] Even Atiyah, who accepts that the trend in modern law is to recognise benefit based obligations, appears to question the theoretical case for treating benefit as a source of obligation unless there has also been reliance.[6]

In other words the danger is that either reliance is made a sub-category of benefit or enrichment, or that benefit or enrichment is made a sub-category of reliance. Both may marginalise obligations based on 'consent'. My purpose is to question the first type of reductionism which is present in both the English books on Restitution.[7] I shall also seek to indicate how one might map out the appropriate territory for the concepts of 'enrichment', 'reliance', and 'consent'. Although present in Goff and Jones, this form of reduction is most clearly evident in the important and illuminating contribution to our understanding of restitution by Birks.[8] The question is not a new one. Thus, Fuller and Purdue point out that:

> The inescapable flexibility of the concept 'benefit' means that drawing the line between the reliance and the restitution interests is in the end rather an arbitrary affair. By substituting for 'benefit' a stricter term like 'enrichment' we shift the line in one direction; by substituting a looser term like 'performance received by the promisor' we shift it in the other.[9]

My concern is with services and the extent to which remedies given in respect of services rendered or received should be seen as based on the unjust enrichment of the defendant or as recompense for reliance losses. The question of whether services rendered should give rise to a remedy and, if so, how to classify that remedy has proved a difficult one to answer. This is because in the case of the rendering of services as opposed to the payment of money, 'the identity and value of the resulting benefit to the recipient may be debatable'.[10] Remedies for unrequested services have been refused for a number of reasons. These include the fact that services cannot be restored: 'one cleans another's shoes; what can the other do but put them on?'[11] It is also said that 'liabilities are not to be forced upon people behind their backs'.[12] In short, English law has generally adhered to the position that individuals should only pay for services they chose to have rendered. Even where there is an undoubted benefit to a person he will generally be allowed to 'subjectively devalue' it by saying that he did not want it or believed the service was being offered gratuitously.[13] Where a remedy is granted in respect of services rendered—and this is less exceptional than it once was—one must consider the basis of such remedy. Unrequested services may take many forms and the question is whether one explanation can sufficiently account for the remedy given whatever form the service takes.

The main forms which services may take are:

(i) those that *result* in improvements to property or in a marketable residuum in the hands of the defendant;

(ii) those where, although there is no marketable residuum, a necessary expense of the defendant is anticipated or avoided[14] (as where a debt is paid or other obligation met by the plaintiff);

(iii) those with no marketable residuum in the hands of the recipient but an increase in his human capital (as where a teacher gives a lesson to an able pupil),[15] and;

(iv) those where there is neither marketable residuum nor increase in human capital (as where an actor or a musician performs his art or where the teacher's lesson falls on deaf ears).

I shall concentrate on (iii) and (iv) which are forms of 'pure' service. Both Birks and Goff and Jones treat certain pure services as within the category of enrichment. According to Birks the function of conceptual analysis, definition, and differentiation is to reveal the skeleton of principle which holds a subject together.[16] Once this is done it can be subjected to critical review and the complex adjustments and refinements which are an inevitable feature of a mature legal subject. 'The key [he says] is a sensible balance between conceptual purity and convenience.'[17] Is the treatment of services justified by these criteria? I hope that what follows will not be dismissed as an arid exercise in categorisation for it is my belief, as I shall illustrate, that there are important practical consequences for the types of rules adopted, the arguments that will be relevant in a given case, and the relationship of obligations in respect of services with rules of contract and tort law.

But the theory comes first. At the outset something needs to be said about two relationships: that between 'restitution' and 'unjust enrichment' and that between 'restitution' or 'unjust enrichment' and other legal categories. There are basically two approaches to these relationships. As far as the relationship between restitution and unjust enrichment is concerned, the first approach equates the two and states that the law of Restitution is the law relating to all claims which are founded on the principle of unjust enrichment.[18] Its adherents recognize that the principle of unjust enrichment may also operate within other categories, for instance contract and tort, [19] but this corrective or subordinate role is distinct from the independent and primary right to restitution based on unjust enrichment. The second approach does not accept the equation between unjust enrichment and restitution for one of two reasons. One is that while unjust enrichment exerts interstitial influence over many areas it is not a complete explanation of any and there is not therefore a coherent law of Restitution.[20] The other is that in a number of situations commonly treated as 'Restitutionary' there is no *enrichment* in any ordinary sense of the word[21] and that restitutionary remedies in fact may operate as loss-splitting devices, aids to the unwinding of a contract, deterrents against unfair conduct, or methods of protecting certain relationships of dependence.

The division between those who favour the equation of restitution and unjust enrichment and those who recognise the importance of benefit-based liabilities but do not believe in a Law of Restitution based on such liabilities obviously influences the approaches to the second relationship, that between restitution or unjust enrichment and other legal categories. Dawson and Atiyah consider that unjust enrichment contributes insight and corrects doctrines framed without primary reference to it and its remedies.[22] In other words it is a supplementary or parasitic principle to be deployed to ensure 'equity' where other principles do not. Goff and Jones and Birks, on the other hand, see it as an independent category of claim.[23] These differences appear to reflect different views of the utility of conceptualizing legal principles rather than different views as to whether there should be a remedy (and if so its extent) on the facts of any given case. . . .

[1] Dawson, [*Unjust Enrichment* (1951)] p. 23; Birks, [*Introduction*] pp. 23, 40–4, 313–14, 347–55.

[2] This familiar term is used although it has been criticised; see Burrows, (1983) 99 LQR 217, 219–20 who describes the interest concerned with compensation for harm as the 'status quo' interest.

[3] Birks, Goff & Jones. There is a change of approach in the 3rd edition of Goff & Jones. In the second edition it was recognised that recompense for services rendered in an emergency might not be based on benefit to or enrichment of the defendant but now, reflecting Jones, (1980) 18 UWOntLR 447, it is also recognised that recompense for services rendered in anticipation of a contract which does not materialise may also not always be based on benefit or enrichment; see pp. 22, 341–3 (emergency) and Ch. 24 (anticipated contracts). But the implications of this for the structure of the subject are not considered, e.g. in the section (pp; 16–22) on the character of the benefit.

[4] See Atiyah, *Rise and Fall; Promises, Morals and the Law* (1981), hereafter *Promises;* S. Levmore, 'Explaining Restitution' (1985) 71 Va L Rev 65; H. Collins, *The Law of Contract* (1986) pp. 51–2.
[5] 'The Reliance Interest in Contract Damages' (1936) 46 Yale LJ 52, 55.
[6] *Promises*, pp. 34–6.
[7] Reductionism is not inevitable; it is avoided by Stoljar, where, albeit in language which is not particularly clear ('proprietary' and 'contractual') the different strands of liability are kept separate. See also Childres & Garamella, (1969) 64 NwULR 433.
[8] *An Introduction to the Law of Restitution* (1985). The paperback edition (1989) contains a number of end notes including a short response to the points made in the original version of this essay.
[9] (1936) 46 Yale LJ 52, 72.
[10] *BP Exploration Co. (Libya) Ltd* v *Hunt (No. 2)* [1979] 1 WLR 783, 799 (Robert Goff J).
[11] *Taylor* v *Laird* (1856) 25 LJ Ex 329, 332 (Pollock CB).
[12] *Falcke* v *Scottish Imperial Insurance Co.* (1886) 34 ChD 234, 248 (Bowen LJ).
[13] Birks, pp. 109–14.
[14] See pp. 32, 33 below.
[15] Mill distinguished (iii) and (iv) because in the second, the only utility is in the mere service rendered; it is not fixed or embodied in any object (material or human): *Principles of Political Economy* (2nd ed., 1849), vol. 1, pp. 57–8. Both are distinguished from services that result in utilities fixed and embodied in external objects. Only services that result in such utilities are treated by Mill as wealth although he does recognise that where the service results in human capital it might be (although it is not usually) spoken of as wealth; ibid. 59–61.
[16] p. 1.
[17] *Principles of Political Economy* (end ed., 1849), vol. 1, p. 72.
[18] Goff & Jones, pp. 3, 5, n. 9; Lord Wright in *Fibrosa* [1943] AC, at 61; Birks, pp. 23, 26, 40–1, 133. For Dawson (pp. 39–40) the fact that unjust enrichment as an independent motive for judicial action is apt to be recognised late in any legal system means that it is unlikely to have much territory that is exclusively its own since many of the problems are dealt with by other motives already expressed in doctrine.
[19] This is, in effect, the point of Birks's second category of enrichment, enrichment by wrongdoing, which seeks to explain when and how it can do this.
[20] Atiyah, *Rise and Fall*, pp. 764 ff. (equating the principle of unjust enrichment and the concept of benefit-based liability); S. Hedley, 'Unjust enrichment as the basis of Restitution—an overworked concept' (1981) 5 LegStud 56, 57–8, 60, 61–2, 66.
[21] J. P. Dawson, 'Restitution without Enrichment' (1981) 61 Boston ULRev 563; S. J. Stoljar, 'Negotiorum Gestio' Ch. 17 of *Int. Encycl. of Comparative Law*, vol. X, pp. 11–13, 17; S. Hedley, op. cit.
[22] Dawson, pp. 116–7; Atiyah, *Rise and Fall; Promises.*
[23] Although *n.b.* Goff & Jones's refusal (p. 13) to engage in the *definition of concepts.*

A. Burrows, 'Free Acceptance and the Law of Restitution' (1988) 104 *Law Quarterly Review* 576, at 578–80

. . . *Free acceptance establishing enrichment*[11]

The general question of when a defendant is benefited is surprisingly complex; but in order to challenge the role of free acceptance it is necessary to give some indication straightaway of an approach to the answer.[12] It is submitted that as a matter of fact a person may be benefited either negatively—that is by being saved an expense—or positively—that is by making a gain—and that as a matter of policy one may judge the issue on a range from total subjectivity (solely through the defendant's own eyes) through to total objectivity (solely through the eyes of the reasonable man, which in this context means the market). The problem with a purely subjective approach is that one can never be sure what the defendant is thinking and, in any event, one would probably not wish to prejudice the plaintiff according to the eccentricities of the defendant. On the other hand, the problem with a purely objective approach is that it may involve a complete sacrifice of the individual's values for those of society. It would seem therefore that the best approach is one that takes a line somewhere between these two extremes.

Half of Goff & Jones' and Birks' approach to the problem of benefit sits happily with this suggestion. Hence the concept of an 'incontrovertible benefit,'[13] which Birks amplifies as resting on a 'no reasonable man' test,[14] is vitally important and stresses that the courts do largely take an approach between the two extremes. So, for example, the receipt of a sum of money by a defendant is regarded as a benefit because no reasonable man would deny that a sum of money benefits him. Any subjective devaluation argument by the defendant to the effect that the receipt of money is of no benefit to him is therefore ignored. Similarly a defendant who has had legally required expenses paid by the plaintiff is regarded as being benefited even though he may argue that he would not have paid those expenses. No reasonable man would make that argument. Clearly at its parameters the concept of an incontrovertible benefit is open-textured and allows a more or less objective approach to be adopted. So, for example, necessary expenses saved can range from legally to mere factually necessary expenses.[15] Similarly positive incontrovertible gains can range from those which have been *realised* to those which are merely *realisable*.[16] But the importance of the concept should not be obscured by its open-textured nature.

However, the other half of Goff and Jones' and Birks' approach to benefit is free acceptance. Even where a defendant is not incontrovertibly benefited, they regard him as benefited where he freely accepts the plaintiff's goods or services. But why is this thought correct? The answer would appear to be that free acceptance shows that the defendant regards himself as benefited, and therefore ordering him to pay does not undermine respect for the individuality of values. But the problem with this is that, even accepting that the defendant's inner wishes must be judged according to his outward conduct,[17] there is no reason why one should assume that a freely accepting defendant actually regards himself as being benefited by what the plaintiff has conferred. On the contrary a defendant is just as likely to accept what the plaintiff is conferring on him where he considers it neither beneficial nor detrimental as where he considers it beneficial.

So if we return to Birks' window-cleaning example [see Birks, *Introduction*, 265], the fact that the householder freely accepts does not establish that he regards himself as being better off by having his windows cleaned. For even if it is a fair inference that he would have stopped the window-cleaning if he had regarded the cleaning of his windows as detrimental to him, he is acting perfectly rationally if he allows the cleaning to continue on the grounds that he is neither being benefited nor harmed. In short, he may be indifferent to the cleaning of his windows. Free acceptance cannot therefore be regarded as establishing the defendant's enrichment.[18]

An alternative way of looking at this is to ask whether the defendant would have otherwise paid for goods or services of the kind provided by the plaintiff so that the plaintiff's intervention has now saved him incurring that expense. It is submitted that free acceptance gives no sound indication that the defendant would have otherwise been willing to pay for the goods or services provided, and hence does not establish that the defendant has been benefited by being saved expense. . . .

[11] See Beatson [1987] *Current Legal Problems* 71. His paper mounts an attack on the approach to benefit taken by Goff and Jones and Birks which is not totally dissimilar to that made in this article. In particular he also regards free acceptance as failing to establish that the defendant has been enriched and to that extent his and my views are in agreement. However we markedly differ

not only in the approach which leads us to that conclusion but also in the consequences we draw from it. Moreover he does not recognise anything akin to the 'bargained for' principle of benefit put forward in this article.

[12] For the suggested actual answer to the question see below.

[13] Goff and Jones, *The Law of Restitution* (3rd ed., 1986) (hereinafter referred to as *Law of Restitution*), pp. 19–23.

[14] *Introduction*, pp. 116–124.

[15] *Ibid*, at pp. 118–121.

[16] Contrast *Introduction*, pp. 121–124 (taking the narrower 'realised' view) with *Law of Restitution*, pp. 19, 147–8 (taking the wider 'realisable' view).

[17] This aspect of objectivity should not be confused with that used earlier in this paragraph and in the preceding one where it refers to judging benefit by the values of the reasonable man in contrast to the values of the individual.

[18] Even if free acceptance is regarded as showing the defendant's subjective benefit this does not in any event obviate the need to overcome the defendant's own values to at least some degree. For a defendant may have freely accepted so long as he merely knew that the plaintiff expected to be paid something: yet he may well be ordered to pay far more at the valuation stage than what he thought the plaintiff would want. For example, the householder may hang back behind the curtains thinking that the window cleaner will expect to be paid £1.50, which is what he last paid for window cleaning. In fact at the valuation stage he may be ordered to pay the objective current market value of the services which is, let us say, £3. Therefore even if free acceptance is regarded as indicating the defendant's subjective benefit it is far from being finely tuned to his own values.

Note

See generally Burrows, *Restitution*, 7–16; Birks, *Introduction*, 109–32; Beatson, *Unjust Enrichment*, 21–44; Goff and Jones, 16–35.

The receipt of money is always beneficial and satisfies the enrichment inquiry. Problems arise with goods and services. Here the plaintiff is met with an argument lucidly termed by Professor Birks the argument of 'subjective devaluation' (Birks, *Introduction*, 109–14): 'I liked my windscreen dirty'; 'I did not want double glazing installed in my house while I was on holiday'. More famously: 'One cleans another's shoes, what can the other do but put them on?' (*per* Pollock CB in *Taylor* v *Laird* (1856) 25 LJ Ex 329, at 332); and 'Liabilities are not to be forced upon people behind their backs any more than you can confer a benefit upon a man against his will' (*per* Bowen LJ in *Falcke* v *Scottish Imperial Insurance Co.* (1886) 34 Ch D 234, at 238). Such personal preferences have to be respected. The enrichment issue in respect of goods and services received has to be resolved in a way which respects such interests. Simple recourse to an objective test of value would negate free choice and would also result in serious tensions with the principles and policies of the law of contract.

The tests suggested in the text books are controversial and are not yet fully tested and accepted in the case law. Various tests advanced include:

(a) free acceptance;
(b) incontrovertible benefit; and
(c) other, miscellaneous tests.

A: *Free acceptance*

This has the effect of negating the defendant's recourse to subjective notions of value. In the words of the leading text, a person will be enriched by the receipt of services 'if he, as a reasonable man, should have known that the plaintiff who rendered the services expected to be paid for them, and yet did not take a reasonable opportunity open to him to reject the proffered services' (Goff and Jones, 19). Moreover, the same argument applies to goods which have been consumed or retained. Reliance on the argument from subjective devaluation is *a fortiori* impermissible where the defendant has *requested* the goods or services.

While supported by Goff and Jones and Professor Birks, free acceptance is rejected by Professor Burrows, who prefers a '*bargained for*' test of benefit. Where it can be shown that the defendant had shown a positive willingness to pay for goods and services a rebuttable presumption arises that the defendant was enriched by receipt (Burrows, *Restitution*, 11–15). Also ranged against free acceptance is Professor Beatson, who believes that the receipt of 'pure services' is not enriching and instead suggests an '*exchange-value*' test (Beatson, *The Use and Abuse of Unjust Enrichment*, 21–44.)

Note also that Birks also employs a concept of '*limited acceptance*' to explain the award of restitution in some cases where there has been part-performance of ineffective contracts (Birks, *Introduction*, 126–7, 232, 238–41, 250–51).

Further reading

Birks, *Introduction*, 114–16; Goff and Jones, 18–22, 26; Birks, 'In Defence of Free Acceptance' in Burrows (ed.), *Essays on the Law of Restitution*, 105, 127–43; Garner, 'The Role of Subjective Benefit in the Law of Unjust Enrichment' (1990) 10 OJLS 42.

B: *Incontrovertible benefit*

'There is much to be said for the view that a person has been incontrovertibly benefited if a reasonable person would conclude that he has been saved an expense which he otherwise would necessarily have incurred or where he has, in consequence of the plaintiff's acts, a realisable financial gain.' (Goff and Jones, 23.) The first half of the test, the saving of necessary expense, illustrates that restitution encompasses *negative* benefits, as well as *positive* accretions to the defendant's wealth (compare *Phillips* v *Homfray* (1883) 24 Ch D 439 in Chapter 6, Section 1; Birks, *Introduction*, 129). With regard to the second half of the test, Professor Birks prefers a narrower *realised* in money test (Birks, *Introduction*, 121–4).

Again the test has rarely been expressly addressed in the case law (an exception is *Proctor & Gamble Philippine Manufacturing Corp.* v *Peter Cremer GmbH & Co., The 'Manila'* [1988] 3 All ER 843), but it is regarded as the most plausible explanation of leading cases such as *Greenwood* v *Bennett* [1973] QB 195 (Chapter 2, Section 3), *Craven-Ellis* v *Canons Ltd* [1936] 2 KB 403 (Chapter 4, Section 4) and *China Pacific SA* v *Food Corporation of India, The 'Winson'* [1982] AC 939 (Chapter 3, Section 5).

Further reading

Burrows, *Restitution*, 9–11; Birks, *Introduction*, 116–24; Goff and Jones, 22–6, 26–7.

C: *Miscellaneous*

Apart from the two main tests of *free acceptance* and *incontrovertible benefit*, we have already alluded to Birks's '*limited acceptance*' test and Burrows's '*bargained for*' test of benefit. To these can be added the '*reprehensible seeking-out*' test applicable against wrongdoers (Burrows, *Restitution*, 15–16) and Professor Birks's observation that where the court insists upon counter-restitution as a precondition to restitution, the measure of counter-restitution is usually objectively valued (Birks, *Introduction*, 124–6).

Proctor & Gamble Philippine Manufacturing Corp. v *Peter Cremer GmbH & Co., The 'Manila'*
[1988] 3 All ER 834 (QBD (Commercial Court))

Under two international sales contracts the sellers agreed to ship from the Philippines two lots of copra cake c.i.f. Rotterdam. The bills of lading incorrectly stated that shipment had taken place during the contractual period. Before the ship sailed the shipowners become insolvent. The buyers therefore decided to pay the shipowners additional freight to ensure that the vessel made the voyage. When the vessel arrived in Rotterdam the buyers rejected the cargo and terminated the contract. The arbitration board of appeal held this was legitimate and awarded the buyers restitution of sums paid under the contract of sale. In addition the sellers were held liable to reimburse the buyers for the additional freight paid to the shipowners.

HIRST J: . . . I now turn to the issue of restitution which I can consider very much more shortly. It turns on the conclusions set out in the supplemental award, which arose as a result of an order of Webster J which required further elucidation of the award as follows:

(a) Stating the Board's reasons for holding that the 'Sellers are liable to repay to buyers the additional freight contributed to the Buyers as Bill of Lading holders to finance M.V. 'Manila' proceeding to Rotterdam as a result of owners' bankruptcy' dealing in particular with causation and remoteness or forseeability of damage; and (b) Making such findings of fact as will enable the Court to decide whether the Board's reasons given under (a) above are correct in law.

The supplemental award responded as follows:

(i) The owner of the 'Manila' was a company called Maritime Company of the Phillipines (M.C.P.).

(ii) After the 'Manila' was loaded and after the insurance of the Bills of Lading, M.C.P. was found to be in financial difficulties.

(iii) On the 26th April 1984, as a result of the 'Manila' failing to sail with its cargo, the cargo interests instructed Recourse & Recovery Bureau M.V. of Rotterdam (R.R.B.) to conduct an investigation into the reasons for the vessel failing to sail and to consider solutions to the problems found by them.

(iv) R.R.B. found in its report that the vessel owners, M.C.P., were hopelessly insolvent and that therefore the ship could not sail. On behalf of the cargo interests, they considered a number of possible alternatives, including local sales of the cargo, and they concluded that the best solution was for the vessel to be sailed to Rotterdam at the expense of the cargo interests and the Banks involved.

(v) This course of action was followed with the result that the vessel duly arrived at Rotterdam on 8th July 1984 as above stated.

(vi) The Buyers' contribution as holders of the two Bills of Lading before mentioned amounted to US $28,500·00, which they duly paid.

(vii) *WE FIND* that this payment by the Buyers which was to enable the holder of the Bills of Lading to obtain the goods in Rotterdam was for the benefit and protection of the holder (whoever he may be) of the Bills of Lading. As we have found by our said Award that the Buyers were entitled to reject the Bills of Lading, it follows in our view that the Buyers are entitled to be reimbursed for this sum as it was paid for the benefit of goods which we hold they can now reject and further that as between the Buyers and the Sellers, the Buyers are entitled to be put in the position in which they would have been had they been able to reject the documents on presentation.

(viii) Our Award in this respect is on the principle of Restitution on the grounds that the payment made by the Buyers under (vi) above was commercially justified and for the benefit of the goods and the holder of the Bills of Lading. Consequently, 'causation and remoteness or foreseeability of damage' do not arise and are not applicable.

It is thus manifest that the supplemental award was based wholly and exclusively on restitution and not at all on common law damages for breach of contract.

The relevant principles are common ground between the two parties, and are conveniently set out in the leading textbook on the law of restitution, Goff and Jones *The Law of Restitution* (3rd edn, 1986) p. 148, as follows:

> The general principle should be that restitution should always be granted when, as a result of the plaintiff's services, the defendant has gained a financial benefit readily realisable without detriment to himself or has been saved expense which he inevitably must have incurred.

This forms part of a section headed 'Restitutionary Claims; where the defendant has gained an incontrovertible benefit', a neat phrase which in my judgment epitomises the whole doctrine under consideration here.

Counsel for the buyers submits that the board of appeal have found, and rightly found, that the sellers did indeed obtain an incontrovertible benefit, in that, as a result of the buyers' funding the extra freight, they had the advantage of being able to sell the goods in Rotterdam rather than locally, and were saved expense.

In my judgment this is not a proper interpretation of the supplemental award. I am unable to derive any findings from it that an incontrovertible benefit was conferred; at most it amounted to the finding that, in the difficult circumstances of the shipowners' insolvency, RRB, on behalf of the (presumably European) cargo interests collectively, formed the view that, to make the best of a bad job, the most favourable solution all round was for the vessel to sail to Rotterdam. This falls far short even of a general finding of incontrovertible benefit, still less of a finding (which in my judgment would be essential to justify relief under this heading) that the present sellers viewed in isolation received an incontrovertible benefit. It is not surprising that the board of appeal did not focus on this critical point, since the question of restitution was, it seems clear, never argued before them. Nor is there any finding that the sellers were saved any expense which they would 'inevitably have incurred'; indeed it is by no means clear that such was the case, since, as a corporation themselves based in the Philippines, they might well have thought it prudent from their own point of view to withdraw the cargo there in the hope of an upturn in the market. It follows, in my judgment, that there was no proper basis for the award based on restitution. . . .

Question

What was the unjust factor or ground for restitution in this case? (See McKendrick [1989] LMCLQ 401.)

2 MISTAKE

Benefits conferred by mistake constitute a large and important concern of a modern law of restitution. The ground for recovery is that the transferor of value would not have enriched the recipient had he or she been in possession of the full facts. Mistaken payments are the subject of a large number of authorities and are considered in Sections 1 and 2, which explore the distinction currently drawn in English law between mistakes of fact and mistakes of law. The former as a general rule give rise to a right to restitution, whereas the the latter generally do not. Section 3 considers the possibility of restitutionary claims by mistaken improvers of real or personal property, and especially the difficulty in that context of satisfying the requirement of enrichment. The first three sections concern benefits not transferred pursuant to valid contracts. In contrast, Section 4 deals with the difficult rules which govern the unravelling of contracts tainted by misrepresentation or mistake, and considers the extent to which restitutionary principles inform the solutions developed by the courts. Section 5 considers whether 'ignorance' is a restitutionary cause of action distinct from mistake.

The recipient of value following a mistake is characteristically one who acts in good faith. Many of the cases in this chapter also give rise to questions of applicable defences, especially bona fide purchase for value and bona fide change of position. The recent judicial recognition of the latter defence may well lead to a more generous approach to questions of prima facie liability, therefore this chapter can profitably be studied alongside the discussion of defences in Chapter 8.

Section 1: money paid under a mistake of fact

See generally Burrows, *Restitution*, 95–109.

A: The classic 'liability mistake' authorities

Kelly* v *Solari
(1841) 9 M & W 54; 152 ER 24 (Exchequer)

Action for money had and received

In 1836, Angelo Solari took out an insurance policy on his own life. He died in October 1840, not having paid the quarterly premium which had fallen due the previous month. In November the insurance office marked its copy of the policy 'lapsed'. In February 1841, Madame Solari, the widow and executrix, claimed under the policy. The directors of the insurance company paid her £987 10s, having forgotten that the policy had lapsed. One of the directors claimed restitution on the ground that the payment was made under a mistake of fact. *Held*: it was not a defence to a claim for the return of money honestly but mistakenly paid, that the plaintiff had the means of knowledge of the truth.

LORD ABINGER CB: I think the defendant ought to have had the opportunity of taking the opinion of the jury on the question whether in reality the directors had a knowledge of the facts, and therefore that there should be a new trial, and not a verdict for the plaintiff; although I am now prepared to say that I laid down the rule too broadly at the trial, as to the effect of their having had means of knowledge. That is a very vague expression, and it is difficult to say with precision what it amounts to; for example, it may be that the party may have the means of knowledge on a particular subject, only by sending to and obtaining information from a correspondent abroad. In the case of *Bilbie* v *Lumley* (1802) 2 East 469, the argument as to the party having means of knowledge was used by counsel, and adopted by some of the judges; but that was a peculiar case, and there can be no question that if the point had been left to the jury, they would have found that the plaintiff had actual knowledge. The safest rule however is, that if the party makes the payment will full knowledge of the facts, although under ignorance of the law, there being no fraud on the other side, he cannot recover it back again. There may also be cases in which, although he might by investigation learn the state of facts more accurately, he declines to do so, and chooses to pay the money notwithstanding; in that case there can be no doubt that he is equally bound. Then there is a third case, and the most difficult one,—where the party had once a full knowledge of the facts, but has since forgotten them. I certainly laid down the rule too widely to the jury, when I told them that if the directors once knew the facts they must be taken still to know them, and could not recover by saying that they had since forgotten them. I think the knowledge of the facts which disentitles the party from recovering, must mean a knowledge existing in the mind at the time of payment. I have little doubt in this case that the directors had forgotten the fact, otherwise I do not believe they would have brought the action; but as Mr Platt certainly has a right to have that question submitted to the jury, there must be a new trial.

PARKE B: I entirely agree in the opinion just pronounced by my Lord Chief Baron, that there ought to be a new trial. I think that where money is paid to another under the influence of a mistake, that is, upon the supposition that a specific fact is true, which would entitle the other to the money, but which fact is untrue, and the money would not have been paid if it had been known to the payer that the fact was untrue, an action will lie to recover it back, and it is against conscience to retain it; though a demand may be necessary in those cases in which the party receiving may have been ignorant of the mistake. The position that a person so paying is precluded from recovering by laches, in not availing himself of the means of knowledge in his power, seems, from the cases cited, to have been founded on the dictum of Mr Justice Bayley, in the case of *Milnes* v *Duncan* 6 B & C 761; and with all respect to that authority, I do not think it can be sustained in point of law. If, indeed, the money is intentionally paid, without reference to the truth or falsehood of the fact, the plaintiff meaning to waive all inquiry into it, and that the person receiving shall have the money at all events, whether the fact be true or false, the latter is certainly entitled to retain it; but if it is paid under the impression of the truth of a fact which is untrue, it may, generally speaking, be recovered back, however careless the party paying may have been, in omitting to use due diligence to inquire into the fact. In such a case the receiver was not entitled to it, nor intended to have it.

Note

This is the leading case for the proposition that restitution is available to a payer who supposes himself to be under a contractual or other liability to the payee. 'Liability' mistakes are the most common category of mistaken payments (see Birks, *Introduction*, 149–55 and Burrows, *Restitution*, 95–7). It also establishes that negligence by the payer in making the mistake is no defence for the payee. *Bilbie* v *Lumley* is the leading case on mistake of law and is considered in Section 2.

Aiken v *Short*

(1856) 1 H & N 210; 156 ER 1180 (Exchequer Chamber)

Action for money had and received

The facts appear from the judgment of Pollock CB.

POLLOCK CB: . . . The defendant's testator, Short, had a claim on Carter,—a bond and a security on property which Carter afterwards mortgaged to the Bank. The defendant, who was the executrix of Short, applied to Carter for payment. He referred her to the Bank, who, conceiving that the defendant had a good equitable charge, paid the debt, as they reasonably might do, to get rid of the charge affecting their interest. In consequence of the discovery of a later will of Edwin Carter, it turned out that the defendant had no title. The Bank had paid the money in one sense without any consideration, but the defendant had a perfect right to receive the money from Carter, and the bankers paid for him. They should have taken care not to have paid over the money to get a valueless security; but the defendant has nothing to do with their mistake. Suppose it was announced that there was to be a dividend on the estate of a trader, and persons to whom he was indebted went to an office and received instalments of the debts due to them, could the party paying recover back the money if it turned out that he was wrong is supposing that he had funds in hand? The money was, in fact, paid by the Bank, as the agents of Carter.

PLATT B: . . . The action for money had and received lies only for money which the defendant ought to refund ex æquo et bono. Was there any obligation here to refund? There was a debt due to Short, secured by a bond and a supposed equitable charge by way of collateral security. The property on which Short had the charge was conveyed by Carter to the Bank. Short having died, the defendant, his executrix, applied to George Carter for payment of the debt due to her husband, the testator. Carter referred her to the Bank, who paid the debt, and the bond was satisfied. The money which the defendant got from her debtor was actually due to her, and there can be [no] obligation to refund it.

BRAMWELL B: . . . In order to entitle a person to recover back money paid under a mistake of fact, the mistake must be as to a fact which, if true, would make the person paying liable to pay the money; not where, if true, it would merely make it desirable that he should pay the money. Here, if the fact was true, the bankers were at liberty to pay or not, as they pleased. But relying on the belief that the defendant had a valid security, they, having a subsequent legal mortgage, chose to pay off the defendant's charge. It is impossible to say that this case falls within the rule. The mistake of fact was, that the Bank thought that they could sell the estate for a better price. It is true that if the plaintiff could recover back this money from the defendant, there would be no difficulty in the way of the defendant suing Carter. . . .

Note

The plaintiffs' mistake here was that it thought it had valuable security. The judgment of Bramwell B is often cited in favour of the view that it is a requirement of a restitutionary claim that the mistake is one as to a *supposed liability*. In contrast, Pollock CB and Platt B stress that the bank paid as Carter's agent. The consequence is that the defendant's *valid* debt was discharged. Goff and Jones therefore argue that this case was decided by the majority on the basis that the defendant was entitled to rely upon a defence of change of position (Goff and Jones 134–5). Goff and Jones appear to have changed their view on this: in the third edition the case was explained as turning on the defence of bona fide purchase (*The Law of Restitution*, 3rd ed., 108–9, 716).

B: Liability to a third party

R. E. Jones Ltd* v *Waring and Gillow Ltd
[1926] AC 670 (HL)

Action for money had and received

Bodenham, an 'accomplished rogue' with expensive tastes, owed the respondents £5,000 for furniture and other goods. Bodenham called at the offices of the appellants, claiming to be the representative of 'International Motors'. He produced a brochure for a car called the 'Roma' and offered to appoint the appellants as regional distributors of the car. The appellants signed an agency agreement requiring them to buy at least 500 cars and to pay a deposit of £10 per car. The appellants were reluctant to hand over the money to Bodenham, but he informed them that the financial backers of International Motors were the respondents, the 'well-known Oxford Street firm'. The appellants were satisfied and gave Bodenham two cheques, one for £2,000 and one for £3,000, both payable to the respondents. Bodenham handed the cheques to the respondents as payment for his furniture. The respondents' chief accountant noticed the cheques were defective and phoned the appellants to arrange for a fresh cheque for £5,000. No mention was made of the purpose of the payment. When Bodenham's fraud was discovered, the appellants sought restitution of the £5,000 from the respondents. The House of Lords held unanimously that prima facie the appellants were entitled to recover on the principle of *Kelly* v *Solari*. By a majority of 3 to 2, it was held the respondents could not rely upon the defence of estoppel.

LORD SUMNER: [having held that the appellants could recover and no relevant defence applied, continued:] The real grievance of the respondents is, that it is hard to make them suffer because Jones, Ld., made a mistake. If it is any satisfaction to them, I am willing to say that I think it is, but such is the law. It might be a good thing if the Statutes of Limitation were amended, so as to cut down to a very short period the time within which actions such as *Kelly* v *Solari* 9 M & W 54 and others may be brought; but the present case at any rate was very promptly begun, and intrinsically the hardship is not as great as it seems to be at first sight. It is the peculiar character of coin or currency that gives rise to this idea. If a tradesman misdelivers goods, so that the wrong person gets them, many laymen and all lawyers recognise at once that they do not thereby become the property of the receiver, for passing of property is a question of intention, and obviously the tradesman never meant in such circumstances to make his goods the property of the wrong man. When goods are found, the maxim that finding is keeping attracts many people, but not without a strong subconsciousness of guilt. In the case of payments of money, however, the notion is common that, if some one pays me money when he need not do so, it is my windfall, for I am not bound to keep his accounts for him. This is where the fallacy comes in. I may not be bound to know the payer's accounts but I ought to know my own. The executrix of Solari ought to have known, and probably did, that the company had cancelled the policy, and was making a mistake in paying again. If so, there was no real intention on the company's part to enrich her. So here: Waring & Gillow Ld., must be taken to have known that Jones, Ld., were not their debtors. If so, and without more, there was no intention of making the 5000*l.* theirs in any event. Doubtless when that plausible person, Mr Bodenham, brought them two cheques with an attractive tale, they honestly and readily concluded that he was deserving of more credit than they had supposed, and, as good tradesmen must, they proceeded with his business in a spirit of trust and not in one of suspicion, but at bottom they took Bodenham's story for what it was worth, and cashed the cheque at their own peril. . . .

Note

In this extract Lord Sumner took his hostility to restitution to the extreme of attempting to redefine *Kelly* v *Solari* as depending on the bad faith of the recipient. However, it seems that the strict liability approach, once a qualifying mistake is established, is now entrenched in English law. Lord Sumner's suggestion that the limitation period for restitutionary claims should be shortened is eminently sensible, but so far has not been taken up by the legislature. (For limitation as a defence to restitutionary claims, see Burrows, *Restitution*, 439–50). For the estoppel point see Chapter 8, Section 2.

C: *'Fundamental' mistake*

Norwich Union Fire Insurance Society Ltd* v *W. H. Price Ltd
[1934] AC 455 (PC)

600 bushels of lemons were insured under a marine insurance policy for a voyage from Messina to Sydney. The ship, but not the lemons, was damaged by a collision with a submerged object, necessitating repairs. The lemons were found to be ripening and so were disposed of at Gibraltar. The insurers, believing the lemons to have been damaged by reason of an insured risk, paid the owners of the goods £453 11s 3d in return for the owners signing a letter assigning to them all rights in the goods and their proceeds. *Held*: there had been a mistake of fact fundamental to the transaction which entitled the insurers to restitution of the sum paid.

LORD WRIGHT: . . . Their Lordships agree with the trial judge and with the majority of the Full Court that for purposes of this appeal the mistake was one of fact and was fundamental to the transaction. On the assumptions on which this appeal proceeds, the misconception under which the payment was made was that there had been a loss by perils insured against; unless that were so, there was no liability under the policy: save for that misconception no payment could have been claimed and no payment would have been made. The facts which were misconceived were those which were essential to liability and were of such a nature that on well-established principles any agreement concluded under such mistake was void in law, so that any payment made under such mistake was recoverable. The mistake, being of the character that it was, prevented there being that intention which the common law regards as essential to the making of an agreement or the transfer of money or property. Thus in *Kelly* v *Solari* 9 M & W 54, where money was paid under a mistake of fact, Baron Parke concludes his well-known statement of the law with these words: 'If it (the money) is paid under the impression of the truth of a fact which is untrue, it may, generally speaking be recovered back, however careless the party paying may have been in omitting to use due diligence to inquire into the fact. In such a case the receiver was not entitled to it, nor intended to have it.' The 'fact' which Baron Parke is referring to is one 'which would entitle the other to the money' if true. The reference to intention is crucial. In the same sense, in *R. E. Jones, Ld* v *Waring & Gillow, Ld.* [1926] AC 670, 696, Lord Sumner says of *Kelly* v *Solari*: 'The executrix of Solari ought to have known, and probably did, that the company had cancelled the policy and was making a mistake in paying again. If so, there was no real intention on the company's part to enrich her.' Lord Sumner had just pointed out that passing of property is a question of intention, and just as much so in the case of payment of money as in the transfer of a chattel. To the same effect, Lord Shaw in the same case says in respect of mistakes: 'The true facts may not have been known to the grantor, or may have been misrepresented with such a result that the mind of the grantor does not go with the transaction at all; his mind goes with another transaction, and he is meaning to give effect to that other transaction, depending on facts different from those which were the true facts.' Thus, in the present case the only transaction with which the mind of the appellants went was payment of a claim on the basis of the truth of facts which constituted a loss by perils insured against: they never intended to pay on the basis of facts inconsistent with any such loss by perils insured against.

The mistake was as vital as that in *Cooper* v *Phibbs* (1867) LR 2 HL 149, 170 in respect of which Lord Westbury used these words: 'If parties contract under a mutual mistake and misapprehension as to their relative and respective rights, the result is, that that agreement is liable to be set aside as having proceeded upon a common mistake.' At common law such a contract (or simulacrum of a contract) is more correctly described as void, there being in truth no intention to contract. Their Lordships find nothing tending to contradict or overrule these established principles in *Bell* v *Lever Bros., Ld.* [1932] AC 161.

It is true that in general the test of intention in the formation of contracts and the transfer of property is objective; that is, intention is to be ascertained from what the parties said or did. But proof of mistake affirmatively excludes intention. It is, however, essential that the mistake relied on should be of such a nature that it can be properly described as a mistake in respect of the underlying assumption of the contract or transaction or as being fundamental or basic. Whether the mistake does satisfy this description may often be a matter of great difficulty. Applying these principles to the present case, their Lordships find themselves so far in agreement with the opinions of the Courts below that the money paid is recoverable at common law. . . .

Question

Was this case concerned with rescission of a contract by reason of mistake, or with restitution of money paid under a mistake, or both?

Notes

1. Burrows criticises this case for its amalgamation of the rules relating to mistake in respect of rescission of contract, restitution of money and vitiation of intention to transfer property (Burrows, *Restitution*, 106–7). In fact all three matters were relevant in the case, if the payment in return for the letter of assignment is seen as a new contract. It also appeared that the mistake was common to insurer and goods owner (see [1934] AC 455, at 460–1). This may explain the reference to *Bell* v *Lever Bros Ltd* [1932] AC 161. However, *Norwich Union* v *Price* does seem to ignore the vital distinction between the relevant principles governing contractual and restitutionary claims. The courts are far more willing to grant relief in respect of an extra-contractual payment, than to release parties from an otherwise sound bargain. 'Sanctity of contract' is a more compelling policy than 'security of receipt'.

2. For an explanation of the case using the concept of an 'implied settlement', see Andrews, 'Mistaken settlements of disputable claims' [1989] LMCLQ 431, at 445–7.

Morgan* v *Ashcroft
[1938] 1 KB 49 (CA)

Action for money had and received

The plaintiff bookmaker claimed to recover an overpayment made to the defendant publican as part of their account in respect of bets placed by the latter. The mistake was that of the plaintiff's clerk in settling the account. *Held*: first, that to award restitution would frustrate the policy of the Gaming Act 1845, s.18, which makes gaming debts unenforceable, and secondly, the mistake was not sufficient to entitle the plaintiff to restitution. Sir Wilfrid Greene MR discussed the *dictum* of Bramwell B in *Aiken* v *Short*, Lord Sumner's speech in *R. E. Jones Ltd* v *Waring and Gillow Ltd* and *Norwich Union Fire Insurance Society* v *William H. Price Ltd* and continued:

SIR WILFRID GREENE MR: . . . It is, I think, instructive to consider the words of Bramwell B referred to above in the light of these authorities. In the first case which he mentions, namely, that where the supposed fact if true would have made the person paying liable to pay the money, the mistake is a mistake as to the nature of the transaction. The payer thinks that he is discharging a legal obligation whereas in truth and in fact he is making a purely voluntary payment. Such a mistake is to my mind unquestionably fundamental or basic and may be compared, at least by way of analogy, with the class of case in which mistakes as to the nature of the transaction negatives intention in the case of contract. But the second case which he mentions, namely, that where the supposed fact would, if true, merely make the payment desirable from the point of view of the payer, is very different. In that case the payment is intended to be a voluntary one and a voluntary payment it is whether the supposed fact be true or not. It appears to me that a person who intends to make a voluntary payment and thinks that he is making one kind of voluntary payment whereas upon the true facts he is making another kind of voluntary payment, does not make the payment under a mistake of fact which can be described as fundamental or basic. The essential quality of the payment, namely its voluntary character, is the same in each case. If a father, believing that his son has suffered a financial loss, gives him a sum of money, he surely could not claim repayment if he afterwards discovered that no such loss had occurred; and (to take the analogous case of contract) if instead of giving him money, he entered into a contract with his son, he surely could not claim that the contract was void. To hold the contrary would almost amount to saying that motive and not mistake was the decisive matter.

I come therefore to the conclusion that the observations of Bramwell B, supported as they are by much weight of judicial opinion, are, so far as regards the class of mistake with which he was dealing, in agreement with the more recent authorities, and I propose to follow them. It was said on behalf of the respondent that these observations do not correctly state the law. I do not agree, although I am disposed to think that they cannot be taken as an exhaustive statement of the law but must be confined to cases where the only mistake is as to the nature of the transaction. For example, if A makes a voluntary payment of money to B under the mistaken belief that he is C, it may well be that A can recover it. Bramwell B was not dealing with a case such as that, since he was assuming that there was no such error in persona. If we are to be guided by the analogous case of contract, where mistake as to the person contracted with negatives the intention to contract, the mistake in the case which I have mentioned ought to be held to negative the intention to pay the money and the money should be recoverable.

But it is not necessary to pursue this matter further. It is sufficient to say that in my opinion the present case falls within principles laid down both by Bramwell B and in the more recent authorities. In making the payment the respondent was, it is true, under a mistake as to the nature of the transaction. He thought that a wagering debt was due from himself to the appellant, whereas in fact it was not. But if the supposed fact had been true, the respondent would have been under no liability to make the payment which therefore was intended to be a voluntary payment. Upon the true facts the payment was still a voluntary payment; and there is in my opinion no such fundamental or basic distinction between the one voluntary payment and the other that the law can for present purposes differentiate between them and say that there was no intention to make the one because the intention was to make the other. . . .

SCOTT LJ: . . . Before adding what little I have to add to my Lord's discussion upon the essential nature of the action for money had and received when based on a mistake of fact, I will consider the particular argument advanced by Mr Micklethwait [counsel for the defendant]. The well known passage in Bramwell B's judgment in *Aiken* v *Short* 25 LJ (Ex) 321, 324 is perhaps the strongest statement of the proposition upon which he relied, but I agree with the Master of the Rolls that the facts of that case were not such as to make what the learned Baron there said the necessary basis of decision in that case. Indeed I do not think that this limiting proposition of the law about mistake of fact as one basis of the action for money had and received has ever been the direct subject of decision, although it has been frequently stated almost as if it were an accepted rule of law. I venture to think that the mind of the Court was in all the cases where the statement has been made concentrated on the particular circumstances under discussion, and was expressing a conclusion appropriate to the facts before it rather than attempting to lay down any absolute or general rule of law. But as counsel for the appellant in the present appeal contended that there is such a rule of law, it is desirable to quote some of the leading expressions of judicial opinion upon which he relies, and all the more so as they are expressed in rather definite language. [Scott LJ then discussed authorities including *Kelly* v *Solari*, *Aiken* v *Short* and *Maskell* v *Horner* [1915] 3 KB 106 and continued:] In none of the above cases, as I have already said, not even in *Aiken* v *Short* 1 H & N 210; 25 LJ (Ex) 321, was there a decision of the Court that the action failed simply because the mistake did not induce a belief of liability. And indeed in *Kerrison* v *Glyn, Mills, Currie & Co.* 15 Com Cas 1; 17 Com Cas 41 it was definitely decided by Hamilton J and by the House of Lords that the plaintiff was entitled to recover a payment made to the defendants for the purpose of meeting an anticipated liability although he then knew that no actual liability had yet attached to him. The decision of the House of Lords seems to me conclusive that the rule as stated in *Aiken* v *Short* cannot be regarded as final and exhaustive in the sense that no mistake, which does not induce in the mind of the payer a belief that payment will discharge or reduce his liability, can ground an action for money had and received. It is, of course, obvious that such a belief must in fact have been induced in a very high percentage of mistaken payments giving rise to a dispute; in human affairs the vast majority of payments made without any fresh consideration are made to perform an obligation or discharge a liability; and I doubt not that performance of an obligation would be accounted discharge of a liability for the purpose of the *Aiken* v *Short* proposition. For this reason of human nature, that proposition is very often—and perhaps usually—a crucial test of the question whether the payment was in truth made by reason of a mistake or was merely voluntary and therefore irrecoverable. But I agree with the view of the Master of the Rolls that the final demarcation of the boundaries of the old action of money had and received has not yet been achieved, and that their final delineation can only be worked out as concrete cases arise and bring up new points for decision. And in refusing assent to the appellant's argument that the *Aiken* v *Short* proposition is of itself necessarily sufficient to fix the boundary, I desire to keep clearly open the possibility of the common law treating other types of payment in mistake as falling within the scope of the action for money had and received. Without expressing any opinion, I recognise, for instance, the possibility that there may be cases of charitable payments or other gifts made under a definite mistake of person to be benefited, or of the substantial nature of the transaction, where on consideration the old principles of the action might still, in spite of limiting decisions, be held to cover such circumstances. [Scott LJ then made the observations quoted in Chapter 1, Section 1 and concluded:] But I am in complete agreement with the Master of the Rolls that there is a plain principle applicable to all those cases of payments in mistake of fact, and that is that the mistake must be in some aspect or another fundamental to the transaction. On the facts of this case there was no fundamental mistake. To pay 24*l.* for a betting debt is just as much in the eye of the law a purely voluntary gift as a wedding present of 24*l.*: the law prevents the plaintiff from saying that he intended anything but a present. I agree that the appeal must be allowed.

Question

Why did (a) Sir Wilfrid Greene MR, (b) Scott LJ not think the plaintiff's mistake was of the sort which entitled him to restitution?

Note

Scott LJ discussed the House of Lords case of *Kerrison* v *Glyn, Mills & Currie* (1911) 81 LJ KB 465, which he attempts to explain as a case of 'anticipated liability'. There the plaintiff had forwarded £500 to the defendant bank, the London agents of a New York bank, Kessler & Co., for the purpose of providing finance for a Mexican silver-mining venture of which he was part-owner. This was done in ignorance of the fact that Kessler & Co. had committed an act of bankruptcy. In the words of Lord Atkinson (at 470): 'If not commercially dead, they were at least in a state of suspended animation, utterly incapable of carrying on business, making advances, or of doing the very things he lodged this money to their credit to enable them to accomplish'. Kessler & Co. were heavily indebted to the defendant bank who claimed to be entitled to retain the money. The House of Lords unanimously held that the plaintiff was entitled to recover the money on the ground of mistake of fact. The case is puzzling and would best be described as a *misprediction* rather than a mistake. Perhaps the cause of action was failure of consideration. (See Birks, *Introduction*, 147–8.)

D: Non-legal liability

Larner* v *London County Council
[1949] 2 KB 683 (CA)

The defendant local authority employed the plaintiff as an ambulance driver. The authority resolved to pay all its men who went to war the difference between their service pay and their civil wage. Employees were required to advise of any change in service pay, which the plaintiff failed to do. The authority overpaid the plaintiff, and on discovering its mistake started to make deductions from his civilian wage after he was demobbed. The plaintiff challenged the authority's right to do so, and the defendant counter-claimed for the balance of £52 10s overpaid.

DENNING LJ: When the men went to the war, many local authorities made up to them the difference between their war service pay and their civil pay. Sometimes overpayments were made and the question is whether the men are bound to repay the excess.

The real question in this case arises on the counterclaim: Are the council entitled to recover from Mr Larner the sums which they overpaid him? Overpay him they certainly did. That is admitted. And the overpayment was due to a mistake of fact. That is also admitted. They were mistaken as to the amount of his service pay. But it is said that they were voluntary payments, which were not made in discharge of any legal liability, and cannot therefore be recovered back. For this proposition reliance was placed on the dictum of Bramwell B in *Aiken* v *Short* 1 H & N 210, 215; but that dictum, as Scott LJ pointed out in *Morgan* v *Ashcroft* [1938] 1 KB 49, 73–74, cannot be regarded as an exhaustive statement of the law. Take this case. The London County Council, by their resolution, for good reasons of national policy, made a promise to the men which they were in honour bound to fulfil. The payments made under that promise were not mere gratuities. They were made as a matter of duty: see *National Association of Local Government Officers* v *Bolton Corporation* [1943] AC 166, 180, 187. Indeed that is how both sides regarded them. They spoke of them as sums 'due' to the men, that is, as sums the men were entitled to under the promise contained in the resolution. If then, owing to a mistake of fact, the council paid one of the men more than he was entitled to under the promise, why should he not repay the excess, at any rate if he has not changed his position for the worse? It is not necessary to inquire whether there was any consideration for the promise so as to enable it to be enforced in a court of law. It may be that, because the men were legally bound to go to the war, there was in strictness no consideration for the promise. But that does not matter. It is not a question here of enforcing the promise by action. It is a question of recovering overpayments made in the belief that they were due under the promise, but in fact not due. They were sums which the council never promised Mr Larner and which they would never have paid him had they known the true facts. They were paid under a mistake of fact, and he is bound to repay them unless he has changed his position for the worse because of them. . . .

Question

What sort of obligation did the local authority suppose itself to be under?

E: *Causative mistake*

Barclays Bank Ltd* v *W.J. Simms, Son & Cooke (Southern) Ltd
[1980] QB 677 (QBD)

The defendant company entered into a written contract with a housing association in respect of construction work. The housing association drew a cheque for £24,000 upon the plaintiff, Barclays Bank, in favour of the defendant. The next day the defendant was placed in receivership. The housing association, learning of this, instructed Barclays not to pay when the cheque was presented, in the belief that it was entitled to do so under the building contract. The receiver, who did not know about the stop instruction, presented the cheque at the company's bank. An employee of Barclays overlooked the stop instruction and paid the cheque. Barclays claimed the money back from the company or the receiver on the basis of a mistake of fact. *Held*: they were entitled to restitution.

ROBERT GOFF J: This case raises for decision the question whether a bank, which overlooks its customer's instructions to stop payment of a cheque and in consequence pays the cheque on presentation, can recover the money from the payee as having been paid under a mistake of fact. The point is one on which there is no decision in this country; and it is a point, I was told, of considerable importance to bankers, not only because it is an everyday hazard that customers' instructions may be overlooked, but because modern technology, rather than eliminating the risk, has if anything increased it. . . .

1. *The principles upon which money is recoverable on the ground that it has been paid under a mistake of fact.*

Nearly 40 years ago, Asquith J stated that 'it is notoriously difficult to harmonise all the cases dealing with payment of money under a mistake of fact,': see *Weld-Blundell* v *Synott* [1940] 2 KB 107, 112. This is indeed true, and it does not make easy the task of the trial judge, whose duty it is both to search for guiding principles among the authorities, and to pay due regard to those authorities by which he is bound. I have however come to the conclusion that it is possible for me, even in this field, to achieve both these apparently irreconcilable objectives. The key to the problem lies, in my judgment, in a careful reading of the earliest and most fundamental authorities, and in giving full effect to certain decisions of the House of Lords. It is necessary therefore for me to review the leading authorities. [Robert Goff J then considered the authorities, including *Kelly* v *Solari* (1841) 9 M & W 54, 152 ER 24; *Aiken* v *Short* (1856) 1 H & N 210; 156 ER 1180; *Colonial Bank* v *Exchange Bank of Yarmouth, Nova Scotia* (1885) 11 App Cas 84 (PC); *Kleinwort, Sons & Co.* v *Dunlop Rubber Co.* (1907) 97 LT 263 (HL); *Kerrison* v *Glyn, Mills, Currie & Co.* (1911) 81 LJ KB 465 (HL) and *R. E. Jones Ltd* v *Waring and Gillow Ltd* [1926] AC 670 (HL), and continued:]

From this formidable line of authority certain simple principles can, in my judgment, be deduced: (1) If a person pays money to another under a mistake of fact which causes him to make the payment, he is prima facie entitled to recover it as money paid under a mistake of fact. (2) His claim may however fail if (a) the payer intends that the payee shall have the money at all events, whether the fact be true or false, or is deemed in law so to intend; or (b) the payment is made for good consideration, in particular if the money is paid to discharge, and does discharge, a debt owed to the payee (or a principal on whose behalf he is authorised to receive the payment) by the payer or by a third party by whom he is authorised to discharge the debt; or (c) the payee has changed his position in good faith, or is deemed in law to have done so.

To these simple propositions, I append the following footnotes: (a) *Proposition* 1. This is founded upon the speeches in the three cases in the House of Lords, to which I have referred. It is also consistent with the opinion expressed by Turner J. in *Thomas* v *Houston Corbett & Co.* [1969] NZLR 151, 167. Of course, if the money was due under a contract between the payer and the payee, there can be no recovery on this ground unless the contract itself is held void for mistake (as in *Norwich Union Fire Insurance Society Ltd* v *Wm. H. Price Ltd* [1934] AC 455) or is rescinded by the plaintiff. (b) *Proposition* 2 (a). This is founded upon the dictum of Parke B in *Kelly* v *Solari*, 9 M & W 54. I have felt it necessary to add the words 'or is deemed in law so to intend' to accommodate the decision of the Court of Appeal in *Morgan* v *Ashcroft* [1938] 1 KB 49, a case strongly relied upon by the defendants in the present case, the effect of which I shall have to consider later in this judgment. (c) *Proposition* 2 (b).

This is founded upon the decision in *Aiken* v *Short* 1 H & N 210, and upon dicta in *Kerrison* v *Glyn, Mills, Currie & Co.*, 81 LJKB 465. However, even if the payee has given consideration for the payment, for example by accepting the payment in discharge of a debt owed to him by a third party on whose behalf the payer is authorised to discharge it, that transaction may itself be set aside (and so provide no defence to the claim) if the payer's mistake was induced by the payee, or possibly even where the payee, being aware of the payer's mistake, did not receive the money in good faith: cf *Ward & Co.* v *Wallis* [1900] 1 QB 675, 678–679, *per* Kennedy J. (d) *Proposition* 2 (c). This is founded upon the statement of principle of Lord Loreburn LC in *Kleinwort, Sons & Co.* v *Dunlop Rubber Co.*, 97 LT 263. I have deliberately stated this defence in broad terms, making no reference to the question whether it is dependent upon a breach of duty by the plaintiff or a representation by him independent of the payment, because these matters do not arise for decision in the present case. I have however referred to the possibility that the defendant may be deemed in law to have changed his position, because of a line of authorities concerned with negotiable instruments which I shall have to consider later in this judgment, of which the leading case is *Cocks* v *Masterman,* 9 B & C 902. (e) I have ignored, in stating the principle of recovery, defences of general application in the law of restitution, for example where public policy precludes restitution. (f) The following propositions are inconsistent with the simple principle of recovery established in the authorities: (i) That to ground recovery, the mistake must have induced the payer to believe that he was liable to pay the money to the payee or his principal. (ii) That to ground recovery, the mistake must have been 'as between' the payer and the payee. Rejection of this test has led to its reformulation (notably by Asquith J in *Weld-Blundell* v *Synott* [1940] 2 KB 107 and by Windeyer J in *Porter* v *Latec Finance (Qld) Pty Ltd* (1964) 111 CLR 177, 204) in terms which in my judgment mean no more than that the mistake must have caused the payment.

In the case before me, Mr Evans Lombe submitted on behalf of the defendants that I could not proceed on the basis of the simple principles I have stated, because I was precluded from so doing by binding authority, viz, the decision of the Court of Appeal in *Morgan* v *Ashcroft* [1938] 1 KB 49. That case came on appeal from the county court. The respondent was a bookmaker, with whom the appellant was in the habit of making bets. The respondent claimed that his clerk mistakenly credited the appellant twice over with a sum of £24 2s 1d, and claimed to recover that sum from the appellant as having been paid under a mistake of fact. The county court judge held that the respondent was entitled to recover the money. The Court of Appeal allowed the appeal, holding that the money was not recoverable. The first ground of the court's decision was that, in order to ascertain whether there had been an overpayment, it would be necessary for the court to examine the state of account between the parties, and that the court could not do, by reason of the Gaming Act 1845. However the court also held that the money was in any event not recoverable as having been paid under a mistake of fact. Mr Evans Lombe relied in particular on a passage in the judgment of Sir Wilfrid Greene MR, in which he stated, at p. 66:

> . . . a person who intends to make a voluntary payment and thinks that he is making one kind of voluntary payment whereas upon the true facts he is making another kind of voluntary payment, does not make the payment under a mistake of fact which can be described as fundamental or basic.

That passage Mr Evans Lombe identified as being the crucial passage in Sir Wilfrid Greene MR's judgment on this point; and he submitted further that the expression 'voluntary payment' must here be understood as a payment made without legal obligation, so that, generally speaking, a person who makes a payment without the intention of discharging a legal obligation cannot recover the money from the payee although it has been paid under a mistake of fact except possibly in circumstances where the mistake can be described as fundamental, for example where the mistake is as to the identity of the payee.

It is legitimate to observe the consequences of Mr Evans Lombe's submission. If he is right, money would be irrecoverable in the following, by no means far-fetched, situations. (1) A man, forgetting that he has already paid his subscription to the National Trust, pays it a second time. (2) A substantial charity uses a computer for the purpose of distributing small benefactions. The computer runs mad, and pays one beneficiary the same gift one hundred times over. (3) A shipowner and a charterer enter into a sterling charterparty for a period of years. Sterling depreciates against other currencies; and the charterer decides, to maintain the goodwill of the shipowner but without obligation, to increase the monthly hire payments. Owing to a mistake in his office, the increase in one monthly hire payment is paid twice over. (4) A Lloyd's syndicate gets into financial difficulties. To maintain the reputation of Lloyd's, other underwriting syndicates decide to make gifts of money to assist the syndicate in difficulties. Due to a mistake, one syndicate makes its gift twice over. It would not be difficult to construct other examples. The consequences of Mr Evans Lombe's submission are therefore so far-reaching that it is necessary to examine the ratio decidendi of this part of the decision in *Morgan* v *Ashcroft* to ascertain whether it produces the result for which Mr Evans Lombe contends.

Only two judges sat to hear the appeal in *Morgan* v *Ashcroft* [1938] 1 KB 49—Sir Wilfrid Greene MR and Scott LJ. Furthermore, there are considerable differences between their two judgments on this part of the case. First, there was a difference in the basic philosophy expounded by the two judges. Sir Wilfrid Greene MR favoured the so-called 'implied contract' theory as the basis of recovery of money paid under a mistake of fact. Citing a well-known dictum of Lord Sumner from *Sinclair* v *Brougham* [1914] AC 398, 452, he rejected the principle of unjust enrichment and stated that the claim was based upon an imputed promise to repay: [1938] 1 KB 49, 62. Scott LJ adopted a less restricted view. While accepting that the moral principle of unjust enrichment had been rejected as a universal or complete legal touchstone whereby to test the cause of action, he referred to passages from the works of eminent jurists and concluded, at p. 76, that his citations emphasised:

> the importance of trying to find some common positive principles upon which these causes of action called 'implied contracts' can be said to rest, and which will not altogether exclude that of unjust enrichment embodied in those citations.

Scott LJ's approach has been amply vindicated by subsequent developments in the law, as is shown in particular by authoritative statements of principle in the House of Lords by Lord Atkin in *United Australia Ltd* v *Barclays Bank Ltd* [1941] AC 1, 28–29 and by Lord Wright in *Fibrosa Spolka Akcyjna* v *Fairbairn Lawson Combe Barbour Ltd* [1943] AC 32, 61.

How far Sir Wilfrid Greene MR's narrower philosophic approach affected his analysis in *Morgan* v *Ashcroft* [1938] 1 KB 49 is difficult to tell; but there was a further difference between him and Scott LJ, in their view of the nature of the mistake which will ground recovery of money paid under a mistake of fact. Again, Sir Wilfrid Greene MR adopted a more restricted view. He founded himself upon the dictum of Bramwell B in *Aiken* v *Short*, 1 H & N 210, which he accepted as an authoritative statement of law 'so far as regards the class of mistake with which he was dealing,' i.e. in 'cases where the only mistake is as to the nature of the transaction.' From that dictum he deduced the conclusion on which Mr Evans Lombe relied before me, viz. that if a person thinks that he is making one kind of voluntary payment, whereas on the true facts he is making another kind of voluntary payment, his mistake is not fundamental or basic and therefore cannot ground recovery: see pp. 65–67 of the report. Scott LJ, on the other hand, was not prepared to accept Bramwell B's dictum as authoritative; in particular, he referred to *Kerrison* v *Glyn, Mills, Currie & Co.*, 81 LJKB 465 and said that the decision of the House of Lords in that case seemed to him 'conclusive that the rule as stated in *Aiken* v *Short* 1 H & N 210 cannot be regarded as final and exhaustive in the sense that no mistake, which does not induce in the mind of the payer a belief that payment will discharge or reduce his liability, can ground an action for money had and received': see pp. 73–74 of the report. In these circumstances it is by no means easy to determine the ratio decidendi of this part of the case. It may well be found in the opinion of both judges that an overpayment of betting debts by a bookmaker is not made under a mistake of fact sufficiently fundamental to ground recovery, apparently on the basis that the payment is in any event intended to be a purely voluntary gift, because 'the law prevents the plaintiff from saying that he intended anything but a present" (see p. 77, *per* Scott LJ), and the plaintiff is therefore deemed in law to intend that the payee shall be entitled to retain the money in any event. . . .

Question

A sells goods to B who pays the price by cheque. The goods are in perfect conformity with the contract, but B changes his mind about the wisdom of his purchase and therefore he instructs his bank to stop the cheque. A, unaware of B's change of mind, presents the cheque which the bank pays by mistake. Can the bank recover the money from A?

Notes

1. The above question was posed and answered in the negative by Professor Goode in 'The Bank's Right to Recover Money Paid on a Stopped Cheque' (1981) 97 LQR 254 (describing the result in *Barclays Bank* v *Simms* as 'astonishing'). Professor Goode's criticisms were not concerned with the cause of action, but rather with the payee's defences. Having held the bank prima facie entitled to recover, Robert Goff J went on to hold that where a bank overlooks a countermand and pays a cheque it acts outside its mandate. Therefore it is not entitled to debit its customer's account and the debt owed to the payee is not discharged. Professor Goode argues this concentrates on the bank's *actual* authority as an agent for its customer, but ignores the payee's reliance upon the bank's *apparent* authority. Because there was apparent authority to make payment, the debt owed to the payee was effectively discharged. The payee was a bona fide purchaser. (See (1981) 97 LQR 254, at 258–9.) Professor Goode also argues that the payee can rely upon change of position in giving up the cheque to the bank (at 259–60). As a procedural matter, in a suit by the payee against the housing association, it would be possible to obtain speedy summary judgment by suing upon the contract embodied in the cheque (the bill of exchange contract) rather than upon the underlying building contract: the possible defences are very restricted in the former case (see Sime, *A Practical Approach to Civil Procedure* (London: Blackstone Press, 2nd ed., 1995), at 167–8). Perhaps this suggested defence is better rationalised as one of no restitution without counter-restitution, rather than change of position. See, for a defence of *Barclays Bank* v *Simms*, Goff and Jones, 138–41; see also Burrows, *Restitution*, 103 and Matthews [1982] JBL 281.

2. The problems with defences apart, *Barclays Bank* v *Simms* is the leading authority for the proposition that a mistake of fact which *causes* a payment to be made is sufficient to entitle the payer to restitution. There is no need to show that the mistake was 'fundamental' or as to the basis of the transaction. This simple causation-based strategy for liability, subject to generous defences, is largely supported in the academic writing (Birks, *Introduction*, 153–9; Burrows, *Restitution*, 99–103), but is thoroughly criticised by Paul Matthews ((1980) 130 NLJ 587), who argues that *Kelly* v *Solari*, *Aiken* v *Short* and *Barclays Bank* v *Simms* are better explained as cases where the cause of action is failure of consideration, not mistake. (For a similar analysis see Butler, 'Mistaken Payments, Change of Position and Restitution' in Finn (ed), *Essays*, 87–137.)

3. For an economic analysis of this area of law see Beatson and Bishop, 'Mistaken Payments in the Law of Restitution' (1986) 36 *University of Toronto LJ* 149 (see also the interesting critique of Beatson and Bishop's 'law and economics' approach and economic insights on law in general in Sutton, 'Mistaken Payments: An Inner Logic Infringed?' (1987) 37 *University of Toronto LJ* 389) now reprinted as Essay 6 in Beatson, *Unjust Enrichment*, 137–73 with a Postscript replying to Professor Sutton at 173–6. Beatson and Bishop's economic perspective suggests an efficient test would be one based on the nature and identity of the parties, that is, one which effected a sensitive allocation of the social costs of mistake by encouraging cost-effective precautions.

Avon County Council* v *Howlett
[1983] 1 WLR 605 (CA)

Howlett was employed by the plaintiff council as a physical education teacher in a school in Bristol. Howlett was injured in a classroom accident in January 1974 and was therefore unable to work, except for a short period, before his retirement in October 1976. Under his contract of employment he was entitled to full pay for the first six months of any absence due to illness, half-pay for the subsequent six months and nothing thereafter. In fact he received full pay until September 1974, and half-pay until August 1975. In total he was overpaid some £1,007. The council sought restitution of that sum.

SLADE LJ: Where an employer has a large pay-roll, there must always exist the risk that, due to error or inadvertence, an employee may be paid either greater or lesser sums than those to which he is strictly entitled under his contract of service. There are many potential sources of such error and the advent of computerisation has introduced yet another one. The present is such a case. Harold Ellis Howlett, the defendant in the action, has been overpaid in a sum of £1,007 by his former employers, Avon County Council, who are the plaintiffs in the action. . . .

The case raises difficult and important questions of law concerning the principles governing the recovery of money paid under a mistake and the relevance of the doctrine of estoppel in this context. . . .

Mistake

I now turn to consider whether the excessive payments totalling £1,007 made by the plaintiffs to the defendant were made under a mistake and if so what was the nature of that mistake. It is common ground that the onus of proving that there was a mistake lies upon the plaintiffs: see, for example, *Holt* v *Markham* [1923] 1 KB 504, 511, *per* Warrington LJ. Furthermore, it is common ground that the mistake in question must be one which can be properly categorised as being a mistake of fact rather than a mistake of law, since payment made under what is properly categorised as a mistake of law are not generally recoverable.

Parke B authoritatively stated the principles governing the recovery of money paid under a mistake of fact in *Kelly* v *Solari* (1841) 9 M & W 54, 58–59:

> I think that where money is paid to another under the influence of a mistake, that is, upon the supposition that a specific fact is true, which would entitle the other to the money, but which fact is untrue, and the money would not have been paid if it had been known to the payer that the fact was untrue, an action will lie to recover it back, and it is against conscience to retain it; though a demand may be necessary in those cases in which the party receiving may have been ignorant of the mistake. . . . If, indeed, the money is intentionally paid, without reference to the truth or falsehood of the fact, the plaintiff meaning to waive all inquiry into it, and that the person receiving shall have the money at all events, whether the fact be true or false, the latter is certainly entitled to retain it; but if it is paid under the impression of the truth of a fact which is untrue, it may, generally speaking, be recovered back, however careless the party may have been, in omitting to use due diligence to inquire into the fact. In such a case the receiver was not entitled to it, nor intended to have it.

This statement of the relevant principles were cited with approval by Lord Shaw of Dumfermline and Lord Carson in *R. E. Jones Ltd* v *Waring and Gillow Ltd* [1926] AC 670, 688 and 698. Its correctness has not been challenged in the present case. In this instance the evidence of Mr Hewlett in my opinion clearly establishes on the balance of probabilities that the extra moneys were paid to the defendant under a mistake of some kind on the part of the plaintiffs or their servants or agents. This is not a case where, to quote the words of Parke B in *Kelly* v *Solari*, 9 M & W 54, 59:

> the money is intentionally paid, without reference to the truth or falsehood of the fact, the plaintiff meaning to waive all inquiry into it, and that the person receiving shall have the money at all events, whether the fact be true or false.

And Mr Bowyer, as I understood his argument, did not seek so to contend.

On this aspect of the case, his argument has been substantially founded on the propositions (i) that the plaintiffs have not proved by their evidence that the relevant mistakes were mistakes of fact rather than of law and (ii) that if these were mistakes of law, the plaintiffs would not be entitled to recover the money. . . .

On the substantial issues, I have come to the conclusion that there was sufficient evidence before the judge to support the inference that, on the balance of probabilities, the mistakes which led to the relevant overpayments were mistakes of fact and not mistakes of law. Though there is no precise evidence to this effect, I think it a reasonable inference from the evidence as a whole that any pay clerk employed by the plaintiffs would have been likely to know the simple fact that an employee of the plaintiffs, such as the defendant, while absent from work following an accident, was under his conditions of service entitled to be paid at full rates of pay for the first six months of his absence, at half rates for the next six months of absence, and to no pay thereafter. Accordingly, on the evidence, I think it a fair inference on the balance of probabilities that the reason why the plaintiffs continued to pay the defendant at full rates after the end of the first six months of his absence from work was that the pay clerks concerned were unaware or had forgotten that more than six months had elapsed since the defendant's accident and for this reason failed to give the appropriate instructions to the computer, which would have led to the appropriate reduction in the defendant's pay at the appropriate time. This was in my view plainly a mistake of fact rather than one of law.

Other errors clearly occurred, which were not explored by either side in evidence at the trial. In particular the defendant continued to be paid half pay for seven months after January 1975 when he should have been paid nothing at all. A comparison of the two schedules referred to earlier in the judgment reveals a number of further discrepancies (for example relating to deductions for sick benefit) between the amounts which he actually received and those which he should have received. Mr Bowyer urged that they might have been caused by a misinterpretation of documents, such as the relevant regulations setting out the entitlement of the plaintiffs' employees while absent from work. He submitted that such misinterpretation would have constituted a mistake of law: see, for example, *Holt* v *Markham* [1923] 1 KB 504 and *Ministry of Health* v *Simpson* [1951] AC 251, 269–273. However, nothing appearing from the evidence or submitted in argument leads me to think there is any real likelihood that these errors were caused by mistakes of law rather than of fact. On the evidence, I think it a fair inference that the reason why the plaintiffs continued to pay the defendant after the end of the first 12 months of his absence from work was that the pay clerks concerned were unaware or had forgotten that this 12 month period had expired. The other errors in my opinion are similarly likely to have occurred simply through incorrect factual data having been fed into the plaintiffs' computers. Thus in my opinion, albeit by a fairly narrow margin, the plaintiffs have discharged the onus which falls upon them of showing that the overpayments were made under mistakes of fact.

However, since this is a test case, I would like to add the following observations before leaving this aspect of it. Though in the present instance the incorrect final figures were produced by computers, it has not been suggested that the fault was that of the computers themselves. It was human error that gave rise to the mistakes, by feeding the computers with the wrong data. In the present instance it has not been possible for the plaintiffs to identify the individual person or persons who were responsible for the errors. However, in other similar cases the court might well expect the responsible individuals to be identified and called as witnesses. Employers who pay their employees under a computerised system should not in my opinion assume from the decision of this court in the present case that, if they overpay their employees through some kind of mistake, they are entitled to recover it simply for the asking, provided only that they are not barred by estoppel or some other special defence. The borderline between mistakes of law and mistakes of fact is not clearly defined in the cases. Decisions such as *Cooper* v *Phibbs* (1867) LR 2 HL 149 and *Allcard* v *Walker* [1896] 2 Ch 369 suggest that the courts are not quick to extend the former category.

The distinction has been the subject of some criticism. The authors of *Goff and Jones, The Law of Restitution*, 2nd ed. (1978), p. 91 express the view that the principle in *Bilbie* v *Lumley* (1802) 2 East 469 should only preclude recovery of money which was paid in settlement of an honest claim and that any other payment made under a mistake of law should be recoverable, if it would have been recoverable had the mistake been one of fact. Nevertheless the distinction still exists in English law. I think the burden will still fall on an employer who seeks to recover an overpayment from an overpaid employee to satisfy the court that, on the balance of probabilities in all the circumstances of the case, it was a mistake of fact which gave rise to the overpayment. The plaintiffs in the present instance in my opinion succeed in relation to this issue only because they have discharged this burden on the particular facts of the case. . . .

Note

For discussion of the defence of estoppel as it applied to this claim, see Chapter 8, Section 2.

Rover International Ltd v Cannon Film Sales Ltd
[1989] 1 WLR 912 (CA)

'Rover' appeal

Rover and Thorn EMI (who were subsequently taken over by Cannon) entered into a purported agreement in the nature of a joint venture for the dubbing and distribution of the latter's films, including 'Highlander', in Italian cinemas. The arrangement provided for gross receipts to be split between the parties in agreed proportions. Rover were to pay Thorn EMI/Cannon an advance of $1,500,000 in instalments. The purported contract was dated 5 December 1985. However, Rover was not incorporated and therefore had no legal existence until 6 February 1986. Rover then paid five instalments totalling $312,500 before a dispute arose. It was then discovered that the underlying agreement was void *ab initio* due to Rover's incapacity at the relevant time. Rover claimed restitution of the instalments paid on the ground of mistake of fact.

KERR LJ: . . . In my view Rover are equally entitled to recover these instalments as having been paid to Cannon under a mistake of fact. As already mentioned, we concluded that this submission was open to Rover although it had only been touched upon in argument below and was not referred to in the judgment. Mr Pardoe submitted faintly that there was no evidence to prove that the instalments had in fact been paid under a mistake, but the facts speak for themselves. It is obvious that the payments would not have been made unless Mr de Rossi and Mrs Karlin had believed that there was a binding contract between Rover and Thorn EMI, and Mr Pardoe rightly did not suggest that this mistaken belief involved a mistake of law. . . .

DILLON LJ: . . . So far as the five instalments in issue are concerned, the claim by Rover for repayment is put on alternative grounds; it is said that, as there was in truth never any contract between Rover and Cannon because the supposed contract had been entered into before Rover had been incorporated in the Channel Islands, the instalments are recoverable either as money paid under a mistake of fact or as money paid for a consideration that has wholly failed.

On the facts this is, in my judgment, a classic case of money paid under a mistake of fact. The instalments were paid because Rover mistakenly believed—as did Cannon—that there was a contract between them, and in order to satisfy Rover's obligations under that contract. It is impossible to suggest any other reason for the payments. Prima facie, therefore, Rover is entitled to recover the payments: see the very valuable explanation of the cases by Robert Goff J in *Barclays Bank Ltd* v *W. J. Simms Son & Cooke (Southern) Ltd* [1980] QB 677, and especially the passage he there cites from the judgment of Parke B in *Kelly* v *Solari*, 9 M & 54, 58–59. . . .

Question

Was Mr Pardoe (counsel for Cannon) right to concede that Rover's mistake was not one of law?

Note

Kerr LJ also held the fact that Rover's incorporators had been at fault in mistakenly believing it had capacity to enter the contract was irrelevant, because the leading case of *Kelly* v *Solari* decided 'a genuine mistake is not vitiated by carelessness'.

Section 2: money paid under a mistake of law

See Burrows, *Restitution*, 109–20.

A: The General Bar on Recovery

Bilbie* v *Lumley

(1802) 2 East 469; 102 ER 448 (KB)

Action for money had and received

The defendant insured failed to disclose to the plaintiff insurer a material letter relating to the time of sailing of a ship before a policy of marine insurance was entered into. This rendered the policy liable to be avoided for non-disclosure at the election of the insurer. There was a claim for a loss as by capture. Before the loss was adjusted and any payment made, all the relevant papers, including the letter, were given to the underwriters. *Then* the plaintiff paid the defendant £100. The plaintiff claimed to recover the money as paid under a mistake of law, that he was not aware at the time of payment that he had a complete defence to any claim on the policy. The defendant argued that the plaintiff had full knowledge or full means of knowledge of all the circumstances at the time of payment. At York Assizes, Rooke J gave judgment for the plaintiff. The Court of King's Bench reversed him, holding that a payment made under a mistake of law was irrecoverable.

LORD ELLENBOROUGH CJ: asked the plaintiff's counsel whether he could state any case where if a party paid money to another voluntarily with a full knowledge of all the facts of the case, he could recover it back again on account of his ignorance of the law? [No answer being given, his Lordship continued:] The case of *Chatfield* v *Paxton* is the only one I ever heard of where Lord Kenyon at Nisi Prius intimated something of that sort. But when it was afterwards brought before this Court on a motion for a new trial, there were some other circumstances of fact relied on; and it was so doubtful at last on what precise ground the case turned that it was not reported. Every man must be taken to be cognizant of the law; otherwise there is no saying to what extent the excuses of ignorance might not be carried. It would be urged in almost every case. In *Lowrie* v *Bourdieu*, Dougl 467, money paid under a mere mistake of the law (was endeavoured to be recovered back), and there Buller J observed that ignorantia juris non excusat, &c.

Note

This case is usually cited as authority for the proposition that payments made under a mistake of law are irrecoverable. Goff and Jones argue (at 142–4) that the case rather supports a narrower principle, that a payment made in submission to an honest claim is irrecoverable. This upholds the policy in favour of settlements (see also Goff and Jones 50–4). See Andrews, 'Mistaken settlements of disputable claims' [1989] LMCLQ 431, who argues for the recognition of a concept of 'implied settlement' to explain cases such as *Bell* v *Lever Bros Ltd* [1932] AC 161, and further that restitutionary principles should not be allowed to subvert the contractual policy of upholding settlements as a way of allocating risks between parties in dispute. See, for another view, Arrowsmith, 'Mistake and the Role of "Submission to an Honest Claim"', Essay 2 in Burrows, *Essays*, 17–38.

Brisbane v *Dacres*

(1813) 5 Taunt 143; 128 ER 641 (Common Pleas)

Action for money had and received

The plaintiff, the commander of HMS *Arethusa*, was ordered by Admiral Dacres to carry 700,000 dollars of government bullion from Jamaica to Portsmouth. The plaintiff received £850 from the Treasury for this service. In accordance with established naval practice the plaintiff, in 1808, paid a proportion of this sum to his admiral, in the belief that in the circumstances the admiral had a legal right to the sum. In *Montagu* v *Janverin* (1811) 3 Taunt 442, 128 ER 175 it had been decided that the practice was not legally binding, although it had been assumed to be in previous cases. However, as a matter of fact the admirals continued to receive a share. The plaintiff sought restitution from the widow and executrix of Admiral Dacres.

GIBBS J: . . . We must take this payment to have been made under a demand of right, and I think that where a man demands money of another as a matter of right, and that other, with a full knowledge of the facts upon which the demand is founded, has paid a sum, he never can recover back the sum he has so voluntarily paid. It may be, that upon a further view he may form a different opinion of the law, and it may be, his subsequent opinion may be the correct one. If we were to hold otherwise, I think many inconveniences may arise; there are many doubtful questions of law: when they arise, the defendant has an option, either to litigate the question, or to submit to the demand, and pay the money. I think, that by submitting to the demand, he that pays the money gives it to the person to whom he pays it, and makes it his, and closes the transaction between them. He who receives it has a right to consider it as his without dispute: he spends it in confidence that it is his; and it would be most mischievous and unjust, if he who has acquiesced in the right by such voluntary payment, should be at liberty, at any time within the statute of limitations, to rip up the matter, and recover back the money. He who received it is not in the same condition: he has spent it in the confidence it was his, and perhaps has no means of repayment. I am aware cases were cited at the bar, in which were dicta that sums paid under a mistake of the law might be recovered back, though paid with a knowledge of the facts; but there are none of these cases which may not be supported on a much sounder ground. In the case of *Farmer* v *Arundel*, 2 Bl Rep 825, De Grey CJ indeed says: 'When money is paid by one man to another on a mistake either of fact, or of law, or by deceit, this action (of money had and received) will certainly lie.' Now the case did not call for this proposition so generally expressed; and I do think, that doctrine, laid down so very widely and generally, where it is not called for by the circumstances of the case, is but little to be attended to; at least it is not entitled to the same weight in a case where the attention of the Court is not called to a distinction, as it is in a case where it is called to the distinction. . . . Among all the practitioners of the Court of King's Bench, where questions of this sort very frequently arise on insurance transactions, we were universally of this opinion, that where the money was paid with a knowledge of the facts, it could not be recovered back. One underwriter chose to pay, rather than resist, another resisted and succeeded; in all similar cases it would be very easy to say, 'I paid this without a knowledge of the law, and therefore may recover it back.' Our only question, then, in all cases was, whether the facts were known: this was the universal practice, till *Bilbie* v *Lumley*, 2 East 469, occurred: that case was tried at York, before Rooke J, who ruled differently: after the report was read, Lord Ellenborough asked Wood B, then of counsel for the plaintiff, whether he could find any case which would support it; and he cited none. Lord Ellenborough said he never heard of any, except *Chatfield* v *Paxton*, and that it was so doubtful at last upon what precise ground that case turned, that it was not reported, and the rule was made absolute for a new trial. Now this was a direct decision upon the point, certainly without argument; but the counsel, whose learning we all know, and who was never forward to give up a case which he thought he could support, abandoned it. In *Herbert* v *Champion*, 1 Campb 134, a distinction is clearly taken between an adjustment on a policy, and a payment on the adjustment; and Lord Ellenborough says, that if the money has been paid, it cannot be recovered back without proof of fraud. I am therefore of opinion this money cannot be recovered back. I think on principle that money which is paid to a man who claims it as his right, with a knowledge of all the facts, cannot be recovered back. I think it on principle, and I think the weight of the authorities is so, and I think the dicta that go beyond it, are not supported or called for by the facts of the cases. *Bilbie* v *Lumley*, I think, is a decision to that effect; and for these reasons, I am of opinion, the plaintiff is not entitled to recover.

MANSFIELD CJ: . . . I find nothing contrary to æquum et bonum, to bring it within the case of *Moses* v *Macfarlane*, in his retaining it. So far from its being contrary to æquum et bonum, I think it would be most contrary to æquum et bonum, if he were obliged to repay it back. For see how it is! If the sum be large, it probably alters the habits of his life, he increases his expenses, he has spent it over and over again; perhaps he cannot repay it at all, or not without great distress: is he then, five years and eleven months after, to be called on to repay it? The case of *Farmer* v *Arundel*, and De Grey's maxim there, is cited: it certainly is very hard upon a Judge, if a rule which he generally lays down, is to be taken up and carried to its full extent. This is sometimes done by counsel, who have nothing else to rely on; but great caution ought to be used by the Court in extending such maxims to cases which the Judge who uttered them never had in contemplation. If such is the use to be made of them, I ought to be very cautious how I lay down general maxims from this bench. . . .

Note

Brisbane v *Dacres* confirmed that *Bilbie* v *Lumley* had laid down a rule that money paid under a mistake of law was irrecoverable. The judgments of Gibbs J and Sir James Mansfield CJ contain the most explicit judicial discussion of concern about what Professor Birks has termed the policy of 'security of receipt'. However, as Professor Birks observes, the only consideration in Gibbs J's discussion of payments under a mistake of law which does not equally apply to payments under a mistake of fact is 'the greater prevalence of "doubtful questions of law"' (Birks, *Introduction*, 165).

Holt v _Markham_
[1923] 1 KB 504 (CA)

Action for money had and received

Upon demobilisation after the First World War, RAF officers were entitled to a gratuity. The defendant was on the Emergency List, which meant that according to the regulations he was entitled to a gratuity at less than the usual rate. The plaintiff paid the defendant the usual gratuity, in ignorance both of the fact that the defendant was on the Emergency List, and of the legal significance of the defendant being on that list. *Held*: that the plaintiff had failed to establish an operative mistake of fact. The mistake, if any, was one of law arising from the misapplication or misconstruction of the relevant regulations in respect of the defendant's special circumstances. Therefore the plaintiff was not entitled to restitution.

B: Exceptions to the Rule of Non-Recovery

In re Diplock, Diplock v _Wintle_
[1948] Ch 465 (CA); affd *sub nom.* **_Ministry of Health_ v _Simpson_**
[1951] AC 251 (HL)

Caleb Diplock died in 1936 and by his will left his residuary estate to be distributed to 'such charitable institution or institutions or other charitable or benevolent object or objects' as his executors saw fit. Over the next three years the executors paid out over £200,000 to 139 charities of their choice. In 1940, Diplock's next-of-kin challenged the will and the House of Lords in an earlier judgment held it to be wholly invalidated by the use of the fatal disjunctive 'or benevolent'. The claims of the next-of-kin against the executors were compromised, and the next-of-kin then brought these actions against various recipient charities. Claims were pursued both on an *in personam* and an *in rem* basis. The extracts relate only to the claim *in personam*.

Court of Appeal

LORD GREENE MR (giving the judgment of the Court): . . . Now upon the question whether the mistake here made was one of fact or of law we think the learned judge was clearly right in deciding that it was the latter and we cannot usefully add anything to what fell from him upon that point. Equally we agree with him that as regards common law claims for money had and received the action will not lie where the money has been paid under a mistake of law. It may, we think, be taken to be clearly established that the common law claim is founded upon an implied promise to pay and that—whether by an application of the principle 'igorantia juris non excusat' or on other grounds—no such promise will be implied where the payment was made under mistake of the general law. It is no doubt true that for certain purposes (for example the purposes of the application of the Statutes of Limitation) the direct equitable claim by the unpaid beneficiary against the wrongly or overpaid recipient of part of the testator's estate—for it is conceded that in certain circumstances such direct claims will lie—has hitherto been regarded as analogous to the common law claim for money had and received. Both are, after all, money claims. But the common law claim, as may now be taken to be established, is in no sense derived from equity, but has a lineage altogether independent of it. And as the appellants forcibly pressed upon us in argument, in other respects there are marked and important differences between the claim here put forward on the part of the appellants and a claim at common law for money had and received. In the latter the proper claimant is normally the person who originally made the payment or is that person's principal or representative: and the claim is made against him who received the money or his representative. It is indeed difficult to see how, save between the parties to the original transaction or between parties linked by a relationship such as that of principal and agent, any implied promise to repay could be imported. In the present case the payments were originally made by the executors and it is in our judgment impossible to say that in making the payments the executors were acting as agents or in any way on behalf of the next-of-kin, of whose rights and existence the executors were entirely ignorant. Plainly, nothing that the next of kin have done can be said to have involved any ratification or acceptance on their part of the executors' acts. Further whatever may have been the nature of the mistakes made by the executors, the next-of-kin have never made any mistake at all whether of law or of fact.

For these reasons it seems to us that in approaching the question of the existence and characteristics of the direct equitable cause of action there is not, unless the authorities otherwise establish, any necessity in logic for regarding the claim as being clothed, as it were, with all the attributes or limitations appropriate to the common law action for money had and received. Nor, on similar grounds, does it appear that there is any conflict involved between law and equity. Equity here, as in other places, comes in, as Maitland has observed, 'not to destroy the common law but to filfil it.' Since (for so runs the appellants' argument) the common law can only recognise the two parties to the transaction, payer and payee, or at most third parties asserting the rights of one or other of them, the common law does not, to borrow again from the language of Maitland 'comprehend the whole truth.' For the payers in the present case (namely the executors) were handling not their own money but the money of others who had a proprietary interest unknown to and unrecognised by the executors and who, from the moment when they became aware of their own rights and the transactions of the executors, immediately challenged and repudiated what the executors had done.

Nevertheless, if the claim in equity exists it must be shown to have an ancestry founded in history and in the practice and precedents of the courts administering equity jurisdiction. It is not sufficient that because we may think that the 'justice' of the present case requires it, we should invent such a jurisdiction for the first time. [Lord Greene MR then undertook a comprehensive review of the authorities which the Court took 'to illustrate a coherent and continuous development of an equitable jurisdiction of which the foundation was firmly laid by Lord Nottingham in the year 1682' (in *Noel* v *Robinson* (1682) 1 Vern 90, 23 ER 334) and concluded:]

What then is the conclusion to be drawn on this part of the appellants' claim from what we fear has been a long citation of the authorities? It is not, we think, necessary or desirable that we should attempt any exhaustive formulation of the nature of the equity invoked which will be applicable to every class of case. But it seems to us, first, to be established and that the equity may be available equally to an unpaid or underpaid creditor, legatee, or next-of-kin. Second, it seems to us that a claim by a next-of-kin will not be liable to be defeated merely (a) in the absence of administration by the court: or (b) because the mistake under which the original payment was made was one of law rather than fact; or (c) because the original recipient, as things turn out, had no title at all and was a stranger to the estate; though the effect of the refund in the last case will be to dispossess the original recipient altogether rather than to produce equality between him and the claimant and other persons having a like title to that of the recipient. In our judgment there is no authority either in logic or in the decided cases for such limitations to the equitable right of action. In our judgment also there is no justification for such limitations to be found in the circumstances which gave rise to the equity. And as regards the conscience of the defendant upon which in this as in other jurisdictions equity is said to act, it is prima facie at least a sufficient circumstance that the defendant, as events have proved, has received some share of the estate to which he was not entitled. 'A party' said Sir John Leach in *David* v *Frowd* 1 My & K 200, 211 'claiming under such circumstances has no great reason to complain that he is called upon to replace what he has received against his right.'

On the other hand, to such a claim by an unpaid beneficiary, there is, in our judgment, at least in circumstances such as the present, one important qualification. Since the original wrong payment was attributable to the blunder of the personal representatives, the right of the unpaid beneficiary is in the first instance against the wrongdoing executor or administrator: and the beneficiary's direct claim in equity against those overpaid or wrongly paid should be limited to the amount which he cannot recover from the party responsible. In some cases the amount will be the whole amount of the payment wrongly made, e.g., where the executor or administrator is shown to be wholly without assets or is protected from attack by having acted under an order of the court. . . .

Note

Lord Greene MR then held that the sum recovered from the executors under the compromise ought to be credited rateably amongst the 139 charities, and that the respondent charities should be ordered to repay the money received subject to that qualification.

House of Lords

LORD SIMONDS: [His Lordship stated 'I think that the reasoning and conclusion of the Court of Appeal are unimpeachable' and turned to consider the main argument of the appellant charity (the Westminster Hospital) that the principle of recovery was inapplicable where the payment was made because of an error of law:] . . . It was that the equitable remedy was subject at least to this qualification, that it was not applicable where the wrongful payment was made in error of law. It was said that in every case where it had been applied the wrongful payment had been made under a mistake of fact and that wherever the principle had been stated without any such qualification, it must be read, nevertheless, as subject to it. I think, my Lords, that this argument which found favour with the judge is misconceived.

In the first place, though in almost all the reported cases the probability is that the wrongful payment was made under a mistake of fact, that is not true of all of them and in many of them, while the probability is in one direction, there can be no certainty without further information which is not now available. This leads directly to the second reason. In not one of the many cases where the equity was applied was any suggestion made in argument or judgment that the issue depended on the nature of the mistake under which the wrongful payment had been made. It is not credible that, if the distinction between mistake of fact and law was relevant, it would never have been mentioned, particularly at a time when in the courts of common law it was being established. And here it may be observed that the equitable doctrine was well settled before that event took place: for such cases as *Farmer* v *Arundel* 2 W Bl 824; *Bize* v *Dickason* 1 Term Rep 285; *Brisbane* v *Dacres* 5 Taunt 143; *Bilbie* v *Lumley* 2 East 469, show that up to the end of the eighteenth century there were in high places doubts as to the validity of the distinction in the common law.

In the third place the most satisfactory reason for the distinction rests in the maxim, itself probably taken from the criminal law, ignorantia juris neminem excusat: see *Baylis* v *Bishop of London* [1913] 1 Ch 127. The man who makes a wrong payment because he has mistaken the law may not plead his own ignorance of the law and so cannot recover what he has wrongfully paid. It is difficult to see what relevance this distinction can have, where a legatee does not plead his own mistake or his own ignorance but, having exhausted his remedy against the executor who has made the wrongful payment, seeks to recover money from him who has been wrongfully paid. To such a suit the executor was not a necessary party and there was no means by which the plaintiff could find out whether his mistake was of law or of fact or even whether his wrongful act was mistaken or deliberate. He could guess and ask the court to guess but he could prove nothing. I reject therefore the suggestion that the equitable remedy in such circumstances was thus restricted and repeat that it would be a strange thing if the Court of Chancery, having taken upon itself to see that the assets of a deceased person were duly administered, was deterred from doing justice to creditor, legatee or next-of-kin because the executor had done him wrong under a mistake of law. If in truth this were so, I think that the Father of Equity would not recognise his child. . . .

Notes

1. For discussion of the *in rem* claim, see Chapter 7, Section 2.

2. The mistake of law was on the part of the executors, not the next-of-kin. The case is also a three party, rather than a two party configuration. As an instance of strict personal liability in equity (albeit arising in the specialised context of the administration of estates) it is crucial to Professor Birks's creative re-interpretation of a large body of case law as evidencing a general cause of action in unjust enrichment which he terms 'ignorance'. For development of this argument see Birks, *Introduction*, 143–5; Birks, 'Misdirected Funds – Restitution from the Recipient' [1989] LMCLQ 296 and see below, Section 5.

3. *In re Diplock* is also crucial to Birks's theory of 'interceptive subtraction' (see Birks, *Introduction*, 142–3). For a thorough rejection of this analysis and a defence of the requirement that the next-of-kin's remedies must be exhausted against the executors (of which Birks is critical), see Smith, 'Three-Party Restitution: A Critique of Birks's Theory of Interceptive Subtraction' (1991) 11 OJLS 481, especially at 497–500. (See further Burrows, *Restitution*, 51–3.)

Kiriri Cotton Co. Ltd* v *Dewani
[1960] AC 192 (PC)

Action for money had and received

The defendant leased to the plaintiff a flat in Salisbury Road, Kampala, at 300 shillings a month. The plaintiff was required to pay a premium ('key money') of 10,000 shillings to the defendant as a condition of the defendant entering into the lease. Such premiums were prohibited by the Ugandan Rent Restriction Ordinance. Neither party appreciated this. The plaintiff sought restitution of the money.

LORD DENNING: . . . The issue thus becomes: Was the plaintiff in pari delicto with the defendant? Mr Elwyn Jones, for the appellant, said they were both in pari delicto. The payment was, he said, made voluntarily, under no mistake of fact, and without any extortion, oppression or imposition, and could not be recovered back. True, it was paid under a mistake of law, but that was a mistake common to them both. They were both equally supposed to know the law. They both equally mistook it and were thus in pari delicto. In support of this argument the appellant referred to such well-known cases as *Harse* v *Pearl Life Assurance Co.* [1904] 1 KB 558; *William Whiteley Ltd* v *The King* (1909) 26 TLR 19; *Evanson* v *Crooks* (1911) 28 TLR 123; and particularly to *Sharp Brothers & Knight* v *Chant* [1917] 1 KB 771, 776.

Their Lordships cannot accept this argument. It is not correct to say that everyone is presumed to know the law. The true proposition is that no man can excuse himself from doing his duty by saying that he did not know the law on the matter. Ignorantia juris neminem excusat. Nor is it correct to say that money paid under a mistake of law can never be recovered back. The true proposition is that money paid under a mistake of law, by itself and without more, cannot be recovered back. James LJ pointed that out in *Rogers* v *Ingham* (1876) 3 ChD 351, 355. If there is something more in addition to a mistake of law—if there is something in the defendant's conduct which shows that, of the two of them, he is the one primarily responsible for the mistake—then it may be recovered back. Thus, if as between the two of them the duty of observing the law is placed on the shoulders of the one rather than the other—it being imposed on him specially for the protection of the other—then they are not in pari delicto and the money can be recovered back; see *Browning* v *Morris* (1778) 2

Cowp 790, 792, by Lord Mansfield. Likewise, if the responsibility for the mistake lies more on the one than the other—because he has misled the other when he ought to know better—then again they are not in pari delicto and the money can be recovered back; see *Harse* v *Pearl Life Assurance Co.* [1904] 1 KB 558, 564, by Romer LJ. These propositions are in full accord with the principles laid down by Lord Mansfield relating to the action for money had and received. Their Lordships have in mind particularly his judgment in *Smith* v *Bromley* (1760) 2 Doug 696 in notis, which he delivered when he sat at Guildhall in April, 1760: and his celebrated judgment three or four weeks later, on May 19, 1760, in *Moses* v *Macferlan* (1760) 2 Burr 1005, when he sat in banco. Their Lordships were referred to some cases 30 or 40 years ago where disparaging remarks were made about the action for money had and received: but their Lordships venture to suggest that these were made under a misunderstanding of its origin. It is not an action on contract or imputed contract. If it were, none such could be imputed here, as their Lordships readily agree. It is simply an action for restitution of money which the defendant has received but which the law says he ought to return to the plaintiff. This was explained by Lord Wright in *Fibrosa Spolka Akcyjna* v *Fairbairn Lawson Combe Barbour Ltd* [1943] AC 32, 62–64. All the particular heads of money had and received, such as money paid under a mistake of fact, paid under a consideration that has wholly failed, money paid by one who is not in pari delicto with the defendant, are only instances where the law says the money ought to be returned.

In applying these principles to the present case, the most important thing to observe is that the Rent Restriction Ordinance was intended to protect tenants from being exploited by landlords in days of housing shortage. One of the obvious ways in which a landlord can exploit the housing shortage is by demanding from the tenant 'key-money.' Section 3(2) of the Rent Restriction Ordinance was enacted so as to protect tenants from exploitation of that kind. This is apparent from the fact that the penalty is imposed only on the landlord or his agent and not upon the tenant. It is imposed on the person who 'asks for, solicits or receives any sum of money,' but not on the person who submits to the demand and pays the money. It may be that the tenant who pays money is an accomplice or an aider and abettor (see *Johnson* v *Youden* [1950] 1 KB 544 and section 3 of the Rent Restriction (Amendment) Ordinance, 1954), but he can hardly be said to be in pari delicto with the landlord. The duty of observing the law is firmly placed by the Ordinance on the shoulders of the landlord for the protection of the tenant: and if the law is broken, the landlord must take the primary responsibility. Whether it be a rich tenant who pays a premium as a bribe in order to 'jump the queue,' or a poor tenant who is at his wit's end to find accommodation, neither is so much to blame as the landlord who is using his property rights so as to exploit those in need of a roof over their heads. . . .

R* v *Tower Hamlets London Borough Council, ex parte Chetnik Developments Ltd
[1988] AC 858 (HL)

Chetnik, the applicant development company, paid rates upon a warehouse to the council, before they realised that they had a complete defence to the claim because at the time they were prohibited by law from occupying those premises. They sought restitution of the sum paid under s. 9(1) of the General Rate Act 1967, which provides: '. . . where it is shown to the satisfaction of a rating authority that any amount paid in rates, and not recoverable apart from this section, could properly be refunded on the ground that . . . (e) the person who made the payment in respect of rates was not liable to make that payment, the rating authority may refund that amount or a part thereof.' The council refused to refund on a number of grounds, including *inter alia* that the payment was made under a mistake of law and that the company had suffered no hardship. The company sought a judicial review of the council's decision.

LORD BRIDGE OF HARWICH: . . . The rule that money paid under a mistake of law is irrecoverable is said to stem from the principle that there must be an end to litigation. But there is an instructive line of authority showing circumstances in which the court will not permit the rule to be invoked.

In *Ex parte James* (1874) LR 9 Ch App 609, a judgment creditor had levied execution in satisfaction of a judgment debt against a debtor subsequently adjudicated bankrupt. The judgment creditor later paid over the proceeds of the execution to the trustee in bankruptcy mistakenly believing that he was legally obliged to do so. The trustee in bankruptcy claimed to retain this sum for the benefit of the general body of unsatisfied creditors on the ground that it had been paid under a mistake of law. Rejecting this claim, James LJ said, at p. 614:

> I am of opinion that a trustee in bankruptcy is an officer of the court. He has inquisitorial powers given him by the court, and the court regards him as its officer, and he is to hold money in his hands upon trust for its equitable distribution among the creditors. The court, then, finding that he has in his hands money which in equity belongs to someone else, ought to set an example to the world by paying it to the person really entitled to it. In my opinion the Court of Banruptcy ought to be as honest as other people.

Ex parte Simmonds (1885) 16 QBD 308 was another case of a trustee in bankruptcy claiming to retain money paid to him under a mistake of law. Lord Esher MR said, at p. 312:

> When I find that a proposition has been laid down by a Court of Equity or by the Court of Bankruptcy which strikes me as a good, a righteous, and a wholesome one, I eagerly desire to adopt it. Such a proposition was laid down by James LJ in *Ex parte James*, LR 9 Ch App 609. A rule has been adopted by courts of law for the purpose of putting an end to litigation, that, if one litigant party has obtained money from the other erroneously, under a mistake of law, the party who has paid it cannot afterwards recover it. But the court has never intimated that it is a high-minded thing to keep money obtained in this way; the court allows the party who has obtained it to do a shabby thing in order to avoid a greater evil, in order that is, to put an end to litigation. But James LJ laid it down in *Ex parte James* that, although the court will not prevent a litigant party from acting in this way, it will not act so itself, and it will not allow its own officer to act so. It will direct its officer to do that which any high-minded man would do, viz., not to take advantage of the mistake of law.

[Lord Bridge considered *Blackpool and Fleetwood Tramroad Co.* v *Bispham with Norbreck Urban District Council* [1910] 1 KB 592 and continued:]

So it emerges from these authorities that the retention of moneys known to have been paid under a mistake at law, although it is a course permitted to an ordinary litigant, is not regarded by the courts as a 'high-minded thing' to do, but rather as a 'shabby thing' or a 'dirty trick' and hence is a course which the court will not allow one of its own officers, such as a trustee in bankruptcy, to take. If the *Blackpool* case [1910] 1 KB 592 was rightly decided, the same principle applies to prevent a rating authority enforcing a liability for current rates without giving credit for a past overpayment of rates made under a mistake of law. Yet this seems to produce an anomaly in effectively permitting a ratepayer to recover a mistakenly overpaid rate by way of set off against a subsequent rate liability, when the ordinary rule of law precludes any direct right of recovery.

It was, as I understand their reasoning, from this anomalous position and in consideration of the legitimate sense of grievance which might be felt by the ratepayer who, like the present respondents, is in no position to avail himself of a right of set off, that the Court of Appeal derived their view of the purpose of section 9 of the Act of 1967 as stated in the passage I have earlier quoted from their judgment.

I in no way dissent from this reasoning, but I should myself have been content to derive the same conclusion from the broader consideration that Parliament must have intended rating authorities to act in the same high principled way expected by the court of its own officers and not to retain rates paid under a mistake of law, or in paragraph (a) upon an erroneous valuation, unless there were, as Parliament must have contemplated there might be in some cases, special circumstances in which a particular overpayment was made such as to justify retention of the whole or part of the amount overpaid.

I agree with the Court of Appeal that the rating authority's decision not to refund the rates overpaid by the respondents was made in disregard of the legislative purpose of section 9 and that the reasons given in the letter of 8 November 1983 were irrelevant to the question how the discretion conferred by the section should be exercised. . . .

It was argued that in exercising discretion under section 9 the rating authority could take account of the financial circumstances both of the applicant and of their body of ratepayers and of the financial constraints to which the authority are subject in providing much needed services for the residents in their area. The London Borough of Tower Hamlets, your Lordships were told, are an indigent, rate-capped authority. These considerations are irrelevant to the justice or injustice of retaining rates mistakenly overpaid in the circumstances of any particular case and therefore irrelevant in the exercise of the discretion under section 9.

A much more formidable argument, which has caused me considerable difficulty, is that the principle underlying the line of decided cases to which I have referred and justifying the conclusion that it falls short of the highest standards of probity and fair dealing to retain money paid under a mistake of law has no application to a case where for any reason the recipient no longer has the amount mistakenly paid 'in hand.' It is pointed out, first, that a rating authority may have expended its entire rate income, including the amount mistakenly overpaid in one year, in the provision of services in its area in that year, but will be obliged to rely, as the source of any refund, on its rate income provided by the body of ratepayers in its area in the year when the refund has to be made. It is contended, therefore, that a relevant consideration to the exercise of the discretion under section 9 is whether the overpayment has contributed to any reserve fund held by the rating authority so that the rating authority may be said to 'retain' the overpayment. It is pointed out, secondly, that a substantial proportion of the rating authority's rate income in this case in the years in which the respondents' mistaken payments were made was levied to meet precepts issued to the rating authority by other authorities, notably the G.L.C., pursuant to section 12 of the Act of 1967. Hence a proportion of the amounts mistakenly paid by the respondents, it is said, ought properly to be regarded as having been received on behalf of those precepting authorities and at least pro tanto this must afford a conclusive reason for refusing to refund the amount mistakenly paid.

I was initially much impressed by this second line of argument. But on reflection I have reached the conclusion that the argument is really self defeating. The legislature must have been well aware, when enacting the provisions now contained in section 9 of the Act of 1967, that rating authorities levy rates not only on their own behalf but also on behalf of precepting authorities. This was the norm under the two tier system of local government in the 1960s. If it is legitimate to start from the premise that the primary objective of section 9 is to remedy what would otherwise ordinarily be the injustice of denying repayment to a ratepayer who has mistakenly paid an amount in excess of his liability, it is difficult to see any rational ground for making a distinction between rates levied for the rating authority's own purposes and rates levied to meet precepts by other authorities. At all events, if the legislature intended to make such a distinction in connection with the discretion to refund overpayments, I would expect to find express provision requiring or authorising precepting authorities to contribute directly or indirectly to the refund. Alternatively, if any amount of the overpayment referrable to precepts had been intended to be left out of account in deciding the amount of a refund, it seems to me inconceivable that the statute would not have expressly so provided. The absence of any provision to either effect leads to the conclusion that the intention of section 9 was that the mistaken overpayments should be treated as having been made to a single indivisible fund in the hands of the rating authority and this is re-enforced by the very use in the section of the word 'refund.' The eventual accounting process as between rating authorities and precepting authorities pursuant to rules made under section 14 of the Act of 1967 (currently the Rate Product Rules 1981 (SI 1981 No. 327)) is a very complex one. To have introduced some provision for apportionment between authorities of contributions towards any refund under section 9 of a mistaken overpayment would have added a further complication and this, to my mind, affords a very probable explanation why no such provision has been made. If mistaken overpayments are intended to be treated under section 9 as having been made to a single indivisible fund, I think it must follow a fortiori that the justice or injustice of making a refund in any particular case cannot depend on the rating authority's internal finances affecting the state of the fund as between one year and another.

The most difficult aspect of the problem is to give guidance as to the positive factors relevant to the exercise of the discretion under section 9 which may be considered in whole or in part to displace the prima facie justice of refunding overpayments. I think such factors can only arise from the circumstances in which the overpayment came to be made in any particular case. The conduct of the person making the payment considered in relation to those circumstances will be of primary relevance. The Court of Appeal have given only one example, which may be thought rather extreme, of the person fraudulently representing himself to be in occupation, when in fact he was not. I can do no more than offer two further illustrations, which may be a little less extreme. Suppose a ratepayer has initially disputed his liability to pay an amount demanded in respect of rates on a debatable legal ground, but after correspondence with the rating authority's solicitor has either agreed a compromise payment or even met the claim in full rather than incur the cost of litigation. Subsequently a decision of the courts in litigation between other parties establishes that the ratepayer's original contention disputing his liability was well-founded. He applies for a refund of the amount he paid under a mistake of law. Here the ratepayer has made the payment in full knowledge of a possible ground on which to contest his liability and in consequence of a deliberate decision not to do so. Suppose again that a residential property is overvalued in the valuation list. The value in the list enables the owner to let the property free of rent restriction. He lets the property at a high inclusive rent and, by agreement, he pays the rates. At the end of the tenancy the owner moves into occupation and immediately makes a successful proposal to reduce the value in the list and applies for a refund in respect of past years under section 9(1)(a) which is supported by a certificate from the valuation officer under section 9(3). The circumstances justify the inference that the owner deliberately took advantage of the excessive valuation. In either of these cases there would be relevant reasons for the rating authority or a Crown Court on appeal to refuse the application for a refund. These illustrations are not, of course, intended to cover the ground exhaustively, which it would be foolish to attempt and impossible to achieve. But I hope they may be of some assistance to rating authorities and Crown Courts in any future case arising under section 9 as indicating the kind of considerations which may and should be taken into account as relevant to the justice of the application for a refund in the circumstances of any particular case. . . .

LORD GOFF OF CHIEVELEY: My Lords, I agree that the appeal should be dismissed for the reasons given by my noble and learned friend, Lord Bridge of Harwich. I wish only to add a few words regarding the guidance which my noble and learned friend has given to assist those who may in future have to consider the exercise of the discretion conferred by section 9 of the Act of 1967.

Section 9 confers on rating authorities a statutory power to refund an amount paid in respect of rates, which is not recoverable apart from the section, where it is shown to their satisfaction that the amount could properly be refunded on certain specified grounds. As my noble and learned friend has pointed out, putting aside paragraph (a), the amount paid would not be recoverable apart from the section because it was paid under a mistake of law and, on the law as it stands at present (which is much criticised, especially by comparative lawyers, since no comparable rule is to be found in continental legal systems—see, in particular, *Zweigert and Kotz, Introduction to Comparative Law*, 2nd ed. (1987), vol. 2. pp. 260–268), money so paid is generally irrecoverable in English law. Effectively, therefore, the section creates a statutory remedy of restitution, in the circumstances specified by the section, to prevent the unjust enrichment of the rating authority at the expense of the ratepayer.

In these circumstances, it should be of assistance to those considering the exercise of the discretion, conferred by the section, to have regard to the general principles of the law of restitution in their search for guidance in the exercise of the power, though always bearing in mind that those principles may be modified, expressly or impliedly, by the terms of the statute. This approach is, as I see it, entirely consistent with (though broader than) the specific examples given by my noble and learned friend. He has first anxiously considered whether the fact that the rating authority will have, for example, employed a substantial part of its rate income to meet precepts by other authorities, would provide a good reason for denying, at least in part, a ratepayer's claim for refund under section 9. This is no more than an inquiry whether it would be right for the local authority to invoke the restitutionary defence of change of position. Generally speaking, I would have thought this to have been an appropriate ground for declining to make a refund; but I nevertheless agree with my noble and learned friend that to do so would be inconsistent with the legislative intention as revealed by the section. Again, he has considered the case of a claim by a ratepayer who has made the payment 'in full knowledge of a possible ground on which to contest liability and in consequence of a deliberate decision not to do so;' such a payment would be irrecoverable in restitution, even on the ground of mistake of fact: see *Kelly* v *Solari* (1841) 9 M & W 54, 58, *per* Lord Abinger CB. Finally, he has considered the case where a ratepayer deliberately takes advantage of an excessive valuation; in such a case, there would of course be no basis for recovery in restitution. It therefore follows, in my opinion, that the general principles of the law of restitution can provide useful guidance in these cases.

Note

There are a number of supposed exceptions to the mistake of law bar. First, it does not apply to payments made to or made by an officer of the court, such as a liquidator or a trustee-in-bankruptcy. Secondly, it does not apply to claims made by the beneficiaries after payments have been made by personal representatives or trustees under a mistake of law, as was held in *Re Diplock* [1948] Ch 465 (CA), affd [1951] AC 251 (HL) (above). Thirdly, mistakes of foreign law are treated as mistakes of fact (*Lazard Bros & Co.* v *Midland Bank Ltd* [1933] AC 289). Fourthly, recently in *Gibbon* v *Mitchell* [1990] 3 All ER 338 Millett J said 'the proposition that equity will never relieve against mistakes of law is clearly too widely stated' (at 343). He set aside a deed entered into by the plaintiff under a mistake as to its effect, even though it appeared to be a mistake of law. This equitable jurisdiction appears to be wider than the law of restitution: see *Cooper* v *Phibbs* (1867) LR 2 HL 149 and *Solle* v *Butcher* [1950] 1 KB 671 discussed in Section 4 below. For these exceptions to the general rule of non-recovery see Burrows, *Restitution*, 111–6. Note also the restrictive tendency towards characterising mistakes as ones as to law. For example, in *Cooper* v *Phibbs*, where the plaintiff mistakenly bought property which he already owned, the House of Lords granted rescission. They distinguished the general law and private rights of ownership. The latter were characterised as matters of fact.

C: *Reform of the Rule*

David Securities Pty Ltd v Commonwealth Bank of Australia
(1992) 175 CLR 353 (High Court of Australia)

The appellant property development companies defaulted in respect of a number of secured borrowing facilities. When the bank sought to recover money due under the contracts of loan, the appellants sought a set-off, alleging that clause 8(b) of the contracts was void as contrary to s. 261 of the Income Tax Assessment Act 1936 (Australia), which prohibited provisions which sought to impose the obligation of paying income tax on the interest paid under a mortgage upon the mortgagor. The bank argued that any such payments were made under a mistake of law.

MASON CJ, DEANE, TOOHEY, GAUDRON AND McHUGH JJ: . . .
The traditional rule
The *Restatement of the Law of Restitution* states[45]:

Until the nineteenth century no distinction was made between mistake of fact and mistake of law and restitution was freely granted both in law and in equity to persons who had paid money to another because of a mistake of law.

In *Farmer* v *Arundel* De Grey CJ stated[46]:

> When money is paid by one man to another on a mistake either of fact or of law, or by deceit, this action [i.e. assumpsit] will certainly lie.

However, in *Bilbie* v *Lumley*[47], Lord Ellenborough CJ refused recovery of moneys paid under a mistake of law. An underwriter sought recovery of moneys from a successful insurance claimant whom he had paid, unaware that non-disclosure by the insured of essential facts at the time of entering the insurance contract relieved the insurer from liability. The underwriter was in possession of all the facts which would have allowed him to deny liability. After counsel was unable to name a case in which recovery had been allowed to a plaintiff who was aware of all relevant facts, Lord Ellenborough CJ denied recovery on the basis of a maxim wholly inapplicable to the case, namely, ignorantia juris non excusat. This approach appears to have been based on an obiter dictum in the judgment of Buller J in *Lowry* v *Bourdieu*[48]. On its facts, the decision in *Bilbie* v *Lumley* was probably correct because the payment appears to have been made voluntarily and not under any mistake at all. Only a few years before, in *Cartwright* v *Rowley*, Lord Kenyon CJ had stated[49]:

> This action cannot be maintained, nor the money recovered back again by it: it has been paid by the plaintiff voluntarily; and where money has been so paid, it must be taken to be properly and legally paid; nor can money be recovered back again by this form of action, unless there are some circumstances to shew that the plaintiff paid it through mistake, or in consequence of coercion.

This was not a case of mistake of law. The plaintiff had employed the defendant, an engine-maker, to make engines under the plaintiff's patent. While work was in progress, the plaintiff advanced money to the defendant, which he then sought to recover because the defendant had caused the plaintiff to miss a business opportunity by taking too long to complete the work. The plaintiff's payment was 'voluntary' in the sense that he had known all the relevant circumstances and yet had chosen to pay the defendant rather than withhold payment or dismiss him. A similar concept of voluntariness was adopted by Chambre J, in dissent, in *Brisbane* v *Dacres*[50], where he concluded that the plaintiff was entitled to recover money paid under a mistake of law because he could not be said to have waived inquiry and chosen to settle the claim. In the same case, Gibbs J took a similar approach in principle, holding that, if a person paid money in response to a claim when fully aware of all the facts, he or she was deemed to have submitted to the demand[51].

It is on the basis of such opinions as this that it has been suggested that *Bilbie* v *Lumley* is authority for the limited proposition that payment made in settlement of an honest claim is irrecoverable[52]. However, rather than being confined to its facts, *Bilbie* v *Lumley* became recognised as authority for the broad proposition that recovery will not be ordered of moneys paid under a mistake of law. It was followed by the majority in *Brisbane* v *Dacres* where Gibbs J said[53]:

> [W]here a man demands money of another as a matter of right, and that other, with a full knowledge of the facts upon which the demand is founded, has paid a sum, he never can recover back the sum he has so voluntarily paid.

Bilbie v *Lumley* was distinguished in *Kelly* v *Solari*[54], a case allowing recovery of moneys paid under a mistake of fact. It thereby became entrenched as a decision denying recovery because the mistake of the plaintiff was one of law. Despite its dubious foundation, the principle gained such acceptance that Croom-Johnson J said of it that it was 'beyond argument at this period in our legal history'[55].
[The judges of the High Court then considered a number of Australian authorities and continued:]

An important feature of the relevant judgments in these three cases is the emphasis on voluntariness or election by the plaintiff. The payment is voluntary or there is an election if the plaintiff chooses to make the payment even though he or she believes a particular law or contractual provision requiring the payment is, or may be, invalid, or is not concerned to query whether payment is legally required; he or she is prepared to assume the validity of the obligation, or is prepared to make the payment irrespective of the validity or invalidity of the obligation, rather than contest the claim for payment. We use the term 'voluntary' therefore to refer to a payment made in satisfaction of an honest claim, rather than a payment not made under any form of compulsion or undue influence. If such qualifying, factual circumstances are considered relevant, the sweeping principle that money paid under a mistake of law is irrecoverable or even the Federal Court's modification of that principle to the effect that mistake of law does not on its own found an action for the recovery of money paid is broader and more preclusive than is necessary. As the authorities cited earlier in explanation of the term 'mistake of law' make clear, the concept includes cases of sheer ignorance as well as cases of positive but incorrect belief. To define 'mistake' as the supposition that a specific fact is true, as Parke B did in *Kelly* v *Solari*[64], which was a mistake of fact case, leaves out of account many fact situations. A narrower principle, founded firmly on the policy that the law wishes to uphold bargains and enforce compromises freely entered into, would be more accurate and equitable.

The identification and acceptance of such a narrow principle is strongly supported by the difficulty and illogicality of seeking to draw a rigid distinction between cases of mistake of law and mistake of fact. The artificiality of this distinction and the numerous exceptions to it[65] lie behind many of the calls for abolition of the traditional rule. Judge Learned Hand called it 'that most unfortunate doctrine'[66]. The Supreme Court of Canada indicated its willingness to abolish the rule in its recent decision of *Air Canada* v *British Columbia*, following the 'thorough, scholarly and damning analysis of the mistake of law doctrine'[67] by Dickson J in his dissenting judgment in the earlier case of *Hydro Electric Commission of Nepean* v *Ontario Hydro*[68]. Western Australia and New Zealand have abolished the rule by legislation[69]. The Law Reform Committee of South Australia[70] and the Law Reform Commissions of New South Wales[71] and British Columbia[72] have recommended abolition of the rule, as has most recently the English Law Commission[73]. Also very recently, the House of Lords has had occasion to refer to the strong criticism to which the traditional rule has been subjected[74].

Commentators have been highly critical of both the fact versus law distinction and the traditional rule precluding recovery. Goff and Jones reject the rule and seek to reconcile the cases with a narrower principle[75]. Palmer is unable to find any reason to support treating restitution in cases of mistake of law any differently from cases of mistake of fact[76]. Birks considers that the old rule cannot be justified and that recovery should be permitted in certain cases where there is a mistake of law[77]. In Canada, the authors of a recent text on the law of restitution condemn the traditional rule and conclude that it is unnecessary to distinguish between mistakes of law and of fact in order to fulfil the policy in favour of the finality of dispute resolution[78]. As the same authors say, it 'would be difficult to identify another private law doctrine which has been so universally condemned'[79].

The criticism gains added impetus in Australia by virtue of the recognition by this Court in *Pavey & Matthews Pty Ltd* v *Paul* of the 'unifying legal concept' of unjust enrichment[80]. As Dickson J stated in *Ontario Hydro*[81].

> Once a doctrine of restitution or unjust enichment is recognised, the distinction as to mistake of law and mistake of fact becomes simply meaningless.

If the ground for ordering recovery is that the defendant has been unjustly enriched, there is no justification for drawing distinctions on the basis of how the enrichment was gained, except in so far as the manner of gaining the enrichment bears upon the juctice of the case.

For the reasons stated above, the rule precluding recovery of moneys paid under a mistake of law should be held not to form part of the law in Australia. In referring to moneys paid under a mistake of law, we intend to refer to circumstances where the plaintiff pays moneys to a recipient who is not legally entitled to receive them. It would not, for example, extend to a case where the moneys were paid under a mistaken belief that they were legally due and owing under a particular clause of a particular contract when in fact they were legally due and owing to the recipient under another clause or contract[82].

Having rejected the so-called traditional rule denying recovery in cases of payments made under a mistake of law, it is necessary to consider what principle should be put in its place. It would be logical to treat mistakes of law in the same way as mistakes of fact[83], so that there would be a prima facie entitlement to recover moneys paid when a mistake of law or fact has caused the payment. Jurisdictions which have abolished the traditional rule by legislation have done so by stating that recovery should be allowed in cases of mistake of law in the same circumstances as it would be were the mistake one of fact (Western Australia and New Zealand). . . .

45 American Law Institute, (1937), p. 179.
46 (1772) 2 W Bl 824, at p. 825 [96 ER 485, at p. 486].
47 (1802) 2 East 469 [102 ER 448].
48 (1780) 2 Doug 468, at p. 471 [99 ER 299, at p. 300]; cf. the view Lord Ellenborough adopted in the later case, *Perrott* v *Perrott* (1811) 14 East 423, at p. 440 [104 ER 665, at p. 671].
49 (1799) 2 Esp 723, at p. 723 [170 ER 509, at p. 510].
50 (1813) 5 Taunt 143, at pp. 159–160 [128 ER 641, at pp. 647–648].
51 ibid., at pp. 152–153 [p. 645].
52 Goff & Jones, *Law of Restitution*, 3rd ed. (1986), pp. 118–119.
53 (1813) 5 Taunt, at p. 152 [128 ER, at p. 645].
54 (1841) 9 M & W 54 [152 ER 24].
55 *Sawyer & Vincent* v *Window Brace Ltd*, [1943] KB 32, at p. 34.
64 (1841) 9 M & W, at p. 58 [152 ER, at p. 26].
65 Goff & Jones, op. cit., pp. 124–125.
66 *St. Paul Fire & Marine Ins. Co.* v *Pure Oil Co.* (1933), 63 F (2d) 771, at p. 773.
67 [1989] 1 SCR, at p. 1199; (1989) 59 DLR (4th) 161, at p. 191, *per* La Forest J.
68 [1982] SCR 347, at pp. 357–370; (1982) 132 DLR (3d) 193, at pp. 201–215.
69 *Property Law Act* 1969 (WA), ss. 124 and 125 (s. 124 was applied in *Inn Leisure* v *D. F. McCloy* (1991) 28 FCR 151); *Judicature Act* 1908 (NZ), ss. 94a and 94b.
70 *Report Relating to the Irrecoverability of Benefits Obtained by Reason of Mistake of Law*, Report 84, (1984).
71 *Restitution of Benefits Conferred Under Mistake of Law*, Report LRC 53 (1987).

[72] *Report on Benefits Conferred Under a Mistake of Law*, Report LRC 51 (1981).

[73] *Restitution of Payments made Under a Mistake of Law*, Consultation Paper No. 120 (1991).

[74] *Woolwich Building Society* v *Inland Revenue Commissioners*, [1993] AC 142, at pp. 153–154, *per* Lord Keith of Kinkel; pp. 164–165, *per* Lord Goff of Chieveley; pp. 199–200, *per* Lord Slynn of Hadley.

[75] op. cit., p. 119.

[76] *Law of Restitution* (1978), vol. 3, §14.27.

[77] *An Introduction to the Law of Restitution* (1989), pp. 166–167.

[78] Maddaugh and McCamus, *The Law of Restitution* (1990), p. 255.

[79] ibid., p. 256.

[80] (1987) 162 CLR 221, at pp. 256–257, *per* Deane J (with whom Mason and Wilson JJ agreed); see also *Australia & New Zealand Banking Group Ltd* v *Westpac Banking Corporation* (1988), 164 CLR 662, at p. 673.

[81] [1982] SCR, at p. 367; (1982) 132 DLR (3d), at p. 209.

[82] *Barclays Bank Ltd* v *W. J. Simms, Son & Cooke (Southern) Ltd*, [1980] QB 677, at p. 695, *per* Robert Goff J: 'Of course, if the money was due under a contract between the payer and the payee, there can be no recovery on this ground.'

[83] See *Barclays Bank* v *W. J. Simms Ltd; Australia & New Zealand Banking Group Ltd* v *Westpac Banking Corporation*.

Notes

1. The High Court rejected tests requiring either a 'liability' mistake or a 'fundamental' mistake and adopted Robert Goff J's 'causative' mistake formulation in *Barclays Bank* v *W. J. Simms Ltd* [1980] QB 677, at 695, as appropriate for both mistakes of fact and mistakes of law. The case was remitted to the trial judge to determine whether the appellant could prove a relevant mistake.

2. See the notes in [1993] CLJ 225 (Jones) and [1993] LMCLQ 145 (Watts) for discussion.

3. For the Canadian position see *Air Canada* v *British Columbia* (1989) 59 DLR (4th) 161 (Supreme Court of Canada) noted in (1990) 106 LQR 28 (Arrowsmith).

4. In *Woolwich Equitable Building Society* v *Inland Revenue Commissioners (No. 2)* [1993] AC 70, different opinions were expressed in *dicta* as to the status of the mistake of law bar. At least one member of the House of Lords thought that it could be judicially abrogated (*per* Lord Slynn at 199), whereas Lord Keith in his dissenting speech opined that it could be removed only by legislation (at 154). The rule has now been held not to be part of the law of Scotland: *Morgan Guaranty Trust Co. of New York* v *Lothian Regional Council* [1995] SLT 299 (Inner House of the Court of Session); noted Laurie (1995) 111 LQR 379.

5. The Law Commission has now recommended the abolition of the mistake of law rule and proposed draft legislation: Law Commission, *Restitution: Mistakes of Law and Ultra Vires Public Authority Receipts and Payments* (HMSO, Law Com. No. 227, 1994). For discussion see Beatson, [1995] *Restitution Law Review* 280 and Virgo, 'Striking the Balance in the Law of Restitution' [1995] LMCLQ 362.

DRAFT RESTITUTION (MISTAKES OF LAW) BILL

1. Claims to which Act applies

(1) In this Act 'mistake claim' means a claim made in any proceedings for restitution of a sum in respect of an act done under mistake.

(2) In this Act 'act' includes anything which may found a claim for restitution, that is to say, the making of a payment, the conferring of a non-pecuniary benefit or the doing of work.

2. Abrogation of mistake of law rule

The classification of a mistake as a mistake of law or as a mistake of fact shall not of itself be material to the determination of a mistake claim; and no such claim shall be denied on the ground that the alleged mistake is a mistake of law.

3. Effect on mistake claim of judicial change in the law

(1) An act done in accordance with a settled view of the law shall not be regarded as founding a mistake claim by reason only that a subsequent decision of a court or tribunal departs from that view.

(2) A view of the law may be regarded for the purpose of this section as having been settled at any time notwithstanding that it was not held unanimously or had not been the subject of a decision by a court or tribunal.

Section 3: services rendered under a mistake

See Burrows, *Restitution*, 120–6.

A: Common law authority on restitution for services

Upton-on-Severn Rural District Council v *Powell*
[1942] 1 All ER 220 (CA)

Powell's Dutch barn caught fire. He phoned his local police station at Upton to ask for 'the fire brigade' to be sent. The police sent for the Upton fire brigade who came and dealt with the fire. All the parties were unaware that although the farm was in the Upton police district, it was in the Pershore, not the Upton, fire district. Powell would have been entitled to the services of the Pershore fire brigade for free, whereas the Upton fire brigade were entitled to make contracts and charge for services performed outside their area. *Held*: Upton fire brigade were entitled to remuneration for the services performed for Powell upon an 'implied promise'.

Question

Who was enriched by the services of the Upton fire brigade?

Notes

1. This case is irreconcilable with ordinary contractual principles. As counsel for Powell argued in vain, neither party had any relevant contractual

intention. The Upton fire brigade thought they were rendering gratuitous services in the normal course of their duty. Powell thought he was receiving the services of the appropriate brigade without charge (Treitel, *Contract*, 34).
2. Despite the reference in the brief judgment of Lord Greene MR to an 'implied promise', the case is also difficult to reconcile with restitutionary principles. Powell did not request or accept services which he knew he would be expected to pay for. Goff and Jones think it unlikely Powell was incontrovertibly benefited since he was entitled to the Pershore fire brigade's services for free (at 178, n.78). The better view is that the Pershore fire brigade were enriched by Upton's mistaken discharge of their (Pershore's) duty to extinguish Powell's fire; in which case the wrong person was made liable. See Burrows, *Restitution*, 124–5.

Greenwood v *Bennett*
[1973] QB 195 (CA)

Bennett, the manager of a garage, required some repairs to be done to a Jaguar car before selling it in the course of trade. The car was worth between £400 and £500. Bennett entrusted the car to Searle to do the necessary repairs at a cost of £85. Searle, while driving the car for his own purposes, crashed it and decided to sell it in its unrepaired state. Harper bought the car from him for £75, a fair price in its damaged state. Harper made good the damage to the tune of £226 in labour and materials and then sold the car to Prattle for £450. Subsequently the police took possession of the car and Searle was convicted of theft. The Chief Constable brought an interpleader summons to determine title to this car. The county court judge ordered the car to be returned to Bennett who then sold it for £400. It was accepted on appeal that Bennett's garage owned the car, but Harper claimed from Bennett £226 for the improvements to the car.

LORD DENNING MR: . . . To decide this case, I think it helpful to consider the legal position as if the police had not taken possession of the car, but it had remained in Mr Prattle's possession.

In the first place, if Mr Bennett's company had brought an action against Mr Harper for conversion of the car (relying on his purchase of it from Mr Searle for £75 as the act of conversion), then the damages would be £75 as its value at that time: whereas, if they had brought an action for conversion (relying on his sale of it to the finance company as the act of conversion) the damages would be its improved value at the time of sale, but the company would have to give credit for the work which Mr Harper had done on it: see *Munro* v *Willmott* [1949] 1 KB 295. So I suppose they would recover again about £75.

In the second place, if Mr Bennett's company had brought an action in detinue against Mr Prattle (while it was still in his possession) they could have recovered from him the value of the car at the time of judgment, that is, as improved by Mr Harper's work: see *Rosenthal* v *Alderton & Sons Ltd* [1946] KB 374 and *General and Finance Facilities Ltd* v *Cooks Cars (Romford) Ltd* [1963] 1 WLR 644, 650 by Diplock LJ. But

Mr Prattle would have a claim against the finance company (for breach of condition as to title), which the finance company could pass on to Mr Harper: and the damages recoverable by them from Mr Harper would be £450, the value of the car as he sold it to them. In those circumstances, I should think that justice would require that Mr Harper should be able to recover the cost of his work from Mr Bennett's company. Otherwise, you would get the very odd result that the company, by suing Mr Prattle in detinue, could—by this indirect means—recover from Mr Harper more than they could by suing him directly in conversion.

In the third place, if Mr Bennett's company had brought an action against Mr Prattle for specific delivery of the car, it is very unlikely that an order for specific delivery of the car would be made. But if it had been, no court would order its delivery unless compensation was made for the improvements. There is a valuable judgment by Lord Macnaghten in *Peruvian Guano Co.* v *Dreyfus Brothers & Co.* [1892] AC 166, 176, where he said:

> I am not aware of any authority upon the point, but I should doubt whether it was incumbent upon the court to order the defendant to return the goods in specie where the plaintiff refused to make a fair and just allowance.

So if this car was ordered to be returned to Mr Bennett's company, I am quite clear the court in equity would insist upon a condition that payment should be made to Mr Harper for the value of the improvements which he put on it.

Applying the principles stated by Lord Macnaghten, I should have thought that the county court judge here should have imposed a condition on the plaintiffs. He should have required them to pay Mr Harper the £226 as a condition of being given delivery of the car.

But the judge did not impose such a condition. The plaintiffs have regained the car, and sold it. What then is to be done? It seems to me that we must order the plaintiffs to pay Mr Harper the £226; for that is the only way of putting the position right.

Upon what principle is this to be done? Mr Rawlins has referred us to the familiar cases which say that a man is not entitled to compensation for work done on the goods or property of another unless there is a contract express or implied, to pay for it. We all remember the saying of Pollock CB: 'One cleans another's shoes; what can the other do but put them on?': *Taylor* v *Laird* (1856) 25 LJ Ex 329, 332. That is undoubtedly the law when the person who does the work knows, or ought to know, that the property does not belong to him. He takes the risk of not being paid for his work on it. But it is very different when he honestly believes himself to be the owner of the property and does the work in that belief. (That distinction is drawn in the mining cases such as *Wood* v *Morewood* (1841) 3 QB 440 and *Livingstone* v *Rawyards Coal Co.* (1880) 5 App Cas 25.) Here we have an innocent purchaser who bought the car in good faith and without notice of any defect in the title to it. He did work on it to the value of £226. The law is hard enough on him when it makes him give up the car itself. It would be most unjust if the company could not only take the car from him, but also the value of the improvements he has done to it—without paying for them. There is a principle at hand to meet the case. It derives from the law of restitution. The plaintiffs should not be allowed unjustly to enrich themselves at his expense. The court will order the plaintiffs, if they recover the car, or its improved value, to recompense the innocent purchaser for the work he has done on it. No matter whether the plaintiffs recover it with the aid of the courts, or without it, the innocent purchaser will recover the value of the improvements he has done to it.

In my opinion, therefore, the judge ought not to have released the car to the plaintiffs except on condition that the plaintiffs paid Mr Harper the £226. But now that it has been released to them and they have sold it, we should order Mr Bennett's company to pay Mr Harper £226 in respect of the improvements he made to the car. I would allow the appeal accordingly.

PHILLIMORE LJ: I agree. This was a case in which I should have thought that in the ordinary way no order for specific restitution of the chattel would have been made, because this was an ordinary commercial article; but the judge has, in effect, dealt with it as if by an order of specific restitution in allowing Mr Bennett to take the car back. In those circumstances it seems to me perfectly clear that on equitable principles someone who has improved the car since it was originally converted and who is not himself a wrongdoer—and it is not suggested that Mr Harper was in any way a wrongdoer—should be credited with the value of the work which he had put into the car by way of improving it. It was not seriously disputed in this case that the £226 had improved the value of the car, making its value far above what it was; and I entirely agree with Lord Denning MR that the judge having failed to allow Mr Harper's claim to be repaid his £226 as a condition of Mr Bennett recovering the motor car, the only course which this court can now take is to make an order that Mr Bennett should pay directly to Mr Harper that sum which indeed ought to have been a condition of Mr Bennett being allowed to take possession.

I agree therefore that this appeal should succeed to that extent.

CAIRNS LJ: I agree. The main issue in this appeal is one on which there is no authority directly in point. The matter has been very well argued on both sides in this court. If the car had, before any proceedings were brought, reached the hands of Mr Bennett, it is difficult to see that Mr Harper could have had any claim against him for the expenditure that he was put to in making the repairs to it. If, on the other hand, the car had remained in the possession of Mr Prattle, and Mr Bennett had sued Mr Harper, then it appears to me that probably the action would have had to be in conversion, and that in assessing the damages for conversion a deduction would have to be made for the expenditure that Mr Harper had incurred. Alternatively, if there could have been an action for detinue against Mr Harper, then similarly, on the principles laid down in *Munro* v *Willmott* [1949] 1 KB 295 and in the speech of Lord Macnaghten in *Peruvian Guano Co.* v *Dreyfus Brothers & Co.* [1892] AC 166, 175–177, Mr Harper's expenditure would have had to be allowed. It appears to me that in interpleader proceedings similar considerations come into play as those which would affect an action for detinue; and an order for delivery of the car to Mr Bennett now having been made and carried out, it seems to me that the result must be that Mr Harper ought to receive from Mr Bennett the amount of his expenditure on the car. I agree, therefore, that the appeal should be allowed and that the order proposed ought to be made.

Questions

1. If the car had been returned to the possession of Bennett without proceedings being brought, which of the judges would have allowed Harper a direct claim for the cost of the repairs against Bennett?

2. The judges do not expressly discuss the question of enrichment. Was Bennett enriched? Which tests of enrichment, if any, are satisfied on the facts of this case? (For tests of enrichment see Chapter 1, Section 3.)

TORTS (INTERFERENCE WITH GOODS) ACT 1977

3. Form of judgment where goods are detained

(7) Where under subsection (1) or subsection (2) of section 6 an allowance is to be made in respect of an improvement of the goods, and an order is made under subsection (2)(a) or (b), the court may assess the allowance to be made in respect of the improvement, and by the order require, as a condition for delivery of the goods, that allowance to be made by the claimant.

6. Allowance for improvement of the goods

(1) If in proceedings for wrongful interference against a person (the 'improver') who has improved the goods, it is shown that the improver acted in the mistaken but honest belief that he had a good title to them, an allowance shall be made for the extent to which, at the time as at which the goods fall to be valued in assessing damages, the value of the goods is attributable to the improvement.

(2) If, in proceedings for wrongful interference against a person ('the purchaser') who has purported to purchase the goods—

(a) from the improver, or

(b) where after such a purported sale the goods passed by a further purported sale on one or more occasions, on any such occasion, it is shown that the purchaser acted in good faith, an allowance shall be made on the principle set out in subsection (1).

For example, where a person in good faith buys a stolen car from the improver and is sued in conversion by the true owner the damages may be reduced to reflect the improvement, but if the person who bought the stolen car from the improver sues the improver for failure of consideration, and the improver acted in good faith, subsection (3) below will ordinarily make a comparable reduction in the damages he recovers from the improver.

(3) If in a case within subsection (2) the person purporting to sell the goods acted in good faith, then in proceedings by the purchaser for recovery of the purchase price because of failure of consideration, or in any other proceedings founded on that failure of consideration, an allowance shall, where appropriate, be made on the principle set out in subsection (1).

(4) This section applies, with the necessary modifications, to a purported bailment or other disposition of goods as it applies to a purported sale of goods.

Notes

1. Section 6 of the 1977 Act adopts the passive claim which forms the *ratio* of *Greenwood* v *Bennett*, but is silent on the question of the possibility of an active claim as favoured by Lord Denning. This therefore remains a matter for the common law. For an excellent case note on *Greenwood* v *Bennett*, see Weir, 'Doing Good by Mistake – Restitution and Remedies' [1973] CLJ 23. Weir suggests persuasive reasons why there should be an asymmetry between causes of action (active claims) and defences (passive claims), relying upon an analogy with *Central London Property Trust Ltd* v *High Trees House Ltd* [1947] KB 130, concluding 'not every shield-bearer has a sword'. For a thorough libertarian critique of *Greenwood* v *Bennett*, see Paul Matthews, 'Freedom, Unrequested Improvements and Lord Denning' (1981) 40 CLJ 340, who contrasts the philosophy of the case with that of *Falcke's* case

(1886) 34 Ch D 234 (see Chapter 3, Section 5). Arguments in favour of the active claim are marshalled by Burrows, *Restitution*, 120–2.
2. On enrichment see Ewan McKendrick, 'Restitution and the misuse of chattels – the need for a principled approach' in Palmer and McKendrick (eds), *Interests in Goods* (London: Lloyd's of London Press, 1993), 599, especially at 603–6, and Birks, *Introduction*, 121–5.

Rover International Limited v *Cannon Film Sales Ltd*
[1989] 1 WLR 912 (CA)

'Rover' appeal: Quantum meruit
As part of the joint venture arrangement discussed above in Section 1, it was agreed that Rover would arrange for the dubbing of the films into Italian, related art work and other expenses. The films themselves would remain the property of Cannon at all times. The work done was to be taken into account in apportioning the profits under the purported agreement. The underlying contract being void for lack of capacity, Rover claimed a *quantum meruit* in respect of the valuable services it, and its sister company Monitor, had performed.

KERR LJ: . . . It had by then [the opening of the appeal] evidently become apparent to Cannon's legal adviser, in my view quite rightly, that Rover's claim for something by way of a *quantum meruit* was irresistible in principle. In the face of the common mistaken belief held by both parties until about 25 July 1986 that the agreement was binding, subject only to the unfounded allegations of breaches made from the side of Cannon to which I have already referred, the task of the court—to put it broadly for the moment—was clearly to carry out a process of equitable restitution. Admittedly, the responsibility for the invalidity of the agreement must rest on the Italian side, since they should have ensured that Rover was incorporated before the agreement was executed. But while this might ground some claim for breach of warranty of authority against Mr Luigi de Rossi, who purported to sign on behalf of Rover, it is irrelevant for present purposes. So also is the fact that the repayment of the instalments sought to be recovered was made under a mistake of fact which Mr de Rossi and Mrs Karlin had the means of avoiding by using greater care: see the leading case, *Kelly* v *Solari* (1841) 9 M & W 54 which decided that a genuine mistake is not vitiated by carelessness. In these circumstances, and perhaps also because Harman J may not have appreciated that the entire gross receipts would now go to Cannon, Mr Pardoe made it clear that he did not seek to uphold the correctness of the judge's out-and-out rejection of a quantum meruit on the grounds stated by him [1987] BCLC 540, 545H–546A. The decision in *In re English and Colonial Produce Co. Ltd* [1906] 2 Ch 435 was clearly distinguishable, since it related solely to services purportedly rendered to a company before its incorporation. Mr Cordara rightly did not press any claim for a quantum meruit for anything done on the Italian side prior to 6 February 1986 when Rover were incorporated, and in any event virtually all Monitor's services were rendered thereafter. In relation to these Mr Pardoe also abandoned any suggestion that he could support the judge's conclusion based on the absence of any requests by Cannon to Rover to which he referred in this passage, and we did not have to consider whether anything in the nature of any express or implied request was indeed necessary to found a claim for a quantum meruit in circumstances like the present. I therefore say no more about these matters than that in my view Mr Pardoe was right to concede, as he did at an early stage of the appeal, that Rover were entitled to a quantum meruit for the services which generated the gross receipts for Cannon, and that this must include an element of reasonable remuneration. . . .

Question

What was the ground for restitution in respect of the services provided in this case?

Note

The passage quoted from Kerr LJ's judgment faintly suggests that it was the parties' common mistake in believing that they were bound by a valid contract which made the claim 'irresistible'.

Peter Birks, *Restitution – The Future*
(Sydney: Federation Press, 1992), 86–7

Historically the materials of the law of restitution have been strongly divided according to the form in which the enrichment is received, whether as money, as a benefit procured by money paid to a third party, as work, as goods, and so on. This division has had two associated effects. First, even allowing for the long neglect of the whole law of restitution, it has left in relative obscurity the law relating to restitution of value transferred other than as money. The non-money side thus remains almost completely undeveloped. Secondly, it has created the illusion that the grounds for restitution actually differ according to the form in which value is received, which is plainly nonsense. Once there is a finding that the defendant was enriched at the plaintiff's expense, the unjust factors must be the same for all value received. The word 'symmetry' here refers to that imperative.

In the coming decades, the asymmetrical benefit-based classification of the law must be eliminated or, more precisely, demoted to a much humbler role. In relation to the single issue of establishing the defendant's enrichment, the difference between money received and value received in other forms cannot but remain relevant. Symmetry is essential in the all important inquiry into the unjust. That is to say, the unjust factors must be the same for all cases. Nobody denies that the inquiry into enrichment must make sensitive distinctions between one kind of benefit and another. . . .

Note

Professor Birks goes on to criticise the Court of Appeal in *Rover* v *Cannon* for failing to promote the cause of symmetry in respect of money and non-money claims. In particular the Court failed to make sufficiently explicit the cause of action in relation to the *quantum meruit* claim. Their excuse was that counsel conceded the point. But the passage quoted from Kerr LJ's judgment suggests that the inquiry, if it had taken place, may have been in terms of express and implied requests. See Birks, *The Future*, at 87–91 for a concise and valuable account of the historical forms of action colouring the judgments in this case, and at 91–6 for discussion of *Rover* v *Cannon* itself. Professor Birks picks up on Kerr LJ's passing reference to the Law Reform

(Frustrated Contracts) Act 1943 and comments upon the striking similarity of *Rover* v *Cannon* and *BP Exploration Co. (Libya) Ltd* v *Hunt (No. 2)* [1979] 1 WLR 783 (QBD), affd [1983] 2 AC 352 (HL), the leading case on the Act which is discussed in Chapter 4, Section 2. See further Birks [1990] 2 JCL 227.

B: *The equitable doctrine of acquiescence ('proprietary estoppel')*

Ramsden v *Dyson*
(1866) LR 1 HL 129 (HL)

A tenant took leases over two plots of land in Huddersfield and built on them, spending in excess of £1,800. The tenant knew he had tenancies only from year to year or tenancies at will, but believed that by building he became entitled to call for a 60-year lease. The landlord's successor sought to eject the tenant. *Held*: on the evidence there was no encouragement or conduct on the part of the landlord which would justify equitable intervention, either to resist the ejection or to compensate the tenant for his improvements.

LORD CRANWORTH LC: . . . If a stranger begins to build on my land supposing it to be his own, and I, perceiving his mistake, abstain from setting him right, and leave him to persevere in his error, a Court of equity will not allow me afterwards to assert my title to the land on which he had expended money on the supposition that the land was his own. It considers that, when I saw the mistake into which he had fallen, it was my duty to be active and to state my adverse title; and that it would be dishonest in me to remain wilfully passive on such an occasion, in order afterwards to profit by the mistake which I might have prevented.

But it will be observed that to raise such an equity two things are required, first, that the person expending the money supposes himself to be building on his own land; and, secondly, that the real owner at the time of the expenditure knows that the land belongs to him and not to the person expending the money in the belief that he is the owner. For if a stranger builds on my land knowing it to be mine, there is no principle of equity which would prevent my claiming the land with the benefit of all the expenditure made on it. There would be nothing in my conduct, active or passive, making it inequitable in me to assert my legal rights.

It follows as a corollary from these rules, or, perhaps, it would be more accurate to say it forms part of them, that if my tenant builds on land which he holds under me, he does not thereby, in the absence of special circumstances, acquire any right to prevent me from taking possession of the land and buildings when the tenancy has determined. He knew the extent of his interest, and it was his folly to expend money upon a title which he knew would or might soon come to an end. . . .

LORD WENSLEYDALE: . . . If a stranger build on my land, supposing it to be his own, and I, knowing it to be mine, do not interfere, but leave him to go on, equity considers it to be dishonest in me to remain passive and afterwards to interfere and take the profit. But if a stranger build knowingly upon my land, there is no principle of equity which prevents me from insisting on having back my land, with all the additional value which the occupier has imprudently added to it. If a tenant of mine does the same thing, he cannot insist on refusing to give up the estate at the end of his term. It was his own folly to build. . . .

LORD KINGSDOWN (dissenting on the facts): . . . The rule of law applicable to the case appears to me to be this: If a man, under a verbal agreement with a landlord for a certain interest in land, or, what amounts to the same thing, under an expectation, created or encouraged by the landlord, that he shall have a certain interest, takes possession of such land, with the consent of the landlord, and upon the faith of such promise or expectation, with the knowledge of the landlord, and without objection by him, lays out money upon the land, a Court of equity will compel the landlord to give effect to such promise or expectation. . . .

If, on the other hand, a tenant being in possession of land, and knowing the nature and extent of his interest, lays out money upon it in the hope or expectation of an extended term or an allowance for expenditure, then, if such hope or expectation has not been created or encouraged by the landlord, the tenant has no claim which any Court of law or equity can enforce. . . .

Notes

1. The tenant made no mistake about his present rights, but was simply in error about the future conduct of the landlord. It was therefore only what Professor Birks calls a *misprediction*, which ordinarily does not entitle a plaintiff to relief (Birks, *Introduction*, 277–9).

2. See Goff and Jones, 167–71 on restitutionary claims arising from mistaken improvements to land.

Willmott v *Barber*
(1880) 15 Ch D 96 (Ch D)

The defendant Barber sub-let a piece of land to Willmott, which adjoined the latter's saw-mill. The agreement gave Willmott an option to purchase all of Barber's interest in the adjoining land. Barber's own lease with the defendant Bowyer contained a covenant against assignment or sub-letting without the written consent of the landlord. Willmott took possession of the land and spent considerable sums converting it into a timber-yard and improving his own saw-mill. He then purported to exercise his option, but Bowyer refused his consent. Willmott claimed Bowyer had acquiesced in his expenditure. *Held*: Bowyer was himself ignorant of his legal rights and did not know about Willmott's mistake so the doctrine of acquiescence could not avail the plaintiff against Bowyer's legal rights.

FRY J: . . . It has been said that the acquiescence which will deprive a man of his legal rights must amount to fraud, and in my view that is an abbreviated statement of a very true proposition. A man is not to be deprived of his legal rights unless he has acted in such a way as would make it fraudulent for him to set up those rights. What, then, are the elements or requisites necessary to constitute fraud of that description? In the first place the plaintiff must have made a mistake as to his legal rights. Secondly, the plaintiff must have expended some money or must have done some act (not necessarily upon the defendant's land) on the faith of his mistaken belief. Thirdly, the defendant, the possessor of the legal right, must know of the existence of his own right which is inconsistent with the right claimed by the plaintiff. If he does not know of it he is in the same position as the plaintiff, and the doctrine of acquiescence is founded upon conduct with a knowledge of your legal rights. Fourthly, the defendant, the possessor of the legal right, must know of the plaintiff's mistaken belief of his rights. If he does not, there is nothing which calls upon him to assert his own rights. Lastly, the defendant, the possessor of the legal right, must have encouraged the plaintiff in his expenditure of money or in the other acts which he has done, either directly or by abstaining from asserting his legal right. Where all these elements exist, there is fraud of such a nature as will entitle the Court to restrain the possessor of the legal right from exercising it, but, in my judgment, nothing short of this will do. . . .

Note

Fry J goes on to say 'when the plaintiff is seeking relief, not on a contract, but on the footing of a mistake of fact, the mistake is not less a ground for relief because he had the means of knowledge'. There are echoes here of *Kelly* v *Solari* (1841) 9 M & W 54, the leading mistaken payment case, and suggests carelessness by the mistaken party will be irrelevant whatever the character of the benefit.

Amalgamated Investment & Property Co. Ltd v *Texas Commerce International Bank Ltd*
[1982] QB 84 (QBD and CA)

Queen's Bench Division

ROBERT GOFF J: . . . Of all doctrines, equitable estoppel is surely one of the most flexible. True, from time to time distinguished judges have enunciated statements of principle concerning aspects of the doctrine; as, for example, the statements of Lord Cranworth LC in *Ramsden* v *Dyson* LR 1 HL 129, 140–141; of Thesiger LJ in *De Bussche* v *Alt*, 8 ChD 286, 314 and of Fry J in *Willmott* v *Barber* (1880) 15 Ch D 96, 105–106, concerning what is usually called the doctrine of acquiescence; the statement of Lord Kingsdown in *Ramsden* v *Dyson*, at pp. 170–171, on what may be called the doctrine of encouragement; and the statement of Lord Cairns LC in *Hughes* v *Metropolitan Railway Co.*, 2 App Cas 439, 448, and Denning J in *Central London Property Trust Ltd* v *High Trees House Ltd* [1947] KB 130, 134, on promissory estoppel. But all these have been statements of aspects of a wider doctrine; none has sought to be exclusive. It is no doubt helpful to establish, in broad terms, the criteria which, in certain situations, must be fulfilled before an equitable estoppel can be established; but it cannot be right to restrict equitable estoppel to certain defined categories, and indeed some of the categories proposed are not easy to defend. Thus, in *Snell's Principles of Equity*, 27th ed. (1973), chapter 7, the editors isolate two categories of equitable estoppel, promissory estoppel and proprietary estoppel. It may be possible nowadays to identify the former with some degree of precision; but the latter is much more difficult to accept as a separate category. The cases concerned appear to derive from two distinct principles; the principle stated by Lord Cranworth LC in *Ramsden* v *Dyson*, LR 1 HL 129, and the principle stated by Lord Kingsdown in the same case—the former being concerned with an estoppel precluding a person, who stands by and allows another to incur expenditure or otherwise act on the basis of a mistaken belief as to his rights, from thereafter asserting rights inconsistent with that mistaken belief (commonly called the doctrine of acquiescence); and the other being concerned with an estoppel precluding a person who has encouraged another to improve his, the encourager's property in the expectation that he will receive an interest in it, from denying that he is entitled to that interest. It is to be observed that the first of these principles appears to be directed towards preventing a person from fraudulently taking advantage of another's error, whereas the latter appears to derive rather from encouragement or representation. As a separate category, proprietary estoppel may perhaps be regarded as an amalgam of doubtful utility; and it is not surprising to find that the use of this term has been the subject of some criticism: see, for example, *Spencer Bower and Turner, Estoppel by Representation*, 3rd ed. (1977), para. 308. Indeed there are cases, in particular cases concerned with the acquisition of easements, and with the legal effect of contracts, which are not easy to accommodate within any of the current classifications. It is not, therefore, surprising to discover a tendency in the more recent authorities to reject any rigid classification of equitable estoppel into exclusive and defined categories. The authorities on the subject have recently been reviewed by Oliver J in his judgment in two related actions, *Taylors Fashions Ltd* v *Liverpool Victoria Trustees Co. Ltd* and *Old & Campbell Ltd* v *Liverpool Victoria Friendly Society* [(1979) [1982] QB 133 (note)] . . . and on the basis of his analysis of the cases, which I gratefully adopt, he rejected an argument founded upon rigid categorisation. The argument was that a clear distinction must be drawn between cases of proprietary estoppel and estoppel by acquiescence on the one hand, and promissory estoppel or estoppel by representation (whether express or by conduct) on the other; and that in the former class of cases it was essential that the party alleged to be estopped himself knew the true position (that is, that he knew that the other party was acting under a mistake as to his rights), the fourth of the five criteria laid down by Fry J in *Willmott* v *Barber*, 15 Ch D 96, as necessary to establish estoppel by acquiescence. Oliver J, however, while recognising that the strict *Willmott* v *Barber* criteria may be necessary requirements in cases where all that has happened is that the party alleged to be estopped has stood by without protest while his rights have been infringed, concluded that the recent authorities supported a much wider jurisdiction to interfere in cases where the assertion of strict legal rights is found by the court to be unconscionable. The cases before him were concerned with a situation where both parties had proceeded on the same mistaken assumption; and he concluded that the inquiry which he had to make was simply whether, in all the circumstances of the cases before him, it was unconscionable for the defendants to seek to take advantage of the mistake which, at the material time, all parties shared. . . .

Note

Equitable estoppel has developed considerably since *Ramsden* v *Dyson*. For discussion from the contractual point of view, see Treitel, *Contract*, 100–15; 120–37. The important question here is to what extent does estoppel belong within the law of restitution? On first principles, the answer is only to the extent that estoppel reverses unjust enrichment. Lord Cranworth LC's statement of principle (often labelled 'the doctrine of acquiescence') can be reconciled with restitutionary aims. In contrast Lord Kingsdown's statement has given rise to a sequence of cases, often labelled 'proprietary estoppel', which seem more concerned with fulfilling parties' expectations, a function commonly associated with the law of contract. The remedial flexibility of equitable intervention has been criticised (Birks, *Introduction*, 290–3) but the judiciary has been reluctant to allow any rigid classification of its flexible friend. In addition to Robert Goff J's doubt about the usefulness of proprietary estoppel as a category, see also *Crabb* v *Arun District Council* [1976] Ch 179, at 187 (CA) *per* Lord Denning MR ('there are estoppels and estoppels') and at 193 *per* Scarman LJ ('I do not find helpful the distinction between promissory and proprietary estoppel'). An important discussion here is Beatson, 'Unfinished Business: Integrating Equity', Essay 9 in Beatson, *Unjust Enrichment*, 244–58.

Professor Beatson discusses the problems which arise from equity's historic role as a supplement or gloss to the common law, using a more diverse range of principles than simply unjust enrichment and injurious reliance. Beatson cites the important work of Elias in analysing another equitable technique. In Elias, *Explaining Constructive Trusts* (Oxford: Oxford University Press, 1990), the author classifies constructive trusts as furthering one of three aims: (i) 'perfection'; (ii) 'restitution'; or (iii) 'reparation'. Elias rejects earlier theories which see all constructive trusts as restitutionary (typified by Waters, *Constructive Trusts*, 1964), or which support what he calls the 'sceptical' thesis that there is no single rationale for the imposition of the remedy (Oakley, *Constructive Trusts*, 2nd ed. (London: Sweet & Maxwell, 1987) provides a good example of this approach). Such a classification might also bring some order to the case law on estoppel. However, it seems likely that most of the modern cases are concerned with what Elias terms the 'perfection' aim, for example *Crabb* v *Arun District Council* itself. Perhaps it is safer to agree with Burrows's sceptical conclusion that it is wrong to see the statements of principle in *Ramsden* v *Dyson* as yielding a 'rich seam of cases awarding restitution for mistaken land improvement' (Burrows, *Restitution*, 123).

Section 4: rescission for misrepresentation and mistake

See Burrows, *Restitution*, 126–38 and for reference Goff and Jones, 183–222.

A: Rescission for misrepresentation

Rescission, or the unwinding of the contract, has been a common and appropriate response of the courts to misstatements made by one of the parties causing the other to enter into the bargain. At the end of the twentieth century the victim of a misrepresentation might almost be embarrassed by the wealth of remedies available. For detail see Cartwright, *Unequal Bargaining* (Oxford: Clarendon Press, 1991), 61–148; Treitel, *Contract*, 307–73. Our principal concern is with whether rescission, one of these remedies, is a species of restitutionary relief; but it is necessary to bear in mind the other possible forms of relief provided by the law of obligations in general.

The representor's state of mind

It is commonplace now to divide this into three categories:

(a) *Fraudulent*: the representor knew the statement was false or was reckless, not caring about its truth or falsity.

(b) *Negligent*: the representor honestly but unreasonably believed the statement was true; that is, the representor failed to use reasonable care in checking the accuracy of the statement.

(c) *Innocent*: the representor honestly and reasonably believed the statement was true.

Availability of damages

The division between possible states of mind of the representor (b) and (c) is comparatively recent. Until the 1960s the only necessary distinction was between fraudulent (class (a)) and non-fraudulent (including negligent) misstatements (classes (b) and (c)), the latter in the older cases being indiscriminately described as *innocent*. The significance of this was that it had been established by the end of the Victorian period that damages were available only if fraud could be proved (under the tort of deceit: *Derry* v *Peek* (1887) 14 App Cas 337 (HL)), whereas rescission was available where the other necessary conditions were made out for all misstatements, including the wholly innocent.

Two developments in the 1960s made tortious damages available for negligent misrepresentations generally. First, in the case where a contract resulted from the misstatement, under the Misrepresentation Act 1967, s. 2(1)). Secondly, at common law damages were made available where no contract resulted in the seminal case of *Hedley Byrne & Co. Ltd* v *Heller & Partners Ltd* [1964] AC 465 (HL), which was extended to contractual cases in *Esso Petroleum Co.* v *Mardon* [1975] QB 819 (CA). So damages may now be available either for the tort of deceit (state of mind (a)), or under the statutory tort or the tort of negligent misstatement (head (b)). Such damages protect what Fuller and Perdue described as the plaintiff's *reliance interest* in their classic article 'The Reliance Interest in Contract Damages' (1936) 46 Yale LJ 52, 373 at 54. That is, they aim to compensate the plaintiff for any loss suffered by acting on the faith of the defendant's statement or promise. This can be contrasted with the plaintiff's *restitution interest* which is protected by making the defendant disgorge any benefit he had received from the plaintiff as a result of his statement or promise. It is the latter which seems to be protected by rescission. The two measures are similar in being backward-looking, but the former is measured by loss to the plaintiff, whereas the latter is measured by benefit to the defendant. (Both can therefore be contrasted with the availability in principle of the forward-looking *expectation measure* by the device of pleading that the misstatement has been incorporated into the resulting contract and suing for breach of the contractual warranty, the appropriate measure in principle being as if the contract had been performed, i.e. as if the statement were true: compare the cases of *Oscar Chess Ltd* v *Williams* [1957] 1 WLR 370 and *Dick Bentley Productions Ltd* v *Harold Smith (Motors) Ltd* [1965] 1 WLR 623; Treitel, *Contract*, 326–30.) The backward-looking measures may not reach precisely the same results on the same facts. Services may have been rendered which cannot be restored. There may have been a deterioration in the quality of the subject-matter of the contract.

Whereas damages aim to place the plaintiff precisely back in *status quo ante*, in rescinding the transaction the courts aim to do what is 'practically just'. See *Erlanger* v *New Sombrero Phosphate Company* (1878) 3 App Cas 1218 and *Newbigging* v *Adam* (1886) 34 Ch D 582 (below).

While rescission is in principle available whether the representor's state of mind be fraudulent, negligent or wholly innocent, the distinction between fraudulent (head (a)) and innocent (heads (b) and (c)) may still be relevant. First, where the misrepresentation is fraudulent the courts may be reluctant to find the right to rescind is barred (*Spence* v *Crawford* [1939] 3 All ER 271). Secondly, where the misrepresentation is non-fraudulent the courts now have a discretion not to rescind the contract and to award damages instead (Misrepresentation Act 1967, s. 2(2)).

Statement of fact

The statement must be one of fact, therefore an innocent misstatement of law will not suffice although a fraudulent misstatement of law will. More importantly, a statement of opinion is not sufficient. A misrepresentation of present intention will suffice, however, for as Bowen LJ once laconically remarked: 'There must be a misstatement of an existing fact: but the state of man's mind is as much a matter of fact as the state of his digestion' (*Edgington* v *Fitzmaurice* (1885) 29 Ch D 459 (CA) (tort of deceit)). Therefore a statement by the directors of a company that money raised by the sale of debentures would be used to acquire new assets and develop the company's business when in fact it was to be used to pay off pre-existing debts, was a misstatement of fact. In contrast, it has been held that a statement that land had the capacity to carry 2,000 sheep was a statement of opinion, where the land had never been used for rearing sheep and both vendor and purchaser were capable of forming an opinion on its capacity (*Bisset* v *Wilkinson* [1927] AC 177 (PC)). In addition, and most obviously, the statement must be false.

The misstatement must 'induce' the contract: materiality and reliance

The statement must be '*a* cause' but need not be '*the* cause' of the representee entering into the contract (*Edgington* v *Fitzmaurice* (1885) 29 Ch D 459 (CA) (tort of deceit)).

Redgrave v *Hurd*
(1881) 20 Ch D 1 (CA)

Rescission

The plaintiff solicitor advertised for a partner who would be willing as part of the same transaction to purchase his house from him for £1,600. The defendant responded and was told by the plaintiff that the practice was worth about £300 per year. The defendant was shown papers showing less than £200 worth of business and was told that the rest of the business was accounted for by another pile of documents. The defendant did not inspect those other documents but agreed to the transaction and paid £100 deposit on the house. In fact the business was worth only about £200 per year. Subsequently, when the defendant learnt the true state of affairs he refused to complete. The plaintiff claimed specific performance of the contract, and the defendant counterclaimed for rescission. *Held*: the defendant was entitled to rely upon the plaintiff's statement, it being no defence that the representee could have with reasonable diligence discovered the truth, and consequently the defendant was entitled to rescission and restitution of the £100.

SIR GEORGE JESSEL MR: . . . when a person makes a material representation to another to induce him to enter into a contract, and the other enters into that contract, it is not sufficient to say that the party to whom the representation is made does not prove that he entered into the contract, relying upon the representation. If it is a material representation calculated to induce him to enter into the contract, it is an inference of law that he was induced by the representation to enter into it, and in order to take away his title to be relieved from the contract on the ground that the representation was untrue, it must be shewn either that he had knowledge of the facts contrary to the representation, or that he stated in terms, or shewed clearly by his conduct, that he did not rely on the representation. If you tell a man, 'You may enter into partnership with me, my business is bringing in between £300 and £400 a year,' the man who makes that representation must know that it is a material inducement to the other to enter into the partnership, and you cannot investigate as to whether it was more or less probable that the inducement would operate on the mind of the party to whom the representation was made. Where you have neither evidence that he knew facts to shew that the statement was untrue, or that he said or did anything to shew that he did not actually rely upon the statement, the inference remains that he did so rely, and the statement being a material statement, its being untrue is a sufficient ground for rescinding the contract. . . .

Note

Materiality and reliance are not two disjunctive aspects of inducement; both are relevant to the causal inquiry, but their main effect is on the burden of proof. If the representee can show the statement was material, that is it would induce a reasonable man to enter into the contract, this will suffice, unless the representor can prove that the representee did not in fact rely upon the statement. In other words, by proving materiality the representee shifts the burden of proof on causation onto the representor. However it is not an inference of law as stated by Jessel MR, but an inference of fact: *Smith* v *Chadwick* (1884) 9 App Cas 187, 196 *per* Lord Blackburn. If the representation was not material, it is still open to the representee affirmatively to prove that he did in fact enter the contract in reliance upon it. For discussion see John Cartwright, *Unequal Bargaining* (Oxford: Clarendon Press, 1991), at 81–4 and Goff and Jones, 196–8.

Limitations on the right to rescind

If it has been established that a false statement of fact has been made rescission may still be unavailable if any one of five bars applies:

(a) there must be *restitutio in integrum*, translated by Professor Birks as 'counter-restitution essential' or 'no restitution without counter-restitution';

(b) if *third party rights* have intervened the remedy is barred (perhaps related to the defence of bona fide purchase);

(c) *lapse of time*: the representee must act promptly if the remedy sought is the unwinding of the contract. This bar, it seems, is distinct from statutory limitation periods or the equitable doctrine of laches;

(d) *affirmation*: if the representee, with knowledge of the facts giving rise to the right to rescind and knowledge of his legal right, chooses to continue with the contract rescission is unavailable;

(e) the Misrepresentation Act 1967, s. 2(2) gives the court a discretion to award damages instead of rescission; the Court of Appeal suggested circumstances in which it would have been willing to exercise that discretion in the recent case of *William Sindall plc* v *Cambridgeshire County Council* [1994] 1 WLR 1016.

For discussion see Goff and Jones, 198–210 and Burrows, *Restitution*, 132–7. The following cases discuss aspects of one or more of these bars.

Erlanger v *New Sombrero Phosphate Company*
(1878) 3 App Cas 1218 (HL)

Rescission

A syndicate headed by the Parisian banker Emile Erlanger purchased a partially-expired 21-year lease for Sombrero island in the West Indies for £55,000. Erlanger and the other appellants then arranged for the formation of the respondent company with the object of exploiting the island's phosphate reserves. The island was sold a few days later by the syndicate to the company for £110,000. The inflated price was not disclosed to the investors. The House of Lords unanimously held that the appellants as promoters of the company stood in a fiduciary position towards it and owed a duty to the company to make a full disclosure of the circumstances of its acquisition of the property. By failing to disclose that they had acquired the lease for £55,000 and only a few days later sold it to the company for £110,000, the appellants were in breach of that duty. Therefore the company was entitled to rescission of the contract and it was ordered that the appellants were obliged to repay the purchase price with interest to the company, and that upon their doing so, the company should give up possession of the island and pay over any profits that might have been made. Their Lordships rejected arguments that counter-restitution was impossible and that rescission was barred by the lapse of 14 months between the contract and the commencement of proceedings (although on the questions of counter-restitution and lapse of time Lord Cairns LC expressed doubts).

LORD BLACKBURN: . . . It is, I think, clear on principles of general justice, that as a condition to a rescission there must be a *restitutio in integrum*. The parties must be put *in statu quo*. See *per* Lord Cranworth in *Addie* v *The Western Bank* Law Rep 1 HL Sc 165. It is a doctrine which has often been acted upon both at law and in equity. But there is a considerable difference in the mode in which it is applied in Courts of Law and Equity, owing, as I think, to the difference of the machinery which the Courts have at command. I speak of these Courts as they were at the time when this suit commenced, without inquiring whether the Judicature Acts make any, or if any, what difference.

It would be obviously unjust that a person who has been in possession of property under the contract which he seeks to repudiate should be allowed to throw that back on the other party's hands without accounting for any benefit he may have derived from the use of the property, or if the property, though not destroyed, has been in the interval deteriorated, without making compensation for that deterioration. But as a Court of Law has no machinery at its command for taking an account of such matters, the defrauded party, if he sought his remedy at law, must in such cases keep the property and sue in an action for deceit, in which the jury, if properly directed, can do complete justice by giving as damages a full indemnity for all that the party has lost: see *Clarke* v *Dixon* EB & E 148, and the cases there cited.

But a Court of Equity could not give damages, and, unless it can rescind the contract, can give no relief. And, on the other hand, it can take accounts of profits, and make allowance for deterioration. And I think the practice has always been for a Court of Equity to give this relief whenever, by the exercise of its powers, it can do what is practically just, though it cannot restore the parties precisely to the state they were in before the contract. And a Court of Equity requires that those who come to it to ask its active interposition to give them relief, should use due diligence, after there has been such notice or knowledge as to make it inequitable to lie by. And any change which occurs in the position of the parties or the state of the property after such notice or knowledge should tell much more against the party *in morâ*, than a similar change before he was *in morâ* should do.

In *Lindsay Petroleum Company* v *Hurd* Law Rep 5 PC 239, it is said:

> The doctrine of laches in Courts of Equity is not an arbitrary or a technical doctrine. Where it would be *practically unjust* to give a remedy, either because the party has, by his conduct done that which might fairly be regarded as equivalent to a waiver of it, or where, by his conduct and neglect he has, though perhaps not waiving that remedy, yet put the other party in a situation in which it would not be reasonable to place him if the remedy were afterwards to be asserted, in either of these cases lapse of time and delay are most material. But in every case if an argument against relief, which otherwise would be just, is founded upon mere delay, that delay of course not amounting to a bar by any statute of limitations, the validity of that defence must be tried upon principles substantially equitable. Two circumstances always important in such cases are the length of the delay and the nature of the acts done during the interval, which might affect either party and cause a balance of justice or injustice in taking the one course or the other, so far as relates to the remedy.

I have looked in vain for any authority which gives a more distinct and definite rule than this; and I think, from the nature of the inquiry, it must always be a question of more or less, depending on the degree of diligence which might reasonably be required, and the degree of change which has occurred, whether the balance of justice or injustice is in favour of granting the remedy or withholding it. The determination of such a question must largely depend on the turn of mind of those who have to decide, and must therefore be subject to uncertainty; but that, I think, is inherent in the nature of the inquiry. . . .

Question

The company's main claim was to a remedy which involved setting the contract aside and mutual restitution of benefits received under it. In the alternative it claimed restitution of £55,000, the difference between the sum paid by the syndicate and that paid by the company. In the light of the view taken of the main relief sought, this question never arose. Would such an award be possible? (See *Gluckstein* v *Barnes* [1900] AC 240 (Chapter 5, Section 3) and especially Lord Macnaghten's discussion of the earlier case of *Hichens* v *Congreve* (1828) 4 Russ 562.)

Note

Although this case concerns rescission for non-disclosure and the exploitation of unfair advantage by a fiduciary, it is authorative for rescission for mistake and misrepresentation in general. For discussion of the limited categories where English law grants remedies for non-disclosure similar to those for actual misstatements (the two main examples being contracts of insurance and transactions with fiduciaries), see Goff and Jones, 189–95 and Burrows, *Restitution*, 137–8.

Newbigging v *Adam*

(1886) 34 Ch D 582 (CA)

Rescission

The plaintiff was induced to enter into a partnership with the defendants by non-fraudulent misrepresentations as to the state of the business. The plaintiff therefore gave up his army commission in India, returned to England and contributed £9,700 to the partnership and discharged partnership debts amounting to £324 2s 7d. *Held*: the plaintiff was entitled to rescission, comprising restitution of the sums he contributed and the amount of the liabilities he discharged, less some £750 he had received from the partnership, being a total of £9,279 6s, together with an indemnity from the defendants against partnership debts and liabilities.

COTTON LJ: . . . Undoubtedly the statements made, as I have already stated, by the Adams were not such as would enable the plaintiff to recover damages in an action of deceit, and Mr Rigby contended that it would not be right in an action of this kind to make the Defendants, whose misstatement had enabled the Plaintiff to set aside the contract, undertake liabilities for which they were never subject antecedently to the contract, for that this was really giving damages in another way. I differ from that proposition. In my opinion it is not giving damages in consequence of the deceit, it is working out the proper result of setting aside a contract in consequence of misrepresentation. This is a very different thing, because although the damages which would have been obtained in an action of deceit if the misstatement had been made fraudulently, or with such reckless negligence as to bring about the same consequence, might have been the same as what the Plaintiff will get under the indemnity, they might have been much more. The Plaintiff here does not recover damages as in an action of deceit, but gets what is the proper consequence in equity of setting aside the contract into which he has been induced to enter. In my opinion it cannot be said that he is put back into his old position unless he is relieved from the consequences and obligations which are the result of the contract which is set aside. That is a very different thing from damages. The Plaintiff may have been induced by these misstatements to give up a commission in the army, and if the misstatements had been such that an action of deceit would lie he could have recovered damages for the loss of his commission, but he could not in such an action as the present obtain any relief in respect of it. The indemnity to which he is entitled is only an indemnity against the obligations which he has contracted under the contract which is set aside, and, in my opinion, the requiring the Defendant whose misstatements, though not fraudulent, have been the cause of setting aside the contract, to indemnify the Plaintiff from those obligations, is the only way in which the Plaintiff can be restored to his old position in an action like this, but I entirely disclaim any intention of giving damages in an action of this nature. . . .

BOWEN LJ: . . . Now, in the first place, in considering the question to what extent Mr Newbigging is entitled to demand an indemnity from Adam & Co., one must consider the doctrine of equity as to the relief which will be given in cases of fraud and misrepresentation. A contract obtained by fraud, being voidable and not void, remains until it is set aside, and when it is set aside it is treated both at law and in equity as non-existing. It appears that equity, as has been pointed out in the case of *Peek* v *Gurney* Law Rep 13 Eq 79; 6 HL 377, has a concurrent jurisdiction with law to give relief in cases of fraud. Common law recognised a rescission if the case shaped itself so that a Court of Common Law had jurisdiction to decide whether there should be a rescission or not, but, besides this, the common law gave damages for deceit, and in my opinion gave them, not as an alternative remedy, but as an alternative or cumulative remedy as the case might be. The Court of Chancery had a concurrent jurisdiction, and in cases of fraud, so far as I know, there can be no doubt that complete indemnity could be given by a Court of Equity to the person who had been defrauded, so as to protect him as fully in equity as he could have been protected in law.

If we turn to the question of misrepresentation, damages cannot be obtained at law for misrepresentation which is not fraudulent, and you cannot, as it seems to me, give in equity any indemnity which corresponds with damages. If the mass of authority there is upon the subject were gone through I think it would be found that there is not so much difference as is generally supposed between the view taken at common law and the view taken in equity as to misrepresentation. At common law it has always been considered that misrepresentations which strike at the root of the contract are sufficient to avoid the contract on the ground explained in *Kennedy* v *Panama, New Zealand, and Australian Royal Mail Company* Law Rep 2 QB 580; but when you come to consider what is the exact relief to which a person is entitled in a case of misrepresentation it seems to me to be this, and nothing more, that he is entitled to have the contract rescinded, and is entitled accordingly to all the incidents and consequences of such rescission. It is said that the injured party is entitled to be replaced *in statu quo*. It seems to me that when you are dealing with innocent misrepresentation you must understand that proposition that he is to be replaced *in statu quo* with this limitation—that he is not to be replaced in exactly the same position in all respects, otherwise he would be entitled to recover damages, but is to be replaced in his position so far as regards the rights and obligations which have been created by the contract into which he has been induced to enter. . . .

[Bowen LJ then discussed the judgment of Jessel MR in *Redgrave* v *Hurd* (1881) 20 Ch D 1, 12–13 where the Master of the Rolls spoke of the relief as being the giving back by the misrepresentor of the advantages he obtained by the contract, and continued:] Now those advantages may be of two kinds. He may get an advantage in the shape of an actual benefit, as when he receives money; he may also get an advantage if the party with whom he contracts assumes some burthen in consideration of the contract. In such a case it seems to me that complete rescission would not be effected unless the misrepresenting party not only hands back the benefits which he has himself—but also re-assumes the burthen which under the contract the injured person has taken upon himself. Speaking only for myself I should not like to lay down the proposition that a person is to be restored to the position which he held before the misrepresentation was made, nor that the person injured must be indemnified against loss which arises out of the contract, unless you place upon the words 'out of the contract' the limited and special meaning which I have endeavoured to shadow forth. Loss arising out of the contract is a term which would be too wide. It would embrace damages at common law, because damages at common law are only given upon the supposition that they are damages which would naturally and reasonably follow from the injury done. I think *Redgrave* v *Hurd* 20 ChD 1 shews that it would be too wide, because in that case the Court excluded from the relief which was given the damages which had been sustained by the plaintiff in removing his business, and other similar items. There ought, as it appears to me, to be a giving back and a taking back on both sides, including the giving back and taking back of the obligations which the contract has created, as well as the giving back and the taking back of the advantages. . . .

FRY LJ: . . . The only other point upon which I will say anything is with regard to the indemnity, and in this case it is obvious that my learned Brothers, although arriving at the same conclusion, have arrived at that conclusion by different roads. It is perhaps enough to say that I agree in their conclusion, and so escape from an inquiry of a very nice and subtle kind. I will only say this, that the inclination of my opinion is towards the view of Lord Justice Cotton; that I am inclined to hold that the Plaintiff is entitled to an indemnity in respect of all obligations entered into under the contract when those obligations are within the necessary or reasonable expectation of both of the contracting parties at the time of the contract. I hesitate to adopt the view of Lord Justice Bowen, that the obligations must be created by the contract, and I feel a little doubt whether the obligation in question in the present suit can be said to have been so created.

It appears to me, however, to be plain that the Plaintiff having been induced by the Defendants to enter into the contract of partnership, it must have been in the contemplation of the contracting parties that the new partner would under that new contract of partnership become liable to the ordinary partnership obligations, and the obligations against which indemnity is sought are such ordinary partnership obligations. . . .

Note

An appeal to the House of Lords was dismissed: *Adam* v *Newbigging* (1888) 13 App Cas 308. There counsel for the plaintiff accepted that there were no outstanding partnership debts, therefore their Lordships declined to express an opinion on the possible availability of an indemnity against the general liabilities of the firm.

Question
Whose formulation of the nature of the indemnity do you prefer: Cotton LJ's, Bowen LJ's or Fry LJ's?

Notes
1. Rescission is arguably a central case example of a restitutionary remedy. Some writers would prefer to consider the setting aside of the contract as a matter for contract law, whereas the restoration of benefits such as goods, or land or money is the concern of restitution (Burrows, *Restitution*, 31–5). Another view is that each party has a right to performance under the contract from the other and therefore holds a *chose in action*, a species of property, owed by the other party. Rescission involves each party giving up their claim on the other. The benefits which are restored are not just tangible ones such as money or goods, but also the intangible *chose in action*: the right to the other side's performance. This view finds support in the language of Bowen LJ.
2. *Newbigging* v *Adam* illustrates the narrow but vital distinction between restitution and compensation. Cotton LJ's wide formulation ('relieved from the consequences and obligations which are the *result* of the contract') may tend to elide that distinction. The same criticism can be made of Fry LJ's judgment. Therefore Bowen LJ's narrower formulation ('rights and obligations which have been *created* by the contract') is to be preferred. The plaintiff is not entitled to be replaced in *status quo ante*, but is entitled to relief from possible burdens which he assumed under the contract, in this case future partnership debts. See Goff and Jones, 210–12 and Burrows, *Restitution*, 130–2.

Whittington* v *Seale-Hayne
(1900) 82 LT 49 (Ch D)

Rescission
The plaintiffs entered into a lease for premises which they wished to use for the purpose of breeding prize poultry. They were induced to enter into the contract by representations that the premises were in good repair and in a sanitary condition, which they were not. The water supply was poisoned, causing illness and death to the poultry and making the plaintiffs' manager ill. The plaintiffs claimed to be indemnified under paragraph 11 of the Statement of Claim for poultry lost due to the insanitary conditions, loss of profit, loss of breeding season and other incidental expenses. *Held*: they were entitled to rescission but not to an indemnity in respect of the losses claimed under paragraph 11.

FARWELL J: The point is one of some nicety. The plaintiffs' action is one for the rescission of a lease on the ground of innocent misrepresentation, and the claim also asks for damages and an indemnity against all costs and charges incurred by the plaintiffs in respect of the lease and the insanitary condition of the premises. The suggestion was made that I should assume for the purpose of argument that innocent misrepresentations were made sufficient to entitle the plaintiffs to rescission. The question then arises to what extent the doctrine, that a plaintiff who succeeds in an action for rescission on the ground of innocent misrepresentation is entitled to be placed *in statu quo ante*, is to be applied. Counsel for the plaintiffs say that in such a case the successful party is to be placed in exactly the same position as if he had never entered into the contract. The defendant admits liability so far as regards anything which was paid under the contract, but not in respect of any damages incurred by reason of the contract; and I think the defendant's view is the correct one. The question is one of some difficulty, because the various authorities have left the point to be decided rather at large. Lord Watson, in *Adam* v *Newbigging* (59 LT Rep 267; 13 App Cas 308, at p. 320), stated it to be one of great nicety and some difficulty. When the plaintiffs say they are entitled to have the misrepresentations made good, it may mean one of two things. It may mean that they are entitled to have the whole of the injury incurred by their entering into the contract made good, or that they are entitled to be repaid what they have paid under their contract–*e.g.*, to make good in the present case would mean to have the drains put right, but to make good by way of compensation for the consequences of the misrepresentations is the same thing as asking for damages. Having regard to *Derry* v *Peek* [(1889) 14 App Cas 337, 58 LJ Ch 864], it is doubtful whether the old doctrine that damages occasioned by misrepresentation should be made good can be enforced now. . . . This brings me back to the case of *Newbigging* v *Adam*, and the difficulty which I have is that the judgments in the Court of Appeal do not agree, and I have therefore to choose between them. I think Bowen, LJ's is the correct view. [Farwell J then discussed the judgments of Bowen and Cotton LJJ in *Newbigging* v *Adam* and continued:] Having regard to the fact that it was only a question of indemnity which was being considered in *Newbigging* v *Adam* (*ubi sup.*), I do not think that Cotton, LJ intended to go further than Bowen, LJ. If he did, I prefer to agree with Bowen, LJ. But Fry, LJ certainly went further. [Farwell J then discussed Fry LJ's judgment and concluded:] Fry, LJ was pointing at cases under the head of damages. His is an entirely different proposition to what Bowen, LJ puts, and he says so. This being so, the point I have here to consider is what is the limit of the liabilities which are within the indemnity. Mr Hughes admits that the rents, rates, and repairs under the covenants in the lease ought to be made good; but he disputes, and I agree with him, that the plaintiff is entitled to what is claimed by paragraph 11 of the statement of claim, which is really damages pure and simple.

Boyd & Forrest v *Glasgow and South-Western Railway Company* [1915] SC(HL) 20 (HL (Scotland))

Rescission; quantum meruit

The railway company invited tenders for construction of a line and disclosed to prospective tenderers details of boring work it had carried out on the proposed route. The pursuers were successful in bidding and entered into a fixed price contract for £243,690 for construction of the railway. The contract expressly stated that the railway company did not guarantee the accuracy of the data it had supplied on boring. The contractors encountered more rock and hard substances than they had anticipated. It turned out the railway company's engineer had in good faith mistakenly transcribed the results of the boring operations. The pursuers sought to rescind the contract and claimed to recover the sum of £106,688 13s 11d for the extra work necessitated by the conditions on a *quantum meruit*. *Held*: the engineer's report being honestly compiled there was no effective misrepresentation, neither had the pursuers discharged the burden of showing they had been induced to enter the contract by the representation. In any event, if there had been a misrepresentation rescission was unavailable because *restitutio in integrum* was impossible.

LORD ATKINSON: . . . The pursuers cannot take back what they gave, their work, though they might restore what they got, the money they received; that, however, is precisely what they are not required to do. The work was done; the parties cannot in any sense be restored, in relation to this contract, to the position they occupied before the contract was entered into. If they had succeeded on their allegation of fraud, they could have got damages in an action for deceit sufficient to cover their loss; but they have not sued for damages either for deceit or breach of contract, and they cannot get damages for an innocent representation made outside the contract, though inducing to it.—*Derry* v *Peek* (1887) 14 App Cas 337. . . .

There is no case in either country which I can find,—we certainly were not referred to any,—where it has even been suggested, much less held, that it is competent for a person, bound to restore what he has got under a contract which he asks to have set aside, to put a money value on the thing to be restored by him and pay over or allow credit for that sum instead of returning the thing itself. If any such rule prevailed, *restitutio in integrum* might be satisfied in the case of a sale of a chattel by putting a money value on some article delivered instead of the article purchased when the former had been destroyed, lost, or re-sold, and setting off this sum *pro tanto* against the price of the article purchased, thereby reducing the thing to what Lord Dundas describes in this case as 'a mere adjustment of disputed accounts.' Yet it has again and again been decided that this cannot be done. For instance, in *Wallis, Son, & Wells* v *Pratt & Haynes* [1910] 2 KB 1003, affirmed on appeal [1911] AC 394, where seed indistinguishable from that purchased, but much inferior in quality and less valuable, was delivered instead of the seed purchased, it was admitted that the contract could not be rescinded because the inferior seed had been re-sold by the plaintiff and he therefore could not deliver it to the vendors. If this new mode of carrying out restitution were legitimate, the plaintiff could have put a money value on the inferior seed, and the contract of sale should have been rescinded on the terms of setting off *pro tanto* that sum against the contract price. . . .

Notes

1. Lord Atkinson's *dicta* stridently assert that where the contractual performance takes the form of services rescission is always impossible. Lord Shaw of Dunfermline in the same case concurred: 'The railway is there, the bridges are built, the excavations are made, the rails are laid, and the railway itself was in complete working two years before this action was brought. Accounts cannot obliterate it, and unless the railway is obliterated *restitutio in integrum* is impossible.'

This insistence on precise restitution *in specie* and rejection of the substitution of money for services rendered is criticised as 'undesirable' and 'productive of injustice' by Goff and Jones, at 212. It may now be open to reconsideration in the light of the courts' willingness to allow substitution of money in contexts such as undue influence, for example in the case of *O'Sullivan* v *Management Agency and Music Ltd* [1985] QB 428 (Chapter 8, Section 3). See Birks, *Introduction*, 415–24 and 475 and Burrows, *Restitution*, 132–7.

2. The courts' reluctance to set aside the contract with its price fixed by a tendering procedure and to substitute for it a reasonable sum in the light of how difficult the work actually was and how long it eventually took, is consistent with the courts' general philosophy on the contractual allocation of risks. The contract insisted that the preliminary boring data should not be relied upon. The House of Lords was extremely reluctant to unravel such a contract where contractors usually take the risk of unanticipated difficulties and delay by agreeing to a fixed price, especially after the work had been completed for two years. Lapse of time may also have been an appropriate bar. It also seems the pursuers accepted an additional sum from the railway company in respect of the excavation. Compare, also in the context of construction work, the frustration case of *Davis Contractors Ltd* v *Fareham Urban District Council* [1956] AC 696 (HL).

Armstrong v *Jackson*
[1917] 2 KB 822 (KBD)

Rescission

The plaintiff in 1910 instructed the defendant stockbroker to purchase shares for him in a company. The defendant produced a contract note purporting to show he had purchased 600 shares for the plaintiff at nearly £3 per share. In fact the defendant never purchased any shares for the plaintiff, but rather transferred to him 600 shares which the defendant had acquired as a promoter of the company. At the date of action the shares were worth 5s each (25p). *Held*: the plaintiff was entitled to rescission and restitution of the sums he had paid to the defendant less £45 for dividends received, and upon payment of those sums by the defendant the plaintiff must transfer the shares back to the defendant.

McCARDIE J: [rejected an argument that rescission was barred because the contract was fully executed because the misrepresentation here was fraudulent (compare now Misrepresentation Act 1967, s. 1) and continued:] . . . I turn now to the second contention of Mr Disturnal with respect to the claim for rescission. He argued that no decree should be granted inasmuch as the circumstances had changed through the lapse of time and that the plaintiff could not restore in 1917 that which he had received from the defendant in 1910. The shares in 1910 stood at nearly 3*l*. for each 5*s*. share. They are now worth 5*s*. only, or slightly less, and at such a price they have been standing at and since the issue of the writ. But in my view this second contention fails also, although, of course, it is clear law that restitutio in integrum is essential to a claim for rescission. The plaintiff still holds the shares he bought in 1910. He can hand them back to the defendant. The company is the same as in 1910. Its name only has been changed. The objects of the company have not changed though the assets of the company may have varied. The market valuation of the shares has greatly dropped, but the shares are the same shares. . . . The phrase 'restitutio in integrum' is somewhat vague. It must be applied with care. It must be considered with respect to the facts of each case. Deterioration of the subject- matter does not, I think, destroy the right to rescind nor prevent a restitutio in integrum. Indeed, it is only in cases where the plaintiff has sustained loss by the inferiority of the subject-matter or a substantial fall in its value that he will desire to exert his power of rescission. Such was the state of things in *Rothschild* v *Brookman* 5 Bli (NS) 165. Such, I infer, was the state of things in *Gillet* v *Peppercorne* 3 Beav 78, where the plaintiff alleged that he had paid extravagant prices for the shares. Such too, I infer, was the state of things in *Oelkers* v *Ellis* [1914] 2 KB 139. If mere deterioration of the subject-matter negatived the right to rescind, the doctrine of rescission would become a vain thing. . . .

The extent to which the requirement of restitutio in integrum may be limited in its application is strikingly illustrated by the decision in *Adam* v *Newbigging* (1888) 13 App Cas 308.

I may point out that mere lapse of time is no answer to a plea of rescission. Here some six years elapsed before the plaintiff claimed to rescind. But in *Rothschild* v *Brookman* 5 Bli (NS) 165 and in *Oelkers* v *Ellis* [1914] 2 KB 139 six years had also elapsed; and in *York Buildings Co.* v *Mackenzie* 3 Pat App Cas 378 eleven years had elapsed, in *Gillet* v *Peppercorne* 3 Beav 78 fourteen years had elapsed, and in *Oliver* v *Court* 8 Price 127 fifteen years had elapsed before the plaintiffs respectively commenced their proceedings to set aside the transaction complained of. In cases like the present the right of the party defrauded is not affected by the mere lapse of time so long as he remains in ignorance of the fraud: see *per* Lord Westbury in *Rolfe* v *Gregory* (1865) 4 DJ & S 576, 579. If, however, he delays his claim to rescission until after the lapse of six years from his discovery of the fraud, then the Court will (apart from any other point) act by analogy to the Statute of Limitations and refuse to grant relief: see *Oelkers* v *Ellis* [1914] 2 KB 139, 151. . . .

Spence* v *Crawford
[1939] 3 All ER 271 (HL (Scotland))

Rescission

Crawford sold his shareholding in a private company to Spence. Later Crawford sought to have the contract set aside alleging fraudulent misrepresentations by Spence as to the company's profitability and assets by deliberate under-valuation of stock. Under the contract of purchase Spence had discharged Crawford's guarantee to the bank of the company's liabilities and released Crawford's securities which had been pledged to the bank for that purpose. Spence argued that this was a contractual benefit which could not be restored, therefore *restitutio in integrum* was impossible. Since the purchase there had been an increase in the issued share capital of the company and the financial prospects of the company had improved. *Held*: Crawford was entitled to rescission and restitution of the shares.

LORD WRIGHT: . . . On the basis that the fraud is established, I think that this is a case where the remedy of rescission, accompanied by *restitutio in integrum*, is proper to be given. The principles governing that form of relief are the same in Scotland as in England. The remedy is equitable. Its application is discretionary, and, where the remedy is applied, it must be moulded in accordance with the exigencies of the particular case. [Lord Wright then discussed *Erlanger* v *New Sombrero Phosphate Company* (above) and continued:] In that case, Lord Blackburn is careful not to seek to tie the hands of the court by attempting to form any rigid rules. The court must fix its eyes on the goal of doing 'what is practically just.' How that goal may be reached must depend on the circumstances of the case, but the court will be more drastic in exercising its discretionary powers in a case of fraud than in a case of innocent misrepresentation. This is clearly recognised by Lindley MR, in the *Lagunas* case [[1899] 2 Ch 392]. There is no doubt good reason for the distinction. A case of innocent misrepresentation may be regarded rather as one of misfortune than as one of moral obliquity. There is no deceit or intention to defraud. The court will be less ready to pull a transaction to pieces where the defendant is innocent, whereas in the case of fraud the court will exercise its jurisdiction to the full in order, if possible, to prevent the defendant from enjoying the benefit of his fraud at the expense of the innocent plaintiff. Restoration, however, is essential to the idea of restitution. To take the simplest case, if a plaintiff who has been defrauded seeks to have the contract annulled and his money or property restored to him, it would be inequitable if he did not also restore what he had got under the contract from the defendant. Though the defendant has been fraudulent, he must not be robbed, nor must the plaintiff be unjustly enriched, as he would be if he both got back what he had parted with and kept what he had received in return. The purpose of the relief is not punishment, but compensation. The rule is stated as requiring the restoration of both parties to the *status quo ante*, but it is generally the defendant who complains that restitution is impossible. The plaintiff who seeks to set aside the contract will generally be reasonable in the standard of restitution which he requires. However, the court can go a long way in ordering restitution if the substantial identity of the subject-matter of the contract remains. Thus, in the *Lagunas* case, though the mine had been largely worked under the contract, the court held that, at least if the case had been one of fraud, it could have ordered an account of profits or compensation to make good the change in the position. In *Adam* v *Newbigging* [(1888) 13 App Cas 308 (HL); (1886) 34 ChD 582 (CA)], where the transaction related to the sale of a share in a partnership, which had become insolvent since the contract, the court ordered the rescission and mutual restitution, though the misrepresentation was not fraudulent, and gave ancillary directions so as to work out the equities. These are merely instances. Certainly in a case of fraud the court will do its best to unravel the complexities of any particular case, which may in some cases involve adjustments on both sides. . . .

Note

In the event the parties agreed on the final state of account between them. Crawford owed the purchase price he had received and made allowance for subsequent losses incurred by Spence. Spence had to account for the dividends he received in the interim, leaving a balance in favour of Crawford at £1,936 6s 10d. (See the summary of the agreement in the speech of Lord Thankerton [1939] 3 All ER 271, at 284.)

MISREPRESENTATION ACT 1967

2. Damages for misrepresentation

(2) Where a person has entered into a contract after a misrepresentation has been made to him otherwise than fraudulently, and he would be entitled, by reason of the misrepresentation, to rescind the contract, then, if it is claimed, in any proceedings arising out of the contract, that the contract ought to be or has been rescinded, the court or arbitrator may declare the contract subsisting and award damages in lieu of rescission, if of opinion that it would be equitable to do so, having regard to the nature of the misrepresentation and the loss that would be caused by it if the contract were upheld, as well as to the loss that rescission would cause to the other party.

(3) Damages may be awarded against a person under subsection (2) of this section whether or not he is liable to damages under subsection (1) thereof, but where he is so liable any award under the said subsection (2) shall be taken into account in assessing his liability under the said subsection (1).

B: Rescission for mistake

Professor Birks draws a distinction between 'induced mistake' and 'spontaneous mistake' (Birks, *Introduction*, 146–7). Where benefits are not conferred pursuant to a binding contract the courts have rarely worried about the reason for the error. As we saw in Section 1 a mistake, as long as it is one of fact, will usually suffice. The distinction is important where as a precondition to restitution a valid contract must be set aside. The policy of sanctity of bargain requires the courts to respect the parties' own allocation of risks. A defect in the formation of the contract may vitiate one party's intention to transfer wealth, however – for example, if one party exerts duress to force the other into the bargain – and the courts may intervene. Similarly, it can be said that informational asymmetry, that is one of the parties being better informed or more intelligent than the other, is a feature of all bargaining. The courts will usually avoid a contract only where the asymmetry was procured by one of the parties. If the representor lied, or even unintentionally misled, rescission, where sought promptly, is usually available. Such 'induced mistakes' have already been considered under the traditional heading 'Misrepresentation'.

The courts are less sympathetic where the mistake which causes a party to contract is wholly spontaneous. It seems to be safe to assert that a unilateral mistake, without more, will never suffice to invalidate a contract in English law. (It may be the case that no contract is ever validly formed in accordance with the principle of objective construction because one party knows or ought to know of the other's mistake: *Hartog* v *Colin & Shields* [1939] 3 All ER 566; *Paal Wilson & Co. A/S* v *Partenreederei Hannah Blumenthal, The 'Hannah Blumenthal'* [1983] 1 AC 854.) The controversial common law doctrine of mistake requires brief consideration. In the 'mistakes as to person' cases occasionally the courts have held the contract void at common law. But here the fundamental defect has been caused by the fraudulent misrepresentations of a rogue as to his identity: see *Cundy* v *Lindsay* (1878) LR 3 App Cas 459 (HL) and *Ingram* v *Little* [1961] 1 QB 31 (CA). These are therefore cases of induced mistake. Where a mistake is *shared* by both parties the contract has been held void, for example where the subject-matter did not exist (*Couturier* v *Hastie* (1856) 5 HL Cas 673; 10 ER 1065) or where the subject-matter is *radically* different from what both parties thought it to be (compare *Bell* v *Lever Bros Ltd* [1932] AC 161 with *Associated Japanese Bank (International)* v *Credit du Nord SA* [1989] 1 WLR 255). Where a contract is held to be void at common law for mistake, restitutionary relief may follow. (For reference see Treitel, *Contract*, 262–87.)

The extent of any *equitable* doctrine providing relief for spontaneous mistakes is more controversial. Goff and Jones describe the jurisdiction of the Court of Chancery in this area as of 'respectable antiquity', but go on to say that the early decisions yield no 'coherent . . . doctrine' (at 213). *Cooper* v *Phibbs* (1867) LR 2 HL 149 is a remarkable decision in extending the equitable rules. The appellant took a lease of a fishery which in fact already belonged to him. Neither party knew of the true facts. The House of Lords set the lease aside upon terms. This case was much relied upon by Denning LJ in his bold judgment in *Solle* v *Butcher* [1950] 1 KB 671, where he sought to synthesise authorities on both induced and spontaneous mistakes to declare a wide power to intervene where the mistake is common, fundamental and the party seeking to have the contract set aside is not at fault.

The status of Lord Denning's views remains uncertain despite the Master of the Rolls reiterating them in *Magee* v *Pennine Insurance Co. Ltd* [1969] 2 QB 507 and support in the first instance cases of *Grist* v *Bailey* [1967] Ch 532 and *Laurence* v *Lexcourt Holdings Ltd* [1978] 1 WLR 1128. Recently the Court of Appeal has signalled a return to sanctity of bargain, marginalising the equitable doctrine, and insisting on respect for the contractual allocation of risks and sensitivity to general rules such as *caveat emptor* in the context of the sale of land (*William Sindall plc* v *Cambridgeshire County Council* [1994] 1 WLR 1016, where Hoffmann LJ disapproved of the results in *Grist* v *Bailey* and *Laurence* v *Lexcourt Holdings Co. Ltd*).

Rescission, or setting aside the contract, in equity for spontaneous mistakes (whatever the status of the doctrine) is clearly wider than restitutionary principle requires, going beyond reversing unjust enrichments. This is clearly brought out by the terms imposed on the parties as a condition of setting the contract aside in the leading cases of *Cooper* v *Phibbs* and *Solle* v *Butcher*. (For discussion see Burrows, *Restitution*, 128–30; for reference see Treitel, *Contract*, 287–302.)

Section 5: is 'ignorance' a restitutionary cause of action?

Professor Birks has cogently and consistently argued that the English case law yields an as yet innominate category of restitutionary claim conceptually distinct from traditional 'mistake' cases. Whereas in mistake cases the reason for restitution is that the plaintiff's error vitiates his intention to transfer value, in these cases the plaintiff claims restitution because his wealth has been diminished without his knowledge. That is, there was never any intention to benefit the defendant. Birks gives simple examples from the case law where a defendant steals or otherwise subtracts the plaintiff's wealth while the latter remains blissfully unaware of what is going on. See, for example, *Neate* v *Harding* (1851) 6 Ex 349, 155 ER 577 and *Moffatt* v *Kazana* [1969] 2 QB 152. However, Professor Birks goes further and seeks to apply this reasoning to cases of indirect recipients, or triangular fact configurations, and here his analysis becomes controversial.

'Ignorance' would therefore be the ground for restitution in unusual cases where *tracing at common law* has yielded an *action for money had and received*, of which *Lipkin Gorman* v *Karpnale Ltd* [1991] 2 AC 548 (HL) is now the most distinguished example. Further, it would encompass some cases presently categorised as cases of mistake of fact (*Agip (Africa) Ltd* v *Jackson* [1990] Ch 265, affd [1991] Ch 547 (CA)). Cases on liability to account in equity as a constructive trustee on the ground of *knowing receipt* also yield to this analysis, although the insistence of some of the authorities on knowledge or fault on the part of the defendant sits rather unhappily with the common law's strict liability approach. Also on the equity side *In re Diplock* [1948] Ch 465 (CA), affd [1951] AC 251 (HL) can be said to be a case of ignorance giving rise to strict personal liability, rather than an exception to the mistake of law bar.

For extracts from *Lipkin Gorman* v *Karpnale*, *Agip* v *Jackson* and cases on tracing at common law, tracing in equity and knowing receipt in general see Chapter 7, Sections 1 and 2. For the detail of Professor Birks's arguments see Birks, *Introduction*, 140–6, and especially the magisterial essay Birks, 'Misdirected Funds – Restitution from the Recipient' [1989] LMCLQ 296. On *Lipkin Gorman* in the House of Lords see Birks, 'The English Recognition of Unjust Enrichment' [1991] LMCLQ 473, at 473–97. See further Burrows, *Restitution*, 139–60.

Ranged against Professor Birks's elegant arguments are, first, the fact that no English case explicitly acknowledges 'ignorance' as a ground for restitution. Secondly, Professor Jones in the latest edition of Goff and Jones has rejected the Birks thesis, preferring to include many of the cases in a wide definition of 'mistake' (at 107–08). Thirdly, Professor Burrows argues that the three party cases which are central to Birks's argument are best explained on a 'property' analysis: see Burrows, 'Misdirected Funds – A Reply' (1990) 106 LQR 20 and Burrows, *Restitution*, 139–60. Fourthly, at least on the Chancery Division side of the High Court, the judges are still insisting on fault, and often a high degree of fault, on the part of the defendant before awarding restitution (see the discussion of 'knowing receipt' in Chapter 7, Section 2). Fifthly, on the Queen's Bench Division side, the recent emergence of 'no consideration' as a possible restitutionary cause of action threatens to subvert the established category of mistake and the not-yet-established category of 'ignorance' (see the discussion of the 'Swaps' cases in Chapter 5, Section 2).

3 COMPULSION

Compulsion takes many forms in relation to the law of unjust enrichment. The acquisition of benefits by means of compulsion presents one of the strongest claims for a restitutionary response. Requiring the party who has exercised the pressure to disgorge any benefits received protects individuals' right to a free and fair choice in disposing of their wealth. A key question for the law is to distinguish the exercise of pressure which is normal in a healthy, competitive society from pressure which crosses the line, being coercive and extortionate (see Birks, *Introduction*, 173–4). The first two sections of this chapter divide on the old jurisdictional grounds, considering, first, the common law's approach to duress and, secondly, equity's intervention in transactions clouded by undue influence. Section 3 considers the difficult question of to what extent the law interferes in transactions tainted by exceptional inequality, where no actual compulsion can be shown. Similarly, Sections 4 and 5 are not concerned with pressure exerted by the recipient. Section 4 considers legal compulsion as a ground for restitution. Ordinarily benefits extracted by due process of law are irrecoverable in the interests of legal certainty. However, there is an exception deriving from the old cases under the *action for money paid* which allows a person who has paid another's debt under legal compulsion to recover from the person primarily liable. Section 5 considers the position of those who interfere uninvited in other people's business. English law generally is hostile to such persons, but there is a body of cases which suggests that an intervener who acts by reason of *necessity* may maintain a restitutionary claim for his expenses.

Section 1: benefits conferred under duress

Historically an 'interests'-based analysis may help explain the common law approach to compulsion. Traditionally the judges took the robust view that transactions would be unwound only on the ground of 'duress to the person'. For example, if X threatens to kill Y unless Y signs a deed, even the old common lawyers saw that the deed and its consequences should be unscrambled. Therefore the interest in bodily integrity was fully protected. A person's interest in personal property was not so secure. If carrier A refused to deliver up B's goods unless B paid extra remuneration over and above the contract price, the law made a curious distinction. If B paid up, the money was recoverable in restitution, but if B simply promised to pay and took the goods, A could enforce the contract. This bizarre anomaly seems now to have been discarded. A further exciting development, largely prompted by restitution scholars, has been the rise of 'economic duress' as a vitiating factor in contract and as a cause of action in unjust enrichment. Recent cases suggest that even non-proprietary economic interests now require protection against coercive behaviour. Renegotiation is the usual context. A threatened breach of contract induces the other contracting party to promise some extra performance or to hand over benefits in return for continued cooperation. The rise of economic duress as a means of policing such disputes has coincided with the marginalisation (or possible discarding) of the contractual doctrine of consideration as a tool for resolving such questions.

The basic structure of a duress claim is the same for all three types of interests: bodily integrity, proprietary rights and economic interests. First, there must be *pressure*, usually in the form of threats, although the judges have been adept at recognising implicit as well as explicit threatening behaviour. Secondly, in view of the need to distinguish coercion from everyday or usual pressures the law uses the touchstone of *illegitimacy*. This will usually take the form of a threat to commit a legal wrong. For example, 'I will have you killed' (crime of homicide), or 'Your family is not safe' (at least assault), or 'I will not release your cargo unless you pay me more' (tort of wrongful interference with goods). The recognition of economic duress means that a breach of contract can be a relevant legal wrong for this purpose. But illegitimate is wider than unlawful, leaving scope for the law to develop to encapsulate more subtle forms of persuasion. The third component is causation: the pressure must *induce* the victim to enter the deal or cause him to transfer wealth. The causal inquiry in the context of 'economic duress' has been clouded by the obfuscatory term 'coercion of the will so as to vitiate consent'. The meaning of this obscure phrase has proved elusive and there are signs that it is being jettisoned in favour of more concrete evidential factors: Did the victim protest? Did the victim repudiate the deal in good time? Did the victim have independent advice?

On the pressures giving rise to restitution see Birks, *Introduction*, 174–9 and for more general discussion see Burrows, *Restitution*, 161–8. It is also worth recording here the observation of Lord Goff of Chieveley in *Woolwich Equitable Building Society* v *Inland Revenue Commissioners* [1993] 1 AC 70 at 165:

> I would not think it right, especially bearing in mind the development of the concept of economic duress, to regard the categories of compulsion for present purposes as closed.

A: *Duress to the person*

See Burrows, *Restitution*, 168–70.

Duke de Cadaval* v *Collins

(1836) 4 Ad & E 858; 111 ER 1006 (KB)

Action for money had and received

The plaintiff, a Portuguese nobleman, arrived at Falmouth in July 1834 and was very soon after arrested by Collins. Collins claimed to be owed £16,200 by the Duke and one of his countrymen. The Duke understood little English, but signed an agreement agreeing to pay £500 pending the trial of the action in return for being released and free from future arrest. The Duke paid £500 and was released. Collins's writ for the supposed debt was set aside for irregularity, and subsequently the Duke in this action claimed the return of the £500. The jury found that Collins knew he had no claim on the Duke. *Held*: the money was recoverable. Lord Denman CJ said 'the arrest was fraudulent; and the money was parted with under the arrest, to get rid of the pressure'.

Barton* v *Armstrong

(1973) [1976] AC 104 (PC)

Landmark Corporation was a company whose principal activity was developing land near Surfers' Paradise in Queensland. There was a struggle for control of the company between its chairman, Armstrong, and its managing director, Barton. By a deed executed on 17 January 1967, Barton agreed to buy out Armstrong's holding in the company. A year later Barton sought to have the deed set aside on the ground of duress. The threats alleged included regular telephone calls to Barton in the middle of the night, consisting of heavy breathing and the occasional utterance 'You will be killed' and Armstrong shouting at Barton in the board room, 'You stink; you stink. I will fix you'. There was even a suggestion that Armstrong had hired a Yugoslavian to kill Barton. Barton bought a rifle, and moved into a hotel with his wife and son until the documents were executed. The judge found that the threats had been made, *but* that the predominant reason for Barton's entering into the agreement was commercial necessity. The majority of the Court of Appeal of New South Wales (Jacobs JA dissenting) dismissed the appeal. The Privy Council by a majority of 3:2 allowed Barton's appeal and held the deed was 'void'. Lords Wilberforce and Simon of Glaisdale dissented, holding it was not appropriate for an appellate court to interfere in what were essentially issues of fact.

LORD CROSS OF CHELSEA: . . . It is hardly surprising that there is no direct authority on the point, for if A threatens B with death if he does not execute some document and B, who takes A's threats seriously, executes the document it can be only in the most unusual circumstances that there can be any doubt whether the threats operated to induce him to execute the document. But this is a most unusual case and the findings of fact made below do undoubtedly raise the question whether it was necessary for Barton in order to obtain relief to establish that he would not have executed the deed in question but for the threats. In answering this question in favour of Barton, Jacobs JA relied both on a number of old common law authorities on the subject of 'duress' and also—by way of analogy—on later decisions in equity with regard to the avoidance of deeds on the ground of fraud. Their Lordships do not think that the common law authorities are of any real assistance for it seems most unlikely that the authors of the statements relied on had the sort of problem which has arisen here in mind at all. On the other hand they think that the conclusion to which Jacobs JA came was right and that it is supported by the equity decisions. The scope of common law duress was very limited and at a comparatively early date equity began to grant relief in cases where the disposition in question had been procured by the exercise of pressure which the Chancellor considered to be illegitimate—although it did not amount to common law duress. There was a parallel development in the field of dispositions induced by fraud. At common law the only remedy available to the man defrauded was an action for deceit but equity in the same period in which it was building up the doctrine of 'undue influence' came to entertain proceedings to set aside dispositions which had been obtained by fraud: see *Holdsworth, A History of English Law,* vol. V (1924), pp. 328-9. There is an obvious analogy between setting aside a disposition for duress or undue influence and setting it aside for fraud. In each case—to quote the words of Holmes J in *Fairbanks* v *Snow* (1887) 13 NE 596, 598—'the party has been subjected to an improper motive for action.' Again the similarity of the effect in law of metus and dolus in connection with dispositions of property is noted by Stair in his *Institutions of the Law of Scotland,* New ed. (1832), Book IV, title 40.25. Had Armstrong made a fraudulent misrepresentation to Barton for the purpose of inducing him to execute the deed of January 17, 1967, the answer to the problem which has arisen would have been clear. If it were established that Barton did not allow the representation to affect his judgment then he could not make it a ground for relief even though the representation was designed and known by Barton to be designed to affect his judgment. If on the other hand Barton relied on the misrepresentation Armstrong could not have defeated his claim to relief by showing that there were other more weighty causes which contributed to his decision to execute the deed, for in this field the court does not allow an examination into the relative importance of contributory causes.

'Once make out that there has been anything like deception, and no contract resting in any degree on that foundation can stand.': *per* Lord Cranworth LJ in *Reynell* v *Sprye* (1852) 1 De GM & G 660, 708—see also the other cases referred to in *Cheshire and Fifoot's Law of Contract,* 8th ed. (1972), pp. 250–251. Their Lordships think that the same rule should apply in cases of duress and that if Armstrong's threats were 'a' reason for Barton's executing the deed he is entitled to relief even though he might well have entered into the contract if Armstrong had uttered no threats to induce him to do so.

. . . If Barton had to establish that he would not have made the agreement but for Armstrong's threats, then their Lordships would not dissent from the view that he had not made out his case. But no such onus lay on him. On the contrary it was for Armstrong to establish, if he could, that the threats which he was making and the unlawful pressure which he was exerting for the purpose of inducing Barton to sign the agreement and which Barton knew were being made and exerted for this purpose in fact contributed nothing to Barton's decision to sign. The judge has found that during the 10 days or so before the documents were executed Barton was in genuine fear that Armstrong was planning to have him killed if the agreement was not signed. His state of mind was described by the judge as one of 'very real mental torment' and he believed that his fears would be at end when once the documents were executed. It is true that the judge was not satisfied that Vojinovic had been employed by Armstrong but if one man threatens another with unpleasant consequences if he does not act in a particular way, he must take the risk that the impact of his threats may be accentuated by extraneous circumstances for which he is not in fact responsible. It is true that on the facts as their Lordships assume them to have been Armstrong's threats may have been unnecessary; but it would be unrealistic to hold that they played no part in making Barton decide to execute the documents. The proper inference to be drawn from the facts found is, their Lordships think, that though it may be that Barton would have executed the documents even if Armstrong had made no threats and exerted no unlawful pressure to induce him to do so the threats and unlawful pressue in fact contributed to his decision to sign the documents and to recommend their execution by Landmark and the other parties to them. It may be, of course, that Barton's fear of Armstrong had evaporated before he issued his writ in this action but Armstrong—understandably enough—expressly disclaimed reliance on the defence of delay on Barton's part in repudiating the deed.

In the result therefore the appeal should be allowed and a declaration made that the deeds in question were executed by Barton under duress and are void so far as concerns him. . . .

LORD WILBERFORCE AND LORD SIMON OF GLAISDALE (dissenting on the facts): . . . The action is one to set aside an apparently complete and valid agreement on the ground of duress. The basis of the plaintiff's claim is, thus, that though there was apparent consent there was no true consent to the agreement: that the agreement was not voluntary.

This involves consideration of what the law regards as voluntary, or its opposite; for in life, including the life of commerce and finance, many acts are done under pressure, sometimes overwhelming pressure, so that one can say that the actor had no choice but to act. Absence of choice in this sense does not negate consent in law: for this the pressure must be one of a kind which the law does not regard as legitimate. Thus, out of the various means by which consent may be obtained—advice, persuasion, influence, inducement, representation, commercial pressure—the law has come to select some which it will not accept as a reason for voluntary action: fraud, abuse of relation of confidence, undue influence, duress or coercion. In this the law, under the influence of equity, has developed from the old common law conception of duress—threat to life and limb—and it has arrived at the modern generalisation expressed by Holmes J— 'subjected to an improper motive for action': *Fairbanks* v *Snow,* 13 NE Reporter 596, 598.

In an action such as the present, then, the first step required of the plaintiff is to show that some illegitimate means of persuasion was used. That there were threats to Barton's life was found by the judge, though he did not accept Barton's evidence in important respects. We shall return to this point in detail later.

The next necessary step would be to establish the relationship between the illegitimate means used and the action taken. For the purposes of the present case (reserving our opinion as to cases which may arise in other contexts) we are prepared to accept, as the formula most favourable to the appellant, the test proposed by the majority, namely, that the illegitimate means used was a reason (not the reason, nor the *predominant* reason nor the *clinching* reason) why the complainant acted as he did. We are also prepared to accept that a decisive answer is not obtainable by asking the question whether the contract would have been made even if there had been no threats because, even if the answer to this question is affirmative, that does not prove that the contract was not made because of the threats.

Assuming therefore that what has to be decided is whether the illegitimate means used was a reason why the complainant acted as he did, it follows that his reason for acting must (unless the case is one of automatism which this is not) be a conscious reason so that the complainant can given evidence of it: 'I acted because I was forced.' If his evidence is honest and accepted, that will normally conclude the issue. If, moreover, he gives evidence, it is necessary for the court to evaluate his evidence by testing it against his credibility and his actions. . . .

Note

Compare the causal test in the fraudulent misrepresentation case of *Edgington* v *Fitzmaurice* (1885) 29 Ch D 459 (CA): misstatement must be *a* cause, not *the* cause of the representee entering into the transaction (discussed in Chapter 2, Section 4). All the members of the Privy Council accepted this straightforward 'but for' strategy. Note the view of the majority that once duress is shown, the burden of proof on the causal question shifts to the person making the threats to show that they did not induce the contract.

B: *Duress of goods*

See Burrows, *Restitution*, 170–2.

Astley* v *Reynolds
(1731) 2 Str 915; 93 ER 939 (KB)

Action for money had and received

The plaintiff pawned plate to the defendant for a loan of £20 over three years. At the end of that period the defendant claimed £10 interest. The plaintiff offered £4, which lesser sum was greater than the maximum legally-permitted interest. The defendant refused. A similar offer and rejection happened four months later, the defendant still insisting on £10. So the plaintiff paid and the defendant released his goods. *Held*: the plaintiff could recover the amount paid which exceeded the legally due interest. *Per curiam*: '. . . this is a payment by compulsion; the plaintiff might have such an immediate want of his goods, that an action of trover will not do his business . . . we must take it that he paid the money relying on his legal remedy to get it back.'

Note

Whether the plaintiff has an alternative course of action other than submitting is an issue in all compulsion cases. Here it was decided that the legal remedy of trover (now termed wrongful interference with goods) was not necessarily an efficacious option.

Skeate v *Beale*

(1841) 11 Ad & E 983; 113 ER 688 (KB)

Skeate claimed that Beale was in arrears with regard to rent. Therefore he seized goods belonging to Beale as distress (a self-help remedy entitling a landlord to take property on the tenant's premises as security for arrears). Beale then signed an agreement undertaking to pay £3 immediately and to pay the remainder of the arrears, some £16, within one month, in return for Skeate withdrawing the distress. Skeate sought to enforce that agreement. Beale claimed that only £3 was owing, but that Skeate had wrongfully seized goods worth £20 and had menaced him, threatening to dispose of the goods unless he entered into the agreement. Beale further alleged that the agreement was made under protest and that Skeate must have known only the smaller amount of rent was due. *Held*: the agreement was not void for duress of goods.

LORD DENMAN CJ: . . . We consider the law to be clear, and founded on good reason, that an agreement is not void because made under duress of goods. There is no distinction in this respect between a deed and an agreement not under seal; and, with regard to the former, the law is laid down in 2 Inst. 483, and Sheppard's Touchstone, p. 61, and the distinction pointed out between duress of, or menace to, the person, and duress of goods. The former is a constraining force, which not only takes away the free agency, but may leave no room for appeal to the law for a remedy: a man, therefore, is not bound by the agreement which he enters into under such circumstances; but the fear that goods may be taken or injured does not deprive any one of his free agency who possesses that ordinary degree of firmness which the law requires all to exert. It is not necessary now to enter into the consideration of cases in which it has been held that money paid to redeem goods wrongfully seized, or to prevent their wrongful seizure, may be recovered back in an action for money had and received: for the distinction between those cases and the present, which must be taken to be that of an agreement, not compulsorily but voluntarily entered into, is obvious. . . .

Note

The illogical distinction drawn here between payments and agreements to pay has not survived the modern cases on economic duress, although the case has never been formally overruled.

Maskell v *Horner*

[1915] 3 KB 106 (CA)

Action for money had and received

Maskell carried on business as a dealer in produce on the fringes of Spitalfields Market. The owner of the market demanded tolls from Maskell, threatening to seize goods if they were not paid. Maskell refused to pay and his goods were seized. Having consulted a solicitor, Maskell decided to pay the tolls, but under protest. Payment was made from September 1900 to June 1912, but always under protest and with the threat of seizure always in the background. In time the repetition of the protests became something of a joke. *Attorney-General* v *Horner (No. 2)* [1913] 2 Ch 140 decided that the tolls were unlawfully demanded. *Held*: (Pickford LJ doubting) Maskell was entitled to restitution on the ground that the payments were not voluntarily made, subject to a defence of limitation barring recovery of payments made over six years before the writ was issued.

LORD READING CJ: [rejected a claim based on mistake and continued . . .] Upon the second head of claim the plaintiff asserts that he paid the money not voluntarily but under the pressure of actual or threatened seizure of his goods, and that he is therefore entitled to recover it as money had and received. If the facts proved support this assertion the plaintiff would, in my opinion, be entitled to succeed in this action.

If a person with knowledge of the facts pays money, which he is not in law bound to pay, and in circumstances implying that he is paying it voluntarily to close the transaction, he cannot recover it. Such a payment is in law like a gift, and the transaction cannot be reopened. If a person pays money, which he is not bound to pay, under the compulsion of urgent and pressing necessity or of seizure, actual or threatened, of his goods he can recover it as money had and received. The money is paid not under duress in the strict sense of the term, as that implies duress of person, but under the pressure of seizure or detention of goods which is analogous to that of duress. Payment under such pressure establishes that the payment is not made voluntarily to close the transaction *per* Lord Abinger CB and *per* Parke B in *Atlee* v *Backhouse* 3 M & W 633, 646, 650. The payment is made for the purpose of averting a threatened evil and is made not with the intention of giving up a right but under immediate necessity and with the intention of preserving the right to dispute the legality of the demand (*per* Tindal CJ in *Valpy* v *Manley* 1 CB 594, 602, 603). There are numerous instances in the books of successful claims in this form of action to recover money paid to relieve goods from seizure. Other familiar instances are cases such as *Parker* v *Great Western Ry. Co.* 7 Man & G 253, where the money was paid to the railway company under protest in order to induce them to carry goods which they were refusing to carry except at rates in excess of those they were legally entitled to demand. These payments were made throughout a period of twelve months, always accompanied by the assertion that they were made under protest, and it was held that the plaintiffs were entitled to recover the excess payments as money had and received, on the ground that the payments were made under the compulsion of urgent and pressing necessity. That case was approved in *Great Western Ry. Co.* v *Sutton* LR 4 HL 226, 249, when the judges were summoned to the House of Lords to give their opinion. Willes J, in stating his view of the law, said: 'When a man pays more than he is bound to do by law for the performance of a duty which the law says is owed to him for nothing, or for less than he has paid, there is a compulsion or concussion in respect of which he is entitled to recover the excess by condictio indebiti, or action for money had and received. This is every day's practice as to excess freight.' That is a clear and accurate statement in accordance with the views expressed by Blackburn J in the same case and adopted by the House of Lords. It treats such claims made in this form of action as matters of ordinary practice and beyond discussion. (See also *per* Lord Chelmsford in *Lancashire and Yorkshire Ry. Co.* v *Gidlow* LR 7 HL 517, 527.)

This principle of law is so well settled that it cannot be challenged, and I find nothing in *Brisbane* v *Dacres* 5 Taunt 143 to the contrary. Indeed the general proposition of law is not disputed; but it was contended, and the learned judge found, that the plaintiff had not brought himself within it, mainly because (1) the payments were not accompanied by a declaration or assertion to the defendant that the plaintiff did not intend to give up his right to recover the money, and (2) the protests for a period of years had degenerated into a sort of grumbling acquiescence and were ineffective. I doubt whether Rowlatt J intended to find that there must be anything in the shape of an express notice or declaration to the defendant of the plaintiff's intention to keep alive his right to recover. It is clear, and was indeed admitted at the Bar, that no express words are necessary and that the circumstances attending the payments and the conduct of the plaintiff when making them may be a sufficient indication to the defendant that the payments were not made with the intention of closing the transactions. I do not think that the mere fact of a payment under protest would be sufficient to entitle the plaintiff to succeed; but I think that it affords some evidence, when accompanied by other circumstances, that the payment was not voluntarily made to end the matter. . . .

Note
See also the recent cases of *The 'Siboen' and the 'Sibotre'* and *The 'Alev'*, discussed below under the heading of 'economic duress'.

C: *Economic duress*

See Burrows, *Restitution*, 174–85.

D & C Builders Ltd v *Rees*
[1966] 2 QB 617 (CA)

The plaintiff company was owned by two jobbing builders. The defendant owed them £480. While the defendant was ill with flu, his wife offered £300 in settlement. The company was in desperate financial straits so the builders decided to accept, otherwise it was feared the company would go bankrupt. Later the company sued for the balance. *Held*: the company could recover the balance applying the rule in *Foakes* v *Beer* (1884) 9 App Cas 605 (HL). *Per* Lord Denning MR:

> The debtor's wife held the creditor to ransom. The creditor was in need of money to meet his own commitments, and she knew it . . . she was putting undue pressure on the creditor. She was making a threat to break a contract (by paying nothing) and she was willing to do it so as to compel the creditor to do what he was unwilling to do (to accept £300 in settlement): and she succeeded. That was on recent authority a case of intimidation: see *Rookes* v *Barnard* [1964] AC 1129 and *Stratford (J.T.) & Son Ltd* v *Lindley* [1964] 2 WLR 1002, 1015.

Occidental Worldwide Investment Corporation v *Skibs A/S Avanti, The 'Siboen' and the 'Sibotre'*
[1976] 1 Lloyd's Rep 293 (QBD (Commercial Court))

Rescission
The vessels '*Siboen*' and '*Sibotre*' were both oil/bulk ore carriers belonging to the defendant owners. They were time-chartered for a period of three

years to the plaintiff charterers, a subsidiary company of the well-known oil company, under a contract dated 3 August 1970. The hire rate was agreed at $4.40 per ton per month, the then prevailing market rate. Subsequently the charter market became depressed, and the financial position of the Occidental group as a whole worsened. In March 1972, the charterers sent notices to the owners purporting to cancel the charterparties, alleging frustration. This allegation was without foundation. As a result representatives of both parties met in Paris on 26 March 1972. Representatives of the charterers gave the owners' representatives the impression that the company had suffered losses of $120 million, that it had virtually no assets and was dependent on its parent company for survival, and that the parent company was willing to let the charterers go bankrupt if there was no reduction in hire rates. This was a 'gross distortion' of the truth. Consequently, Captain Tschudi, the manager of the owners, agreed to a variation of the charters contained in written 'addenda' setting a reduced hire rate of $4.10 in return for an unconditional guarantee by the parent company of the charterers' liabilities. The charterers sought a further reduction and in arbitration achieved a new rate of $3.95 in August 1972. On 27 April 1973, Captain Tschudi sent an angry telex to the charterers claiming that the variation had been 'unlawfully forced' on him. Both ships were then withdrawn in May 1973. In this action the plaintiff charterers claimed damages for wrongful withdrawal, and the defendant owners counterclaimed for rescission on the grounds of misrepresentation or duress. *Held*: the variation of the charters could be rescinded on the ground of misrepresentation, but the plea of duress failed. Therefore the defendant owners could claim hire at the original rate up to the time of withdrawal.

KERR J: . . . I then turn to Mr Goff's primary submission on duress. He agreed that for this purpose it had to be assumed that the charterers were in fact liable to go bankrupt if the various owners did not reduce their rates, without any misrepresentation having been made on this or any other subject. He submitted that the cancellation notices constituted threatened breaches of the charters, and with this I agree. He also submitted that if the charterers were liable to go bankrupt if the owners did not reduce their rates, then the owners would be left without any effective legal remedy in the face of these threatened breaches. He accordingly submitted that the defence of duress is made out whenever one party to a contract threatens to commit a breach of it and the other party agrees to vary or cancel the contract under this threat because it has no effective legal remedy in respect of the threatened breach and has in this sense been compelled to agree. For good measure, though again I do not think that this makes any difference, he added that duress must a fortiori be a defence when the party threatening to break the contract is putting foward some justification for doing so without any bona fides.

I think that this submission is much too wide. On the other hand, Mr Lloyd's counter-submissions were in their turn in my view too narrow. These fell under two main heads. First, he submitted that English law only knows duress to the person and duress to goods, and that a case like the present falls into neither category, with the result that this defence must fail in limine. Secondly, he submitted that although money paid under duress to goods is recoverable, a contract can only be set aside for duress to the person but not in any other case of duress. He said that in every case in which a party enters into a contract otherwise than under duress to the person, any payment or forbearance pursuant to such contract is regarded as voluntary, whatever may have been the nature or degree of compulsion, short of violence to the person, which may have caused him to enter into the contract. He relied mainly on a line of authority in which *Skeate* v *Beale,* (1841) 2 Ad & E 983 is the leading case.

I do not think that English law is as limited as submitted by Mr Lloyd, though there are statements in some of the cases which support his submissions. For instance, if I should be compelled to sign a lease or some other contract for a nominal but legally sufficient consideration under an imminent threat of having my house burnt down or a valuable picture slashed, though without any threat of physical violence to anyone, I do not think that the law would uphold the agreement. I think that a plea of coercion or compulsion would be available in such cases. The latter is the term used in a line of Australian cases of strong persuasive authority to which I was referred: *Nixon* v *[Furphy],* (1925) 25 NSW 151 and in the High Court of Australia in 37 CLR 161, in *Re Hooper & Grass' Contract,* (1949) VLR 269 and *T. A. Sundell & Sons Pty. Ltd* v *Emm Yannoulatos (Overseas) Pty. Ltd,* [1956] SR (NSW) 323. These judgments also state that the degree of compulsion or duress is not necessarily limited to cases of threats to the person or duress in relation to goods. Further, I think that there are indications in *Skeate* v *Beale* itself and in other cases that the true question is ultimately whether or not the agreement in question is to be regarded as having been concluded voluntarily; but it does not follow that every agreement concluded under some form of compulsion is ipso facto to be regarded as voluntary with the solitary exception of cases involving duress to the person. In *Wakefield* v *Newton,* (1844) 6 QB 276, Lord Denman referred to cases such as *Skeate* v *Beale* as

> . . . that class where the parties have come to a voluntary settlement of their concerns, and have chosen to pay what is found due.

In *Kaufman* v *Gerson,* (1904) 1 KB 591 the Court of Appeal refused to enforce a written contract signed by the defendant which was valid under French law because the consideration for the defendant's promise to pay sums of money to the plaintiff had been that the plaintiff would not prosecute the defendant's husband in France, he having apparently committed a criminal offence under French law. The reason for the refusal to enforce the contract was duress or coercion. The Judge at first instance held the contract to be enforceable because there was no threat of physical violence. But this was reversed unanimously, and Sir Richard Henn Collins, MR, significantly asked: 'What does it matter what particular form of coercion is used as long as the will is coerced?' The same approach is strongly supported by the judgments of Lord Denning, MR., and Lord Justice Danckwerts in *D. & C. Builders Ltd* v *Rees,* [1966] 2 QB 617. The plaintiffs were owed about £480 by the defendant and were in desperate financial straits. They were in effect told that unless they settled for £300 they would get nothing, and when they unwillingly decided to accept the sum of £300 the defendant's wife insisted on their signing a receipt 'in completion of the account'. In the action they were nevertheless held entitled to recover the balance of £180. There were two grounds for the decision of Lord Denning and Lord Justice Danckwerts. First, that there was no consideration for the settlement, which was the only point dealt with in the concurring judgment of Lord Justice Winn, the third member of the Court. Secondly, that there was no 'true accord' because (in the words of Lord Denning at p. 265) 'no person can insist on a settlement procured by intimidation'. It is true that in that case, and in all the three Australian cases, it was held that there had been no consideration for the settlement which the Courts reopened. But I do not think that it would have made any difference if the defendants in these cases had also insisted on some purely nominal but legally sufficient consideration. If the contract is void the consideration would be recoverable in quasi-contract; if it is voidable equity could rescind the contract and order the return of the consideration. The anomaly of the position for which Mr Lloyd contends as a matter of principle is helpfully discussed in Goff and Jones, 'The Law of Restitution' at p. 150.

But even assuming, as I think, that our law is open to further development in relation to contracts concluded under some form of compulsion not amounting to duress to the person, the Court must in every case at least be satisfied that the consent of the other party was overborne by compulsion so as to deprive him of any animus contrahendi. This would depend on the facts of each case. One relevant factor would be whether the party relying on duress made any protest at the time or shortly thereafter. Another would be to consider whether or not he treated the settlement as closing the transaction in question and as binding upon him, or whether he made it clear that he regarded the position as still open. All these considerations are mentioned in the Australian judgments, and the question whether or not there was any intention to close the transaction is also referred to in the judgments of Lord Reading, CJ, and Lord Justice Buckley in *Maskell* v *Horner,* [1915] 3 KB 106. But the facts of the present case fall a long way short of the test which would in law be required to make good a defence of compulsion or duress. Believing the statements about the charterers' financial state to be true, as must for this purpose be assumed, Captain Tschudi made no protest about having to conclude the addenda, either at the Paris meeting on March 26, 1972, or at any time before the telex of April 28, 1973. He repeatedly said in his evidence that he regarded the agreement then reached as binding and sought to uphold it in the subsequent arbitration. He was acting under great pressure, but only commercial pressure, and not under anything which could in law be regarded as a coercion of his will so as to vitiate his consent. I therefore hold that the plea of duress fails. . . .

Notes

1. This was the first case to state explicitly that duress was no longer confined to the traditional categories of duress to the person and duress of goods. However, it does not really clarify what distinguishes 'economic duress' from 'commercial pressure'. Counsel for the charterers' (now Lord Lloyd of Berwick) account of the existing law was rejected as 'too narrow', whereas counsel for the shipowners' (now Lord Goff of Chieveley) bold submissions were rejected as 'too wide'. This leaves the difficult test that the 'consent of the other party was overborne by compulsion so as to deprive him of any *animus contrahendi*' (intention to contract). The Australian cases mentioned by Kerr J more helpfully suggest that relevant questions are, first, was there any protest and, secondly, was the settlement treated as conclusive? The reference to Goff and Jones is to the first edition (*The Law of Restitution*, London: Sweet & Maxwell, 1966); see now the fourth edition, 240–2.

2. Kerr J held that the parent company's guarantee was 'ample consideration' for the reduction in the charter hire. Economic duress is often linked with the contractual doctrine of consideration in the cases. Consideration requires some exchange of value before a contract is enforced. From *Stilk* v

Myrick (1809) 2 Camp 317, 170 ER 1168 to *D & C Builders Ltd* v *Rees* [1966] 2 QB 617, the courts manipulated consideration as a blunt means of distinguishing extorted promises from genuine ones. It was an inappropriate tool to do this sensitive work. The following cases demonstrate the nascent doctrine of economic duress superseding it.

North Ocean Shipping Co. Ltd v *Hyundai Construction Co. Ltd The 'Atlantic Baron'*
[1979] QB 705 (QBD (Commercial Court))

Action for money had and received
The Hyundai Yard agreed to build a vessel subsequently named the '*Atlantic Baron*' for the prospective owners under a contract dated 10 April 1972. The price was US$30,950,000 payable in five instalments. In February 1973, the US dollar was devalued by 10 per cent so the Yard requested that the value of the four unpaid instalments should be increased by 10 per cent on account of the devaluation. Initially the owners refused to pay, but it became clear that the Yard did not intend to complete the contract unless the increase was made. Meanwhile, unknown to the Yard, the owners had agreed to a lucrative three-year time charter for the vessel with Shell starting upon its completion. By a telex of 28 June 1973 the owners agreed to the Yard's demands but 'without prejudice to our rights'. The owners made no further protest but paid the increased instalments. The owners after delivery claimed the increase was obtained by duress and sought restitution of the sums overpaid. The arbitrators stated a special case for the opinion of the court. *Held*: the variation of the contract was procured by economic duress, but the subsequent conduct of the owners amounted to affirmation.

MOCATTA J: . . . First, I do not take the view that the recovery of money paid under duress other than to the person is necessarily limited to duress to goods falling within one of the categories hitherto established by the English cases . . . Secondly, from this it follows that the compulsion may take the form of 'economic duress' if the necessary facts are proved. A threat to break a contract may amount to such 'economic duress'. Thirdly, if there has been such a form of duress leading to a contract for consideration, I think that contract is a voidable one which can be avoided and the excess money paid under it recovered.

I think the facts found in this case do establish that the agreement to increase the price by 10 per cent reached at the end of June 1973 was caused by what may be called 'economic duress.' The Yard were adamant in insisting on the increased price without having any legal justification for so doing and the owners realised that the Yard would not accept anything other than an unqualified agreement to the increase. The owners might have claimed damages in arbitration against the Yard with all the inherent unavoidable uncertainties of litigation, but in view of the position of the Yard vis-à-vis their relations with Shell it would be unreasonable to hold that this is the course they should have taken: see *Astley* v *Reynolds* (1731) 2 Str 915. The owners made a very reasonable offer of arbitration coupled with security for any award in the Yard's favour that might be made, but this was refused. They then made their agreement, which can truly I think be said to have been made under compulsion, by the telex of June 28 without prejudice to their rights. I do not consider the Yard's ignorance of the Shell charter material. It may well be that had they known of it they would have been even more exigent.

If I am right in the conclusion reached with some doubt earlier that there was consideration for the 10 per cent increase agreement reached at the end of June 1973, and it be right to regard this as having been reached under a kind of duress in the form of economic pressure, then what is said in *Chitty on Contracts,* 24th ed. (1977), vol. 1, para. 442, p. 207, to which both counsel referred me, is relevant, namely, that a contract entered into under duress is voidable and not void:

> . . . consequently a person who has entered into a contract under duress, may either affirm or avoid such contract after the duress has ceased; and if he has so voluntarily acted under it with a full knowledge of all the circumstance he may be held bound on the ground of ratification, or if, after escaping from the duress, he takes no steps to set aside the transaction, he may be found to have affirmed it.

On appeal in *Ormes* v *Beadel,* 2 De GF & J 333 and in Kerr J's case [1976] 1 Lloyd's Rep 293 there was on the facts action held to amount to affirmation or acquiescence in the form of taking part in an arbitration pursuant to the impugned agreement. There is nothing comparable to such action here.

On the other hand, the findings of fact in the special case present difficulties whether one is proceeeding on the basis of a voidable agreement reached at the end of June 1973, or whether such agreement was void for want of consideration, and it were necessary in consequence to establish that the payments were made involuntarily and not with the intention of closing the transaction.

I have already stated that no protest of any kind was made by the owners after their telex of June 28, 1973, before their claim in this arbitration on July 30, 1975, shortly after in July of that year the *Atlantic Baroness,* a sister ship of the *Atlantic Baron,* had been tendered, though, as I understand it, she was not accepted and arbitration proceedings in regard to her are in consequence taking place. There was therefore a delay between November 27, 1974, when the *Atlantic Baron* was delivered and July 30, 1975, before the owners put forward their claim.

The owners were, therefore, free from the duress on November 27, 1974, and took no action by way of protest or otherwise between their important telex of June 28, 1973, and their formal claim for the return of the excess 10 per cent paid of July 30, 1975, when they nominated their arbitrator. One cannot dismiss this delay as of no significance, though I would not consider it conclusive by itself . . . However, by the time the *Atlantic Baron* was due for delivery in November 1974, market conditions had changed radically, as is found in paragraph 39 of the special case and the owners must have been aware of this. The special case finds in paragraph 40, as stated earlier, that the owners did not believe that if they made any protest in the protocol of delivery and acceptance that the Yard would have refused to deliver the vessel or the *Atlantic Baroness* and had no reason so to believe. Mr Longmore naturally stressed that in the rather carefully expressed findings in paragraphs 39 to 44 of the special case, there is no finding that if at the time of the final payments the owners had withheld payment of the additional 10 per cent the Yard would not have delivered the vessel. However, after careful consideration, I have come to the conclusion that the important points here are that since there was no danger at this time in registering a protest, the final payments were made without any qualification and were followed by a delay until July 31, 1975, before the owners put forward their claim, the correct inference to draw, taking an objective view of the facts, is that the action and inaction of the owners can only be regarded as an affirmation of the variation in June 1973 of the terms of the original contract by the agreement to pay the additional 10 per cent. In reaching this conclusion I have not, of course, overlooked the findings in paragraph 45 of the special case, but I do not think that an intention on the part of the owners not to affirm the agreement for the extra payments not indicated to the Yard can avail them in the view of their overt acts. As was said in *Deacon* v *Transport Regulation Board* [1958] VR 458, 460 in considering whether a payment was made voluntarily or not: 'No secret mental reservation of the doer is material. The question is—what would his conduct indicate to a reasonable man as his mental state.' I think this test is equally applicable to the decision this court has to make whether a voidable contract has been affirmed or not, and I have applied this test in reaching the conclusion I have just expressed.

I think I should add very shortly that having considered the many authorities cited, even if I had come to a different conclusion on the issue about consideration, I would have come to the same decision adverse to the owners on the question whether the payments were made voluntarily in the sense of being made to close the transaction. . . .

Question

Mocatta J held that a threat to break a contract could constitute economic duress. What other forms of conduct could amount to economic duress?

Notes

1. Once again in this case absence of contractual consideration was pleaded in the alternative to duress. Mocatta J found consideration in the request by the owners that a letter of credit in their favour which guaranteed their right to repayment of instalments in the event of default by the Yard should be correspondingly increased by 10 per cent and the Yard's acceptance of this condition of the variation. However, the judge was impatient with what he clearly regarded as a formalistic issue, and devoted most of his attention to the substantive question of compulsion.

2. Mocatta J held, it is submitted correctly, that duress renders a contract voidable not void. Compare the views of Lord Cross in *Barton* v *Armstrong* [1976] AC 104 and Kerr J in *The 'Siboen' and the 'Sibotre'* [1976] 1 Lloyd's Rep 293 (although nothing seemed to turn on the issue of whether the contract was void or voidable in those cases). There is therefore a close analogy with rescission for misrepresentation, and it seems that similar bars to relief apply; for example, as this case demonstrates, affirmation and lapse of time were both considered relevant.

3. Mocatta J referred approvingly to an influential article by Beatson, 'Duress as a Vitiating Factor in Contract' (1974) 33 CLJ 97. In this article it was argued, first, that there was no justification for the so-called rule in *Skeate* v *Beale* (1841) 11 Ad & E 983, 113 ER 688 that, whereas money paid under duress of goods was recoverable, a contract entered into as a result of duress was enforceable; secondly, that duress was not limited to the traditional person and goods cases, but that threatened breach of contract could constitute duress, concluding that 'in a modern society there is no justification for the assumption that physical coercion is more potent than economic coercion'. Professor Beatson has now updated and expanded his seminal article, 'Duress, Restitution and Contract Renegotiation' as Essay 5 in Beatson, *Unjust Enrichment*, 95–136.

Pao On v *Lau Yiu Long*
[1980] AC 614 (PC)

The plaintiffs owned all the shares in Shing On, a private company which owned the Wing On building in Hong Kong. The defendants were the majority shareholders in Fu Chip, an investment company which had recently gone public and wished to acquire more property. By the main agreement between the *plaintiffs* and *Fu Chip*, dated 27 February 1973, the former sold all their shares in Shing On to Fu Chip in return for 4.2 million shares in Fu Chip. The plaintiffs agreed to retain at least 60 per cent of their holding in Fu Chip until 30 April 1974, in order to preserve the new public company's share price. By a subsidiary agreement of the same date between the *plaintiffs* and the *defendants*, the plaintiffs agreed to sell to the defendants their shareholding in Fu Chip for $2.50 per share. This was a bad bargain for the plaintiffs, because although it guaranteed them against any fall in Fu Chip's share price, if the share price rose they had deprived themselves of any profit. Everyone confidently expected share prices to increase. Therefore in April 1973 the plaintiffs made it clear to the first defendant that unless the subsidiary agreement was changed they would refuse to complete the main agreement. Having taken advice and considered the possibility of specific performance to enforce the main agreement, the defendants, concerned about the public image of Fu Chip, agreed to the cancellation of the subsidiary agreement and signed a written contract of guarantee with the plaintiffs undertaking to indemnify them if the value of the shares fell below $2.50 per share on 30 April 1974. The market slumped and on that date shares in Fu Chip had fallen to $0.36 per share. The plaintiffs sued to enforce the indemnity. *Held*: the indemnity was supported by valid consideration, and the new contract was not procured by economic duress, only commercial pressure.

LORD SCARMAN: . . . Duress, whatever form it takes, is a coercion of the will so as to vitiate consent. Their Lordships agree with the observation of Kerr J in *Occidental Worldwide Investment Corporation* v *Skibs A/S Avanti* [1976] 1 Lloyd's Rep 293, 336 that in a contractual situation commercial pressure is not enough. There must be present some factor 'which could in law be regarded as a coercion of his will so as to vitiate his consent.' This conception is in line with what was said in this Board's decision in *Barton* v *Armstrong* [1976] AC 104, 121 by Lord Wilberforce and Lord Simon of Glaisdale—observations with which the majority judgment appears to be in agreement. In determining whether there was a coercion of will such that there was no true consent, it is material to inquire whether the person alleged to have been coerced did or did not protest; whether, at the time he was allegedly coerced into making the contract, he did or did not have an alternative course open to him such as an adequate legal remedy; whether he was independently advised; and whether after entering the contract he took steps to avoid it. All these matters are, as was recognised in *Maskell* v *Horner* [1915] 3 KB 106, relevant in determining whether he acted voluntarily or not.

In the present case there is unanimity amongst the judges below that there was no coercion of the first defendant's will. In the Court of Appeal the trial judge's finding (already quoted) that the first defendant considered the matter thoroughly, chose to avoid litigation, and formed the opinion that the risk in giving the guarantee was more apparent than real was upheld. In short, there was commercial pressure, but no coercion. Even if this Board was disposed, which it is not, to take a different view, it would not substitute its opinion for that of the judges below on this question of fact.

It is, therefore, unnecessary for the Board to embark upon an inquiry into the question whether English law recognises a category of duress known as 'economic duress.' But, since the question has been fully argued in this appeal, their Lordships will indicate very briefly the view which they have formed. At common law money paid under economic compulsion could be recovered in an action for money had and received: *Astley* v *Reynolds* (1731) 2 Str 915. The compulsion had to be such that the party was deprived of 'his freedom of exercising his will' (see p. 916). It is doubtful, however, whether at common law any duress other than duress to the person sufficed to render a contract voidable: see *Blackstone's Commentaries,* Book 1, 12th ed. pp. 130–131 and *Skeate* v *Beale* [1841] 11 Ad & E 983. American law (*Williston on Contracts,* 3rd ed.) now recognises that a contract may be avoided on the ground of economic duress. The commercial pressure alleged to constitute such duress must, however, be such that the victim must have entered the contract against his will, must have had no alternative course open to him, and must have been confronted with coercive acts by the party exerting the pressure: *Williston on Contracts,* 3rd ed., vol. 13 (1970), section 1603. American judges pay great attention to such evidential matters as the effectiveness of the alternative remedy available, the fact or absence of protest, the availability of independent advice, the benefit received, and the speed with which the victim has sought to avoid the contract. Recently two English judges have recognised that commercial pressure may constitute duress the pressure of which can render a contract voidable: Kerr J in *Occidental Worldwide Investment Corporation* v *Skibs A/S Avanti* [1976] 1 Lloyds Rep 293 and Mocatta J in *North Ocean Shipping Co. Ltd* v *Hyundai Construction Co. Ltd* [1979] QB 705. Both stressed that the pressure must be such that the victim's consent to the contract was not a voluntary act on his part. In their Lordships' view, there is nothing contrary to principle in recognising economic duress as a factor which may render a contract voidable, provided always that the basis of such recognition is that it must amount to a coercion of will, which vitiates consent. It must be shown that the payment made or the contract entered into was not a voluntary act. . . .

Notes

1. The advice of the Privy Council in this case was the first appellate recognition of the developing economic duress doctrine. Lord Scarman appears to prefer the approach of Kerr J to that of Mocatta J, and insists that there must be 'coercion of the will so as to vitiate consent' (this phrase does not appear in Mocatta J's judgment). This convoluted test lacks clarity, but Lord Scarman goes on to specify four concrete factors which inform the duress inquiry: (i) was there any protest? (ii) did the victim have any alternative course, including adequate legal remedies? (iii) was the victim independently advised? (iv) what subsequent steps were taken to avoid the contract? The important factor in this case was the trial judge's finding that the defendants took a 'calculated risk' in giving the guarantee, assuming that the stock market would be more likely to rise than fall.

2. Note that the threatened breach of contract did not relate to a contract with the victim, but rather related to a breach of contract with the public company in which the defendants were interested.

Universe Tankships Inc. of Monrovia v *International Transport Workers' Federation, The 'Universe Sentinel'*
[1983] 1 AC 366 (HL)

Action for money had and received; resulting trust

The International Transport Workers' Federation ('ITF') waged a long-running campaign of 'blacking' ships sailing under 'flags of convenience' in order to improve the employment conditions of crews on board such ships. As part of the campaign the appellant owners' vessel, which flew the Liberian flag and had a predominantly Asian crew, was prevented from sailing away from Milford Haven because the tugboat crews, on the instructions of the ITF, refused to render the necessary assistance. Negotiations between the shipowners and the ITF resulted in the owners acceding to the ITF's demands, including a demand to pay a $6,480 contribution to its welfare fund. After the ship sailed away the owners sought restitution of that sum. *Held*: by a majority of 3:2, that there had been illegitimate pressure so as to entitle the shipowners to restitution of the $6,480. There was no public policy bar to recovery, by analogy with the Trade Unions and Labour Relations Act 1974, on the facts of this particular case because the pressure complained of was insufficiently connected with the terms and conditions of the employment of the crew.

LORD DIPLOCK: . . . It is not disputed that the circumstances in which ITF demanded that the shipowners should enter into the special agreement and the typescript agreement and should pay the moneys of which the latter documents acknowledge receipt, amounted to economic duress upon the shipowners; that is to say, it is conceded that the financial consequences to the shipowners of the *Universe Sentinel* continuing to be rendered off-hire under her time charter to Texaco, while the blacking continued, were so catastrophic as to amount to a coercion of the shipowners' will which vitiated their consent to those agreements and to the payments made by them to ITF. This concession makes it unnecessary for your Lordships to use the instant appeal as the occasion for a general consideration of the developing law of economic duress as a ground for treating contracts as voidable and obtaining restitution of money paid under economic duress as money had and received to the plaintiffs' use. That economic duress may constitute a ground for such redress was recognised, albeit obiter, by the Privy Council in *Pao On* v *Lau Yiu Long* [1980] AC 614. The Board in that case referred with approval to two judgments at first instance in the commercial court which recognised that commercial pressure may constitute duress: one by Kerr J in *Occidental Worldwide Investment Corporation* v *Skibs A/S Avanti* [1976] 1 Lloyd's Rep 293, the other by Mocatta J in *North Ocean Shipping Co*

Ltd v *Hyundai Construction Co. Ltd* [1979] QB 705, which traces the development of this branch of the law from its origin in the eighteenth and early nineteenth-century cases.

It is, however, in my view crucial to the decision of the instant appeal to identify the rationale of this development of the common law. It is not that the party seeking to avoid the contract which he has entered into with another party, or to recover money that he has paid to another party in response to a demand, did not know the nature or the precise terms of the contract at the time when he entered into it or did not understand the purpose of which the payment was demanded. The rationale is that his apparent consent was induced by pressure exercised upon him by that other party which the law does not regard as legitimate, with the consequence that the consent is treated in law as revocable unless approbated either expressly or by implication after the illegitimate pressure has ceased to operate on his mind. It is a rationale similar to that which underlies the avoidability of contracts entered into and the recovery of money exacted under colour of office, or under undue influence or in consequence of threats of physical duress.

Commercial pressure, in some degree, exists wherever one party to a commercial transaction is in a stronger bargaining position than the other party. It is not, however, in my view, necessary, nor would it be appropriate in the instant appeal, to enter into the general question of the kinds of circumstances, if any, in which commercial pressure, even though it amounts to a coercion of the will of a party in the weaker bargaining position, may be treated as legitimate and, accordingly, as not giving rise to any legal right of redress. . . .

The use of economic duress to induce another person to part with property or money is not a tort per se; the form that the duress takes may, or may not, be tortious. The remedy to which economic duress gives rise is not an action for damages but an action for restitution of property or money exacted under such duress and the avoidance of any contract that had been induced by it; but where the particular form taken by the economic duress used is itself a tort, the restitutional remedy for money had and received by the defendant to the plaintiff's use is one which the plaintiff is entitled to pursue as an alternative remedy to an action for damages in tort.

In extending into the field of industrial relations the common law concept of economic duress and the right to a restitutionary remedy for it which is currently in process of development by judicial decisions, this House would not, in my view, be exercising the restraint that is appropriate to such a process if it were so to develop the concept that, by the simple expedient of 'waiving the tort,' a restitutionary remedy for money had and received is made enforceable in cases in which Parliament has, over so long a period of years, manifested its preference for a public policy that a particular kind of tortious act should be legitimised in the sense that I am using that expression.

It is only in this indirect way that the provisions of the Trade Union and Labour Relations Act 1974 are relevant to the duress point. The immunities from liability in tort provided by sections 13 and 14 are not directly applicable to the shipowners' cause of action for money had and received. Nevertheless, these sections, together with the definition of trade dispute in section 29, afford an indication, which your Lordships should respect, of where public policy requires that the line should be drawn between what kind of commercial pressure by a trade union upon an employer in the field of industrial relations ought to be treated as legitimised despite the fact that the will of the employer is thereby coerced, and what kind of commercial pressure in that field does amount to economic duress that entitles the employer victim to restitutionary remedies. . . .

LORD SCARMAN (dissenting on public policy): . . . It is, I think, already established law that economic pressure can in law amount to duress; and that duress, if proved, not only renders voidable a transaction into which a person has entered under its compulsion but is actionable as a tort, if it causes damage or loss: *Barton* v *Armstrong* [1976] AC 104 and *Pao On* v *Lau Yiu Long* [1980] AC 614. The authorities upon which these two cases were based reveal two elements in the wrong of duress: (1) pressure amounting to compulsion of the will of the victim; and (2) the illegitimacy of the pressure exerted. There must be pressure, the practical effect of which is compulsion or the absence of choice. Compulsion is variously described in the authorities as coercion or the vitiation of consent. The classic case of duress is, however, not the lack of will to submit but the victim's intentional submission arising from the realisation that there is no other practical choice open to him. This is the thread of principle which links the early law of duress (threat to life or limb) with later developments when the law came also to recognise as duress first the threat to property and now the threat to a man's business or trade. The development is well traced in Goff and Jones, *The Law of Restitution*, 2nd ed. (1978), chapter 9.

The absence of choice can be proved in various ways, e.g., by protest, by the absence of independent advice, or by a declaration of intention to go to law to recover the money paid or the property transferred: see *Maskell* v *Horner* [1915] 3 KB 106. But none of these evidential matters goes to the essence of duress. The victim's silence will not assist the bully, if the lack of any practicable choice but to submit is proved. The present case is an excellent illustration. There was no protest at the time, but only a determination to do whatever was needed as rapidly as possible to release the ship. Yet nobody challenges the judge's finding that the owner acted under compulsion. He put it thus [1981] ICR 129, 143:

> It was a matter of the most urgent commercial necessity that the plaintiffs should regain the use of their vessel. They were advised that their prospects of obtaining an injunction were minimal, the vessel would not have been released unless the payment was made, and they sought recovery of the money with sufficient speed once the duress had terminated.

The real issue in the appeal is, therefore, as to the second element in the wrong duress: was the pressure applied by the I.T.F. in the circumstances of this case one which the law recognises as legitimate? For, as Lord Wilberforce and Lord Simon of Glaisdale said in *Barton* v *Armstrong* [1976] AC 104, 121D: 'the pressure must be one of a kind which the law does not regard as legitimate.'

As the two noble and learned Lords remarked at p. 121D, in life, including the life of commerce and finance, many acts are done 'under pressure, sometimes overwhelming pressure': but they are not necessarily done under duress. That depends on whether the circumstances are such that the law regards the pressure as legitimate.

In determining what is legitimate two matters may have to be considered. The first is as to the nature of the pressure. In many cases this will be decisive, though not in every case. And so the second question may have to be considered, namely, the nature of the demand which the pressure is applied to support.

The origin of the doctrine of duress in threats to life or limb, or to property, suggests strongly that the law regards the threat of unlawful action as illegitimate, whatever the demand. Duress can, of course, exist even if the threat is one of lawful action: whether it does so depends upon the nature of the demand. Blackmail is often a demand supported by a threat to do what is lawful, e.g. to report criminal conduct to the police. In many cases, therefore, 'What [one] has to justify is not the threat, but the demand. . .': see *per* Lord Atkin in *Thorne* v *Motor Trade Association* [1937] AC 797, 806. . . .

Questions

1. Are Lord Scarman and Lord Diplock in agreement about the nature of the action for money had and received on the ground of economic duress?

2. Which torts, if any, were committed by the ITF?

3. Does the cause of action arise in autonomous unjust enrichment or is it a case of restitution for wrongs?

Notes

1. See Birks, *Introduction*, 178–9 and 336–7 and Burrows, *Restitution*, 163 and 182–4. For restitution for wrongs and in particular 'waiver of tort' see Chapter 6, Section 1. For public policy as a defence to a restitutionary claim see Chapter 8, Section 4 for further discussion of *The 'Universe Sentinel'*.

2. In addition to the *action for money had and received*, the money was claimed alternatively in equity on the basis of a *resulting trust*. At first instance before Parker J in the Commercial Court ([1981] ICR 129) both causes of action succeeded. Somewhat artificially, for the purpose of this argument it was assumed the contribution to the fund was voluntary (in the sense of not being vitiated by duress) but was advanced on the basis that the contribution was void because the fund was a non-charitable purpose trust. The House of Lords unanimously rejected this argument, holding that the fund was governed by contract (the rules of the ITF) and had not been constituted by means of a trust. No attempt was made to promote symmetry between the causes of action at law and in equity. The ground for the resulting trust was not made explicit, but appeared to be analogous to a common law claim for (total) failure of consideration. In Birks's terminology it would be a case of *qualified* intention, not *vitiated* intention. For an argument that the resulting trust is a restitutionary remedy see Birks, *Introduction*, 60–4 and Birks, 'Restitution and Resulting Trusts' in Goldstein (ed.), *Equity and Contemporary Legal Developments* (1992), 355.

B & S Contracts and Design Ltd* v *Victor Green Publications Ltd
[1984] ICR 419 (CA)

The plaintiffs agreed to erect stands for the defendants for a five-day exhibition at Olympia for the price of £11,731.50. The plaintiffs decided to use employees from their insolvent subsidiary company, who had recently been given notice. When the workers arrived at Olympia they went on strike demanding severance pay. The plaintiffs' cash-flow was poor, so Mr Barnes, of the defendants, offered to pay to Mr Fenech, of the plaintiffs, £4,500 of the contract price in advance. This was rejected, Mr Fenech making it clear that the plaintiffs would not perform under the contract unless the workers could be persuaded to do the work. For this he required an additional payment, not just an advance. Mr Barnes paid up. When the work was done the defendants sent a cheque for the contract price less £4,500 to the plaintiffs. The plaintiffs sued for the £4,500. *Held*: the promise of the extra £4,500 had been procured by duress.

EVELEIGH LJ: . . . The matters that have to be established in order to substantiate a claim for the return of money on the ground that it was paid under duress have been stated in a number of different ways. We have been referred to a number of cases and indeed we have been taken through the history of the common law on duress, so thoroughly set out in the judgment of Mocatta J in *North Ocean Shipping Co. Ltd* v *Hyundai Construction Co. Ltd* [1979] QB 705. It is not necessary to consider these cases: for the purpose of my judgment all I require to read is a passage from the speech of Lord Diplock in *Universe Tankships Inc. of Monrovia* v *International Transport Workers Federation* [1982] ICR 262. He said, referring to the law on duress, at pp. 272–3:

> The rationale is that his apparent consent was induced by pressure exercised upon him by that other party which the law does not regard as legitimate, with the consequence that the consent is treated in law as revocable unless approbated either expressly or by implication after the illegitimate pressure has ceased to operate on his mind. It is a rationale similar to that which underlies the avoidability of contracts entered into and the recovery of money exacted under colour of office, or under undue influence or in consequence of threats of physical duress.

It is not necessary to consider precisely the meaning of the word 'legitimate' in that context. For the purpose of this case it is sufficient to say that if the claimant has been influenced against his will to pay money under the threat of unlawful damage to his economic interest he will be entitled to claim that money back, and as I understand it that proposition was not dissented from.

In this case the plaintiffs say that there was no threat; that Mr Fenech was really stating the obvious, stating the factual situation, namely, that unless they could retain the workforce they would be unable to perform their contract. I have had some difficulty in deciding whether or not the evidence in this case did disclose a threat, but on a full reading of the evidence of Mr Fenech and Mr Barnes and the cross-examination of Mr Fenech I have come to the conclusion that the judge was right in the way in which he put it. There was here, as I understand the evidence, a veiled threat although there was no specific demand, and this conclusion is very much supported, as I see it, by Mr Barnes's reaction, which must have been apparent to Mr Fenech when Mr Barnes said, 'You have got me over a barrel.' On 18 April what was happening was this. Mr Fenech was in effect saying, 'We are not going on unless you are prepared to pay another £4,500 in addition to the contract price,' and it was clear at that stage that there was no other way for Mr Barnes to avoid the consequences that would ensue if the exhibition could not be held from his stands than by paying the £4,500 to secure the workforce. . . .

GRIFFTHS LJ: I agree. The law on economic pressure creating a situation which will be recognised as duress is in the course of development, and it is clear that many difficult decisions lie ahead of the courts. Many commercial contracts are varied during their currency because the parties are faced with changing circumstances during the performance of the contract, and it is certainly not on every occasion when one of the parties unwillingly agrees to a variation that the law would consider that he had acted by reason of duress. The cases will have to be examined in the light of their particular circumstances. But two recent decisions of the highest authority—the decision of the Privy Council in *Pao On* v *Lau Yiu Long* [1980] AC 614 and *Universe*

Tankships Inc. of Monrovia v *International Transport Workers Federation* [1982] ICR 262—establish that a threatened breach of contract may impose such economic pressure that the law will recognise that a payment made as a result of the threatened breach is recoverable on the grounds of duress.

The facts of this case appear to me to be as follows. The plaintiffs intended to break their contract, subject to the effect of the force majeure clause, by allowing their workforce to walk off the job in circumstances in which they could not possibly replace it with another workforce. The defendants offered to advance the sum of £4,500 on the contract price, which would have enabled the plaintiffs to pay the men a sufficient extra sum of money to induce them to remain on the job. The plaintiffs refused this sum of money. There is no question that they refused to pay as a matter of principle. They refused to pay because they did not want to reduce the sum they would receive for the contract. They said to the defendants, 'If you will give us £4,500 we will complete the contract.' The defendants, faced with this demand, were in an impossible position. If they refused to hand over the sum of £4,500 they would not be able to erect the stands in this part of the exhibition, which would have clearly caused grave damage to their reputation and I would have thought might have exposed them to very heavy claims from the exhibitors who had leased space from them and hoped to use those stands in the ensuing exhibition. They seem to me to have been placed in the position envisaged by Lord Scarman in the Privy Council decision, *Pao On* v *Lau Yiu Long* [1980] AC 614, in which they were faced with no alternative course of action but to pay the sum demanded of them. It was submitted to us that there was no overt demand, but it was implicit in negotiations between the parties that the plaintiffs were putting the defendants into a corner and it was quite apparent to the defendants, by reason of the plaintiffs' conduct, that unless they handed over £4,500 the plaintiffs would walk off the job. This is, in my view, a situation in which the judge was fully entitled to find in the circumstances of this case that there was duress. As the defendants' director said, he was over a barrel, he had no alternative but to pay; he had no chance of going to any other source of labour to erect the stands. . . .

KERR LJ: . . . the plaintiffs were clearly saying in effect, 'This contract will not be performed by us unless you pay an additional sum of £4,500.' This faced the defendants with a disastrous situation in which there was no way out for them, and in the face of this threat—which is what it was—they paid the £4,500. In the light of the authorities it is perhaps important to emphasise that there is no question in this case of the defendants having subsequently approbated this payment or failed to seek to avoid it, which in some cases (such as the *North Ocean Shipping Co. Ltd* v *Hyundai Construction Co. Ltd* [1979] QB 705, a decision of Mocatta J, to which Eveleigh LJ has referred) would be fatal. In the present case the defendants took immediate action by deducting that £4,500 from the invoice price.

I also bear in mind that a threat to break a contract unless money is paid by the other party can, but by no means always will, constitute duress. It appears from the authorities that it will only constitute duress if the consequences of a refusal would be serious and immediate so that there is no reasonable alternative open, such as by legal redress, obtaining an injunction, etc. I think that this is implicit in the authorities to which we have been referred, of which the most recent one is *Universe Tankships Inc. of Monrovia* v *International Transport Workers Federation* [1982] ICR 262. . . .

Notes

1. Kerr LJ, revisiting this subject, makes it clear that a threat to break a contract '*can*, but by no means always *will*, constitute duress'. This is surely correct, but the difficulty is how the line is to be drawn. Griffiths LJ says the particular circumstances of each case are important, but that does not take us much further. It is clear, as Sir John Donaldson MR confirmed in *Hennessy* v *Craigmyle & Co. Ltd* [1986] ICR 461 (CA), that economic duress is a question of fact for the first instance judge.

2. Compare the similar facts and differing result in *Williams* v *Roffey Bros & Nicholls (Contractors) Ltd* [1991] 1 QB 1 (CA) below.

Vantage Navigation Corporation v *Suhail and Saud Bahwan Building Materials LLC, The 'Alev'*

[1989] 1 Lloyd's Rep 138 (QBD (Commercial Court))

The plaintiff shipowners time-chartered their vessel, the *'Alev'* to Alsa, a German company. Alsa were on the brink of insolvency, therefore although they paid some of the hire due under the charterparty, they soon defaulted. A cargo of steel worth $3.3 million was loaded and bills of lading were issued in respect of the goods providing for their carriage to Muscat. The bills were marked 'freight prepaid' and made no reference to the charterparty. During the voyage Alsa declared themselves bankrupt. The shipowners were owed about $200,000 by Alsa in unpaid hire, but under the bills of lading they were contractually obliged to deliver the steel to the defendant cargo-owners without any right to further remuneration from them. In negotiations the shipowners made it clear to the cargo-owners that unless they agreed to pay a sum in respect of port expenses and discharging costs, they would not get their cargo. The cargo-owners urgently needed the steel and there was little hope of obtaining steel from elsewhere. Therefore the cargo-owners signed an agreement to pay those sums under protest, but upon discharge of the cargo they repudiated the agreement. *Held*: the agreement was obtained by duress of goods and economic duress; there had been an illegitimate threat to interfere with the cargo-owners' interest in the goods and the shipowners knew the threat was illegitimate.

Notes

1. Duress of goods and economic duress were both proved in this case: the shipowners' conduct amounted to both a threat to commit the tort of conversion (wrongful interference with goods) in respect of the defendants' steel and a threat to break the contract to deliver the steel evidenced by the bills of lading. Compare *The 'Atlantic Baron'* (above), where the property in the vessel probably did not pass until delivery.

2. The defendants further pleaded 'no consideration' for the agreement, but Hobhouse J rejected this argument, saying the question was a 'formality' and that technically there was consideration. On the relationship between the two doctrines he observed:

> Now that there is a properly developed doctrine of the avoidance of contracts on the grounds of economic duress, there is no warrant for the

Court to fail to recognise the existence of some consideration even though it may be insignificant and even though there may have been no mutual bargain in any realistic use of that phrase.

Atlas Express Ltd* v *Kafco (Importers and Distributors) Ltd
[1989] QB 833 (QBD)

Kafco received a large order to supply basketware to Woolworths. Kafco therefore made a contract with the plaintiff haulage firm for delivery of the basketware to branches of Woolworths. The price was agreed at £1.10 per carton. The rate has been worked out by the manager of one of the plaintiffs' depots after seeing samples of the cartons used, assuming that each lorry could carry 400–600 cartons. Kafco were not informed of this basis of calculation. On the first delivery it was discovered that only around 200 cartons would constitute a full load. The plaintiffs' manager realised the deal was not financially viable and therefore sought to renegotiate. He made it plain to one of Kafco's directors that unless they agreed to pay £440 per trailer no further deliveries would be made. It would have been difficult, if not impossible, for Kafco to find alternative carriers in time to meet their delivery dates. The plaintiffs' manager sent a trailer to Kafco's premises instructing the driver to load the trailer only if the defendants signed a document agreeing to new terms. One of Kafco's directors signed, but felt 'over a barrel'. They feared losing the business with Woolworths and being sued for loss of profit. *Held*: the document was signed under compulsion as a result of pressure amounting to 'economic duress'. Further, there was no consideration for the agreement which was unenforceable.

Question
In this case Tucker J held that 'it was essential to the defendants' success and to their commercial survival that they should be in a position to make deliveries' and that the plaintiffs' manager knew of this. Is knowledge of the victim's economic circumstances on the part of the person exerting pressure *essential* to a successful plea of economic duress?

Williams* v *Roffey Bros & Nicholls (Contractors) Ltd
[1991] 1 QB 1 (CA)

The defendant building contractors entered into a contract with the Shepherd's Bush Housing Association to refurbish 27 flats. The defendants sub-contracted the carpentry work to the plaintiff for a fixed price of £20,000. During the work the sub-contractor ran into financial difficulties, partly because, as was recognised by the defendants' surveyor, the sub-contract price was too low. The defendants, wanting to get the carpentry work finished on time because of a liquidated damages clause in the main contract, agreed to pay the sub-contractor an extra £575 per completed flat on top of the original price. The sub-contractor then substantially completed the work and claimed the extra sums promised. *Held*: there was consideration for the defendants' promise to pay more in the factual benefit of having the work completed.

Question

In this case Russell LJ observed that there was 'no hint' in the pleaded defence of any duress. Why did the defendants in this case not choose to rely on economic duress?

Notes

1. Professor Birks says that this case 'drives a fatal nail into the doctrine of consideration' (see his excellent discussion of the policy issues in this case, 'The Travails of Duress' [1990] LMCLQ 342, at 344–7). Birks identifies two competing policies in this context. One favours accommodation between the parties, upholding reasonable renegotiations. The other fosters responsibility in bidding and tendering by upholding the original contract price (a view firmly articulated in the frustration case of *Davis Contractors Ltd* v *Fareham Urban District Council* [1956] AC 696 (HL)). The former policy would mean that compulsion would not easily be found, but the latter would result in more successful pleas of economic duress. Birks advocates the more explicit recognition of these issues and abandoning the concealed discretion given to judges by the obscure 'coercion of the will' test. He favours a test which requires proof of bad faith or malice: the deliberate exploitation of difficulties. This is consistent with the finding of fact by Hobhouse J in *The 'Alev'* that the shipowners *knew* that the threat was illegitimate, and the finding of Tucker J in *Atlas Express* v *Kafco* that the road hauliers' manager knew of Kafco's dependence upon their performing their contract.

2. All three members of the Court of Appeal seemed satisfied that economic duress was not made out on the facts. Glidewell LJ said of economic duress: '. . . this concept may provide another answer in law to the question of policy which has troubled the courts since before *Stilk* v *Myrick* (1809) 2 Camp 317, 170 ER 1168, and no doubt led at the date of that decision to a rigid adherence to the doctrine of consideration.' Purchas LJ said: 'The modern cases tend to depend more upon the defence of duress in a commercial context rather than lack of consideration for the second agreement. In the present case the question of duress does not arise.' Purchas LJ even opined that it was 'open to the plaintiff to be in deliberate breach of the contract in order to "cut his losses" commercially'. So what takes this case outside of compulsion? Professor Treitel notes that the initiative for the renegotiation seems to have come from the defendants (Treitel, *Contract*, 90). Therefore it seems that no pressure or threat was applied by the plaintiff; there was simply a laconic 'I cannot go on'. The conclusion must be that the relative bargaining positions of the parties are relevant to the 'factual matrix' of the duress inquiry. A weaker party is unlikely to be found guilty of duress.

Dimskal Shipping Co. SA v *International Transport Workers' Federation, The 'Evia Luck' (No. 2)*
[1992] 2 AC 152 (HL)

The facts were very similar to those in *The 'Universe Sentinel'* except the events took place in the Swedish port of Uddevalla. The '*Evia Luck*' sported a Panamanian flag and its crew consisted of Greeks and Filipinos. Under threat of 'blacking', the shipowners signed contracts expressed to be governed by English law undertaking to pay compensation for the crew's past low wages, and to enter into new contracts of employment with the crew. The shipowners sought declarations that the agreements were void on the ground of duress and sought restitution of $111,743 paid to the ITF. *Held*: by a majority of 4:1 that as a matter of the conflict of laws, the question whether economic pressure amounted to duress was a question for the proper law of the contract. Therefore, although the conduct of the ITF was lawful in Sweden, its legitimacy fell to be determined according to English law where such 'secondary industrial action' was outside the scope of trade unions' statutory immunity for tort (since the Employment Act 1980). Accordingly the shipowners were entitled to avoid the contracts and to restitution of moneys paid.

LORD GOFF OF CHIEVELEY: . . . It was common ground between the parties before your Lordships that the money in respect of which the owners claimed restitution was paid to the I.T.F. under a contract, albeit a contract which the owners claim to have been voidable by them, and indeed to have been avoided by them, on the ground of duress. It follows that, before the owners could establish any right to recover the money, they had first to avoid the relevant contract. Until this was done, the money in question was paid under a binding contract and so was irrecoverable in restitution. But once the contract was avoided, the money paid under it was recoverable in restitution, on the ground either of duress or possibly of failure of consideration. It was not, in my opinion, necessary for the owners, even if the duress relied upon by them was in fact tortious, to base their claim on waiver of tort (see the note by Ewan McKendrick in [1990] ILJ 195), nor have they done so. The present case is, however, concerned with the anterior question whether the pressure exerted by the I.T.F. constituted duress enabling the owners to avoid the contract on that ground, as they claim to have been entitled to do.

We are here concerned with a case of economic duress. It was at one time thought that, at common law, the only form of duress which would entitle a party to avoid a contract on that ground was duress of the person. The origin for this view lay in the decision of the Court of Exchequer in *Skeate* v *Beale* (1841) 11 Ad & El 983. However, since the decisions of Kerr J in *Occidental Worldwide Investment Corporation* v *Skibs A/S Avanti (The Siboen and The Sibotre)* [1976] 1 Lloyds Rep 293, of Mocatta J in *North Ocean Shipping Co. Ltd* v *Hyundai Construction Co. Ltd* [1979] QB 705, and of the Judicial Committee of the Privy Council in *Pao On* v *Lau Yiu Long* [1980] AC 614, that limitation has been discarded; and it is now accepted that economic pressure may be sufficient to amount to duress for this purpose, provided at least that the economic pressure may be characterised as illegitimate and has constituted a significant cause inducing the plantiff to enter into the relevant contract (see *Barton* v *Armstrong* [1976] AC 104, 121, *per* Lord Wilberforce and Lord Simon of Glaisdale (referred to with approval in *Pao On* v *Lau Yiu Long* [1980] AC 614, 635, *per* Lord Scarman) and *Crescendo Management Pty. Ltd* v *Westpac Banking Corporation* (1988) 19 NSWLR 40, 46, *per* McHugh JA). It is sometimes suggested that the plaintiff's will must have been coerced so as to vitiate his consent. This approach has been the subject of criticism: see Beatson, *The Use and Abuse of Unjust Enrichment* (1991), pp. 113-117; and the notes by Professor Atiyah in (1982) 98 LQR 197–202, and by Professor Birks in [1990] 3 LMCLQ 342–351. I myself, like McHugh JA, doubt whether it is helpful in this context to speak of the plaintiff's will having been coerced. It is not however necessary to explore the matter in the present case. Nor is it necessary to consider the broader question of what constitutes illegitimate economic pressure, for it is accepted that blacking or a threat of blacking, such as occurred in the present case, does constitute illegitimate economic pressure in English law, unless legitimised by statute. . . .

Questions

1. Does Lord Goff think that the causation test is different in cases of economic duress to that established in duress to the person?

2. Lord Templeman (dissenting) in discussing *The 'Universe Sentinel'* expressed the view that Lord Diplock stated 'there is no difference between tort and restitution'. Do you agree that this is what Lord Diplock said?

Note

This case is usefully discussed by O'Dair [1992] LMCLQ 145. The private international law aspects of restitution are under-developed. See the discussion of Burrows, *Restitution*, 487–500, especially 498–500, on *The 'Evia Luck'*. The first edition of Goff and Jones had a short chapter on 'Restitution and the Conflicts of Laws' (*The Law of Restitution*, London: Sweet & Maxwell, 1966, at 505–8), but this has not re-appeared. Detailed reference should now be made to *Dicey and Morris* on the *Conflict of Laws*, 12th ed. (London: Stevens & Son, 1993), Ch. 34 and Rose (ed.), *Restitution and the Conflict of Laws* (Oxford: Mansfield Press, 1995).

D: *'Lawful act' duress?*

CTN Cash and Carry Ltd* v *Gallaher Ltd
[1994] 4 All ER 714 (CA)

The plaintiffs owned 'cash and carry' warehouses in six Lancashire towns. The defendants, who supplied the plaintiffs with cigarettes under separate contracts made from time to time, were the sole distributors in England of 'Silk Cut' and 'Benson & Hedges'. As a result of an error by the defendants a consignment of cigarettes was sent to the plaintiffs' warehouse in Burnley, when in fact they were ordered for delivery to Preston. While the cigarettes were in Burnley they were stolen. The defendants, mistakingly believing that the risk in the cigarettes had passed to the plaintiffs, demanded the price of £17,000 saying that otherwise they would not in the future grant credit to the plaintiffs. In fact, the defendants were not, and were never, entitled to payment for the goods. The plaintiffs paid for the stolen goods, regarding that as the lesser of the two evils. *Held*: the plaintiffs were not entitled to restitution of the £17,000 on the ground of duress. In a commercial context a plea of 'lawful act' duress would only rarely succeed.

STEYN LJ: A buyer paid a sum of money to his supplier. The sum of money was in truth not owed by the buyer to the supplier. The buyer paid the sum as a result of the supplier's threat to stop the buyer's credit facilities in their future dealings if the sum was not paid. The supplier acted in the bona fide belief that the sum was owing. Does the doctrine of economic duress enable the buyer to recover the payment? . . .

The present dispute does not concern a protected relationship. It also does not arise in the context of dealing between a supplier and a consumer. The dispute arises out of arm's length commercial dealings between two trading companies. It is true that the defendants were the sole distributors of the popular brands of cigarettes. In a sense the defendants were in a monopoly position. The control of monopolies is, however, a matter for Parliament. Moreover, the common law does not recognise the doctrine of inequality of bargaining power in commercial dealings (see *National Westminster Bank plc* v *Morgan* [1985] AC 686). The fact that the defendants were in a monopoly position cannot therefore by itself convert what is not otherwise duress into duress.

A second characteristic of the case is that the defendants were in law entitled to refuse to enter into any future contracts with the plaintiffs for any reason whatever or for no reason at all. Such a decision not to deal with the plaintiffs would have been financially damaging to the defendants, but it would have been lawful. A fortiori it was lawful for the defendants, for any reason or for no reason, to insist that they would no longer grant credit to the plaintiffs. The defendants' demand for payment of the invoice, coupled with the threat to withdraw credit, was neither a breach of contract nor a tort.

A third, and critically important, characteristic of the case is the fact that the defendants bona fide thought that the goods were at the risk of the plaintiffs and that the plaintiffs owed the defendants the sum in question. The defendants exerted commercial pressure on the plaintiffs in order to obtain payment of a sum which they bona fide considered due to them. The defendants motive in threatening withdrawal of credit facilities was commercial self-interest in obtaining a sum that they considered due to them.

Given the combination of these three features, I take the view that none of the cases cited to us assist the plaintiffs' case. Miss Heilbron accepted that there is no decision which is in material respects on all fours with the present case. It is therefore unnecessary to disinter all those cases and to identify the material distinctions between each of those decisions and the present case. But Miss Heilbron rightly emphasised to us that the law must have a capacity for growth in this field. I entirely agree.

I also readily accept that the fact that the defendants have used lawful means does not by itself remove the case from the scope of the doctrine of economic duress. Professor Birks, in *An Introduction to the Law of Restitution* (1989) p.177, lucidly explains:

> Can lawful pressures also count? This is a difficult question, because, if the answer is that they can, the only viable basis for discriminating between acceptable and unacceptable pressures is not positive law but social morality. In other words, the judges must say what pressures (though lawful outside the restitutionary context) are improper as contrary to prevailing standards. That makes the judges, not the law or the legislature, the arbiters of social evaluation. On the other hand, if the answer is that lawful pressures are always exempt, those who devise outrageous but

> technically lawful means of compulsion must always escape restitution until the legislature declares the abuse unlawful. It is tolerably clear that, at least where they can be confident of a general consensus in favour of their evaluation, the courts are willing to apply a standard of impropriety rather than technical unlawfulness.

And there are a number of cases where English courts have accepted that a threat may be illegitimate when coupled with a demand for payment even if the threat is one of lawful action (see *Thorne* v *Motor Trade Association* [1937] AC 797 at 806–807, *Mutual Finance Ltd* v *John Wetton & Sons Ltd* [1937] 2 KB 389 and *Universe Tankships Inc. of Monrovia* v *International Transport Workers' Federation* [1983] 1 AC 366 at 384, 401). On the other hand, Goff and Jones *Law of Restitution* (3rd edn. 1986) p. 240 observed that English courts have wisely not accepted any general principle that a threat not to contract with another, except on certain terms, may amount to duress.

We are being asked to extend the categories of duress of which the law will take cognisance. That is not necessarily objectionable, but it seems to me that an extension capable of covering the present case, involving 'lawful act duress' in a commercial context in pursuit of a bona fide claim, would be a radical one with far-reaching implications. It would introduce a substantial and undesirable element of uncertainty in the commercial bargaining process. Moreover, it will often enable bona fide settled accounts to be reopened when parties to commercial dealings fall out. The aim of our commercial law ought to be to encourage fair dealing between parties. But it is a mistake for the law to set its sights too highly when the critical inquiry is not whether the conduct is lawful but whether it is morally or socially unacceptable. That is the inquiry in which we are engaged. In my view there are policy considerations which militate against ruling that the defendants obtained payment of the disputed invoice by duress.

Outside the field of protected relationships, and in a purely commercial context, it might be a relatively rare case in which 'lawful act duress' can be established. And it might be particularly difficult to establish duress if the defendant bona fide considered that his demand was valid. In this complex and changing branch of the law I deliberately refrain from saying 'never'. But as the law stands, I am satisfied that the defendants' conduct in this case did not amount to duress.

It is an unattractive result, inasmuch as the defendants are allowed to retain a sum which at the trial they became aware was not in truth due to them. But in my view the law compels the result. . . .

Questions

1. In this case Sir Donald Nicholls V-C observed that there was no evidence that the defendant company's belief was unreasonable. Should the reasonableness of a party's belief be relevant?

2. Was this an example of a 'submission to an honest claim'?

Notes

1. Sir Donald Nicholls V-C agreed with Steyn LJ that restitution on the grounds of duress was unavailable, but suggested that prima facie there was a case that it was 'unconscionable for the defendant company to insist on retaining the money now' and that in 'broad terms' they were 'unjustly enriched'. The judge did not pursue the point, but he seems to be alluding to a claim based on unconscionable retention of benefits, i.e. when the defendants learnt the true state of facts and only then a restitutionary cause of action arose. With respect to the learned Vice-Chancellor, claims based on 'unconscionability' should be concerned with 'unconscientiousness' at the time of receipt, not with knowledge acquired subsequent to receipt.

2. At first instance the judge found that when the pressure was exerted the plaintiffs paid because they regarded it as the lesser of two evils. It seems to have been accepted both there and in the Court of Appeal that this finding satisfied the causal question. Compare Holmes J in the American case of *Union Pacific Railway Company* v *Public Service Commission of Missouri* (1918) 248 US 67 at 70: 'It always is for the interest of a party under duress to choose the lesser of two evils. But the fact that a choice was made according to interest does not exclude duress. It is the characteristic of duress properly so called'. The *CTN Cash and Carry* case failed because of the absence of illegitimacy, not because of any failure to prove causation.

3. If the category of 'lawful act' duress is to have any content, the most obvious candidates for inclusion are cases where threats are made (usually against vulnerable relatives) to prosecute a member of the family unless certain demands are complied with. In *Williams* v *Bayley* (1866) LR 1 HL 200 ('it is a case of transportation for life') the resulting mortgage was set aside, and in *Mutual Finance Ltd* v *John Wetton & Sons Ltd* [1937] 2 KB 389 the resulting guarantee was also set aside. Obviously threats to prosecute the criminally culpable are not unlawful, but the coupling with a demand for benefits renders the conduct illegitimate. Both these cases were decided as ones of actual undue influence, indeed in the latter Porter J would have 'unhesitatingly' said the facts did not amount to common law duress. Such a conclusion has been doubted since the expansion of duress over the last few decades: see Birks, *Introduction*, 185 and Burrows, *Restitution*, 185–8.

Section 2: benefits obtained as a result of undue influence

Undue influence is an equitable supplement to the common law of duress, developed by the Chancellors to cope with more subtle forms of exploitation. It is properly classified as a cause of action belonging to the group 'compulsion'. Its concern is victimisation: see Lindley LJ in *Allcard* v *Skinner* (1887) 36 Ch D 145 (CA) (below). It has two basic forms: actual and presumed. The former category exists where it can be shown that influence was actually exerted and caused the disposal of wealth. The latter category covers situations where a relationship of dependence, or trust and confidence exists between transferor and transferee. This creates a rebuttable presumption that any resulting transaction was not free and fair. In this situation the transferee must show that the other had the opportunity to exercise independent judgment to escape restitutionary obligations. So both categories are concerned with more subtle forms of pressure, but in the latter the evidential burden is shifted. Professor Birks prefers to categorise presumed undue influence as a species of 'inequality'. This argument will be assessed in Section 3.

A further important division which cuts across the actual/presumed divide is that between relatively simple two party cases and more difficult three party cases where the person exerting influence (or presumed to be in a relationship of influence) is not the same person as the recipient of the benefit. The question arises: when is the recipient infected by the conduct of the influencer? A recent House of Lords case (*Barclays Bank plc* v *O'Brien* [1994] 1 AC 180) has greatly clarified the issues in this area.

A wrong turning was taken in *Bank of Credit and Commerce International SA* v *Aboody* [1990] 1 QB 923, where the Court of Appeal held that 'manifest disadvantage' was essential to a plea of either actual or presumed undue influence, In fact it is only an evidential factor which, amongst other factors, can give rise to a presumption of undue influence. Therefore it is irrelevant where undue influence has actually been exerted. Actual undue influence is a clear case of compulsion, not a case of gross inequality. The victim should therefore be able to set the transaction aside as of right. This error was corrected by the House of Lords in *CIBC Mortgages plc* v *Pitt* [1994] 1 AC 200.

Allcard* v *Skinner
(1887) 36 Ch D 145 (CA)

In 1868, the plaintiff was introduced by the Rev. Mr Nihill to the defendant, who was the Superior of an Anglican sisterhood. In 1871, the plaintiff joined the sisterhood as a full member, taking vows of poverty, chastity and obedience. The sisterhood's rules also forbade the seeking of advice of outsiders without the leave of the Superior and stated 'the voice of thy Superior is the voice of God'. The plaintiff made a will in favour of the sisterhood, and when she later came into wealth, made substantial gifts of money and property to the defendant. Subsequently the plaintiff left the sisterhood and joined the Roman Catholic church in 1879, but she made no claim for the return of her property until 1885. At first instance the judge refused restitution of all the benefits received by the defendant. The plaintiff appealed, but only in respect of some railway company shares still in the hands of the defendant. *Held*: the circumstances of the relationship between the plaintiff and the defendant together with her spiritual adviser gave rise to the presumption of undue influence, therefore the plaintiff was prima facie entitled to restitution. However, by a majority (Cotton LJ dissenting on this point) the plaintiff's claim was defeated by laches (she became free of the influence in 1879, but made no claim until more than six years later) and by acquiescence.

COTTON LJ (dissenting on laches): The question is—Does the case fall within the principles laid down by the decisions of the Court of Chancery in setting aside voluntary gifts executed by parties who at the time were under such influence as, in the opinion of the Court, enabled the donor afterwards to set the gift aside? These decisions may be divided into two classes—First, where the Court has been satisfied that the gift was the result of influence expressly used by the donee for the purpose; second, where the relations between the donor and donee have at or shortly before the execution of the gift been such as to raise a presumption that the donee had influence over the donor. In such a case the Court sets aside the voluntary gift, unless it is proved that in fact the gift was the spontaneous act of the donor acting under circumstances which enabled him to exercise an independent will and which justifies the Court in holding that the gift was the result of a free exercise of the donor's will. The first class of cases may be considered as depending on the principle that no one shall be allowed to retain any benefit arising from his own fraud or wrongful act. In the second class of cases the Court interferes, not on the ground that any wrongful act has in fact been committed by the donee, but on the ground of public policy, and to prevent the relations which existed between the parties and the influence arising therefrom being abused.

Both the Defendant and Mr Nihill have stated that they used no influence to induce the Plaintiff to make the gift in question, and there is no suggestion that the Defendant acted from any selfish motive, and it cannot be contended that this case comes under the first class of decisions to which I have referred. The question is whether the case comes within the principle of the second class, and I am of opinion that it does. At the time of the gift the Plaintiff was a professed sister, and, as such, bound to render absolute submission to the Defendant as superior of the sisterhood. She had no power to obtain independent advice, she was in such a position that she could not freely exercise her own will as to the disposal of her property, and she must be considered as being (to use the words of Lord Justice Knight Bruce in *Wright* v *Vanderplank* 8 DM & G 137) 'not, in the largest and amplest sense of the term—not, in mind as well as person—an entirely free agent.' We have nothing to do with the Plaintiff's reasons for leaving the sisterhood; but, in my opinion, when she exercised her legal right to do this she was entitled to recover so much of the fund transferred by her as remained in the hands of the Defendant, on the ground that it was property the beneficial interest in which she had never effectually parted with. . . .

LINDLEY LJ: . . . What then is the principle? Is it that it is right and expedient to save persons from the consequences of their own folly? or is it that it is right and expedient to save them from being victimised by other people? In my opinion the doctrine of undue influence is founded upon the second of these two principles. Courts of Equity have never set aside gifts on the ground of the folly, imprudence, or want of foresight on the part of donors. The Courts have always repudiated any such jurisdiction. *Huguenin* v *Baseley* 14 Ves 273 is itself a clear authority to this effect. It would obviously be to encourage folly, recklessness, extravagance and vice if persons could get back property which they foolishly made away with, whether by giving it to charitable institutions or by bestowing it on less worthy objects. On the other hand, to protect people from being forced, tricked or misled in any way by others into parting with their property is one of the most legitimate objects of all laws; and the equitable doctrine of undue influence has grown out of and been developed by the necessity of grappling with insidious forms of spiritual tyranny and with the infinite varieties of fraud.

As no Court has ever attempted to define fraud so no Court has ever attempted to define undue influence, which includes one of its many varieties. The undue influence which Courts of Equity endeavour to defeat is the undue influence of one person over another; not the influence of enthusiasm on the enthusiast who is carried away by it, unless indeed such enthusiasm is itself the result of external undue influence. But the influence of one mind over another is very subtle, and of all influences religious influence is the most dangerous and the most powerful, and to counteract it Courts of Equity have gone very far. They have not shrunk from setting aside gifts made to persons in a position to exercise undue influence over the donors, although there has been no proof of the actual exercise of such influence; and the Courts have done this on the avowed ground of the necessity of going this length in order to protect persons from the exercise of such influence under circumstances which render proof of it impossible. The Courts have required proof of its non-exercise, and, failing that proof, have set aside gifts otherwise unimpeachable. . . .

Note

There are a number of established categories of relationship where the presumption has been held to exist: parent and child, solicitor and client, doctor and patient, trustee and beneficiary, guardian and ward, and spiritual adviser and devotee. (See Birks, *Introduction*, 207.) Here the presumption arises automatically because of the nature of the relationship. It is also possible to establish the presumption on the facts of a particular relationship. See, for example, *O'Sullivan* v *Management Agency and Music Ltd* [1985] QB 428 (manager and young pop musician, discussed in Chapter 8, Section 3) and the next case.

Lloyds Bank Ltd v *Bundy*
[1975] QB 326 (CA)

The defendant, an elderly farmer, mortgaged his only asset, Yew Tree Farm, for £1,500 to the plaintiff bank to secure an overdraft for his son's plant hire business. Following advice from his solicitor the plaintiff subsequently increased the mortgage to £6,000, in May 1969. However, the son's business continued to struggle and in December 1969 the son and the local branch's new assistant manager called on the defendant. The bank was prepared to continue the business's existing overdraft of £10,000 on the condition that the plaintiff increased the bank's security to £11,000, more than the value of the house. The plaintiff signed a further mortgage. When the son's business failed the bank sought possession of Yew Tree Farm. *Held*: the documents signed in December 1969 would be set aside for undue influence. In the exceptional circumstances a presumption of confidentiality arose, and the bank had failed to discharge the burden upon it of showing that the defendant was independently advised.

Notes

1. This is an extreme case. The relationship of banker and customer does not normally give rise to a presumption of undue influence, but a presumption was established on the particular facts here: the son and father were both customers for a long time; the home visit with documents ready-prepared and no opportunity for independent advice or reflection; the confidence and trust reposed by the defendant in the bank's officials; the fact that the bank knew of the defendant's solicitor and knew that he advised the defendant on important matters including the earlier charge. Lord Denning MR in his judgment stressed the fact that the transaction was all one-sided. The bank was only promising to continue the overdraft at its existing level, it was not providing further sums. In fact it made detailed proposals for repayment. Lord Denning went further than the other judges and synthesised from the case of undue influence and other categories, such as duress of goods and salvage agreements, a new principle of 'inequality of bargaining power'. See Section 3.

2. Here the bank was itself fixed with the presumption of undue influence, in a straightforward two party scenario. The relationship between father and son provided only the background for this finding. Therefore, as stressed by the House of Lords in the subsequent case of *National Westminster Bank* v *Morgan* [1985] AC 686, *Lloyds Bank* v *Bundy* turned on its 'very special facts'. In *National Westminster* v *Morgan* the law lords rejected a plea by a wife that her bank procured the execution of her signature to a remortgage of the matrimonial home in circumstances giving rise to the presumption of undue influence following a 20-minute home visit by the manager. Lord Scarman said:

> . . . the relationship between banker and customer is not one which ordinarily gives rise to a presumption of undue influence: and that in the ordinary course of banking business a banker can explain the nature of the proposed transaction without laying himself open to a charge of undue influence.

After the victory of the bank in *National Westminster* v *Morgan* the focus in the cases shifted away from two party cases to the three-party case question: when can a bank or other third party be infected by pressure or undue influence of another? In other words, the shadowy figures of the son in *Bundy* and the husband in *Morgan* took centre stage alongside the bank and the party allegedly influenced.

3. While a useful corrective in confining *Lloyds Bank* v *Bundy* to its special facts, *National Westminster* v *Morgan* sowed several seeds of doubt and prompted further expensive litigation. First, certain *dicta* of Lord Scarman which suggested that it was necessary to show 'dominating influence' before the presumption was raised, had to be explained away by the Court of Appeal in *Goldsworthy* v *Brickell* [1987] Ch 378. Secondly, the very structure of Lord Scarman's speech caused confusion about the relevance and role of 'manifest disadvantage' which was only clarified, and the law put back on a proper footing, in *CIBC Mortgages plc* v *Pitt* [1994] 1 AC 200.

Bank of Credit and Commerce International SA v *Aboody* [1990] 1 QB 923 (CA)

Mr Aboody ran a textile importing business in Manchester which was in financial difficulties. His wife (by an arranged marriage) was also a director and shareholder of the family business, but in name only. Mrs Aboody owned the matrimonial home and entered into several guarantees and mortgages of the home to secure the company's massive borrowing. When the company collapsed she challenged the bank's claim on the ground that her husband had exerted actual undue influence to procure her signature. In particular in respect of the most recent charge, she had been taken to the bank by her husband. Mrs Aboody was then taken to a private room in the bank where she received advice from a solicitor who warned her not to enter into the transaction, but she said she wanted to go ahead with it anyway. Mr Aboody then burst into the room shouting at the solicitor 'Why the hell don't you get on with what you are paid to do and witness her signature?'. Mrs Aboody was reduced to tears, but signed nonetheless. *Held*: the bank had *actual* notice of Mr Aboody's *actual* undue influence, but Mrs Aboody was not entitled to relief because she had failed to show that any of the transactions were manifestly disadvantageous to her.

Questions

1. What is the function of insisting on 'manifest disadvantage' as an ingredient of the cause of action of undue influence?

2. If it was clear that Mrs Aboody would have signed regardless of any advice she received, could it still be said that her husband's undue influence induced her to enter the transaction? (See *Aboody* [1990] 1 QB 923, at 971.)

Note

This was a clear case of *actual* notice (for this purpose the solicitor was treated as an agent of the bank) of *actual* undue influence, but Mrs Aboody was refused relief because she failed to clear the hurdle of showing 'manifest disadvantage'. This holding, that manifest disadvantage is essential even to a plea of *actual* undue influence, involves a confusion between *procedural* fairness (where, for example, compulsion or lies are proved) and *substantive* fairness (where the concern is with the parties' respective status, their relationship and the reasonableness of the terms of the bargain, in other words 'inequality'). But the Court of Appeal felt constrained to hold it was essential after minute analysis of Lord Scarman's speech in *National Westminster* v *Morgan* (and see the identical opinions expressed in five other Court of Appeal cases discussed in *Aboody* [1990] 1 QB 923, at 959–60). See now *CIBC Mortgages plc* v *Pitt* [1994] 1 AC 200, below.

Barclays Bank plc v O'Brien
[1994] 1 AC 180 (HL)

Rescission

LORD BROWNE-WILKINSON: My Lords, in this appeal your Lordships for the first time have to consider a problem which has given rise to reported decisions of the Court of Appeal on no less than 11 occasions in the last eight years and which has led to a difference of judicial view. Shortly stated the question is whether a bank is entitled to enforce against a wife an obligation to secure a debt owed by her husband to the bank where the wife has been induced to stand as surety for her husband's debt by the undue influence or misrepresentation of the husband. . . .

Policy considerations

The large number of cases of this type coming before the courts in recent years reflects the rapid changes in social attitudes and the distribution of wealth which have recently occurred. Wealth is now more widely spread. Moreover a high proportion of privately owned wealth is invested in the matrimonial home. Because of the recognition by society of the equality of the sexes, the majority of matrimonial homes are now in the joint names of both spouses. Therefore in order to raise finance for the business enterprises of one or other of the spouses, the jointly owned home has become a main source of security. The provision of such security requires the consent of both spouses.

In parallel with these financial developments, society's recognition of the equality of the sexes has led to a rejection of the concept that the wife is subservient to the husband in the management of the family's finances. A number of the authorities reflect an unwillingness in the court to perpetuate law based on this outmoded concept. Yet, as Scott LJ in the Court of Appeal rightly points out [1993] QB 109, 139, although the concept of the ignorant wife leaving all financial decisions to the husband is outmoded, the practice does not yet coincide with the ideal. In a substantial proportion of marriages it is still the husband who has the business experience and the wife is willing to follow his advice without bringing a truly independent mind and will to bear on financial decisions. The number of recent cases in this field shows that in practice many wives are still subjected to, and yield to, undue influence by their husbands. Such wives can reasonably look to the law for some protection when their husbands have abused the trust and the confidence reposed in them.

On the other hand, it is important to keep a sense of balance in approaching these cases. It is easy to allow sympathy for the wife who is threatened with the loss of her home at the suit of a rich bank to obscure an important public interest viz., the need to ensure that the wealth currently tied up in the matrimonial home does not become economically sterile. If the rights secured to wives by the law renders vulnerable loans granted on the security of matrimonial homes, institutions will be unwilling to accept such security, thereby reducing the flow of loan capital to business enterprises. It is therefore essential that a law designed to protect the vulnerable does not render the matrimonial home unacceptable as security to financial institutions.

Undue influence

A person who has been induced to enter into a transaction by the undue influence of another ('the wrongdoer') is entitled to set that transaction aside as against the wrongdoer. Such undue influence is either actual or presumed. In *Bank of Credit and Commerce International SA* v *Aboody* [1990] 1 QB 923, 953, the Court of Appeal helpfully adopted the following classification.

Class 1: Actual undue influence

In these cases it is necessary for the claimant to prove affirmatively that the wrongdoer exerted undue influence on the complainant to enter into the particular transaction which is impugned.

Class 2: Presumed undue influence

In these cases the complainant only has to show, in the first instance, that there was a relationship of trust and confidence between the complainant and the wrongdoer of such a nature that it is fair to presume that the wrongdoer abused that relationship in procuring the complainant to enter into the impugned transaction. In Class 2 cases therefore there is no need to produce evidence that actual undue influence was exerted in relation to the particular transaction impugned: once a confidential relationship has been proved, the burden then shifts to the wrongdoer to prove that the complainant entered into the impugned transaction freely, for example by showing that the complainant had independent advice. Such a confidential relationship can be established in two ways, viz.,

Class 2(A)
Certain relationships (for example solicitor and client, medical advisor and patient) as a matter of law raise the presumption that undue influence has been exercised.

Class 2(B)
Even if there is no relationship falling within Class 2(A), if the complainant proves the de facto existence of a relationship under which the complainant generally reposed trust and confidence in the wrongdoer, the existence of such relationship raises the presumption of undue influence. In a Class 2(B) case therefore, in the absence of evidence disproving undue influence, the complainant will succeed in setting aside the impugned transaction merely by proof that the complainant reposed trust and confidence in the wrongdoer without having to prove that the wrongdoer exerted actual undue influence or otherwise abused such trust and confidence in relation to the particular transaction impugned.

As to dispositions by a wife in favour of her husband, the law for long remained in an unsettled state. In the 19th century some judges took the view that the relationship was such that it fell into Class 2(A) i.e. as a matter of law undue influence by the husband over the wife was presumed. It was not until the decisions in *Howes* v *Bishop* [1909] 2 KB 390 and *Bank of Montreal* v *Stuart* [1911] AC 120 that it was finally determined that the relationship of husband and wife did not as a matter of law raise a presumption of undue influence within Class 2(A). . . .

Conclusions
(a) Wives
. . . A wife who has been induced to stand as a surety for her husband's debts by his undue influence, misrepresentation or some other legal wrong has an equity as against him to set aside that transaction. Under the ordinary principles of equity, her right to set aside that transaction will be enforceable against third parties (e.g., against a creditor) if either the husband was acting as the third party's agent or the third party had actual or constructive notice of the facts giving rise to her equity. Although there may be cases where, without artificiality, it can properly be held that the husband was acting as the agent of the creditor in procuring the wife to stand as surety, such cases will be of very rare occurrence. The key to the problem is to identify the circumstances in which the creditor will be taken to have had notice of the wife's equity to set aside the transaction.

The doctrine of notice lies at the heart of equity. Given that there are two innocent parties, each enjoying rights, the earlier right prevails against the later right if the acquirer of the later right knows of the earlier right (actual notice) or would have discovered it had he taken proper steps (constructive notice). In particular, if the party asserting that he takes free of the earlier rights of another knows of certain facts which put him on inquiry as to the possible existence of the rights of that other and he fails to make such inquiry or take such other steps as are reasonable to verify whether such earlier right does or does not exist, he will have constructive notice of the earlier right and take subject to it. Therefore where a wife has agreed to stand surety for her husband's debts as a result of undue influence or misrepresentation, the creditor will take subject to the wife's equity to set aside the transaction if the circumstances are such as to put the creditor on inquiry as to the circumstances in which she agreed to stand surety.

It is at this stage that, in my view, the 'invalidating tendency' or the law's 'tender treatment' of married women, becomes relevant. As I have said above in dealing with undue influence, this tenderness of the law towards married women is due to the fact that, even today, many wives repose confidence and trust in their husbands in relation to their financial affairs. This tenderness of the law is reflected by the fact that voluntary dispositions by the wife in favour of her husband are more likely to be set aside than other dispositions by her: a wife is more likely to establish presumed undue influence of Class 2(B) by her husband than by others because, in practice, many wives do repose in their husbands trust and confidence in relation to their financial affairs. Moreover the informality of business dealings between spouses raises a substantial risk that the husband has not accurately stated to the wife the nature of the liability she is undertaking i.e., he has misrepresented the position, albeit negligently.

Therefore in my judgment a creditor is put on inquiry when a wife offers to stand surety for her husband's debts by the combination of two factors: (a) the transaction is on its face not to the financial advantage of the wife; and (b) there is a substantial risk in transactions of that kind that, in procuring the wife to act as surety, the husband has committed a legal or equitable wrong that entitles the wife to set aside the transaction.

It follow that unless the creditor who is put on inquiry takes reasonable steps to satisfy himself that the wife's agreement to stand surety has been properly obtained, the creditor will have constructive notice of the wife's rights.

What, then are the reasonable steps which the creditor should take to ensure that it does not have constructive notice of the wife's rights, if any? Normally the reasonable steps necessary to avoid being fixed with constructive notice consist of making inquiry of the person who may have the earlier right (i.e. the wife) to see whether such right is asserted. It is plainly impossible to require of banks and other financial institutions that they should inquire of one spouse whether he or she has been unduly influenced or misled by the other. But in my judgment the creditor, in order to avoid being fixed with constructive notice, can reasonably be expected to take steps to bring home to the wife the risk she is running by standing as surety and to advise her to take independent advice. As to past transactions, it will depend on the facts of each case whether the steps taken by the creditor satisfy this test. However for the future in my judgment a creditor will have satisfied these requirements if it insists that the wife attend a private meeting (in the absence of the husband) with a representative of the creditor at which she is told of the extent of her liability as surety, warned of the risk she is running and urged to take independent legal advice. If these steps are taken in my judgment the creditor will have taken such reasonable steps as are necessary to preclude a subsequent claim that it had constructive notice of the wife's rights. I should make it clear that I have been considering the ordinary case where the creditor knows only that the wife is to stand surety for her husband's debts. I would not exclude exceptional cases where a creditor has knowledge of further facts which render the presence of undue influence not only possible but probable. In such cases, the creditor to be safe will have to insist that the wife is separately advised. . . .

(b) Other Persons

I have hitherto dealt only with the position where a wife stands surety for her husband's debts. But in my judgment the same principles are applicable to all other cases where there is an emotional relationship between cohabitees. The 'tenderness' shown by the law to married women is not based on the marriage ceremony but reflects the underlying risk of one cohabitee exploiting the emotional involvement and trust of the other. Now that unmarried cohabitation, whether heterosexual or homosexual, is widespread in our society, the law should recognise this. Legal wives are not the only group which are now exposed to the emotional pressure of cohabitation. Therefore if, but only if, the creditor is aware that the surety is cohabiting with the principal debtor, in my judgment the same principles should apply to them as apply to husband and wife.

In addition to the cases of cohabitees, the decision of the Court of Appeal in *Avon Finance Co. Ltd* v *Bridger* [1985] 2 All ER 281 shows (rightly in my view) that other relationships can give rise to a similar result. In that case a son, by means of misrepresentation, persuaded his elderly parents to stand surety for his debts. The surety obligation was held to be unenforceable by the creditor inter alia because to the Bank's knowledge the parents trusted the son in their financial dealings. In my judgment that case was rightly decided: in a case where the creditor is aware that the surety reposes trust and confidence in the principal debtor in relation to his financial affairs, the creditor is put on inquiry in just the same way as it is in relation to husband and wife.

Summary
I can therefore summarise my views as follows. Where one cohabitee has entered into an obligation to stand as surety for the debts of the other cohabitee and the creditor is aware that they are cohabitees: (1) the surety obligation will be valid and enforceable by the creditor unless the suretyship was procured by the undue influence, misrepresentation or other legal wrong of the principal debtor; (2) if there has been undue influence, misrepresentation or other legal wrong by the principal debtor, unless the creditor has taken reasonable steps to satisfy himself that the surety entered into the obligation freely and in knowledge of the true facts, the creditor will be unable to enforce the surety obligation because he will be fixed with constructive notice of the surety's right to set aside the transaction; (3) unless there are special exceptional circumstances, a creditor will have taken such reasonable steps to avoid being fixed with constructive notice if the creditor warns the surety (at a meeting not attended by the principal debtor) of the amount of her potential liability and of the risks involved and advises the surety to take independent legal advice.

I should make it clear that in referring to the husband's debts I include the debts of a company in which the husband (but not the wife) has a direct financial interest.

The decision of this case
Applying those principles to this case, to the knowledge of the bank Mr and Mrs O'Brien were man and wife. The bank took a surety obligation from Mrs O'Brien, secured on the matrimonial home, to secure the debts of a company in which Mr O'Brien was interested but in which Mrs O'Brien had no direct pecuniary interest. The bank should therefore have been put on inquiry as to the circumstances in which Mrs O'Brien had agreed to stand as surety for the debt of her husband. If the Burnham branch had properly carried out the instructions from Mr Tucker of the Woolwich branch, Mrs O'Brien would have been informed that she and the matrimonial home were potentially liable for the debts of a company which had an existing liability of £107,000 and which was to be afforded an overdraft facility of £135,000. If she had been told this, it would have counteracted Mr O'Brien's misrepresentation that the liability was limited to £60,000 and would last for only three weeks. In addition according to the side letter she would have been recommended to take independent legal advice.

Unfortunately Mr Tucker's instructions were not followed and to the knowledge of the bank (through the clerk at the Burnham branch) Mrs O'Brien signed the documents without any warning of the risks or any recommendation to take legal advice. In the circumstances the bank (having failed to take reasonable steps) is fixed with constructive notice of the wrongful misrepresentation made by Mr O'Brien to Mrs O'Brien. Mrs O'Brien is therefore entitled as against the bank to set aside the legal charge on the matrimonial home securing her husband's liability to the bank. . . .

CIBC Mortgages plc v *Pitt*
[1994] 1 AC 200 (HL)

Rescission

This is a tale of the 1980s. Mr and Mrs Pitt had been married for 22 years and they jointly owned a house valued at £270,000 with an outstanding mortgage of only £16,700. Mr Pitt wanted to re-mortgage the house in order to invest on the stock market. Mrs Pitt was reluctant, but Mr Pitt exerted what the trial judge held was undue influence to make her comply. Mrs Pitt signed all the necessary forms without reading them. No one suggested she take independent advice. The purpose of the loan was stated to be a joint advance to purchase a second home. They received over £130,000 which Mr Pitt promptly invested. He speculated heavily, charging his securities to buy more shares. At one stage he was a millionaire on paper. In October 1987 the stock market crashed. Mr Pitt fell into arrears. The plaintiff sought possession. By the time of trial the property slump had intervened. The arrears then stood at £219,000, more than the value of the house. *Held*: Mrs Pitt was entitled to set aside the transaction as against her husband, because it was not necessary to prove manifest disadvantage once *actual* undue influence had been made out. However, Mrs Pitt was not entitled to set aside the transaction as against the plaintiff lender, as there was nothing in this transaction to suggest it was anything other than a normal advance to husband and wife for their joint benefit.

LORD BROWNE-WILKINSON: . . . In the present case, the Court of Appeal as they were bound to, applied the law laid down in *National Westminster Bank Plc* v *Morgan* [1985] AC 686 as interpreted by the Court of Appeal in *Bank of Credit and Commerce International SA* v *Aboody* [1990] 1 QB 923: a claim to set aside a transaction on the grounds of undue influence whether presumed (*Morgan*) or actual (*Aboody*) cannot succeed unless the claimant proves that the impugned transaction was manifestly disadvantageous to him. Before your Lordships, Mrs Pitt submitted that the Court of Appeal in *Aboody* erred in extending the need to show manifest disadvantage in cases of actual, as opposed to presumed, undue influence. Adopting the classification used in *O'Brien's* case [*Barclays Bank Plc* v *O'Brien* [1994] 1 AC 180], p. 189C–G, it is argued that although *Morgan's* case decides that the claimant must show that the impugned transaction was disadvantageous to him in order to raise the presumption of undue influence within Class 2(A) or (B), there is no such requirement where it is proved affirmatively that the claimant's agreement to the transaction was actually obtained by undue influence within Class 1.

In the *Morgan* case it was alleged that Mrs Morgan had been induced to grant security to the bank by the undue influence of one of the bank's managers. Mrs Morgan did not allege actual undue influence within Class 1, but relied exclusively on a presumption of undue influence within Class 2. It was held that the bank manager had never in fact assumed such a role as to raise any presumption of undue influence. However, in addition, it was held that Mrs Morgan could not succeed because she had not demonstrated that the transaction was manifestly disadvantageous to her. Lord Scarman (who delivered the leading speech) rejected a submission that the presumption of undue influence was based on any public policy requirements. In reliance on the judgment of Lindley LJ in *Allcard* v *Skinner* [1887] 36 Ch D 145 and the decision of the Privy Council in *Poosathurai* v *Kannappa Chettiar* (1919) LR 47 Ind App 1, he laid down the following proposition [1985] AC 686, 704:

> Whatever the legal character of the transaction, the authorities show that it must constitute a disadvantage sufficiently serious to require evidence to rebut the presumption that in the circumstances of the relationship between the parties it was procured by the exercise of undue influence. In my judgment, therefore, the Court of Appeal erred in law in holding that the presumption of undue influence can arise from the evidence of the relationship of the parties without also evidence that the transaction itself was wrongful in that it constituted an advantage taken of the person subjected to the influence which, failing proof to the contrary was explicable only on the basis that undue influence had been exercised to procure it.

In the *Aboody* case [1990] 1 QB 923 the claimant had established that actual undue influence within Class 1 had been exercised to induce her to enter into the impugned transaction. That transaction was not manifestly disadvantageous to her. The Court of Appeal, following a number of dicta in the Court of Appeal and a first instance decision subsequent to *Morgan* [1985] AC 686, held that the decision in *Morgan* applied as much to cases of Class 1 actual indue influence as to Class 2 presumed undue influence. They placed reliance on certain passages in Lord Scarman's speech in *Morgan* which indicated a view that the demonstration of a manifest disadvantage was essential even in a Class 1 case. The Court of Appeal were initially impressed by a submission that, if manifest disadvantage had to be shown in all cases, an old lady who had unduly influenced by her solicitor to sell him her family house but had been paid the full market price for it, would be unable to recover. However, they were satisfied that in such a case the old lady would have a remedy under what they regarded as a wholly separate doctrine of equity, viz., the right to set aside transactions obtained in abuse of confidence.

My Lords, I am unable to agree with the Court of Appeal's decision in *Aboody.* I have no doubt that the decision in *Morgan* does not extend to cases of actual undue influence. Despite two references in Lord Scarman's speech to cases of actual undue influence, as I read his speech he was primarily concerned to establish that disadvantage had to be shown, not as a constituent element of the cause of action for undue influence, but in order to raise a presumption of undue influence with Class 2. That was the only subject matter before the House of Lords in *Morgan* and the passage I have already cited was directed solely to that point. With the exception of a passing reference to *Ormes* v *Beadel* (1980) 2 Gif 166, all the cases referred to by Lord Scarman were cases of presumed undue influence. In the circumstances, I do not think that this House can have been intending to lay down any general principle applicable to all claims of undue influence, whether actual or presumed.

Whatever the merits of requiring a complainant to show manifest disadvantage in order to raise a Class 2 presumption of undue influence, in my judgment there is no logic in imposing such a requirement where actual undue influence has been exercised and proved. Actual undue influence is a species of fraud. Like any other victim of fraud, a person who has been induced by undue influence to carry out a transaction which he did not freely and knowingly enter into is entitled to have that transaction set aside as of right. No case decided before *Morgan* was cited (nor am I aware of any) in which a transaction proved to have been obtained by actual undue influence has been upheld nor is there any case in which a court has even considered whether the transaction was, or was not, advantageous. A man guilty of fraud is no more entitled to argue that the transaction was beneficial to the person defrauded than is a man who has procured a transaction by misrepresentation. The effect of the wrongdoer's conduct is to prevent the wronged party from bringing a free will and properly informed mind to bear on the proposed transaction which accordingly must be set aside in equity as a matter of justice.

I therefore hold that a claimant who proves actual undue influence is not under the further burden of proving that the transaction induced by undue influence was manifestly disadvantageous: he is entitled as of right to have it set aside. . . .

Notes

1. See Cretney, 'Mere Puppets, Folly and Imprudence: Undue Influence for the Twenty First Century' [1994] *Restitution Law Review* 3 for critical discussion of *Barclays Bank* v *O'Brien*, *CIBC Mortgages* v *Pitt* and other recent cases in this area. *Massey* v *Midland Bank plc* is now reported at [1995] 1 All ER 929 (CA). See also *Banco Exterior Internacional* v *Mann* [1995] 1 All ER 936 and *TSB Bank plc* v *Camfield* [1995] 1 All ER 951 for applications of the *O'Brien* guidelines.

2. See further Birks and Chin, 'On the Nature of Undue Influence' in Beatson and Friedmann (eds), *Fault and Good Faith in Contract* (Oxford: Oxford University Press, 1995).

Section 3: inequality

Mere inequality is not a sufficient factor to give rise to a right to restitution. Professor Birks has cautioned that 'inequality' is necessarily an abbreviation for 'exceptional or abnormal inequality' (Birks, *Introduction*, 204). Unsurprisingly it was Lord Denning MR who took the judicial lead in *Lloyds Bank Ltd* v *Bundy* [1975] QB 326 (the facts of which have been outlined in Section 2 above) where he examined five categories of case. The first category consisted of 'duress of goods' (e.g., *Astley* v *Reynolds* (1731) 2 Stra 915; 93 ER 939) and the '*colore officii*' cases (e.g., *Steele* v *Williams* (1853) 8 Exch 625, 155 ER 1502). The second category was 'unconscionable transactions' (e.g., *Fry* v *Lane* (1888) 40 Ch D 312). Third, 'undue influence' (e.g., *Allcard* v *Skinner* (1887) 36 Ch D 145 (CA)) and fourth, 'undue pressure' (e.g., the actual undue influence case of *Williams* v *Bayley* (1886) LR 1 HL 200 and *D & C Builders Ltd* v *Rees* [1966] 2 QB 617). The fifth category was 'salvage agreements' (e.g., *The Port Caledonia and the Anna* [1903] P 184, where the 'rescuer' issued the ultimatum '£1,000 or no rope'). Lord Denning continued:

> Gathering all together, I would suggest that through all these instances there runs a single thread. They rest on 'inequality of bargaining power.' By virtue of it, the English Law gives relief to one who, without indepen-

dent advice, enters into a contract upon terms which are very unfair or transfers property for a consideration which is grossly inadequate, when his bargaining power is grievously impaired by reason of his own needs or desires, or by his own ignorance or infirmity, coupled with undue influences or pressures brought to bear on him by or for the benefit of the other. When I use the word 'undue' I do not mean to suggest that the principle depends on proof of any wrongdoing. The one who stipulates for an unfair advantage may be moved solely by his own self-interest, unconscious of the distress he is bringing to the other. I have also avoided any reference to the will of the one being 'dominated' or 'overcome' by the other. One who is in extreme need may knowingly consent to a most improvident bargain, solely to relieve the straits in which he finds himself. Again, I do not mean to suggest that every transaction is saved by independent advice. But the absence of it may be fatal. With these explanations, I hope this principle will be found to reconcile the cases. . . .

Despite his lordship's reliance on cases such as *Astley* v *Reynolds* and *Allcard* v *Skinner*, where there were no contracts and restitution was the only issue, the reference to 'bargaining power' gave this synthesis a contractual flavour. As Lord Scarman (in *National Westminster Bank* v *Morgan* [1985] AC 686, also discussed in Section 2 above) later observed, the language is not apt 'to cover transactions of gift where there is no bargain'. Lord Scarman went on to question the necessity of such a generalisation:

. . . And even in the field of contract I question whether there is any need in the modern law to erect a general principle of relief against inequality of bargaining power. Parliament has undertaken the task—and it is essentially a legislative task—of enacting such restrictions upon freedom of contract as are in its judgment necessary to relieve against the mischief: for example, the hire-purchase and consumer protection legislation, of which the Supply of Goods (Implied Terms) Act 1973, Consumer Credit Act 1974, Consumer Safety Act 1978, Supply of Goods and Services Act 1982 and Insurance Companies Act 1982 are examples. I doubt whether the courts should assume the burden of formulating further restrictions.

So, as a super-category which encompass all the doctrines discussed in Sections 1 and 2 of this chapter, 'inequality' has been authoritatively rejected.

Has 'inequality' any remaining utility? Professor Birks uses the concept as an organising device to gather together specific instances where the law has intervened, in the absence of proof of compulsion, simply on the grounds of gross inequality. Therefore presumed undue influence properly analysed is a case of '*inequality*' in the sub-category 'vulnerable relationships' (unlike its cousin 'actual' undue influence which is a species of '*compulsion*'). The category of inequality also includes 'easily exploited transactions', such as extortionate credit bargains, penalty and forfeiture clauses, and cases of 'personal disadvantage'. (See Birks, *Introduction*, 205–18.)

One part of the miscellany, transactions with minors, might be more happily classified as 'incapacity' and is so analysed by Burrows, *Restitution*, 322–6. At the other extreme of the 'seven ages of man' is the problem of transactions with the elderly and others who are mentally infirm. With Alzheimer's disease common but misunderstood, an increasingly elderly population and the current predilection for 'care in the community', this is one of the most difficult and sensitive questions faced by lawyers in this field. It is here that the Privy Council has recently re-affirmed the common law rule that where a contract is made with a person of unsound mind who was ostensibly sane, the transaction cannot be called into question on the ground of incapacity unless the other knew or ought to have known of the lack of mental capacity. In *Hart* v *O'Connor* [1985] AC 1000, Lord Brightman, giving the advice of the Judicial Committee, went on to make some remarks of wider significance:

> If a contract is stigmatised as 'unfair', it may be unfair in one of two ways. It may be unfair by reason of the unfair manner in which it was brought into existence; a contract induced by undue influence is unfair in this sense. It will be convenient to call this 'procedural unfairness.' It may also, in some contexts, be described (accurately or inaccurately) as 'unfair' by reason of the fact that the terms of the contract are more favourable to one party than to the other. In order to distinguish this 'unfairness' from procedural unfairness, it will be convenient to call it 'contractual imbalance.' The two concepts may overlap. Contractual imbalance may be so extreme as to raise a presumption of procedural unfairness, such as undue influence or some other form of victimisation. Equity will relieve a party from a contract which he has been induced to make as a result of victimisation. Equity will not relieve a party from a contract on the ground only that there is contractual imbalance not amounting to unconscionable dealing.

The Privy Council disapproved of developments in New Zealand law evidenced by *Archer* v *Cutler* [1980] 1 NZLR 386, which had established a jurisdiction to unwind transactions in this context on the ground of substantive unfairness above. For discussion of that case and the unreported case of *Ayres* v *Hazelgrove* (9 February 1984) see Birks, *The Future*, 50–52.

Hart v *O'Connor* and *CIBC Mortgages plc* v *Pitt* [1994] 1 AC 200 together provide ammunition for the view that the judiciary are much more comfortable intervening in transactions where there has been a procedural defect in the intention to transfer, than in cases where the allegation is merely contractual imbalance. Non-statutory examples of substantive unfairness are taking on an increasingly marginal appearance. The cases of 'unconscionable bargains' already have an archaic flavour and seem out-of-date in a less class-conscious age. The jurisdiction to relieve 'expectant heirs' of their folly in selling reversionary interests was skilfully curtailed by the majority of the House of Lords in *O'Rorke* v *Bolingbroke* (1877) 2 App Cas 814 (see especially the robustly individualist speech of Lord Blackburn). At the other end of the social scale, intervention of behalf of the 'poor and ignorant' (as in *Fry* v *Lane* (1888) 40 Ch D 312) briefly raised its head again in *Cresswell* v *Potter* (1968) [1978] 1 WLR 255 where Megarry J substituted for the traditional test the proto-politically correct language of 'a member of the lower income group' and 'less highly educated'. (See Burrows, *Restitution*, 199–203.) The safest conclusion seems to be that of Lord Scarman, that regulating substantively unfair bargains is a matter for Parliament, rather than for the application of the nebulous idea of 'unconscionability'.

See generally Burrows, *Restitution*, 189–204. For discussion see Beatson, 'Unconscionability: Placebo or Pill?' (1981) 1 OJLS 426; Beale, 'Inequality of Bargaining Power' (1986) 6 OJLS 123; Bamforth, 'Unconscionability as a vitiating factor' [1995] LMCLQ 538.

Section 4: legal compulsion

If a person resorts to legal process, with all the coercive power of the State behind it, to extract benefits from another, and does so in bad faith, we saw above in Section 1 that the coerced party may be entitled to restitution (for example, in *Duke de Cadaval* v *Collins* (1836) 4 Ad & E 858, 111 ER 1006; see Goff and Jones, 234–9). However, there is also a public interest in ensuring finality in litigation, so where legal process is resorted to in good faith the law encourages compromise, and in restitution it has been argued that the law recognises a defence of 'submission to an honest claim'. (See Goff and Jones, 50–54, 268–72; Andrews, 'Mistaken settlements of disputable claims' [1989] LMCLQ 431; but compare Arrowsmith, 'Mistake and the role of the "Submission to an Honest Claim"' in Burrows, *Essays*, 17–38.) Similarly, where process has resulted in judgment the issue cannot be re-opened in subsequent litigation: the defence of *res judicata* applies (see Goff and Jones, 763–4; the great case of *Moses* v *Macferlan* (1760) 2 Burr 1005, 97 ER 676 appears to ignore this principle). Restitution is therefore generally not available. There is a significant exception where more than one person is liable to legal compulsion. In these cases restitution is allowed not between debtor and creditor, but between those liable to a common claimant. Where one party is a principal debtor and the other's liability was only an accessory one, the latter can recover the full amount of the benefit conferred. These cases were the main subject-matter of the old *action for money paid* and are commonly termed cases of 'recoupment' nowadays. A distinct group of cases concern persons with a shared liability, for example where multiple tortfeasors all to some extent caused the injured party's losses. Various specific instances of contribution claims were known to the common law. Most instances are now governed by statute (the Civil Liability (Contribution) Act 1978), which gives the courts the power to apportion responsibility amongst persons who are jointly liable.

A: *Recoupment*

See Burrows, *Restitution*, 207–19 and Birks, *Introduction*, 185–9.

Exall v *Partridge*
(1799) 8 TR 308; 101 ER 1405 (KB)

Action for money paid

Exall left his carriage upon the premises of Partridge, a coach-maker (presumably for repairs to be done). The carriage was lawfully seized by Partridge's landlord as distress (a landlord's self-help remedy) for rent arrears. In order to get his carriage back, Exall paid the arrears to the landlord. Exall now claimed that sum from Partridge and his two fellow tenants who had assigned their interest in the premises to Partridge.

LORD KENYON CJ: Some propositions have been stated, on the part of the plaintiff, to which I cannot assent. It has been said, that where one person is benefited by the payment of money by another, the law raises an assumpsit against the former; but that I deny: if that were so, and I owed a sum of money to a friend, and an enemy chose to pay that debt, the latter might convert himself into my debtor, nolens volens. Another proposition was, that the assignment from two of the defendants to the third, was not evidence against the plaintiff, because he was no party to it, that also I deny: it surely was evidence to shew in what relation the parties stood to this estate. I admit that where one person is surety for another, and compellable to pay the whole debt, and he is called upon to pay, it is money paid to the use of the principal debtor, and may be recovered in an action against him for money paid, even though the surety did not pay the debt by the desire of the principal: but none of those points affect the present question. As the plaintiff put his goods on the premises, knowing the interests of the defendants, and thereby placed himself in a situation where he was liable to pay this money, without the concurrence of two of the defendants, I thought at the trial that it was money paid to the use of the other defendants only; but on that point I have since doubted; and I rather think that the opinion I gave at the trial was not well founded.

GROSE J: The question is, whether the payment made by the plaintiff, under these circumstances, were such an one from which the law will imply a promise by the three defendants to repay? I think it was. All the three defendants were originally liable to the landlord for the rent: there was an express covenant by all, from which neither of them was released. One of the defendants only being in the occupation of these premises, the plaintiff put his goods there, which the landlord distrained for rent, as he had a right to do; then, for the purpose of getting back his goods, he paid the rent to the landlord, which all the three defendants were bound to pay. The plaintiff could not have relieved himself from the distress without paying the rent: it was not therefore a voluntary, but a compulsory payment. Under these circumstances, the law implies a promise by the three defendants to repay the plaintiff; and, on this short ground, I am of opinion that the action may be maintained.

LAWRENCE J: One of the propositions stated by the plaintiff's counsel certainly cannot be supported, that whoever is benefited by a payment made by another, is liable to an action of assumpsit by that other; for one person cannot, by a voluntary payment, raise an assumpsit against another: but here was a distress for rent, due from the three defendants; the notice of distress expressed the rent to be due from them all; the money was paid by the plaintiff in satisfaction of a demand on all, and it was paid by compulsion; therefore I am of opinion that this action may be maintained against the three defendants. The justice of the case indeed is, that the one who must ultimately pay this money, should alone be answerable here: but as all the three defendants were liable to the landlord for the rent in the first instance, and as by this payment made by the plaintiff, all the three were released from the demand of the rent, I think that this action may be supported against all of them.

Note

See also *Johnson* v *Royal Mail Steam Packet Co.* (1867) LR 3 CP 38, where the mortgagees of two ships who had paid the crews' past wages which were due from the defendants, because the crews had exercised their martime lien over the vessels to secure their claims, were entitled to reimbursement from the defendants who were primarily liable for the wages, on the ground of compulsion of law in an *action for money paid.* Willes J stated that a claim of this nature was 'independent of contract'.

Moule v *Garrett*
(1872) LR 7 Ex 101 (Exchequer Chamber)

The plaintiff was the lessee of premises under a lease containing a covenant to repair. He assigned the lease to Bartley, who in turn assigned the lease to the defendants. Both assignments contained express covenants to indemnify the immediate assignor against any subsequent breaches of the repairing covenant. The landlord sued and recovered £75 for breach of the repairing covenant from the plaintiff in respect of dilapidations which occurred while the defendants were in possession. The plaintiff sought recoupment from the defendants.

COCKBURN CJ: I am of opinion that the judgment of the Court of Exchequer is right, and that it must be affirmed. The defendants are the ultimate assignees of a lease, and the plaintiff, who is suing them for indemnity against the consequence of a breach of a covenant contained in that lease, is the original lessee. There is no doubt that the breach of covenant is one in respect of which the defendants, as such assignees, are liable to the lessor, and that they have acquired by virtue of mesne assignments the same estate which the plaintiff originally took. And I think that taking this estate from the assignee of the plaintiff, their own immediate assignor, they must be taken to have acquired it, subject to the discharge of all the liabilities which the possession of that estate imposed on them under the terms of the original lease, not merely as regards the immediate assignor, but as regards the original lessee.

Another ground on which the judgment below may be upheld, and, as I think, a preferable one, is that, the premises which are the subject of the lease being in the possession of the defendants as ultimate assignees, they were the parties whose duty it was to perform the covenants which were to be performed upon and in respect of those premises. It was their immediate duty to keep in repair, and by their default the lessee, though he had parted with the estate, became liable to make good to the lessor the conditions of the lease. The damage therefore arises through their default, and the general proposition applicable to such a case as the present is, that where one person is compelled to pay damages by the legal default of another, he is entitled to recover from the person by whose default the damage was occasioned the sum so paid. This doctrine, as applicable to cases like the present, is well stated by Mr Leake in his work on Contracts, p. 41:

> Where the plaintiff has been compelled by law to pay, or, being compellable by law, has paid money which the defendant was ultimately liable to pay, so that the latter obtains the benefit of the payment by the discharge of his liability; under such circumstances the defendant is held indebted to the plaintiff in the amount.

Whether the liability is put on the ground of an implied contract, or of an obligation imposed by law, is a matter of indifference: it is such a duty as the law will enforce. The lessee has been compelled to make good an omission to repair, which has arisen entirely from the default of the defendants, and the defendants are therefore liable to reimburse him.

WILLES J: I am of the same opinion, on the ground that where a party is liable at law by immediate privity of contract which contract also confers a benefit, and the obligation of the contract is common to him and to the defendant, but the whole benefit of the contract is taken by the defendant; the former is entitled to be indemnified by the latter in respect of the performance of the obligation.

Note

If there had only been one assignment of the lease to Bartley and the dilapidations had occurred during his possession, reimbursement of Moule could be explained on ordinary contractual principles. Where there are subsequent assignments, however, a restitutionary analysis is required because of the doctrine of privity of contract. For a recent application of the principle see *Re Healing Research Trustee Co. Ltd* [1992] 2 All ER 481, where Harman J affirmed that *Moule* v *Garrett* liability is 'independent of contract'.

Bonner* v *Tottenham and Edmonton Permanent Investment Building Society

[1899] 1 QB 161 (CA)

Action for money paid

Moore, the owner of two houses in North London, leased them to the plaintiffs for 99 years at £20 rent per year. Some years later the plaintiffs assigned the remainder of the lease to Price, who covenanted to pay the rent and indemnify the plaintiffs. Price in turn mortgaged his interest in the premises to the defendant building society by way of a sub-lease. The defendants covenanted with Price that if they should enter into possession and receive the rents and profits, they would pay the rent due under the original lease. Price became bankrupt, the building society entered into possession and received the rents and profits, but did not pay the rent due to Moore. Moore recovered the rent from the plaintiffs under their original covenant, therefore the plaintiffs sought to recover those sums from the building society.

A.L. SMITH LJ: . . .It is clear that no contract or privity of estate exists between the plaintiffs and the defendants, or between the original lessor, Moore, and the defendants; and, unless there be circumstances from which a request to pay can be implied, or, in other words, a contract can be implied between the defendants and the plaintiffs that the defendants would indemnify the plaintiffs if they paid to their landlord the rent accruing whilst they, the defendants, were in possession, there are no circumstances which will support an action by the plaintiffs against the defendants to recover the amount so paid. It is true that Moore could sue the plaintiffs, his lessees, upon their covenant with him in the lease. It is also true that the plaintiffs, the lessees, could sue their assignee, Price, upon his covenant with them. It is also true that Price could sue the defendants, his underlessees, upon their covenant with him. But how can the plaintiffs sue the defendants? I omit Price's trustee in bankruptcy, for he, in my opinion, does not affect this case. It is said that the case of *Moule* v *Garrett* LR 5 Ex 132; 7 Ex 101 shews that the plaintiffs can sue the defendants to recover what they have been compelled to pay to their lessor, and that this case falls within the principle of that case. Now what was the case of *Moule* v *Garrett*? It was a case in which there had been two assignments of the term, the defendants being the second assignees thereof. First of all there was, as here, a lease from a lessor to the lessee, Moule, the plaintiff in the action, containing the usual covenants by a lessee. Moule afterwards assigned the term to Bartley, who afterwards assigned the term to the defendants, Garrett & Co., who then committed breaches of covenants in the lease. Moule, having been compelled under his covenant with his lessor to pay to him damages for these breaches committed by the defendants, Garrett & Co., the assignees of Bartley, sued Garrett & Co, to recover the amount so paid by him, Moule, to his lessor. It was held that, inasmuch as both the plaintiff and the defendants were compellable to pay to the original lessor the damages accruing to him for the breaches of covenant by the defendants whilst assignees of the term, the former by reason of his covenant with the original lessor and the latter by reason of their being assignees of the term and having committed the breaches whilst assignees, and inasmuch as the plaintiff had been compelled to pay damages to his lessor for these breaches of covenant by the defendants, for which the defendants were also compellable under privity of estate to pay to the lessor, they, the defendants, were liable to indemnify the plaintiff in respect of these payments of which the defendants had had the benefit. For, as Willes J put it in *Roberts* v *Crowe* (1872) LR 7 CP 629, at p. 637, the lessee is liable for breaches of covenant committed by the assignee, but being only secondarily liable he has his remedy over against the person primarily liable—that is, the assignee. The ratio decidendi of *Moule* v *Garrett* is this: If A is compellable to pay B damages which C is also compellable to pay B, then A, having been compelled to pay B, can maintain an action against C for money so paid, for the circumstances raise an implied request by C to A to make such payment in his ease. In other words, A can call upon C to indemnify him. See the notes to *Lampleigh* v *Brathwait* 1 Sm LC 9th ed. 151, p. 160, and cases there cited. To raise this implied request, both A and C must, in my judgment, be compellable to pay B; otherwise, as it seems to me, the payment by A to B so far as regards C is a voluntary payment, which raises no implication of a request by C to A to pay. If Cockburn CJ, in his alternative reason in *Moule* v *Garrett* LR 7 Ex 101 for holding the defendants liable meant this by the expression 'by the legal default of another,' I agree; but, if it means by a default for which they were not compellable to pay in that case to the original lessor, I do not agree, and one of the other learned judges who decided that case adopted what Cockburn CJ then said, and indeed, Willes J expressly points out that the obligation of the contract must be common to the plaintiff and the defendant, and that the whole benefit was taken by the defendants. In the present case the defendants are underlessees of an assignee of the term, and are not liable at all to the original lessor for rent whenever it accrued, there being between them and the original lessor neither contract nor privity of estate, and there is no suggestion that there were goods upon the demised premises available for distress other than the goods of the mortgagor Price, even if this would have sufficed to maintain the action, about which I say nothing, for it is not before me. The above, in my judgment, is what was decided in *Moule* v *Garrett,* and the present case, as it appears to me, is an attempt to stretch the decision of that case, and to say that the principle therein laid down applies equally to the case of an underlessee of an assignee who is not compellable to pay the original lessor as to the case of an assignee who is compellable to pay the original lessor. It will be seen upon looking at the case of *Penley* v *Watts* 7 M & W 601, at p. 608 that Parke B deals with this exact point. He says: 'The lessee and his assignee are liable to precisely the same extent, and the assignee is a surety for the lessee, but that is not the case in a sub-lease.' And, again in *Moule* v *Garrett* LR 7 Ex 101, at p. 102, in the Exchequer Chamber, when it was suggested that the case of an underlessee of an assignee and an assignee of an assignee were the same, Blackburn J said: 'No, because the underlessee has never come under any obligation to the lessor, but here the defendant, by taking the same estate which the plaintiff had, has become liable to the same obligation,' and this is the foundation of the judgment of the Court of Exchequer delivered by Channell B, and the ground upon which the judgment was upheld in the Exchequer Chamber. The fact that in this case the defendants covenanted with Price, the assignee, that if they, the defendants, became mortgagees in possession they would pay the rent, gives Price a remedy against them subject to any set-off which may exist between him and them and does not give the present plaintiffs a right of action against them. . . .

RIGBY LJ: The only question in this case is as to the liability of the defendants, who are mortgagees by sub-lease of an assignee of a lease originally granted to the plaintiffs, to indemnify the plaintiffs in respect of rent recovered by the lessor against them on their covenant in the lease. The mortgagees entered into possession of the leasehold property by virtue of their sub-term in 1890, and the assignee became bankrupt in 1891.

Now prima facie a sub-lessee of a lessee or assignee of a term comes under no liability to the original lessor either for payment of rent or performance of covenants in the original lease. This is true whether the sub-lease be by way of sale or by way of mortgage, and entry into possession of the sub-term does not make the sub-lessee liable to the lessor. But it is said that the present case is distinguishable from the ordinary case by the fact that the mortgagees expressly covenanted with their mortgagor (assignee of the lease) that, if they entered into possession, they would out of the rents and profits received by them (among other things) pay the rent, and that they have been, as they have, in possession during the whole time during which the rents recovered by the lessor against the plaintiffs, original lessees, have been accruing. The argument is that they are thus placed in the position of the defendants in *Moule* v *Garrett* LR 5 Ex 132; 7 Ex 101, who were held liable to repay to the plaintiff money which the latter had been compelled to pay to the original lessors for breach of covenant in the original lease. In that case the plaintiff, like the plaintiffs here, was an original lessee who had assigned the term before the breach on which he was sued; but the defendants were not, like the defendants here, holders of a sub-term, but were the actual holders at the time of the breach of puisne assignment of the whole of the original term, and in that capacity liable by privity of estate to the original lessors for the very damages which had been recovered by them against the original lessee, who in the action was seeking to recover them over. Both plaintiff and defendants were under a direct obligation to pay the rent to the lessors; but the defendants reaped all the benefit of the payment. It was treated as plain that, as between the plaintiff and defendants, the liability of the defendants to the original lessors by privity of estate was in the nature of a primary liability, that of the plaintiff by privity of contract being secondary; and on this ground the plaintiff was held entitled to recover over against the defendants, as though he were in a manner surety for them for payment of their debt. Here there is no privity either of estate or contract between the defendants and either the original lessor or the plaintiffs in this action, so that there can be nothing analogous to the relation of principal and surety between them. The reasoning in *Moule* v *Garrett*, therefore, has no application.

If the assignee had been solvent, the plaintiffs would have had a sufficient remedy in recourse to him. The fact of his having become bankrupt can give no right of action against the defendants on the principle of *Moule* v *Garrett* which did not otherwise exist. . . .

Edmunds v *Wallingford*
(1885) 14 QBD 811 (CA)

Action for money paid

A father bought an ironmongery business in his own name for his two sons. However, he took the lease of the premises and the bank account of the business in his own name, and took a regular interest in the conduct of the business. A judgment creditor of the father seized some stock of the business as security for its debt. The sons' claim for return of the goods against the sheriff was barred, and the goods were sold realising £1,300. Subsequently the sons became bankrupt. The plaintiff, their trustee-in-bankruptcy, entered into an agreement with the father, whereby the latter promised in consideration of the seizure of the stock to pay £300 per year to the trustee until he had paid enough to satisfy the sons' creditors. The trustee sought to enforce the agreement, or in the alternative to recover for money paid. Huddleston B gave judgment for £1,200. The father appealed. *Held*: even if the promise was unenforceable, the claim succeeded because the father's conduct had led to the seizure, the goods of the sons had been lawfully taken and therefore the father was bound to indemnify the sons.

LINDLEY LJ: . . . The first question is the liability incurred by the defendant to his sons by reason of the seizure of what he has deliberately asserted to be their goods for his debt. That as between the father and the sons, the goods were theirs, we consider established by the father's own statements. Speaking generally, and excluding exceptional cases, where a person's goods are lawfully seized for another's debt, the owner of the goods is entitled to redeem them and to be reimbursed by the debtor against the money paid to redeem them, and in the event of the goods being sold to satisfy the debt, the owner is entitled to recover the value of them from the debtor. The authorities supporting this general proposition will be found collected in the notes to *Lampleigh* v *Brathwait* 1 Sm LC 151 and *Dering* v *Winchelsea* 1 W & T (LC) 106. As instances illustrating its application, reference may be made to the case of a person whose goods are lawfully distrained for rent due from some one else, as in *Exall* v *Partridge* 8 TR 308; to the case of a surety paying the debt of his principal; to the case where the whole of a joint debt is paid by one only of the joint debtors; to the case where the joint property of a firm is seized for the separate debt of one of the partners. The right to indemnity or contribution in these cases exists, although there may be no agreement to indemnify or contribute, and although there may be, in that sense, no privity between the plaintiff and the defendant: see *Johnson* v *Royal Mail Steam Packet Co.* Law Rep 3 CP 38. But it is obvious that the right may be excluded by contract as well as by other circumstances. . . .

Another exception to the general rule has been held to exist, where the owner of the goods has left them for his own convenience, where they could be lawfully seized for the debt of the person from whom he seeks indemnity: *England* v *Marsden* Law Rep 1 CP 529. The plaintiff in that case seized the defendant's goods under a bill of sale, but did not remove them from the defendant's house. The plaintiff left them there for his own convenience, and they were afterwards distrained by the defendant's landlord. The plaintiff paid the rent distrained for, and brought an action to recover the money from the defendant. The Court, however, held that the action would not lie as the plaintiff might have removed his goods before, and could not under the circumstances be considered as having been compelled to pay the rent. This appears to us a very questionable decision. The evidence did not show that the plaintiff's goods were left in the defendant's house against his consent; and although it is true that the plaintiff only had himself to blame for exposing his goods to seizure, we fail to see how he thereby prejudiced the defendant, or why, having paid the defendant's debt in order to redeem his own goods from lawful seizure, the plaintiff was not entitled to be reimbursed by the defendant. This decision has been questioned before by Thesiger, LJ, in 15 Ch D 417, and by the late Vaughan Williams, J., in the notes to the last edition of Wms. Saunders, vol. 1, p. 361, and we think the decision ought not to be followed. Be the case of *England* v *Marsden*, however, right or wrong, it is distinguishable in its facts from the case now before us.

In order to bring the present case within the general principle alluded to above, it is necessary that the goods seized shall have been lawfully seized; and it was contended before us that the sons' goods were in this case wrongfully seized, and that the defendant, therefore, was not bound to indemnify them. But when it is said that the goods must be lawfully seized, all that is meant is that as between the owner of the goods and the person seizing them, the latter shall have been entitled to take them. It is plain that the principle has no application, except where the owner of the goods is in a position to say to the debtor that the seizure ought not to have taken place; it is because as between them the wrong goods have been seized that any question arises. Now, in this case it has been decided between the owners of the goods seized (i.e., the sons), and the sheriff seizing them, that the goods were rightfully seized; and although the defendant is not estopped by this decision, and is at liberty, if he can, to shew that the seizure was one which the sheriff was not justified in making, he has not done so. Indeed, the defendant's connection with his sons' business was such as to justify the inference that the sheriff had a right to seize the goods for the defendant's debt, and if, in truth, any mistake was made by the sheriff, the defendant had only himself to thank for it. His own conduct led to the seizure and although he did not in fact request it to be made, he brought the seizure about, and has wholly failed to show that the seizure was wrongful on the part of the sheriff.

The case, therefore, stands thus: goods which the defendant has admitted in writing to be his sons', have, owing to his conduct, been legally taken in execution for his debt, and the proceeds of sale have been impounded as a security for what is due from him to the execution creditors. The defendant, therefore, was liable to repay to his sons the amount realized by the sale of the goods. This liability the plaintiff, as the sons' trustee in bankruptcy, was in a position to enforce, and he has never released it or agreed so to do except upon payment of £1200. The plaintiff is in a position now to enforce that liability, if the defendant succeeds in shewing that his express promise to pay £1200 is not legally binding upon him. The plaintiff is content to take the

£1200 expressly promised to be paid instead of insisting on his right to the £1300; and Huddleston, B, has properly given the plaintiff judgment accordingly. . . .

Gebhardt v Saunders
[1892] 2 QB 452 (QBD)

Action for money paid

The plaintiff was a tenant of a dwelling in which a public nuisance arose by reason of water and sewage collecting in the cellar due to a blockage in the drains. It was impossible to tell whether the nuisance was caused by a structural defect (the defendant landlord's responsibility), or by improper use by the tenant. The relevant sanitary authority served notice under s. 4(1) of the Public Health (London) Act 1891, directed to the owner or occupier requiring the nuisance to be abated. The plaintiff did the necessary work and it was then discovered that the nuisance was caused by a structural defect. The plaintiff therefore sought reimbursement from his landlord.

DAY J: . . . The action is brought by the occupier of a house to recover from the defendants, who are the owners and landlords, the costs necessarily incurred by him in abating a nuisance caused by a structural defect in the drains, and the plaintiff was nonsuited by the learned judge by reason of a defect in the service of notices under the Act. I think that that nonsuit was wrong, and that the plaintiff may recover as of right without proof of the matters relied on on behalf of the defendants. There can be no doubt that in consequence of the defective construction of the drains a serious nuisance did exist in the plaintiff's house, to which the plaintiff very properly called the attention of the sanitary authority; the officer of the authority went to the house and satisfied himself of the existence of a nuisance requiring immediate abatement. Being unable to determine at the time whether the nuisance arose from defective construction of the drains or from their mismanagement by the plaintiff, the officer took a sound view of the position; he saw that there was an accumulation of sewage in the lower part of the house dangerous to health and possibly to life, and he immediately served a notice on the premises requiring the owner or occupier (he not being then in a position to say whether the owner or the occupier might subsequently turn out to be responsible) to forthwith abate the nuisance arising from the defect in or stoppage of the drain. In that notice he does not define whether the nuisance is caused by the drain being defective or by its being stopped; but it was due to one of the two. The plaintiff had already very properly given notice of the defective state of the drain to the defendants, who however, did nothing; common sense and the necessity of the case made it necessary for something to be done forthwith, and as either the plaintiff or the defendants was bound to do that something the plaintiff proceeded to do it; had he not done so he would have been liable under s. 4, sub-s. 4, of the Act of 1891 to a penalty of 10*l*. He then brings this action to recover the expenses from the defendants.

The difficulty in the present case is no greater than that which one ordinarily expects to find in the construction of a modern statute. The gist of the enactment is this: where there is a nuisance injurious to life or health measures are to be taken to secure its speedy abatement; the expenses of abating the nuisance are cast on the person who caused it by his acts or defaults. This is a reasonable scheme; is it carried out by the different sections of the statute? In my opinion, whatever criticisms may be passed upon their wording, the sections do contain such a provision. By s. 4, sub-s. 1. a notice is to be served on the occupier or owner, and, by sub-s. 4, disobedience to such notice entails a fine of 10*l.* a day. It is urged on behalf of the defendants that if the occupier does the work which the owner ought to have done, and the owner has not been served at his place of abode with a notice under sub-s. 3 requiring him to abate the nuisance, the occupier must do it at his own cost. I have rarely heard a proposition so unreasonable. The gist of s. 11 is that, if the occupier does the work in order to abate a nuisance for which the owner is responsible, he may recover from the latter the expenses incurred in doing it. It is true that the section provides in terms only for the expenses incurred in carrying 'the order' into effect, and that one would have expected it to have said 'the notice or the order'; but the word 'order' must clearly be taken to include 'notice,' for disobedience to the notice entails a penalty; the section, therefore, applies to the expenses incurred in carrying out the notice or order in the sense of doing the work. If two people are required to do certain work under a penalty in case of disobedience, and one does the work, and it turns out afterwards that the other ought to have done it, the expenses are properly money paid at the request of the person who was primarily liable, but who neglected to do the work. There are no merits in this defence; and as the technical points upon which the defence was based have failed, judgment must be entered for the plaintiff.

CHARLES J: . . . The first question is, Was the plaintiff legally compellable to do this work? I think he was. It seems that there was in the plaintiff's house a drainage defect which, being latent, was one of which the sanitary authority may reasonably be held to be unable to find the author; they were, therefore, warranted in serving notice under s. 4, sub-s. 1, on the occupier or owner to abate the nuisance. Such a notice was served upon the plaintiff's premises, requiring the abatement of the nuisance forthwith. Did that notice impose upon the plaintiff the legal liability to obey it. Having regard to the provisions of sub-s. 4, for the imposition of a penalty for default in compliance, I am clearly of opinion that it did. It is contended, however, that the plaintiff was not legally liable to do the work, because in the result it turned out that the defects were structural. Now, there is no doubt that under the proviso in s. 4, sub-s. 3, where the defects are structural, notice is to be served on the owner; it turned out in the present case that they were structural; hence the defendants' contention. It is impossible, having regard to the language of sub-s. 1, to assent to this argument; looking at that sub-section it seems clear that, if on inspection the cause of the nuisance cannot be found, it is right to serve the notice on the occupier. The first question must, therefore, be answered in the affirmative.

The second question is whether the defendants were legally compellable to do the work. The jury found that the nuisance was caused by a structural defect; the moment that that defect was discovered the defendants were the proper persons to do the work, and were bound to do it. I think, therefore, that it having been proved that a nuisance existed, and that it arose from a structural defect in the drain, the defendants were legally compellable to set it right. In my opinion the ordinary principle of law is applicable to this case apart from the statute, the principle applicable to cases where one man has been legally compelled to expend money on what another man ought to have done, and, without having recourse to s. 11, the plaintiff is entitled to recover from the defendants as having been legally compelled to incur expense in abating a nuisance which the defendants themselves ought to have abated. As to the construction of s. 11, I agree with my brother Day. It is a difficult section to construe; but I think that a reasonable construction to place upon it is that where no order for the abatement of a nuisance is actually made, but the nuisance is abated in obedience to a notice from the sanitary authority, the expenses of abatement must be borne by the person causing the nuisance. Beyond all doubt the owners are here the persons responsible for the existence of this nuisance, and ought to pay for its abatement. It is contended that the section only applies where a nuisance order has been obtained; but I feel no difficulty in reading it otherwise so as to apply it to the expenses of serving a notice and carrying the notice into effect. In a sense, indeed, the notice is an order, for it is a requirement that certain things shall be done. I think, therefore, that both apart from and in accordance with s. 11, the plaintiff has proved his case.

Question

What was the ground for restitution in this case? (See Birks, *Introduction*, 191.)

Brook's Wharf and Bull Wharf Ltd v *Goodman Brothers*
[1937] 1 KB 534 (CA)

Action for money paid

The defendant furriers imported from Russia a consignment of squirrel skins. Of the consignment, ten packages were stored in the plaintiffs' warehouse from where they were stolen but not due to any negligence on the part of the plaintiffs. The plaintiffs as bonded warehousemen were compelled by s. 85 of the Customs Consolidation Act 1876 to pay import duties on those packages out of their own pocket. The plaintiffs claimed to be reimbursed the £824 they had been compelled to pay.

LORD WRIGHT MR: . . .Under these circumstances the plaintiffs claim that they are entitled to recover from the defendants the amount which they have paid to the Customs in respect of duties due on the defendants' goods. They make their claim as for money paid to the defendants' use on the principle stated in Leake on Contracts. The passage in question is quoted in the Exchequer Chamber by Cockburn CJ in *Moule* v *Garrett* LR 7 Ex 101, 104 and is in these terms: 'Where the plaintiff has been compelled by law to pay, or, being compellable by law, has paid money which the defendant was ultimately liable to pay, so that the latter obtains the benefit of the payment by the discharge of his liability; under such circumstances the defendant is held indebted to the plaintiff in the amount.' This passage remains, with a slight verbal alteration, in the eighth edition of Leake on Contracts at p. 46.

The principle has been applied in a great variety of circumstances. Its application does not depend on privity of contract. Thus in *Moule* v *Garrett*, which I have just cited, it was held that the original lessee who had been compelled to pay for breach of a repairing covenant was entitled to recover the amount he had so paid from a subsequent assignee of the lease, nothwithstanding that there had been intermediate assignees. In that case the liability of the lessee depended on the terms of his covenant, but the breach of covenant was due to the default of the assignee, and the payment by the lessee under legal compulsion relieved the assignee of his liability.

That class of case was discussed by Vaughan Williams LJ in *Bonner* v *Tottenham and Edmonton Permanent Investment Building Society* [1899] 1 QB 161, where *Moule* v

Garrett was distinguished. The essence of the rule is that there is a liability for the same debt resting on the plaintiff and the defendant and the plaintiff has been legally compelled to pay, but the defendant gets the benefit of the payment, because his debt is discharged either entirely or pro tanto, whereas the defendant is primarily liable to pay as between himself and the plaintiff. The case is analogous to that of a payment by a surety which has the effect of discharging the principal's debt and which, therefore, gives a right of indemnity against the principal.

I need not refer to more than two of the numerous cases in which this principle has been applied. In *Pownal* v *Ferrand* 6 B & C 439, an endorser of a bill had been compelled on default by the acceptor to make a payment on account to the holder. He sued the acceptor for the money so paid as money paid to his use. The money so paid was a part only of the amount of the bill. He was held entitled to recover. Lord Tenterden CJ said: 'I am of opinion that he is entitled to recover upon the general principle, that one man, who is compelled to pay money which another is bound by law to pay, is entitled to be reimbursed by the latter.' As an instance of money payable under a statute I may refer to *Dawson* v *Linton* (1822) 5 B & Ald 521, 523, where a tax was due from the landlord, but there was power to enforce payment by distress, if necessary, from the tenant. Abbott CJ said: 'It is clear that this tax must ultimately fall on the landlord, and that the plaintiff has paid his money in discharge of it; he has therefore a right to call upon the landlord to repay it to him.'

These statements of the principle do not put the obligation on any ground of implied contract or of constructive or notional contract. The obligation is imposed by the Court simply under the circumstances of the case and on what the Court decides is just and reasonable, having regard to the relationship of the parties. It is a debt or obligation constituted by the act of the law, apart from any consent or intention of the parties or any privity of contract.

It is true that in the present case there was a contract of bailment between the plaintiffs and the defendants, but there is no suggestion that the obligation in question had ever been contemplated as between them or that they had ever thought about it. The Court cannot say what they would have agreed if they had considered the matter when the goods were warehoused. All the Court can say is what they ought as just and reasonable men to have decided as between themselves. The defendants would be unjustly benefited at the cost of the plaintiffs if the latter, who had received no extra consideration and made no express bargain, should be left out of pocket by having to discharge what was the defendants' debt.

I agree with the learned judge in holding that this principle applies to the present case. As I have explained, the duties were due from the importer. There is nothing in the machinery of the Customs Act which had removed this liability from him when the warehousemen paid the duties, as they were compelled to do under s. 85. The payment relieved the importer of his obligation. The plaintiffs were no doubt liable to pay the Customs, but, as between themselves and the defendants, the primary liability rested on the defendants. The liability of the plaintiffs as warehousemen was analogous to that of a surety. It was imposed in order to facilitate the collection of duties in a case like the present, where there might always be a question as to who stood in the position of importer. The defendants as actual importers have obtained the benefit of the payment made by the plaintiffs and they are thus discharged from the duties which otherwise would have been payable by them. It may also be noted that the goods which were stolen were the defendants' goods and the property remained in them after the theft. If the goods had been recovered, the defendants could have claimed them as their own and would have been free to apply them for home use without further payment of duty. . . .

Owen v *Tate*
[1976] QB 402 (CA)

In 1965, Elizabeth and John Tate obtained a loan from Lloyds Bank which was secured by a legal mortgage upon Miss Lightfoot's property. In 1969, Miss Lightfoot, who was concerned that her deeds were being held by the bank, consulted Mr Owen, her former employer, who offered to help her. Owen therefore deposited £350 with the bank and signed a guarantee in respect of moneys owed by the Tates to the bank up to £350. Owen did not consult the Tates and they did not ask him to do this. Indeed, at first the Tates protested when they heard that the mortgage over Miss Lightfoot's property was to be released. In 1970, the bank applied the £350 deposited with them in support of the guarantee. Owen sought reimbursement from the Tates.

SCARMAN LJ: . . . A right of indemnity is a right of restitution. It can arise, as the cases reveal, notwithstanding the absence of any consensual basis. For instance, in *Moule* v *Garrett* (1872) LR 7 Ex 101 an original lessee, who was of course in privity of contract with his lessor, was compelled to pay for a breach of a repairing covenant by a subsequent assignee. He was held to be entitled to an indemnity notwithstanding the absence of any privity of contract between him and the subsequent assignee.

In the two cases to which I have already referred, *Exall* v *Partridge*, 8 Term Rep 308 and *England* v *Marsden*, LR 1 CP 529 the courts were faced with the owner of goods who had deposited them on the land of another, and that other had failed to pay either rates or rent, with the result that a distraint was levied, and the owner in order to release his goods paid their value to the distrainer. In *Exall* v *Partridge* Lord Kenyon CJ was at pains to discover in the circumstances an implied request or authority from the mere fact that the goods were on the land with the consent of the occupier. In *England* v *Marsden* no such consent was spelt out by implication by the court. But in *Edmunds* v *Wallingford*, 14 QBD 811 Lindley LJ said it should have been. We can, therefore, take that class of case as an illustration of where the law will grant a right of indemnity notwithstanding the absence really of any consensual basis. In the *Brook's Wharf* case [[1937] 1 KB 534] a warehouseman who paid import duties for which his customer—the owner of the goods—was primarily liable, and did so because of an obligation imposed by statute and without any prior request from the owner of the goods, was also held to be entitled to an indemnity.

These cases, to my mind, amply support the proposition that a broad approach is needed to the question whether in circumstances such as these a right of indemnity arises, and that broad approach requires the court to look at all the circumstances of the case. It follows that the way in which the obligation came to be assumed is a relevant circumstance. If, for instance, the plaintiff has conferred a benefit upon the defendant behind his back in circumstances in which the beneficiary has no option but to accept the benefit, it is highly likely that the courts will say that there is no right of indemnity or reimbursement. But (to take the other extreme) if the plaintiff has made a payment in a situation not of his own choosing, but where the law imposes an obligation upon him to make the payment on behalf of the principal debtor, then clearly the right of indemnity does arise. Not every case will be so clear-cut: the fundamental question is whether in the circumstances it was reasonably necessary in the interests of the volunteer or the person for whom the payment was made, or both, that the payment should be made—whether in the circumstances it was 'just and reasonable' that a right of reimbursement should arise. . . .

Adopting this broad approach, I now come to consider in more detail than I have yet done the two phases of the transaction of guarantee which appear to me to be of critical importance. The first phase consists of the circumstances in which the plaintiff entered into the guarantee; the second phase consists of the circumstances in which the plaintiff made the payment.

It is enough to refer to the judge's findings of fact to know that the plaintiff assumed the obligation of a guarantor behind the back of the defendants, against their will, and despite their protest. At that moment he was interested, as the judge has found, not to confer a benefit upon the defendants; he was interested to confer a benefit upon Miss Lightfoot. Using the language of the old common law, I would say that the plaintiff was as absolute a volunteer as one could conceivably imagine anyone to be when assuming an obligation for the debt of another.

What of the second phase? Mr Unwin [counsel for Mr Owen], rightly I think, relied strongly on two letters; and Mr Stephenson, also rightly, I think, invited us to consider a third. I now turn to those letters. The first letter on which Mr Unwin relied was a letter of July 1, 1970, addressed by the defendants' solicitors to the bank, who at the time held not only the plaintiff's signed guarantee, but the deposit of £350. Mr Unwin invited the court to read that letter as one in which the defendants were pressing the bank to clear their overdraft by recourse to the money deposited by the plaintiff: and there is no doubt that that is exactly what the defendants at that moment were doing. On November 10 they once more invited the bank to clear their overdraft by recourse to the plaintiff. Mr Unwin submits that if one looks at those two letters, and at the whole history of the case, once reaches this situation: that by the time those letters were written the defendants were well aware, although they had not known it at first, that the plaintiff had guaranteed their account up to the sum of £350 and had deposited this sum with the bank. The defendants' case, of course, is that this was an uncovenanted benefit, if benefit it was, and the fact that the plaintiff had conferred this benefit imposed upon them no duty to indemnify him when he made the payment. But, says Mr Unwin, if that is their position, they had a perfectly good opportunity in 1970 of telling the bank that on no account was it to have recourse to the plaintiff; that the plaintiff had interfered without their consent in their affairs, and that they proposed to deal with the matter of their overdraft without the support of the plaintiff's guarantee. No doubt had they either paid off the overdraft or made some suitable arrangements for securing it, the bank would not have had recourse to the plaintiff. But they chose at that moment to encourage the bank to have recourse to the plaintiff.

Mr Unwin has, as one might expect, put his point in a number of different verbal ways: authority, ratification, adoption—all terms really borrowed from different transactions and different legal situations. But he is entitled to make the point under the general principle to which I have referred; he is entitled to rely on the circumstances of payment as part of the total circumstances of the case and to use them to support an argument that it would in all the circumstances be just and reasonable for the plaintiff to have his right of indemnity. But these letters have to be looked at in all the circumstances; and the circumstances, of course, include the earlier history. We learn from the third letter which was introduced before us by Mr Stephenson [counsel for the Tates], and to which I need not refer in terms, something of the earlier history. When the defendants learnt that the bank were proposing to release Miss Lightfoot's deeds because they had accepted a guarantee and a cash deposit, the defendants strongly objected. The bank, no doubt quite properly, did not tell the defendants that the guarantor was the plaintiff—who was, of course, a stranger to the Lightfoot/Tate transaction. When the Tates protested strongly, the bank replied that they were, as no doubt they were, entitled to disregard the protest, and were going to release, as in fact they did release, to Miss Lightfoot the deeds and rely upon the guarantee and deposit. At the time there was nothing to suggest to the defendants who the guarantor was, or that he was a stranger to the previous transaction. That being the case, must one read the subsequent letters to the bank to which I have referred as an adoption by the defendants of a benefit conferred upon them by the plaintiff? They never wished to lose the security of Miss Lightfoot's deeds. They lost it through circumstances outside their control and notwithstanding their protest. When the bank decided to call in the debt the defendants no longer had the security for the overdraft which was acceptable to them: they had to put up with a security which without their consent or authority had been substituted by the plaintiff for that which was, or had been, acceptable to them and agreed by them. I do not criticise the defendants, nor do I think they can be reasonably criticised, for making the best of the situation in which they then found themselves, a situation which they did not desire, and one which I doubt ever appeared to them as beneficial.

Looking, therefore, at the circumstances as a whole, and giving weight to both phases of the transaction, I come to the conclusion that the plaintiff has failed to make out a case that it would be just and reasonable in the circumstances to grant him a right to reimbursement. Initially he was a volunteer; he has, as I understand the findings of fact of the judge and as I read the documents in the case, established no facts, either initially when he assumed the obligation, or later when he was called upon to make the payment, such as to show that it was just and reasonable that he should have a right of indemnity. I think, therefore, that on the facts as found this appeal fails.

In my judgment, the true principle of the matter can be stated very shortly, without reference to volunteers or to the compulsions of the law, and I state it as follows. If without an antecedent request a person assumes an obligation or makes a payment for the benefit of another, the law will, as a general rule, refuse him a right of indemnity. But if he can show that in the particular circumstances of the case there was some necessity for the obligation to be assumed, then the law will grant him a right of reimbursement if in all the circumstances it is just and reasonable to do so. In the present case the evidence is that the plaintiff acted not only behind the backs of the defendants initially, but in the interests of another, and despite their protest. When the moment came for him to honour the obligation thus assumed, the defendants are not to be criticised, in my judgment, for having accepted the benefit of a transaction which they neither wanted nor sought. . . .

Note

'It is difficult to conceive of any intervention more voluntary than that of the plaintiff in *Owen* v *Tate*' wrote Oakley [1975] CLJ 202, at 204. See Goff and Jones, 350–5 for discussion of 'officiousness' in this context. See also (1975) 39 MLR 563 (Cornish); Burrows, *Restitution*, 213–16 and Birks, *Introduction*, 189–92, 311–12 for discussion of this controversial case. The difficulty with this area of restitution is the related uncertainty over the question when, if ever, is a debt validly discharged by payment by a person other than the debtor. Current authority suggests the debt is discharged only if that payment is authorised or ratified by the *debtor*, or where the payment was made in circumstances of compulsion arising from a secondary liability or, after *Owen* v *Tate*, necessity. So it has been held that a mistaken payment does not usually discharge the debt of a third party: *Barclays Bank Ltd* v *W. J. Simms, Son and Cooke* [1980] QB 677. For detailed discussion of this intractable topic see Birks and Beatson, 'Unrequested Payment of Another's Debt' (1976) 92 LQR 188, now updated in Beatson, *Unjust Enrichment*, 177–205. For an argument that both the authorities and principle favour a rule of 'automatic discharge' see Burrows, *Restitution*, 222–30 (and compare Friedmann, 'Payment of Another's Debt' (1983) 99 LQR 534).

The 'Zuhal K' and 'Selin'
[1987] 1 Lloyd's Rep 151 (QBD (Admiralty Court))

A cargo of grapefruit was damaged while being carried on the '*Selin*' from Turkey to Shoreham. The ship then sailed to Rotterdam where she was arrested by the cargo-owners. The '*Selin*' was required to sail to Antwerp the next day to collect a new cargo, therefore the shipowners wanted her released from arrest immediately. Therefore they instructed Oceanus, their P & I Club (a shipowners' mutual indemnity insurance association) to obtain the release of the '*Selin*' by providing security. The cargo-owners refused to accept a letter of undertaking from Oceanus, as they feared it might be unable to meet its financial commitments. Therefore Mr Pelling of Oceanus arranged for the Home Insurance Co. to enter into a bond guarantee in respect of the shipowner's liabilities up to £30,000. Subsequently Home Insurance paid £23,560 to the cargo-owners under the bond in settlement for their claim. Home Insurance claimed the £23,560 from the defendant shipowners. *Held*: Oceanus had actual, or at least ostensible, authority to arrange for Home Insurance to enter into the guarantee. It was reasonably necessary to secure the release of the ship, therefore the shipowners, who were primarily liable to the cargo-owners, were obliged to reimburse Home Insurance, the guarantors.

SHEEN J: . . . The plaintiffs contend that if the bond was given by Home without any prior request by the defendants and the defendants did not subsequently adopt the guarantee and require payment of their debt to the cargo-owners by Home, they are nevertheless entitled to recover the sum of £23,560 from the defendants because they are able to show (1) that they were compelled by law to make the payment; (2) that they did not officiously expose themselves to the liability to make the payment; (3) that their payment discharged a liability of the defendants. (See the Law of Restitution by Goff and Jones, 2nd ed. p. 244 [see now 4th ed. Goff and Jones, 343-4].) The plaintiffs contend that these three elements are established. As to (1) Home were compelled to pay the cargo-owners by reason of the bond of guarantee. As to (2), Home did not officiously expose themselves to this liability because they were asked to Mr Pelling to undertake it. As to (3), it cannot be disputed that the defendants were under a liability to pay damages to the cargo-owners by virtue of the terms of settlement.

The only answer advanced by Mr Longmore [counsel for the shipowners] to the claim put in this way was that the transaction with Home was carried out for the benefit of Oceanus and was without the consent of the defendants. Mr Longmore submitted that the facts of this case are strikingly similar to the facts in *Owen* v *Tate*, [1976] QB 402. That was a bold submission. I have to confess that although Counsel referred me to the judgments in *Owen* v *Tate* on several occasions during the course of their submissions it did not strike me that the facts of that case were similar to the facts of the case with which I am now concerned. It is, of course, true that when the facilities provided by Home were enlisted, the owners of *Selin* were unaware of the fact that their debt was being guaranteed by Home. But their agent who was seeking to secure the immediate release of their ship was well aware that Home was being asked to assist by providing a bond of guarantee. It was the only practicable way he could secure the immediate release of the ship. Any delay would have been very costly for the defendants. On p. 409 of the report of *Owen* v *Tate* Lord Justice Scarman said:

> The fundamental question is whether in the circumstances it was reasonably necessary on the interests of the volunteer or the person for whom the payment was made, or both, that the payment should be made—whether in the circumstances it was 'just and reasonable' that a right of reimbursement should arise.

If that question is asked, there can be no doubt that it was reasonably necessary in the interests of the shipowners that the guarantee should be given. Pursuant to that guarantee payment had to be made. To my mind it is clearly just and reasonable that a right of reimbursement should arise. . . .

Note

The case is noted by Watts [1989] LMCLQ 7, where it is suggested that there is no need to have recourse to the law of restitution to deal with the problem of intervening guarantors. Rather the law of contract usually gives rise to an implied right for the guarantor to be subrogated to the creditor's debt. With respect this seems to be either a return to implied contract reasoning, or a more convoluted way of saying that restitution should have been awarded.

Esso Petroleum Co. v *Hall, Russell & Co. Ltd, The 'Esso Bernicia'*

[1989] AC 643 (HL (Scotland))

Subrogation

The eponymous vessel was involved in an accident at Sullom Voe in the Shetland Islands, and as a result large quantities of bunker oil escaped her, causing pollution. The owners, Esso, were a party to the Tanker Owners Voluntary Agreement Concerning Liability for Oil Pollution ('TOVALOP') and under the terms of this agreement paid over £500,000 to crofters in respect of damage to their sheep caused by oil on the foreshore. Subsequently Esso sued Hall Russell, the builders of a tug involved in the accident, claiming that their negligence in designing and building the tug had caused the accident. As one of the heads of loss, Esso claimed reimbursement of the sums paid to the crofters. *Held*: first, the sums were irrecoverable under the doctrine of subrogation; secondly, the payments to the crofters were voluntary and gratuitous, and were therefore irrecoverable in the tort of negligence as they constituted pure economic loss. The extract relates to the subrogation claim.

LORD GOFF OF CHIEVELEY: . . . The primary submission of Mr Cameron [counsel for Esso] was that Esso was entitled to be subrogated to the crofters' claims in tort against Hall Russell, and further that Esso was entitled to pursue such claims against Hall Russell in its own name. In my opinion, this submission is not well founded.

In considering this submission, I proceed on the basis (which appears to have been common ground throughout the case) that there is for present purposes no material distinction between Scots law and English law. Now, let it be assumed that the effect of Esso's payment to the crofters was to indemnify the crofters in respect of loss or damage suffered by them by reason of the wrongdoing of Hall Russell. If such a payment were made under a contract of indemnity between Esso and the crofters, there can be no doubt that Esso would upon payment be subrogated to the crofters' claims against Hall Russell. This would enable Esso to proceed against Hall Russell in the names of the crofters; but it would not enable Esso to proceed, without more, to enforce the crofters' claims by an action in its own name against Hall Russell.

The reason for this is plain. It is that Esso's payment to the crofters does not have the effect of discharging Hall Russell's liability to them. That being so, I do not see how Esso can have a direct claim against Hall Russell in respect of its payment. I put on one side Esso's claim against Hall Russell in negligence: that I will consider in a moment. There can of course be no direct claim by Esso against Hall Russell in restitution, if only because Esso has not by its payment discharged the liability of Hall Russell, and so has not enriched Hall Russell; if anybody has been enriched, it is the crofters, to the extent that they have been indemnified by Esso and yet continue to have vested in them rights of action against Hall Russell in respect of the loss or damage which was the subject matter of Esso's payment to them. All that is left is the fact that the crofters' rights of action against Hall Russell continued to exist (until the expiry of the relevant limitation period), and that it might have been inequitable to deny Esso the opportunity to take advantage of them—which is the classic basis of the doctrine of subrogation in the case of contracts of indemnity (see *Castellain* v *Preston* (1883) 11 QBD 380). In normal cases, as for example under contracts of insurance, the insurer will on payment request the assured to sign a letter of subrogation, authorising the insurer to proceed in the name of the assured against any wrongdoer who has caused the relevant damage to the assured. If the assured refuses to give such authority, in theory the insurer can bring proceedings to compel him to do so. But nowadays the insurer can short-circuit this cumbrous process by bringing an action against both the assured and the third party, in which (1) he claims an order that the assured shall authorise him to proceed against the third party in the name of the assured, and (2) he seeks to proceed (so authorised) against the third party. But it must not be thought that, because this convenient method of proceeding now exists, the insurer can without more proceed in his own name against the third party. He has no right to do so, so long as the right of action he is seeking to enforce is the right of action of the assured. Only if that right of action is assigned to him by the assured can he proceed directly against the third party in his own name (see, e.g., *Compania Colombiana de Seguros* v *Pacific Steam Navigation Co.* [1965] 1 QB 101). I have no doubt that the like principles apply in the present case. It follows that Esso could only proceed directly in its own name against Hall Russell in respect of the crofters' claims against Hall Russell if, on paying the crofters, it received from them a valid and effective assignation of their claims. I cannot think that, in practice, Esso would have met with difficulty if it had, at the time of payment to the crofters, asked each of them for a receipt which operated either as an assignation or as an authority to proceed against the third party in the name of the crofters concerned; if any such practical difficulty should exist, it could surely be overcome in future by an appropriate amendment to TOVALOP.

Question

Would the reasoning be the same if the crofters had recovered substantial sums in damages from Hall Russell?

Note

For discussion see Weir [1989] LMCLQ 1.

B: *Contribution*

See Burrows, *Restitution*, 219–22. This subject is considered only briefly here: for detailed discussion see Goff and Jones, 299–342.

Dering v *Earl of Winchelsea*

(1787)1 Cox 318; 29 ER 1184 (Exchequer)

Contribution

Three persons, including the plaintiff, by three separate bonds became guarantors or sureties of the obligations to the Crown in respect of custom duties collected of Thomas Dering, younger brother of the plaintiff. Thomas Dering became insolvent (apparently as a result of gambling) and left the country and his debts behind. Judgment was obtained against the plaintiff in respect of those debts, and the plaintiff in turn sought contribution from his co-sureties.

EYRE CB: . . . The real point is whether a contribution can be demanded between the obligors of distinct and separate obligations under the circumstances of this case. It is admitted that if there had been only one bond in which the three sureties had joined for £12,000, there must have been a contribution amongst them to the extent of any loss sustained; but it is said, that that case proceeds on the contract and privity subsisting amongst the sureties, which this case excludes; that this case admits of the supposition that the three sureties are perfect strangers to each other, and each of them might be ignorant of the other sureties, and that it would be strange to imply any contract as amongst the sureties in this situation; that these are perfectly distinct undertakings without connection with each other, and it is added, that the contribution can never be *eodem modo*, as in the three joining in one bond for £12,000, for there, if one of them become insolvent, the two others would be liable to contribute in moieties to the amount of £6000 each, whereas here it is impossible to make them contribute beyond the penalty of the bond. *Mr Madocks* has stated what is decisive, if true, that nobody is liable to contribute who does not appear on the face of the bond; if this means only that there is no contract, then it comes back to the question, whether the right of contribution is founded on contract. If we take a view of the cases both in law and equity, we shall find that contribution is bottomed and fixed on general principles of justice, and does not spring from contract; though contract may qualify it, as in *Swain* v *Wall*, 1 Cha Rep 149. . . . In *Sir William Harbert's* case, 3 Co. 11 *b*, many cases of contribution are put; and the reason given in the books is, that in *equali jure* the law requires equality; one shall not bear the burthen in ease of the rest, and the law is grounded in great equity. *Contract* is never mentioned. Now the doctrine of equality operates more effectually in this Court, than in a Court of law. The difficulty in *Coke's Cases* was how to make them contribute; they were put to their *audita querela*, or *scire facias*. In equity there is a string of cases in 1 *Eq. Ca. abr. tit.* 'Contribution and average.' Another case occurs in *Harg. Law Tracts* on the right of the King on the prisage of wine. The King is entitled to one ton before the mast, and one ton behind, and in that case a right of contribution accrues; for the King may take by his prerogative any two tons of wine he thinks fit, by which one man might suffer solely; but the contribution is given of course on general principles which govern all these cases. Now to come to the particular case of sureties; it is clear that one surety may compel a contribution from another, towards payment of a debt to which they are jointly bound. On what principle? Can it be necessary to resort to the circumstance of a joint bond? What, if they are jointly and severally bound? What difference will it make if they are severally bound, and by *different* instruments, but for the *same* principal, and the *same* engagement? In all these cases the sureties have a common interest, and a common burthen; they are joined by the common end and purpose of their several obligations, as much as if they were joined in one instrument, with this difference only, that the penalties will ascertain the proportion in which they are to contribute, whereas if they had joined in one bond, it must have depended on other circumstances. In this case the three sureties are all bound that Mr Dering shall account for the monies he receives; this is a common burthen; all the bonds are forfeited at law; and in this Court, as far as the balance due: the balance might have been so great as to have exhausted all the penalties, and then the obligee forces them all to pay; but here the balance is something less than one of the penalties. Now who ought to pay this? the one who is sued must pay it to the Crown, as in the case of prisage, but, as between themselves, there shall be a contribution, for they are in *equali jure*. This is carried a great way, where they are joined in one obligation, for if one should pay the whole £12,000 and the second were insolvent, the third shall contribute a moiety, though he certainly never meant to be liable for more than a third; this circumstance, and the possibility of one being liable for the whole, if the other two should prove insolvent, suggested the mode of entering into separate bonds; but this does not vary the reason for contribution, for there is the same principal and the same engagement; all are equally liable to the obligee to the extent of the penalty of the bonds when they are not all exhausted; if, as in the common case of a joint bond, no distinction is to be made, why shall not the same rule govern here? As in the case of average of cargo in a Court of law, *qui sentit commodum sentire debet et onus*. This principle has a direct application here, for the charging one surety, discharges the other, and each therefore ought to contribute to the *onus*. In questions of average there is no contract or privity in ordinary cases, but it is the result of general justice from the equality of burthen and benefit: then there is no difficult or absurdity in making a contribution take place in this case, if not founded on contract, nor any difficulty in adjusting the proportions in which they are to contribute; for the penalties will necessarily determine this. . . .

CIVIL LIABILITY (CONTRIBUTION) ACT 1978

1. Entitlement to contribution

(1) Subject to the following provisions of this section, any person liable in respect of any damage suffered by another person may recover contribution from any other person liable in respect of the same damage (whether jointly with him or otherwise). . . .

2. Assessment of contribution

(1) Subject to subsection (3) below, in any proceedings for contribution under section 1 above the amount of the contribution recoverable from any person shall be such as may be found by the court to be just and equitable having regard to the extent of that person's responsibility for the damage in question.

. . .

6. Interpretation

(1) A person is liable in respect of any damage for the purposes of this Act if the person who suffered it (or anyone representing his estate or dependants) is entitled to recover compensation from him in respect of that damage (whatever the legal basis of his liability, whether tort, breach of contract, breach of trust or otherwise).

. . .

Section 5: necessity or moral compulsion

'Danger invites rescue' said Cardozo CJ in *Palsgraf* v *Long Island Railroad* 248 NY 339, 162 NE 99 (1928), albeit in the context of tort, not restitution. There is no general principle in English law that those who render necessary services or other necessary benefits in an emergency or other necessitous circumstances to the advantage of another have a right to reimbursement for their efforts. There are, however, pockets of case law from disparate contexts – maritime salvage, burial, care of the mentally incompetent and agency of necessity – where something akin to restitution has been awarded. Restitution scholars have sought to generalise from these single instances. In contrast, there are a number of authorities hostile to uninvited intervener, robustly defending the instinctive individualism of the common law, of which the most famous is *Falcke's case* (1866) 34 Ch D 234, below. Classification is not consistent. Goff and Jones (363–84) and Burrows (*Restitution*, 231–49) keep necessity distinct from compulsion. In contrast Professor Birks prefers a heading of 'moral compulsion' (Birks, *Introduction*, 193–202).

A: *Authorities favouring restitution*

Agency of necessity

Great Northern Railway Co. v *Swaffield*
(1874) LR 9 Ex 132 (Exchequer)

The facts appear from the judgment of Kelly CB.

KELLY CB: . . . It appears that the defendant caused a horse to be sent by the plaintiffs' railway to Sandy station; but the horse was not directed to be taken to any particular place. The owner ought to have had some one ready to receive the horse on his arrival and take him away; but no one was there. It does not appear that there was at the station any stable or other accommodation for the horse; and the question arises, what was it, under those circumstances, the plaintiffs' duty, and consequently what was it competent for them to do? I think we need do no more than ask ourselves, as a question of common sense and common understanding, had they any choice? They must either have allowed the horse to stand at the station—a place where it would have been extremely improper and dangerous to let it remain; or they must have put it in safe custody, which was what in fact they did in placing it in the care of the livery stable keeper. Presently the defendant's servant comes and demands the horse. He is referred to the livery stable keeper, and it may be (I do not say it is so) that upon what passed on that occasion the defendant might have maintained an action against the plaintiffs for detaining the horse. But next day the defendant comes himself; the charges now amount to 2*s.* 6*d.*; an altercation takes place about this trumpery sum, and ultimately the station-master offers to pay the charges himself if the defendant will take the horse away; but the defendant refuses and leaves the horse at the stable. Then a correspondence ensues between the parties, in which the defendant is told that he can have the horse without payment if he sends for it, but he refuses, and says that unless the horse is sent to him with 30*s.* for expenses and loss of time by tomorrow morning he will not accept it at all; and he never sends for the horse. Meanwhile the plaintiffs run up a bill of 17*l.* with the livery stable keeper with whom they placed the horse, which they ultimately have to pay; and at last they send the horse to the defendant, who receives it; and they now sue him for the amount so paid.

I am clearly of opinion that the plaintiffs are entitled to recover. My Brother Pollock has referred to a class of cases which is identical with this in principle, where it has been held that a shipowner who, through some accidental circumstance, finds it necessary for the safety of the cargo to incur expenditure, is justified in doing so, and can maintain a claim for reimbursement against the owner of the cargo. That is exactly the present case. The plaintiffs were put into much the same position as the shipowner occupies under the circumstances I have described. They had no choice, unless they would leave the horse at the station or in the high road to his own danger and the danger of other people, but to place him in the care of a livery stable keeper, and as they are bound by their implied contract with the livery stable keeper to satisfy his charges, a right arises in them against the defendant to be reimbursed those charges which they have incurred for his benefit.

PIGOTT B: I am of the same opinion. I do not think we have to deal with any question of lien. We have only to see whether the plaintiffs necessarily incurred this expense in consequence of the defendant's conduct in not receiving the horse, and then whether under these circumstances, the defendant is under an implied obligation to reimburse them. I am clearly of opinion that he is. The horse was necessarily put in the stable for a short time before the defendant's man arrived. I give no opinion on what then passed, whether the man was right, or whether the plaintiffs were right; I think it is not material. On the following day the defendant comes himself; and the basis of my judgment is, that at that time the station master offered, rather than the defendant should go away without the horse, to pay the charge out of his own pocket; but the defendant declared he would have nothing to do with it, and went away. That I understand to be the substance of what was proved; and if that be so, it shews to me that there was a leaving of the horse by the defendant in the possession of the carriers, and a refusal to take it. Then what were the carriers to do? They were bound, from ordinary feelings of humanity, to keep the horse safely and feed him; and that became necessary in consequence of the defendant's own conduct in refusing to receive the animal at the end of the journey according to his contract. Then the defendant writes and claims the price of the horse; and then again, in answer to the plaintiffs' offer to deliver the horse without payment of the charges, he requires delivery at his farm and the payment of 30*s.*; in point of fact, he again refuses the horse. Upon the whole, therefore, I come to the conclusion that, whoever was right on the night when the horse arrived, the defendant was wrong when, on the next day, he refused to receive him; that the expense was rightly incurred by the plaintiffs; and that there was, under these circumstances, an implied contract by the defendant entitling the plaintiff's to recover the amount from him.

POLLOCK B: . . . Now, in my opinion it was the duty of the plaintiffs, as carriers, although the transit of the horse was at an end, to take such reasonable care of the horse as a reasonable owner would take of his own goods; and if they had turned him out on the highway, or allowed him to go loose, they would have been in default. Therefore they did what it was their duty to do. Then comes the question, Can they recover any expenses thus incurred against the owner of the horse? As far as I am aware, there is no decided case in English law in which an ordinary carrier of goods by land has been held entitled to recover this sort of charge against the consignee or consignor of goods. But in my opinion he is so entitled. It had been long debated whether a shipowner has such a right, and gradually, partly by custom and partly by some opinions of authority in this country, the right has come to be established. It was clearly held to exist in the case of *Notara* v *Henderson* Law Rep 7 QB 225, at pp. 230–5, where all the authorities on the subject are reviewed with very great care; and that case, with some others, was cited and acted upon by the Privy Council in the recent case of *Cargo ex Argos* Law Rep 5 PC 134. The Privy Council is not a Court whose decisions are binding on us sitting here, but it is a Court to whose decisions I should certainly on all occasions give great weight; and their judgment on this point is clearly in accordance with reason and justice. It was there said (after referring to the observations of Sir James Mansfield, CJ, in *Christy* v *Row* 1 Taunt 300). 'The precise point does not seem to have been subsequently decided, but several cases have since arisen in which the nature and scope of the duty of the master, as agent of the merchant, have been examined and defined.' Then, after citing the cases, the judgment proceeds: 'It results from them, that not merely is a power given, but a duty is cast on the master, in many cases of accident and emergency, to act for the safety of the cargo in such manner as may be best under the circumstances in which it may be placed; and that, as a correlative right, he is entitled to charge its owner with the expenses properly incurred in so doing.' That seems to me to be a sound rule of law. That the duty is imposed upon the carrier, I do not think any one has doubted; but if there were that duty without the correlative right, it would be a manifest injustice. Therefore, upon the whole of the circumstances, I come to the conclusion that the claim of the company was a proper one, and that the judgment of the learned judge of the county court must be reversed.

Prager* v *Blatspiel, Stamp and Heacock Ltd
[1924] 1 KB 566 (KBD)

The plaintiff in Bucharest was furrier to the Romanian Court. The defendant fur merchants based in London acted as agents in buying and dressing skins, and had done so on behalf of the plaintiff for many years. Their relationship was not interrupted by the outbreak of the Great War, and in 1915–1916 the defendants purchased numerous skins – skunk, leopard, marten, opossum, ermine and silver fox — worth £1,900 on behalf of the plaintiff. The plaintiff paid substantially the whole of this sum, but wartime conditions made delivery difficult. In 1916, Germany invaded Romania, rendering it an enemy country. During the remainder of the war the defendants sold the skins which had increased in value. At the end of the war the plaintiff sought his goods. He brought an action for conversion, and the defendants pleaded agency of necessity. *Held*: agency of necessity was a general principle not confined to carriage of goods by sea and bills of exchange. But on the facts the defence failed because there was no necessity: dressed furs were not perishable goods and the sellers had not acted bona fide.

McCARDIE J: . . . Now the first question of law is this: Can the facts as I have outlined them afford a possible legal basis on which to rest an agency of necessity? The defendants say yes; the plaintiff says no. The doctrine of agency of necessity doubtless took its rise from marine adventure. Hence the numerous decisions set out in Carver's Carriage by Sea, 6th ed., s. 294, and following sections. The substance of the matter as stated in that book is that in cases of necessity the master of a ship has power and it is his duty to sell the goods in order to save their value or some part of it: see s. 297. In *Hawtayne* v *Bourne* (1841) 7 M & W 595 Parke B expressed a view that agency of necessity could not arise save in the case of a master of a ship and of the acceptor of a bill of exchange for the honour of the drawer. He added that: 'The authority of the master of a ship rests upon the peculiar character of his office.' In *Gwilliam* v *Twist* [1895] 2 QB 84, 87 Lord Esher said: 'I am very much inclined to agree with the view taken by Eyre CJ in the case of *Nicholson* v *Chapman*, (1793) 2 H Bl 254, and by Parke B in the case of *Hawtayne* v *Bourne* 7 M & W 599, to the effect that this doctrine of authority by reason of necessity is confined to certain well-known exceptional cases, such as those of the master of a ship or the acceptor of a bill of exchange for the honour of the drawer.' If the dicta I have cited be correct then the defendants in the case now before me cannot justify their acts of sale. In my humble opinion, however, those dicta are not the law today. In *Great Northern Ry. Co.* v *Swaffield* (1874) LR 9 Ex 132, more than twenty years before the dictum of Lord Esher, the Court of Exchequer (Kelly CB, Pigott, Pollock and Amphlett BB) had applied the doctrine of agency of necessity to a land carrier. They applied to him the principle of the shipping cases. I think too that *London and North Western Ry.* v *Duerden* (1916) 32 Times LR 315 is in substance an application of the same principle. In *Sims & Co.* v *Midland Ry. Co.* [1913] 1 KB 103—the sale of butter case—the Divisional Court (Ridley and Scrutton JJ) again recognised that the principle of the shipping cases might apply to land carriers. See also Macnamara on Carriers by Land, 2nd ed., art. 189 (n.). In *Springer* v *Great Western Ry.* [1921] 1 KB 257 the Court of Appeal approved the principle stated in *Sims' Case*.

The decisions I have already cited show that the dictum of Lord Esher in *Gwilliam* v *Twist* is not the law of today. Agency of necessity is not confined to shipmaster cases and to bills of exchange. I may next point out that in the well-known judgment of the Court of Appeal in *De Bussche* v *Alt* (1878) 8 Ch D 286 the Court stated that unforeseen emergencies may arise which impose on an agent the necessity of employing a substitute, and the authority to do so which he would not otherwise possess. That case related to the sale of a ship in the East, and it shows an appreciation by the Court of Appeal in 1878 of a principle which, in its application, could not be confined to carriers or acceptors of bills of exchange. The object of the common law is to solve difficulties and adjust relations in social and commercial life. It must meet, so far as it can, sets of fact abnormal as well as usual. It must face and deal with changing or novel circumstances. Unless it can do that it fails in its function and declines in its dignity and value. An expanding society demands an expanding common law. A dozen decisions could be cited to illustrate the remarks I have just made. I mention only the words of Bankes LJ in *Rex* v *Electricity Commissioners* (1923)

39 Times LR 715, 718; [1924] 1 KB 171, 192 when he said: 'It has, however, always been the boast of our common law that it will, whenever possible, and where necessary, apply existing principles to new sets of circumstances.' I respectfully agree, and I venture to add that it would be well if those words were more often remembered and applied. In my view there is nothing in the existing decisions which confines the agency of necessity to carriers whether by land or sea, or to the acceptors of bills of exchange. The basic principle I think is a broad and useful one. It lies at the root of the various classes of cases of which the carrier decisions are merely an illustration. . . .

I must refer briefly to several other features of the doctrine of agency of necessity in a case where, as here, the agent has, without orders, sold the goods of his principal. In the first place, it is, of course, clear that agency of necessity does not arise if the agent can communicate with his principal. This is established by all the decisions: see Carver on Carriage by Sea, 6th ed., arts. 295, 299; Scrutton on Charterparties, 11th ed., art. 98; and *Springer* v *Great Western Ry.* [1921] 1 KB 257. The basis of this requirement is, I take it, that if the principal's decision can be obtained the agent should seek it ere acting. In the present case it is admitted that the agents could not communicate with the principal. In the next place it is essential for the agent to prove that the sale was necessary. What does this mean? In *Cannon* v *Meaburn* (1823) 1 Bing 243, 247 Park J said: 'The master cannot sell except in a case of inevitable necessity.' In *Australian Steam Navigation Co.* v *Morse* (1872) LR 4 PC 222, 230, however, Sir Montague Smith said: 'The word "necessity," when applied to mercantile affairs, where the judgment must, in the nature of things, be exercised, cannot of course mean an irresistible compelling power—what is meant by it in such cases is, the force of circumstances which determine the course a man ought to take.' Later on he refers to 'commecial necessity.' In *Acatos* v *Burns* (1878) 3 Ex D 282, 290 Brett LJ uses the words 'unless there is an urgent necessity for the sale.' In *Atlantic Mutual Insurance Co.* v *Huth* (1880) 16 Ch D 474, 481 Cotton LJ says: 'It lies on those who claim title to cargo, as purchasers from the captain, to prove that this necessity clearly existed; further . . . . it is not sufficient to prove that the master thought he was doing the best for all concerned, or even that the course adopted was, so far as can be ascertained, the best for all concerned.' In *Sims & Co.* v *Midland Ry. Co.* [1913] 1 KB 103, 112 Scrutton J, as he then was, said that the question was whether 'necessity justified the sale.' In *Springer's Case* [1921] 1 KB 257, 267, already quoted, Scrutton LJ said that the defendants must show 'that a sale was in the circumstances the only reasonable business course to take.' With this may be compared art. 97 of Scrutton on Charterparties, 11th ed. In substance I may say that the agent must prove an actual and definite commercial necessity for the sale. In the third place, I think that an alleged agent of necessity must satisfy the Court that he was acting bona fide in the interests of the parties concerned. In *Ewbank* v *Nutting* (1849) 7 CB 797, 804 Coltman J said during the argument: 'Does not the authority of the master extend to acts such as he, in the exercise of an honest judgment, thinks the best for the interest of the owner of both ship and goods?' . . .

Note

McCardie J then applied the principles to the facts and held that this was not a case of agency of necessity.

Jebara v *Ottoman Bank*

[1927] 2 KB 254 (CA); reversed [1928] AC 269 (HL)

The facts are not relevant.

SCRUTTON LJ: . . . But considerable difficulties arise on the question of agent of necessity in English law. Until recently it was treated as limited to certain classes of agents of whom masters of ships were the most prominent. High authorities had doubted whether it could be extended. I refer to the observations of Lord Esher MR in *Gwilliam* v *Twist* [1895] 2 QB 84; to the judgment of Parke B in *Hawtayne* v *Bourne* (1841) 7 M & W 595, 599, but especially to the careful judgment of Eyre CJ in *Nicholson* v *Chapman* 2 H Bl 254, 257. Many of the authorities are collected in a recent judgment of McCardie J in *Prager's* case [1924] 1 KB 566. He there finds the facts so as not to raise any question of action by an agent of necessity, but discusses what the law would be, if he had found the facts differently. He takes the view that judges should expand the common law to meet the needs of expanding society, and proceeds to expand the doctrine of agent of necessity without clearly defining the limits, if any, of its expansion. The difficulty may be seen by considering the case of the finder of perishable goods or chattels which need expenditure to preserve them. If the finder incurs such expenditure, can he recover it from the true owner when he finds him, as his 'agent of necessity'? Eyre CJ raises this difficulty in the case above cited, and cites *Binstead* v *Buck* (1777) 2 W Bl 1117, the case of the pointer dog. The pointer dog was lost, and his finder fed him for twenty weeks, and claimed the cost from his owner when he appeared, but the claim was treated as unarguable. The expansion desired by McCardie J becomes less difficult when the agent of necessity develops from an original and subsisting agency, and only applies itself to unforeseen events not provided for in the original contract, which is usually the case where a shipmaster is agent of necessity. But the position seems quite different when there is no pre-existing agency, as in the case of a finder of perishable chattels or animals, and still more difficult when there is a pre-existing agency, but it has become illegal and void by reason of war, and the same reason will apply to invalidate any implied agency of necessity. How can one imply a duty in an enemy to protect the property of his enemy? Will he not be violating his duty to his own country? I do not feel strong enough to expand the common law to this extent, and I do not see that McCardie J has considered the effect of illegality and invalidity by reason of war in his doctrine. . . .

Question

Do you think that the 'pointer dog case' (*Binstead* v *Buck* (1777) 2 W Bl 1117, 96 ER 660) cited by Scrutton LJ was rightly decided?

China Pacific SA v *Food Corporation of India, The 'Winson'* [1982] AC 939 (HL)

The '*Winson*', carrying a full cargo of wheat from the US to India, became stranded on the North Danger Reef in the South China Sea. China Pacific, who were professional salvors, entered into a salvage agreement on the Lloyd's open form with the ship's managing agents in Hong Kong, who acted on behalf of the shipowner and cargo owner. As part of the operation it was necessary to lighten the vessel by off-loading part of the cargo into barges. 15,429 tonnes of wheat were as a result taken to Manila, where the salvors arranged for and paid for suitable storage facilities to prevent their rapid deterioration. It was accepted by the cargo-owners that this expenditure was necessary and reasonable, but they denied liability for the initial period of storage. *Held*: the direct relationship of bailor and bailee existed between the salvors and cargo-owners, and consequently the former were entitled to be re-imbursed for the whole period of storage.

LORD DIPLOCK: . . . My Lords, with modern methods of communication and the presence of professional salvors within rapid reach of most parts of the principal maritime trade routes of the world, nearly all salvage of merchant ships and their cargoes nowadays is undertaken under a salvage contract in Lloyd's open form. The contract is one for the rendering of services; the services to be rendered are of the legal nature of salvage and this imports into the contractual relationship between the parties to the contract by necessary implication a number of mutual rights and obligations attaching to salvage of vessels and their cargo under common law, except in so far as such rights and obligations are inconsistent with express terms of the contract.

Lloyd's open form is expressed by clause 16 to be signed by the master 'as agent for the vessel her cargo and freight and the respective owners thereof and binds each (but not the one for the other or himself personally) to the due performance thereof.' The legal nature of the relationship between the master and the owner of the cargo aboard the vessel in signing the agreement on the latter's behalf is often though not invariably an agency of necessity. It arises only when salvage services by a third party are necessary for the preservation of the cargo. Whether one person is entitled to act as agent of necessity for another person is relevant to the question whether circumstances exist which in law have the effect of conferring on him authority to create contractual rights and obligations between that other person and a third party that are directly enforceable by each against the other. It would, I think, be an aid to clarity of legal thinking if the use of the expression 'agent of necessity' were confined to contexts in which this was the question to be determined and not extended, as it often is, to cases where the only relevant question is whether a person who without obtaining instructions from the owner of goods incurs expense in taking steps that are reasonably necessary for their preservation is in law entitled to recover from the owner of the goods the reasonable expenses incurred by him in taking those steps. Its use in this wider sense may, I think, have led to some confusion in the instant case, since where reimbursement is the only relevant question all of those conditions that must be fulfilled in order to entitle one person to act on behalf of another in creating direct contractual relationships between that other person and a third party may not necessarily apply.

In the instant case it is not disputed that when the Lloyd's open form was signed on January 22, 1975, the circumstances that existed at that time were such as entitled the master to enter into the agreement on the cargo owner's behalf as its agent of necessity. The rendering of salvage services under the Lloyd's open agreement does not usually involve the salvor's taking possession of the vessel or its cargo from the shipowner; the shipowner remains in possession of both ship and cargo while salvage services are being carried out by the salvors on the ship. But salvage services may involve the transfer of possession of cargo from the shipowner to the salvors, and will do so in a case of stranding as respects part of the cargo if it becomes necessary to lighten the vessel in order to refloat her. Where in the course of salvage operations cargo is off-loaded from the vessel by which the contract of carriage was being performed and conveyed separately from that vessel to a place of safety by means (in the instant case, barges) provided by the salvor, the direct relationship of bailor and bailee is created between cargo owner and salvor as soon as the cargo is loaded on vessels provided by the salvor to convey it to a place of safety; and all the mutual rights and duties attaching to that relationship at common law apply, save in so far as any of them are inconsistent with the express terms of the Lloyd's open agreement.

. . . the bailment which up to the conclusion of the salvage services had been a bailment for valuable consideration became a gratuitous bailment; and so long as that relationship of bailor and bailee continued to subsist the salvors, under the ordinary principles of the law of bailment too well known and too well-established to call for any citation of authority, owed a duty of care to the cargo owner to take such measures to preserve the salved wheat from deterioration by exposure to the elements as a man of ordinary prudence would take for the preservation of his own property. For any breach of such duty the bailee is liable to his bailor in damages for any diminution in value of the goods consequent upon his failure to take such measures; and if he fulfils that duty he has, in my view, a correlative right to charge the owner of the goods with the expenses reasonably incurred in doing so.

My Lords, as I have already said, there is not any direct authority as to the existence of this correlative right to reimbursement of expenses in the specific case of a salvor who retains possession of cargo after the salvage services rendered by him to that cargo have ended; but Lloyd J discerned what he considered to be helpful analogous applications of the principle of the bailee's right to reimbursement in *Cargo ex Argos* (1873) LR 5 PC 134, from which I have taken the expression 'correlative right,' and in *Great Northern Railway Co.* v *Swaffield* (1874) LR 9 Ex 132. Both these were cases of carriage of goods in which the carrier/bailee was left in possession of the goods after the carriage contracted for had terminated. Steps necessary for the preservation of the goods were taken by the bailee in default of any instructions from owner/bailor to do otherwise. To these authorities I would add *Notara* v *Henderson* (1872) LR 7 QB 225, in which the bailee was held liable in damages for breach of his duty to take steps necessary for the preservation of the goods, and the Scots case of *Garriock* v *Walker* (1873) 1 R 100 in which the bailee recovered the expenses incurred by him in taking such steps. Although in both these cases, which involved carriage of goods by sea, the steps for the prevention of deterioration of the cargo needed to be taken before the contract voyage was completed, the significance of the Scots case is that the cargo owner was on the spot when the steps were taken by the carrier/bailee and did not acquiesce in them. Nevertheless, he took the benefit of them by taking delivery of the cargo thus preserved at the conclusion of the voyage.

In the instant case the cargo owner was kept informed of the salvors' intentions as to the storage of the salved wheat upon its arrival in Manila; it made no alternative proposals; it made no request to the salvors for delivery of any of the wheat after its arrival at Manila, and a request made by the salvors to the cargo owner through their solicitors on February 25, 1975, after the arrival of the second of the six parcels, to take delivery of the parcels of salved wheat on arrival at Manila remained unanswered and uncomplied with until after notice of abandonment of the charter voyage had been received by the cargo owner from the shipowner.

The failure of the cargo owner as a bailor to give any instructions to the salvors as its bailee although it was fully apprised of the need to store the salved wheat under cover on arrival at Manila if it was to be preserved from rapid deterioration was, in the view of Lloyd J, sufficient to attract the application of the principle to which I have referred above and to entitle the salvors to recover from the cargo owner their expenses in taking measures necessary for its preservation. For my part I think that in this he was right and the Court of Appeal, who took the contrary view, were wrong. It is, of course, true that in English law a mere stranger cannot compel an owner of goods to pay for a benefit bestowed upon him against his will; but this latter principle does not apply where there is a pre-existing legal relationship between the owner of the goods and the bestower of the benefit, such as that of bailor and bailee, which imposes upon the bestower of the benefit a legal duty of care in respect of the preservation of the goods that is owed by him to their owner.

In the Court of Appeal Megaw LJ, as I understand his judgment, with which Bridge and Cumming-Bruce LJJ expressed agreement, was of opinion that, in order to entitle the salvors to reimbursement of the expenses incurred by them in storing the salvaged wheat at Manila up to April 24, 1975, they would have to show not only that, looked at objectively, the measures that they took were necessary to preserve it from rapid deterioration, but, in addition, that it was impossible for them to communicate with the cargo owner to obtain from him such instructions (if any) as he might want to give. My Lords, it may be that this would have been so if the question in the instant case had been whether the depositaries could have sued the cargo owner directly for their contractual storage charges on the ground that the cargo owner was party as principal to the contracts of storage made on its behalf by the salvors as its agents of necessity; for English law is economical in recognising situations that give rise to agency of necessity. In my view, inability to communicate with the owner of the goods is not a condition precedent to the bailee's own right to reimbursement of his expenses. The bailor's failure to give any instructions when apprised of the situation is sufficient. . . .

Note

For recent discussion of the 'agency of necessity' doctrine, albeit *obiter dicta*, see *In re F (Mental Patient: Sterilisation)* [1990] 2 AC 1, at 74–6, *per* Lord Goff of Chieveley.

Burial cases

Jenkins* v *Tucker

(1788) 1 H Bl 90; 126 ER 55 (Common Pleas)

Action for money paid

Tucker married Jenkins's daughter. Some time later he left for his estate in Jamaica, leaving his wife behind in England with an infant child, in bad health and much in want of money. She died during his absence and Jenkins brought this action to recover the expenses he had incurred after his daughter's death, including an undertaker's bill of £141.

LORD LOUGHBOROUGH: . . . I think there was a sufficient consideration to support this action for the funeral expenses, though there was neither request nor assent on the part of the defendant, for the plaintiff acted in discharge of a duty which the defendant was under a strict legal necessity of himself performing, and which common decency required at his hands; the money therefore which the plaintiff paid on this account, was paid to the use of the defendant. A father also seems to be the proper person to interfere in giving directions for his daughter's funeral in the absence of her husband. There are many cases of this sort, where a person having paid money which another was under a legal obligation to pay, though without his knowledge or request, may maintain an action to recover back the money so paid: such as in the instance of goods being distrained by the commissioners of the land-tax, if a neighbour should redeem the goods, and pay the tax for the owner, he might maintain an action for the money against the owner.

GOULD J: It appears from this demurrer, that the defendant was possessed of a plantation in Jamaica, from the time he left his wife, till her death, which annually produced above 120 hogsheads of sugar, the value of which, at a moderate estimation, amounted to near 3000l. a year. He was therefore bound to support her in a manner suitable to his degree; and the expenses were such as were suitable to his degree and situation in life. The law takes notice of things suitable to the degree of the husband in the paraphernalia of the wife, and in other respects. In the present case, the demurrer admits that the money was expended on account of the wife, and being for things suitable to the degree of the husband, the law raises a consideration, and implies a promise to pay it.

WILSON J: If the plaintiff in this case had declared as having himself buried the deceased, the husband clearly would have been liable; and as the case stands at present, the plaintiff having defrayed the expenses of the funeral, the husband is in justice equally liable to repay those expenses, and in him the law will imply an assumpsit for that purpose.

Rogers v Price
(1829) 3 Y & J 28; 148 ER 1080 (Exchequer)

Quantum meruit

Davis died at the house of his brother in Wales. Rogers, the plaintiff undertaker, was sent for, and he arranged the funeral. It was admitted that the funeral was suitable to the degree of the deceased. Rogers brought this action against the executor of Davis for work and labour as an undertaker and for materials furnished at the funeral.

GARROW B: It would, in my opinion, have been more satisfactory, if this case had been submitted to the consideration of a jury, to inquire upon whose credit the funeral was provided; but, that course not having been pursued, we must dispose of this rule in its present form. I am of opinion that the plaintiff is entitled to recover, and that therefore this rule must be made absolute. The simple question is, notwithstanding many ingenious views of the case have been presented, who is answerable for the expenses of the funeral of this gentleman. In my opinion, the executor is liable. Suppose a person to be killed by accident at a distance from his home; what, in such a case ought to be done? The common principles of decency and humanity, the common impulses of our nature, would direct every one, as a preliminary step, to provide a decent funeral, at the expense of the estate; and to do that which is immediately necessary upon the subject, in order to avoid what, if not provided against, may become an inconvenience to the public. It is necessary in that or any other case to wait until it can be ascertained whether the deceased has left a will, or appointed an executor; or, even if the executor be known, can it, where the distance is great, be necessary to have communication with that executor before any step is taken in the performance of those last offices which require immediate attention? It is admitted here that the funeral was suitable to the degree of the deceased, and upon this record it must be taken that the defendant is executor with assets sufficient to defray this demand; I therefore think that, if the case had gone to the jury, they would have found for the plaintiff, and that therefore this rule should be made absolute.

Necessaries for mental incompetents

In re Rhodes
(1890) 44 Ch D 94 (CA)

The facts appear in the judgment of Cotton LJ:

COTTON LJ: . . . The case raises several questions, one of which is of considerable importance; and, although in the view which we take, that question is not necessary to the decision of the case, yet, as it has been fully argued, we think we ought to express our opinion upon it. That question is, whether there can be an implied contract on the part of a lunatic not so found by inquisition to repay out of her property sums expended for necessaries supplied to her. Now the term 'implied contract' is a most unfortunate expression, because there cannot be a contract by a lunatic. But whenever necessaries are supplied to a person who by reason of disability cannot himself contract, the law implies an obligation on the part of such person to pay for such necessaries out of his own property. It is asked, can there be an implied contract by a person who cannot himself contract in express terms? The answer is, that what the law implies on the part of such a person is an obligation, which has been improperly termed a contract, to repay money spent in supplying necessaries. I think that the expression 'implied contract' is erroneous and very unfortunate. In one case which was before the Court of Appeal, *In re Weaver* 21 Ch D 615, the question whether there could be what has been called an implied contract by a lunatic, was left undecided by the Court, and one of the Judges said that it was difficult to see how there could be an implied contract on the part of a lunatic if he was himself incompetent to make an express contract.

But we all agree with the view that I have thus expressed in order to prevent any doubt from arising in consequence of our having declined to settle the question in the case to which I have alluded.

But, then, although there may be an implied obligation on the part of the lunatic, the necessaries must be supplied under circumstances which would justify the Court in implying an obligation to repay the money spent upon them.

I have no difficulty as to the question of the expenditure being for necessaries, for the law is well established that when the necessaries supplied are suitable to the position in life of the lunatic an implied obligation to pay for them out of his property will arise. But then the provision of money or necessaries must be made under circumstances which would justify the Court in implying an obligation. Here the lady, who was never found a lunatic, was confined in a private asylum, in 1855, at a cost of £140 a year, and her brother from that time down to the time of his death supplied her with the sums required to make good the necessaries for her maintenance. After his death the Appellant, who was his father's executor, and his brother and sisters, contributed towards the expense of her maintenance. I do not so much rely on the circumstance that there is no evidence to show that the father intended this to be a debt. But we must look to the facts of the case in order to see whether the payments for the lunatic were made with the intention of constituting thereby a debt against the lunatic's estate. It is said that the father and the brother and sisters always intended to be recouped. And, no doubt, at the time the payments were made, the persons making them were the next of kin, or some of the next of kin, of the lady, and it is very probable that, although they did it as relations, they, no doubt, in making such payments did look to the fact that, as next of kin, they would ultimately come into the lunatic's property. No books have been produced, but we must assume that the Appellant kept no account between himself and his brother and sisters. And the observation occurs that, if it had been intended by the Appellant that these payments should constitute an obligation in his favour, as against the estate of the lunatic, he would not have asked his brother and sisters to contribute, but would have paid the money himself. The certificate has, no doubt, found that the sisters had no intention of making a gift, and this in favour of the Appellant. But although they had no particular intention of making a gift, they contributed the money; and, if they intended to be repaid, it is very strange that they make no claim on their own behalf, but leave their brother to make it for them. In my opinion, the true effect of the evidence is that all these persons—the Appellant, and his brother and sisters, and the father—did provide this money under circumstances from which no implied obligation could arise.

LINDLEY LJ: . . . The question whether an implied obligation arises in favour of a person who supplies a lunatic with necessaries is a question of law, and in *In re Weaver* 21 Ch D 615 a doubt was expressed whether there is any obligation on the part of the lunatic to repay. I confess I cannot participate in that doubt. I think that that doubt has arisen from the unfortunate terminology of our law, owing to which the expression 'implied contract' has been used to denote not only a genuine contract established by inference, but also an obligation which does not arise from any real contract, but which can be enforced as if it had a contractual origin. Obligations of this class are called by civilians *obligationes quasi ex contractu.*

But that a lunatic's estate may be made liable for necessaries was treated as settled as long ago as *Manby* v *Scott* 1 Sid 112, where three learned Judges, after holding that an infant might be bound for necessaries provided for him, said, 'and what has been said of an infant is applicable to an idiot in case of housekeeping.'

I do not doubt that the cost of necessaries can be recovered against a lunatic's estate in a proper case.

Then we come to the question of fact. Now, in order to raise an obligation to repay, the money must have been expended with the intention on the part of the person providing it that it should be repaid. I think that that intention is not only not proved, but is expressly negatived in the present case. I do not believe that the brother ever intended to constitute himself a creditor of his sister so as to render her estate liable to repay him. He was a kind and affectionate brother; but if he had had any such an intention, being a man of business, he would naturally have kept some kind of account between himself and his sister. There is no real ground for saying that he ever dreamt of repayment. Since his death his children maintained this lady by contribution, and, while there is no direct evidence to shew that the money contributed was a gift, there is still less evidence to show any intention to be repaid.

Upon the facts, then, I come to the conclusion that the constitution of a debt between themselves and the lunatic was the last thing that the persons who made the payments contemplated.

Note

For criticism of the requirement of an intention to be repaid see Birks, *Introduction*, 199.

Services rendered by a liquidator

In re Berkeley Applegate (Investment Consultants) Ltd (in liquidation)

[1989] Ch 32 (Ch D)

An investment company went into voluntary liquidation. The cost of liquidation was considerable and was likely to exceed the company's free assets. The question arose whether the liquidator could claim any part of his expenses and remuneration out of trust assets managed by the company. It was argued that the court had the power to award these sums out of the trust assets belonging to the investors.

EDWARD NUGEE QC (sitting as a deputy High Court judge): . . . Mr Mann [counsel for the liquidator] submitted that the source of the jurisdiction was to be found first in the maxim that he who seeks equity must do equity, and secondly in the inherent jurisdiction to promote the proper administration of trusts, which includes the doctrine of salvage; and he submitted that these two sources are not distinct but overlap. *In re Marine Mansions Co.* LR 4 Eq 601 and subsequent cases in which the liquidator had been allowed the costs incurred in preserving mortgaged property, might be seen as based on the maxim or on the jurisdiction to promote the proper administration of trusts, but reimbursement of expenses was not enough for his purposes: what he sought was an order authorising reasonable remuneration for the liquidator. He submitted that the court's jurisdiction to award compensation for services rendered was supported by two comparatively recent cases, *Phipps* v *Boardman* [1964] 1 WLR 993 and *In re Duke of Norfolk's Settlement Trusts* [1982] Ch 61.

In *Phipps* v *Boardman* [1964] 1 WLR 993 trustees of a will held shares in a company. Mr Boardman, who was the solicitor to the trustees, and Mr Phipps, who was a beneficiary, obtained confidential information about the company by acting as self-appointed agents for the trustees. With the aid of that information they made a take-over bid on their own behalf for the oustanding shares in the company, so as to obtain control and, by a liquidation of assets, make a repayment of capital to the shareholders. The assets of the company proved to be worth far more than the amount paid for the shares. The trustees made a handsome profit on their shares, and Mr Boardman and Mr Phipps an even larger one on theirs. Wilberforce J held that they must account to the beneficiaries for the profit they had made, less their expenditure incurred to enable it to be realised. He continued, at p. 1018:

> But, in addition to expenditure, should not the defendants be given an allowance or credit for their work and skill? This is a subject on which authority is scanty; but Cohen J in *In re Macadam* [1946] Ch 73, 82, gave his support to an allowance of this kind to trustees for their services in acting as directors of a company. It seems to me that this transaction, i.e., the acquisition of a controlling interest in the company, was one special character calling for the exercise of a particular kind of professional skill. If Boardman had not assumed the role of seeing it through, the beneficiaries would have had to employ (and would, had they been well advised, have employed) an expert to do it for them. If the trustees had come to the court asking for liberty to employ such a person, they would in all probability have been authorised to do so, and to remunerate the person in question. It seems to me that it would be inequitable now for the beneficiaries to step in and take the profit without paying for the skill and labour which has produced it.

Wilberforce J's decision was affirmed in the Court of Appeal [1965] Ch 992, where Lord Denning MR equated the case to an action for restitution of the kind described in *Fibrosa Spolka Akcyjna* v *Fairbairn Lawson Combe Barbour Ltd* [1943] AC 32, 61, and said that the claim for restitution should not be allowed to extend further than the justice of the case demanded, and that generous remuneration should be allowed to the agents; and in the House of Lords [1967] 2 AC 46, where Lord Cohen and Lord Hodson, at pp. 104 and 112 respectively, agreed with Wilberforce J that payment should be allowed on a liberal scale in respect of the work and skill employed in obtaining the shares and the profit therefrom. . . .

[Nugee QC then discussed *In re Duke of Norfolk's Settlement Trusts* [1982] Ch 61 (CA) and other authorities and continued: . . .] It is true that the legal title to the mortgages and to the clients' accounts is not vested in the liquidator but remains in the company; but the investors still need the assistance of a court of equity to secure their rights. In this respect their position is different from that of the claimant in *Falcke* v *Scottish Imperial Insurance Co.*, 34 Ch D 234, where Bowen LJ said, at p. 251: 'It is not even a case where the owner of the saved property requires the assistance of a court of equity . . . to get the property back.' As a condition of giving effect to their equitable rights, the court has in my judgment a discretion to ensure that a proper allowance is made to the liquidator. His skill and labour may not have added directly to the value of the underlying assets in which the investors have equitable interests; but he has added to the estate in the sense of carrying out work which was necessary before the estate could be realised for the benefit of the investors. As was the case in *Scott* v *Nesbitt*, 14 Ves Jun 438, if the liquidator had not done this work, it is inevitable that the work, or at all events a great deal of it, would have had to be done by someone else, and on an application to the court a receiver would have been appointed whose expenses and fees would necessarily have had to be borne by the trust assets. On the evidence before me the beneficial interests of the investors could not have been established without some such investigation as has been carried out by the liquidator.

The allowance of fair compensation to the liquidator is in my judgment a proper application of the rule that he who seeks equity must do equity.

> That . . . is a rule of unquestionable justice, but which decides nothing in itself: for you must first inquire what are the equities which the defendant must do, and what the plaintiff ought to have: *Neesom* v *Clarkson* (1845) 4 Hare 97, 101 *per* Wigram V–C.
>
> The rule means that a man who comes to seek the aid of a court of equity to enforce a claim must be prepared to submit in such proceedings to any directions which the known principles of a court of equity may make it proper to give; he must do justice as to the matters in respect of which the assistance of equity is asked: *Halsbury's Laws of England*, 4th ed., vol. 16 (1976), p. 874, para. 1303, which in my judgment correctly states the law.

The authorities establish, in my judgment, a general principle that where a person seeks to enforce a claim to an equitable interest in property, the court has a discretion to require as a condition of giving effect to that equitable interest that an allowance be made for costs incurred and for skill and labour expended in connection with the administration of the property. It is a discretion which will be sparingly exercised; but factors which will operate in favour of its being exercised include the fact that, if the work had not been done by the person to whom the allowance is sought to be made, it would have had to be done either by the person entitled to the equitable interest (as in *In re Marine Mansions Co.* LR 4 Eq 601 and similar cases) or by a receiver appointed by the court whose fees would have been borne by the trust property (as in *Scott* v *Nesbitt*, 14 Ves Jun 438); and the fact that the work has been of substantial benefit to the trust property and to the persons interested in it in equity (as in *Phipps* v *Boardman* [1964] 1 WLR 993). In my judgment this is a case in which the jurisdiction can be exercised.

It seems to me that this principle is entirely consistent with the basis upon which the Court of Appeal acted in *In re Duke of Norfolk's Settlement Trusts* [1982] Ch 61. What the Court of Appeal held in that case was that, if the increase of the trustees' remuneration was beneficial to the trust administration, there was an inherent jurisdiction to require the beneficiaries to accept, as a condition of effect being given to their equitable interests, that such an increase in remuneration should be authorised. The court there was concerned with the good administration of a settlement of a conventional kind; but the jurisdiction which was held to be exercisable in that case is in my judgment equally exercisable in other cases in which a person seeks to enforce an interest in property to which he is entitled in equity. The principles on which a court of equity acts are not divided into watertight compartments but from a seamless whole, however necessary it may be for the purposes of exposition to attempt to set them out under distinct headings. I have already referred to the way in which Kekewich J in *In re Staffordshire Gas and Coke Co.* [1893] 3 Ch 523 treated expenditure on the preservation of trust property as coming under the head of 'salvage,' and the petitioning creditor in *In re Anglo-Austrian Printing and Publishing Union* [1895] 2 Ch 891 sought to persuade Vaughan Williams J to do the same. It is of interest that in *In re Duke of Norfolk's Settlement Trusts* [1979] Ch 37, 59B–C, Walton J regarded the cases in which the court authorises additional remuneration in order to secure the services of a particular trustee as also being 'closely analogous to "salvage".' I think this can fairly be regarded as confirmation of the underlying unity of the inherent jurisdiction which is exercised in such diverse circumstances as those which existed in *In re Marine Mansions Co.* LR 4 Eq 601; *Scott* v *Nesbitt*, 14 Ves Jun 438; *Phipps* v *Boardman* [1964] 1 WLR 993 and *In re Duke of Norfolk's Settlement Trusts* [1982] Ch 61. . . .

The particular aspect of the inherent jurisdiction which is sometimes referred to as 'salvage' was said by Evershed MR and Romer LJ in *In re Downshire Settled Estates* [1953] Ch 218, 235, to be exercisable

> where a situation has arisen in regard to the [trust] property (particularly a situation not originally foreseen) creating what may be fairly called an 'emergency'—that is a state of affairs which has to be presently dealt with, by which we do not imply that immediate action then and there is necessarily required—and such that it is for the benefit of everyone interested under the trusts that the situation should be dealt with by the exercise of the administrative powers proposed to be conferred for the purpose.

The situation which existed in the present case immediately before the commencement of the winding up could similarly fairly be called an emergency; and although the observations of Evershed MR and Romer LJ were directed to the court's jurisdiction to confer administrative powers upon trustees, the cases to which I have referred show that the inherent jurisdiction is wider than this and extends to making an allowance for costs incurred and skill and labour expended by those who have acted without obtaining the prior authority of the court. . . .

Question

Can the situation in this case fairly be described as an emergency? (See Goff and Jones, 369.)

B: *Authorities hostile to restitution*

The limits of maritime salvage

Nicholson* v *Chapman

(1793) 2 H Bl 254; 126 ER 536 (Common Pleas)

Nicholson's timber was secured in a dock by the Thames, but the ropes holding it fast became loose. The timber was carried by the tide as far as

Putney, where it was left at low water upon a tow path within the manor of Wimbledon. Chapman, under instructions from the bailiff of the manor, carried the timber in his waggon to a nearby place of safety beyond the reach of the tide. When Nicholson demanded his timber, Chapman refused to restore it unless he was remunerated for his efforts. Nicholson refused to pay. *Held*: Chapman held no lien upon the timber and was liable in trover for not handing it over.

EYRE CJ: The only difficulty that remained with any of us, after we had heard this case argued, was upon the question whether this transaction could be assimilated to salvage? The taking care of goods left by the tide upon the banks of a navigable river, communicating with the sea, may in a vulgar sense be said to be salvage; but it has none of the qualities of salvage, in respect of which the laws of all civilised nations, the laws of Oleron, and our own laws in particular, have provided that a recompence is due for the saving, and that our law has also provided that this recompence should be a lien upon the goods which have been saved. Goods carried by sea are necessarily and unavoidably exposed to the perils which storms, tempests and accidents (far beyond the reach of human foresight to prevent) are hourly creating, and against which, it too often happens that the greatest diligence and the most strenuous exertions of the mariner cannot protect them. When goods are thus in imminent danger of being lost, it is most frequently at the hazard of the lives of those who save them, that they are saved. Principles of public policy dictate to civilised and commercial countries, not only the propriety, but even the absolute necessity of establishing a liberal recompence for the encouragement of those who engage in so dangerous a service.

Such are the grounds upon which salvage stands . . . But see how very unlike this salvage is to the case now under consideration. In a navigable river within the flux and reflux of the tide, but at a great distance from the sea, pieces of timber lie moored together in convenient places; carelessness, a slight accident, perhaps a mischievous boy, casts off the mooring rope, and the timber floats from the place where it was deposited, till the tide falls and leaves it again somewhere upon the banks of the river. Such as event as this, gives the owner the trouble of employing a man, sometimes for an hour, and sometimes for a day, in looking after it till he finds it, and brings it back again to the place from whence it floated. If it happens to do any damage, the owner must pay for that damage; it will be imputable to him as carelessness, that his timber in floating from its moorings is found damage-feasant, if that should happen to be the case. But this is not a case of damage-feasance; the timber is found lying upon the banks of the river, and is taken into the possession, and under the care of the Defendant, without any extraordinary exertions, without the least personal risk, and in truth, with very little trouble. It is therefore a case of mere finding, and taking care of the thing found (I am willing to agree) for the owner. This is a good office, and meritorious, at least in the moral sense of the word, and certainly intitles the party to some reasonable recompence from the bounty, if not from the justice of the owner; and of which, if it were refused, a court of justice would go as far as it could go, towards enforcing the payment. So it would if a horse had strayed, and was not taken as an estray by the Lord under his manorial rights, but was taken up by some good-natured man and taken care of by him, till at some trouble, and perhaps at some expense, he had found out the owner. So it would be in every other case of finding that can be stated (the claim to the recompence differing in degree, but not in principle); which therefore reduces the merits of this case to this short question, whether every man who finds the property of another, which happens to have been lost or mislaid, and voluntarily puts himself to some trouble and expense to preserve the thing, and to find out the owner, has a lien upon it for the casual, fluctuating and uncertain amount of the recompence which he may reasonably deserve? It is enough to say, that there is no instance of such a lien having been claimed and allowed; the case of the pointer-dog [*Binstead* v *Buck* (1777) 2 W Bl 1117; 96 ER 660], was a case in which it was claimed and disallowed, and it was thought too clear a case to bear an argument. Principles of public policy and commercial necessity support the lien in the case of salvage. Not only public policy and commercial necessity do not require that it should be established in this case, but very great inconvenience may be apprehended from it, if it were to be established. The owners of this kind of property, and the owners of craft upon the river which lie in many places moored together in large numbers, would not only have common accidents from the carelessness of their servants to guard against, but also the wilful attempts of ill-designing people to turn their floats and vessels adrift, in order that they might be paid for finding them. I mentioned in the course of the cause another great inconvenience, namely, the situation in which an owner seeking to recover his property in an action of trover will be placed, if he is at his peril to make a tender of a sufficient recompence, before he brings his action: such an owner must always pay too much, because he has no means of knowing exactly how much he ought to pay, and because he must tender enough. I know there are cases in which the owner of property must submit to this inconvenience; but the number of them ought not to be increased: perhaps it is better for the public that these voluntary acts of benevolence from one man to another, which are charities and moral duties, but not legal duties, should depend altogether for their reward upon the moral duty of gratitude. But at any rate, it is fitting that he who claims the reward in such case should take upon himself the burthen of proving the nature of the service which he has performed, and the quantum of the recompence which he demands, instead of throwing it upon the owner to estimate it for him, at the hazard of being nonsuited in an action of trover.

Note

Birks takes the view that this case is hostile only to a proprietary claim (a lien, that is a legally imposed security, entitling a person to keep a possession of personal property until an obligation is discharged) but not to a purely personal claim: '*Negotiorum Gestio* and the Common Law' [1971] CLP 110, at 111–12.

The 'Goring'
[1988] AC 831 (HL)

Around midnight on 14 September 1984 the '*Goring*', a passenger vessel, broke free of her moorings on the River Thames, just up-river of Reading Bridge. She floated unmanned downriver in danger of colliding with other vessels, heading inexorably for the bridge and Reading Weir beyond. Five enterprising members of a club based on De Montford Island in the middle of the river managed to get one of their number aboard the vessel, and therefore got a rope from her and hauled her to the island where she was made fast. The five sought remuneration for the services provided in the Admiralty Court. Two issues were agreed. First, the Thames above

Reading bridge is non-tidal. Secondly, the services constituted the classic ingredients of a salvage claim: the claimants were volunteers who had rendered services to a ship in danger and had been successful in saving her from that danger.

LORD BRANDON OF OAKBROOK: [His lordship made a comprehensive survey of the history of the salvage jurisdiction and the statutory statements and extensions of that jurisdiction from 1840 to 1982, concluding that the jurisdiction did not extend to non-tidal inland waters. He continued:] My Lords, counsel for the appellants submitted that, even if the cause of action for salvage had not up till now been extended to services rendered in navigable non-tidal waters, it should now be so extended, by way of analogy and for reasons of public policy, by the process of judicial decision. In support of that submission reliance was placed on certain observations contained in the judgments of Sheen J and Sir John Donaldson MR [1987] QB 687. Sheen J said, at p. 693:

> If a ship or her cargo is in danger in non-tidal waters it is highly desirable, as a matter of public policy, that other ships should be encouraged to go to her assistance without hesitation.

Sir John Donaldson MR said, at pp. 706–707:

> In the end I believe that I have to seek a rational basis of confining the cause of action to tidal waters and I can find one. It is, of course, a maritime remedy and the public policy considerations which support it are directed at commercial shipping and seagoing vessels. But that said, I can see no sense in a cause of action which will remunerate the salvors of an ocean-going vessel inward bound for Manchester up to the moment when the vessel enters the Manchester Ship Canal, but no further. Some of the perils facing the vessel in the canal may be different from those facing it at sea, but many, such as fire, will be the same. The need to encourage assistance otherwise than under contract may be greater at sea, but the skills required of the salvors will be the same or at least similar. The vessel is not intended to sail only on tidal waters. The voyage over tidal and non-tidal waters is a single maritime adventure and should not attract wholly different rights and obligations by reference to the tidality of the water in which the vessel is for the time being sailing.

These are forceful passages. The majority in the Court of Appeal, however, took a different view, expressed with similar force. Their view was that, since salvage was a cause of action peculiar to the maritime law, and unknown to the common law in respect of services voluntarily rendered to property in danger on land, it would be wrong to extend its scope to non-tidal waters. They further considered that the need for such an extension for reasons of public policy had not been established.

In my view, since the scope of the cause of action for salvage has to be determined by reference to the statutory provisions which I examined earlier, it is not open to your Lordships' House, if it concludes that those provisions have the effect of limiting the scope of that cause of action to services rendered at sea or in tidal waters, to extend that scope by the process of judicial decision. If any such extension is to be made, it must, in my opinion, be left to the legislature to make it. . . .

Note

For discussion of this wasted opportunity to rationalise the law see Rose, 'Restitution for the Rescuer' (1989) 9 OJLS 167. The detail of the law of maritime salvage is beyond the scope of this book, but it has been rationalised as being concerned with the reversal of unjust enrichment: see Burrows, *Restitution*, 236–8; Birks, *Introduction*, 304–8; Goff and Jones, 385–99.

Non-maritime authority hostile to restitution for necessary preservation of property

Falcke* v *Scottish Imperial Insurance Company
(1886) 34 Ch D 234 (CA)

In 1879, Emanuel purchased a life insurance policy, which he mortgaged several times including once to Falcke. In 1883, Emanuel petitioned for bankruptcy and entered into a composition with his creditors. His interest in the policy was not subject to that agreement, so when he was discharged from bankruptcy later in 1883 he was the ultimate owner of the equity of redemption in the policy, subject to the various charges. In that year Emanuel paid the annual premium which fell due in the belief that without it the policy would be lost. In 1885, Mrs Falcke, who was her husband's executrix, sought to enforce her security against the insurance company and others, including Emanuel. The policy was realised for £4,000 which was paid into court. Emanuel brought a summons seeking reimbursement of the £1,212 he had paid as the premium. *Held*: Falcke was not entitled to a lien over the money.

COTTON LJ: . . . Now let us see what the general law is. It is not disputed that if a stranger pays a premium on a policy that payment gives him no lien on the policy. A man by making a payment in respect of property belonging to another, if he does so without request, is not entitled to any lien or charge on that property for such payment. If he does work upon a house without request he gets no lien on the house for the work done. If the money has been paid or the work done at the request of the person entitled to the property, the person paying the money or doing the work has a right of action against the owner for the money paid or for the work done at his request. If here there had been circumstances to lead to the conclusion that there was a request by Falcke that this premium should be paid by Emanuel, then there would be a claim against Falcke or his representative for the money, and I do not say that there might not be a lien on the policy. But in my opinion there is no evidence upon which we should be justified in coming to the conclusion that there was any request expressed or implied by Falcke to Emanuel to pay this money. An express request is not suggested. Was there an implied request? I think that in a case of this sort, when money is paid in order to keep alive property which belongs to another, a request to make that payment might be implied from slight circumstances, but in my opinion there is no circumstance here in evidence from which such a request can be implied. . . .

But what was the position of Emanuel at the time? He was, in my opinion, owner of the ultimate equity of redemption. Does that give him a right to have this sum paid by him for premium repaid to him out of the moneys arising from the policy? In my opinion it does not. It would be strange indeed if a mortgagor expending money on the mortgaged property could establish a charge in respect of that expenditure in priority to the mortgage. It is true that here the mortgagor, the ultimate owner of the equity of redemption, was no longer personally liable to pay the sums charged on the policy and was not bound by the covenant to pay the premium, but he pays it as the owner of the equity of redemption entitled to the ultimate interest in the property, although not personally bound to pay the debt or provide for the premium. It must be considered, in my opinion, that he paid it not so as to get any claim in priority to the incumbrancer, but in order to retain the benefit of the interest which would come to him if the property proved sufficient to pay off the previous incumbrancers. In my opinion it would be utterly wrong to say that a mortgagor, the owner of the equity of redemption, can under those circumstances defeat the incumbrancers on the estate. Suppose the mortgaged property is a mine, and the owner of the equity of redemption were to spend large sums of money in order to prevent the mine being flooded or otherwise destroyed, could he have in respect of that expenditure a lien on the estate as against the persons having charges and mortgages on that estate? In my opinion, no. . . .

BOWEN LJ: I am of the same opinion. The general principle is, beyond all question, that work and labour done or money expended by one man to preserve or benefit the property of another do not according to English law create any lien upon the property saved or benefited, nor, even if standing alone, create any obligation to repay the expenditure. Liabilities are not to be forced upon people behind their backs any more than you can confer a benefit upon a man against his will.

There is an exception to this proposition in the maritime law. I mention it because the word 'salvage' has been used from time to time throughout the argument, and some analogy is sought to be established between salvage and the right claimed by the Respondents. With regard to salvage, general average, and contribution, the maritime law differs from the common law. That has been so from the time of the Roman law downwards. The maritime law, for the purposes of public policy and for the advantage of trade, imposes in these cases a liability upon the thing saved, a liability which is a special consequence arising out of the character of mercantile enterprises, the nature of sea perils, and the fact that the thing saved was saved under great stress and exceptional circumstances. No similar doctrine applies to things lost upon land, nor to anything except ships or goods in peril at sea.

With regard to ordinary goods upon which labour or money is expended with a view of saving them or benefiting the owner, there can, as it seems to me, according to the common law be only one principle upon which a claim for repayment can be based, and that is where you can find facts from which the law will imply a contract to repay or to give a lien. It is perfectly true that the inference of an understanding between the parties—which you may translate into other language by calling it an implied contract—is an inference which will unhesitatingly be drawn in cases where the circumstances plainly lead to the conclusion that the owner of the saved property knew that the other party was laying out his money in the expectation of being repaid. In other words, you must have circumstances from which the proper inference is that there was a request to perform the service. It comes to the same thing, but I abstain the [from] using the word 'request' more than is necessary, for fear of plunging myself into all the archaic embarrassments connected with the cases about requests. But wherever you find that the owner of the property saved knew of the service being performed, you will have to ask yourself (and the question will become one of fact) whether under all the circumstances there was either what the law calls an implied contract for repayment or a contract which would give rise to a lien?

Now in the present case how can it be said that Mr Falcke, whose representative is claiming the benefit of this policy, so conducted himself as to justify an inference of the kind on the part of Mr Emanuel? There is absolutely no fact from which any such inference, as it seems to me, can be drawn at common law.

But then it is said that though at the time there may have been no such implied contract, nevertheless the subsequent attempt on the part of Mr Falcke's representative to take the benefit of the preserved policy makes her, by virtue of something in the nature of adoption or ratification, liable to repay the money expended. There is nothing more vague than the way in which the word 'adoption' is used in arguments at law, and sometimes ambiguous language used about adoption is imported into arguments about ratification. There is no such thing in law as adopting or ratifying anything except where there is the sanctioning of an act professedly done on your behalf in such a sense as to make you liable for it. A man can ratify that which purports to be done for him, but he cannot ratify a thing which purports to be done for somebody else. Ratification only takes effect in law from its being equivalent to a previous authority, and a previous authority is an incident which only arises in the relation of principal and agent. There have been many attempts to make people liable by what is called adoption of a contract, or of some other act which never purported to be made or done on their behalf, and such attempts have failed. I may instance as a leading type of that class of cases the attempts that have been made of late to make companies liable for contracts entered into by promoters.

Now the first observation with regard to the attempt to make Mr Falcke's estate liable on the ground that his respresentative has taken the benefit of what Emanuel has done, is that what Emanuel did was not done for Falcke's estate. Still, if he or his representative took the benefit of it under such circumstances as raise the proper inference of a fresh contract to pay, that would be altogether a different matter. But when we come to examine the case there is not a single fact which raises the slightest presumption that there was any intention at any time, either before Mr Falcke's death or afterwards, on the part of those who were negotiating with Mr Emanuel, to ask him to pay this sum of money. So much, therefore, for the idea of a lien or even of a right to be repaid this sum at common law.

Now in equity what is there here to give rise to any such right? The cases in equity were examined by Lord Justice Fry in *In re Leslie* 23 Ch D 552, and the general rule is the same in equity as at law. What have we here to take this case out of the general rule? Mr Emanuel was the owner of the equity of redemption. Does the mere fact that the owner of the equity of redemption paid premiums to keep alive the policy give him a right against the mortgagees to have the moneys which he so expended paid in priority to their debt? He paid in his own interest; he did not pay in the interest of the mortgagees. There can be no question here of acquiescence. The mortgagor does not pay under a mistake of fact or any mistake as to his own title. The mortgagee does not stand by and allow him to pay under such a mistake, and as regards any notion that he was allowed to pay under the expectation that he would be repaid again, or would have a lien for the money upon the policy, I have examined that already in the first part of the observations I have been making. If there were any acquiescence of this last kind, it would be an acquiescence from which in common law you would draw the inference of a contract; but, as I said before, there is no fact that leads to that.

Then, what equity is there than can be relied upon? It is not even a case where the owner of the saved property requires the assistance of a Court of Equity, or the name of the person who has paid that money to get the property back. Here the simple question is whether there are any facts from which we can say that it is unjust or inequitable that Mr Falcke's representatives should be allowed to have that which is their own? If you state the case in that way the answer is obvious, that one cannot see anything of the kind.

Note
For criticism see Birks, *Introduction*, 193–5 and Goff and Jones, 369–71.

C: *A general principle?*

Question
Fred's house is burgled while he is on a caravanning holiday in France. The thieves gained access by smashing the kitchen window. A storm is brewing. What legal remedies are there if:

(a) Fred's neighbour George pays a glazier to repair the window?
(b) Fred's neighbour Henry, who is himself a professional glazier, repairs the window?

Note
For academic advocacy of a generalisation of the right to restitution for the necessitous intervener see Birks, '*Negotiorum Gestio* and the Common Law' [1971] CLP 110 and Rose, 'Restitution for the Rescuer' (1989) 9 OJLS 167. See also the discussion in Birks, *Introduction*, 193–202, Burrows, *Restitution*, 231–49 and Goff and Jones, 363–84. Civilian systems, whose philosophy kept more in touch with the Roman law tradition than our own common law, have been more sympathetic to uninvited interveners. As a result this topic has attracted an excellent comparative literature. See, for example, Stoljar, '*Negotiorum Gestio*', Vol. X, Ch. 17, *International Encyclopedia of Comparative Law* and Dawson, '*Negotiorum Gestio*: The Altruistic Intermeddler' (1960–61) 74 Harv LR 817 and 1073.

4 FAILURE OF CONSIDERATION

Failure of consideration is the appropriate restitutionary cause of action where a benefit is transferred by A to B on the basis that B will in turn do some requested counter-performance or upon the happening of a future contingent event. If B fails to effect the counter-performance or the event does not occur, the reason for A's transfer is gone, and there is a good reason why A should get the benefit, or its value, back: the transfer was conditional upon obtaining the reciprocal performance by B or upon the event happening. In the language of Professor Birks, the reason for restitution is not that A's intention to transfer was *vitiated* (as in cases of mistake or compulsion), rather the intention was *qualified*. The distinction between *vitiation* and *qualification* is the central divide within Birks's analysis of non-voluntary transfers: Birks, *Introduction*, 219. It can be seen that most of the case law has a contractual flavour, at least that in which the language of 'failure of consideration' is explicitly used. For example, where contracts are discharged by termination for breach or frustration. The flavour is less prominent where an anticipated contract never materialises, or a contract is held to be void. To take an example of the former, suppose an intending house purchaser, keen to complete, pays the would-be vendor a deposit, as a token of good faith. All negotiations are 'subject to contract' and the deal falls through. The would-be purchaser can recover the money paid (*Chillingworth* v *Esche* [1924] 1 Ch 97). Cases such as this prompt Professor Birks to argue that the focus on contractual contexts is misconceived. Failure of consideration, or failure of basis, is a general principle of the law of transactions. Support is found in the equity case law concerning resulting trusts. These cases are not considered in detail here, partly for reasons of space, partly because they do not use the same language as the common law authorities. For discussion see Birks, *Introduction*, 219–20, 223–6; Birks, 'Restitution and Resulting Trusts' in Goldstein (ed.), *Equity and Contemporary Legal Developments* (1992), 335 especially at 347–59. This generalisation of 'failure of consideration' has so far failed to convince the judiciary. Hobhouse J stated recently:

> The phrase 'failure of consideration' is one which in its terminology presupposes that there has been at some stage a valid contract which has been partially performed by one party. It is essentially a concept for use in the law of contract and provides a common law remedy governed by rigid rules granted as of right where the contract becomes ineffective through breach or otherwise. (*Westdeutsche Landesbank Girozentrale* v *Islington London Borough Council* [1994] 4 All ER 891, at 924.)

(For further discussion of this case see Chapter 5, Section 2.)

Birks's generalisation of failure of consideration is attractive, but so far the case law has proceeded in a more haphazard way. While Birks's account eschews any obvious link with contractual doctrine, the majority of decisions which explicitly use 'failure of consideration' reasoning arise in a contractual context. The bulk of decisions concern contracts discharged by reason of termination for breach or frustration. The common law insisted on two preconditions for relief. First, the contract must be discharged (this is in accordance with general principles as discussed in Chapter 1). Secondly, the failure must be total. This second condition is much criticised and has been reversed by statute in relation to frustrated contracts. Another criticism of the common law was that it seemed concerned only with money whereas, in principle, failure of consideration could apply to other types of benefit. Again this point is accepted by statute in relation to frustrated contracts. Sections 1 and 2 below deal respectively with contracts discharged by termination for breach and frustration.

Sections 3 and 4 deal respectively with restitutionary techniques in the context of pre-contractual liability and in the sphere of void and unenforceable contracts. Where one party has conferred a benefit upon another, either in anticipation of remuneration under a contract not yet come to fruition, or under a contract rendered void or enforceable for reasons of policy, the other may be called upon to make restitution in respect of that benefit. Professor Burrows has convincingly argued that while the language of failure of consideration is not used by the judges, it is the best explanation of the restitutionary cause of action in many of the cases (Burrows, *Restitution*, 293–4, 304). That lead is followed here. Section 5 considers an alternative way of explaining many of the same cases: by using the concept of *free acceptance* as an unjust factor.

See Burrows, *Restitution*, 250–61, especially 253–7 and 259–61, discussing the requirement that the failure of consideration must be *total*.

Section 1: contracts discharged by breach

The law might have developed so that the remedies available upon a failure of contractual performance were entirely within the province of the law of contract. The remedies provided by that branch of the law are familiar. Most characteristically, every breach gives rise to a right to damages. Usually such damages are calculated according to the formula 'the victim of breach is to be placed in the position as if the contract had been performed' (commonly known as the *expectation* measure after Fuller and Perdue's seminal article 'The Reliance Interest in Contract Damages' (1936) 46 Yale LJ 36, 373, or more simply the contract measure). Damages are the primary remedy. Exceptionally the courts may be willing to order specific performance of contractual obligations if damages are likely to be inadequate, for example if the subject-matter of a contract of sale is unique, such as a Renoir or a Ming vase. A third remedy, important in practice because it is a self-help remedy, is the right to terminate for breach. Here the innocent party can elect to bring the contract to an end, to discharge both his own and the other party's obligations to perform. This remedy is prospective, operating only from the time of election, and is therefore distinct from remedies which seek to rescind the contract *ab initio*, for example, because of misrepresentation or duress. We have now moved from the realm of defective *formation* to the realm of defective *performance*. To determine whether termination for breach is available the courts utilise two distinct techniques. First, the courts characterise the parties' obligations. Some terms, either as a matter of positive law (because classified as such by statute, most famously the Sale of Goods Act, or by previous judicial exegesis) or as a matter of construction of the particular contract, are characterised as *fundamental terms*, or more classically *conditions*. Every breach of such a term gives rise to a right to terminate. If this process does not resolve the question of whether the innocent party can quit, the second stage is to examine the nature, seriousness and consequences of the breach. If the failure in performance is so serious that it deprives the innocent party of 'substantially the whole benefit which was the intention of the parties as expressed in the contract that he should obtain as the consideration' for his own performance, he is entitled to terminate (*Hong Kong Fir Shipping Ltd* v *Kawasaki Kishen Kaisha* [1962] 2 QB 26, at 66 *per* Diplock LJ). This combination of *term* analysis and *breach* analysis exhaustively determines the existence of the right to terminate (see generally *Photo Production Ltd* v *Securicor Ltd* [1980] AC 827, at 848–50 *per* Lord Diplock; *Bunge Corp. New York* v *Tradax Export SA, Panama* [1981] 1 WLR 711, at 717 *per* Lord Scarman).

What role is there for restitution in this essentially contractual scheme? It could be argued none, and that the availability of damages and the possibility of termination protect the innocent parties' interests and expectations. In fact the resulting picture is nowhere near so tidy. Consider the example of a straightforward high street contract of sale. Jill buys a consumer durable, perhaps a video camcorder, perhaps a brand new car. The product turns out to be defective. What does Jill want? Often she wants her money back. The mutual restitution of benefits received is an everyday way of unwinding unsatisfactory contracts. Such a course of action is usually willingly agreed to by businesses, keen on safeguarding reputation. In our increasingly consumer-driven society it is a surprising fact that our 100-odd year old Sale of Goods Act codification makes no mention of this straightforward remedy. Such consensual unwinding of defective consumer bargains may be common in practice, but when is it available as a matter of legal right? Here the law imposes two important preconditions. First, the contract must be discharged before any claim can be made in restitution. An important theme of this chapter will be concern with sanctity of contract, provoked by fears that restitutionary relief may subvert that principle by allowing parties to escape from bad bargains. Secondly, in order to recover it must be possible to show that there has been a *total* failure of consideration. To revert to our consumer sale example, what if Jill had had the benefit of the camcorder for two weeks on a Greek holiday before the defect manifested itself, or had driven the car for several months before its latent problems became apparent? Restitution may not be available as a matter of legal right where there has been intermediate use of the subject-matter of the contract. English law has resolutely set its face against adjustment or insisting on counter-restitution as a precondition of relief in this context. However, the strains are beginning to show and implausible judicial findings of *total* failure abound.

Moving away from our consumer sales example, money is not the only benefit which may have been conferred before the contract is discharged. Goods and services claims have arisen. History forces their separate treatment. The prospective nature of the remedy of termination means that property will usually have passed any goods transferred prior to discharge. Services give rise to their usual intractable problems in restitution. It is also necessary to distinguish the rights of the innocent party from the even more attenuated situation of the party in breach. It is far from clear when the party in breach will be able to claim in restitution. If such a claim is possible, it seems the ground for restitution is still failure of consideration.

A: Recovery of money by innocent party

See Burrows, *Restitution*, 262–6.

The requirement of total failure

Giles **v** ***Edwards***

(1797) 7 Term Rep 181; 101 ER 920 (KB)

Action for money had and received

On 6 June 1791, the defendant agreed to sell to the buyer all the cordwood growing in Tredgodoer, Shropshire, the wood to be removed by Michaelmas 1792, and the money to be paid on 1 March 1792. The custom was for the seller to cut off the boughs and trunks, and then cord it; the buyer would then re-cord it, after which it became his property. The defendant cut 60 cords, ten of which he corded, and the plaintiff re-corded half a cord and measured the rest. On 8 March 1792 the plaintiff paid the defendant 20 guineas, but the defendant failed to cord the rest of the wood. Therefore the plaintiff sought repayment of 20 guineas. Lord Kenyon CJ said: '. . . this was an entire contract; and as by the defendant's default the plaintiff could not perform what they had undertaken to do, they had a right to put an end to the whole contract and recover back the money that they had paid under it; they were not bound to take part of the wood only'.

Hunt v *Silk*

(1804) 5 East 449; 102 ER 1142 (KB)

Action for money had and received

On 31 August, 1802 Silk agreed that within ten days he would grant Hunt a 19-year lease of a dwelling-house at £93 per year, and Hunt agreed to pay £10 at the time of executing the lease. It was agreed that Hunt should have immediate possession. Silk agreed to make certain alterations and to make sure the premises were in a state of complete repair by the time the lease was executed. Hunt took possession and paid the £10 assuming the repairs would be done within ten days, but despite many requests Silk did not do the work. Some days after the ten-day deadline elapsed, Hunt left the house and claimed the £10 back.

LORD ELLENBOROUGH CJ: Without questioning the authority of the case cited [*Giles* v *Edwards* (1797) 7 Term Rep 181; 101 ER 920], which I admit to have been properly decided, there is this difference between that and the present; that there by the terms of the agreement the money was to be paid antecedent to the cording and delivery of the wood, and here it was not to be paid till the repairs were done and the lease executed. The plaintiff there had no opportunity by the terms of the contract of making his stand to see whether the agreement were performed by the other party before he paid his money, which the plaintiff in this case had: but instead of making his stand, as he might have done, on the defendant's non-performance of what he had undertaken to do, he waved his right, and voluntarily paid the money; giving the defendant credit for his future performance of the contract; and afterwards continued in possession notwithstanding the defendant's default. Now where a contract is to be rescinded at all, it must be rescinded in toto, and the parties put in statu quo. But here was an intermediate occupation, a part execution of the agreement, which was incapable of being rescinded. If the plaintiff might occupy the premises two days beyond the time when the repairs were to have been done and the lease executed, and yet rescinded the contract, why might he not rescind it after a twelvemonth on the same account. This objection cannot be gotten rid of: the parties cannot be put in statu quo.

LAWRENCE J: In the case referred to, where the contract was rescinded, both parties were put in the same situation they were in before. For the defendant must at any rate have corded his wood before it was sold. But that cannot be done here where the plaintiff has had an intermediate occupation of the premises under the agreement. If indeed the 101. had been paid specifically for the repairs, and they had not been done within the time specified, on which the plaintiff had thrown up the premises, there might have been some ground for the plaintiff's argument that the consideration had wholly failed: but the money was paid generally on the agreement, and the plaintiff continued in possession after the ten days, which can only be referred to the agreement.

Rowland v *Divall*

[1923] 2 KB 500 (CA)

Action for money had and received

In April 1922, Divall bought an 'Albert' motor car, which on 19 May he re-sold to Rowland, a car dealer, for £334. Rowland repainted the car and placed it on display in his showroom. In July, a Colonel Railsdon purchased it for £400. In September, the police took possession of the car. It turned out to have been stolen by the person who had sold it to Divall. Rowland repaid the colonel £400 and sought restitution of £334 from Divall. Bray J held that because of the intermediate use between May and September there had been no total failure of consideration, and therefore Rowland was confined to his remedy in damages. Rowland, the plaintiff, appealed.

SCRUTTON LJ: The discussion which this case has received in the course of the argument has made it reasonably clear to me that the learned judge below came to a wrong conclusion. The plaintiff purchased a car from the defendant for 334*l*. He drove it from Brighton, where he bought it, to the place where he had a garage, painted it and kept it there for about two months. He then sold it to a third person who had it in his possession for another two months. Then came the police, who claimed it as the stolen car for which they had been looking. It appears that it had been stolen before the defendant became possessed of it, and consequently he had no title that he could convey to the plaintiff. In these circumstances the plaintiff sued the defendant for the price he paid for the car as on a total failure of consideration. Now before the passing of the Sale of Goods Act there was a good deal of confusion in the authorities as to the exact nature of the vendor's contract with respect to his title to sell. It was originally said that a vendor did not warrant his title. But gradually a number of exceptions crept in, till at last the exceptions became the rule, the rule being that the vendor warranted that he had title to what he purported to sell, except in certain special cases, such as that of a sale by a sheriff, who does not so warrant. Then came the Sale of Goods Act, which re-enacted that rule, but did so with this alteration: it re-enacted it as a condition, not as a warranty. Section 12 says in express terms that there shall be 'An implied condition on the part of the seller that . . . he has a right to sell the goods.' It being now a condition, wherever that condition is broken the contract can be rescinded, and with the rescission the buyer can demand a return of the purchase money, unless he has, with knowledge of the facts, held on to the bargain so as to waive the condition. But Mr Doughty [counsel for Divall] argues that there can never be a rescission where a restitutio in integrum is impossible, and that here the plaintiff cannot rescind because he cannot return the car. To that the buyer's answer is that the reason of his inability to return it—namely, the fact that the defendant had no title to it—is the very thing of which he is complaining, and that it does not lie in the defendant's mouth to set up as a defence to the action his own breach of the implied condition that he had a right to sell. In my opinion that answer is well founded, and it would, I think, be absurd to apply the rule as to restitutio in integrum to such a state of facts. No doubt the general rule is that a buyer cannot rescind a contract of sale and get back the purchase money unless he can restore the subject matter. There are a large number of cases on the subject, some of which are not very easy to reconcile with others. Some of them make it highly probable that a certain degree of deterioration of the goods is not sufficient to take away the right to recover the purchase money. However I do not think it necessary to refer to them. It certainly seems to me that, in a case of rescission for the breach of the condition that the seller had a right to sell the goods, it cannot be that the buyer is deprived of his right to get back the purchase money because he cannot restore the goods which, from the nature of the transaction, are not the goods of the seller at all, and which the seller therefore has no right to under any circumstances. For these reasons I think that the plaintiff is entitled to recover the whole of the purchase money as for a total failure of consideration, and that the appeal must be allowed.

ATKIN LJ: I agree. It seems to me that in this case there has been a total failure of consideration, that is to say that the buyer has not got any part of that for which he paid the purchase money. He paid the money in order that he might get the property, and he has not got it. It is true that the seller delivered to him the de facto possession, but the seller had not got the right to possession and consequently could not give it to the buyer. Therefore the buyer, during the time that he had the car in his actual possession had no right to it, and was at all times liable to the true owner for its conversion. Now there is no doubt that what the buyer had a right to get was the property in the car, for the Sale of Goods Act expressly provides that in every contract of sale there is an implied condition that the seller has a right to sell; and the only difficulty that I have felt in this case arises out of the wording of s. 11, sub-s. 1(c) [Sale of Goods Act 1979, s. 11(4)], which says that: 'Where a contract of sale is not severable, and the buyer has accepted the goods . . . the breach of any condition to be fulfilled by the seller can only be treated as a breach of warranty, and not as a ground for rejecting the goods and treating the contract as repudiated, unless there be a term of the contract, express or implied, to that effect.' It is said that this case falls within that provision, for the contract of sale was not severable and the buyer had accepted the car. But I think that the answer is that there can be no sale at all of goods which the seller has no right to sell. The whole object of a sale is to transfer property from one person to another. And I think that in every contract of sale of goods there is an implied term to the effect that a breach of the condition that the seller has a right to sell the goods may be treated as a ground for rejecting the goods and repudiating the contract notwithstanding the acceptance, within the meaning of the concluding words of sub-s. 1(c); or in other words that the sub-section has no application to a breach of that particular condition. It seems to me that in this case there must be a right to reject, and also a right to sue for the price paid as money had and received on failure of the consideration, and further that there is no obligation on the part of the buyer to return the car, for ex hypothesi the seller had no right to receive it. Under those circumstances can it make any difference that the buyer has used the car before he found out that there was a breach of the condition? To my mind it makes no difference at all. The buyer accepted the car on the representation of the seller that he had a right to sell it, and inasmuch as the seller had no such right he is not entitled to say that the buyer has enjoyed a benefit under the contract. In fact the buyer has not received any part of that which he contracted to receive—namely, the property and right to possession—and, that being so, there has been a total failure of consideration. The plaintiff is entitled to recover the 334*l.* which he paid.

Questions

1. Was there a *total* failure of consideration in this case?

2. Assuming that the intermediate enjoyment of the car did constitute a benefit, at whose expense was the plaintiff Rowland enriched?

Note

The background to this case is the rule of personal property, *nemo dat quod non habet* (a non-owner cannot give good title to chattels). It has been well-observed that the *action for money had and received* is 'not properly integrated' into the Sale of Goods Act codification: see Bridge, 'The evolution of modern sales law' [1991] LMCLQ 52, at 64–6.

Butterworth v _Kingsway Motors_
[1954] 1 WLR 1286 (Liverpool Assizes)

Miss Rudolph had possession of a 'Jowett Javelin' motor car under a contract of hire-purchase with Bowmaker Ltd. Before she had completed payment of the instalments and exercised her option to buy the car under the agreement, she wrongfully sold it, and by a sequence of further sales it reached the possession of the defendant car dealers. They in turn sold the car to Butterworth for £1,275 on 30 August 1951. The price was in part made up by the part-exchange of a 'Standard' car valued at £725. Butterworth made full use of the car from 30 August until 16 July 1952, when he received a letter from Bowmaker informing him that they were the owners and requiring possession. In the alternative Bowmaker offered Butterworth the opportunity to acquire the car lawfully upon payment of Miss Rudolph's unpaid instalments. Butterworth immediately wrote to Kingsway Motors terminating the contract and demanding £1,275. He made no further use of the car (although it remained on his premises). By July 1952 it was worth £800, and by the date of trial only £450. By that time the defendants had perfected their title to the car. Pearson J held that Butterworth was entitled to restitution of the £1,275 on the authority of *Rowland* v *Divall* [1923] 2 KB 500, but described the claim as 'somewhat lacking in merits'.

Notes

1. See also *Warman* v *Southern Counties Car Finance Corporation* [1949] 2 KB 576.

2. Part III of the Hire Purchase Act 1964 would now probably ensure that a private purchaser of a motor car, buying in good faith and without notice of the hire-purchase agreement, would obtain good title, as an exception to the general rule *nemo dat quod non habet*. This does not however affect the restitutionary right. See *Barber* v *NWS Bank plc* [1996] 1 All ER 906 (CA).

Yeoman Credit Ltd v _Apps_
[1962] 2 QB 508 (CA)

Goodbody, a car dealer, in April 1959 took a second-hand 1954 'Ford Zephyr' to the house of Apps late at night for Apps to have a run in it. It being dark Apps was unable to inspect the car, but took it for a short drive. He noticed that the windows were cracked, and pointed this out to Goodbody who promised that they would be replaced and that the car would have a complete overhaul. That night Goodbody persuaded Apps to sign a hire-purchase agreement with Yeoman Credit in respect of the car. The agreement stipulated an initial payment of £125, which Apps paid, and for 30 monthly instalments of £15. On 5 May, Goodbody left the car outside Apps's house, again at night, in the same state of disrepair. The car was 'unusable, unroadworthy and unsafe'. It took 1½ hours to drive three or four miles. It required repairs estimated at between £70 and £120. Apps paid the May, June and July instalments under the agreement, but failed to pay in August and September. Consequently in October Yeoman Credit terminated the contract. The car had to be towed away and was resold for £210. By now Goodbody was bankrupt. Yeoman Credit (the plaintiff) sued for the unpaid instalments, but Apps (the defendant) counterclaimed the money he had paid upon a total failure of consideration.

HOLROYD PEARCE LJ: . . . The defendant was plainly entitled to reject the car, to accept the plaintiff's repudiation of the contract by their delivery of such a car, and to rescind the contract. Had he done so, there would have been a total failure of consideration, and he would have recovered the sums paid. But, as the judge found, he made no serious effort to return the car. He kept it for five or six months, and approbated the contract by paying three instalments. He intended (to quote his evidence) 'to keep the car, and hoped Goodbody would pay half the cost.' He tried to find out from the plaintiffs what he could do to make Goodbody carry out the work. In those circumstances he was at that stage continuing with the agreement while protesting against the state of the car which was due to a breach of condition by the plaintiffs. This is not a case like *Rowland* v *Divall* [1923] 2 KB 500, CA where title was lacking, and the defendant never had lawful possession. Here the defendant had the possession of the car and its use, such as it was. In evidence he said: 'That month I got copy of agreement. I had had the car by that time. I had been able to drive it—very poor.' Admittedly the use was of little (if any) value, but in my view that use, coupled with possession, and his continuance of the hiring agreement with the intention of keeping the car and getting Goodbody to pay half the repairs, debars the defendant from saying that there was total failure of consideration. . . .

Note

Contrast *Rogers* v *Parish (Scarborough) Ltd* [1987] 2 All ER 232, where the plaintiff purchased a brand new Range Rover at a cost of £16,000. The vehicle proved unsatisfactory due to faulty oil seals, engine, gearbox and bodywork defects. The Court of Appeal held the vehicle was unmerchantable under s. 14 of the Sale of Goods Act 1979 (now amended by the Sale and Supply of Goods Act 1994). Despite the fact that the car had been driven 5,500 miles and had been used over a period of months, it had been validly rejected by the plaintiff who was entitled to recover the money paid for the vehicle, together with the value of a vehicle traded in part-exchange, and damages for breach of contract. The defendant company had failed to plead that the plaintiff was precluded from rejecting by their conduct; presumably this would have raised the question whether the intermediate enjoyment of the vehicle amounted to an acceptance of the car under s. 35 of the 1979 Act (also subsequently amended by the 1994 Act). Compare the less consumer-friendly decision of *Bernstein* v *Pamson Motors (Golders Green) Ltd* [1987] 2 All ER 220, which suggests that a motorist has only days (or possibly weeks) to reject the car, even when there is a serious latent defect potentially affecting its safe use. In *Rogers* v *Parish* there was no suggestion that any allowance should be made for the plaintiff's intermediate enjoyment.

Linz v *Electric Wire Company of Palestine Ltd*
[1948] AC 371 (PC)

Action for money had and received
Linz bought preference shares in a company which she then sold to a third party for substantially less than she had paid for them. It subsequently appeared that the shares were invalid, so Linz sought restitution alleging that 'she did not receive the consideration which she bargained for or any consideration'. *Held*: she was not entitled to restitution. Viscount Simonds:

> Their Lordships would at once dismiss as irrelevant to the determination of this question the fact that the appellant spontaneously offered in a certain event to refund to the bank the money which she received on the sale of her shares. Equally irrelevant is the fact that she obtained substantially less than she had paid for the shares. . . . [H]aving been duly registered as a shareholder and having parted for value with her shares by a sale which the company recognised by issue of a share certificate to, and registration of, her transferee, she got exactly that which she bargained for.

Notes
1. This case has been criticised as anomalous, the benefit received from the third party transferee being irrelevant to the question whether Linz received any consideration from the company (Goff and Jones, 402; and see Birks, *Introduction*, 248).
2. Here the plaintiff was seeking to escape a bad (and defective) bargain. Ignoring the defect in the shares in this particular case, should English law allow a plaintiff to escape a bad bargain by seeking restitution on the ground of total failure of consideration? Restitutionary relief may circumvent the rule that in damages for breach of contract a plaintiff is entitled to recover in the *expectation* measure: that is to be placed in the position that they would have been in had the contract been performed, and as recently suggested, not in a better position than if the contract had been performed (*C & P Haulage* v *Middleton* [1983] 1 WLR 1461 (CA) and *CCC Films (London) Ltd* v *Impact Quadrant Films Ltd* [1985] QB 16). There is no clear authority. The American case of *Bush* v *Canfield* 2 Conn 495 (1818) suggests that one can escape from bad bargains in this way. Canfield agreed to sell Bush 2,000 barrels of wheat flour at $7 a barrel by a contract made in February, delivery to be on or before 1 May. Bush paid a $5,000 deposit. Canfield bizarrely failed to deliver, even though the price had fallen to $5.50 on 1 May. Bush was awarded restitution of his $5,000. See Burrows, *Restitution*, 265–6.

Baltic Shipping Co. v *Dillon, The 'Mikhail Lermontov'*
(1993) 111 ALR 289 (High Court of Australia)

Action for money had and received
Mrs Dillon booked a 14–day cruise in the South Pacific aboard the '*Mikhail Lermontov*' and paid Australian $2,205 in advance. On the tenth

day of the cruise the vessel struck a rock off Cape Jackson, on the north-eastern tip of South Island, New Zealand, was holed and sank. Mrs Dillon lost some of her possessions and suffered personal injuries. The shipping company repaid part of the advance payment. Mrs Dillon sued in the Admiralty Division of the Supreme Court of New South Wales for damages for breach of contract and restitution of the remainder of her fare. The trial judge awarded both restitution of the fare and damages for breach of contract, including damages for mental distress. The Court of Appeal of New South Wales agreed. The shipping company appealed to the High Court. *Held*: Mrs Dillon was entitled to recover damages for breach of contract, but was not entitled to restitution of the fare.

MASON CJ: . . .

Is the fare recoverable on the grounds of total failure of consideration or otherwise? . . .

The question whether an advance payment, not being a deposit or earnest of performance, is absolute or conditional is one of construction. In determining that question it is material to ascertain whether the payee is required by the contract to perform work and incur expense before completing this performance of his or her obligations under the contract. If the payee is so required then, unless the contract manifests a contrary intention, it would be unreasonable to hold that the payee's right to retain the payment is conditional upon performance of the contractual obligations.[24]

I have come to the conclusion in the present case that the respondent is not entitled to recover the cruise fare on either of the grounds just discussed. The consequence of the respondent's enjoyment of the benefits provided under the contract during the first eight full days of the cruise is that the failure of consideration was partial, not total. I do not understand how, viewed from the perspective of failure of consideration, the enjoyment of those benefits was 'entirely negated by the catastrophe which occurred upon departure from Picton',[25] to repeat the words of the primary judge.

Nor is there any acceptable foundation for holding that the advance payment of the cruise fare created in the appellant no more than a right to retain the payment conditional upon its complete performance of its entire obligations under the contract. As the contract called for performance by the appellant of its contractual obligations from the very commencement of the voyage and continuously thereafter, the advance payment should be regarded as the provision of consideration for each and every substantial benefit expected under the contract. It would not be reasonable to treat the appellant's right to retain the fare as conditional upon complete performance when the appellant is under a liability to provide substantial benefits to the respondent during the course of the voyage. After all, the return of the respondent to Sydney at the end of the voyage, though an important element in the performance of the appellant's obligations, was but one of many elements. In order to illustrate the magnitude of the step which the respondent asks the court to take, it is sufficient to pose two questions, putting to one side cl. 9 of the printed ticket terms and conditions. Would the respondent be entitled to a return of the fare if, owing to failure of the ship's engines, the ship was unable to proceed on the last leg of the cruise to Sydney and it became necessary to airlift the respondent to Sydney? Would the fare be recoverable if, owing to a hurricane, the ship was compelled to omit a visit to one of the scheduled ports of call? The answer in each case must be a resounding negative. . . .

The combination of a claim for restitution and a claim for damages

In view of my conclusion that the respondent cannot succeed in her restitutionary claim for recoupment of the fare, there is no necessity for me to consider whether the two claims can be maintained. However, as the question has been argued, I should record my view of the question. There is authority to suggest that the claims are alternative and not cumulative.[30] But Lord Denning MR was clearly of the view that the claims may be concurrent. In *Heywood* v *Wellers*, he said:[31]

> [The plaintiff] could recover the £175 as money paid on a consideration which had wholly failed. She was, therefore, entitled to recover it as of right. And she is entitled to recover as well damages for negligence. Take this instance. If you engage a driver to take you to the station to catch a train for a day trip to the sea, you pay him £2—and then the car breaks down owing to his negligence. So that you miss your holiday. In that case you can recover not only your £2 back but also damages for the disappointment, upset and mental distress which you suffered.

Lord Denning was speaking of negligence in the sense of breach of a contractual obligation of due care. He noted a qualification to the entitlement to maintain the two claims:[32] 'Some reduction should be made for the fact that if the [defendants] had done their duty . . . it would have cost her something.' That reduction was accordingly made to the damages for breach of contract.

Similarly, in *Millar's Machinery Co. Ltd* v *David Way and Son*,[33] the Court of Appeal dismissed an appeal from a decision of Branson J in which such a dual award was made. The case concerned a contract for supply of machinery. It was held that there had been a total failure of consideration and that the purchasers were entitled to recover the amount paid on account. In addition, the purchasers were held to be entitled to damages, the proper measure of which was:[34]

> . . . the sum which the [purchasers] had to spend to put themselves in the position which they would have been if the [suppliers] had carried out their contract.

That amount was the difference between the contract price and the amount which they had to pay to another supplier for a similar machine.

And Treitel says in relation to claims for loss of bargain, reliance loss and restitution:[35]

> There is sometimes said to be an inconsistency between combining the various types of claim . . .
>
> The true principle is not that there is any logical objection to combining the various types of claim, but that the plaintiff cannot combine them so as to recover more than once for the same loss . . . The point has been well put by Corbin: '*full* damages and *complete* restitution . . . will not both be given for the same breach of contract'.[36]

The action to recover money paid on a total failure of consideration is on a common money count for money had and received to the use of the plaintiff.[37]

[Mason CJ then considered the history of the form of action and concluded:]

Conclusion: the respondent cannot recover the fare and damages for breach of contract

The old forms of action cannot provide the answer today. But, in my view, *Walstab* v *Spottiswoode* and the earlier cases support the view expressed by Corbin and Treitel that full damages and complete restitution will not be given for the same breach of contract. There are several reasons. First, restitution of the contractual consideration removes, at least notionally, the basis on which the plaintiff is entitled to call on the defendant to perform his or her contractual obligations. More particularly, the continued retention by the defendant is regarded, in the language of Lord Mansfield, as 'against conscience' or, in the modern terminology, as an unjust enrichment of the defendant because the condition upon which it was paid, namely, performance by the defendant may not have occurred.[61] But, equally, that performance, for deficiencies in which damages are sought, was conditional on payment by the plaintiff. Recovery of the money paid destroys performance of that condition. Secondly, the plaintiff will almost always be protected by an award of damages for breach of contract, which in appropriate cases will include an amount for substitute performance or an amount representing the plaintiff's reliance loss. It should be noted that nothing said here is inconsistent with *McRae* v *Commonwealth Disposals Commission*.[62]

I would therefore conclude that, even if the respondent had an entitlement to recover the cruise fare, Carruthers J and the majority of the court of Appeal erred in allowing restitution of the balance of the fare along with damages for breach of contract. . . .

[24] See *Hyundai Shipbuilding & Heavy Industries Co. Ltd* v *Pournaras* [1978] 2 Lloyds's Rep 502; *Hyundai Heavy Industries Co. Ltd* v *Papadopoulos* [1980] 1 WLR 1129, and the discussion in Beatson, [*The Use and Abuse of Unjust Enrichment*], pp. 56–7.

[25] (1989) 21 NSWLR, at 668; 92 ALR 331 at 381.

[30] eg, *Walstab* v *Spottiswoode* (1846) 15 M & W 501, *per* Pollock CB at 514; 153 ER 947, at 953.

[31] [1976] QB 446, at 458.

[32] ibid, at 459.

[33] (1935) 40 Com Cas 204.

[34] ibid, at 208.

[35] *The Law of Contract*, 8th ed. (1991), p. 834 [see now Treitel, *The Law of Contract* (9th ed., 1995), 850]. However, elsewhere he appears to treat the claims as alternatives: pp. 932–3 [see 9th ed., at 949–50].

[36] *Corbin on Contracts*, §1221 (emphasis added by Treitel).

[37] *Fibrosa* [1943] AC, at 61–3. To the extent that it is necessary to say so, this decision correctly reflects the law in Australia and, to the extent that it is inconsistent, should be preferred to the decision of this court in *Re Continental C & G Rubber Co. Pty Ltd* (1919) 27 CLR 194.

[61] See *Fibrosa* [1943] AC, *per* Lord Wright at 65–7.

[62] (1951) 84 CLR 377.

Question

Was an award of restitution of the passenger fare in this case logically incompatible with an award of damages for breach of contract?

Kit Barker, 'Restitution of Passenger Fare'

[1993] *Lloyd's Martime and Commercial Law Quarterly* 291, at 294–6.

. . . Discharge for breach: the relationship between contract and restitution

The High Court appears to have offered two lines of justification for its conclusion that Mrs Dillon could not successfully maintain both an action for damages for breach of contract and an action to recover her fare. One was that the two forms of action were logically inconsistent on the facts; the other that they could not be combined for reasons of policy.

Logical inconsistency

At one point, it was suggested that an award of compensation for breach eradicates a plaintiff's restitutionary cause of action: since damages for breach of contract represent a form of substitute performance or 'consideration', it is not open to a plaintiff who has received them to argue that the consideration for her payment has totally failed. She *has* received something for her money—namely, damages.[21]

A mirror argument, that an award of restitution extinguishes a plaintiff's contractual cause of action, was also used.[22] Since Mrs Dillon's right to demand performance from Baltic was itself conditional upon the payment of her fare, restitution of the fare removed her entitlement to demand contract performance and, with it, the right to recover compensatory damages for breach.

Both of these arguments are misconstrued. The first overlooks the fact that Mrs Dillon wanted primary performance (a cruise), not secondary performance (damages). To obtain compensation is never *to receive part of* that for which one has bargained; it is to have one's *loss* of bargain made good. The second argument plays tricks with time. If Mrs Dillon had a contractual cause of action at the time the *Mikhail Lermontov* sank (which she did), it cannot be that giving her money back would retroactively eradicate this ground of complaint. The wrong done to her at the time would do nothing, in other words, to 'rectify' or 'extinguish' the contractual wrong. Moreover, the consequences of the second argument would be ludicrous. To take an extreme example, the recovery of a 50p bus-fare would automatically preclude a passenger from suing in contract for spinal injuries caused to her by the driver's culpable negligence.

A third argument sometimes put is not so much that contract damages eradicate the restitutionary cause of action, as that the objectives of compensatory and restitutionary remedies are incompatible. Damages for breach are designed to 'enforce' a contract, taking the plaintiff 'forward' to a notional post-performance position, while restitution forms part of the process of its 'rescission', and aims to restore a plaintiff to the pre-contractual position. One cannot, it is said, go forwards and backwards at the same time. Logical though this proposition may seem, it is founded upon artificial considerations.[23] For one thing, contract damages do not always take the plaintiff 'forward', since reliance damages aim to restore the plaintiff to the position he would have been in if the contract had never been made. More generally, the perceived contrast between 'enforcement' and 'restitution' is largely the product of loose thinking. Contract damages, remember, do not, 'enforce' a contract in any real sense; they compensate a loss.[24] So the appropiate principles to compare, when deciding upon the logical compatibility of damages and the action for money had and received, are not the principles of 'enforcement' and 'rescission' (whatever these may mean) but those of 'compensation' and 'restitution'; the rectification of unjust losses and the restoration of unjust gains. Once this is realised, and the misleading imagery of a plaintiff's moving forwards and backwards in time is removed, it becomes apparent that the two actions are not incompatible at all. It is quite feasible, on one set of facts, both to eradicate a loss and to restore a gain, though one must always be careful that, in so doing, the plaintiff is not compensated twice.

The logical compatibility of restitutionary awards and contract damages appears now to have been widely acknowledged.[25]

Policy

The more popular reservation about combining the two remedies is that this may contravene the law's policy against double recovery for the same loss. This is always a danger in cases such as the present, because there is at least a partial correspondence between the plaintiff's loss and the defendant's gain. If Mrs Dillon were awarded both 'full' (gross) compensation and restitution of her fare, she would 'have the equivalent of performance of the contractual promise without having borne the expense which

. . . she had agreed to pay for it'.[26] Her fare might be recovered once within the restitutionary award, and again as part of the loss occasioned by the defendant's breach. The argument is nonetheless strictly limited. It holds true only if the plaintiff's loss of bargain is valued gross; that is, without subtracting from the award the amount she would have had to pay to secure the promised performance. Provided losses are assessed net of this sum, compensation and restitution are perfectly compatible. The policy argument does not debar combined claims for restitution and contract damages at all. It merely requires a downward adjustment of the latter to take account of the former.

[21] 'it would be quite wrong to say [in such a case] . . . that the promise and the recovery of compensatory damages for its breach can realistically be seen as representing no consideration at all:' [(1993) 111 ALR 289] at p. 316, *per* Deane and Dawson, JJ.

[22] See Mason, CJ, at p. 300. It is particularly surprising that Mason CJ, ran this argument, given his apparent acceptance of the views of Professor Treitel, *infra*, fn. 23.

[23] See Treitel, *Remedies for Breach of Contract* (1988), 98–100; *Corbin on Contracts*, s. 1223.

[24] Albeit that this loss may be assessed by reference to different notional positions: pre-contractual and post-contractual. The only real 'enforcement' remedy in this context is specific performance.

[25] See, Treitel, *supra*, fn. 23; Corbin, *supra*, fn. 23; *Heywood* v *Wellers* [1976] QB 446, 458, *per* Lord Denning, MR; *Millar's Machinery Co. Ltd* v *David Way & Son* (1935) 40 Com Cas 204. Combined awards are also acknowledged in the US Uniform Commercial Code, s. 2–711(1).

[26] At p. 316, *per* Deane and Dawson, JJ.

Note

The reasoning of the High Court of Australia is at first blush very attractive, although, as Barker's criticisms make clear, their conclusions were not ineluctable. Perhaps the High Court succumbed too easily to an elegant solution. It is not easy to point to English authority pointing either way after seriously addressing the question. However, as a matter of practice it seems likely that English courts have awarded combinations of restitution and compensation, oblivious of any theoretical difficulties. To take one example, consider the award in *Rogers* v *Parish (Scarborough) Ltd* [1987] 2 All ER 232 (discussed above).

A three-party configuration

Pan Ocean Shipping Co. Ltd* v *Creditcorp Ltd, The 'Trident Beauty'
[1994] 1 WLR 161 (HL)

Pan Ocean chartered the vessel '*Trident Beauty*' from Trident under a time charter dated 19 April 1991. Hire for the ship at US $6,400 per day was payable 15 days in advance. In order to finance its operations, Trident arranged credit facilities with Creditcorp. As part of this arrangement Trident assigned its right to hire from the vessel to Creditcorp. On 21 May, Trident informed Pan Ocean that all hire payments should be made directly to Creditcorp. Accordingly on 31 May, Pan Ocean paid $93,600 to Creditcorp. However, throughout the period to which this payment was referable, the vessel was rendered off-hire, because she was undergoing repairs in Singapore. On 12 June the vessel was withdrawn, so on 10 July Pan Ocean terminated the charterparty, accepting Trident's conduct as repudiatory. Pan Ocean sought restitution of $93,600 from *Creditcorp* on the ground of total failure of consideration.

LORD GOFF OF CHIEVELEY: . . . To consider the question whether Pan Ocean is entitled to recover the money from Creditcorp on this ground, it is necessary first to turn to the time charter which governed the relationship between Trident and Pan Ocean. Under the charter the hire was, as normal, payable in advance—here 15 days in advance. Provision was made, also as normal, for the vessel to be off-hire in certain specified circumstances. . . .

Now, given the circumstances that the charter hire was payable in advance and that the vessel might be off-hire under one or other of the relevant clauses during a period in respect of which hire had been paid, it was inevitable that, from time to time, there might have to be an adjustment of the hire so paid. Such adjustments are a normal feature of the administration of time charters. The usual practice is, I understand, for an adjustment to be made when the next instalment of hire falls due, by making a deduction from such instalment in respect of hire previously paid in advance which has not been earned. . . .

Sometimes, the event which gives rise to the charterer being deprived of the services of the vessel, in whole or in part, which in its turn renders the vessel off hire under one of the applicable clauses, may constitute a breach of contract by the shipowner. If so, the charterer will have a claim for damages for breach of contract, which may embrace the amount of hire paid in advance in respect of the period during which the vessel was off hire. But this need not be so; and in any event the charter will usually make express provision for the repayment of hire which has been overpaid. In the present charter, such a provision is to be found in clause 18 of the printed form, which provides that 'any overpaid hire' is 'to be returned at once.' This provision gives rise to a contractual debt payable in the relevant circumstances by the shipowner to the charterer. But even in the absence of any such express contractual provision, advance hire which proves to have been paid in respect of a period during which the vessel was rendered off hire under a term of the contract must ordinarily be repaid, and if necessary a term will be implied into the contract to that effect. That such an implied obligation may arise is implicit in such early cases as *Tonnelier* v *Smith* (1897) 2 Com Cas 258, and *C. A. Stewart & Co.* v *Phs. Van Ommeren (London) Ltd* [1918] 2 KB 560. This will of course be dealt with in the ordinary case as a matter of administration of the time charter; if any dispute should persist, it will fall to be resolved by arbitration.

All this is important for present purposes, because it means that, as between shipowner and charterer, there is a contractual regime which legislates for the recovery of overpaid hire. It follows that, as a general rule, the law of restitution has no part to play in the matter; the existence of the agreed regime renders the imposition by the law of a remedy in restitution both unnecessary and inappropriate. Of course, if the contract is proved never to have been binding, or if the contract ceases to bind, different considerations may arise, as in the case of frustration (as to which see *French Marine* v *Compagnie Napolitaine d'Eclairage et de Chauffage par le Gaz* [1921] 2 AC 494, and now the Law Reform (Frustrated Contracts) Act 1943). With such cases as these, we are not here concerned. Here, it is true, the contract was prematurely determined by the acceptance by Pan Ocean of Trident's repudiation of the contract. But, before the date of determination of the contract, Trident's obligation under clause 18 to repay the hire instalment in question had already accrued due; and accordingly that is the relevant obligation, as between Pan Ocean and Trident, for the purposes of the present case.

It follows that, in the present circumstances and indeed in most other similar circumstances, there is no basis for the charterer recovering overpaid hire from the shipowner in restitution on the ground of total failure of consideration. It is true that sometimes we find in the cases reference to there having been in such circumstances a failure of consideration (see, e.g., *C. A. Stewart & Co.* v *Phs. Van Ommeren (London) Ltd* [1918] 2 KB 560, 563, *per* Scrutton LJ). But it should not be inferred that such statements refer to a quasi-contractual, as opposed to a contractual, remedy. Consistently with this view, the remedy is not limited to the recovery of money paid for a consideration which has *wholly* failed. A contractual remedy is not, of course, so circumscribed and so, in *C. A. Stewart & Co.* v *Phs. Van Ommeren (London) Ltd* itself, overpaid hire was recoverable where it was recognised that there had been a partial failure of consideration—see p. 562, *per* R.A. Wright KC arguendo.

It is against this background that we have to consider Pan Ocean's claim now made against Creditcorp for repayment of the hire instalment paid to it as assignee of the charter hire. First, although the benefit of the contract debt had been assigned to Creditcorp, with the effect that payment to Creditcorp by Pan Ocean constituted a good discharge of the debt, nevertheless the burden of the contract remained upon Trident. From this it follows that Trident remained contractually bound to repay to Pan Ocean any overpaid hire, notwithstanding that such hire had been paid not to Trident but to Creditcorp as assignee. Mr Hirst, for Pan Ocean, accepted in argument that this was so; but he nevertheless maintained that Pan Ocean had alternative courses of action open to it—either to proceed against Trident in contract, or to proceed against Creditcorp in restitution. His argument proceeded on the basis that, in ordinary circumstances, a charterer has alternative remedies against the shipowner for the recovery of overpaid hire, either in contract or in restitution; and that here, since the hire had been paid to Creditcorp as assignee, Pan Ocean's remedy in restitution lay against Creditcorp in place of Trident. However, for the reasons I have already given, I am unable to accept this argument. This is because, in my opinion, Pan Ocean never had any remedy against Trident in restitution on the ground of failure of consideration in the present case, its only remedy against Trident lying under the contract. . . .

I am of course well aware that writers on the law of restitution have been exploring the possibility that, in exceptional circumstances, a plaintiff may have a claim in restitution when he has conferred a benefit on the defendant in the course of performing an obligation to a third party (see, e.g., *Goff and Jones on the Law of Restitution*, 4th ed. (1993), pp. 55 et seq., and (for a particular example) *Burrows on the Law of Restitution*, (1993) pp. 271–272). But, quite apart from the fact that the existence of a remedy in restitution in such circumstances must still be regarded as a matter of debate, it is always recognised that serious difficulties arise if the law seeks to expand the law of restitution to redistribute risks for which provision has been made under an applicable contract. Moreover, it would in any event be unjust to do so in a case such as the present where the defendant, Creditcorp, is not the mere recipient of a windfall but is an assignee who has purchased from Trident the right to receive the contractual debt which the plaintiff, Pan Ocean, is now seeking to recover from Creditcorp in restitution despite the facts that the relevant contract imposes on the assignor (Trident) an obligation of repayment in the circumstances in question, and that there is nothing in the assigment which even contemplates, still less imposes, any additional obligation on the assignee (Creditcorp) to repay. This is the point which, as I understand it, concerned Neill LJ in the Court of Appeal, when he said that 'Creditcorp were in a position analogous to that of a bona fide purchaser for value:' see [1993] 1 Lloyd's Rep 443, 449.

LORD WOOLF: . . . It is one thing to require the other party to the contract to repay if he does not provide the consideration which under the contract he was under obligation to supply, it is another to make the assignee, who was never intended to be under any obligation to supply the consideration liable to make the repayment. It is conceded that there is no right to trace moneys which are paid to an assignee and there is never any question of there being any restriction on the assignee preventing him dealing with the money as his own. There is no justification for subjecting an assignee, because he has received a payment in advance, to an obligation to make a repayment because of the non-performance of an event for which he has no reponsibility. . . .

Question

What is the *ratio decidendi* of this case?

Note

The reasoning in this case is rigorously criticised by Barker [1994] LMCLQ 305.

B: *Recovery of non-money benefits by the innocent party*

See Burrows, *Restitution*, 267–72.

Planché v *Colburn*
(1831) 8 Bing 14; 131 ER 305 (Common Pleas)

Quantum meruit

The defendants commenced a periodical publication entitled 'The Juvenile Library' and commissioned Planché to write a volume on costume and ancient armour for the series for £100. Planché did a considerable amount of the work, made one journey to inspect a collection of ancient armour and made some drawings of the collection. The author was ready and willing to complete and tender the manuscript, but had neither offered it nor delivered it. The reason was that the defendants refused to publish it; the earlier volumes of the library not having been successful, they had abandoned the project. Planché at the trial attempted to argue that there was a fresh contract, but this was rejected by the jury, who nevertheless found it was the defendants who had abandoned the original contract and awarded Planché £50. The defendants sought to have that judgment set aside.

TINDAL CJ: In this case a contract had been entered into for the publication of a work on Costume and Ancient Armour in 'The Juvenile Library.' The considerations by which an author is generally actuated in undertaking to write a work are pecuniary profit and literary reputation. Now, it is clear that the latter may be sacrificed, if an author, who has engaged to write a volume of a popular nature, to be published in a work intended for a juvenile class of readers, should be subject to have his writings published as a separate and distinct work, and therefore liable to be judged of by more severe rules than would be applied to a familiar work intended merely for children. The fact was, that the Defendants not only suspended, but actually put an end to,

'The Juvenile Library;' they had broken their contract with the Plaintiff; and an attempt was made, but quite unsuccessfully, to shew that the Plaintiff had afterwards entered into a new contract to allow them to publish his book as a separate work.

I agree that, when a special contract is in existence and open, the Plaintiff cannot sue on a quantum meruit: part of the question here, therefore, was, whether the contract did exist or not. It distinctly appeared that the work was finally abandoned; and the jury found that no new contract had been entered into. Under these circumstances the Plaintiff ought not to lose the fruit of his labour; and there is no ground for the application which has been made.

BOSANQUET J: The Plaintiff is entitled to retain his verdict. The jury have found that the contract was abandoned; but it is said that the Plaintiff ought to have tendered or delivered the work. It was part of the contract, however, that the work should be published in a particular shape; and if it had been delivered after the abandonment of the original design, it might have been published in a way not consistent with the Plaintiff's reputation, or not at all.

Question

Were the defendants enriched in this case?

Note

It is a matter of some controversy whether *Planché* v *Colburn* can be explained on restitutionary principles. See Burrows, *Restitution*, 8–9, 267, who regards the case as one awarding damages for breach of contract, in either the expectation or reliance measure; Birks, *Introduction*, 126–7, 232, 286–7, who believes the case does belong within restitution, explicable as a case of failure of consideration (unjust factor) coupled with 'limited acceptance' (as a test of enrichment); Beatson prefers to explain the case on the basis of a principle of injurious reliance (Beatson, *Unjust Enrichment*, 35); see also Goff and Jones, 20–21, 425–6.

De Bernardy v *Harding*

(1853) 8 Ex 822; 155 ER 1586 (Exchequer Chamber)

Quantum meruit; action for money paid

Harding planned to erect some seats over the Opera Colonnade in order to let them for viewing the procession of the state funeral of the Duke of Wellington. He engaged De Bernardy as foreign agent, to promote the event and sell tickets abroad. It was agreed that De Bernardy would be remunerated by a 10 per cent share of tickets sold. De Bernardy expended money on advertising, accommodation and clerks, but before he had sold any tickets, Harding requested him not to do so as he would sell them all on the spot. De Bernardy accordingly sent all applicants to Harding and after the funeral submitted a bill to Harding for his work and expenses. Harding paid the printers and others employed by De Bernardy, but refused him any remuneration for work done. De Bernardy sued, but at the trial Alderson B held he could not recover on a *quantum meruit* but ought to have sued for breach of the contract. He accordingly entered judgment for the defendant and withdrew the question from the jury. De Bernardy sought a re-trial.

POLLOCK CB: This rule must be absolute. It was a question for the jury, whether, under the circumstances, the original contract was not abandoned, and whether there was not an implied understanding between the parties that the plaintiff should be paid for the work actually done as upon a quantum meruit.

ALDERSON B: I also think that it ought to have been left to the jury to say whether the special contract was abandoned. Where one party has absolutely refused to perform, or has rendered himself incapable of performing, his part of the contract, he puts it in the power of the other party either to sue for a breach of it, or to rescind the contract and sue on a quantum meruit for the work actually done.

Boomer v *Muir*

24 P 2d 570 (1933) (District Court of Appeal of California)

Quantum meruit

Muir was the main contractor for a large hydro-electric project in the mountains on the tributaries of the Feather River. In May 1926, Boomer was appointed sub-contractor for the construction of the Buck's Creek dam. Work was to be completed by 1 December 1927. Boomer was to receive monthly progress payments based on 90 per cent of the value of work done the previous month. Friction and dispute arose between the parties almost as soon as work began. This continued for 18 months. In December 1927, Boomer left the site leaving the work unfinished, though near completion. There was evidence that the main contractor did not supply materials as quickly as Boomer needed them, and that this slowed up Boomer's progress and increased his costs. Boomer elected to sue upon a *quantum meruit* rather than claim damages for breach. *Held*: Boomer was entitled to quit the job because of the main contractor's failure to furnish materials. He was further entitled to recover the reasonable value of the work done under the contract, even though such recovery might exceed the contract price. Therefore Boomer recovered over $250,000 on the *quantum meruit* when only $20,000 remained due under the contract. Dooling J said:

> To hold that payments under the contract may limit recovery where the contract is afterwards rescinded through the defendant's fault seems to us to involve a confusion of thought. A rescinded contract ceases to exist for all purposes. How can it then be looked to for one purpose, the purpose of fixing the amount of the recovery? . . . [T]he defendant by his own wrong having put an end to the contract, cannot insist on its terms to limit the recovery, even though part payments have been made for part performance because the payments are received as satisfaction only on condition that the entire contract be performed according to its terms; but that, the contract having been rescinded through the defendant's fault, he should place the plaintiff as nearly as possible *in statu quo* by paying the reasonable value of the plaintiff's performance.

Notes

1. See *Lodder* v *Slowey* [1904] AC 442, where the Privy Council reached a similar conclusion, although without explicit consideration of the 'contract ceiling' question. For discussion see Burrows, *Restitution*, 268–71.

2. The reasoning of the District Court of Appeal of California appears to rest on an extreme view of the effect of rescission (or termination for breach) upon the contract. At least in the English jurisidiction the remedy operates prospectively, not retrospectively (*Johnson* v *Agnew* [1980] AC 367, at 392–3 *per* Lord Wilberforce; and see *Photo Production Ltd* v *Securicor Transport Ltd* [1980] AC 827, at 848–50 *per* Lord Diplock).

C: Recovery of money by the party in breach

See Burrows, *Restitution*, 272–6.

Howe* v *Smith
(1884) 27 Ch D 89 (CA)

Under a contract for the sale of land the purchaser paid £500 out of the purchase price of £12,500 as a deposit. The sale did not go ahead due to delay on the part of the purchaser, who was refused a decree of specific performance. The purchaser then sought restitution of the £500. Clause 8 of the contract provided:

> If the purchaser shall fail to comply with this agreement the vendors shall be at liberty to resell the premises in any manner, and the deficiency on such second sale thereof, together with all expenses attending the same, shall be made good by the defaulter at this present sale. . . .

Held: the purchaser was in breach and was not entitled to restitution.

COTTON LJ: . . . In *Palmer* v *Temple* 9 Ad & E 508, undoubtedly, the Judges did say that independently of contract the vendor cannot on the default of the purchaser retain the deposit, and there are similar expressions in other cases. There is a similar expression of opinion in *Hinton* v *Sparkes* Law Rep 3 CP 161, and I think similar expressions of opinion in other cases at Common Law. But that, as I understand the expression used by Lord St. Leonards, in his book on Vendors and Purchasers, is not in accordance with his view; for he says there, 'Where a purchaser is in default and the seller has not parted with the subject of the contract, it is clear that the purchaser could not recover the deposit; for he cannot, by his own default, acquire a right to rescind the contract.' Then he goes on and states his opinion that the mere re-sale of the estate after the purchaser's default cannot in any way affect the right of the vendor to retain the deposit.

Then we have a case of *Collins* v *Stimson* 11 QBD 142, 143 in which Baron Pollock refused to order the return of the deposit under circumstances somewhat different from this. What he says is this, 'According to the law of vendor and purchaser the inference is that such a deposit is paid as a guarantee for the performance of the contract, and where the contract goes off by default of the purchaser, the vendor is entitled to retain the deposit.' That was the principle of his decision.

But the case does not quite stop there. There is a decision under somewhat different circumstances from the present case in *Depree* v *Bedborough* 4 Giff 479, where there was a purchase under a sale by decree of the Court. I will not refer further to that case, but it is in accordance with a subsequent decision of the Court of Appeal in *Ex parte Barrell* Law Rep 10 Ch 512, where the purchaser had become bankrupt, and the trustee in bankruptcy had disclaimed the contract under which he sought to recover the deposit. That was refused. What Lord Justice James says is this, 'The trustee in this case has no legal or equitable right to recover the deposit. The money was paid to the vendor as a guarantee that the contract should be performed. The trustee refuses to perform the contract, and then says, Give me back the deposit. There is no ground for such a claim.'

There is a variance, no doubt, in the expressions of opinion, if not in the decisions, with reference to the return of the deposit, but I think that the judgment of Lord Justice James gives us the principle on which we should deal with the case. What is the deposit? The deposit, as I understand it, and using the words of Lord Justice James, is a guarantee that the contract shall be performed. If the sale goes on, of course, not only in accordance with the words of the contract, but in accordance with the intention of the parties in making the contract, it goes in part payment of the purchase-money for which it is deposited; but if on the default of the purchaser the contract goes off, that is to say, if he repudiates the contract, then, according to Lord Justice James, he can have no right to recover the deposit.

I do not say that in all cases where this Court would refuse specific performance, the vendor ought to be entitled to retain the deposit. It may well be that there may be circumstances which would justify this Court in declining, and which would require the Court, according to its ordinary rules, to refuse to order specific performance, in which it could not be said that the purchaser had repudiated the contract, or that he had entirely put an end to it so as to enable the vendor to retain the deposit. In order to enable the vendor so to act, in my opinion there must be acts on the part of the purchaser which not only amount to delay sufficient to deprive him of the equitable remedy of specific performance, but which would make his conduct amount to a repudiation on his part of the contract. In those circumstances, in my opinion, the rule is correctly laid down in Lord Justice James's judgment (of course the case there was stronger than the one we have to deal with) where the representatives of the purchaser had neither in law nor in equity the right to the return of the deposit.

BOWEN LJ: . . . The question as to the right of the purchaser to the return of the deposit money must, in each case, be a question of the conditions of the contract. In principle it ought to be so, because of course persons may make exactly what bargain they please as to what is to be done with the money deposited. We have to look to the documents to see what bargain was made. . . .

In the present case we have in the first place, turning to the language of the instrument, a description of the manner in which the money is staked or deposited. It is a deposit, and it is to be both a deposit and in the nature of part payment, and there is further a special clause in the contract at which we ought to look to see if any light is thrown by it on the language of the provision that the money is deposited as a deposit.

We may however pass by that special clause, for I think it does not really deprive the deposit in this case of the character which it would bear if there were no special clause—because, in my opinion, that clause merely fixes the amount which the vendor is to receive in the event of his insisting on his rights under the special clause. We have therefore to consider what in ordinary parlance, and as used in an ordinary contract of sale, is the meaning which business persons would attach to the term 'deposit.' Without going at length into the history, or accepting all that has been said or will be said by the other members of the Court on that point, it comes shortly to this, that a deposit, if nothing more is said about it, is, according to the ordinary interpretation of business men, a security for the completion of the purchase. But in what sense is it a security for the completion of the purchase? It is quite certain that the purchaser cannot insist on abandoning his contract and yet recover the deposit, because that would be to enable him to take advantage of his own wrong. Mr Pearson [counsel for the purchaser] said the rule is different when the purchaser does not insist on abandoning his contract, but, on the contrary, is desirous, at the moment he appears before the Court, of completing it, and therefore neither the principle nor the decisions apply—that this is not a case where the purchaser is receding from the contract, but on the contrary he is seeking to enforce it. It seems to me the answer to that argument is that although in terms in a case like the present the purchaser may appear to be insisting on his contract, in reality he has so conducted himself under it as to have refused, and has given the other side the right to say that he has refused, performance. He may look as if he wished to perform, but in reality he has put it out of his power to do so—he has, in the language of the Roman law, receded from his contract.

In every case at law, it seems to me, the question whether time is of the essence of the contract must depend, just as the question of the deposit must depend, on the contract itself. It is not necessary in the present instance to consider whether under this special contract time was of the essence of the contract or not; because the Judicature Act has placed the matter as regards such proposition on the footing on which it would have been treated in Equity before the Judicature Act. But it is obvious that the party may lose his right to insist on specific performance before an equitable tribunal, without at the same time having necessarily so acted as to justify the other side in saying the contract is altogether at an end. As I understand, speaking with a due consciousness of my own ignorance on the point, all that a Court of Equity does when it refuses specific performance on the ground of lapse of time is to leave the parties to their remedy at law. It refuses it because it would be unfair that the relief should be given. It does not follow as a matter of law on principle that because specific performance is refused therfore the whole contract is at an end in law. We have to look to the conduct of the parties and to the contract itself, and, putting the two things together, to see whether the purchaser has acted not merely so as to break his contract, but to entitle the other side to say he has repudiated and no longer stands by it.

Now, looking to see whether the conduct of the purchaser has not in the present instance brought him within that definition, I think it is impossible, viewing the case from first to last, to doubt that he has so dealt with his bargain as to give the vendor a right to allege, if he chooses so to say, that the contract is at an end, that the purchaser has receded from the bargain, and that the deposit money is liable to be retained by the vendor. Therefore the appeal fails.

FRY LJ: . . . Money paid as a deposit must, I conceive, be paid on some terms implied or expressed. In this case no terms are expressed, and we must therefore inquire what terms are to be implied. The terms most naturally to be implied appear to me in the case of money paid on the signing of a contract to be that in the event of the contract being performed it shall be brought into account, but if the contract is not performed by the payer it shall remain the property of the payee. It is not merely a part payment, but is then also an earnest to bind the bargain so entered into, and creates by the fear of its forfeiture a motive in the payer to perform the rest of the contract. . . .

Dies v *British and International Mining and Finance Corporation Ltd* [1939] 1 KB 724 (KBD)

Action for money had and received

Quintana agreed to buy Mauser rifles and ammunition at a price of £270,000 from the defendant company. The contract contained a *force majeure* clause which provided that £13,500 would be forfeited by the buyer if the contract became impossible of performance. Quintana paid £100,000 in advance, but subsequently, in breach of the contract, failed to accept delivery of the goods. The company elected to treat the contract as terminated. Quintana assigned his rights under the contract to Dies. Dies and Quintana claimed restitution. *Held*: the plaintiffs were entitled to restitution of the £100,000. The *force majeure* clause applied only if the contract had become impossible of performance. Further, the defendant company was entitled to set off against the £100,000, damages for Dies's breach of contract.

STABLE J: . . . The form of declaration or count which it was said embraced a claim of this nature was the old common count for money had and received. A considerable amount of discussion centred round the precise area of legal right covered by an action framed in this particular way. No doubt in the earlier stages of our law, when forms of action were few in number and restricted in their scope, no person obtained a remedy in the common-law Courts of this country unless he could bring his particular grievance within the ambit of some recognised form of pleading. The result was that the existence of a right depended on the existence of some recognised writ or form of pleading in which the claim could be comprised. It was therefore the object of the pleader, and to some extent of the Courts, in cases where it was found that the then existing forms were too narrow to meet the changing conditions of life, to devise new forms or adapt old ones so that just claims should not fall to the ground by reason of the defects of the system rather than any lack of merit in the litigant. Under these circumstances the count for money had and received came into being, and was developed and expanded by Lord Mansfield. I was referred to a number of cases in which the origin and the ambit of this particular remedy were discussed, and in particular the celebrated opinion of Lord Sumner in the case of *Sinclair* v *Brougham* [1914] AC 398, 453 et seq. Lord Sumner pointed out that the basis of the action was an implied or notional or fictitious promise to pay. The actual decision in *Sinclair* v *Brougham* on this particular point was that a depositor who had banked with a company carrying on a banking business that was wholly ultra vires could not recover that money in any action based on a notional promise to repay, inasmuch as, if there had been an express promise in fact, it would have been ultra vires, and a notional promise could not have any greater efficacy than that of the real promise, if real promise there had been. . . .

In my judgment, the question whether the right exists cannot be determined by inquiring whether the action for money had and received is the appropriate form of plea. If the right exists, the form of plea is appropiate enough. If the right does not exist, it cannot be enforced, no matter how attractively it be disguised by the pleader.

The question is not now one of the appropriate form in which to clothe the right, but whether or not the right exists, although the absence of any clothing that fits may be an indication of the non-existence of the right. . . .

In the present case, neither by the use of the word 'deposit' or otherwise, is there anything to indicate that the payment of 100,000*l*. was intended or was believed by either party to be in the nature of a guarantee or earnest for the due performance of the contract. It was a part payment of the price of the goods sold and was so described.

On behalf of the defendant corporation it was contended that on the true construction of the contract the part payment was agreed to be regarded as an earnest for the performance of the contract, inasmuch as, since the clause which I have already read provided for the return of a part of the payment to the plaintiffs in one event only, it must have been the intention of the parties that in every other event the money was to be retained by the defendant corporation.

I do not so construe the contract. The clause, in my judgment, deals with one situation, and one situation only—namely, the frustration of the performance of the contract. It was, as I have already said, designed to confer on the defendant corporation certain rights additional to the rights which the law alone in the absence of agreement would have given in the event of the performance of the contract being frustrated. Beyond that field its implications ought not to be extended, and the doctrine 'expressum facit cessare tacitum' has no application. The argument under this head is double-edged, since it might be argued on behalf of the plaintiffs that, as the contract expressly conferred on the corporation the right in one event to retain 13,500*l*., it cannot have been intended that in another event they were to have the right of retaining 100,000*l*.

It was said further that the rule which under certain circumstances enables a purchaser in default to recover a payment or part payment of the purchase price is a rule applicable to the sale of land only and must not be extended to the sale of goods, but no authority for this latter proposition was cited to me, and I was referred to certain passages in the Seventh Edition of Benjamin on Sale, at pp. 989, 994 and 995, which state the rule as being of general application.

At p. 989 the principle is summarised in these words: 'In ordinary circumstances, unless the contract otherwise provides, the seller, on rescission following the buyer's default, becomes liable to repay the part of the price paid.'

If this passage accurately states the law as, in my judgment, it does where the language used in a contract is neutral, the general rule is that the law confers on the purchaser the right to recover his money, and that to enable the seller to keep it he must be able to point to some language in the contract from which the inference to be drawn is that the parties intended and agreed that he should.

The argument on behalf of the defendant corporation was supported by the submission that the action for money had and received would not lie, since on the present facts the only possible basis was a total failure of consideration, which basis was ruled out by the fact that it was the purchaser who had made default. . . .

I was, however, quite satisfied that in the present case the foundation of the right, if right there be, is not a total failure of consideration. There was no failure of consideration, total or partial. It was not the consideration that failed but the party to the contract.

This objection, in my judgment, really goes to a question of form and not of substance, for if under the present circumstances there is a right in the buyer to recover a payment he has made in part, it is wholly immaterial in point of form whether the basis of right depends on a total failure of consideration, or something else. In my judgment, the real foundation of the right which I hold exists in the present case is not a total failure of consideration but the right of the purchaser, derived from the terms of the contract and the principle of law applicable; to recover back his money.

I am fortified in the view I have formed by the consideration that, in cases where the parties have agreed that a certain sum shall in the event of a breach represent the liquidated damages to be paid, the Court can, if satisfied that the agreed amount is not damages but a penalty, relieve one or other of the parties against his inequitable and improvident bargain. In my judgment there would be a manifest defect in the law if, where a buyer had paid for his goods but was unable to accept delivery, the vendor could retain the goods and the money quite irrespective of whether the money so retained bore any relation to the amount of the damage, if any, sustained as a result of the breach. The seller is already amply protected, since he can recover such damage as he has sustained and can, it seems, set off his claim for damages against the claim for the return of the purchase price. . . .

Note

Stable J's reluctance to base recovery explicitly upon the ground of failure of consideration was probably due to the currency at that time of the rule in *Chandler* v *Webster* [1904] 1 KB 493 (which applied in relation to frustrated contracts). Stable J went on in his judgment to distinguish that case. The fallacy in *Chandler* v *Webster* was exposed soon after by the House of Lords in *Fibrosa Spolka Akcyjna* v *Fairbairn Lawson Combe Barbour Ltd* [1943] AC 32 (see below in Section 2) and Stable J's reticence in relying upon failure of consideration as the cause of action would now be unnecessary. (Contrast Birks, *Introduction*, 236–7.)

Hyundai Heavy Industries Co. Ltd* v *Papadopoulos
[1980] 1 WLR 1129 (HL)

A Liberian company (the 'buyer') entered into a contract with the shipbuilders Hyundai, whereby the latter agreed to build and deliver a multi-purpose cargo ship for US $14,300,000. The price was to be paid by five instalments, the first two each being 2.5 per cent of the total price ($357,500). The first instalment was paid, but the buyer failed to pay the second instalment in accordance with the timetable set out in the contract. Therefore Hyundai elected, under an express term (article 11) to cancel the contract. At the same time as the contract between the buyer and Hyundai, the appellants agreed to guarantee the obligations of the buyer to Hyundai in the following terms: 'in accordance with the terms of the contract of all sums due or to become due by the buyer to you under the contract, and in case the buyer is in default of any such payment we will forthwith make the payment in default on behalf of the buyer.' Hyundai sued the appellant guarantors for the amount of the second instalment. Lloyd J and the Court of Appeal awarded Hyundai summary judgment. *Held*: first (Lord Russell of Killowen and Lord Keith of Kinkel doubting), the guarantors were liable because under the contract between the buyer and Hyundai, cancellation did not affect the accrued right to payment of the second instalment; secondly and unanimously, in any event the guarantors were liable under the express terms of the guarantee contract to Hyundai in the amount of the second instalment.

LORD EDMUND-DAVIES: . . . It has to be said, at the outset, that the assertion that the builders' exercise of their undoubted right to cancel the ship contract terminated it for *all* purposes and, in particular, rendered the second instalment no longer exigible, is an irrational assumption unsupported by any direct authority. It is true that upon cancellation the builders acquired a right to recover damages for such injury flowing from the buyers' default as, in due course and upon proper accounts being taken and a balance struck, the builders could establish. But there is no warrant for saying that such right was acquired in *substitution* for their accrued right to recover the due but unpaid second instalment. On the contrary, having regard to what Lord Wilberforce once called 'the matrix of facts' (*Prenn* v *Simmonds* [1971] 1 WLR 1381, 1384A), there are sound commercial reasons for holding that a vested and indubitable right to prompt payment on a specified date of a specified sum, expressly provided for in the contract, should *not* be supplanted by or merged in or substituted by a right to recover at some future date such indefinite sum by way of damages as, on balance and on proof, might be awarded to the builders, following upon a scrutiny of the parties' respective rights and obligations under the contract as a whole.

In my judgment there is ample authority and judicial support for the proposition stated in Treitel, *The Law of Contract*, 5th ed. (1979), p. 641 that:

> Rescission . . . releases the party in breach for the future from his primary obligations to perform. But he is not released from primary obligations already due at the time of rescission, and he also comes under a secondary liability to pay damages. His liability may thus relate both to breaches committed before rescission and to losses suffered by the victim as a result of the defaulting party's repudiation of future obligations.

In *McDonald* v *Dennys Lascelles Ltd* (1933) 48 CLR 457, 476, Dixon J said, in a judgment unanimously approved of by this House in *Johnson* v *Agnew* [1980] AC 367, 396:

> When a party to a simple contract, upon a breach by the other contracting party of a condition of the contract, elects to treat the contract as no longer binding upon him, the contract is not rescinded as from the beginning. Both parties are discharged from the further performance of the contract, but rights are not divested or discharged which have already been unconditionally acquired. Rights and obligations which arise from the partial execution of the contract and causes of action which have accrued from its breach alike continue unaffected.

Despite an attempt by Mr Curry [counsel for the guarantors] to show that hire-purchase agreements are to be distinguished from the ship contract with which this House is presently concerned, they clearly fall within the general proposition propounded by Dixon J. It is true that in such cases the hirer has received consideration in the shape of use for a limited period of the subject matter of the contract, but that is taken care of by the limited nature of his payment towards the ultimate purchase-price. It has become well established that in such contracts the finance company is entitled not only to retain instalments paid at the time of cancellation but also to recover instalments accrued due before that date: see Guest, *The Law of Hire Purchase* (1966), paras. 431 and 473. So in *Brooks* v *Beirnstein* [1909] 1 KB 98, 102, Bigham J held that, when the owners of furniture, hired out with an option to purchase, retook possession under the terms of the contract where the hirer had defaulted in payment of the agreed monthly rent:

> The agreement, in so conferring the right to retake possession on a breach by the hirer, does not take away any other rights which the law gives to the owners, among which rights is that of suing for monthly rent which had already accrued.

And in *Chatterton* v *Maclean* [1951] 1 All ER 761, where the hirer of a car defaulted under a hire-purchase agreement and the owners exercised their right to repossess, Parker J said, at p. 764:

> The hirer remains under any liability that has already accrued at the date of the acceptance of the repudiation. That is put beyond all doubt by *Brooks* v *Beirnstein*.

That the legal position is similar in relation to a time charterparty was common ground between counsel and manifestly approved of by Greer J in *Leslie Shipping Co.* v *Welstead* [1921] 3 KB 420.

In the light of the foregoing I have been led to the conclusion that, notwithstanding the notice of cancellation of the ship contract given by the builders on September 6, 1976, when they issued their writ against the guarantors on March 6, 1978, under that contract the second instalment of $357,500 was still due from the buyers to the builders.

But, my Lords, what if I am wrong so far—that is to say, what if, although the second instalment was undoubtedly due from the buyers until September 6, 1976, the builders' notice of cancellation of the ship contract on that date destroyed the builders' right to recover the sum and replaced it by a right to sue the buyers for damages? In those circumstances, would the guarantors nevertheless be liable under their letter of guarantee? Upon that hypothesis, can it still be said, that, after September 6, 1976, the guarantors were still under an obligation to pay 'forthwith' $357,500 to the builders? It is to those questions that I now turn.

The appellants sought to place reliance on the decision of Stable J in *Dies* v *British and International Mining and Finance Corporation Ltd* [1939] 1 KB 724, a decision which has been described as 'not easy to reconcile with earlier authority': see Goff and Jones, *The Law of Restitution*, 2nd ed. (1978), p. 381. But in my judgment, the exiguous nature of the known facts in the present case renders it wholly unrealistic to think that a single payment of a mere 2.5 per cent of the contract price of the vessel could bring about the sort of case dealt with in the *Dies* case, and I am in respectful agreement with Roskill LJ in *Hyundai Shipbuilding & Heavy Industries Co. Ltd* v *Pournaras* [1978] 2 Lloyd's Rep 502, 508, that the avowed object of the letter of guarantee was:

> to enable the yard to recover from the guarantors the amount due irrespective of the position between yard and buyers, so that the yard gets its money from the guarantors without difficulty if the yard cannot get it from the buyers.

LORD FRASER OF TULLYBELTON: . . . The provision in article 11(b)(iv) that instalments 'already paid' are to be retained and applied by the builders is not matched by any provision as to other instalments. Other instalments are not mentioned at all, but nobody has suggested that future instalments (that is, instalments which have not fallen due for payment by the date of cancellation of the contract) are payable. It is, I think, clear that they cease to be payable as instalments, and are replaced by the buyer's obligation to pay any deficiency brought out in the final accounting. But the position is less clear in the case of instalments which had accrued and become due for payment before the date of cancellation of the contract. Counsel for the guarantors drew our attention to article 10(e) of the shipbuilding contract which is headed 'Refund' and which includes a provision that 'The payments made by the buyer to the builder prior to delivery of the vessel shall constitute *advances* to the builder' (my italics). That shows that such payments, which would of course have included the second instalment if it had been paid, are not earnests of ability to pay but advances of part of the price. But, said counsel, once the contract has been cancelled the price must cease to be payable; the purchaser can no longer be liable to pay the price for a vessel which the builder is no longer obliged to sell to him, and which he has said he has no intention of selling to him. The argument was supported by reference to a statement by Lord Denman CJ in *Palmer* v *Temple* (1839) 9 A & E 508, 520–521, where he said:

> But the very idea of payment falls to the ground when both [parties] have treated the bargain as at an end; and from that moment the vendor holds the money advanced to the use of the purchaser.

Palmer v *Temple* was a case where the plaintiff had contracted to purchase landed property and had paid a sum 'by way of deposit, and in part of £5,500,' which was the purchase price, and had then failed to pay the balance of the price or to complete the contract. He was held to be entitled to recover his deposit, but the actual decision turned on the terms of the particular contract. In *Dies* v *British and International Mining and Finance Corporation Ltd* [1939] 1 KB 724, where a passage from Lord Denman's judgment in *Palmer* v *Temple* including the statement that I have quoted was relied on by Stable J at pp 740 to 742, the contract was again purely one of sale—in that case of rifles and ammunition. The vendor was a merchant or middleman who had intended to buy the goods from the manufacturer and to resell them to the purchaser at a profit. Stable J held that the purchaser who had paid a large sum as an advance of the purchase price, and who had then failed to complete payment or to take delivery of the goods, was entitled to recover his advance payment under deduction of an agreed sum of liquidated damages. Counsel for the guarantors in the instant case argued that if the buyer in the *Dies* case was entitled to recover an advance which had already been paid, then a fortiori the buyer in the instant case could not be liable to make an advance that was due but unpaid; if he did make it, said counsel, he would be entitled to immediate repayment of it.

I do not accept that argument. In my opinion the *Dies* case [1939] 1 KB 724 and *Palmer* v *Temple*, 9 A & E 508 are both distinguishable from the present case because in both these cases the contracts were simply contracts of sale which did not require the vendor to perform any work or incur any expense on the subjects of sale. But the contract in the instant case is not of that, [comparatively] simple character. The obligations of the buyer were not confined to selling the vessel but they included designing and building it and there were special provisions (article 2) that the contract price 'shall include payment for services in the inspection, tests, survey and classification of the vessel' and also 'all costs and expenses for designing and supplying all necessary drawings for the vessel in accordance with the specifications.' Accordingly the builder was obliged to carry out work and to incur expense, starting from the moment that the contract had been signed, including the wages of designers and workmen, fees for inspection and for cost of purchasing materials. It seems very likely that the increasing proportions of the contract price represented by the five instalments bore some relation to the anticipated rate of expenditure, but we have no information on which to make any nice comparison between the amount of expenses that the builder would have to bear from time to time, and the amounts of the instalments payable by the buyer. I do not think that such comparisons are necessary. It is enough that the builder was bound to incur considerable expense in carrying out his part of the contract long before the actual sale could take place. That no doubt is the explanation for the provision in article 10 (b) of the shipbuilding contract that:

> . . . all payments under the provisions of this article shall not be delayed or withheld by the buyer due to any dispute of whatever nature arising between the builder and the buyer hereto, unless the buyer shall have claimed to cancel the contract under the terms thereof. . . .

The importance evidently attached by the parties to maintaining the cash flow seems to support my view of the contract.

There was no evidence either way as to whether the builders had in fact carried out their obligations to start designing and building the vessel, but in my opinion we must assume, in the absence of evidence or averment to the contrary, that they had carried out their part of the bargain up till the date of cancellation.

Much of the plausibility of the argument on behalf of the guarantors seemed to me to be derived from the assumption that the *contract* price was simply a *purchase* price. That is not so, and once that misconception has been removed I think it is clear that the shipbuilding contract has little similarity with a contract of sale and much more similarity, so far as the present issues are concerned, with contracts in which the party entitled to be paid had either performed work or provided services for which payment is due by the date of cancellation. In contracts of the latter class, which of course includes building and construction contracts, accrued rights to payment are not (in the absence of express provisions) destroyed by cancellation of the contract. . . .

In the instant case the buyer has not actually enjoyed any benefit from the work which the builder has performed, but it has been performed, (or at least we must so assume, in the absence of evidence to the contrary) on the faith of the buyer's promise to pay the instalments on the due dates. The builder had acquired a vested right to the debt which was owed by the buyer at the date of cancellation and I see no reason for holding it to be cancelled. . . .

Question

Can you reconcile the result in *Hyundai* with the result in *Dies*?

Notes

1. The first part of the decision in *Hyundai*, that the second instalment was still due from the buyer, with the necessary implication that if the instalment had been paid it would be irrecoverable in restitution on the ground of failure of consideration, is criticised by Professor Burrows (Burrows, *Restitution*, 256–7) but is defended by Professor Birks (Birks, *Introduction*, 237–8). Birks's defence turns upon the nature of the contract. This was not a discrete sale. The instalments were equivalent to progress payments. As Viscount Dilhorne stressed in his speech ([1980] 1 WLR 1129, at 1134):

> . . . it was a contract to 'build, launch, equip and complete' a vessel and 'to deliver and sell' her. The contract price included 'all costs and expenses for designing and supplying all necessary drawings for the vessel . . .' It was a contract which was not simply one of sale but which so far as the construction of the vessel was concerned, resembled a building contract.

However, for Burrows, the first holding is inconsistent with his 'beneficial performance view' of total failure of consideration (Burrows, *Restitution*, 253–7).

2. The most comprehensive account of *Dies* and *Hyundai* is provided by Professor Beatson, 'Discharge for Breach: The Position of Instalments, Deposits and Other Payments due before Completion' (1981) 97 LQR 389 (now updated in Beatson, *Unjust Enrichment*, 45–77). Beatson concludes that the cases are best explained by an approach which rests primarily upon the *construction* of the contract. Therefore reliance expenditure will be protected, in a rough-and-ready fashion, by holding that where the expenditure was envisaged as part of the contract price, any advance payment is irrecoverable or remains due. This construction approach can be supplemented by restitutionary principles which can make sure that the party incurring expenditure does not thereby receive a windfall. This is consistent with the general tenor of Professor Beatson's work which is sensitive in ensuring that restitutionary principles do not subvert sound contractual doctrines or the parties' own allocation of risk.

Rover International Ltd v *Cannon Film Sales Ltd*
[1989] 1 WLR 912 (CA)

'Proper' appeal

Proper Film Ltd, a Guernsey company, entered into a contract with Thorn EMI (who were subsequently taken over by Cannon) for the television screening in Italy of nine feature films, including 'A Passage to India'. The rights to that film had previously been assigned to a third party, so Cannon had to arrange to buy those rights back. The total fee was US $1,800,000 payable in three instalments. Owing to disputes the third instalment of $900,000 was not paid on 30 September 1986 (the due date), so Cannon elected on 3 October 1986 to treat the contract as terminated. Cannon claimed the $900,000 from Proper.

KERR LJ: . . . The issue is whether Cannon are entitled to claim this instalment notwithstanding the fact that they rescinded the contract, on the ground of Proper's breach, as it is now accepted they were entitled. Proper contend that if they had paid this instalment before rescission then it would now be recoverable by them, and that a fortiori they cannot now be held liable to pay it. They have not claimed repayment of the $900,000 paid under the first and second instalments, and we are not concerned with that aspect. But they deny their liability to pay the final instalment and contend that Cannon are restricted to a claim for damages, if any. Harman J upheld Cannon's counterclaim [[1987] BCLC 540], at p. 547E–F, and Proper now appeal against that part of his judgment.

The relevant principles were stated by Dixon J in the High Court of Australia in *McDonald* v *Dennys Lascelles Ltd* (1933) 48 CLR 457, 476–478. Part of this judgment was cited by Lord Edmund-Davies in *Hyundai Heavy Industries Co. Ltd* v *Papadopoulos* [1980] 1 WLR 1129, 1141, but for present purposes it is helpful to quote a fuller extract:

> When a party to a simple contract, upon a breach by the other contracting party of a condition of the contract, elects to treat the contract as no longer binding upon him, the contract is not rescinded as from the beginning. Both parties are discharged from the further performance of the contract, but rights are not divested or discharged which have already been unconditionally acquired. Rights and

obligations which arise from the partial execution of the contract and causes of action which have accrued from its breach alike continue unaffected. . . . But when a contract, which is not void or voidable at law, or liable to be set aside in equity, is dissolved at the election of one party because the other has not observed an essential condition or has committed a breach going to its root, the contract is determined so far as it is executory only and the party in default is liable for damages for its breach. . . . *It does not, however, necessarily follow from these principles that when, under an executory contract for the sale of property, the price or part of it is paid or payable in advance, the seller may both retain what he has received, or recover overdue instalments, and at the same time treat himself as relieved from the obligation of transferring the property to the buyer.* When a contract stipulates for payment of part of the purchase money in advance, the purchaser relying only on the vendor's promise to give him a conveyance, the vendor is entitled to enforce payment before the time has arrived for conveying the land; yet his title to retain the money has been considered not to be absolute but conditional upon the subsequent completion of the contract. 'The very idea of payment falls to the ground when both have treated the bargain as at an end; and from that moment the vendor holds the money advanced to use of the purchaser' (*Palmer* v *Temple* (1839) 9 Ad & E 508, 521).... *It is now beyond question that instalments already paid may be recovered by a defaulting purchaser when the vendor elects to discharge the contract* (*Mayson* v *Clouet* [1924] AC 980). . . . (Emphasis added.)

Subject to Mr Pardoe's [counsel for Cannon] reliance on the *Hyundai* decision, to which I turn in a moment, it is clear from the passages which I have emphasised that if Proper had paid the disputed instalment of $900,000, and if the contract had thereafter been rescinded by Cannon for whatever reason, Proper would have been entitled to recover this sum; and if the reason for the rescission of the contract had been a breach on the part of Proper, then Cannon would still not have been entitled to retain this sum but would have been limited to a claim in damages. The fact that the present contract is not one of sale cannot affect the position in principle.

In the present case Proper do not claim repayment, but Cannon claim that the liability to pay survives the rescission of the contract. Clearly that cannot make any difference to the outcome; on the contrary, it must be a fortiori from the point of view of Proper, who are merely resisting Cannon's claim. Dixon J in *McDonald* v *Dennys Lascelles Ltd*, 48 CLR 457, dealt with this situation a little later on when he said, at p. 479:

It appears to me inevitably to follow from the principles upon which instalments paid are recoverable that an unpaid overdue instalment ceases to be payable by the purchasers when the contract is discharged.

The situation envisaged by Dixon J in the main passage, at pp. 476–478, which I have quoted, arose in *Dies* v *British and International Mining and Finance Corporation Ltd* [1939] 1 KB 724. The defendants had contracted to sell certain rifles and ammunition for a total sum of £270,00. The buyer paid £100,000 but was thereafter in breach by failing to make any further payments and declining to take delivery. The defendant sellers elected to treat the contract as at an end. The purchaser then sued to recover the £100,000 which he had paid, and succeeded. Stable J stated the contention which he accepted as follows, relying inter alia on *Palmer* v *Temple* (1839) 9 Ad & E 508 to which Dixon J had also referred, at pp. 736–737:

Where there is a contract for the sale of goods, and a part payment for the goods is made, but no goods are delivered or tendered by reason of the default of the buyer,

> the seller's only remedy is to recover damages for the default, while the buyer, notwithstanding that it is by reason of his default that the contract has not been performed, is entitled to recover the purchase price that he has paid, subject possibly to the right of the seller to set off against that claim the damages to which he can establish his title.

He went on to point out that if this were not so, then the seller would be entitled to keep the advance as well as to claim damages for the buyer's breach.

That decision was distinguished by a majority of the House of Lords in *Hyundai Heavy Industries Co. Ltd* v *Papadopoulos* [1980] 1 WLR 1129. The case arose from a ship building contract which provided that the builders should 'build, launch, equip and complete' the vessel and that its construction should proceed continuously from keel laying to delivery. The price was payable by instalments and it was a term that the builders' yard should have the right to cancel the contract in the event of the buyers' failure to pay an instalment. That is what happened. The builders thereupon brought an action against the guarantor, on the same lines as Cannon's claim against Monitor in the present case, and the House of Lords held unanimously that the defendant was liable under the terms of the guarantee irrespective of the liability of the buyers. But three of their Lordships also dealt with the question whether the buyers' liability to pay the instalment in question survived the consequent cancellation of the contract by the builders. They held that it did, in effect because this was not a contract which merely provided for the sale and delivery of the ship, but because it was in the nature of a building contract under which the yard was obliged to continue with the construction of the vessel throughout. By continuing to work upon the ship during the period since the payment of the previous instalment, the builders had accordingly provided consideration for the instalment in question, with the result that it remained due despite the builders' cancellation of the contract.

The issue in the present case, as I see it, is accordingly whether it falls on the side of cases such as *Dies* v *British and International Mining and Finance Corporation Ltd* [1939] 1 KB 724, or whether the terms of the contract and the facts lead to the conclusion that it is to be assimilated to the situation in *Hyundai Heavy Industries Co. Ltd* v *Papadopoulos* [1980] 1 WLR 1129. Had Thorn EMI/Cannon provided any consideration under the contract for which the instalment of $900,000 was payable, or was this instalment payable merely as an advance for the obligations which Thorn EMI/Cannon had agreed to perform thereafter? When referring to the provision of consideration in this context, in the same way as in the context of a failure of consideration discussed earlier in the Rover appeal, one is not referring to the original promise to perform the contract. The question is whether there was any consideration in the nature of part performance for which the instalment was payable, as in *Hyundai Heavy Industries Co. Ltd* v *Papadopoulos* [1980] 1 WLR 1129, or whether the instalment was payable in advance of any performance which was required from Thorn EMI/Cannon.

In my view the present case falls clearly into the latter category and is indistinguishable in principle from the situations examined by Dixon J in *McDonald* v *Dennys Lascelles Ltd.*, 48 CLR 457, and the decision in *Dies* v *British and International Mining and Finance Corporation Ltd.* It is true that *Dies* appears to have been a contract for the sale of unascertained goods whereas the present contract deals with specific films in relation to which Thorn EMI/Cannon had to possess or to acquire the necessary rights. It is also true that they were precluded from transferring these right to anyone other than Proper. But that is not a situation whereby Thorn EMI/Cannon provided anything in the nature of part performance under the contract. It merely meant that they had to arrange matters so as to enable them to perform their contractual obligations at the time when these would become due. Thus, it is clear from *Palmer* v *Temple*, 9 Ad & E 508, and the judgment of Dixon J in *McDonald* v *Dennys Lascelles Ltd.*, 48 CLR 457, that the principle that advance payments made on account of the price are recoverable applies even where the contract relates to a specific piece of land which the vendor must either acquire or retain in order to perform the contract. The fact that he is bound to the contract in that way does not alter the character of the payment being in the nature of an advance for a consideration to be provided in the future.

In the present case it is entirely clear, in my view, that this instalment was payable in advance of any consideration for the payment which fell to be provided from the side of Thorn EMI/Cannon. Indeed, when Proper declined to pay it, it was rightly pointed out on behalf of Cannon that nothing in the way of performance was as yet due from their side. This instalment would accordingly have been recoverable by Proper if it had been paid, and it is therefore irrecoverable by Cannon for the same reason. The only claim open to them would have been a claim for damages if they had shown that they had suffered any as the result of the termination of the contract. It follows that Cannon's counterclaim should in my view have been dismissed, and that Proper's appeal should also be allowed.

Notes

1. For the failure of consideration point in the 'Rover' appeal, see Section 4 below.

2. For discussion see Birks, 'Restitution after Ineffective Contracts: Issues for the 1990s' (1990) 2 JCL 227, at 233–5.

Relief against forfeiture?

Stockloser v _Johnson_

[1954] 1 QB 476 (CA)

The buyer entered into contracts for the purchase of plant and machinery used in certain lime quarries. The price was payable in instalments and the contracts provided that if the buyer should fail to pay any instalment within 28 days of it falling due, the seller could retake possession of the machinery and the instalments already paid were forfeit. Bad weather made the enterprise less profitable than the buyer anticipated and he was soon in default. The buyer did not claim he was ready and willing to perform, rather he claimed restitution of the instalments already paid.

DENNING LJ: There was acute contest as to the proper legal principles to apply in this case. On the one hand, Mr Neil Lawson urged us to hold that the buyer was entitled to recover the instalments at law. He said that the forfeiture clause should be ignored because it was of a penal character; and once it was ignored, it meant that the buyer was left with a simple right to repayment of his money on lines of *Dies* v *British and International Mining and Finance Corporation* [1939] 1 KB 724, subject only to a cross-claim for damages. In asking us to ignore the forfeiture clause, Mr. Lawson relied on the familiar tests which are used to distinguish between penalties and liquidated damages, and said that these tests had been applied in cases for the repayment of money, citing *Barton* v *Capewell* (1893) 68 LT 857 and *Commissioner of Public Works* v *Hills* [1906] AC 368. In neither of those cases, however, was the point argued or discussed, and I do not think they warrant Mr. Lawson's proposition. There is, I think, a plain distinction between penalty cases, strictly so called, and cases like the present.

It is this: when one party seeks to exact a penalty from the other, he is seeking to exact payment of an extravagant sum either by action at law or by appropriating to himself moneys belonging to the other party, as in *Commissioner of Public Works* v *Hills*. The claimant invariably relies, like Shylock, on the letter of the contract to support his demand, but the courts decline to give him their aid because they will not assist him in an act of oppression: see the valuable judgments of Somervell and Hodson LJJ in *Cooden Engineering Co.* v *Stanford* [1953] 1 QB 86; [1952] 2 TLR 822; [1952] 2 All ER 915.

In the present case, however, the seller is not seeking to exact a penalty. He only wants to keep money which already belongs to him. The money was handed to him in part payment of the purchase price and, as soon as it was paid, it belonged to him absolutely. He did not obtain it by extortion or oppression or anything of that sort, and there is an express clause—a forfeiture clause, if you please—permitting him to keep it. It is not the case of a seller seeking to enforce a penalty, but a buyer seeking restitution of money paid. If the buyer is to recover it, he must, I think, have recourse to somewhat different principles from those applicable to penalties, strictly so called.

On the other hand, Mr Beney urged us to hold that the buyer could only recover the money if he was able and willing to perform the contract, and for this purpose he ought to pay or offer to pay the instalments which were in arrear and be willing to pay the future instalments as they became due; and he relied on *Mussen* v *Van Dieman's Land Co.* [1938] Ch 253. I think that this contention goes too far in the opposite direction. If the buyer was seeking to re-establish the contract, he would of course have to pay up the arrears and to show himself willing to perform the contract in the future, just as a lessee, who has suffered a forfeiture, has to do when he seeks to re-establish the lease. So, also, if the buyer were seeking specific performance he would have to show himself able and willing to perform his part. But the buyer's object here is not to re-establish the contract. It is to get his money back, and to do this I do not think that it is necessary for him to go so far as to show that he is ready and willing to perform the contract.

I reject, therefore, the arguments of counsel at each extreme. It seems to me that the cases show the law to be this: (1) *When there is no forfeiture clause*. If money is handed over in part payment of the purchase price, and then the buyer makes default as to the balance, then, so long as the seller keeps the contract open and available for perfomance, the buyer cannot recover the money; but once the seller rescinds the contract or treats it as at an end owing to the buyer's default, then the buyer is entitled to recover his money by action at law, subject to a cross-claim by the seller for damages: see *Palmer* v *Temple* (1839) 9 Ad & E 508; *Mayson* v *Clouet* [1924] AC 980; 40 TLR 678; *Dies* v *British and International Co.* [1939] 1 KB 724; Williams on Vendor and Purchaser, 4th ed., p. 1006. (2) *But when there is a forfeiture clause or the money is expressly paid as a deposit (which is equivalent to a forfeiture clause)*, then the buyer who is in default cannot recover the money at law at all. He may, however, have a remedy in equity, for, despite the express stipulation in the contract, equity can relieve the buyer from forfeiture of the money and order the seller to repay it on such terms as the court thinks fit. That is, I think, shown clearly by the decision of the Privy Council in *Steedman* v *Drinkle* [1916] 1 AC 275, where the Board consisted of a strong three, Viscount Haldane, Lord Parker and Lord Sumner.

The difficulty is to know what are the circumstances which give rise to this equity, but I must say that I agree with all that Somervell LJ has said about it, differing herein from the view of Romer LJ. Two things are necessary: first, the forfeiture clause must be of a penal nature, in this sense, that the sum forfeited must be out of all proportion to the damage, and, secondly, it must be unconscionable for the seller to retain the money. Inasmuch as the only case in which this jurisdiction has been exercised is *Steedman* v *Drinkle*, I have examined the record and would draw attention to the circumstances of the case. The agreement was in effect a hire-purchase agreement of land. The purchase-money was payable by instalments over six years, completion to be at the end of the six years, and meanwhile the purchasers were to be let into possession of the land as tenants with the instalments ranking as rent. In case of default the vendor was at liberty to cancel the contract and retain the payments which had been made. The purchasers paid the first instalment and went into possession, but they failed to pay the second instalment which was due at the end of the first year. The value of the land had risen greatly during that year and the vendor seized upon the purchaser's default as giving him the opportunity to rescind the contract. Without previous warning, the vendor gave notice cancelling the contract. The purchasers at once tendered the amount due but the vendor refused to accept it. The purchasers issued a writ for specific performance and meanwhile remained in possession of the land taking the crops off it. They failed to get specific performance in the first court, then succeeded in the Court of Appeal, but failed again in the Privy Council on the ground that time was expressly of the essence of the contract. Nevertheless, the Privy Council relieved the purchasers from forfeiture of the sums already paid. The purchasers would no doubt have to give credit for the crops they had taken from the land during the three years or more that they had been in possession, but subject to that credit they would get their money back.

In the later case of *Mussen* v *Van Dieman's Land Co.* Farwell J said that the whole basis of the decision in *Steedman* v *Drinkle* was that the purchasers were ready and willing to perform the contract; but I think that that is much too narrow an explanation. Readiness and willingness is essential in specific performance, and in relief from forfeiture of leases, but not in relief from forfeiture of sums paid. The basis of the decision in *Steedman* v *Drinkle* was, I think, that the vendor had somewhat sharply exercised his right to rescind the contract and retake the land, and it was unconscionable for him also to forfeit the sums already paid. Equity could not specifically enforce the contract, but it could and would relieve against the forfeiture.

In the course of the argument before us Somervell LJ put an illustration which shows the necessity for this equity even though the buyer is not ready and willing to perform the contract. Suppose a buyer has agreed to buy a necklace by instalments, and the contract provides that, on default in payment of any one instalment, the seller is entitled to rescind the contract and forfeit the instalments already paid. The buyer pays 90 per cent of the price but fails to pay the last instalment. He is not able to perform the contract because he simply cannot find the money. The seller thereupon rescinds the contract and retakes the necklace and resells it at a higher price. Surely equity will relieve the buyer against forfeiture of the money on such terms as may be just.

Again, suppose that a vendor of property, in lieu of the usual 10 per cent deposit, stipulates for an initial payment of 50 per cent of the price as a deposit and a part payment; and later, when the purchaser fails to complete, the vendor resells the property at a profit and in addition claims to forfeit the 50 per cent deposit. Surely the court will relieve against the forfeiture. The vendor cannot forestall this equity by describing an extravagant sum as a deposit, any more than he can recover a penalty by calling it liquidated damages.

These illustrations convince me that in a proper case there is an equity of restitution which a party in default does not lose simply because he is not able and willing to perform the contract. Nay, that is the very reason why he needs the equity. The equity operates, not because of the plaintiff's default, but because it is in the particular case unconscionable for the seller to retain the money. In short, he ought not unjustly to enrich himself at the plaintiff's expense. This equity of restitution is to be tested, I think, not at the time of the contract, but by the conditions existing when it is invoked. Suppose, for instance, that in the instance of the necklace, the first instalment was only 5 per cent of the price; and the buyer made default on the second instalment. There would be no equity by which he could ask for the first instalment to be repaid to him any more than he could claim repayment of a deposit. But it is very different after 90 per cent has been paid. Again, delay may be very material. Thus in *Mussen's* case the court was much influenced by the fact that the purchaser had allowed nearly six years to elapse before claiming restitution. He had already had a good deal of land conveyed to him and, during his six years delay, values had so greatly changed that it may be that he had had his money's worth. At any rate, it was not unconscionable for the defendant to retain the money.

Applying these principles to the present case, even if one regards the forfeiture clause as of a penal nature—as the judge did and I am prepared to do—nevertheless I do not think that it was unconscionable for the seller to retain the money. The buyer seems to have gambled on the royalties being higher than they were. He thought that they would go a long way to enable him to pay the instalments; but owing to bad weather they turned out to be smaller than he had hoped and he could not find the additional amount necessary to pay the instalments. The judge summarised the position neatly when he said that the purchaser 'is in the position of a gambler who has lost his stake and is now saying that it is for the court of equity to get it back for him.' He said, 'if it is a question of what is unconscionable, or, to use a word with a less legal flavour, unfair, I can see nothing whatever unfair in the defendant retaining the money.' With that finding of the judge I entirely agree and think that it disposes of the purchaser's claim to restitution. . . .

ROMER LJ: . . . Generally speaking, courts of equity have never interfered with contracts merely by reason of their being improvident. 'The Chancery,' as Lord Nottingham said in *Maynard* v *Moseley* (1676) 3 Swanst 651, 655, 'mends no man's bargain.' To this rule exceptions were made, notably in favour of expectant heirs and borrowers, to whom equity manifested some tenderness, on the supposition that the sale or mortgaging of their inheritances or properties was usually induced by the pressure of financial need. Such persons were regarded as being to some extent at the mercy of persons who were willing, on terms, to enter into financial relations with them, and the court frequently intervened so as to relieve them from the strict letter of their obligations upon such conditions as it considered fair and just. The equity of redemption which mortgagors have enjoyed for over 300 years had its origin in this exceptional jurisdiction and may be taken as an example of it.

In general, however, as I have said, people were expected to abide by their contracts, and if a man made a foolish or improvident one so much the worse for him. The question, then, is whether a purchaser who freely and voluntarily negotiates and executes a contract of sale upon terms that the price is to be paid by instalments and that, on default by him of payment of any instalments, the vendor may rescind the contract and retain any instalments previously paid, is entitled to relief in equity if he finds himself unable to comply with his bargain. It is to be observed that, in such a case, no element of pressure or duress exists and no question of the purchaser acting under the stress of economic necessity; both parties to the contract are on terms of bargaining equality with each other, the one desiring to exchange cash for property, the other, desiring to exchange property for cash. I confess that, in these circumstances, I am unable to see what ground there is for interference by a court of equity if it ultimately turns out that the terms on which these exchanges are mutually agreed operate hardly on either vendor or purchaser. If one of the terms which the vendor requires is disagreeable to the purchaser he is under no compulsion to accept it; he can either keep his money and forgo the property or he can purchase a similar property from some other vendor who is more tolerant in his approach to the conditions of sale.

If a man agrees to buy property by instalments which he will forfeit to the vendor if he cannot continue them to completion, he knows perfectly well the risk which he is taking and I do not know what right he has to appeal to equity if that risk does in fact ripen into actuality. [Romer LJ then discussed the authorities and concluded: . . .]

There is, in my judgment, nothing inequitable per se in a vendor, whose conduct is not open to criticism in other respects, insisting upon his contractual right to retain instalments of purchase-money already paid. In my judgment, there is no sufficient ground for interfering with the contractual rights of a vendor under forfeiture clauses of the nature which are now under consideration, while the contract is still subsisting, beyond giving a purchaser who is in default, but who is able and willing to proceed with the contract, a further opportunity of doing so; and no relief of any other nature can properly be given, in the absence of some special circumstances such as fraud, sharp practice or other unconscionable conduct of the vendor, to a purchaser after the vendor has rescinded the contract.

My brother Denning in his judgment has referred to the hypothetical case which was suggested during the argument of a purchaser who buys a pearl necklace on terms that the purchase price is to be payable by instalments and that the vendor is to be entitled to get the necklace back and retain all previous payments if the purchaser makes default in the punctual payment of any instalment, even the final one. It would certainly seem hard that the purchaser should lose both the necklace and all previous instalments owing to his inability to pay the last one. But that is the bargain into which the purchaser freely entered and the risk which he voluntarily accepted. The court would doubtless, as I have already indicated, give him further time to find the money if he could establish some probability of his being able to do so, but I do not know why it should interfere further; nor would it be easy to determine at what point in his failure to pay the agreed instalments the suggested equity would arise. In any event I venture to suggest that it is extremely unlikely that such a case would occur in practice; for a purchaser who had paid, say, nine-tenths of the agreed price for the necklace would have little difficulty in borrowing the remaining one-tenth on the security of his interest therein.

It will appear from what I have already said that in my opinion *Mussen's* case was rightly decided and that I agree with the grounds and reasoning upon which the decision was based, namely, that subject to the exceptions or qualifications to which I have referred (and which Farwell J in terms recognised), there is no 'equity . . . in favour of a purchaser who has failed to complete his contract through no fault of the vendor.' For my part I share the reluctance which Farwell J expressed to sponsor such an equity; it seems to me that in the long run it is much better that people who freely negotiate and conclude a contract of sale should be held to their bargain rather than that the judges should intervene by substituting, each according to his own individual sense of fairness, terms which are contrary to those which the parties have agreed upon for themselves. Agreeing as I do with Farwell J's judgment, no useful purpose would be served by further considering the case beyond emphasising (possibly ex abundanti cautela) that the decision of Farwell J was not directed to relief from penalties in the strict sense, but from the forfeiture of sums which the purchaser had paid in pursuance of the contract and in part payment of the purchase-money for the property agreed to be sold. . . .

Question

Whose statement of principle do you prefer, Denning LJ's or Romer LJ's?

Note

For sensitive analysis see Birks, *Introduction*, 211–6 discussing the merits of a jurisdiction to relieve against forfeiture and classifying it as a species of recovery based either upon 'inequality' or as a 'policy-motivated factor'. See further, Treitel, *Contract* 908–10

Unreasonable deposits

Workers Trust & Merchant Bank Ltd* v *Dojap Investments Ltd
[1993] AC 573 (PC)

The bank sold land to Dojap at an auction at a price of Jamaican $11.5 million. The contract provided for a 25 per cent deposit, and accordingly $2,875,000 was paid. The balance was to be paid within 14 days, the contract stating that time was of the essence and that if the buyer defaulted the deposit was forfeit. Dojap tendered a cheque for the balance seven days late. This was returned, the bank terminating the contract and purporting to forfeit the deposit. Dojap sought restitution of the deposit.

LORD BROWNE-WILKINSON: . . . In general, a contractual provision which requires one party in the event of his breach of the contract to pay or forfeit a sum of money to the other party is unlawful as being a penalty, unless such provision can be justified as being a payment of liquidated damages being a genuine pre-estimate of the loss which the innocent party will incur by reason of the breach. One exception to this general rule is the provision for the payment of a deposit by the purchaser on a contract for the sale of land. Ancient law has established that the forfeiture of such a deposit (customarily 10 per cent of the contract price) does not fall within the general rule and can be validly forfeited even though the amount of the deposit bears no reference to the anticipated loss to the vendor flowing from the breach of contract.

This exception is anomalous and at least one textbook writer has been surprised that the courts of equity ever countenanced it: see Farrand, *Contract and Conveyance*, 4th ed. (1983), p. 204. The special treatment afforded to such a deposit derives from the ancient custom of providing an earnest for the performance of a contract in the form of giving either some physical token of earnest (such as a ring) or earnest money. The history of the law of deposits can be traced to the Roman law of arra, and possibly further back still: see *Howe* v *Smith* (1884) 27 Ch D 89, 101–102, *per* Fry LJ. Ever since the decision in *Howe* v *Smith*, the nature of such a deposit has been settled in English law. Even in the absence of express contractual provision, it is an earnest for the performance of the contract: in the event of completion of the contract the deposit is applicable towards payment of the purchase price; in the event of the purchaser's failure to complete in accordance with the terms of the contract, the deposit is forfeit, equity having no power to relieve against such forfeiture.

However, the special treatment afforded to deposits is plainly capable of being abused if the parties to a contract, by attaching the label 'deposit' to any penalty, could escape the general rule which renders penalties unenforceable. There are two authorities which indicate that this cannot be done. In *Stockloser* v *Johnson* [1954] 1 QB 476, Denning LJ in considering the power of the court to relieve against forfeiture said, obiter, at p. 491:

> Again, suppose that a vendor of property, in lieu of the usual 10 per cent deposit, stipulates for an initial payment of 50 per cent of the price as a deposit and part payment; and later, when the purchaser fails to complete, the vendor resells the property at a profit and in addition claims to forfeit the 50 per cent deposit. Surely the court will relieve against the forfeiture. The vendor cannot forestall this equity by describing an extravagant sum as a deposit, any more than he can recover a penalty by calling it liquidated damages.

In *Linggi Plantations Ltd* v *Jagatheesan* [1972] 1 MLJ 89 Lord Hailsham of St. Marylebone LC delivered the judgment of the Board which upheld the claim to forfeit a normal 10 per cent deposit even though the vendor had in fact suffered no loss. He referred on a number of occasions to a requirement that the amount of a deposit should be 'reasonable' and said, at p. 94:

> It is also no doubt possible that in a particular contract the parties may use language normally appropriate to deposits properly so-called even to forfeiture which turn out on investigation to be purely colourable and that in such a case the real nature of the transaction might turn out to be the imposition of a penalty, by purporting to render forfeit something which is in truth part payment. This no doubt explains why in some cases the irrecoverable nature of a deposit is qualified by the insertion of the adjective 'reasonable' before the noun. But the truth is that a reasonable deposit has always been regarded as a guarantee of performance as well as a payment on account, and its forfeiture has never been regarded as a penalty in English law or common English usage.

In the view of their Lordships these passages accurately reflect the law. It is not possible for the parties to attach the incidents of a deposit to the payment of a sum of money unless such sum is reasonable as earnest money. The question therefore is whether or not the deposit of 25 per cent in this case was reasonable as being in line with the traditional concept of earnest money or was in truth a penalty intended to act in terrorem.

. . . In order to be reasonable a true deposit must be objectively operating as 'earnest money' and not as a penalty. To allow the test of reasonableness to depend upon the practice of one class of vendor, which exercises considerable financial muscle, would be to allow them to evade the law against penalties by adopting practices of their own.

However although their Lordships are satisfied that the practice of a limited class of vendors cannot determine the reasonableness of a deposit, it is more difficult to define what the test should be. Since a true deposit may take effect as a penalty, albeit one permitted by law, it is hard to draw a line between a reasonable, permissible amount of penalty and an unreasonable, impermissible penalty. In their Lordships' view the correct approach is to start from the position that, without logic but by long continued usage both in the United Kingdom and formerly in Jamaica, the customary deposit has been 10 per cent. A vendor who seeks to obtain a larger amount by way of forfeitable deposit must show special circumstances which justify such a deposit. . . .

The question therefore arises whether the court has jurisdiction to relieve against the express provision of the contract that the deposit of 25 per cent was to be forfeited. Although there is no doubt that the court will not order the payment of a sum contracted for (but not yet paid) if satisfied that such sum is in reality a penalty, it was submitted that the court could not order, by way of relief, the repayment of sums already paid to the defendant in accordance with the terms of the contract which, on breach, the contract provided should be forfeit. The basis of this submission was the view expressed in a considered obiter dictum of Romer LJ in *Stockloser* v *Johnson* [1954] 1 QB 476.

In that case there was a contract for the sale of quarry machinery to the plaintiff, the purchase price to be paid by instalments. The contract provided that in the event of a default in payment of the instalments, the vendor could retake the machinery and all instalments of the price previously paid should be forfeit. Pursuant to the contract, the plaintiff took possession and used the machinery but defaulted in payment of an instalment. The defendant forfeited the instalments already paid. In the action, the plaintiff sought to recover the instalments, alleging that their forfeiture was a penalty. The Court of Appeal unanimously held that the forfeiture did not constitute a penalty on the facts of that case but went on to express conflicting views, obiter, as to whether, if the forfeiture had been a penalty, the court had jurisdiction to order repayment. Somervell LJ and Denning LJ expressed the view that there was such jurisdiction. Romer LJ held that there was no general right in equity to mend the parties' bargain and that, even where there was jurisdiction to relieve from forfeiture, that could only be exercised by allowing a late completion to a party who was in default in performance but willing and able to carry out the terms of the contract belatedly.

Their Lordships do not find it necessary to decide which of those two views is correct in a case where a party is seeking relief from forfeiture for breach of contract to pay a price by instalments, the party in default having been let into possession in the meantime. This is not such a case. In the view of their Lordships, since the 25 per cent deposit was not a true deposit by way of earnest, the provision for its forfeiture was a plain penalty. There is clear authority that in a case of a sum paid by one party to another under the contract as security for the performance of that contract, a provision for its forfeiture in the event of non-performance is a penalty from which the court will give relief by ordering repayment of the sum so paid, less any damage actually proved to have been suffered as a result of non-completion: *Commissioner of Public Works* v *Hills* [1906] AC 368. Accordingly, there is jurisdiction in the court to order repayment of the 25 per cent deposit. . . .

Note

For a note on this case and very useful discussion of this controversial area of law see Beale, 'Unreasonable Deposits' (1993) 109 LQR 524.

D: Recovery of non-money benefits by the party in breach

See generally Burrows, *Restitution*, 276–81.

Sumpter* v *Hedges
[1898] 1 QB 673 (CA)

Quantum meruit; quantum valebat

A builder contracted to erect two houses and stables upon the defendant's land for £565. The builder did work worth £333, and received part of the price, but then informed the defendant that he had no money and could not complete. It was found as a fact that the builder had abandoned the contract. The defendant finished the work himself, using materials the builder had left behind. The builder sued for work done and materials provided. The judge awarded the builder the value of the materials, but nothing in respect of work done. The builder appealed.

A. L. SMITH LJ: In this case the plaintiff, a builder, entered into a contract to build two houses and stables on the defendant's land for a lump sum. When the buildings were still in an unfinished state the plaintiff informed the defendant that he had no money, and was not going on with the work any more. The learned judge has found as a fact that he abandoned the contract. Under such circumstances, what is a building owner to do? He cannot keep the buildings on his land in an unfinished state for ever. The law is that, where there is a contract to do work for a lump sum, until the work is completed the price of it cannot be recovered. Therefore the plaintiff could not recover on the original contract. It is suggested however that the plaintiff was entitled to recover for the work he did on a quantum meruit. But, in order that that may be so, there must be evidence of a fresh contract to pay for the work already done. With regard to that, the case of *Munro* v *Butt* 8 E & B 738 appears to be exactly in point. That case decides that, unless the building owner does something from which a new contract can be inferred to pay for the work already done, the plaintiff in such a case as this cannot recover on quantum meruit. In the case of *Lysaght* v *Pearson* [*The Times*, 3 March 1879], to which we have been referred, the case of *Munro* v *Butt* does not appear to have been referred to. There the plaintiff had contracted to erect on the defendant's land two corrugated iron roofs. When he had completed one of them, he does not seem to have said that he abandoned the contract, but merely that he would not go on unless the defendant paid him for what he had already done. The defendant thereupon proceeded to erect for himself the second roof. The Court of Appeal held that there was in that case something from which a new contract might be inferred to pay for the work done by the plaintiff. That is not this case. In the case of *Whitaker* v *Dunn* 3 Times LR 602 there was a contract to erect a laundry on defendant's land, and the laundry erected was not in accordance with the contract, but the official referee held that the plaintiff could recover on a quantum meruit. The case came before a Divisional Court, consisting of Lord Coleridge CJ and myself, and we said that the decision in *Munro* v *Butt* applied, and there being no circumstances to justify an inference of a fresh contract the plaintiff must fail. My brother Collins thinks that that case went to the Court of Appeal, and that he argued it there, and the Court affirmed the decision of the Queen's Bench Division. I think the appeal must be dismissed.

CHITTY LJ: I am of the same opinion. The plaintiff had contracted to erect certain buildings for a lump sum. When the work was only partly done, the plaintiff said that he could not go on with it, and the judge had found that he abandoned the contract. The position therefore was that the defendant found his land with unfinished buildings upon it, and he thereupon completed the work. That is no evidence from which the inference can be drawn that he entered into a fresh contract to pay for the work done by the plaintiff. If we held that the plaintiff could recover, we should in my opinion be overruling *Cutter* v *Powell* (1795) 6 TR 320, and a long series of cases in which it has been decided that there must in such a case be some evidence of a new contract to enable the plaintiff to recover on a quantum meruit. There was nothing new in the decision in *Pattinson* v *Luckley* (1875) LR 10 Ex 330, but Bramwell B there pointed out with his usual clearness that in the case of a building erected upon land the mere fact that the defendant remains in possession of his land is no evidence upon which an inference of a new contract can be founded. He says: 'In the case of goods sold and delivered, it is easy to shew a contract from the retention of the goods; but that is not so where work is done on real property.' I think the learned judge was quite right in holding that in this case there was no evidence from which a fresh contract to pay for the work done could be inferred.

COLLINS LJ: I agree. I think the case is really concluded by the finding of the learned judge to the effect that the plaintiff had abandoned the contract. If the plaintiff had merely broken his contract in some way so as not to give the defendant the right to treat him as having abandoned the contract, and the defendant had then proceeded to finish the work himself, the plaintiff might perhaps have been entitled to sue on a quantum meruit on the ground that the defendant had taken the benefit of the work done. But that is not the present case. There are cases in which, though the plaintiff has abandoned the performance of a contract, it is possible for him to raise the inference of a new contract to pay for the work done on a quantum meruit from the defendant's having taken the benefit of that work, but, in order that that may be done, the circumstances must be such as to give an option to the defendant to take or not to take the benefit of the work done. It is only where the circumstances are such as to give that option that there is any evidence on which to ground the inference of a new contract. Where, as in the case of work done on land, the circumstances are such as to give the defendant no option whether he will take the benefit of the work or not, then one must look to other facts than the mere taking the benefit of the work in order to ground the inference of a new contract. In this case I see no other facts on which such an inference can be founded. The mere fact that a defendant is in possession of what he cannot help keeping, or even has done work upon it, affords no ground for such an inference. He is not bound to keep unfinished a building which in an incomplete state would be a nuisance on his land. I am therefore of opinion that the plaintiff was not entitled to recover for the work which he had done. I feel clear that the case of *Whitaker* v *Dunn*, to which reference has been made, was the case which as counsel I argued in the Court of Appeal, and in which the Court dismissed the appeal on the ground that the case was concluded by *Munro* v *Butt*.

Notes

1. See also *Bolton* v *Mahadeva* [1972] 1 WLR 1009 and *Hoenig* v *Isaacs* [1952] 2 All ER 176. For more detail on the contractual doctrines of 'entire obligations' and 'substantial performance' see Treitel, *Contract*, 697–703.

2. For an unsatisfactory reform proposal, rejected and never implemented, see the Law Commission Report on *Pecuniary Restitution on Breach of Contract* (HMSO, Law Com 121, 1983). For discussion see Burrows (1984) 47 MLR 76, Birks, *Introduction*, 259–64 and Burrows, *Restitution*, 280–81.

Hain Steamship Company Ltd v *Tate & Lyle Ltd*
[1936] 2 All ER 597 (HL)

Quantum meruit

Tate & Lyle were cif buyers of a quantity of West Indian sugar. The cif sellers in New York chartered from the shipowners the '*SS Tregenna*' in order to ship sugar from two ports in Cuba and one port in San Domingo. Under the charterparty half the freight was payable by the charterers in New York upon signing of the bills of lading, and half upon delivery of the cargo. Having loaded sugar in Cuba, the master, who had not received a telegram instructing him to proceed to San Domingo, set sail for Queenstown (now Cobh in Eire). The sellers, becoming aware of the mistake, radioed the master to return to San Domingo. This he did, and loaded there a further quantity of sugar. The ship had gone some 265 miles out of its way. Upon leaving San Domingo, the vessel stranded and was seriously damaged. The non-damaged cargo was discharged and transhipped by the shipowners onto another vessel. Tate & Lyle were named as consignees on the bills of lading which were issued by the shipowners. The shipowners required Tate & Lyle to enter into a Lloyd's average bond and to pay a deposit, before receiving their goods. When Tate & Lyle (the respondents) found out about the ship's deviation they claimed for the return of the proportion of the deposit which related to the sugar shipped from Cuba. The shipowners (the appellants) counterclaimed for a general average contribution, and for the freight still owing on the Cuban sugar. *Held*: the unjustified deviation was a breach of contract which entitled the charterers to treat the contract as at an end; however, they waived that breach so the charterparty remained on foot. Tate & Lyle as consignees were not liable under the bill of lading contract to pay contribution or freight, because they were entitled as a result of the deviation to treat the bill of lading contract as at an end, and therefore incurred no further obligations under it. The charterers' waiver of deviation under the charterparty contract had no effect upon the bill of lading contract. Further, while Tate & Lyle were not personally liable under the bill of lading to make a general average contribution, they were liable upon the bond to so contribute. On the *quantum meruit* issue, on the facts there was no obligation on Tate & Lyle to pay the balance of freight, which remained due from the charterers under the charterparty. The extracts are concerned only with the *quantum meruit* issue.

LORD ATKIN: . . . On the ship's claim for the balance of freight in respect of the San Domingo sugar I have come to the conclusion that it must fail. That there is no claim on the express contract—the bill of lading—I have already said. An amendment to claim a *quantum meruit* was however allowed, and this has occasioned me some difficulty. I am not prepared at present to adopt the view of Scrutton, LJ, that in no circumstances can a consignee, whether holder of a bill of lading or not, be liable to pay after a deviation any remuneration for the carriage form which he has benefited. I prefer to leave the matter open, and in those circumstances to say that the opinion of the Court of Appeal to the contrary in this case should not be taken as authoritative. In the present case I find that the balance of freight under the charterparty, and therefore under the bill of lading, was to be paid in New York after advice of right delivery and ascertainment of weight. The terms of the cesser clause do not affect this obligation, and consequently the charterer remained and remains still liable for that freight. In these circumstances I am not satisfied that conditions existed under which a promise should be implied whereby the shippers undertook to give to the ship a further and a different right to receive some part of what would be a reasonable remuneration for the carriage. I think, therefore, that the claim for freight fails. . . .

LORD WRIGHT MR: . . . The respondents claim that by reason of the deviation they are relieved from liability to pay any freight at all. Under the charterparty, the balance of freight, that is the 50 per cent not payable in advance, was payable in cash at New York upon receipt of cable advice of right delivery of the cargo and the net delivered weight ascertained. Clearly there could be no lien for such freight; but, as the charterers had waived the deviation and the cesser clause was only to operate on payment of all freight, the charterers remained liable. The average bond imposed no new liability on the respondents so far as this freight was concerned. The express term of the bond was that delivery should be made 'on payment of the freight payable on delivery, if any.' According to the charterparty no freight was payable on delivery; if the bill of lading contracts applied, no freight was payable on delivery under them: they stipulated that all conditions should be as per charterparty and that the consignees should pay freight, as per charterparty. I paraphrase the actual words which differed at the two ports of shipment in Cuba, but whatever they mean, they do not make any freight payable on delivery.

I have discussed the effect of a deviation in so far as it deprives the shipowner of a right to rely on the contractual exceptions, but a deviation carries wider consequences. I think it is right to say that it abrogates the special contract entirely. By 'special' here is meant the express contract; it is thereby intended to reserve the question of there being any implied contract. But in particular the deviation destroys, as I think, the right to claim the contract freight, even if the voyage is completed and the goods delivered at the contract destination. It is curious that there is no express decision on this point. It has however been held that a deviation discharges provisions in the contract of affreightment for unloading in a fixed time—*United States Shipping Board* v *Bunge y Born* (1925) 31 Com Cas 118. Freight payable at destination under the terms of the contract must be an *a fortiori* case. But the Court of Appeal have denied the appellants' claim to any freight at all on a more fundamental ground: they have held that not only is the contract freight gone, but no freight on a *quantum meruit* can be claimed. Scrutton, LJ, states the proposition quite generally:

> The fact that a volunteer without authority renders services to another man's property does not give him a right to remuneration, or to keep the property unless he gets remuneration. There is no authority on the question; but as a matter of logic, I think the claim for freight fails.

The 'logic' involved is also explained by Greer, LJ, who thinks that after a deviation

> the goods are being carried unlawfully: the shipowner is throughout in unauthorised possession of the goods of whoever may turn out to be the owner, and must deliver them up to the owner on demand without payment for a service which neither the shipper nor the owner ever asked him to perform.

During the argument I was of opinion, like your Lordships, that in the circumstances of this case the claim for freight failed. It was accordingly not necessary to hear argument on this important question of principle: it may be reserved for full argument and decision when, if ever, it arises in that simple and abstract form. I merely add a few observations to explain why as at present advised I feel difficulty about it.

I have myself in my own experience never heard of a case where a shipowner who has carried goods to their destination, but after a deviation, has been refused payment of freight. It is different if the goods have been lost after the deviation, as in *Morrison's* case [1916] 2 KB 783, or if they have been delivered at a port other than the agreed destination. But a sweeping general rule such as the Court of Appeal laid down will, if it be correct, have startling consequences. Let me put a quite possible case: A steamer carrying a cargo of frozen meat from Australia to England deviates by calling at a port outside the usual or permitted route: it is only the matter of a few hours extra steaming: no trouble ensues except the trifling delay. The cargo is duly delivered in England at the agreed port. The goods owner has had for all practical purposes the benefit of all that his contract required; he has had the advantages, of the use of a valuable ship, her crew, fuel, refrigeration and appliances, canal dues, port charges, stevedoring. The shipowner may be technically a wrongdoer in the sense that he has once deviated, but otherwise over a long period he has been performing the exacting and costly duties of a carrier at sea. I cannot help thinking that epithets like 'unlawful' and 'unauthorised' are not apt to describe such services; it may be that by the maritime law the relationship of carrier and goods owner still continues despite the deviation, though subject to the modifications consequent on the deviation. Nor can I help feeling that the court would not be slow to infer an obligation when the goods are received at destination to pay, not indeed the contract freight, but a reasonable remuneration. The observations of the Court of Appeal certainly go beyond such authority as there is. In *Joseph Thorley* v *Orchis* [1907] 1 KB 660 the shipowners, after a deviation, were held liable for the negligence of stevedores in unloading, notwithstanding the exception in the bill of lading. Fletcher Moulton, LJ, said at p. 669:

> In what position, then, does he [the shipowner] stand? He has carried the goods to their place of destination, and is therefore entitled to some remuneration for that service, of which their owner has recieved the benefit. The most favourable position which he can claim to occupy is that he has carried the goods as a common carrier for the agreed freight. I do not say that in all circumstances he would be entitled as of right to be treated even as favourably as this, but in the present case the plaintiffs do not contest his right to stand in that position.

I do not think that Fletcher Moulton, LJ, intended to lay down here precise rules of law. *Morrison's* case shows that the shipowner, after a deviation, cannot claim the protection afforded by law to a common carrier, nor can there be any question of the agreed freight if what is called the special contract (as distinguished from any implied contract) is displaced. Collins, MR, at p. 667, says:

> It may be, no doubt, that, although that condition [so not to deviate] is broken, the circumstances are such as to give rise to an implied obligation on the part of the cargo owner to pay the shipowner the freight . . . from the fact of the carriage of the cargo to its destination.

I may note that in *United States Shipping Board* v *Bunge y Born* the goods owner did not contest the shipowner's right to freight, though the ship had deviated and the terms as to demurrage had gone.

I am not expressing any final opinion because I think the matter does not arise for decision in this case. Here on any view, in my opinion, all the circumstances point against the implication of an agreement to pay a *quantum meruit* freight. By the charterparty, freight was payable by the charterers in New York after delivery: there was no operative cesser clause: it was known to all parties that the charterers were liable throughout for the freight. I can find at this stage no hint that anyone was thinking that the deviation had displaced the contract. The appellants were entitled to freight from the charterers. Under these circumstances the fact that the respondents ordered the ship from the port of call to Greenock and presented the bills of lading and took delivery in the normal way without any mention of freight pointed to the view that freight was no interest of theirs. In fact they had purchased on 'arrived' terms and as against their sellers were entitled to delivery 'freight free.' It is not expressly shown that the appellants were cognisant of the terms of sale, but the terms of the charterparty might be taken to point in that direction and the charterers asked the appellants to send them 'released' bills of lading, so as to obtain payment of the purchase price in London. I am not quite clear of the precise effect of the bill of lading terms, which were in effect 'paying freight and all conditions as per charterparty,' in a case like this, where the charterparty expressly provided for payment in New York, that is, by the charterers at a date afer delivery. But it is, I think, sufficiently clear that at the time neither the respondents nor the appellants had any idea of the respondents paying the freight. The appellants were giving up no lien for freight, because they had none. Above all, in the average bond there was an express promise to pay freight, if any, payable on delivery, and I think that this express agreement excludes the possibility of implying an agreement to pay any other freight. It is, in my opinion, clear that no one thought that the bill of lading contract was gone, still less that if it was gone there might be an implied agreement to pay a reasonable freight against delivery. And finally in fact delivery was made so far as the evidence goes as a matter of course without any freight being paid at all.

Your Lordships gave leave to amend so as to include a claim for freight *quantum meruit*. The respondents can be liable for such freight, if at all, only on the ground that an obligation to pay it ought to be implied from all the circumstances. As I think, reserving all more general questions, that on any view no such obligation can here be implied, the claim for freight should, in my opinion, fail and the appeal under that head be dismissed.

LORD MAUGHAM: [His Lordship discussed the other features of the case before turning to the *quantum meruit* issue . . . :]

Finally, on the general question whether a consignee is liable to pay freight after a deviation which has been treated as putting an end to the contract of affreightment I would only observe that that question does not now arise for decision; but I am strongly inclined to doubt the correctness of the view suggested in the Court of Appeal. As I have already indicated, I do not agree with the proposition that the ship owner (apart from any step taken by the consignee) ought to be regarded as a volunteer or a wrongdoer, and I am of opinion that a claim on the footing of *quantum meruit* must depend on all circumstances of the case, including the question whether the goods have been delivered at the agreed port and without injury or substantial delay. Bearing in mind a well-known adage and your Lordships' abstention from expressing any final opinion on this matter I do not propose to express any further view of my own on it. In the present case the claim for freight on the basis of *quantum meruit* is excluded by the fact that the freight by the terms of the charterparty was payable by the charterers in New York after delivery at Greenock. There was therefore no lien for freight and nothing in the Lloyd's average bond to make the respondents liable to pay it.

Notes

1. This difficult commercial factual configuration gives rise to an important question of principle. The carriage of goods by sea is a valuable service normally rendered under an express contract (either a charterparty or a bill of lading). A deviation from the contractual route is a breach of contract which entitles the cargo interest to treat the contract as at an end and no longer binding on him. (On one view deviation is like any other fundamental breach of contract or breach of condition which gives the innocent party a right to elect to treat the contract as at an end. For example, see Lord Atkin in *Hain* v *Tate & Lyle* [1936] 2 All ER 597, at 601. The more traditional view is that deviation, unlike an ordinary breach of a fundamental term, *automatically discharges* the carriage contract, unless waived by the cargo interest. See the remarks of Lord Wilberforce in *Photo Productions Ltd* v *Securicor Ltd* [1980] AC 827 at 845.) As the example cited by Lord Wright MR above suggests, this means that the cargo-owner might receive the benefit of valuable services to his goods, but have no obligation under an express contract to pay for them. Can restitution come to the aid of the carrier? This question never arose in *Hain* because the House of Lords decided that the contractual scheme always envisaged that the charterers (who were the sellers of the goods) should pay the remuneration under the still binding charterparty. Therefore the discussions extracted above are technically *obiter dicta*. They are, however, interesting in showing that the House of Lords appeared sympathetic to the justice of the carrier's case and rejected the anti-restitution fundamentalism of Scrutton LJ in the Court of Appeal. However, the discussion in the speeches does not take us very far and the usual questions still need to be asked: Is the cargo-owner enriched, and upon which test(s) of enrichment? What is the factor giving rise to a right to restitution? For discussion see Burrows, *Restitution*, 279–80; Birks, *Introduction*, 239–41; Goff and Jones, 442–4.

2. General average contribution was the main concern in this case. This arises where an accident befalls a maritime adventure and expenditure is required, for example, the salvage services after the ship stranded in *Hain* which were necessary to preserve the vessel and the cargo. By rules as ancient as any in our commercial law, all the parties interested in the voyage, ship and cargo are required to contribute in proportion to their interest. In this case Tate & Lyle were personally liable to contribute because they had signed the Lloyd's average bond in return for good consideration. The law of general average contribution (which is not discussed in detail in this book) has also been categorised as concerned with reversing unjust enrichment (Goff and Jones, 333–42).

Section 2: contracts discharged by frustration

A: The common law

See Burrows, *Restitution*, 281–3 for an analysis of the defects of the common law which the Law Reform (Frustrated Contracts) Act 1943 attempted to remedy. For more detail see Goff and Jones, 407–12.

Cutter v *Powell*
(1795) 6 Term Rep 320; 101 ER 573 (KB)

Quantum meruit

A master of a ship signed and delivered a promissory note to Cutter in Jamaica which stated: 'Ten days after the ship '*Governor Parry*', myself master, arrives at Liverpool, I promise to pay Mr T. Cutter the sum of thirty guineas [£31.50], provided he proceeds, continues and does his duty as second mate in the said ship from hence to the port of Liverpool. Kingston, 31 July 1793.' The '*Governor Parry*' embarked from Kingston on 2 August 1793 and arrived in Liverpool on 9 October 1793. Cutter had joined the ship and done his duty until he died during the currency of the voyage on 20 September. The usual wage of a second mate was £4 per month and the usual duration of a voyage from Jamaica to Liverpool was about eight weeks. Cutter's widow sued to recover a proportion of the sum for the work and labour done by Cutter up to his death.

LORD KENYON CJ: I should be extremely sorry that in the decision of this case we should determine against what had been the received opinion in the mercantile world on contracts of this kind, because it is of great importance that the laws by which the contracts of so numerous and so useful a body of men as the sailors are supposed to be guided should not be overturned. Whether these kind of notes are much in use among the seamen, we are not sufficiently informed; and the instances now stated to us from Liverpool are too recent to form any thing like usage. But it seems to me at present that the decision of this case may proceed on the particular words of this contract and the precise facts here stated, without touching marine contracts in general. That where the parties have come to an express contract none can be implied has prevailed so long as to be reduced to an axiom in the law. Here the defendant expressly promised to pay the intestate thirty guineas, provided he proceeded, continued and did his duty as second mate in the ship from Jamaica to Liverpool; and the accompanying circumstances disclosed in the case are that the common rate of wages is four pounds per month, when the party is paid in proportion to the time he serves: and that this voyage is generally performed in two months. Therefore if there had been no contract between these parties, all that the intestate could have recovered on a quantum meruit for the voyage would have been eight pounds; whereas here the defendant contracted to pay thirty guineas provided the mate continued to do his duty as mate during the whole voyage, in which case the latter would have received nearly four times as much as if he were paid for the number of months he served. He stipulated to receive the larger sum if the whole duty were performed, and nothing unless the whole of that duty were performed: it was a kind of insurance. On this particular contract my opinion is formed at present; at the same time I must say that if we were assured that these notes are in universal use, and that the commercial world have received and acted upon them in a different sense, I should give up my own opinion.

ASHHURST J: We cannot collect that there is any custom prevailing among merchants on these contracts; and therefore we have nothing to guide us but the terms of the contract itself. This is a written contract, and it speaks for itself. And as it is entire, and as the defendant's promise depends on a condition precedent to be performed by the other party, the condition must be performed before the other party is entitled to receive any thing under it. It has been argued however that the plaintiff may now recover on a quantum meruit: but she has no right to desert the agreement; for wherever there is an express contract the parties must be guided by it; and one party cannot relinquish or abide by it as it may suit his advantage. Here the intestate was by the terms of his contract to perform a given duty before he could call upon the defendant to pay him any thing; it was a condition precedent, without performing which the defendant is not liable. And that seems to me to conclude the question: the intestate did not perform the contract on his part; he was not indeed to blame for not doing it; but still as this was a condition precedent, and as he did not perform it, his representative is not entitled to recover.

Appleby v *Myers*
(1867) LR 2 CP 651 (Exchequer Chamber)

Quantum meruit; quantum valebat

The plaintiff engineers agreed to erect a steam engine and machinery on the defendant's premises and to keep it in repair for two years. The contract was divided into ten separate stages. It was agreed that the price was to be paid when the work was completed. After some portions of the work were done and while others were in the course of completion, the premises and all the machinery so far installed and some of the plaintiff's materials were destroyed by an accidental fire. The plaintiff claimed £419 in respect of work done and materials supplied.

BLACKBURN J: . . . The whole question depends upon the true construction of the contract between the parties. We agree with the Court below in thinking that it sufficiently appears that the work which the plaintiffs agreed to perform could not be performed unless the defendant's premises continued in a fit state to enable the plaintiffs to perform the work on them; and we agree with them in thinking that, if by any default on the part of the defendant, his premises were rendered unfit to receive the work, the plaintiffs would have had the option to sue the defendant for this default, or to treat the contract as rescinded, and sue on a quantum meruit. But we do not agree with them in thinking that there was an absolute promise or warranty by the defendant that the premises should at all events continue so fit. We think that where, as in the present case, the premises are destroyed without fault on either side, it is a misfortune equally affecting both parties; excusing both from further performance of the contract, but giving a cause of action to neither.

Then it was argued before us, that, inasmuch as this was a contract of that nature which would in pleading be described as a contract for work, labour, and materials, and not as one of bargain and sale, the labour and materials necessarily became the property of the defendant as soon as they were worked into his premises and became part of them, and therefore were at his risk. We think that, as to a great part at least of the work done in this case, the materials had not become the property of the defendant; for, we think that the plaintiffs, who were to complete the whole for a fixed sum, and keep it in repair for two years, would have had a perfect right, if they thought that a portion of the engine which they had put up was too slight, to change it and substitute another in their opinion better calculated to keep in good repair during the two years, and that without consulting or asking the leave of the defendant. But, even on the supposition that the materials had become unalterably fixed to the defendant's premises, we do not think that, under such a contract as this, the plaintiffs could recover anything unless the whole work was completed. It is quite true that materials worked by one into the property of another become part of that property. This is equally true, whether it be fixed or movable property. Bricks built into a wall become part of the house; thread stitched into a coat which is under repair, or planks and nails and pitch worked into a ship under repair, become part of the coat or the ship; and therefore, generally, and in the absense of something to shew a contrary intention, the bricklayer, or tailor, or shipwright, is to be paid for the work and materials he has done and provided, although the whole work is not complete. It is not material whether in such a case the non-completion is because the shipwright did not choose to go on with the work, as was the case in *Roberts* v *Havelock* 3 B & Ad 404 or because in consequence of a fire he could not go on with it, as in *Menetone* v *Athawes* 3 Burr 1592. But, though this is the prima facie contract between those who enter into contracts for doing work and supplying materials, there is nothing to render it either illegal or absurd in the workman to agree to complete the whole, and be paid when the whole is complete, and not till then: and we think that the plaintiffs in the present case had entered into such a contract. Had the accidental fire left the defendant's premises untouched, and only injured a part of the work which the plaintiffs had already done, we apprehend that it is clear the plaintiffs under such a contract as the present must have done that part over again, in order to fulfil their contract to complete the whole and 'put it to work for the sums above named respectively.' As it is, they are, according to the principle laid down in *Taylor* v *Caldwell* 3 B & S 826; 32 LJ (QB) 164, excused from completing the work; but they are not therefore entitled to any compensation for what they have done, but which has, without any fault of the defendant, perished. The case is in principle like that of a shipowner who has been excused from the performance of his contract to carry goods to their destination, because his ship has been disabled by one of the excepted perils, but who is not therefore entitled to any payment on account of the part-performance of the voyage, unless there is something to justify the conclusion that there has been a fresh contract to pay freight pro ratâ.

On the argument, much reference was made to the Civil law. The opinions of the great lawyers collected in the Digest afford us very great assistance in tracing out any question of doubtful principle; but they do not bind us: and we think that, on the principles of English law laid down in *Cutter* v *Powell* 6 TR 320; 2 Smith's LC 1, *Jesse* v *Roy* 1 CM & R 316, *Munroe* v *Butt* 8 E & B 738, *Sinclair* v *Bowles* 9 B & C 92, and other cases, the plaintiffs, having contracted to do an entire work for a specific sum, can recover nothing unless the work be done, or it can be shewn that it was the defendant's fault that the work was incomplete, or that there is something to justify the conclusion that the parties have entered into a fresh contract. . . .

***Whincup* v Hughes**

(1871) LR 6 CP 78 (Common Pleas)

Action for money had and received

The plaintiff apprenticed his son to Hughes, a watchmaker and jeweller, by deed for a term of six years and paid him a £25 premium in respect of instruction, board and so on. The plaintiff's son received instruction for almost a year, when Hughes died. *Held*: the death of the master brought the contract to an end, but the plaintiff could not recover a proportion of the premium from the executrix because the failure of consideration was only partial. Bovill CJ said: 'The general rule of law is, that where a contract has been in part performed no part of the money paid under such contract can be recovered back.'

Fibrosa Spolka Akcyjna v *Fairbairn Lawson Combe Barbour Ltd* [1943] AC 32 (HL)

Action for money had and received

An English seller entered into a written contract dated 12 July 1939 with a Polish buyer for the sale of flax hackling machinery to be delivered to the buyer at Gdynia, Poland. The price was agreed at £4,800, of which a third was to be paid with the order. In fact only £1,000 was paid when the Second World War began in September 1939 and Gdynia was occupied by the Germans. It was held the contract was frustrated by supervening illegality. The buyer claimed for the return of the £1,000 on the ground of total failure of consideration.

VISCOUNT SIMON LC: . . . The locus classicus for the view which has hitherto prevailed is to be found in the judgment of Collins MR in *Chandler* v *Webster* [1904] 1 KB 493. It was not a considered judgment, but it is hardly necessary to say that I approach this pronouncement of the then Master of the Rolls with all the respect due to so distinguished a common lawyer. When his judgment is studied, however, one cannot but be impressed by the circumstance that he regarded the proposition that money in such cases could not be recovered back as flowing from the decision in *Taylor* v *Caldwell* 3 B & S 826. *Taylor* v *Caldwell*, however, was not a case in which any question arose whether money could be recovered back, for there had been no payment in advance, and there is nothing in the judgment of Blackburn J, which, at any rate in terms, affirms the general proposition that 'the loss lies where it falls.' The application by Collins MR of *Taylor* v *Caldwell* to the actual problem with which he had to deal in *Chandler* v *Webster* [1904] 1 KB 493, 499 deserves close examination. He said:

> The plaintiff contends that he is entitled to recover the money which he has paid on the ground that there has been a total failure of consideration. He says that the condition on which he paid the money was that the procession should take place, and that, as it did not take place, there has been a total failure of consideration. That contention does no doubt raise a question of some difficulty, and one which has perplexed the courts to a considerable extent in several cases. The principle on which it has been dealt with is that which was applied in *Taylor* v *Caldwell* 3 B & S 826—namely, that where, from causes outside the volition of the parties something which was the basis of, or essential to the fulfilment of, the contract has become impossible, so that, from the time when the fact of that impossibility has been ascertained, the contract can no further be performed by either party, it remains a perfectly good contract up to that point, and everything previously done in pursuance of it must be treated as rightly done, but the parties are both discharged from further performance of it. If the effect were that the contract were wiped out altogether, no doubt the result would be that money paid under it would have to be repaid as on a failure of consideration. But that is not the effect of the doctrine; it only releases the parties from further performance of the contract. Therefore the doctrine of failure of consideration does not apply.

It appears to me that the reasoning in this crucial passage is open to two criticisms: (a) The claim of a party, who has paid money under a contract, to get money back, on the ground that the consideration for which he paid it has totally failed, is not based on any provision contained in the contract, but arises because, in the circumstances that have happened, the law gives a remedy in quasi-contract to the party who has not got that for which he bargained. It is a claim to recover money to which the defendant has no further right because in the circumstances that have happened the money must be regarded as received to the plaintiff's use. It is true that the effect of frustration is that, while the contract can no further be performed, 'it remains a perfectly good contract up to that point, and everything previously done in pursuance of it must be treated as rightly done,' but it by no means follows that the situation existing at the moment of frustration is one which leaves the party that has paid money and has not received the stipulated consideration without any remedy. To claim the return of money paid on the ground of total failure of consideration is not to vary the terms of the contract in any way. The claim arises not because the right to be repaid is one of the stipulated conditions of the contract, but because, in the circumstances that have happened, the law gives the remedy. It is the failure to distinguish between (1) the action of assumpsit for money had and received in a case where the consideration has wholly failed, and (2) an action on the contract itself, which explains the mistake which I think has been made in applying English law to this subject-matter. Thus, in *Blakeley* v *Muller & Co.* [1903] 2 KB 760n, 761n, Lord Alverstone CJ said, 'I agree that *Taylor* v *Caldwell* applies, but the consequence of that decision is that neither party here could have sued on the contract in respect of anything which was to be done under it after the procession had been abandoned.' That is true enough, but it does not follow that because the plaintiff cannot sue 'on the contract' he cannot sue dehors the contract for the recovery of a payment in respect of which consideration has failed. In the same case, Wills J relied on *Appleby* v *Myers* LR 2 CP 651, where a contract was made for the erection by A of machinery on the premises of B, to be paid for on completion. There was no pre-payment and in the course of the work the premises were destroyed by fire. It was held that both parties were excused from further performance, and that no liability accrued on either side, but the liability referred to was liability under the contract, and the learned judge seems to have thought that no action to recover money in such circumstances as the present could be conceived of unless there was a term of the contract, express or implied, which so provided. Once it is realised that the action to recover money for a consideration that has wholly failed rests, not on a contractual bargain between the parties, but, as Lord Sumner said in *Sinclair* v *Brougham* [1914] AC 398, 452, 'upon a notional or imputed promise to repay,' or (if it is preferred to omit reference to a fictitious promise) upon an obligation to repay arising from the circumstances, the difficulty in the way of holding that a prepayment made under a contract which has been frustrated can be recovered back appears to me to disappear. (b) There is, no doubt, a distinction between cases in which a contract is 'wiped out altogether,' e.g., because it is void as being illegal from the start or as being due to fraud which the innocent party has elected to treat as avoiding the contract, and cases in which intervening impossibility 'only releases the parties from further performance of the contract.' But does the distinction between these two classes of case justify the deduction of Collins MR that 'the doctrine of failure of consideration does not apply' where the contract remains a perfectly good contract up to the date of frustration? This conclusion seems to be derived from the view that, if the contract remains good and valid up to the moment of frustration, money which has already been paid under it cannot be regarded as having been paid for a consideration which has wholly failed. The party that has paid the money has had the advantage, whatever it may be worth, of the promise of the other party. That is true, but it is necessary to draw a distinction. In English law, an enforceable contract may be formed by an exchange of a promise for a promise, or by the exchange of a promise for an act—I am excluding contracts under seal—and thus, in law relating to the formation of contract, the promise to do a thing may often be the consideration, but when one is considering the law of failure of consideration and of the quasi-contractual right to recover money on that ground, it is, generally speaking, not the promise which is referred to as the consideration, but the performance of the promise. The money was paid to secure performance and, if performance fails the inducement which brought about the payment is not fulfilled.

If this were not so, there could never be any recovery of money, for failure of consideration, by the payer of the money in return for a promise of future perfomance, yet there are endless examples which show that money can be recovered, as for a complete failure of consideration, in cases where the promise was given but could not be fulfilled: see the notes in Bullen and Leake's Precedents of Pleading, 9th ed., p. 263. In this connexion the decision in *Rugg* v *Minett* 11 East 210 is instructive. There the plaintiff had bought at auction a number of casks of oil. The contents of each cask were to be made up after the auction by the seller to the prescribed quantity so that the property in a cask did not pass to the plaintiff until this had been done. The plaintiff paid in advance a sum of money on account of his purchases generally, but a fire occurred after some of the casks had been filled up, while the others had not. The plaintiff's action was to recover the money he had paid as money received by the defendants to the use of the plaintiffs. The Court of King's Bench ruled that this cause of action succeeded in respect of the casks which at the time of the fire had not been filled up to the prescribed quantity. A simple illustration of the same result is an agreement to buy a horse, the price to be paid down, but the horse not to be delivered and the property not to pass until the horse had been shod. If the horse dies before the shoeing, the price can unquestionably be recovered as for a total failure of consideration, notwithstanding that the promise to deliver was given. This is the case of a contract de certo corpore where the certum corpus perishes after the contract is made, but, as Vaughan Williams LJ's judgment in *Krell* v *Henry* [1903] 2 KB 740, 748 explained, the same doctrine applies 'to cases where the event which renders the contract incapable of performance is the cessation or non-existence of an express condition or state of things, going to the root of the contract, and essential to its performance.' I can see no valid reason why the right to recover prepaid money should not equally arise on frustration arising from supervening circumstances as it arises on frustration from destruction of a particular subject-matter. The conclusion is that the rule in *Chandler* v *Webster* [1904] 1 KB 493 is wrong, and that the appellants can recover their 1000*l*.

While this result obviates the harshness with which the previous view in some instances treated the party who had made a prepayment, it cannot be regarded as dealing fairly between the parties in all cases, and must sometimes have the result of leaving the recipient who has to return the money at a grave disadvantage. He may have incurred expenses in connexion with the partial carrying out of the contract which are equivalent, or more than equivalent, to the money which he prudently stipulated should be prepaid, but which he now has to return for reasons which are no fault of his. He may have to repay the money, though he has executed almost the whole of the contractual work, which will be left on his hands. These results follow from the fact that the English common law does not undertake to apportion a prepaid sum in such circumstances—contrast the provision, now contained in s. 40 of the Partnership Act, 1890, for apportioning a premium if a partnership is prematurely dissolved. It must be for the legislature to decide whether provision should be made for an equitable apportionment of prepaid moneys which have to be returned by the recipient in view of the frustration of the contract in respect of which they were paid. I move that the appeal be allowed, and that judgment be entered for the appellants.

LORD ATKIN: . . . A sells a horse to B for 50*l*., delivery to be made in a month, the price to be paid forthwith, but the property not to pass till delivery, and B to pay A each week an agreed sum for keep of the horse during the month. The horse dies in a fortnight. A is excused from delivery and B from taking delivery. B is bound to pay the sum due for the fortnight during which the horse was kept. But what is the position as to the 50*l*., the price paid in advance? This is in simple terms the problem in the present case. The answer that I venture to think would occur to most people, whether laymen or lawyers, would be that the buyer ought to get his money back, having had nothing for it, and the lawyer would support the claim by saying that it is money had and received to the use of the buyer, being money paid on a consideration which has wholly failed.

But that is not the answer which was given in similar circumstances in the coronation cases, and it is those decisions that come up for review in the present case. The question arose in the neatest form in *Chandler* v *Webster* [1904] 1 KB 493, where the leading judgment was given in the Court of Appeal by Collins MR, a master of the common law, whose opinion the profession have always rightly held in the greatest respect. In that case the plaintiff had hired a room to view the coronation procession on Thursday, June 26, 1902. On June 10 he wrote to the defendant: 'I beg to confirm my purchase of the first floor room of the Electric Lighting Board at 7, Pall Mall to view the procession on Thursday, June 26, for the sum of 141*l*. 15s., which amount is now due. I shall be obliged if you will take the room on sale, and I authorise you to sell separate seats in the room, for which I will erect a stand.' It became the subject of controversy whether, in view of certain other terms arranged between the parties, the whole sum became due before the procession became impossible, but the courts decided, as was clearly the case, that it did so become due. It may be noted that the defendant had nothing to do under the contract but allow the plaintiff the use of the room. On June 19 the plaintiff paid the defendant 100*l*. on account of the price of the room, but had not paid the balance at the time the procession was abandoned. The plaintiff claimed the return of the 100*l*. on a total failure of consideration, the defendant counterclaimed for the balance of 41*l*. 15s. Collins MR dealing with the contention that there had been a total failure of consideration, after stating that it raised a question of some difficulty, stated that the principle on which it has been dealt with is that which was applied in *Taylor* v *Caldwell* 3 B & S 826, namely, that where the contract has become impossible in the circumstances there stated 'it remains a perfectly good contract up to that point, and everything previously done in pursuance of it must be treated as rightly done, but the parties are both discharged from further performance of it.' So far the statement is unassailable. But the Master of the Rolls proceeded: 'If the effect were that the contract were wiped out altogether, no doubt the result would be that money paid under it would have to be repaid as on a failure of consideration. But that is not the effect of the doctrine: it only releases the parties from further performance of the contract. *Therefore*' (the italics are mine) 'the doctrine of failure of consideration does not apply.' It seems plain that the Master of the Rolls is not repelling the claim for money had and received on the ground that the doctrine as to impossibility of performance itself, as part of its content, excludes the claim. *Taylor* v *Caldwell*, the principle of which he is expressly applying, had nothing to do with money had and received. The claim was for damages in costs of advertisements, etc., for concerts for which the defendants had agreed to let their hall at the Surrey Gardens, a contract which it was impossible to perform because the hall was destroyed by fire after the contract. The Master of the Rolls there is applying the common law rule as to money had and received to a case of a contract where all that had happened was that in law both parties were released from further performance, and in those circumstances he seems to say: 'The doctrine of failure of consideration only applies where the contract is wiped out altogether. In this case it is not. The parties are only discharged from further performance. Therefore, the claim for money had and received must fail.'

My Lords, the difficulty which this decision causes me is to understand how this great lawyer came to the conclusion that the claim for money paid on a consideration which wholly failed could only be made where the contract was wiped out altogether, and I have sought for some construction of his words which stopped short of that absolute statement, but I can find none. I know of no authority for the proposition. It is true that where a party is in a position to rescind a contract he may be able to sue for money which he has paid under the contract now rescinded, but there are numerous cases where there has been no question of rescission where such an action has lain. I may refer to *Giles* v *Edwards* (1797) 7 Term Rep 181 where a contract to deliver wood was prevented by the defendant preventing performance by not loading all the wood; *Rugg* v *Minett* 11 East 210, where the buyer had paid part of the purchase price on a sale of turpentine in casks, where the property in some casks had passed while in seller's warehouse, but in some had not, and the purchaser was entitled to recover as money had and received the proportion properly attributable to the casks in which the property had not passed; *Nockels* v *Crosby* (1825) 3 B & C 814; *Wilson* v *Church* 13 Ch D 1; *National Bolivian Navigation Co.* v *Wilson* 5 App Cas 176; *Johnson* v *Goslett* 3 CB (NS) 569; and *Ashpitel* v *Sercombe* (1850) 5 Ex 147, in all of which the plaintiff had put up money for an adventure which was eventually abandoned by the promoters; *Devaux* v *Conolly* 8 CB 640, where there had been an over-payment in respect of goods delivered. In none of these cases was it suggested that the contract was 'wiped out altogether.' Indeed, in other cases where it is suggested that the contract was 'rescinded,' all that is meant is that the party was entitled to treat himself as no longer bound to perform and to recover what he himself has paid. With great respect, therefore, to the judgment in *Chandler* v *Webster* [1904] 1 KB 493, I do not agree with that part of it which refused to give effect to the plaintiff's claim for return of the sum which he had paid on the ground of total failure of consideration. . . .

That the result of the law may cause hardship when a contract is automatically stayed during performance and any further right to performance is denied to each party is incontrovertible. One party may have almost completed expensive work. He can get no compensation. The other party may have paid the whole price, and if he has received but a slender part of the consideration he can get no compensation. At present it is plain that if no money has been paid on the contract there is no legal principle by which loss can be made good. What is being now decided is that the application of an old-established principle of the common law does enable a man who has paid money and received nothing for it to recover the money so expended. At any rate, it can be said it leaves the man who has received the money and given nothing for it in no worse position than if he had received none. Many commercial contracts provide for various risks. It is always possible to provide for the risk of frustration, but what provision the parties may agree will probably take some time to negotiate. Meanwhile, by the application of a general doctrine which is independent of the special contract and only comes into play when further performance of the latter is precluded, the man who pays money in advance on a contract which is frustrated and receives nothing for his payment is entitled to recover it back. I think, therefore, that the appeal should be allowed.

LORD WRIGHT: [having made the observations cited in Chapter 1, Section 1 considered the authorities and concluded: . . .] but I think it is clear both in English and Scots law that the failure of consideration which justifies repayment is a failure in the contract performance. What is meant is not consideration in the sense in which the word is used when it is said that in executory contracts the promise of one party is consideration for the promise of the other. No doubt, in some cases the recipient of the payment may be exposed to hardship if he has to return the money though before the frustration he has incurred the bulk of the expense and is then left with things on his hands which become valueless to him when the contract fails, so that he gets nothing and has to return the prepayment. These and many other diificulties show that the English rule of recovering payment the consideration for which has failed works a rough justice. It was adopted in more primitive times and was based on the simple theory that a man who has paid in advance for something which he has never got ought to have his money back. It is further imperfect because it depends on an entire consideration and a total failure. Courts of equity have evolved a fairer method of apportioning an entire consideration in cases where a premium has been paid for a partnership which has been ended before its time: Partnership Act, s. 40; contrary to the common law rule laid down in *Whincup* v *Hughes* LR 6 CP 78. Some day the legislature may intervene to remedy these defects. . . .

Question

What were the deficiencies in the common law approach to restitution in relation to frustrated contracts?

Note

What if one or both of the parties renders valuable services or other benefits to the other *after* the contract is discharged. On some facts a new contract might have been agreed. If not, there may still be scope for common law restitutionary relief. In *Société Franco Tunisienne d'Armement* v *Sidermar SPA, The 'Massalia'* [1961] 2 QB 278, Pearson J held that a voyage charterparty for the carriage of iron ore from India to Genoa was frustrated by the closure of the Suez Canal. The vessel had instead proceeded via the Cape of Good Hope, twice the distance of the trip via Suez. The shipowners claimed for a *quantum meruit.* Pearson J discussed *Craven Ellis* v *Canons Ltd* [1936] 2 KB 403 and the *dicta* of Lords Atkin, Wright and Maughan in *Hain Steamship Company Ltd* v *Tate & Lyle Ltd* [1936] 2 All ER 597 and said the present case was *a fortiori*. The shipowners carried the goods 'for the charterers' benefit and with the consent of the charterers. In my view, the law implies or imposes an obligation for the charterers to pay reasonable freight' (at 314). However, *The 'Massalia'* was subsequently overruled by the Court of Appeal in *Ocean Tramp Tankers Corporation* v *V/O Sovfracht, The 'Eugenia'* [1964] 2 QB 226 on the unrelated ground that the charterparty was not frustrated by the closure of the Suez Canal.

B: The Act

For clear discussion see Birks, *Introduction*, 249–58. For reference see Goff and Jones, 447–68 and Treitel, *Frustration and Force Majeure* (London: Sweet & Maxwell, 1994), 537–69.

When is the Act applicable?

LAW REFORM (FRUSTRATED CONTRACTS) ACT 1943

1. Adjustment of rights and liabilities of parties to frustrated contracts

(1) Where a contract governed by English law has become impossible of performance or been otherwise frustrated, and the parties thereto have for that reason been discharged from the further performance of the contract, the following provisions of this section shall, subject to the provisions of section two of this Act, have effect in relation thereto.

. . .

2. Provision as to application of this Act

(3) Where any contract to which this Act applies contains any provision which, upon the true construction of the contract, is intended to have effect in the event of circumstances arising which operate, or would but for the said provision operate, to frustrate the contract, or is intended to have effect whether such circumstances arise or not, the court shall give effect to the said provision and shall only give effect to the foregoing section of this Act to such extent, if any, as appears to the court to be consistent with the said provision.

Money claims

See Burrows, *Restitution*, 283–7.

LAW REFORM (FRUSTRATED CONTRACTS) ACT 1943

1. Adjustment of rights and liabilities of parties to frustrated contracts

. . .

(2) All sums paid or payable to any party in pursuance of the contract before the time when the parties were so discharged (in this Act referred to as 'the time of discharge') shall, in the case of sums so paid, be recoverable from him as money received by him for the use of the party by whom the sums were paid, and, in the case of sums so payable, cease to be so payable:

Provided that, if the party to whom the sums were so paid or payable incurred expenses before the time of discharge in, or for the purpose of, the performance of the contract, the court may, if it considers it just to do so having regard to all the circumstances of the case, allow him to retain or, as the case may be, recover the whole or any part of the sums so paid or payable, not being an amount in excess of the expenses so incurred.

Question

In *Fibrosa* v *Fairbairn* (above) the cost of the machinery was £4,800 and the agreed advance payment was £1,600. In fact only £1,000 was paid by the buyer prior to discharge. It seems that the seller had incurred expenses 'in or for the purpose of the performance of the contract', but that the machines could have been sold elsewhere without loss. What if nobody else wanted machines of those specifications? Applying s. 1(2) to such facts, what would be the result if the seller's proven reliance expenditure had been:

(a) £400?
(b) £1,400?
(c) £4,400?

Gamerco SA v *I.C.M./Fair Warning (Agency) Ltd*
[1995] 1 WLR 1226 (QBD)

The plaintiff pop promotors agreed to arrange a rock concert in Madrid with the defendant group, Guns 'n' Roses, as part of their European tour in 1992. The venue was to be the Vicente Caldéron Stadium, the home of Atlético Madrid, but just days before the concert it was discovered that the stadium could not be safely used. *Held*: the contract was frustrated and the plaintiffs could recover the $412,500 they had paid on account under s. 1(2) of the Law Reform (Frustrated Contracts) Act 1943. In addition it appeared that both sides had incurred expenses. One question was whether the defendant group was able to set off expenses under the proviso to s. 1(2)? It was held that the defendant group's expenses were roughly $50,000. The extract relates to the construction of the proviso.

GARLAND J: . . .

The approach to the proviso

The following have to be established: (1) that the defendants incurred expenses paid or payable (2) before the discharge of the contract on 2 July (3) in performance of the contract (which is not applicable) or (4) for the purposes of the performance of the contract, and (5) that it is just in all the circumstances to allow them to retain the whole or any part of the sums so paid or payable.

The onus of establishing these matters must lie on the defendant. It is, in the broad sense, his case to be made out and I am assisted by the Victorian case of *Lobb* v *Vasey Housing Auxiliary (War Widows Guild)* [1963] VR 239 under the corresponding Victorian Act of 1959, which is in very similar terms to the Act of 1943.

I have already dealt with (1), (2) and (4) so far as the evidence allows. I turn to (5). I take the following matters into consideration. (a) My assumption that the relevant expenses of US $50,000 was undisputed. (b) It was undisputed that the plaintiffs incurred expenses in excess of 52m. pesetas (approximately £285,000 or US $450,000. (c) Neither party conferred any benefit on the other or on a third party, so that subsections (3) and (6) did not apply. (d) The plaintiffs' expenditure was wholly wasted, as was the defendants'. (e) The plaintiffs were concerned with one contract only. The defendants were concerned with the last of 20 similar engagements, neither party being left with any residual benefit or advantage. (f) As already stated, I entirely ignore any insurance recoveries in accordance with subsection (5).

Various views have been advanced as to how the court should exercise its discretion and these can be categorised as follows.

(1) *Total retention.* This view was advanced by the Law Revision Committee in 1939 (Cmd. 6009) on the questionable ground 'that it is reasonable to assume that in stipulating for prepayment the payee intended to protect himself from loss under the contract.' As the editor of *Chitty on Contracts*, 27th ed. (1994), vol. 1, p. 1141, para. 23–060, note 51, (Mr E.G.McKendrick) comments: 'He probably intends to protect himself against the possibility of the other party's insolvency or default in payment.' To this, one can add: 'and secure his own cash flow.'

In *BP Exploration Co. (Libya) Ltd* v *Hunt (No. 2)* [1979] 1 WLR 783 Robert Goff J considered the principle of recovery under subsections (2) and (3). He said, at pp. 799–800:

> The Act is *not* designed to do certain things: (i) It is not designed to apportion the loss between the parties. There is no general power under either section 1(2) or section 1(3) to make any allowance for expenses incurred by the plaintiff (except, under the proviso to section 1(2), to enable him to enforce pro tanto payment of a sum payable but unpaid before frustration); and expenses incurred by the defendant are only relevant in so far as they go to reduce the net benefit obtained by him and thereby limit any award to the plaintiff. (ii) It is not concerned to restore the parties to the position in which they would have been if the contract had been performed. (iii) It is not concerned to restore the parties to the position they were in before the contract was made. A remedy designed to prevent unjust enrichment may not achieve that result; for expenditure may be incurred by either party under the contract which confers no benefit on the other, and in respect of which no remedy is available under the Act.

He then turned to section 1(2) and said:

> There is no discretion in the court in respect of a claim under section 1(2), except in respect of the allowance for expenses; subject to such an allowance . . . the plaintiff is entitled to repayment of the money he has paid. The allowance for expenses is probably best rationalised as a statutory recognition of the defence of change of position. True, the expenses need not have been incurred by reason of the plaintiff's payments; but they must have been incurred in, or for the purpose of, the performance of the contract under which the plaintiff's payment has been made, and for that reason it is just that they should be brought into account.

I do not derive any specific assistance from the *BP Exploration Co.* case. There was no question of any change of position as a result of the plaintiffs' advance payment.

(2) *Equal division.* This was discussed by Professor Treitel in *Frustration and Force Majeure*, pp. 555–556, paras. 15–059 and 15–060. There is some attraction in splitting the loss, but what if the losses are very unequal? Professor Treitel considers statutory provisions in Canada and Australia but makes the point that unequal division is unnecessarily rigid and was rejected by the Law Revision Committee in the 1939 report to which reference has already been made. The parties may, he suggests, have had an unequal means of providing against the loss by insurers, but he appears to overlook subsection (5). It may well be that one party's expenses are entirely thrown away while the other is left with some realisable or otherwise usable benefit or advantage. Their losses may, as in the present case, be very unequal. Professor Treitel therefore favours the third view.

(3) *Broad discretion.* It is self-evident that any rigid rule is liable to produce injustice. The words, 'if it considers it just to do so having regard to all the circumstances of the case,' clearly confer a very broad discretion. Obviously the court

must not take into account anything which is not 'a circumstance of the case' or fail to take into account anything that is and then exercise its discretion rationally. I see no indication in the Act, the authorities or the relevant literature that the court is obliged to incline towards either total retention or equal division. Its task is to do justice in a situation which the parties had neither contemplated nor provided for, and to mitigate the possible harshness of allowing all loss to lie where it has fallen.

I have not found my task easy. As I have made clear, I would have welcomed assistance on the true measure of the defendants' loss and proper treatment of overhead and non-specific expenditure. Because the defendants have plainly suffered some loss, I have made a robust assumption. In all the circumstances, and having particular regard to the plaintiffs' loss, I consider that justice is done by making no deduction under the proviso. . . .

Non-money claims
See Burrows, *Restitution*, 287–93.

LAW REFORM (FRUSTRATED CONTRACTS) ACT 1943

1. Adjustment of rights and liabilities of parties to frustrated contracts

. . .

(3) Where any party to the contract has, by reason of anything done by any other party thereto in, or for the purpose of, the performance of the contract, obtained a valuable benefit (other than a payment of money to which the last foregoing subsection applies) before the time of discharge there shall be recoverable from him by the said other party such sum (if any), not exceeding the value of the said benefit to the party obtaining it, as the court considers just, having regard to all the circumstances of the case and, in particular,—

(a) the amount of any expenses incurred before the time of discharge by the benefited party in, or for the purpose of, the performance of the contract, including any sums paid or payable by him to any other party in pursuance of the contract and retained or recoverable by that party under the last foregoing subsection, and

(b) the effect, in relation to the said benefit, of the circumstances giving rise to the frustration of the contract.

BP Exploration Co. (Libya) Ltd v *Hunt (No. 2)*

[1979] 1 WLR 783 (QBD (Commercial Court));
[1981] 1 WLR 232 (CA); [1983] 2 AC 352 (HL)

Hunt, a Texan oil-man, was granted a concession to develop a potential oil field in the Libyan desert. However, he lacked the resources and experience to explore and develop the field, therefore he entered into a joint venture agreement with BP. Under the agreement Hunt transferred half his interest in the field to BP, and in return BP undertook to explore and develop the field using their own funds, and to transfer to Hunt cash and oil, termed 'farm-in contributions'. BP had no right to claim a contribution from Hunt for the cost of development until the oil came on-stream. The oil was to be shared by BP and Hunt, but three-eighths of Hunt's share would be taken by BP until they received 125 per cent of the 'farm-in contributions' and of Hunt's half-share of the development costs, which ran into many millions of dollars. Once the field came on-stream operating and further development costs would be borne equally. Therefore the risk of not finding oil in commercially worthwhile quantities was on BP. Drilling was successful and the oil field came into production in January 1967. However, following a revolution in Libya, the new régime of Colonel Gaddafi expropriated or 'nationalised' BP's interest in the field in December 1971 and BP's employees were excluded from the facilities. Hunt attempted to carry on operations but in a position of increasing difficulty, and eventually his share of the concession was also expropriated in June 1973. At the time of expropriation of its interest, BP had received about two-thirds of the reimbursement oil it was entitled to under the contract. BP brought a claim under s. 1(3) of the Law Reform (Frustrated Contracts) Act 1943. *Held*: the contract was frustrated in December 1971 and the Act applied as the contract was governed by English law. The extracts concern the principles for applying the Act.

ROBERT GOFF J: . . .

(1) *The principle of recovery*

(a) The principle, which is common to both section 1(2) and (3), and indeed is the fundamental principle underlying the Act itself, is prevention of the unjust enrichment of either party to the contract at the other's expense. It was submitted by Mr Rokison, on behalf of BP, that the principle common to both subsections was one of restitution for net benefits received, the net benefit being the benefit less an appropriate deduction for expenses incurred by the defendant. This is broadly correct so far as section 1(2) is concerned; but under section 1(3) the net benefit of the defendant simply provides an upper limit to the award—it does not measure the amount of the award to be made to the plaintiff. This is because in section 1(3) a distinction is drawn between the plaintiff's performance under the contract, and the benefit which the defendant has obtained by reason of that performance—a distinction about which I shall have more to say later in this judgment; and the net benefit obtained by the defendant from the plaintiff's performance may be more than a just sum payable in respect of such performance, in which event a sum equal to the defendant's net benefit would not be an appropriate sum to award to the plaintiff. I therefore consider it better to state the principle underlying the Act as being the principle of unjust enrichment, which underlies the right of recovery in very many cases in English law, and indeed is the basic principle of the English law of restitution, of which the Act forms part.

(b) Although section 1(2) and (3) is concerned with restitution in respect of different types of benefit, it is right to construe the two subsections as flowing from the same basic principle and therefore, so far as their different subject matters permit, to achieve consistency between them. Even so, it is always necessary to bear in mind the difference between awards of restitution in respect of money payments and awards where the benefit conferred by the plaintiff does not consist of a payment of money. Money has the peculiar character of a universal medium of exchange. By its receipt, the recipient is inevitably benefited; and (subject to problems arising from such matters as inflation, change of position and the time value of money) the loss suffered by the plaintiff is generally equal to the defendant's gain, so that no difficulty arises concerning the amount to be repaid. The same cannot be said of other benefits, such as goods or services. By their nature, services cannot be restored; nor in many cases can goods be restored, for example where they have been consumed or tranferred to another. Furthermore the identity and value of the resulting benefit to the recipient may be debatable. From the very nature of things, therefore, the problem of restitution in respect of such benefits is more complex than in cases where the benefit takes the form of a money payment; and the solution of the problem has been made no easier by the form in which the legislature has chosen to draft section 1(3) of the Act.

(c) The Act is *not* designed to do certain things: (i) It is not designed to apportion the loss between the parties. There is no general power under either section 1(2) or section 1(3) to make any allowance for expenses incurred by the plaintiff (except, under the proviso to section 1(2), to enable him to enforce pro tanto payment of a sum payable but unpaid before frustration); and expenses incurred by the defendant are only relevant in so far as they go to reduce the net benefit obtained by him and thereby limit any award to the plaintiff. (ii) It is not concerned to put the parties in the position in which they would have been if the contract had been performed. (iii) It is not concerned to restore the parties to the position they were in before the contract was made. A remedy designed to prevent unjust enrichment may not achieve that result; for expenditure may be incurred by either party under the contract which confers no benefit on the other, and in respect of which no remedy is available under the Act.

(d) An award under the Act may have the effect of rescuing the plaintiff from an unprofitable bargain. This may certainly be true under section 1(2), if the plaintiff has paid the price in advance for an expected return which, if furnished, would have proved unprofitable; if the contract is frustrated before any part of that expected return is received, and before any expenditure is incurred by the defendant, the plaintiff is entitled to the return of the price he has paid, irrespective of the consideration he would have recovered had the contract been performed. Consistently with section 1(2), there is nothing in section 1(3) which necessarily limits an award to the contract consideration. But the contract consideration may nevertheless be highly relevant to the assessment of the just sum to be awarded under section 1(3); this is a matter to which I will revert later in this judgment.

(2) *Claims under section* 1(2)

Where an award is made under section 1(2), it is, generally speaking, simply an award for the repayment of money which has been paid to the defendant in pursuance of the contract, subject to an allowance in respect of expenses incurred by the defendant. It is not necessary that the consideration for the payment should have wholly failed: claims under section 1(2) are not limited to cases of total failure of consideration, and cases of partial failure of consideration can be catered for by a cross-claim by the defendant under section 1(2) or section 1(3) or both. There is no discretion in the court in respect of a claim under section 1(2), except in respect of the allowance for expenses; subject to such an allowance (and, of course, a cross-claim) the plaintiff is entitled to repayment of the money he has paid. The allowance for expenses is probably best rationalised as a statutory recognition of the defence of change of position. True, the expenses need not have been incurred by reason of the plaintiff's payment; but they must have been incurred in, or for the purpose of the performance of the contract under which the plaintiff's payment has been made, and for that reason it is just that they should be brought into account. No provision is made in the subsection for any increase in the sum recoverable by the plaintiff, or in the amount of expenses to be allowed to the defendant, to allow for the time value of money. The money may have been paid, or the expenses incurred, many years before the date of frustration; but the cause of action accrues on that date, and the sum recoverable under the Act as at that date can be no greater than the sum actually paid, though the defendant may have had the use of the money over many years, and indeed may have profited from its use. Of course, the question whether the court may award interest from the date of the accrual of the cause of action is an entirely different matter, to which I shall refer later in this judgment.

(3) *Claims under section 1(3)*

(a) *General.* In [contrast], where an award is made under section 1(3), the process is more complicated. First, it has to be shown that the defendant has, by reason of something done by the plaintiff in, or for the purpose of, the performance of the contract, obtained a valuable benefit (other than a payment of money) before the time of discharge. That benefit has to be identified, and valued, and such value forms the upper limit of the award. Secondly, the court may award to the plaintiff such sum, not greater than the value of such benefit, as it considers just having regard to all the circumstances of the case, including in particular the matters specified in section 1(3) (a) and (b). In the case of an award under section 1(3) there are, therefore, two distinct stages—the identification and valuation of the benefit, and the award of the just sum. The amount to be awarded is the just sum, unless the defendant's benefit is less, in which event the award will be limited to the amount of that benefit. The distinction between the identification and valuation of the defendant's benefit, and the assessment of the just sum, is the most controversial part of the Act. It represents the solution adopted by the legislature of the problem of restitution in cases where the benefit does not consist of a payment of money; but the solution so adopted has been criticised by some commentators as productive of injustice, and it certainly gives rise to considerable problems, to which I shall refer in due course.

(b) *Identification of the defendant's benefit.* In course of the argument before me, there was much dispute whether, in the case of services, the benefit should be identified as the services themselves, or as the end product of the services. One example canvassed (because it bore some relationship to the facts of the present case) was the example of prospecting for minerals. If minerals are discovered, should the benefit be regarded (as Mr Alexander [counsel for Hunt] contended) simply as the services of prospecting, or (as Mr Rokison contended) as the minerals themselves being the end product of the successful exercise? Now, I am satisfied that it was the intention of the legislature, to be derived from section 1(3) as a matter of construction, that the benefit should in an appopriate case be identified as the end product of the services. This appears in my judgment, not only from the fact that section 1(3) distinguishes between the plaintiff's performance and the defendant's benefit, but also from section 1(3)(b) which clearly relates to the product of the plaintiff's performance. Let me take the example of a building contract. Suppose that a contract for work on a building is frustrated by a fire which destroys the building and which, therefore, also destroys a substantial amount of work already done by the plaintiff. Although it might be thought just to award the plaintiff a sum assessed on quantum meruit basis, probably a rateable part of the contract price, in respect of the work he has done, the effect of section 1(3)(b) will be to reduce the award to nil, because of the effect, in relation to the defendant's benefit, of the circumstances giving rise to the frustration of the contract. It is quite plain that, in section 1(3)(b), the word 'benefit' is intended to refer, in the example I have given, to the actual improvement to the building, because that is what will be affected by the frustrating event; the subsection therefore contemplates that, in such a case, the benefit is the end product of the plaintiff's services, not the services themselves. This will not be so in every case, since in some cases the services will have no end product; for example, where the services consist of doing such work as surveying, or transporting goods. In each case, it is necessary to ask the question: what benefit has the defendant obtained by reason of the plaintiff's contractual performance? But it must not be forgotten that in section 1(3) the relevance of the value of the benefit is to fix a ceiling to the award. If, for example, in a building contract, the building is only partially completed, the value of the partially completed building (i.e. the product of the services) will fix a ceiling for the award; the stage of the work may be such that the uncompleted building may be worth less than the value of the work and materials that have gone into it, particularly as completion by another builder may cost more than completion by the original builder would have cost. In other cases, however, the actual benefit to the defendant may be considerably more than the appropiate or just sum to be awarded to the plaintiff, in which event the value of the benefit will not in fact determine the quantum of the award. I should add, however, that, in a case of prospecting, it would usually be wrong to identify the discovered mineral as the benefit. In such a case there is always (whether the prospecting is successful or not) the benefit of the prospecting itself, i.e. of knowing whether or not the land contains any deposit of the relevant minerals; if the prospecting is successful, the benefit may include also the enhanced value of the land by reason of the discovery; if the prospector's contractual task goes beyond discovery and includes development and production, the benefit will include the further enhancement of the land by reason of the installation of the facilities, and also the benefit of in part transforming a valuable mineral deposit into a marketable commodity.

I add by way of footnote that all these difficulties would have been avoided if the legislature had thought it right to treat the services themselves as the benefit. In the opinion of many commentators, it would be more just to do so; after all, the services in question have been requested by the defendant, who normally takes the risk that they may prove worthless, from whatever cause. In the example I have given of the building destroyed by fire, there is much to be said for the view that the builder should be paid for the work he has done, unless he has (for example by agreeing to insure the works) taken upon himself the risk of destruction by fire. But my task is to construe the Act as it stands. On the true construction of the Act, it is in my judgment clear that the defendant's benefit must, in an appropiate case, be identified as the end product of the plaintiff's services, despite the difficulties which this construction creates, difficulties which are met again when one comes to value the benefit.

(c) *Apportioning the benefit.* In all cases, the relevant benefit must have been obtained by the defendant by reason of something done by the plaintiff. Accordingly, where it is appropriate to identify the benefit with an end product and it appears that the defendant has obtained the benefit by reason of work done both by the plaintiff and by himself, the court will have to do its best to apportion that benefit, and to decide what proportion is attributable to the work done by the plaintiff. That proportion will then constitute the relevant benefit for the purposes of section 1(3) of the Act.

(d) *Valuing the benefit.* Since the benefit may be identified with the product of the plaintiff's performance, great problems arise in the valuation of the benefit. First, how does one solve the problem which arises from the fact that a small service may confer an enormous benefit, and conversely, a very substantial service may confer only a very small benefit? The answer presumably is that at the stage of valuation of the benefit (as opposed to assessment of the just sum) the task of the court is simply to assess the value of the benefit to the defendant. For example, if a prospector after some very simple prospecting discovers a large and unexpected deposit of a valuable mineral, the benefit to the defendant (namely, the enhancement in the value of the land) may be enormous; it must be valued as such, always bearing in mind that the assessment of a just sum may very well lead to a much smaller amount being awarded to the plaintiff. But conversely, the plaintiff may have undertaken building work for a substantial sum which is, objectively speaking, of little or no value—for example, he may commence the redecoration, to the defendant's execrable taste, of rooms which are in good decorative order. If the contract is frustrated before the work is complete, and the work is unaffected by the frustrating event, it can be argued that the defendant has obtained no benefit, because the defendant's property has been reduced in value by the plaintiff's work; but the partial work must be treated as a benefit to the defendant, since he requested it, and valued as such. Secondly, at what point in time is the benefit to be valued? If there is a lapse of time between the date of the receipt of the benefit, and the date of frustration, there may in the meanwhile be a substantial variation in the value of the benefit. If the benefit had simply been identified as the services rendered, this problem would not arise; the court would simply award a reasonable remuneration for the services rendered at the time when they were rendered, the defendant taking the risk of any subsequent depreciation and the benefit of any subsequent appreciation in value. But that is not what the Act provides: section 1(3)(b) makes it plain that the plaintiff is to take the risk of depreciation or destruction by the frustrating event. If the effect of the frustrating event upon the value of the benefit is to be measured, it must surely be measured upon the benefit as at the date of frustration. For example, let it be supposed that a builder does work which doubles in value by the date of frustration, and is then so severely damaged by fire that the contract is frustrated; the valuation of the residue must surely be made on the basis of the value as at the date of frustration. However, does this mean that, for the purposes of section 1(3), the benefit is always to be valued as at the date of frustration? For example, if goods are transferred and retained by the defendant till frustration when they have appreciated or depreciated in value, are they to be valued as at the date of frustration? The answer must, I think, generally speaking, be in the affirmative, for the sake of consistency. But this raises an acute problem in relation to the time value of money. Suppose that goods are supplied and sold, long before the date of frustration; does the principle that a benefit is be to valued as at the date of frustration require that allowance must be made for the use in the meanwhile of the money obtained by the disposal of the goods, in order to obtain a true valuation of the benefit as at the date of frustration? This was one of the most hotly debated matters before me, for the very good reason that in the present case it affects the valuation of the parties' respective benefits by many millions of dollars. It is very tempting to conclude that an allowance should be made for the time value of money, because it appears to lead to a more realistic valuation of the benefit as at the date of frustration; and, as will appear hereafter, an appropriate method for making such an allowance is available in the form of the net discounted cash flow system of accounting. But I have come to the conclusion that, as a matter of construction, this course is not open to me. First, the subsection limits the award to the value of the benefit obtained by the defendant; and it does not follow that, because the defendant has had the money over a period of time, he has in fact derived any benefit from it. Secondly, if an allowance was to be made for the time value of the money obtained by the defendant, a comparable allowance should be made in respect of expenses incurred by the defendant, i.e. in respect of the period between the date of incurring expenditure and the date of frustration, and section 1(3)(a) only contemplates that the court, in making an allowance for expenses, already indicated, no allowance for the time value of money can be made under section 1(2); and it would be inconsistent to make such an allowance under section 1(3) but not under section 1(2).

Other problems can arise from the valuation of the defendant's benefit as the end product; I shall come to these later in the consideration of the facts of the present case. But there is a further problem which I should refer to, before leaving this topic. Section 1(3)(a) requires the court to have regard to the amount of any expenditure incurred before the time of discharge by the benefited party in, or for the purpose of, the performance of the contract. The question arises—should this matter be taken into account at the stage of valuation of the benefit, or of assessment of the just sum? Take a simple example. Suppose that the defendant's benefit is valued at £150, and that a just sum is assessed at £100, but that there remain to be taken into account defendant's expenses of £75: is the award to be £75 or £25? The clue to this problem lies, in my judgment, in the fact that the allowance for expenses is a statutory recognition of the defence of change of position. Only to the extent that the position of the defendant has so changed that it would be unjust to award restitution, should the court make an allowance for expenses. Suppose that the plaintiff does work for the defendant which produces no valuable end product, or a benefit no greater in value than the just sum to be awarded in respect of the work; there is then no reason why the whole of the relevant expenses should not be set off against the just sum. But suppose that the defendant has reaped a large benefit from the plaintiff's work, far greater in value than the just sum to be awarded for the work. In such circumstances it would be quite wrong to set off the whole of the defendant's expenses against the just sum. The question whether the defendant has suffered a change of position has to be judged in the light of all the circumstances of the case. Accordingly, on the Act as it stands, under section 1(3) the proper course is to deduct the expenses from the value of the benefit, with the effect that only in so far as they reduce the value of the benefit below the amount of the just sum which would otherwise be awarded will they have any practical bearing on the award.

Finally, I should record that the court is required to have regard to the effect, in relation to the defendant's benefit, of the circumstances giving rise to the frustration of the contract. I have already given an example of how this may be relevant, in the case of building contracts; and I have recorded the fact that this provision has been the subject of criticism. There may, however, be circumstances where it would not be just to have regard to this factor—for example if, under a building contract, it was expressly agreed that the work in progress should be insured by the building-owner against risks which include the event which had the effect of frustrating the contract and damaging or destroying the work.

(e) *Assessment of the just sum.* The principle underlying the Act is prevention of the unjust enrichment of the defendant at the plaintiff's expense. Where, as in cases under section 1(2), the benefit conferred on the defendant consists of payment of a sum of money, the plaintiff's expense and the defendant's enrichment are generally equal; and, subject to other relevant factors, the award of restitution will consist simply of an order for repayment of a like sum of money. But where the benefit does not consist of money, then the defendant's enrichment will rarely be equal to the plaintiff's expense. In such cases where (as in the case of a benefit conferred under a contract thereafter frustrated) the benefit has been requested by the defendant, the basic measure of recovery in restitution is the reasonable value of the plaintiff's performance—in a case of services, a quantum meruit or reasonable remuneration, and in a case of goods, a quantum valebat or reasonable price. Such cases are to be contrasted with cases where such a benefit has not been requested by the defendant. In the latter class of case, recovery is rare in restitution; but if the sole basis of recovery was that the defendant had been incontrovertibly benefited, it might be legitimate to limit recovery to the defendant's actual benefit—a limit which has (perhaps inappropriately) been imported by the legislature into section 1(3) of the Act. However, under section 1(3) as it stands, if the defendant's actual benefit is less than the just or reasonable sum which would otherwise be awarded to the plaintiff, the award must be reduced to a sum equal to the amount of the defendant's benefit.

A crucial question, upon which the Act is surprisingly silent, is this: what bearing do the terms of the contract, under which the plaintiff has acted, have upon the assessment of the just sum? First, the terms upon which the work was done may serve to indicate the full scope of the work done, and so be relevant to the sum awarded in respect of such work. For example, if I do work under a contract under which I am to receive a substantial prize if successful, and nothing if I fail, and the contract is frustrated before the work is complete but not before a substantial benefit has been obtained by the defendant, the element of risk taken by the plaintiff may be held to have the effect of enhancing the amount of any sum to be awarded. Secondly, the contract consideration is always relevant as providing some evidence of what will be a reasonable sum to be awarded in respect of the plaintiff's work. Thus if a prospector, employed for a fee, discovers a gold mine before the contract under which he is employed is frustrated (for example, by illegality or by his illness or disablement) at a time when his work was incomplete, the court may think it just to make an award in the nature of a reasonable fee for what he has done (though of course the benefit obtained by the defendant will be far greater), and a rateable part of the contract fee may provide useful evidence of the level of sum to be awarded. If, however, the contract had provided that he was to receive a stake in the concession, then the just sum might be enhanced on the basis that, in all the circumstances, a reasonable sum should take account of such a factor: cf. *Way* v *Latilla* [1937] 3 All ER 759. Thirdly, however, the contract consideration, or a rateable part of it, may provide a limit to the sum to be awarded. To take a fairly extreme example, a poor householder or a small businessman may obtain a contract for building work to be done to his premises at considerably less than the market price, on the basis that he cannot afford to pay more. In such a case, the court may consider it just to limit the award to a rateable part of the contract price, on the ground that it was the understanding of the parties that in no circumstances (including the circumstances of the contract being frustrated) should the plaintiff recover more than the contract price or a rateable part of it. Such a limit may properly be said to arise by virtue of the operation of section 2(3) of the Act. But it must not be forgotten that, unlike money, services can never be restored, nor usually can goods, since they are likely to have been either consumed or disposed of, or to have depreciated in value; and since, ex hypothesi, the defendant will only have been prepared to contract for the goods or services on the basis that he paid no more than the contract consideration, it may be unjust to compel him, by an award under the Act, to pay more than that consideration, or a rateable part of it, in respect of the services or goods he has received. It is unnecessary for me to decide whether this will always be so; but it is likely that in most cases this will impose an important limit upon the sum to be awarded—indeed it may well be the most relevant limit to an award under section 1(3) of the Act. The legal basis of the limit may be section 2(3) of the Act; but even if that subsection is inapplicable, it is open to the court, in an appropriate case, to give effect to such a limit in assessing the just sum to be awarded under section 1(3), because in many cases it would be unjust to impose upon the defendant an obligation to make restitution under the subsection at higher than the contract rate.

(4) *The effect of section 2(3) of the Act*

The court has always to bear in mind the provisions of section 2(3) of the Act. It was submitted by Mr Rokison that effect should only be given to this subsection where the relevant contractual provision was *clearly* intended to have effect in the event of the frustrating circumstances. I can see no good reason for so qualifying the express words of the subsection. In my judgment the effect of the subsection depends, as it expressly provides, simply upon applying the ordinary principles of construction. If the contract contains any provision which, upon the true construction of the contract, is intended to have effect in the circumstances specified in the subsection, then the court can only give effect to section 1 of the Act to such extent as is consistent with such provision.

Examples of such provisions may be terms which have the effect of precluding recovery of any award under the Act, or of limiting the amount of any such award, for example, by limiting the award to the contractual consideration or a rateable part thereof. Similarly, the parties may contract upon the terms that the plaintiff shall not be paid until the occurence of an event, and by reason of the frustration of the contract that event does not or cannot occur; then, if upon a true construction of the contract the court concludes that the plaintiff has taken the risk of non-payment in the event of such frustration the court should make no award by virtue of section 2(3) of the Act. Such may be the conclusion if the contract contains an express term imposing upon the plaintiff an obligation to insure against the consequences of the frustrating event. Another example considered in argument was a loan of money advanced to a businessman on the terms that it was to be repaid out of the profits of his business. Such a term should not automatically preclude an award in the event of frustration, for example, if the businessman is incapacitated the day after the loan is made; but if the business consists, for example, of a ship, which strikes a reef and sinks, then it may be that the court, having regard to the terms of the contract and the risk taken thereunder by the lender, would make no award. But in such cases the court should only refuse to make an award if it is satisfied that the plaintiff has, by the contract, taken the risk of the consequences of the frustrating event. The principle is the same as in those cases where the contract consideration controls the amount or basis of the award under the Act—the court should not act inconsistently with the contractual intention of the parties applicable in the events which have occurred. But, such cases apart, the court is free to make an award which differs from the anticipated contractual performance of the defendant. I have already referred to the fact that, under section 1(2) at least, the effect of an award under the Act may be to rescue the plaintiff from a bad bargain. Again, the contract may provide that the plaintiff is to receive goods or services; the court may nevertheless make an award in money. The contract may provide for the plaintiff to receive money at a certain place or in certain currency; frustation may render that impossible (for example, in a case of supervening illegality), and the court may make an award for payment which takes effect at a different place or in a different currency. Most striking of all, in most frustrated contracts under which the claim is made in respect of a benefit other than money, the time for payment will not yet have come—the contract, or a severable part of it, will be 'entire' in the old strict sense of that term; I do not, however, consider that such a provision should automatically preclude an award under section 1(3). If it were intended to do so, there would be few awards under section 1(3), and the matter would surely be the subject of an express provision if it was the intention that so fundamental a qualification was to be imposed upon the power of the court under this subsection. Certainly, no such qualification is imposed in section 1(2), and no such result can be achieved in relation to an award under that subsection since, generally speaking, the plaintiff is entitled to the return of his money. In my judgment, only if upon a true construction of the contract the plaintiff has contracted on the terms that he is to receive no payment in the event which has occurred, will the fact that the contract is 'entire' have the effect of precluding an award under the Act. . . .

Notes

1. Robert Goff J accordingly *identified* Hunt's benefit as *prima facie* the transformation of a bare concession of unknown potential into a giant oilfield in production, in which Hunt had a half interest. However, Hunt's benefit was greatly reduced by the circumstances giving rise to the frustration and was limited to the oil he had received and the value of the settlement Hunt obtained from the Libyan government. With regard to *apportionment*, one-half of that benefit was attributable to BP's efforts and one half was attributable to Hunt's own contribution to the joint venture, namely the oil concession itself. The judge then *valued the benefit* to Hunt, taking into account both his expenses and the circumstances giving rise to frustration of the contract, at US $84,951,000. Robert Goff J held that BP were not entitled to restitution of the benefit received by Hunt, rather the relevance of the benefit under s. 1(3) was to provide a ceiling for the sum to be awarded. Turning to the *calculation of the just sum*, the judge held that the contractual consideration for BP's services in exploring and developing the field provided the best evidence of a reasonable remuneration to be awarded in the circumstances. The contractual consideration contemplated for BP's performance was the transfer of a half interest in the concession and the receipt of reimbursement oil. Therefore if BP had received the whole of the reimbursement oil, in addition to its half share in the concession, no sum would have been awarded under the Act. Here the just sum consisted of the value of BP's actual expenditure on Hunt's account in exploring and developing the field (but only 100 per cent of that cost, not 125 per cent as contemplated by the contract), the value of the 'farm-in contributions' and BP's expenditure in operating the field on Hunt's account after the oil came on-stream. All items were to be valued at the date they were incurred or received. From this sum of $98,105,146 was to be deducted the value of the reimbursement oil already received, some $67,702,000. The total was some $35,403,146, so there was no need to reduce the award, because the benefit ceiling was greater than the just sum.

2. The judgment of Robert Goff J was upheld by the Court of Appeal, although the farm-in contribution in the form of money was held to be recoverable under s. 1(2), not s. 1(3). Otherwise the judgment of the Court of Appeal is summed up in one sentence: 'What is just is what the trial judge thinks is just' ([1981] 1 WLR 232, at 238). Further, with regard to Goff J's view that the concept underlying the Act was preventing unjust enrichment, the Court of Appeal got 'no help from the use of words which are not in the statute' ([1981] 1 WLR 232, at 243). An appeal to the House of Lords principally on the ground that the terms of the contract excluded the operation of the Act pursuant to s. 2(3) was also dismissed ([1983] 2 AC 352). Lord Brandon of Oakbrook concluded (at 372):

> . . . there is nothing in the terms of the contract between the parties, or in the circumstances surrounding the making of it as found by Robert Goff J, to indicate, either expressly or by necessary implication, that the parties, when they made the contract in 1960, had in contemplation political risks,

such as expropriation of the concession in whole or in part by the Libyan government, which would operate to frustrate the contract; or that, having had such risks in contemplation, they included in the contract any provision which, expressly or by necessary implication, was to take effect in the event of such risks materialising.

Questions

1. How would *Appleby* v *Myers* (1867) LR 2 CP 651 (above) be decided under s. 1(3) of the Act?

2. The Law Reform Commission of British Columbia in its 'Report on the Need for Frustrated Contracts Legislation in British Columbia' (Project No. 8) concluded (at p. 7) after consideration of the English 1943 Act that it 'was not well-thought or well-drafted'. Do you agree?

Note

The following extract is from a Commonwealth statute.

FRUSTRATED CONTRACTS ACT 1974 (BRITISH COLUMBIA)

5. Adjustment of rights and liabilities

(1) Subject to section 6, every party to a contract to which this Act applies is entitled to restitution from the other party or parties to the contract for benefits created by his performance or part performance of the contract.

(2) . . .

(3) Where the circumstances giving rise to the frustration or avoidance cause a total or partial loss in value of a benefit to a party required to make restitution under subsection (1), that loss shall be apportioned equally between the party required to make restitution and the party to whom such restitution is required to be made.

(4) In this section, a 'benefit' means something done in the fulfilment of contractual obligations whether or not the person for whose benefit it was done received the benefit.

Note

Two essays, one descriptive, one prescriptive, argue that the concern of the law in this context should be loss apportionment, not unjust enrichment. Haycroft and Waksman, 'Frustration and Restitution' [1984] JBL 207, argue that Robert Goff J was wrong to argue that apportionment was not the principle underlying the Act and conclude (at 225) that the statute 'is designed to provide a flexible machinery for the adjustment of losses'. In contrast, in 'Frustration, Restitution and Loss Apportionment', Essay 6 in Burrows, *Essays*, at 147–70, Professor McKendrick, after careful analysis, largely agrees with Robert Goff J's conclusions on the construction of the Act, but advocates legislative reform to ensure that the question of loss apportionment is dealt with. McKendrick (at 165–9) gives a useful account of Commonwealth statutes (British Columbia, New South Wales and South Australia) which do explicity deal with loss-splitting. See further Stewart and Carter, 'Frustrated Contracts and Statutory Adjustment: The Case for a Reappraisal' [1992] CLJ 66.

Section 3: restitution and pre-contractual liability

Our concern here is with anticipated contracts which never come to fruition. The English law of contract adopts a very black-and-white, contract or no contract approach to contractual responsibility, with its simple concepts of offer, acceptance and counter-offer. In negotiations for large-scale contracts, such as construction projects, or in the context of the sale of interests in real property (by the use of the words 'subject to contract'), the moment when negotiations crystallise into bargain can be postponed almost indefinitely. What if a construction company does invaluable work on the project prior to contract? Or if a prospective tenant does repairs to the property in the expectation of a lease materialising? If the expected contract never eventuates the law of contract provides no redress.

Parties therefore often look outside the resources of the law of contract, and consequently tort, estoppel and restitution concepts have been utilised to ground pre-contractual responsibility. The following cases appear to adopt restitutionary reasoning to ground relief. Two ingredients are often found. First, it is clear that a party's expenditure must be greater than that which is normally risked at the pre-contractual stage. Secondly, the question who was 'responsible' for the breakdown in negotiations may influence the result. A central question is whether these can properly be fitted into the unjust enrichment scheme, or whether to do so would utilise an 'over-inclusive test of benefit' (Beatson, *Unjust Enrichment*, 21, 31–9; see also 5–8). Beatson's view, which is increasingly gaining support, is that what is being protected here is a party's *injurious reliance*. In the seminal language of Fuller and Perdue, 'The Reliance Interest in Contract Damages' (1936) 46 Yale LJ 52, 373, an award in these cases protects a plaintiff's *reliance interest*, not his *restitution interest*. Professor Jones now takes this view and argues in 'Claims Arising Out of Anticipated Contracts Which Do Not Materialize' (1980) 18 *UW Ontario LRev* 447 that many of the cases are more directly analogous to claims in estoppel than claims in restitution. See Burrows, *Restitution*, 293–9.

Way v *Latilla*
[1937] 3 All ER 759 (HL)

Quantum meruit

Way (the appellant) obtained information concerning gold mines and concessions in the Gold Coast Colony on behalf of Latilla (the respondent). Eventually Way obtained a concession as agent for Latilla. Latilla promised Way that in due course he would be rewarded with an interest in the concession. Latilla derived considerable profits from the concession. Way never received any share of the concession.

LORD ATKIN: . . . The question now is, what are Mr Way's rights to remuneration? He originally claimed that there was a completed agreement to give him an interest in the concession, which, by custom, or on a reasonable basis, the court was asked to define as one-third. The trial judge accepted this view, holding he was entitled to assess a reasonable share, and he accordingly awarded him £30,000, as being roughly 3 per cent on the sum of about £1,000,000, which he took to represent Mr Latilla's profits in the transaction. The Court of Appeal rejected this view, and, in my opinion, rightly. There certainly was no concluded contract between the parties as to the amount of the share or interest that Mr Way was to receive, and it appears to me impossible for the court to complete the contract for them. If the parties had proceeded on the terms of a written contract, with a material clause that the remuneration was to be a percentage of the gross returns, but with the figure left blank, the court could not supply the figure. The judge relied upon the decision of this House in *Hillas & Co. Ltd* v *Arcos Ltd* [(1932) 147 LT 503]. But in that case this House was able to find, in the contract to give an option for the purchase of timber in a future year, an intention to be bound contractually, and all the elements necessary to form a concluded contract. There is no material in the present case upon which any court would decide what was the share which the parties must be taken to have agreed. But, while there is, therefore, no concluded contract as to the remuneration, it is plain that there existed between the parties a contract of employment under which Mr Way was engaged to do work for Mr Latilla in circumstances which clearly indicated that the work was not to be gratuitous. Mr Way, therefore, is entitled to a reasonable remuneration on the implied contract to pay him *quantum meruit.* It is on the assessment of this amount that I believe all your Lordships differ from the Court of Appeal. The members of the court appear to have acted on the view that Mr Way had given no evidence as to the value of his services, that the only evidence before the court was the evidence of one or two consulting mining engineers, in particular that of Colonel Lake, on whom the Court of Appeal relied, and that, following this evidence, the proper reward was a fee of 500 guineas. My Lords, this decision appears to me to ignore the real business position. Services of this kind are no doubt usually the subject of an express contract as to remuneration, which may take the form of a fee, but may also take the form of a commission share of profits, or share of proceeds calculated at a percentage, or on some other basis. In the present case, there was no question of fee between the parties from beginning to end. On the contrary, the parties had discussed remuneration on the footing of what may loosely be called a 'participation,' and nothing else. The reference is analogous to the well known distinction between salary and commission. There are many employments the remuneration of which is, by trade usage, invariably fixed on a commission basis. In such cases, if the amount of the commission has not been finally agreed, the *quantum meruit* would be fixed after taking into account what would be a reasonable commission, in the circumstances, and fixing a sum accordingly. This has been an everyday practice in the courts for years. But, if no trade usage assists the court as to the amount of the commission, it appears to me clear that the court may take into account the bargainings between the parties, not with a view to completing the bargain for them, but as evidence of the value which each of them puts upon the services. If the discussion had ranged between 3 per cent on the one side and 5 per cent on the other, all else being agreed, the court would not be likely to depart from somewhere about those figures, and would be wrong in ignoring them altogether and fixing remuneration on an entirely different basis, upon which, possibly, the services would never have been rendered at all. That, in fixing a salary basis, the court may pay regard to the previous conversation of the parties was decided by the Court of Exchequer in 1869, in *Scarisbrick* v *Parkinson* [(1869) 20 LT 175], where the terms of an agreement, invalid under the Statute of Frauds, were held to be admissible as evidence in a *quantum meruit.* This seems to me to be good law, and to give effect to a principle which has been adopted regularly by the courts not only in fixing remuneration for services but also in fixing prices, sums due for use and occupation, and, indeed, in all cases where the court has to determine what is a reasonable reward for the consideration given by the claimant. As I have said, the rule applied in fixing the amount of the remuneration necessarily applies to the basis on which the amount is to be fixed. I have therefore no hesitation in saying that the basis of remuneration by fee should, in this case, on the evidence of the parties themselves, be rejected, and that Mr Way is entitled to a sum to be calculated on the basis of some reasonable participation.

What this should be is a task primarily to be undertaken by the trial judge. He did make an alternative award, and arrived at the sum of £5,000. I see no reason to differ from this. It is true that there is evidence that Mr Latilla made very large profits. On the other hand, this amount was very favourably affected by this country's financial policy in respect of gold, which was altered some time after the services were rendered. Mr Way does not profess to have discovered the line of reef on which the concessions lay, and some of them at least were in respect of abandoned workings. These concessions had to be financed for some years, and other interests had to be satisfied. Mr Way had no reason to contemplate even a participation based on a percentage of profits. A transfer of a substantial number of shares would have been an adequate satisfaction of any contemplated obligation on Mr Latilla's part. I think that the sum of £5,000 which the judge appears to have arrived at on consideration of all the necessary factors would be a reasonable remuneration in all the circumstances. I therefore think that the judgment of the judge should be varied by entering judgment for the plaintiff for £5,000, instead of for £30,000. . . .

LORD WRIGHT: My Lords, I have had the advantage of reading in print the opinion of my noble and learned friend on the woolsack, and agree with it. I add a very few observations, out of respect to the very careful judgments delivered in the Court of Appeal. On the main decision at which the Court of Appeal arrived in reversing the judge, I am in full agreement with the Lords Justices. There was, I think, no justification for making for the parties, as Charles, J, did, a contract which they did not make themselves. It is, however, clear, on the evidence, that the work was done by the appellant and accepted by the respondent on the basis that some remuneration was to be paid to the appellant by the respondent. There was thus an implied promise by the respondent to pay on a *quantum meruit*, that is, to pay what the services were worth. My difference with the Court of Appeal turns on a narrow issue, which is whether the *quantum meruit* should be determined on the footing of a fee as for professional services, or on some other footing. The Court of Appeal took the former view. I cannot, however, with respect, find, on the whole of the evidence in the case, and, in particular, on the discussions between the parties, any sufficient reason for accepting that view. The services of the appellant were, I think, outside the range of his duties as mining engineer, and were those of an agent for purchase, who suggests to his principal a transaction, and negotiates and completes it for him. While it is not unknown that such services should be remunerated by a fee if it is expressly or impliedly so agreed, this is by no means necessarily, and would not generally be, the case. The idea of such a fee being excluded, it follows that the question of the amount to which the appellant is entitled is left at large, and the court must do the best it can to arrive at a figure which seems to it fair and reasonable to both parties, on all the facts of the case. One aspect of the facts to be considered is found in the communings of the parties while the business was going on. Evidence of this nature is admissible to show what the parties had in mind, however indeterminately, with regard to the basis of remuneration. On those facts, the court may be able to infer, or attribute to the parties, an intention that a certain basis of payment should apply. This evidence seems to me to show quite clearly that the appellant was employed on the basis of receiving a remuneration depending on results. If he had been unsuccessful, he would have been entitled to no more than his expenses, but the respondent had led him to believe that, if the concessions he obtained were valuable, his remuneration would be on the basis of some proportion of their value. The realisation of that value was removed from the actual services by the lapse of time (during which large sums of money were expended and adventured), and by many contingencies, and therefore the proper proportion may be comparatively very small, though the fruits of success were very large. The precise figure can be only a rough estimate. If what the court fixes is either too small or too large, the fault must be ascribed to the parties in leaving this important matter in so nebulous a state. But, forming the best judgment I can, I agree with your Lordships that the figure to be awarded to the appellant should be £5,000, which is what Charles, J, was prepared to adopt if his judgment were reversed.

Question

There are numerous explanations of the ground of liability of *Way* v *Latilla*: contractual (Treitel, *Contract*, 951); free acceptance (Birks, *Introduction*, 271–2) and failure of consideration (Burrows, *Restitution*, 294–5). Which do you prefer?

Brewer Street Investments Ltd v *Barclays Woollen Co. Ltd*
[1954] 1 QB 428 (CA)

The plaintiffs were the landlords of premises in the West End of London, and the defendants were prospective tenants. The essential terms of a 21-year lease were agreed between them, including the rent, subject to contract. Negotiations continued, and both parties confidently expected a lease to eventuate. The defendants, anxious to enter as soon as possible, desired certain alterations to be made to the premises. In correspondence they agreed to be responsible for the cost of these. However, negotiations broke down and the alterations, which had considerably progressed, were halted. The plaintiffs paid off the contractors and claimed reimbursement from the defendants. Morris LJ, sitting as an additional High Court judge, held for the plaintiffs. On appeal:

SOMERVELL LJ: . . . if one considers the matter in principle the defendants undertook responsibility for this work at a time when they knew that either side could resile and decide not to conclude a lease.

The only question of law, therefore, would be whether the events which have happened, by reason of some implication, entitle the defendants to put up a defence. The judge below clearly thought that if the matter had gone off because the plaintiffs had changed their mind or had found someone else who would pay more, the defendants would have such a defence. It is unnecessary to decide that point, though there seems to be a strong argument for that view. It is plain that the matter went off because of the defendants' own course of conduct in adhering to the condition that they should get an option when it had been made clear to them that the plaintiffs were not willing to grant an option. If Mr Dare [counsel for the prospective tenants] is right in saying, in the alternative, that the lease went off through circumstances for which neither party can be regarded as responsible, that is in the ordinary course of negotiations and misunderstandings, I still think that that would not afford a good defence to this claim. I wish to guard the words which I use because an earlier case which came before this court shows that the area is somewhat difficult. Each case must be judged on its own circumstances. There might be a case in which the circumstances were such, and the benefits conferred on the landlord if the matter went off were such, that, even although it was not through the deliberate action of the landlord that the matter went off, the defendant still might have a defence. One should not seek to anticipate circumstances which may arise. . . .

DENNING LJ: This case raises questions of considerable interest. The landlords seek to recover from the prospective tenants the moneys which they have had to pay to their own contractors for the work done on the alterations before the negotiations for the lease broke down. The question is whether they can do so.

It is not easy to state the legal basis of the landlords' claim. The difficulty arises because, although the prospective tenants agreed to pay the cost of the alterations, nevertheless those alterations were never completed. The work was abandoned before it was finished. Once the negotiations for a lease broke down, both sides realised that the work must be stopped. It was a very sensible thing to do, but it means that the landlords cannot sue for the price as on a completed contract. Nor can they sue the prospective tenants for damages for breach of contract, because the prospective tenants have not been guilty of breach. Let me give an instance. One item of the work was a lift door to be made, fixed and installed for the lump sum of £48 10s. At the time when the work was abandoned, the lift door had been made in the provinces but it had not been transported to London, let alone fixed or installed. Nevertheless the landlords have had to pay to their contractors the full sum of £48 10s., presumably by way of damages, and they seek to recover it from the prospective tenants. They clearly cannot recover on a quantum meruit as ordinarily understood. The way they put their claim on this item and the others in the statement of claim is money paid on request. The prospective tenants, however, made no request in fact to the landlords to pay the money. Their request, if any, was to pay on completion of the work, and it was not completed. In these circumstances, the proper way to formulate the claim is on a request implied in law, or, as I would prefer to put it in these days, on a claim in restitution.

It is clear on the facts that the parties proceeded on a fundamental assumption—that the lease would be granted—which has turned out to be wrong. The work done has been wasted. The question is: on whom is the loss to fall? The parties themselves did not envisage the situation which has emerged and did not provide for it; and we do not know what they would have provided if they had envisaged it. Only the law can resolve their rights and liabilities in the new situation, either by means of implying terms or, more simply, by asking on whom should the risk fall. This is how the court approached a similar question in *Jennings and Chapman Ld.* v *Woodman, Matthews & Co.* [1952] 2 TLR 409, and I think that we should approach the question in the same way.

Morris LJ gave a reserved judgment in which he put the matter in a way which appeals to me. He asked himself: what was the reason for the negotiations breaking down? If it was the landlords' fault, as, for instance, if they refused to go on with the lease for no reason at all, or because they demanded a higher rent than that which had been already agreed, then they should not be allowed to recover any part of the cost of the alterations. Even if the landlords derived no benefit from the work, they should not be allowed to recover the cost from the prospective tenants, seeing that it was by their fault that the prospective tenants were deprived of it.

On the other hand, if it was the prospective tenants' fault that the negotiations broke down, as, for instance, if they sought a lower rent than that which had been agreed upon, then the prospective tenants ought to pay the cost of the alterations up to the time they were stopped. After all, they did promise to pay for the work, and they should not be able to get out of their promise by their own fault, even though the alterations were not completed. It is a very old principle laid down by Sir Edward Coke that a man shall not be allowed to take advantage of a condition brought about by himself.

I do not think, however, that in the present case it can be said that either party was really at fault. Neither party sought to alter the rent or any other point which had been agreed upon. They fell out on a point which had not been agreed at all. From the very beginning the prospective tenants wanted an option to purchase, whereas the landlords were only ready to give them the first refusal. Each of them in the course of the negotiations sought on this point to get more favourable terms—the prospective tenants to get a firm option to purchase, the landlords to give a first refusal of little value—but their moves in the negotiations can hardly be considered a default by one or other.

What, then, is the position when the negotiations go off without the default of either? On whom should the risk fall? In my opinion the prospective tenants ought to pay all the costs thrown away. The work was done to meet their special requirements and was prima facie for their benefit and not for the benefit of the landlords. If and in so far as the work is shown to have been of benefit to the landlords, credit should be given in such sum as may be just. Subject to such credit, the prospective tenants ought to pay for the cost of the work, because they in the first place agreed to take responsibility for it; and when the matter goes off without the default of either side, they should pay the costs thrown away. There is no finding here that the work was of any benefit to the landlords, and in the circumstances the prospective tenants should, I think, pay the amount claimed.

Mr Waters argued that the test laid down in *Jennings and Chapman Ld.* v *Woodman, Matthews & Co.* [1952] 2 TLR 409 was wrong. It was not right, he said, to ask whose fault it was, or on whom should the risk fall, because each side had an absolute right to withdraw from the negotiations: and could not be said to be at fault in doing so. He referred to *Luxor (Eastbourne) Ld.* v *Cooper* [1941] AC 108, and argued that, even if the landlord, for instance, demanded a higher rent and thus caused the negotiations to fall through, he could still recover the cost of the alterations. I do not think that that is right. Estate agents are employed on the footing that they get a large commission if a sale is completed, but nothing if it is not. They take the risk of the deal falling through. The cases on the subject are, therefore, illustrations of the same test: on whom in all the circumstances should the risk fall?

In the present case I think that the risk should fall on the prospective tenants and that they should pay the costs of the alterations. . . .

ROMER LJ: . . . Taking the whole of the circumstances, the dates, the urgency of the matter, the fact that the defendants themselves paid directly for part of the electrical work without any suggestion of their liability in that regard being conditional, I have no doubt but that in common phraseology they were 'taking the risk' for their own purposes in the hope that they would get the benefit of it if, as they hoped and thought, a lease was finally agreed and granted. As the negotiations failed, solely because the defendants right up to the end insisted on getting that which they had been told already the plaintiffs were unwilling to give, namely, an option, I cannot see how they can escape responsibility by seeking to put the blame on the shoulders of the plaintiffs. It may well be that if, after this work had been done, the plaintiffs got the benefit of it, assuming it to be work which improved the value of the property, and had then said 'We will not grant a lease at all,' the defendants would not have been without remedy. That was not the position in this case. The facts led to an entirely different result. . . .

Question

In what way were the defendant prospective tenants benefited?

Notes

1. Compare *Jennings and Chapman Ltd* v *Woodman, Matthews & Co.* [1952] 2 TLR 409.

2. During argument Romer LJ said: 'Suppose that, whilst parties were in negotiation for a lease, the landlords allowed the prospective tenants to go on the land and spend money on it in anticipation of a lease. If the landlords subsequently broke off negotiations for no reason at all they could not get the benefit of the work without paying for it. Equity would give a remedy.' Denning LJ immediately insisted: 'Whether equity would do so or not, the common law, nowadays, would give the prospective tenants the right to recover the value of the work done in an action for restitution.'

William Lacey (Hounslow) Ltd v *Davis*
[1957] 1 WLR 932 (QBD)

Quantum meruit

The defendant owned war-damaged premises which he wished to redevelop. The plaintiff building company submitted the lowest tender for the reconstruction work, and were led to believe that they would receive the contract. Subsequently, at the request of the defendant they prepared further estimates for the purpose of obtaining necessary licences, for negotiations for a claim from the War Damage Commission and to take into account suggested alterations to the premises. In fact the defendant sold the premises and no contract was ever entered into.

BARRY J: [rejected a claim based on breach of contract and continued: . . .] In elaborating his argument [on the alternative claim] Mr Daniel [counsel for the plaintiff building company] rightly conceded that if a builder is invited to tender for certain work, either in competition or otherwise, there is no implication that he will be paid for the work—sometimes the very considerable amount of work—involved in arriving at his price: he undertakes this work as a gamble, and its cost is part of the overhead expenses of his business which he hopes will be met out of the profits of such contracts as are made as a result of tenders which prove to be successful. This generally accepted usage may also—and I think does also—apply to amendments of the original tender necessitated by bona fide alterations in the specification and plans. If no contract ensues, the builder is, therefore, without a remedy. Mr Daniel, however, contends that no such principle applies if the builder's tender is sought and used not to ascertain the cost of erecting or reconstructing some genuinely contemplated building project, but for some extraneous or collateral purpose for which the building owner may require it. In such circumstances, Mr Daniel suggests that the builder is entitled to recover a reasonable payment for his work. It may also happen—as it certainly did happen in the present case—that when a builder is told that his tender is the lowest and led to believe that the building contract is to be given to him, he, the builder, is prepared to perform other incidential services at the request of the building owner without any intention of charging for them as such. He is not—Mr Daniel suggests—rendering these services gratuitously, but is content to be recompensed for them out of the profit which he will make under the contract. If, without default on the builder's part, no contract supervenes, then, says Mr Daniel, the law will imply a contract to pay a reasonable sum for these services. His contention is that, for one or other of these two reasons, the defendants are under a legal obligation to pay for all the work itemised in the schedule.

Mr Lawson's [counsel for the defendant owner] answer can be put quite shortly. He does not deny that a considerable amount of work was done by the plaintiffs, but he says that it was all done—on [the plaintiffs'] own admission—in the expectation and hope that they would receive the building contract. They did not do so and, although the consequences to them are, of course, unfortunate, there can be no room for an implication that they were to be paid for services for which they never intended to charge.

[His Lordship examined the facts in detail and continued:] Now, on this evidence, I am quite satisfied that the whole of the work covered by the schedule fell right outside the normal work which a builder, by custom and usage, normally performs gratuitously, when invited to tender for the erection of a building. In the absence of any evidence called by the defendants, I can only find that the earlier estimates were given for work which it was never intended to execute. It is possible that, in the very latest stages, the defendant was intending to erect the type of building for which the plaintiffs were giving their quotation, but having obtained, without charge, an initial estimate for a purely notional building, Mr Davis could hardly expect the builders to go on giving free estimates when a state of reality was at last approached. The earlier estimates, as the correspondence shows, were in fact used, and used for some purpose, in the defendant's negotiations with the War Damage Commission and, as an apparent result of the plaintiffs' efforts, not only were the reconstruction plans approved, but a much higher 'permissible amount' was also agreed with the War Damage Commission. It is perhaps justifiable to surmise that these facts, especially the reconstruction plans and the increase in the permissible amount, had at least some influence upon the price of the damaged building which the defendant obtained when it was ultimately sold by him. The work itemised in the schedule which does not relate to estimation, as I think, falls even more clearly outside the type of work which any builder would be expected to do without charge when tendering for a building contract.

The plaintiffs are carrying on a business and, in normal circumstances, if asked to render services of this kind, the obvious inference would be that they ought to be paid for so doing. No one could expect a business firm to do this sort of work for nothing, and again, in normal circumstances, the law would imply a promise to pay on the part of the person who requested the services to be performed. Mr Lawson, however, submits that no such promise can be implied in the circumstances of the present case. The existence, he submits, of a common expectation that a contract would ultimately come into being and that the plaintiffs' services would be rewarded by the profits of that contract leaves no room, in his submission, and, indeed, wholly negatives any suggestion, that the parties impliedly agreed that these services would be paid for in any other way.

This, at first sight, is a formidable argument which, if well founded, would wholly defeat the plaintiffs' alternative claim. If such were the law it would, I think, amount to a denial of justice to the plaintiffs in the present case, and legal propositions which have that apparent effect must always be scrutinised with some care. In truth, I think that Mr Lawson's proposition is founded upon too narrow a view of the modern action for quantum meruit. In its early history it was no doubt a genuine action in contract, based upon a real promise to pay, although that promise had not been expressed in words, and the amount of the payment had not been agreed. Subsequent developments have, however, considerably widened the scope of this form of action, and in many cases the action is now founded upon what is known as quasi-contract, similar, in some ways, to the action for money had and received. In these quasi-contractual cases the court will look at the true facts and ascertain from them whether or not a promise to pay should be implied, irrespective of the actual views or intentions of the parties at the time when the work was done or the services rendered.

The authority which perhaps best illustrates this modern view is a case cited by Mr Lawson for another purpose, *Craven-Ellis* v *Canons Ltd* [1936] 2 KB 403. [Barry J discussed *Craven-Ellis* v *Canons Ltd* [1936] 2 KB 403 (see Section 4 below) and *Upton-On-Severn Rural District Council* v *Powell* [1942] 1 All ER 220 (see Chapter 2, Section 3) and concluded:]

I am unable to see any valid distinction between work done which was to be paid for under the terms of a contract erroneously believed to be in existence, and work done which was to be paid for out of the proceeds of a contract which both parties erroneously believed was about to be made. In neither case was the work to be done gratuitously, and in both cases the party from whom payment was sought requested the work and obtained the benefit of it. In neither case did the parties actually intend to pay for the work otherwise than under the supposed contract, or as part of the total price which would become payable when the expected contract was made. In both cases, when the beliefs of the parties were falsified, the law implied an obligation—and, in this case, I think the law should imply an obligation—to pay a reasonable price for the services which had been obtained. I am, of course, fully aware that in different circumstances it might be held that work was done gratuitously merely in the hope that the building scheme would be carried out and that the person who did the work would obtain the contract. That, I am satisfied, is not the position here. In my judgment, the proper inference from the facts proved in this case is not that this work was done in the hope that this building might possibly be reconstructed and that the plaintiff company might obtain the contract, but that it was done under a mutual belief and understanding that this building was being reconstructed and that the plaintiff company was obtaining the contract. . . .

I have, therefore, come to the conclusion that the defence to the alternative claim fails and that the court should imply a condition or imply a promise that the defendant should pay a reasonable sum to the plaintiffs for the whole of these services which were rendered by them. As to amount, I have considered the plaintiffs' charges as set out in the schedule with some care. On the rather scanty information available to me, I have come to the conclusion that while some of the items may well be undercharged, certain of the larger items cannot be fully justified. The plaintiffs are entitled to a fair remuneration for the work which they have done, but they cannot, in my view, quantify their charges by reference to professional scales. Doing the best I can, I think the plaintiffs would be fairly recompensed if I deducted £100 from the amount claimed, leaving a balance of £250 13s. 5d. . . .

British Steel Corp. v *Cleveland Bridge & Engineering Co.*
(1981) [1984] 1 All ER 504 (QBD (Commercial Court))

Quantum meruit

CBE was involved in the construction of a bank building in Saudi Arabia. The building was to be of an unusual construction, with the main body suspended from four columns, with a steel lattice-work frame. CBE approached BSC with a view to their manufacturing the cast-steel nodes for use at the centre of the lattice-work. On 21 February 1979, CBE sent BSC a 'letter of intent' stating that it was its intention to enter into a sub-contract for the manufacture of the nodes and requesting BSC to commence work immediately pending preparation of the formal contract. BSC commenced manufacture. However, the first nodes cast were unsatisfactory and various alterations to the specifications were agreed. It was only after the first nodes were manufactured that CBE made it clear that it required delivery of the nodes in a particular sequence. The parties were unable to agree the terms of the proposed formal contract, before eventually all the nodes were delivered. CBE refused to pay for the nodes.

ROBERT GOFF J: In this action the plaintiffs, British Steel Corp (whom I shall refer to as BSC), are claiming from the defendants, Cleveland Bridge and Engineering Co Ltd (whom I shall refer to as CBE), the sum of £229,832·70 as the price of 137 cast-steel nodes and other related goods sold and delivered to CBE, or alternatively are claiming the like sum on a quantum meruit. In their defence and counterclaim, CBE admit that the goods were sold and delivered to them, and further admit liability in a sum of £200,853; but that admission is subject to a plea of set-off against the sum of £867,735·68 counterclaimed by them on the ground that BSC had, in breach of contract, delivered the nodes too late and out of sequence. Accordingly CBE's net counterclaim is for the difference between these two sums, viz £666,882·68. . . .

I turn then to the facts of the case. This is a case in which there is no doubt that BSC did in fact manufacture the 137 cast-steel nodes in question at the request of CBE, and did deliver them to CBE. But, despite protracted negotiations between the parties, no formal contract was ever entered into between them. CBE complained that BSC were late in delivering the nodes, and that the causes of delay were (with one minor exception) all within the control of BSC; they also complained that BSC failed to deliver the nodes in the sequence requested by CBE. In these circumstances, two main areas of dispute developed between the parties. First, was there any binding contract between the parties at all, under which the nodes were delivered? CBE contended that there was such a contract, which was to be found in certain documents (including a letter of intent issued by CBE dated 21 February 1979) and the conduct of BSC in proceeding with the manufacture of the nodes. BSC's primary contention was that no binding contract was ever entered into, and that they were entitled to be paid a reasonable sum for the nodes on a quantum meruit, a claim sounding not in contract but in quasi contract. The motives of the parties in putting their cases in these different ways lay primarily in the fact that, unless there was a binding contract between the parties there was no legal basis for CBE's counterclaim for damages in respect of late delivery or delivery out of sequence. So far as delivery was concerned, CBE's submission was that BSC's obligations, under the contract alleged by them to have come into existence, was to deliver the goods in the requested sequence and within a reasonable time. . . .

Now the question whether in a case such as the present any contract has come into existence must depend on a true construction of the relevant communications which have passed between the parties and the effect (if any) of their actions pursuant to those communications. There can be no hard and fast answer to the question whether a letter of intent will give rise to a binding agreement: everything must depend on the circumstances of the particular case. In most cases, where work is done pursuant to a request contained in a letter of intent, it will not matter whether a contract did or did not come into existence, because, if the party who has acted on the request is simply claiming payment, his claim will usually be based on a quantum meruit, and it will make no difference whether that claim is contractual or quasi-contractual. Of course, a quantum meruit claim (like the old actions for money had and received and for money paid) straddles the boundaries of what we now call contract and restitution, so the mere framing of a claim as a quantum meruit claim, or a claim for a reasonable sum, does not assist in classifying the claim as contractual or quasi contractual. But where, as here, one party is seeking to claim damages for breach of contract, the question whether any contract came into existence is of crucial importance.

As a matter of analysis the contract (if any) which may come into existence following a letter of intent may take one of two forms: either there may be an ordinary executory contract, under which each party assumes reciprocal obligations to the other; or there may be what is sometimes called an 'if' contract, i.e. a contract under which A requests B to carry out a certain performance and promises B that, if he does so, he will receive a certain performance in return, usually remuneration for his performance. The latter transaction is really no more than a standing offer which, if acted on before it lapses or is lawfully withdrawn, will result in a binding contract.

[Robert Goff J rejected on the evidence the submissions that negotiations had resulted either in an executory contract or an 'if' contract and concluded: . . .] In my judgment, the true analysis of the situation is simply this. Both parties confidently expected a formal contract to eventuate. In these circumstances, to expedite performance under that anticipated contract, one requested the other to commence the contract work, and the other complied with that request. If thereafter, as anticipated, a contract was entered into, the work done as requested will be treated as having been performed under that contract; if, contrary to their expectation, no contract was entered into, then the performance of the work is not referable to any contract the terms of which can be ascertained, and the law simply imposes an obligation on the party who made the request to pay a reasonable sum for such work as has been done pursuant to that request, such an obligation sounding in quasi contract or, as we now say, in restitution. Consistently with that solution, the party making the request may find himself liable to pay for work which he would not have had to pay for as such if the anticipated contract had come into existence, e.g. preparatory work which will, if the contract is made, be allowed for in the price of the finished work (cf *William Lacey (Hounslow) Ltd* v *Davis* [1957] 2 All ER 712, [1957] 1 WLR 932). This solution moreover accords with authority: see the decision in *Lacey* v *Davis*, the decision of the Court of Appeal in *Sanders & Forster Ltd* v *A. Monk & Co. Ltd* [1980] CA Transcript 35, though that decision rested in part on a concession, and the crisp dictum of Parker J in *OTM Ltd* v *Hydranautics* [1981] 2 Lloyd's Rep 211 at 214, when he said of a letter of intent that 'its only effect would be to enable the defendants to recover on a quantum meruit for work done pursuant to the direction' contained in the letter. I only wish to add to this part of my judgment the footnote that, even if I had concluded that in the circumstances of the present case there was a contract between the parties and that that contract was of the kind I have described as an 'if' contract, then I would still have concluded that there was no obligation under that contract on the part of

BSC to continue with or complete work, and therefore no obligation on their part to complete the work within a reasonable time. However, my conclusion in the present case is that the parties never entered into any contract at all. . . .

[Robert Goff J then held that, even if there were a contractual obligation to deliver within a reasonable time, BSC were not in breach. Judgment for BSC for £229,832.70.]

Question

What would the legal analysis be if the steel nodes had been defectively manufactured, causing the bank building to collapse and resulting in personal injuries or damage to property?

Note

1. For discussion see McKendrick, 'The Battle of the Forms and the Law of Restitution' (1988) 8 OJLS 197, where Professor McKendrick argues that if restitutionary solutions are proposed to solve the problems arising from failed negotiations, the courts ought to be more sensitive in their construction of the terms of any request in order better to protect the interests of the recipient.

2. Compare the robust approach to contract formation taken by Steyn LJ on the very similar facts of *G. Percy Trentham Ltd* v *Archital Luxfer Ltd* [1993] 1 Lloyd's Rep 25. In that case the main contractor had paid but was complaining about defective performance by the sub-contractor.

Regalian Properties plc v *London Dockland Development Corp* [1995] 1 WLR 212 (Ch D)

The plaintiff development company tendered in 1986 for the residential development of land in London's docklands. LDDC accepted their tender, but *'subject to contract'* and other conditions. Negotiations dragged on over two years, delays being caused both by LDDC's difficulties in obtaining vacant possession of parts of the site and disagreements over the eventual price caused by fluctuations in the property market, which initially spiralled and then fell away in 1988. No contract ever materialised. The plaintiff sought restitution of some £3 million representing fees paid to various professional firms in respect of the proposed development and in preparation for the proposed contract.

RATTEE J: [discussed *William Lacey (Hounslow) Ltd* v *Davis* [1957] 1 WLR 932 and continued:]

In my judgment, one important distinction between the facts in that case and those in the present case is that the work for which the plaintiffs claimed in that case was not work done for the purposes of the expected contract, but was rather for what was described in the first passage I have cited, at p. 934, as 'for some extraneous or collateral purpose.' It was for the wholly separate purpose of enabling the defendant to negotiate a claim made by the defendant to the War Damage Commission. In the present case, by contrast, the expenditure for which Regalian claims recompense was, I find, all for the purpose either of satisfying the requirements of the proposed contract as to planning permission and the approval of the designs for the development by LDDC, or of putting Regalian into a position of readiness to start the development in accordance with the terms of the proposed contract. In other words it was expenditure made for the purpose of enabling Regalian to obtain and perform the expected contract.

Although I have to say, with respect, that I do not find the reasoning of Barry J entirely easy to follow, the result seems to me to make perfectly good sense on the facts of that case. At the request of the defendant the plaintiffs had done work which had clearly benefited the defendant, quite outside the ambit of the anticipated contract, and had only not charged for it separately, as one would otherwise have expected them to do, because they thought they would be sufficiently recompensed by what they would be paid by the defendant under the contract. In those circumstances it is not surprising that the law of restitution found a remedy for the plaintiffs when the contract did not materialise. I do not consider that the decision lends any real support to the claim made by Regalian in the present case for compensation for expenditure incurred by it for the purpose of enabling itself to obtain and perform the intended contract at a time when the parties had in effect expressly agreed by the use of the words 'subject to contract' that there should be no legal obligation by either party to the other unless and until a formal contract had been entered into. It was frankly accepted by Mr Goldstone of Regalian that he knew and intended that this should be the effect of the use of the phrase 'subject to contract,' and indeed Regalian admits in its pleadings that those words were not intended to have any unusual meaning in the present case. As Mr Goldstone, whom I found an honest and indeed impressive witness, put it in his evidence, he knew that either party was free to walk away from the negotiations, although he confidently expected that this would not happen.

I should mention at this point the only question of fact on which there was any real issue between the parties. That is whether the expenditure for which Regalian claims recompense produced any benefit for LDDC Regalian contended that the production of designs and obtaining of detailed planning permission for the proposed development did benefit LDDC in that it enhanced the value of the Hermitage sites and also other adjacent land belonging to LDDC. Despite the evidence of Mr Warner, a surveyor called to give expert evidence on behalf of Regalian, I am not satisfied that any such or any other ascertainable benefit accrued to LDDC. LDDC did not own the copyright in the designs. It could not have used them itself or enabled any other developer to do so. More important was the fact that by the time the negotiations between the parties fell through the fall in the residential property market had been such that Regalian was not, and no-one else would have been, interested in buying the land concerned to carry out the sort of development for which designs had been produced.

The second authority on which Mr Coulson relied was a decision of the Supreme Court of New South Wales, *Sabemo Pty. Ltd* v *North Sydney Municipal Council* [1977] 2 NSWLR 880. The facts of that case have a certain similarity to the facts of the present case. The plaintiff company ('Sabemo') tendered for a building lease of land on which the defendant local authority ('the council') wished to carry out development. The council accepted Sabemo's tender and negotiations for the lease followed. According to the headnote (which contains the only statement of the facts of the case):

> It was agreed that the acceptance of the tender did no more than bring the parties together so that they could plan the project until a point was reached where they would enter into a contractual relationship, namely, the proposed building lease.

Sabemo carried out a lot of detailed work on the plans for the proposed development, and at one point actually raised (apparently inconclusively with the council) the question of compensation before it worked on any revised design. Eventually the council decided to abandoned the proposed development scheme altogether. Sabemo sued the council for $426,000 which it said was the cost of work done by it for the council in connection with the proposed development. Sabemo succeeded. Sheppard J said, at pp. 900–901:

> In a judgment of this kind it would be most unwise, and in any event impossible, to fix the limitations which should circumscribe the extent of the right to recover. It is enough for me to say that I think that there is one circumstance here which leads to the conclusion that the plaintiff is entitled to succeed. That circumstance is the fact that the defendant deliberately decided to drop the proposal. It may have had good reasons for doing so, but they had nothing to do with the plaintiff, which, in good faith over a period exceeding three years, had worked assiduously towards the day when it would take a building lease of the land and erect thereon the civic centre which the defendant, during that long period, has so earnestly desired. In the *William Lacey* case, [1957] 1 WLR 932 too, the defendant made a unilateral decision not to go on, but to sell its land instead. I realise that, in looking at the matter in this way, I am imputing a degree of fault to the defendant. To some this may seem to be, at least in English law, somewhat strange. It has long been the law that parties are free to negotiate such contract as they may choose to enter into. Until such contract comes about, they are in negotiation only. Each is at liberty, no matter how capricious his reason, to break off the negotiations at any time. If that occurs that is the end of the matter and, generally speaking, neither party will be under any liability to the other. But the concept that there can be fault in such a situation was adopted both by Somervell and Romer LJJ in the *Brewer Street* case [1954] 1 QB 428, 434, 438, 439 the latter, so it seems to me, basing his judgment upon it. Denning LJ [1954] 1 QB 428, 435, 437 did not in fact find fault in that case, but it would seem that he thought it could sometimes exist in negotiating situations, as distinct from contractual ones, although there had not in fact been fault in the case with which he was immediately concerned. To my mind the defendant's decision to drop the proposal is the determining factor. If the transaction had gone off because the parties were unable to agree, then I think it would be correct, harking back to the expressions used by the judges in the *Jennings* v *Chapman* case [1952] 2 TLR 409, 413, 414, 415, and in the *Brewer Street* case [1954] 1 QB 428, 436, 437, 438, to say that each party had taken a risk, in incurring the expenditure which it did, that the transaction might go off because of the bona fide failure to reach agreement on some point of substance in such a complex transaction. But I do not think it right to say that that risk should be so borne, when one party has taken it upon itself to change its mind about the entirety of the proposal.

Sheppard J described the principle he was applying, at pp. 902–903:

> In my opinion, the better view of the correct application of the principle in question is that, where two parties proceed upon the joint assumption that a contract will be entered into between them, and one does work beneficial for the project, and thus in the interests of the two parties, which work he would not be expected, in other circumstances, to do gratuitously, he will be entitled to compensation or restitution, if the other party unilaterally decides to abandon the project, not for any reason associated with bona fide disagreement concerning the terms of the contract to be

entered into, but for reasons which, however valid, pertain only to his own position and do not relate at all to that of the other party.

Sheppard J appears from other passages in his judgment to have considered that he was applying the decision in *William Lacey (Hounslow) Ltd* v *Davis* [1957] 1 WLR 932. In my judgment *Sabemo's* claim was distinguishable from that in *William Lacey (Hounslow) Ltd* v *Davis* on similar grounds to those on which I have already explained I think Regalian's claim in the present case is distinguishable—namely that in *William Lacey (Hounslow) Ltd* v *Davis* the work the subject matter of the claim was quite outside the ambit of the intended contract.

I will deal a little later in this judgment with the question whether the principle enunciated by Sheppard J in the *Sabemo* case [1977] 2 NSWLR 880 should be held to apply in English law. Irrespective of the answer to that question, in my judgment it would not apply to the facts of the present case, for the reason for the breakdown of negotiations between LDDC and Regalian was their inability to agree on an essential term of the intended contract, namely the price. It was not because one party 'unilaterally decided to abandon the project' in the words of Sheppard J in the *Sabemo* case.

In this context Regalian placed reliance on the letter of 8 July 1987 from Mr Ward, Chief Executive of LDDC, to Mr Goldstone, which I have already quoted, in which Mr Ward said that 'the delay in our providing vacant possession will not create the situation under which we would seek to amend the terms of our disposal of the site to you.' Regalian submitted that in the end that was just what LDDC did try to do—namely increase the price because of the alleged change in market value during the period of delay in LDDC's obtaining vacant possession. I see some force in this submission, despite LDDC's response that in the interim Regalian itself had sought successfully to alter the terms of the deal to take account of the vacant possession problem. However, I cannot see that the submission helps Regalian's claim as formulated in this action, even if the principle enunciated by Sheppard J in the *Sabemo* case is to be applied, for it does not alter the fact that negotiations broke down because the parties could not ultimately agree on price. It may be that the letter of 8 July 1987 could have been relied on as giving rise to some sort of estoppel disentitling LDDC from seeking to renegotiate the price, but no such estoppel is relied on by Regalian for the obvious reason that presumably the result of such a plea, if successful, would be a contract between the parties at the price agreed subject to contract before LDDC tried to increase it and otherwise on the terms agreed between the parties. This would be a result totally unwanted by Regalian, because in the light of market changes since mid-1988 such a contract would be financially very unattractive to Regalian.

The third authority particularly relied on by Mr Coulson is a decision of Judge Peter Bowsher QC sitting on official referees' business in *Marston Construction Co. Ltd* v *Kigass Ltd* (1989) 15 Con LR 116. In that case the defendant had invited tenders for the rebuilding of a factory which had been burned down. The plaintiff tendered for the work. Its tender was accepted. It was made clear by the defendant to the plaintiff that no contract for the rebuilding would be entered into unless and until the defendant had succeeded in obtaining from an insurance claim sufficient money to finance the rebuilding. Both the plaintiff and the defendant confidently expected that sufficient insurance moneys would be forthcoming and that accordingly a contract between them would result. In this confident expectation the plaintiff carried out substantial preparatory works the cost of which, if a contract had materialised, would have been included in the contract price. At one point the plaintiff sought an assurance from the defendant that the plaintiff's costs incurred before the expected contract was signed would be met by the defendant. No such assurance was forthcoming. The defendant's insurance claim did not produce sufficient to cover the cost of the proposed rebuilding and no contract was entered into between the parties. The plaintiff sought recompense for the preparatory works. Judge Bowsher QC referred, at p. 126, to *William Lacey (Hounslow) Ltd* v *Davis* [1957] 1 WLR 932 and cited the passage, at p. 939, which I have already cited from the judgment of Barry J. He then referred to a dictum of Robert Goff J in *British Steel Corporation* v *Cleveland Bridge and Engineering Co. Ltd* [1984] 1 All ER 504, 511, to which I shall refer a little later in this judgment. Then Judge Bowsher QC said, 15 Con LR 116, 127:

> I find that the facts of the present case, although different in important respects are similar in kind to the facts in *William Lacey (Hounslow) Ltd* v *Davis* [1957] 1 WLR 932. There was a request to do work, though the request in respect of the bulk of the work was implied rather than express. It was contemplated that the work would be paid for out of the contemplated contract. Both parties believed that the contract was about to be made despite the fact that there was a very clear condition which had to be met by a third party if the contract was to be made. The defendants obtained the benefit of the work in my judgment, though Mr Raeside submitted that they did not.

Judge Bowsher QC expressed his conclusion in favour of the plaintiff in the following terms, at p. 129:

> The preliminary works requested were undoubtedly done for the benefit of the defendants and were only done for the benefit of the plaintiffs in the sense that they hoped to make a profit out of them. As a result of the works some progress was made towards getting consents and in the end the defendants had in the hands of their agent some designs and working drawings (though not a complete set) together with an implied licence to build to those drawings even though that licence be limited as I think (without having heard argument) to a licence to have the factory built by the plaintiffs. Whether the defendants decide ultimately to build a factory or to sell the land, they have a benefit which is realisable.
>
> *Conclusion.* I therefore conclude that there was no agreement as alleged in paras. 5 to 8 of the statement of claim. I find that there was an express request made by the defendants to the plaintiffs to carry out a small quantity of design works and that there was an implied request to carry out preparatory works in general and that both the express and the implied requests gave rise to a right of payment of a reasonable sum.

I have to say, with all respect for Judge Bowsher QC, that I find this a surprising decision, not least because, as I have recited from his findings of fact, the plaintiff had earlier requested and been refused an assurance that it would be compensated for the preparatory work concerned. In this respect I agree with the critical commentary on Judge Bowsher's decision by the editor of the Building Law Reports (1989) 46 BLR 109. However, whether the decision be right or wrong. I do not feel obliged to apply it in the present case, which is distinguishable on the facts in two particular respects. First, in the present case, unlike the *Marston Construction Co.* case, even if a contract had materialised no part of any costs incurred or work done by Regalian in connection with the contract would have been paid for by LDDC. The only obligation on LDDC would have been to grant the building lease. Secondly, as I have already said, I am not satisfied in the present case that the preparatory works resulted in any benefit to LDDC.

I referred a little earlier to the citation by Judge Bowsher QC in the *Marston Construction Co.* case of a dictum of Robert Goff J in *British Steel Corporation* v *Cleveland Bridge and Engineering Co. Ltd* [1984] 1 All ER 504, 511. I should say a little more about that case. The defendant had successfully tendered for the fabrication of steelwork to be used in the construction of a building. It entered into negotiations with the plaintiff for a sub-contract whereunder the plaintiff would supply certain steel nodes that would form part of the relevant steelworks. It was proposed that the sub-contract would be in a standard form used by the defendant. The defendant requested the plaintiff to commence work on the steel nodes immediately 'pending the preparation and issuing to you of the official form of sub-contract.' The intended formal contract was not entered into because the parties failed to agree certain terms to go into it. The plaintiff produced and delivered to the defendant all but one of the steel nodes. The defendant refused to pay for them, and instead sought to recover from the plaintiff damages for late delivery of the nodes. The plaintiff sued for the value of the nodes it had supplied by way of quantum meruit. The defendant counterclaimed for damages for inter alia late delivery of the nodes, alleging that a binding contract came into being between the parties. Robert Goff J rejected the defendant's argument that a contract existed between the parties. He then considered the plaintiff's quantum meruit claim in these terms, at p. 511:

> In my judgment, the true analysis of the situation is simply this. Both parties confidently expected a formal contract to eventuate. In these circumstances, to expedite performance under that anticipated contract, one requested the other to commence the contract work, and the other complied with that request. If thereafter, as anticipated, a contract was entered into, the work done as requested will be treated as having been performed under that contract; if, contrary to their expectation, no contract was entered into, then the performance of the work is not referable to any contract the terms of which can be ascertained, and the law simply imposes an obligation on the party who made the request to pay a reasonable sum for such work as has been done pursuant to that request, such an obligation sounding in quasi-contract or, as we now say, in restitution. Consistently with that solution, the party making the request may find himself liable to pay for work which he would not have had to pay for as such if the anticipated contract had come into existence, e.g., preparatory work which will, if the contract is made, be allowed for in the price of the finished work (cf. *William Lacey (Hounslow) Ltd* v *Davis* [1957] 1 WLR 932).

I do not consider that this decision lends any real support to Regalian's claim in the present case. I can well understand why Robert Goff J concluded that, where one party to an expected contract expressly requests the other to perform services or supply goods that would have been performable or suppliable under the expected contract when concluded, in advance of the contract, that party should have to pay a quantum meruit if the contract does not materialise. The present case is not analogous. The costs for which Regalian seeks reimbursement were incurred by it not by way of accelerated performance of the anticipated contract at the request of LDDC, but for the purpose of putting itself in a position to obtain and then perform the contract.

Mr Coulson relied on the last part of the dictum of Robert Goff J, at p. 511, which I have cited, in which he pointed out that the application of the principle of restitution which he applied in that case can result in one party to an anticipated contract which does not materialise finding himself liable to pay the other party for preparatory work for which he would not have had to pay under the contract, because under the contract it would have been allowed for in the overall contract price. I do not think the judge had in mind (because he was not concerned with such a claim) that a landowner intending to contract to grant a building lease could find itself liable to pay the intending lessee developer for preparatory work done by the lessee for the purpose of putting itself in a position to obtain and perform the contract.

I must return now to the statement of principle made by Sheppard J in the *Sabemo* case [1977] 2 NSWLR 880, 900–901, 902–903 which I have cited earlier, for the essence of Mr Coulson's submission on behalf of Regalian is that that principle should be applied in the present case. For convenience I repeat here the relevant passage from the judgment of Sheppard J, at pp. 902–903:

> In my opinion, the better view of the correct application of the principle in question is that, where two parties proceed upon the joint assumption that a contract will be entered into between them and one does work beneficial for the project, and thus in the interests of the two parties, which work he would not be expected, in other circumstances, to do gratuitously, he will be entitled to compensation or restitution, if the other party unilaterally decides to abandon the project, not for any reason associated with bona fide disagreement concerning the terms of the contract to be entered into, but for reasons which, however valid, pertain only to his own position and do not relate at all to that of the other party.

I have already said that the principle as so stated would not, in my judgment, apply in any event to the facts of this case, because the reason the contract did not materialise was that the parties could not agree on the price, and not that either party decided to abandon the project. However, in case I am wrong on this, I should say that in my respectful opinion the principle enunciated by Sheppard J in the passage I have cited is not established by any English authority. I appreciate that the English law of restitution should be flexible and capable of continuous development. However I see no good reason to extend it to apply some such principle as adopted by Sheppard J in the *Sabemo* case to facts such as those of the present case, where, however much the parties expect a contract between them to materialise, both enter negotiations expressly (whether by use of the words 'subject to contract' or otherwise) on terms that each party is free to withdraw from the negotiations at any time. Each party to such negotiations must be taken to know (as in my judgment Regalian did in the present case) that pending the conclusion of a binding contract any cost incurred by him in preparation for the intended contract will be incurred at his own risk, in the sense that he will have no recompence for those costs if no contract results. In other words I accept in substance the submission made by Mr Naughton for LDDC to the effect that, by deliberate use of the words 'subject to contract' with the admitted intention that they should have their usual effect, LDDC and Regalian each accepted that in the event of no contract being entered into any resultant loss should lie where it fell.

Regalian, under the leadership of Mr Goldstone, was a very experienced operator in the property development market. To his considerable credit Mr Goldstone did not pretend that he was not aware that LDDC, like any other party to negotiations 'subject to contract,' was free to walk away from those negotiations, however little he expected it to do so. Regalian incurred the costs concerned in that knowledge. Though it is perhaps not strictly relevant, I see nothing inequitable in those circumstances in the loss resulting from the breakdown of negotiations lying where it fell, particularly bearing in mind that, in the light of the slump in the residential property market that followed the attempt by LDDC in May 1988 to renegotiate the price for the proposed building leases, Regalian has good reason to be thankful that it did not find itself having to take those leases on the terms previously proposed.

In my judgment Regalian has failed to make good its claim based on the principles of restitution. . . .

Question

Was the defendant enriched in this case?

Note

Rattee J's judgment helpfully differentiates the questions of risk, benefit and fault. The case is noted by Key (1995) 111 LQR 576 and McKendrick [1995] *Restitution Law Review* 100.

Section 4: void and unenforceable contracts

A: Void contracts

Until recently, where restitution was awarded where there had been partial performance of a void contract, the courts were rarely explicit about the ground for recovery. In most cases commentators suggested that failure of consideration or mistake would explain examples of recovery. However, the cases involving void 'interest rate swap' transactions and local authorities have suggested the basis of mutual restitution should be '*absence of consideration*' or '*no consideration*' rather than either of the two more traditional grounds. See the leading case of *Westdeusche Landesbank Girozentrale* v *Islington London Borough Council* [1994] 4 All ER 890. The 'swaps' cases have been given their own section in Chapter 5, Section 2 below, but clearly what they say has implications for the law relating to void contracts as a whole. For discussion see Birks, 'No Consideration: Restitution After Void Contracts' (1993) 23 UWAL Rev 195.

A major concern is that restitutionary relief should not frustrate the statute or other public policy which rendered the contract void or unenforceable in the first place. See for discussion of public policy, Chapter 8, Section 4.

See generally Burrows, *Restitution*, 304–12.

Craven-Ellis* v *Canons Ltd
[1936] 2 KB 403 (CA)

Quantum meruit

Sir Arthur de Cros and his son, Phillip, wished to engage the services of the plaintiff, Craven-Ellis, a valuer and estate agent, for the development of a building estate. In 1928, Canons Ltd was formed to purchase the estate. Craven-Ellis worked for the company for a time without a formal contract. Then in April 1931 a formal agreement was executed under the company's seal setting out the terms upon which Craven-Ellis was to act as managing director. However, none of the directors, including Craven-Ellis, was capable of making such an agreement as none of them held the necessary qualification shares as required under the articles of association.

Therefore the agreement was void. Craven-Ellis sought remuneration for services rendered.

GREER LJ: . . . The plaintiff in this action sought to recover from the defendant company the remuneration set out in the agreement, and as an alternative, sought to recover for his services on a quantum meruit. Until the company purported to put an end to his engagement he continued to perform all the services mentioned in the agreement.

The company, having had the full benefit of these services, decline to pay either under the agreement or on the basis of a quantum meruit. Their defence to the action is a purely technical defence, and if it succeeds the Messrs. du Cros as the principal shareholders in the company, and the company, would be in the position of having received and accepted valuable services and refusing, for purely technical reasons, to pay for them.

As regards the services rendered between December 31, 1930, and April 14, 1931, there is, in my judgment, no defence to the claim. These services were rendered by the plaintiff not as managing director or as a director, but as an estate agent, and there was no contract in existence which could present any obstacle to a claim based on a quantum meruit for services rendered and accepted.

As regards the plaintiff's services after the date of the contract, I think the plaintiff is also entitled to succeed. The contract, having been made by directors who had no authority to make it with one of themselves who had notice of their want of authority, was not binding on either party. It was, in fact, a nullity, and presents no obstacle to the implied promise to pay on a quantum meruit basis which arises from the performance of the services and the implied acceptance of the same by the company.

It was contended by Mr Croom-Johnson on behalf of the respondents that, inasmuch as the services relied on were purported to be done by the plaintiff under what he and the directors thought was a binding contract, there could be no legal obligation on the defendants on a quantum meruit claim. The only one of the numerous authorities cited by Mr Croom-Johnson that appears to support his contention is the judgment of a Divisional Court in *In re Allison, Johnson & Foster, Ld.; ex parte Birkenshaw* [1904] 2 KB 327. The Court consisted of Lord Alverstone, Wills and Kennedy JJ, and the judgment was delivered by Kennedy J. In giving judgment that learned judge, expressing not merely his own opinion, but that of the other two judges, said [at 330]: 'There can be no implied contract for payment arising out of acceptance of the work done where the work was done upon an express request which turns out to be no request at all, but which down to the time when the whole of the work had been done was supposed by both parties to be valid and operative.' This passage appears to involve the proposition that in all cases where parties suppose there is an agreement in existence and one of them has performed services, or delivered goods in pursuance of the supposititious agreement there cannot be any inference of any promise by the person accepting the service or the goods to pay on the basis of a quantum meruit. This would certainly be strictly logical if the inference of a promise to pay on a quantum meruit basis were an inference of fact based on the acceptance of the services or of the goods delivered under what was supposed to be an existing contract; but in my judgment the inference is not one of fact, but is an inference which a rule of law imposes on the parties where work has been done or goods have been delivered under what purports to be a binding contract, but is not so in fact.

. . . In my judgment, the obligation to pay reasonable remuneration for the work done when there is no binding contract between the parties is imposed by a rule of law, and not by an inference of fact arising from the acceptance of services or goods. It is one of the cases referred to in books on contracts as obligations arising quasi ex contractu, of which a well known instance is a claim based on money had and received. Although I do not hold that the decision of the Court in *Ex parte Birkenshaw* was wrong, I think that the passage I read from the judgment is not a correct statement of the law.

I accordingly think that the defendants must pay on the basis of a quantum meruit not only for the services rendered after December 31, 1930, and before the date of the invalid agreement, but also for the services after that date. I think the appeal should be allowed, and judgment given for such a sum as shall be found to be due on the basis of a quantum meruit in respect of all services rendered by the plaintiff to the company until he was dismissed. The defendants seem to me to be in a dilemma. If the contract was an effective contract by the company, they would be bound to pay the remuneration provided for in the contract. If, on the other hand, the contract was a nullity and not binding either on the plaintiff or the defendants, there would be nothing to prevent the inference which the law draws from the performance by the plaintiff of services to the company, and the company's acceptance of such services, which, if they had not been performed by the plaintiff, they would have had to get some other agent to carry out. . . .

Questions

1. Was the company enriched? If so, which test(s) of enrichment were satisfied?

2. What was the ground for restitution (or unjust factor)?

Notes

1. For discussion see Burrows, *Restitution*, 306–7 and Goff and Jones, 478–80.

2. Compare *In re Cleadon Trust Ltd* [1939] 1 Ch 286 (CA), where a company director expended over £53,000 paying debts owed by the company at the request of the managing director, in the expectation that he would be repaid. A resolution of the board purported to ratify the payments, but this was invalid because the meeting was inquorate. On the company's liquidation the director sought restitution, but the majority of the Court of Appeal held the company was under no obligation either at common law or in equity to reimburse him. Professor Birks would argue that the best explanation of *Craven-Ellis* v *Canons Ltd* is that the unjust factor was *mistake* as to a present fact, whereas in *In re Cleadon Trust Ltd* there was simply a *misprediction*: the director confidently expected to be repaid. See Birks, *Introduction*, 147 and 167.

3. Compare also *Guinness plc* v *Saunders* [1990] 2 AC 663, where a company director received £5.2 million from his company under a contract which was void for want of authority. The House of Lords ordered restitution, Lord Goff accepting a submission that recovery followed 'on the ground of total failure of consideration, or alternatively on the basis that he had received the money as constructive trustee' (at 698). Compare Birks [1990] LMCLQ 330, 332, arguing that the ground of recovery should be regarded as mistaken belief in the existence of a valid contract. For further discussion of this case see Chapter 8, Section 3.

Rover International Ltd v *Cannon Film Sales Ltd* [1989] 1 WLR 912 (CA)

'Rover' appeal

The facts and extracts relating to the claim based on mistake are set out in Chapter 2, Section 1. It will be recalled that Rover had paid instalments under a film distribution contract which was void for non-incorporation of Rover at the relevant time. Rover claimed restitution in the alternative on the ground of total failure of consideration.

KERR LJ: . . .

Total failure of consideration

The claim for repayment of the five instalments of the advance on this ground was rejected by the judge in the following terms [1987] BCLC 540, 546:

> As for the claim for money had and received, the answer is plain. The consideration, if there had been a contract, had not failed at all. Rover has had several films, including 'Highlander,' and distributed them in Italy for payment no doubt of substantial sums. To allow it now to get back the moneys which it paid to Cannon would be grossly unjust. There is no claim in law here for moneys had and received to the use of Rover.

This passage strongly supports my impression that the judge did not have in mind the full financial consequences which would flow from his judgment. But that is of no direct relevance at this juncture. The important point is that in my view the judge could not have expressed himself in this way if his attention had been directed to the correct approach in principle. The question whether there has been a total failure of consideration is not answered by considering whether there was any consideration sufficient to support a contract or purported contract. The test is whether or not the party claiming total failure of consideration has in fact received any part of the benefit bargained for under the contract or purported contract.

The relevant principles are set out in *Chitty on Contracts*, 25th ed. (1983), vol. 1, pp. 1091–1092, para. 1964 and the authorities there cited, to which we understand the judge was not referred. It is convenient to quote the following passages from the text:

> Where money has been paid under a transaction that is or becomes ineffective the payer may recover the money provided that the consideration for the payment has totally failed. Although the principle is not confined to contracts most of the cases are concerned with ineffective contracts. In that context failure of consideration occurs where the payer has not enjoyed the benefit of any part of what he bargained for. Thus, the failure is judged from the payer's point of view and 'when one is considering the law of failure of consideration and of the quasi-contractual right to recover money on that ground, it is generally speaking, not the promise which is referred to as the consideration, but the performance of the promise.' The failure has to be total. . . . Thus, any performance of the actual thing promised, *as determined by the contract*, is fatal to recovery under this heading.
>
> The role of the contractual specification means that it is not true to say that there can be a total failure of consideration only where the payer received no benefit at all in return for the payment. The concept of total failure of consideration can ignore real benefits received by the payer if they are not the benefit bargained for. . . .

The quotation was taken from the speech of Viscount Simon LC in *Fibrosa Spolka Akcyjna* v *Fairbairn Lawson Combe Barbour Ltd* [1943] AC 32, 48. It is not necessary to refer to this or the other authorities cited in support of this passage, but I should refer to two authorities by way of illustration.

In *Rowland* v *Divall* [1923] 2 KB 500 the plaintiff bought a car from the defendants. He had the use of it for several months but then discovered that the seller had no title, with the result that he had to surrender the car to the true owner. He sued for the return of the price on the ground that there had been a total failure of consideration. The defendant denied this, pointing out that the plaintiff had had the use of the car for a substantial time. This contention succeeded at first instance, leaving the plaintiff only with a claim for damages, but this court unanimously upheld the plaintiff's claim. The consideration for which he had bargained was lawful possession of the car and a good title to it, neither of which he got. Although the car had been delivered to him pursuant to the contract and he had had its use and enjoyment for a considerable time, there was a total failure of consideration because he had not got any part of what he had bargained for.

The decision of Finnemore J in *Warman* v *Southern Counties Car Finance Corporation Ltd* [1949] 2 KB 576 was to the same effect. The plaintiff was buying a car on hire purchase when he became aware that a third party was claiming to be the true owner of the car. But he nevertheless went on paying the remaining instalments and then the necessary nominal sum to exercise his option to purchase. When the true owner then claimed the car he surrendered it and sued the finance company for the return of everything he had paid. He succeeded on the ground that there had been a total failure of consideration. He had not bargained for having the use of the car without the option to purchase it.

The position of Rover in the present case is a fortiori to these cases. Admittedly, as the judge said, they had several films from Cannon. But the possession of the films was merely incidental to the performance of the contract in the sense that it enabled Rover/Monitor to render services in relation to the films by dubbing them, preparing them for release on the Italian market and releasing them. These were onerous incidents associated with the delivery of the films to them. And delivery and possession were not what Rover had bargained for. The relevant bargain, at any rate for present purposes, was the opportunity to earn a substantial share of the gross receipts pursuant to clause 6 of the schedule, with the certainty of at least breaking even by recouping their advance. Due to the invalidity of the agreement Rover got nothing of what they had bargained for, and there was clearly a total failure of consideration.

This equally disposes of Mr Pardoe's ingenious attempt to convert his concession of a quantum meruit, in particular the element of reasonable remuneration, into consideration in any relevant sense. Rover did not bargain for a quantum meruit, but for the benefits which might flow from clause 6 of the schedule. That is the short answer to this point.

It follows that in my view Rover's claim for the repayment of the five instalments of the advance totalling $312,500 succeeds on the basis of a total failure of consideration. . . .

Note

In addition the court rejected a 'contract ceiling' argument. See [1989] 1 WLR 912, at 926–8 (Kerr LJ) and 933–4 (Dillon LJ). For discussion see Birks, 'Restitution after Ineffective Contracts: Issues for the 1990s' (1990) 2 JCL 227, at 231–3 and (1989) 105 LQR 179 (Beatson).

B: Contracts unenforceable due to lack of formality

See Burrows, *Restitution*, 299–304.

Pavey & Matthews Pty Ltd v *Paul*

(1987) 162 CLR 221 (High Court of Australia)

Quantum meruit

A licensed building company undertook and completed the renovation of a cottage under an oral contract which contemplated that a reasonable remuneration would be paid. The oral contract was rendered unenforceable on the part of the builder by s. 45 of the Builders Licensing Act 1971 (New South Wales) which required a signed, written contract. The plaintiff building company claimed upon a *quantum meruit* for the balance due.

DEANE J: [referred to Goff and Jones, *The Law of Restitution* (2nd ed., 1978), 320–21 for the proposition: . . .] that the basis of the obligation to make payment for an executed consideration given and received under an unenforceable contract should now be accepted as lying in restitution or unjust enrichment. . . . In such a case, the underlying obligation or debt for the work done, goods supplied, or services rendered does not arise from a genuine agreement at all. It is an obligation or debt imposed by operation of law which 'arises from the defendant having taken the benefit of the work done, goods supplied, or services rendered . . .' (*per* Starke J., *Phillips* v *Ellinson Bros. Pty Ltd* (1941) 65 CLR, at p. 235) and which can be enforced '*as if* it had a contractual origin' (emphasis added) (*In re Rhodes*, *per* Lindley LJ (1890) 44 Ch D 94, at p. 107) and see, among many other relevant works and cases, Lord Wright, ['*Sinclair* v *Brougham*', (1938) *Cambridge Law Journal*, vol. 6, 305], p. 317ff.; R. M. Jackson, *History of Quasi-Contract in English Law* (1936); *Pulbrook* v *Lawes* (1876) 1 QBD, at p. 290 (*per* Blackburn J) (1876) 1 QBD, at pp. 290–291 (*per* Lush J); *Fibrosa Spolka Akcyjna* v *Fairbairn Lawson Combe Barbour Ltd* [1943] AC 32, at pp. 61–62; *Deglman* v *Guaranty Trust* [1954] 3 DLR 785, at pp. 788, 794–795; the judgment of Lord Denning himself (then Denning LJ) in *James* v *Thomas H. Kent & Co. Ltd* [1951] 1 KB 551, at p. 556; and the judgment of the Privy Council, delivered by Lord Denning, in *Kiriri Cotton Co. Ltd* v *Dewani* [1960] AC 192, at pp. 204–205.

It is not necessary to pursue here the question whether, now that the common law is released from the controls of the old forms of action, there is a continuing need for or utility in the traditional approach that any claim which would in previous times have been asserted by a common indebitatus count must be seen as lying either in contract or quasi-contract: see e.g., the discussion of the subject by Lord Wright, op. cit., and by W.S. Holdsworth, 'Unjustifiable Enrichment', *Law Quarterly Review*, vol. 55 (1939), p. 37. It suffices to say that, even accepting that traditional approach, it is clear that the old common indebitatus count could be utilised to accommodate what should be seen as two distinct categories of claim: one to recover a debt arising under a genuine contract, whether express or implied; the other to recover a debt owing in circumstances where the law itself imposed or imputed an obligation or promise to make compensation for a benefit accepted. In the first category of case, the action was brought upon the genuine agreement regardless of whether it took the form of a special or a common count. It follows from what has been said above that the cases in which a claimant has been held entitled to recover in respect of an executed consideration under an agreement upon which the Statute of Frauds precluded the bringing of an action should be seen as falling within the second and not the first category. In that second category of case, the tendency of common lawyers to speak in terms of implied contract rather than in terms of an obligation imposed by law (see, e.g., *per* Salter J, *Scott* v *Pattison* [1923] 2 KB 723, at pp. 727–728) should be recognised as but a reflection of the influence of discarded fictions, buried forms of action and the conventional conviction that, if a common law claim could not properly be framed in tort, it must necessarily be dressed in the language of contract. That tendency should not be allowed to conceal the fact that, in that category of case, the action was not based upon a genuine agreement at all. Indeed, if there was a valid and enforcable agreement governing the claimant's right to compensation, there would be neither occasion nor legal justification for the law to superimpose or impute an obligation or promise to pay a reasonable remuneration. The quasi-contractual obligation to pay fair and just compensation for a benefit which has been accepted will only arise in a case where there is no applicable genuine agreement or where such an agreement is frustrated, avoided or unenforceable. In such a case, it is the very fact that there is no genuine agreement or that the genuine agreement is frustrated, avoided or unenforceable that provides the occasion for (and part of the circumstances giving rise to) the imposition by the law of the obligation to make restitution.

To identify the basis of such actions as restitution and not genuine agreement is not to assert a judicial discretion to do whatever idiosyncratic notions of what is fair and just might dictate. The circumstances in which the common law imposes an enforceable obligation to pay compensation for a benefit accepted under an unenforceable agreement have been explored in the reported cases and in learned writings and are unlikely to be greatly affected by the perception that the basis of such an obligation, when the common law imposes it, is preferably seen as lying in restitution rather than in the implication of a genuine agreement where in fact the unenforceable agreement left no room for one. That is not to deny the importance of the concept of unjust enrichment in the law of this country. It constitutes a unifying legal concept which explains why the law recognises, in a variety of distinct categories of case, an obligation on the part of a defendant to make fair and just restitution for a benefit derived at the expense of a plaintiff and which assists in the determination, by the ordinary processes of legal reasoning, of the question whether the law should, in justice, recognise such an obligation in a new or developing category of case: see *Muschinski* v *Dodds* (1985) 160 CLR 583, at pp. 619–620; Goff & Jones, op. cit., p. 11ff. In a category of case where the law recognises an obligation to pay a reasonable remuneration or compensation for a benefit actually or constructively accepted, the general concept of restitution or unjust enrichment is, as is pointed out subsequently in this judgment, also relevant, in a more direct sense, to the identification of the proper basis upon which the quantum of remuneration or compensation should be ascertained in that particular category of case.

The fact that the action which can be brought on a common indebitatus count consistently with the Statute of Frauds is founded on an obligation arising independently of the unenforceable contract does not mean that the existence or terms of that contract are necessarily irrelevant. In such an action, it will ordinarily be permissible for the plaintiff to refer to the unenforceable contract as evidence, but as evidence only, on the question whether what was done was done gratuitously. In many cases, such as where the claim is for money lent or paid, the obligation to make restitution will plainly involve the obligation to pay the precise amount advanced or paid. In those cases where a claim for a reasonable remuneration or price is involved, the unenforceable agreement may, as Jordan CJ pointed out in *Horton* v *Jones [No. 1]* (1934) 34 SR (NSW), at pp. 368–368, be referred to as evidence, but again as evidence only, on the question of the appropriate amount of compensation. If the unenforceable contract has not been rescinded by the plaintiff or otherwise terminated, the defendant will be free to rely on it as a defence to the claim for compensation in a case where he is ready and willing to perform his obligations under it: see *Thomas* v *Brown* (1876) 1 QBD 714. The defendant will also be entitled to rely on the unenforceable contract, if it has been executed but not rescinded, to limit the amount recoverable by the plaintiff to the contractual amount in a case where that amount is less than what would constitute fair and reasonable remuneration. . . .

Note
This case is noted in (1988) 104 LQR 13 (Beatson) and the historical learning behind the case is thoroughly analysed by Ibbetson, 'Implied Contracts and Restitution: History in the High Court of Australia' (1988) 8 OJLS 312. See, for the public policy issue, Chapter 8, Section 4.

Section 5: free acceptance

The concept of 'free acceptance' made its first appearance in the English law of restitution in the first edition of Goff and Jones, *The Law of Restitution* (London: Sweet & Maxwell, 1966), 30–31, where it states:

> . . . the defendant will not usually be regarded as having been benefited by the receipt of services or goods unless he has accepted them (or, in the case of goods, retained them) with an opportunity of rejection and with actual or presumed knowledge that they were to be paid for. For convenience we shall refer to a person who has so acted as having *freely accepted* the services or goods in question.

This passage clearly relates to establishing the defendant's enrichment. The (somewhat controversial) role of free acceptance as a test for enrichment is discussed above in Chapter 1, Section 3. Here the concern is the distinct question of whether free acceptance can also constitute an unjust factor, or ground for restitution.

The prime advocate of the dual role of free acceptance is Peter Birks. In *An Introduction to the Law of Restitution* Professor Birks established an influential framework for the subject, which posits a law which is primarily concerned with the integrity of the transferor's intention. Therefore in the bulk of the decided cases in *subtractive unjust enrichment*, restitution is awarded because either there was *no intention* to transfer wealth (unjust factor: ignorance), or the intention was *vitiated* (mistake, compulsion, inequality) or the intention was *qualified*, and the condition of transfer was not met (failure of consideration). There is in addition a limited role of *policy-motivated* unjust factors, but most of the law is concerned with the quality of the decision to transfer, or in other words is *plaintiff-sided*. Even the law on duress or induced mistake is consistent with this, as long as the focus is ultimately on the effect on the transferor rather than on the nature of the transferee's wrongdoing. Further, *restitution for wrongs* is distinct from autonomous unjust enrichment and constitutes a remedial response to events which lie outside the substantive law of restitution.

The one exception to the plaintiff-sided analysis within subtractive or autonomous unjust enrichment is free acceptance, a *defendant-sided* factor. The issue is the defendant's state of mind at the time of receipt. It is also unique in Professor Birks's scheme in being bivalent: it is capable on a single set of facts of satisfying the requirement that the defendant be *enriched*, and the requirement that his enrichment should be *unjust*. An example was given (Birks, *Introduction*, 265):

> Suppose that I see a window-cleaner beginning to clean the windows of my house. I know that he will expect to be paid. So I hang back unseen till he has finished the job; then I emerge and maintain that I will not pay for work which I never ordered. It is too late. I have freely accepted the service. I had my opportunity to send him away. I chose instead to let him go on. I must pay him the reasonable value of the work.

For the full development of this argument see Birks, *Introduction*, 265–93. There free acceptance is used to explain the pre-contractual liability cases such as *William Lacey (Hounslow) Ltd* v *Davis* [1957] 1 WLR 932 and *Sabemo Pty Ltd* v *North Sydney Municipal Council* [1977] 2 NSWLR 880 (above, Section 3); cases in equity establishing the doctrine of acquiescence such as *Ramsden* v *Dyson* (1866) LR 1 HL 129 and *Willmott* v *Barber* (1880) 15 Ch D 96 (discussed in Chapter 2, Section 4) and various other cases including *Lamb* v *Bunce* (1815) 4 M & S 275, 105 ER 836 and *Weatherby* v *Banham* (1832) 5 C & P 228, 172 ER 950.

In response, Burrows, 'Free Acceptance and the Law of Restitution' (1988) 104 LQR 576, criticised Birks's reliance upon 'free acceptance' as an unjust factor (and also as a test of enrichment) and advanced the important insight that most of the cases relied upon by Goff and Jones and Birks can be explained on other, less controversial grounds. Most importantly, with regard to ineffective contracts, whether discharged by breach or frustration, or void or incomplete, Burrows argued the ground for restitution is usually 'failure of consideration'. In a recent essay Birks accepts many of those points, but still insists on a (now more limited) role for the concept: 'In Defence of Free Acceptance' in Burrows, *Essays*, 105, at 109–27. See finally Burrows, *Restitution*, 315–20.

5 RESTITUTION AND PUBLIC LAW

Section 1: the *Woolwich* case

Restitution and public law have in the post-war period both undergone an intellectual renaissance. In each field half-forgotten or misunderstood legal techniques with curious names, have been rediscovered and developed into a sophisticated, principled legal régime fit for the twenty-first century. In public law the prerogative writs of *certiorari*, *mandamus* and *prohibition* have evolved into the principles governing judicial review of administrative action. So too in restitution *action for money had and received* and *quantum meruit* are giving ground to 'unjust enrichment' and 'incontrovertible benefit'. *Lipkin Gorman* v *Karpnale Ltd* [1991] 2 AC 548 was an important climax. Then, just over a year later, the House of Lords decided *Woolwich Equitable Building Society* v *Inland Revenue Commissioners* [1993] 1 AC 70, in which the two fields of law come together.

The question in *Woolwich* was one of constitutional principle. The basic constituent of the British constitution is the separation of powers (albeit imperfect) between legislature, executive and judiciary. The constitutional settlement we have inherited – and it took the Civil War to establish it – is that there shall be no taxation without the permission of Parliament. This is enshrined in article 4 of the Bill of Rights 1689: 'That levying for or to the use of the Crowne by pretence of prerogative without grant of Parlyament for longer time or in other manner than the same is or shall be granted is illegal'. What, then, if a purported tax is demanded and paid, when in fact the tax was not lawfully due, either because taxing regulations were *ultra vires* the empowering Act, or the statute or regulations were misconstrued or for some other reason. Can the taxpayer have his money back? Two factors, the unique authority and coercive powers of the State, together with the imperative of the principle of legality (or respect for the 'Rule of Law') would seem to favour restitution. This was the view elegantly advocated by Professor Birks, 'Restitution for the Executive: a Tercentenary Footnote to the Bill of Rights' in Finn, *Essays*, 164. Another view, perhaps more consistent with the constitutional theory of Professor Dicey, was that the same principles should govern relationships between individuals and the State as govern relations between citizens *inter se*. It follows that recovery would be available only if one of the usual grounds for restitution (mistake, compulsion) could be established. This was the view of some of the case law and was articulated by Professor Burrows, 'Public Authorities, *Ultra Vires* and Restitution' in Burrows, *Essays*, 39–69. *Woolwich* provided the opportunity for the House of Lords to resolve the controversy.

Woolwich Equitable Building Society v *Inland Revenue Commissioners*

[1989] 1 WLR 137; [1993] 1 AC 70 (CA and HL)

The Inland Revenue decided to bring the way building societies paid the sums representing income tax on the interest payable to their depositors into line with the scheme of payment by banks. Parliament gave its authority by s. 40 of the Finance Act 1984, which empowered the Inland Revenue to make appropriate secondary legislation. The resulting Income Tax (Building Societies) Regulations 1986 (SI 1986 No. 482) included transitional provisions. These transitional arrangements were objected to by Woolwich who claimed that they involved an element of double taxation. Woolwich brought a judicial review of the regulations. In the meantime, fearing adverse publicity, Woolwich paid the sums claimed, but expressly under protest and without prejudice to their rights. The sums paid totalled some £57 million. Woolwich then issued a writ of summons claiming restitution of the money and interest thereon. On 31 July 1987, Nolan J decided the regulations were *ultra vires* as alleged (*R* v *Inland Revenue Commissioners, ex parte Woolwich Equitable Building Society* [1987] STC 654, affd [1990] 1 WLR 1400 (HL)). The Revenue repaid the money with interest from 31 July 1987. They refused to pay interest for the period prior to Nolan J's judgment. Woolwich's claim to interest for the earlier period under s. 35A of the Supreme Court Act 1981, being some £6.73 million, depended upon whether it had a cause of action to recover the money as a debt from the date upon which it was received by the Revenue. The claim for interest was also heard before Nolan J who rejected it. The Court of Appeal by a majority allowed Woolwich's appeal. *Held* by the House of Lords, by a majority of 3:2, that Woolwich was entitled to restitution, and therefore interest, as of right.

LORD KEITH OF KINKEL (dissenting): . . . The argument for Woolwich starts with the general principle enunciated by Lord Wright in *Fibrosa Spolka Akcyjna* v *Fairbairn Lawson Combe Barbour Ltd* [1943] AC 32, 61:

> The claim was for money paid for a consideration which had failed. It is clear that any civilised system of law is bound to provide remedies for cases of what has been called unjust enrichment or unjust benefit, that is to prevent a man from retaining

> the money of or some benefit derived from another which it is against conscience that he should keep. Such remedies in English law are generically different from remedies in contract or in tort, and are now recognised to fall within a third category of the common law which has been called quasi-contract or restitution.

This general principle has however been circumscribed in various ways by decided cases, not least by the rule that money under a mistake of law is not recoverable, a rule which, though heavily criticised in academic writings and elsewhere, is in my opinion too deeply embedded in English jurisprudence to be uprooted judicially. There is a considerable tract of authority, both in England and in other jurisdictions, which must be examined in order to ascertain whether or not the circumstances of the present case fall within Lord Wright's principle. The earliest case is *Newdigate* v *Davy* (1936) 1 Ld Raym 742, where before the revolution of 1688 the plaintiff had sentence from James II's High Commissioners to pay a sum of money to the defendant and did pay it. After the revolution the plaintiff succeeded in recovering the money on the ground of indebitatus assumpsit. Leaving aside the political implications, the circumstances that the money was paid under the sentence of a court, albeit one that was held to have no jurisdiction, gives the case a flavour of duress, so that it is not a significant authority in Woolwich's favour. Then in *Campbell* v *Hall* (1774) 1 Cowp 204 the plaintiff brought a successful action against the King's Collector to recover duty which he had paid upon sugar exported from the island of Grenada. The question principally debated was whether the duty had been validly imposed by the Sovereign though not consented to by the British Parliament or the local Assembly, and this question was answered in the negative. The nature of the action was thus stated by Lord Mansfield, at p. 205:

> The action is an action for money had and received; and it is brought upon this ground; namely, that the money was paid to the defendant without any consideration; the duty, for which, and in respect of which he received it, not having been imposed by lawful or sufficient authority to warrant the same.

The judgment does not, however, contain any examination of this ground, there being no opposition on the part of the Crown to the duty being recoverable in the event of its being invalid. So no weight can, in my opinion, be attached to the decision.

[Lord Keith then surveyed English and Scottish authorities culminating with *South of Scotland Electricity Board* v *British Oxygen Co. Ltd* [1959] 1 WLR 587 and concluded:]

The foregoing review of the native authorities satisfies me that they afford no support for Woolwich's major proposition. The principle to be derived from them, in my opinion, is that payments not lawfully due cannot be recovered unless they were made as a result of some improper form of pressure. Such pressure may take the form of duress, as in *Maskell* v *Horner* [1915] 3 KB 106. It may alternatively take the form of withholding or threatening to withhold the performance of some public duty or the rendering of some public service unless a payment is made which is not lawfully due or is greater than that which is lawfully due, as was the position in the colore officii cases. The mere fact that the payment has been made in response to a demand by a public authority does not emerge in any of the cases as constituting or forming part of the ratio decidendi. Many of the cases appear to turn upon a consideration of whether the payment was voluntary or involuntary. In my opinion that simply involves that the payment was voluntary if no improper pressure was brought to bear, and involuntary if it was. In the present case no pressure to pay was put upon Woolwich by the revenue. Woolwich paid because it calculated that it was in its commercial interest to do so. It could have resisted payment, and the revenue had no means other than the taking of legal proceedings which it might have used to enforce payment. The threat of legal proceedings is not improper pressure. There was no improper pressure by the revenue and in particular there was no duress.

To give effect to Woolwich's proposition would, in my opinion, amount to a very far reaching exercise of judicial legislation. That would be particularly inappropriate having regard to the considerable number of instances which exist of Parliament having legislated in various fields to define the circumstances under which payments of tax not lawfully due may be recovered, and also in what situations and upon what terms interest on overpayments of tax may be paid. Particular instances are section 33 of Taxes Management Act 1970 as regards overpaid income tax, corporation tax, capital gains tax and petroleum revenue tax; section 24 of the Finance Act 1989 as regards value added tax; section 29 of the Finance Act 1989 as regards excise duty and car tax; section 241 of the Capital Transfer Tax Act 1984 as regards inheritance tax; and section 13(4) of the Stamp Act 1891 (54 & 55 Vict. c. 39) as regards stamp duty. Mention may also be made of section 9 of the General Rate Act 1967 which, as described above was, considered by this House in *Reg.* v *Tower Hamlets London Borough Council, Ex parte Chetnik Developments Ltd* [1988] AC 858. It is to be noted that the section only applies where overpayment of rates is not otherwise recoverable, and it plainly did not occur to the House in that case that the overpayment might be recoverable apart from the section. It seems to me that formulation of the precise grounds upon which overpayments of tax ought to be recoverable and of any exceptions to the right of recovery, may involve nice considerations of policy which are properly the province of Parliament and are not suitable for consideration by the courts. In this connection the question of possible disruption of public finances must obviously be a very material one. Then it is noticeable that existing legislation is restrictive of the extent to which interest on overpaid tax (described as 'repayment supplement') may be recovered. A general right of recovery of overpaid tax could not incorporate any such restriction.

I would add that although in the course of argument some distinction was sought to be drawn between overpayment of tax under regulations later shown to be ultra vires and overpayment due to the erroneous interpretation of a statute, no such distinction can, in my view, properly be drawn. The distinction had particular reference to article 4 of the Bill of Rights 1688 (1 Will. & Mary, sess. 2, c. 2), but I do not consider that this article has any relevance to the present case, being concerned, as it was, with the denial of the right of the executive to levy taxes without the consent of Parliament. . . .

LORD GOFF OF CHIEVELEY: . . . There can be no doubt that this appeal is one of considerable importance. It is certainly of importance to both parties—to the revenue, which is concerned to maintain the traditional position under which the repayment of overpaid tax is essentially a matter for its own discretion; and to Woolwich, which adopted a courageous and independent stance about the lawfulness of the underlying regulations, and now adopts a similar stance about the obligation of the revenue to repay tax exacted without lawful authority. In addition, of course, there is a substantial sum of money at stake. But the appeal is also of importance for the future of the law of restitution, since the decision of your Lordships' House could have a profound effect upon the structure of this part of our law. It is a reflection of this fact that there have been cited to your Lordships not only the full range of English authorities, and also authorities from Commonwealth countries and the United States of America, but in addition a number of academic works of considerable importance. These include a most valuable Consultation Paper (Law Com. No. 120) published last year by the Law Commission, entitled 'Restitution of Payments Made Under A Mistake of Law,' for which we owe much to Mr Jack Beatson and also, I understand, to Dr Sue Arrowsmith; and a series of articles by academic lawyers of distinction working in the field of restitution. I shall be referring to this academic material in due course. But I wish to record at once that, in my opinion, it is of such importance that it has a powerful bearing upon the consideration by your Lordships of the central question in the case.

My first task must be to review the relevant authorities. I am very conscious, however, that this task has already been performed in considerable detail, not only by Ralph Gibson and Glidewell LJJ in the Court of Appeal, but also by my noble and learned friends, Lord Keith of Kinkel and Lord Jauncey of Tullichettle. Rather than once again review the authorities in chronological order, therefore, I propose to encapsulate their effect in a number of propositions which can, I believe, be so stated as to reflect the law as it is presently understood with a reasonable degree of accuracy. The law as so stated has, I think, been so understood for most of this century, at least at the level of the Court of Appeal; but it has been the subject of increasing criticism by academic lawyers, and has been departed from in significant respects in some Commonwealth countries, both by legislation and by judicial development of the law. A central question in the present case is whether it is open to your Lordships' House to follow their judicial brethren overseas down the road of development of the law; and, if so, whether it would be appropriate to do so, and which is the precise path which it would then be appropriate to choose. But the answers to these fundamental questions must follow a review of the law as understood at present, which I would express in the following propositions.

(1) Whereas money paid under a mistake of fact is generally recoverable, as a general rule money is not recoverable on the ground that it was paid under a mistake of law. This principle was established in *Bilbie* v *Lumley* (1802) 2 East 469. It has however been the subject of much criticism, which has grown substantially during the second half of the present century. The principle had been adopted in most, if not all, Commonwealth countries; though in some it has now been modified or abandoned, either by statute or by judicial action. No such principle applies in civil law countries, and its adoption by the common law has been criticised by comparative lawyers as unnecessary and anomalous. This topic is the subject of the Consultation Paper No. 120 published by the Law Commission last year, in which serious criticisms of the rule of non-recovery are rehearsed and developed, and proposals for its abolition are put forward for discussion.

(2) But money paid under compulsion may be recoverable. In particular: (a) money paid as a result of actual or threatened duress to the person, or actual or threatened seizure of a person's goods, is recoverable. For an example of the latter, see *Maskell* v *Horner* [1915] 3 KB 106. Since these forms of compulsion are not directly relevant for present purposes, it is unnecessary to elaborate them; but I think it pertinent to observe that the concept of duress has in recent years been expanded to embrace economic duress.

(b) Money paid to a person in a public or quasi-public position to obtain the performance by him of a duty which he is bound to perform for nothing or for less than the sum demanded by him is recoverable to the extent that he is not entitled to it. Such payments are often described as having been demanded colore officii. There is much abstruse learning on the subject (see, in particular, the illuminating discussion by Windeyer J in *Mason* v *New South Wales*, 102 CLR 108, 139–142), but for present purposes it is not, I think, necessary for us to concern ourselves with this point of classification. Examples of influential early cases are *Morgan* v *Palmer*, 2 B & C 729 and *Steele* v *Williams*, 8 Ex 625; a later example of some significance is *T. and J. Brocklebank Ltd* v *The King* [1925] 1 KB 52.

(c) Money paid to a person for the performance of a statutory duty, which he is bound to perform for a sum less than that charged by him, is also recoverable to the extent of the overcharge. A leading example of such a case is *Great Western Railway Co.* v *Sutton*, LR 4 HL 226; for a more recent Scottish case, also the subject of an appeal to this House, see *South of Scotland Electricity Board* v *British Oxygen Co. Ltd* [1959] 1 WLR 587.

(d) In cases of compulsion, a threat which constitutes the compulsion may be expressed or implied, a point perhaps overlooked in *Twyford* v *Manchester Corporation* [1946] Ch 236.

(e) I would not think it right, especially bearing in mind the development of the concept of economic duress, to regard the categories of compulsion for present purposes as closed.

(3) Where a sum has been paid which is not due, but it has not been paid under a mistake of fact or under compulsion as explained under (2) above, it is generally not recoverable. Such a payment has often been called a voluntary payment. In particular, a payment is regarded as a voluntary payment and so as irrecoverable in the following circumstances.

(a) The money has been paid under a mistake of law: see (1) above. See e.g., *Slater* v *Burnley Corporation*, 59 LT 636 and *National Pari-Mutuel Association Ltd* v *The King*, 47 TLR 110.

(b) The payer has the opportunity of contesting his liability in proceedings, but instead gives way and pays: see e.g., *Henderson* v *Folkestone Waterworks Co.* (1885) 1 TLR 329, and *Sargood Brothers* v *The Commonwealth*, 11 CLR 258, especially at p. 301, *per* Isaacs J. So where money has been paid under pressure of actual or threatened legal proceedings for its recovery, the payer cannot say that for that reason the money has been paid under compulsion and is therefore recoverable by him. If he chooses to give way and pay, rather than obtain the decision of the court on the question whether the money is due, his payment is regarded as voluntary and so is not recoverable: see e.g., *William Whiteley Ltd* v *The King*, 101 LT 741.

(c) The money has otherwise been paid in such circumstances that the payment was made to close the transaction. Such would obviously be so in the case of a binding compromise; but even where there is no consideration for the payment, it may have been made to close the transaction and so be irrecoverable. Such a payment has been treated as a gift: see *Maskell* v *Horner* [1915] 3 KB 106, 118, *per* Lord Reading CJ.

(4) A payment may be made on such terms that it has been agreed, expressly or impliedly, by the recipient that, if it shall prove not to have been due, it will be repaid by him. In that event, of course, the money will be repayable. Such was held to be the case in *Sebel Products Ltd* v *Customs and Excise Commissioners* [1949] Ch 409 (although the legal basis upon which Vaisey J there inferred the existence of such an agreement may be open to criticism). On the other hand, the mere fact that money is paid under protest will not give rise of itself to the inference of such an agreement; though it may form part of the evidence from which it may be inferred that the payee did not intend to close the transaction: see *Maskell* v *Horner* [1915] 3 KB 106, 120, *per* Lord Reading CJ.

The principles which I have just stated had come to be broadly accepted, at the level of the Court of Appeal, at least by the early part of this century. But a formidable argument has been developed in recent years by leading academic lawyers that this system of authority should be the subject of reinterpretation to reveal a different line of thought pointing to the conclusion that money paid to a public authority pursuant to an ultra vires demand should be repayable, without the necessity of establishing compulsion, on the simple ground that there was no consideration for the payment. I refer in particular to the powerful essay by Professor Peter Birks (in the volume *Essays in Restitution* (1990), edited by Professor Finn, at pp. 164 et seq.) entitled 'Restitution from the Executive: a Tercentenary Footnote to the Bill of Rights.' I have little doubt that this essay by Professor Birks, which was foreshadowed by an influential lecture delivered by Professor W. R. Cornish in Kuala Lumpur in 1986 (the first Sultan Azlan Shah Law Lecture (1987) J Mal & Comp L 41), provided the main inspiration for the argument of Woolwich, and the judgments of the majority of the Court of Appeal, in the present case. . . .

I now turn to the submission of Woolwich that your Lordships' House should, despite the authorities to which I have referred, reformulate the law so as to establish that the subject who makes a payment in response to an unlawful demand of tax acquires forthwith a prima facie right in restitution to the repayment of the money. This is the real point which lies at the heart of the present appeal; in a sense, everything which I have said so far has done no more than set the stage for its consideration.

The justice underlying Woolwich's submission is, I consider, plain to see. Take the present case. The revenue has made an unlawful demand for tax. The taxpayer is convinced that the demand is unlawful, and has to decide what to do. It is faced with the revenue, armed with the coercive power of the state, including what is in practice a power to charge interest which is penal in its effect. In addition, being a reputable society which alone among building societies is challenging the lawfulness of the demand, it understandably fears damage to its reputation if it does not pay. So it decides to pay first, asserting that it will challenge the lawfulness of the demand in litigation. Now, Woolwich having won that litigation, the revenue asserts that it was never under any obligation to repay the money, and that it in fact repaid it only as a matter of grace. There being no applicable statute to regulate the position, the revenue has to maintain this position at common law.

Stated in this stark form, the revenue's position appears to me, as a matter of common justice, to be unsustainable; and the injustice is rendered worse by the fact that it involves, as Nolan J pointed out [1989] 1 WLR 137, 140, the revenue having the benefit of a massive interest-free loan as the fruit of its unlawful action. I turn then from the particular to the general. Take any tax or duty paid by the citizen pursuant to an unlawful demand. Common justice seems to require that tax to be repaid, unless special circumstances or some principle of policy require otherwise; prima facie, the taxpayer should be entitled to repayment as of right.

To the simple call of justice, there are a number of possible objections. The first is to be found in the structure of our law of restitution, as it developed during the 19th and early 20th centuries. That law might have developed so as to recognise a condictio indebiti—an action for the recovery of money on the ground that it was not due. But it did not do so. Instead, as we have seen, there developed common law actions for the recovery of money paid under a mistake of fact, and under certain forms of compulsion. What is now being sought is, in a sense, a reversal of that development, in a particular type of case; and it is said that it is too late to take that step. To that objection, however, there are two answers. The first is that the retention by the state of taxes unlawfully exacted is particularly obnoxious, because it is one of the most fundamental principles of our law—enshrined in a famous constitutional document, the Bill of Rights 1688—that taxes should not be levied without the authority of Parliament; and full effect can only be given to that principle if the return of taxes exacted under an unlawful demand can be enforced as a matter of right. The second is that, when the revenue makes a demand for tax, that demand is implicity backed by the coercive powers of the state and may well entail (as in the present case) unpleasant economic and social consequences if the taxpayer does not pay. In any event, it seems strange to penalise the good citizen, whose natural instinct is to trust the revenue and pay taxes when they are demanded of him. The force of this answer is recognised in a much-quoted passage from the judgment of Holmes J in *Atchison, Topeka & Santa Fe Railway Co.* v *O'Connor*, 223 US 280, 285–286, when he said:

> . . . when, as is common, the state has a more summary remedy, such as distress, and the party indicates by protest that he is yielding to what he cannot prevent, courts sometimes perhaps have been a little too slow to recognise the implied duress under which payment is made. But even if the state is driven to an action, if at the same time the citizen is put at a serious disadvantage in the assertion of his legal, in this case of his constitutional, rights, by defence in the suit, justice may require that he should be at liberty to avoid those disadvantages by paying promptly and bringing suit on his side. He is entitled to assert his supposed right on reasonably equal terms.

This particular answer might however point at first sight to a development of the common law concept of compulsion, rather than recognition of the broad principle of justice by which Woolwich contends. This was what in fact occurred in the leading Australian case of *Mason* v *New South Wales*, 102 CLR 108. It is impossible to summarise the effect of that complicated case in a few lines, but in practical terms the High Court of Australia found duress to exist in the possibility that the state might seize the plaintiff's property. A similar tendency to expand the concept of compulsion is to be discovered in the majority judgment of the Supreme Court of Canada in *Eadie* v *Township of Brantford* (1967) 63 DLR (2d) 561 (though events of a more dramatic character have since occurred in that jurisdiction, to which I will refer in a moment). This type of approach has also been advocated by Mr Andrew Burrows in his interesting essay entitled 'Public Authorities, Ultra Vires and Restitution' in *Essays on the Law of Restitution* (1991), edited by Mr Burrows, at pp. 39 et seq. We may expect that in any event the common law principles of compulsion, and indeed of mistake, will continue to develop in the future. But the difficulty with this approach for the present case is that Woolwich was in reality suffering from no mistake at all, so much so that it was prepared to back its conviction that the revenue was acting ultra vires by risking a very substantial amount of money in legal costs in establishing that fact; and, since the possibility of distraint by the revenue was very remote, the concept of compulsion would have to be stretched to the utmost to embrace the circumstances of such a case as this. It is for this reason that Woolwich's alternative claim founded upon compulsion did not loom large in the argument, and is difficult to sustain. In the end, logic appears to demand that the right of recovery should require neither mistake nor compulsion, and that the simple fact that the tax was exacted unlawfully should prima facie be enough to require its repayment.

There is however a second objection to the recognition of such a right of recovery. This is that for your Lordships' House to recognise such a principle would overstep the boundary which we traditionally set for ourselves, separating the legitimate development of the law by the judges from legislation. It was strongly urged by Mr. Glick, in his powerful argument for the revenue, that we would indeed be trespassing beyond that boundary if we were to accept the argument of Woolwich. I feel bound however to say that, although I am well aware of the existence of the boundary, I am never quite sure where to find it. Its position seems to vary from case to case. Indeed, if it were to be as firmly and clearly drawn as some of our mentors would wish, I cannot help feeling that a number of leading cases in your Lordships' House would never have been decided the way they were. For example, the minority view would have prevailed in *Donoghue* v *Stevenson* [1932] AC 562; our modern law of judicial review would have never developed from its old, ineffectual, origins; and *Mareva* injunctions would never have seen the light of day. Much seems to depend upon the circumstances of the particular case. In the present case Mr Glick was fully entitled to, and did, point to practical considerations to reinforce his argument. The first was that a case such as the present was so rare that it could not of itself call for a fundamental reformulation of the underlying principle—a point which I find unimpressive, when I consider that our task is essentially to do justice between the parties in the particular case before us. Second, however, he asserted that, if your Lordships' House were to accept Woolwich's argument, it would be impossible for us to set the appropriate limits to the application of the principle. An unbridled right to recover overpaid taxes and duties subject only to the usual six-year time bar was, he suggested, unacceptable in modern society. Some limits had to be set to such claims; and the selection of such limits, being essentially a matter of policy, was one which the legislature alone is equipped to make.

My reaction to this submission of Mr Glick is to confess (to some extent) and yet to avoid. I agree that there appears to be a widely held view that some limit has to be placed upon the recovery of taxes paid pursuant to an ultra vires demand. I would go further and accept that the armoury of common law defences, such as those which prevent recovery of money paid under a binding compromise or to avoid a threat of litigation, may be either inapposite or inadequate for the purpose; because it is possible to envisage, especially in modern taxation law which tends to be excessively complex, circumstances in which some very substantial sum of money may be held to have been exacted ultra vires from a very large number of taxpayers. It may well therefore be necessary to have recourse to other defences, such as for example short time limits within which such claims have to be advanced. An instructive example of this approach is to be found in German law, in which we find a general right of recovery which is subject to the principle that an administrative act is, even if in fact unlawful, treated as legally effective unless and until it is cancelled, either by the authority itself or by an administrative court. Furthermore a citizen can only enforce the cancellation by making a formal objection within one month of notification; and if that objection is rejected by the authority, the citizen must take legal action within another month. In addition, one citizen cannot benefit from the successful formal objection of another citizen; he must object in due time himself. Such draconian time limits as these may be too strong medicine for our taste; but the example of a general right of recovery subject to strict time limits imposed as a matter of policy is instructive for us as we seek to solve the problem in the present case. . . .

In all the circumstances, I do not consider that Mr Glick's argument, powerful though it is, is persuasive enough to deter me from recognising, in law, the force of the justice underlying Woolwich's case. Furthermore, there are particular reasons which impel me to that conclusion. The first is that this opportunity will never come again. If we do not take it now, it will be gone forever. The second is that I fear that, however compelling the principle of justice may be, it would never be sufficient to persuade a government to propose its legislative recognition by Parliament; caution, otherwise known as the Treasury, would never allow this to happen. The third is that, turning Mr Glick's argument against him, the immediate practical impact of the recognition of the principle will be limited, for (unlike the present case) most cases will continue for the time being to be regulated by the various statutory régimes now in force. The fourth is that, if the principle is to be recognised, this is an almost ideal moment for that recognition to take place. This is because the Law Commission's Consultation Paper is now under active consideration, calling for a fundamental review of the law on this subject, including a fresh look at the various, often inconsistent, statutory règimes under which overpaid taxes and duties either may or must be repaid. The consultation may acquire a greater urgency and sense of purpose if set against the background of a recognised right of recovery at common law. But in addition there is an immediate opportunity for the authorities concerned to reformulate, in collaboration with the Law Commission, the appropriate limits to recovery, on a coherent system of principles suitable for modern society, in terms which can (if it is thought right to do so) embrace the unusual circumstances of the present case. In this way, legislative bounds can be set to the common law principle, as Mr Glick insists that they should. Fifth, it is well established that, if the Crown pays money out of the consolidated fund without authority, such money is ipso facto recoverable if it can be traced: see *Auckland Harbour Board* v *The King* [1924] AC 318. It is true that the claim in such a case can be distinguished as being proprietary in nature. But the comparison with the position of the citizen, on the law as it stands at present, is most unattractive.

There is a sixth reason which favours this conclusion. I refer to the decision of the European Court of Justice, in *Amministrazione delle Finanze dello Stato* v *SpA San Giorgio* (Case 199/82) [1983] ECR 3595, which establishes that a person who pays charges levied by a member state contrary to the rules of Community law is entitled to repayment of the charge, such right being regarded as a consequence of, and an adjunct to, the rights conferred on individuals by the Community provisions prohibiting the relevant charges: see paragraph 12 of the judgment of the court, at p. 3612. The *San Giorgio* case is also of interest for present purposes in that it accepts that Community law does not prevent a national legal system from disallowing repayment of charges where to do so would entail unjust enrichment of the recipient, in particular where the charges have been incorporated into the price of goods and so passed on to the purchaser. I only comment that, at a time when Community law is becoming increasingly important, it would be strange if the right of the citizen to recover overpaid charges were to be more restricted under domestic law than it is under European law.

I would therefore hold that money paid by a citizen to a public authority in the form of taxes or other levies paid pursuant to an ultra vires demand by the authority is prima facie recoverable by the citizen as of right. As at present advised, I incline to the opinion that this principle should extend to embrace cases in which the tax or other levy has been wrongly exacted by the public authority not because the demand was ultra vires but for other reasons, for example because the authority has misconstrued a relevant statute or regulation. It is not however necessary to decide the point in the present case, and in any event cases of this kind are generally the subject of statutory regimes which legislate for the circumstances in which money so paid either must or may be repaid. Nor do I think it necessary to consider for the purposes of the present case to what extent the common law may provide the public authority with a defence to a claim for the repayment of money so paid; though for the reasons I have already given, I do not consider that the principle of recovery should be inapplicable simply because the citizen has paid the money under a mistake of law. It will be a matter for consideration whether the fact that the plaintiff has passed on the tax or levy so that the burden has fallen on another should provide a defence to his claim. Although this is contemplated by the European Court of Justice in the *San Giorgio* case, it is evident from *Air Canada* v *British Columbia*, 59 DLR (4th) 161 that the point is not without its difficulties; and the availability of such a defence may depend upon the nature of the tax or other levy. No doubt matters of this kind will in any event be the subject of consideration during the current consultations with the Law Commission. . . .

LORD BROWNE-WILKINSON: My Lords, in this case your Lordships are all agreed that, as the law at present stands, tax paid under protest in response to an ultra vires demand is not recoverable at common law. The authorities are fully analysed in the speeches of my noble and learned friends, Lord Keith of Kinkel, Lord Jauncey of Tullichettle and Lord Goff of Chieveley, and I agree with those analyses.

The issue which divides your Lordships is whether this House should now reinterpret the principles lying behind the authorities so as to give a right of recovery in such circumstances. On that issue, I agree with my noble and learned friend, Lord Goff of Chieveley, that, for the reasons he gives, it is appropriate to do so.

Although as yet there is in English law no general rule giving the plaintiff a right of recovery from a defendant who has been unjustly enriched at the plaintiff's expense, the concept of unjust enrichment lies at the heart of all the individual instances in which the law does give a right of recovery. As Lord Wright said in *Fibrosa Spolka Akcyjna* v *Fairbairn Lawson Combe Barbour Ltd* [1943] AC 32, 61:

> The claim was for money paid for a consideration which had failed. It is clear that any civilised system of law is bound to provide remedies for cases of what has been called unjust enrichment or unjust benefit, that is to prevent a man from retaining the money of or some benefit derived from another which it is against conscience that he should keep. Such remedies in English law are generically different from remedies in contract or in tort, and are now recognised to fall within a third category of the common law which has been called quasi-contract or restitution.

In the present case, the concept of unjust enrichment suggests that the plaintiffs should have a remedy. The revenue demanded and received payment of the sum by way of tax alleged to be due under regulations subsequently held by your Lordships' House to be ultra vires. The payment was made under protest. Yet the revenue maintains that it was under no legal obligation to repay the wrongly extracted tax and in consequence is not liable to pay interest on the sum held by it between the date it received the money and the date of the order of Nolan J. If the revenue is right, it will be enriched by the interest on money to which it had no right during that period. In my judgment, this is the paradigm of a case of unjust enrichment.

As in so many other fields of English law, the occasions on which recovery is permitted have been built up on a case by case basis. For present purposes there are in my judgment two streams of authority relating to moneys wrongly extracted by way of impost. One stream is founded on the concept that money paid under an ultra vires demand for a tax or other impost has been paid without consideration. The other stream is based on the notion that such payments have been made under compulsion, the relative positions and powers of the two parties being unequal.

The stream based on the concept of payment without consideration stems from what Lord Mansfield said in *Campbell* v *Hall*, 1 Cowp 204 and is reflected in the decision in *Dew* v *Parsons*, 2 B & Ald 562. In *Steele* v *Williams*, 8 Ex 625, 632, Martin B said that the payment in that case was not a voluntary payment but was 'more like the case of money paid without consideration.' In *Queens of the River Steamship Co. Ltd* v *Conservators of the River Thames*, 15 TLR 474, Phillimore J founded his decision on the fact that there was no consideration for the payment. Although this stream seems subsequently to have run into the sand, I find the approach attractive: money paid on the footing that there is a legal demand is paid for a reason that does not exist if that demand is a nullity. There is in my view a close analogy to the right to recover money paid under a contract the consideration for which has wholly failed.

The other stream, based on compulsion, stems from *Morgan* v *Palmer*, 2 B & C 729 and the majority decision in *Steele* v *Williams*. In their inception, these authorities were based on the fact that the payer and payee were not on an equal footing and it was this inequality which gave rise to the right to recovery. However, most of the cases which arose for decision were concerned with payments extracted ultra vires by persons who in virtue of their position could insist on the wrongful payment as a precondition to affording the payer his legal rights i.e. they were payments colore officii. In consequence, the courts came to limit the cases in which recovery of an ultra vires impost was allowed to cases where there had been an extraction colore officii. I can see no reason in principle to have restricted the original wide basis of recovery to this limited class of case. In my judgment, as a matter of principle the colore officii cases are merely examples of a wider principle, viz. that where the parties are on an unequal footing so that money is paid by way of tax or other impost in pursuance of a demand by some public officer, these moneys are recoverable since the citizen is, in practice, unable to resist the payment save at the risk of breaking the law or exposing himself to penalties or other disadvantages. . . .

In cases such as the present both the concept of want of consideration and payment under implied compulsion are in play. The money was demanded and paid for tax, yet no tax was due: there was a payment for no consideration. The money was demanded by the state from the citizen and the inequalities of the parties' respective positions is manifest even in the case of a major financial institution like Woolwich. There are, therefore, in my judgment sound reasons by way of analogy for establishing the law in the sense which Lord Goff proposes. I agree with him that the practical objections to taking this course are not sufficient to prevent this House from establishing the law in accordance with both principle and justice. I, too, therefore would dismiss this appeal.

Questions

1. How would you formulate the ground for restitution relied upon by the majority of the House of Lords?

2. British Gas plc misconstrues the statute which authorises its charges and regulates its prices. As a result thousands of customers are overcharged. Is the *Woolwich* principle applicable?

Notes

1. *Woolwich* has certainly had structural ramifications. The textbooks now have separate chapters on this topic: Burrows, *Restitution*, 345–61; Goff and Jones, 545–53. The case is further discussed by Birks, '"When Money is Paid in Pursuance of a Void Authority . . ." a Duty to Repay?' [1992] PL 580; Beatson, 'Restitution of Taxes, Levies and Other Imposts: Defining the Extent of the *Woolwich* Principle?' (1993) 109 LQR 401, and McKendrick, 'Restitution of Unlawfully Demanded Tax' [1993] LMCLQ 88.

2. The Law Commission, whose Working Paper was referred to by Lord Goff, has now published its Report in the wake of *Woolwich*: *Restitution: Mistake of Law and Ultra Vires Receipts and Payments* (HMSO: Law Com No.

227, 1994). For discussion see Beatson [1995] *Restitution Law Review* 280, at 286–8.
3. On the old *colore officii* cases and the question of whether they have any continuing independent existence after *Woolwich*, see Goff and Jones, 243–50.
4. On the possibility of a defence of 'passing on' see Burrows, *Restitution*, 475–7 and for discussion Rose, 'Passing On' in Birks, *Laundering and Tracing*, 261–87.

Section 2: the 'swaps' cases

Sophisticated modern markets offer a wide range of complex financial products, often termed 'derivatives', such as 'options' and 'futures contracts'. Effectively these allow (enforceable) bets to be made upon a number of future possible events, for example, whether the stock market will go up or down, whether interest rates will rise or fall, the future values of particular currencies, or on the future prices of commodities. Sensibly used, these products enable organisations to 'hedge' risks, by insuring themselves against future market movements. Therefore English travel companies can minimise the risks caused by sharp movements in sterling and thereby avoid the need to surcharge a holiday booked in December one year, but to be taken in July the next. But as the collapse of Britain's oldest merchant bank, Barings, in 1994 illustrated, derivatives, if improperly used or imperfectly understood, can prove catastrophic.

Our particular concern is with attempts by United Kingdom local authorities in the 1980s to circumvent the central Government's restrictions on public expenditure by playing the financial markets. (See generally Loughlin, 'Innovative Financing in Local Government: the Limits of Legal Instrumentalism' [1990] PL 372 and [1991] PL 568.) Fortunately nothing as disastrous as happened in Orange County, California befell Britain's town halls, but the ill-fated exercise has required much expensive legal mopping-up. Here the favoured financial product was 'interest rate swaps'. The mechanics of this type of transaction were described as follows by Lord Templeman in *Hazell* v *Hammersmith and Fulham London Borough Council* [1992] 2 AC 1, at 24:

> an agreement between two parties by which each agrees to pay the other on a specified date or dates an amount calculated by reference to the interest which would have accrued over a given period on the same notional principal sum assuming different rates of interest are payable in each case. For example, one rate may be fixed at 10 per cent, and the other rate may be equivalent to the six month London Inter-bank Offered Rate ('LIBOR'). If the LIBOR rate over the period of the swap is higher than 10 per cent then the party agreeing to receive 'interest' in accordance with LIBOR will receive more than the party entitled to receive 10 per cent. Normally neither party will in fact pay the sums which it has agreed to pay over the period of the swap but instead will make a settlement on a 'net payment basis' under which the party owing the greater amount on any day simply pays the difference between the two amounts due to the other.

The problems arose because the result of the judicial review in *Hazell* was that such transactions were *ultra vires* local authorities, and that the contracts were all void. This threw many established commercial arrangements between local authorities and banks into disarray. Much litigation ensued and it was decided to channel lead cases through a single judge, Hobhouse J in the Queen's Bench Division. These cases will inevitably make a profound contribution to the development of the law of restitution. A number have already been reported, and at least one is on appeal to the House of Lords. Where appropriate these cases have been taken into account in the relevant sections of other chapters of this book. However, it is useful to consider them here together as a sequence.

After *Hazell* came *Kleinwort Benson Ltd* v *Glasgow District Council* [1994] 4 All ER 865, (Hirst J and CA) eventually resolved after a fruitless trip to the ECJ [1996] QB 57, by the CA [1996] 2 All ER 257. This concerned the question of the place of restitutionary obligations in the Brussels Convention on Jurisdictions and Judgments, an aspect of the nascent conflict of law rules on restitution. (See Burrows, *Restitution*, 487–9) Next came two significant cases on the restitutionary cause of action and applicable defences: *Westdeusche Landesbank Girozentrale* v *Islington London Borough Council* [1994] 4 All ER 890 (Hobhouse J and CA), [1994] 1 WLR 938 (CA) (below); and *Kleinwort Benson Ltd* v *South Tyneside Metropolitan Borough Council* [1994] 4 All ER 972 (Hobhouse J) (both noted at first instance by Cowan [1993] LMCLQ 300). Later came *Morgan Grenfell & Co. Ltd* v *Welwyn Hatfield District Council* [1995] 1 All ER 1 (Hobhouse J) (on whether the transactions were illegal gaming contracts), *TSB Bank of Scotland plc* v *Hatfield & Welwyn District Council* (1993) 2 Bank LR 267 (Hobhouse J) (on whether the claim was one in debt or for damages) and *South Tyneside Metropolitan Borough Council* v *Svenska International plc* [1995] 1 All ER 545 (Clarke J) (a valuable new discussion of the defence of change of position extracted in Chapter 8, Section 2). The most significant ruling is that of Hobhouse J in *Westdeusche*, which was affirmed by the Court of Appeal, that the cause of action in restitution was '*no consideration*'. This was based in part upon the speeches of Lord Goff and Lord Browne-Wilkinson in *Woolwich* (extracted in Section 1 above) and in part upon an old line of half-forgotten cases about void annuities in the eighteenth and nineteenth centuries.

Westdeusche Landesbank Girozentrale v *Islington London Borough Council*

[1994] 1 WLR 938 (CA); [1994] 4 All ER 890 (Hobhouse J and CA)

Action for money had and recieved; resulting trust

The council and the bank entered into a 10-year interest rate swap agreement commencing on 18 June 1987, based upon a notional principal sum of £25 million. The bank was to be the fixed ratepayer and the council was to be the floating rate payer. Additionally, the bank paid the council an up-front premium of £2.5 million. The bank entered a parallel transaction as a floating rate payer with another bank in order to 'hedge' its liabilities. The council paid four 'interest' payments pursuant to its liabilities under the contract, totalling £1,354,474.07. No further payments were made after it was discovered that such transactions were *ultra vires* the council and void. The bank sought restitution and the difference between £2.5 million and £1,354,474.07, namely £1,145,525.93. Hobhouse J awarded restitution of that sum together with compound interest from 1 April 1990.

DILLON LJ: . . . it is the council's case that as the council has made four 'interest' payments to the bank—for the purposes of the argument one payment would have been enough—the bank can recover nothing and the council can keep the £1,145,525.93. I find such conclusion repugnant to common sense.

The council's case is, in effect, that common sense or fairness do not come into it because the categories of case in which money can be recovered in quasi-contract as money had and received or on grounds of unjust enrichment have been laid down long ago and the only recognised category which the bank can hope to invoke is that of 'money paid for a consideration which has wholly failed.'

That is of course, a well known category for cases in which the full amount of money paid by one party to a contract or intended contract can be recovered. It applies not merely where the supposed contract has for some reason been void, or was voidable and has been rescinded, but also where there was a valid contract, but there has been a fundamental breach by the other party and so the payer can get his money back instead of merely having to claim damages. It is clear from *Fibrosa Spolka Akcyjna* v *Fairbairn Lawson Combe Barbour Ltd* [1943] AC 32, a case of frustration, that by 'the consideration has wholly failed' is meant that the performance promised has not been provided.

Thus it is said for the council that the performance promised by the council to the bank has in part been satisfied or provided because the council has made the four 'interest' payments to the bank—and one would have been enough—and so the consideration has not wholly failed and so the bank cannot recover the balance of the £2.5m.

The judge held that the balance fell to be repaid on the different ground that, as the swap transaction and the agreement for it were ultra vires and void, there was no consideration for the payment of the £2.5m. by the bank to the council and so, as the bank never intended to make a gift of the money to the council, the money was recoverable as money paid for no consideration.

That is an approach recently developed by the House of Lords in *Woolwich Equitable Building Society* v *Inland Revenue Commissioners* (1993] AC 70. That case concerned a claim by the building society to recover from the revenue money paid to the revenue under protest by the building society which had asserted throughout that the regulation under which the money was claimed by the revenue was ultra vires. Lord Goff of Chieveley referred, at p. 166c, to reinterpretation to reveal a different line of thought pointing to the conclusion that money paid to a public authority pursuant to an ulta vires demand should be repayable, without the necessity of establishing compulsion, on the simple ground that there was no consideration for the payment. In relation to a decision of Lord Mansfield in *Campbell* v *Hall* (1774) 1 Cowp 204, he said, at p. 166g, that 'the simple fact remains that recovery was stated to be founded upon absence of consideration for the payment.' Lord Browne-Wilkinson dealt with the same argument in the *Woolwich* case, at p. 197:

> As in so many other fields of English law, the occasions on which recovery is permitted have been built up on a case by case basis. For present purposes there

are in my judgment two streams of authority relating to moneys wrongly extracted by way of impost. One stream is founded on the concept that money paid under an ultra vires demand for a tax or other impost has been paid without consideration. The other stream is based on the notion that such payments have been made under compulsion, the relative positions and powers of the two parties being unequal. The stream based on the concept of payment without consideration stems from what Lord Mansfield said in *Campbell* v *Hall*, 1 Cowp. 204 and is reflected in the decision in *Dew* v *Parsons* (1819) 2 B & Ald 562. In *Steele* v *Williams* (1853) 8 Ex 625, 632, Martin B said that the payment in that case was not a voluntary payment but was 'more like the case of money paid without consideration.' In *Queens of the River Steamship Co. Ltd* v *Conservators of the River Thames* (1899) 15 TLR 474, Phillimore J founded his decision on the fact that there was no consideration for the payment. Although this stream seems subsequently to have run into the sand, I find the approach attractive: money paid on the footing that there is a legal demand is paid for a reason that does not exist if that demand is a nullity. There is in my view a close analogy to the right to recover money paid under a contract the consideration for which has wholly failed.

The same concept, that a payment can be recovered if there was no consideration for the payment, seems to have been relied on by Robert Goff J in *Barclays Bank Ltd* v *W. J. Simms, Son & Cooke (Southern) Ltd* [1980] QB 677. In that case the bank had honoured its customer's cheque in favour of the defendant, but had done so under a mistake of fact, forgetting that the customer had cancelled its mandate to honour the cheque. It was held that the bank could recover the amount of the cheque from the defendant, because the payment without mandate was not effective to discharge the drawer's obligation on the cheque and—as I understand the case—the payee therefore gave no consideration for the payment.

The *Woolwich* case [1993] AC 70 and *Barclays Bank Ltd* v *W. J. Simms Son & Cooke (Southern) Ltd* [1980] QB 677 were both cases in which it would be more accurate to say that there had been no consideration for the payment than to say that the consideration had wholly failed; the transactions in issue did not obviously involve any consideration or performance, moving from the payee to the plaintiff, in the sense of the phrase 'the consideration has wholly failed.'

In the *Fibrosa* case [1943] AC 32, 64–65 Lord Wright, in referring to the concept that the consideration has wholly failed, spoke of where 'the consideration, if entire, has entirely failed, or where, if it is severable, it has entirely failed as to the severable residue, as in *Rugg* v *Minett* (1809) 11 East 210.' *Rugg* v *Minett* is also referred to by Viscount Simon LC [1943] AC 32, 48, as an instructive decision. Lord Atkin described it, at p. 52, as being a case where the buyer had paid part of the purchase price on a sale of turpentine in casks, where the property in some casks had passed while in the seller's warehouse but some had not (because the casks had not yet been filled) and the purchaser was entitled to recover as money had and received the proportion properly attributable to the casks in which the property had not passed when they were destroyed by fire. Lord Simon's account indicates that the plaintiff's payment in advance had been a sum of money on account of his purchases generally. Plainly there had been no total failure of consideration in respect of the whole of the payment in advance on account of the purchases generally, since the title to the casks which had been filled had passed to the plaintiff. But the court severed the consideration and held that the part attributable to the casks which had not been filled had wholly failed.

Mr Philipson contends that the true interpretation of *Rugg* v *Minett*, 11 East 210 is that the plaintiff had brought separately a number of lots of casks, sold separately at an auction sale, and that he recovered his payments in respect of those lots separately purchased which were destroyed by the fire before they were filled because they had been bought by separate bids and thus separate contracts at the auction. That was not how the case was interpreted by the House of Lords, nor, as I read the report, is it the basis on which the judges who heard the case decided it.

I do not see why a similar process of severance should not be applied where what has happened, in a purely financial matter, is that there has been a payment of money one way and a payment of smaller sums of money the other way. The effect of severance is that there has been a total failure of consideration in respect of the balance of the money which has not come back.

Severance apart, however, to hold that as the interest swap transaction and contract were ultra vires and void there was no consideration for the payment by the bank of the £2·5m and therefore the balance which has not so far been repaid by the council can be recovered by the bank in quasi contract as money had and received or on the grounds of unjust enrichment is warranted by early cases decided under the Annuities Act 1777 (17 Geo. 3, c. 26).

It appears that before that Act was enacted a practice had developed whereby a person desiring to raise money would grant—i.e., sell—an annuity to a grantee in consideration of a capital sum paid to the grantor by the grantee. The Act of 1777 imposed various restrictions on such transactions, including a requirement that a memorial of the document which granted the annuity, containing prescribed details, must be inrolled in the Court of Chancery within 20 days of execution of the document. In default of compliance the document was to be 'null and void to all intents and purposes.'

As a result of the Act of 1777 there were a number of cases and the law was established that if there had been non-compliance the grantor was entitled to have the annuity set aside, but the grantee was entitled to have his capital premium repaid to him with interest, subject to giving credit for the instalments of the annuity which he had received.

In *Hicks* v *Hicks* (1802) 3 East 16, the action was brought by the plaintiff for money had and received to recover the consideration money paid many years ago for an annuity granted by the defendant to the plaintiff which had been paid for several years but had been recently set aside by the court on the application of the defendant for a defect in the memorial of registry. The defendant claimed to set off the payments of the annuity which the plaintiff had received. Lord Ellenborough CJ upheld that claim. He said, at p. 17:

> This was either an annuity or not an annuity. If not an annuity, the sums paid on either side were money had and received by the one party to the other's use. If the consideration of the annuity be money had and received, it must be money had and received with all its consequences; and therefore the defendant must be at liberty to set off his payments as such, on the same score.

What Lord Ellenborough CJ there said was applied by Sir William Grant MR in *Holbrook* v *Sharpey* (1812) 19 VesJun 131. Grant MR also said, at p. 132:

> Either all the payments, made under a void annuity deed, must be considered as purely voluntary, in which case none of them could be recovered back: or they are all money had and received to the use of the grantor, and therefore to be all returned or accounted for.

The payments were not to be considered as purely voluntary because they had been intended to be made for the consideration expressed in the annuity deed. That is equally the case with the payments each way in the present case. Neither party intended to make a gift to the other.

In *Lipkin Gorman* v *Karpnale Ltd* [1991] 2 AC 548, 564 Lord Templeman approved another statement by Lord Ellenborough CJ, in *Hudson* v *Robinson* (1816) 4 M & S 475, 478 that 'an action for money had and received is maintainable wherever the money of one man has, without consideration, got into the pocket of another.'

It must follow, in my judgment, on the authorities referred to, that the bank is entitled to recover the balance of the £2·5m from the council as money had and received, or, as it is now called, as Lord Goff of Chieveley pointed out in *Lipkin Gorman* [1991] 2 AC 548, 572, unjust enrichment at the expense of the owner of the money. It is unnecessary to explore in this case what intricacies there may be in applying the concept of 'money paid for a consideration which has wholly failed' in other cases where the consideration for a payment of money is something other than the payment of other money and is not severable.

The same result can be achieved on equitable, as opposed to common law, grounds. Since, contrary to the expectation of the parties, the swap transaction and contract are, and were from the outset, ultra vires and void, the purpose for which the £2·5m was paid by the bank to the council has wholly failed, and the £2·5m has, from the time the council received it, been held on a resulting trust for the bank: see the speech of Viscount Haldane LC in *Sinclair* v *Brougham* [1914] AC 398, 418 where he referred to the claim of the depositors in the ultra vires banking business of the Birbeck Building Society as 'a claim to . . . recover property with which, in equity at all events, they had never really parted.' He further stated, at pp. 420–421:

> The Court of Chancery could and would declare, even as against the general creditors of the wrongdoer, that there was what it called a charge on the banker's debt to the person whose money had been paid into the latter's bank account in favour of the person whose money it really was. . . . It was, as I think, merely an additional right, which could be enforced by the Court of Chancery in the exercise of its auxiliary jurisdiction, wherever money was held to belong in equity to the plaintiff.

Sinclair v *Brougham* was, so far as is relevant for present purposes, summed up by Lord Greene MR in *In re Diplock* [1948] Ch 465, 540–541, as follows:

> There, a sufficient fiduciary relationship was found to exist between the depositors and the directors by reason of the fact that the purposes for which the depositors had handed their money to the directors were by law incapable of fulfilment.

So interpreted, *Sinclair* v *Brougham* [1914] AC 398 is a direct parallel to the present case. Thus in equity also the bank is entitled to the return of the balance of the £2·5m. . . .

LEGGATT LJ: . . .

Unjust enrichment

The parties believed that they were making an interest swaps contract. They were not, because such a contract was ultra vires the council. So they made no contract at all. The council say that they should receive a windfall, because the purpose of the doctrine of ultra vires is to protect council taxpayers whereas restitution would disrupt the council's finances. They also contended that it would countenance 'unconsidered dealings with local authorities.' If that is the best that can be said for refusing restitution, the sooner it is enforced the better. Protection of council taxpayers from loss is to be distinguished from securing a windfall for them. The disruption of the council's finances is the result of ill-considered financial dispositions by the council and its officers. It is not the policy of the law to require others to deal at their peril with local authorities, nor to require others to undertake their own inquiries about whether a local authority has power to make particular contracts or types of contract. Any system of law, and indeed any system of fair dealing, must be expected to ensure that the council do not profit by the fortuity that when it became known that the contract was ineffective the balance stood in their favour. In other words, in circumstances such as these they should not be unjustly enriched.

It is common ground that the interest swaps and the council's payments were ultra vires the council, and that the contract was therefore void ab initio; that there was no illegality involved; and that the legal property in the money which was paid by the parties to each other under the swap contract passed to the recipient.

Where A has in his possession the money of B under a void transaction, B should be entitled to reimbursement unless some principle of law precludes it. If the transaction was a contract, initially valid, the question will arise whether it has been partially performed. If so, the failure of consideration will not be total. But if the transaction was entered into by both parties in the belief, which proves unfounded, that it was an enforceable contract, in principle the parties ought to be restored to the respective positions from which they started. To achieve that, where there have been mutual payments, the recipient of the larger payment has only to repay the net excess over the payment he has himself made.

The trial judge said (1993) 91 LGR 323, 367:

> In my judgment the correct analysis is that any payments made under a contract which is void ab initio, in the way that an ultra vires contract is void, are not contractual payments at all. They are payments in which the legal property in the money passes to the recipient but in equity the property in the money remains with the payer. The recipient holds the money as a fiduciary for the payer and is bound to recognise his equity and repay the money to him. This relationship and the consequent obligation have been recognised both by courts applying the common law and by Chancery courts. The principle is the same in both courts: it is unconscionable that the recipient should retain the money. Neither mistake nor the contractual principle of total failure of consideration are the basis for the right of recovery.

In my judgment that formulation is wholly accurate, provided that the contract in question is not a borrowing contract. If it were a borrowing contract, it would fall foul, as the judge recognised, of the principle in *Sinclair* v *Brougham* [1914] AC 398 that restitution will not be ordered where to do so would have the effect of enforcing a void contract. That is not the case here. In relation to a contract other than a borrowing contract the effect of restitution is to put the payer into the position in which he would have been if the transaction had never been entered into.

The judge's conclusion was supported, as he found and as Dillon LJ has demonstrated, by the annuity cases. There have been other manifestations of the principle, culminating in *Woolwich Equitable Building Society* v *Inland Revenue Commissioners* [1993] AC 70, although the decision in that case could be treated as confined to cases of money paid pursuant to an unlawful demand by a public authority which is thereby unjustly enriched. But the principle for which the bank contends has been exemplified in *North Central Wagon Finance Co. Ltd* v *Brailsford* [1962] 1 WLR 1288, in which Cairns J held money paid on a bill of sale which was void for non-registration to be recoverable as money had and received after giving proper credits. In *Rowland* v *Divall* [1923] 2 KB 500 the buyer of a car, who had used it for several months, was held entitled, when the seller proved to have had no title to it, to sue for the price paid as money had and received, because the buyer had received no part of what he contracted to receive, namely, the property and right to possession. In *Rover International Ltd* v *Cannon Film Sales Ltd* [1989] 1 WLR 912, 923 Kerr LJ expressed the test as being 'whether or not the party claiming total failure of consideration has in fact received any part of the benefit bargained for under the contract or purported contract.' That seems to me to be the test to apply here.

As the bank submitted, the fact that the payer had received a benefit did not mean that there had been no total failure of consideration, if the payer did not get the benefit for which he bargained. What in this case the bank bargained for were payments which would discharge a contractual obligation and which the bank was entitled lawfully to receive. What it obtained were payments made under a void agreement which in equity remained the property of the council and which even at law it was always entitled to recover back.

The council criticise that formulation as artificial, contending that if the formulation of counsel for the bank in the court below, which appears to have been endorsed by Hobhouse J was that the council must also show absence of consideration, then the argument is circular. The payments by the bank were tainted by 'absence of consideration' because it received payments from the council which were recoverable because the council received payments from the bank which were recoverable by the bank, and so on. The council argued that the bank here did not bargain for the right to receive repayment of its payment to the council. No doubt it hoped to do so. It bargained for participation in a series of risks on specified days in the future on each of which the prevailing LIBOR would be compared with 7·5 per cent and, if the risk favoured the bank, a payment would be made by the council, and vice versa. It bargained for the risk-taking twice a year for 10 years. It got two years. There was no total failure of consideration, only partial. It was so held by Hobhouse J.

There can have been no consideration under a contract void ab initio. So it is fallacious to speak of the failure of consideration having been partial. What is meant is that the parties did, in the belief that the contract was enforceable, part of what they would have been required to do if it had been. As it was, they were not performing the contract even in part: they were making payments that had no legal justification, instead of affording each other mutual consideration for an enforceable contract. In my judgment the payments made are in those circumstances recoverable by the bank, in so far as they exceed the payments made by the council, as money had and received to the use of the bank, by which the council have been unjustly enriched.

The proprietary claim in equity

All of the components of the bank's claim in equity were viewed in a sense favourable to the bank by the House of Lords in *Sinclair* v *Brougham* [1914] AC 398 with the result that: (1) in equity the money remained the property of the bank; (2) mere receipt by the council of money which was not theirs constituted them fiduciaries; (3) the bank's equitable right in relation to the money in the council's hands which remained the bank's was in the nature of an equitable charge; and (4) since the council are solvent, the bank can recover in full. . . .

Question

What is the relationship between 'no consideration' and established unjust factors such as mistake of fact and total failure of consideration?

Notes

1. The Court of Appeal awarded compound interest as from 18 June 1987 when the initial payment was made, rather than from 1 April 1990 when the council made provision for repayment of the sums it had received as followed by the judge. An appeal is pending before the House of Lords on the question of interest.

2. For discussion see Birks, 'No Consideration: Restitution After Void Contracts' (1993) 23 UWAL Rev 195; Swadling, 'Restitution for No Consideration [1994] *Restitution Law Review* 73; Burrows, 'Swaps and the Friction between Common Law and Equity' [1995] *Restitution Law Review* 15.

6 RESTITUTION AND THE LAW OF WRONGS

Inherent in the need for manageable law school courses and for expository textbooks of a reasonable length is a tendency to see the law in boxes. Contract is a first year subject and tort is a second year subject (or *vice versa*) and never the twain shall meet. However, clients' lives are not so neat. Lawyers need to be aware of the possible existence of distinct causes of action arising on the same facts, and the respective advantages and disadvantages of each type of claim. Here we reach an intersection in the law, which reflects the untidiness of everyday life, between restitution and the law of wrongs. For Professor Birks this is the most important division in the law of restitution. Hitherto we have been dealing with *subtractive* or *autonomous* unjust enrichment where 'at the expense of' means by subtraction from the plaintiff. Here, in *restitution for wrongs*, 'at the expense of' means by a wrong done to the plaintiff. (See Birks, *Introduction*, 313 and contrast Beatson, 'The Nature of Waiver of Tort' (1979) 17 UWOL Rev 1, now updated in Beatson, *Unjust Enrichment*, 206–43.) Another way of putting this is to say that we are no longer concerned with the *substantive* side of restitution, but with its *remedial* side, (Birks, *The Future*, 1–25). In restitution for wrongs the cause of action is established by reference to other legal categories. The Birks bifurcation into subtractive unjust enrichment and restitution for wrongs has been approved of in recent case law: see *Macmillan Inc.* v *Bishopsgate Investment Trust plc (No. 3)* [1995] 3 All ER 747, at 757–8 *per* Millett J (reversed on other grounds: [1996] 1 All ER 585 (CA)) and *Halifax Building Society* v *Thomas* [1995] 4 All ER 673, at 677 *per* Peter Gibson LJ. The question here is: for which wrongs do the courts award restitution as a remedy?

What is a wrong? It is submitted (as a matter of description rather than definition) that it typically has three characteristic elements. First, a wrong consists of some *breach of duty* owed by the defendant to the plaintiff (so our concern is with civil, rather than criminal wrongs, although the same fact situation may yield both civil and criminal liability). Secondly, the law of wrongs characteristically protects some *interest* of the plaintiff, whether in bodily integrity, reputation, property, economic assets or some other interest. Therefore the breach of duty commonly consists of a failure by the defendant to respect the plaintiff's interest, by harming that right or otherwise interfering with the enjoyment of some legally recognised interest. Thirdly, so far as the harm done is compensable, the law's response to the harm done typically consists of the payment of a sum of money termed damages as a remedy.

'Wrongs' is deliberately jurisdictionally neutral. The way the cases have developed forces their separate treatment on the basis of the old division between common law and equity. Section 1 deals with restitution and torts. Section 2 with the controversial question whether there can ever be a 'benefit to the defendant' based liability for breach of contract. Section 3 deals with breach of fiduciary duty. Sections 4 and 5 deal respectively with the emerging equitable wrongs of breach of confidence and dishonest accessory liability. There is a refusal to discuss authorities from the other side of the jurisdictional divide in the cases. This is perpetuated by separate textbooks on 'tort' and 'equity'. Historically the Chancery side has been more likely to award a measure of recovery based on the defendant's gain rather than on the plaintiff's loss. At common law compensation for harm caused is viewed as the normal measure of recovery. Exemplary damages have been marginalised (*Rookes* v *Barnard* [1964] AC 1129 (HL); but see now Law Commission Consultation Paper, *Aggravated, Exemplary and Restitutionary Damages* (HMSO, Law Com. 132, 1993)). In Birks, 'Civil Wrongs – A New World', *Butterworths Lectures 1990–1991* (1992), the common law's supposed traditional 'hegemony of compensation' received a sustained critique. The aim of restitution scholars in this context has been to show that reparation for harm caused need only be one of several devices in the judicial armoury for dealing with a breach of duty by a defendant. See generally Jackman, 'Restitution for Wrongs' [1989] CLJ 302; Burrows, *Restitution*, 376–80 and Law Commission Consultation Paper, *Aggravated, Exemplary and Restitutionary Damages*, 155–72.

Section 1: restitution and torts

The common law's traditional response to civil wrongs has been to award a compensation-based monetary remedy. Sometimes, however, it was possible for a plaintiff to seek a benefit-based measure, by the quaintly (and inaccurately) named device of *waiving the tort*. More recently some awards of damages seem to have reflected the defendant's gain rather than the plaintiff's loss. So when is a restitutionary response appropriate? Traditionally, it would have been asked 'what torts could be waived?' Modern theories seeking to explain restitutionary awards incorporate one or more of three basic strategies. First, some theories consider the nature of the wrong committed or the interest it protects. For example, a benefit-based measure might be considered only for *proprietary* torts, or wrongs which protect 'facilitative institutions' (see the approach of Jackman [1989] CLJ 302). Secondly, consider the nature of the defendant's conduct: was it intentional, cynical or exploitative? Thirdly, it might be asked whether a measure which strips the wrongdoers of the profits resulting from breach is appropriate as a deterrent, to discourage such conduct in future. These considerations are appropriate for all wrongs, not just torts.

See Burrows, *Restitution*, 381–97; Beatson, 'The Nature of Waiver of Tort', *Unjust Enrichment*, 206–43; Hedley, 'The Myth of Waiver of Tort' (1984) 100 LQR 653 and Jackman, 'Restitution for Wrongs' [1989] CLJ 302, at 305–11.

A: *Waiver of tort*

Traditionally the torts which could be waived have a proprietary flavour. For example, conversion or wrongful interference with goods (*Hambly* v *Trott* (1776) 1 Cowp 371; 98 ER 1136; *United Australia Ltd* v *Barclays Bank Ltd* [1941] AC 1; *Chesworth* v *Farrar* [1967] 1 QB 407). However, the device has also been used for non-proprietary torts such as deceit (Goff and Jones, 715). Nevertheless the Court of Appeal in *Halifax Building Society* v *Thomas* [1995] 4 All ER 673, has recently ruled that a building society, which was the victim of a mortgage fraud, had no claim, personal or proprietary, to the surplus funds realised after it had enforced its security. It had elected to affirm the transaction rather than avoid it for deceit. Peter Gibson LJ was not satisfied that the fraudster's enrichment was at the building society's expense even within the extended meaning given to that phrase in the context of restitution for wrongs (at 680). The Court of Appeal was particularly reluctant to extend the common law in the light of Parliament's introduction of confiscation orders (which seize the proceeds of crime for the benefit of the State) in Part VI of the Criminal Justice Act 1988. There was no question here of the fraudster being unjustly enriched. The question was one involving competing claims by the State and the defrauded party. The case is noted by Watts (1996) 112 LQR 219 and Birks (1996) 10 *Trusts Law International* 2.

Many of the older cases arise from attempts to circumvent the old common law rule, now abolished, of *actio personalis moritur cum persona* (a personal action dies with the person). This meant that causes of action in tort did not generally survive against the wrongdoer's estate.

Hambly* v *Trott
(1776) 1 Cowp 371; 98 ER 1136 (KB)

This was an 'action for sheep, goats, pigs, oats and cyder converted by injustice to the use of the person of the deceased'. The question was whether the action survived against the estate of the deceased.

LORD MANSFIELD: This was an action of trover against an administrator, with the will annexed. The trover and conversion were both charged to have been committed by the testator in his life-time: the plea pleaded was, that the testator was not guilty. A verdict was found for the plaintiffs, and a motion has been made in arrest of judgment, because this is a tort, for which an executor or administrator is not liable to answer.

The maxim, actio personalis moritur cum persona, upon which the objection is founded, not being generally true, and much less universally so, leaves the law undefined as to the kind of personal actions which die with the person or survive against the executor.

An action of trover being in form a fiction, and in substance founded on property, for the equitable purpose of recovering the value of the plaintiff's specific property, used and enjoyed by the defendant; if no other action could be brought against the executor, it seems unjust and inconvenient, that the testator's assets should not be liable for the value of what belonged to another man, which the testator had reaped the benefit of.

We therefore thought the matter well deserved consideration: we have carefully looked into all the cases upon the subject. To state and go through them all would be tedious, and tend rather to confound than elucidate. Upon the whole, I think these conclusions may be drawn from them.

First, as to actions which survive against an executor, or die with the person, on account of the cause of action. Secondly, as to actions which survive against an executor, or die with the person, on account of the form of action.

As to the first; where the cause of action is money due, or a contract to be performed, gain or acquisition of the testator, by the work and labour, or property of another, or a promise of the testator express or implied; where these are the causes of action, the action survives against the executor. But where the cause of action is a tort, or arises ex delicto . . . supposed to be by force and against the King's peace, there the action dies; as battery, false imprisonment, trespass, words, nuisance, obstructing lights, diverting a water course, escape against the sheriff, and many other cases of the like kind.

Secondly, as to those which survive or die, in respect of the form of action. In some actions the defendant could have waged his law; and therefore, no action in that form lies against an executor. But now, other actions are substituted in their room upon the very same cause, which do survive and lie against the executor.—No action where in form the declaration must be quare vi et armis, et contra pacem, or where the plea must be, as in this case, that the testator was not guilty, can lie against the executor. Upon the face of the record, the cause of action arises ex delicto: and all private criminal injuries or wrongs, as well as all public crimes, are buried with the offender.

But in most, if not in all the cases, where trover lies against the testator, another action might be brought against the executor, which would answer the purpose.—An action on the custom of the realm against a common carrier, is for a tort and supposed crime: the plea is not guilty; therefore, it will not lie against an executor. But assumpsit, which is another action for the same cause, will lie.—So if a man take a horse from another, and bring him back again; an action of trespass will not lie against his executor, though it would against him; but an action for the use and hire of the horse will lie against the executor. . . .

Here therefore is a fundamental distinction. If it is a sort of injury by which the offender acquires no gain to himself at the expence of the sufferer, as beating or imprisoning a man, &c. there, the person injured has only a reparation for the delictum in damages to be assessed by a jury. But where, besides the crime, property is acquired which benefits the testator, there an action for the value of the property shall survive against the executor. As for instance, the executor shall not be chargeable for the injury done by his testator in cutting down another man's trees, but for the benefit arising to his testator for the value or sale of the trees he shall.

So far as the tort itself goes, an executor shall not be liable; and therefore it is, that all public and all private crimes die with the offender, and the executor is not chargeable; but so far as the act of the offender is beneficial, his assets ought to be answerable; and his executor therefore shall be charged. . . .

The form of the plea is decisive, viz. that the testator was not guilty; and the issue is to try the guilt of the testator. And no mischief is done; for so far as the cause of action does not arise ex delicto, or ex maleficio of the testator, but is founded in a duty, which the testator owes the plaintiff; upon principles of civil obligation, another form of action may be brought, as an action for money had and received. Therefore, we are all of opinion that the judgment must be arrested.

Lightly v *Clouston*

(1808) 1 Taunt 112; 127 ER 774 (Common Pleas)

Quantum meruit

The defendant enticed an apprentice of the plaintiff away from the plaintiff's ship in Jamaica, and employed him upon his own ship to assist his voyage back to England. This conduct amounted to the old tort of seduction (which was perhaps an ancestor of the modern tort of interference with contractual relations). The plaintiff sued the defendant for the value of the apprentice's work and labour.

SIR JAMES MANSFIELD CJ: It is difficult upon principle to distinguish this case from those that have arisen on bankruptcies and executions, and in which it has been held that trover may be converted into an action for money had and received, to recover the sum produced by the sale of the goods. I should much doubt the case of *Smith* v *Hodson* [(1791) 4 Term Rep 211; 100 ER 979], but that I remember a case so long back as the time of Lord Chief Justice Eyre in the reign of George the second, in which the same thing was held. I should have thought it better for the law to have kept its course; but it has now been long settled, that in cases of sale, if the Plaintiff chuses to sue for the produce of that sale, he may do it: and the practice is beneficial to the Defendant, because a jury may give in damages for the tort a much greater sum than the value of the goods. In the present case the Defendant wrongly acquires the labour of the apprentice: and the master may bring his action for the seduction. But he may also waive his right to recover damages for the tort, and may say that he is entitled to the labour of his apprentice, that he is consequently entitled to an equivalent for that labour, which has been bestowed in the service of the Defendant. It is not competent for the Defendant to answer, that he obtained that labour, not by contract with the master, but by wrong; and that therefore he will not pay for it. This case approaches as nearly as possible to the case where goods are sold, and the money has found its way into the pocket of the Defendant.

Phillips v *Homfray*

(1883) 24 Ch D 439 (CA)

The defendants, Homfray, Fothergill and Forman, had been working minerals on land adjoining the plaintiffs' farm, and had secretly been transporting coal and ironstone through passages beneath the farm. When the plaintiffs discovered this they brought an action, and in 1870 obtained a decree that Homfray and Fothergill and the estate of the deceased Forman were liable to the plaintiffs for minerals taken by them under the plaintiffs' farm and that Homfray and Fothergill were liable to compensate the plaintiffs for use of the passages. The following inquiries were ordered: (1) as to the quantity of any minerals taken and their value; (2) the quantities of minerals transported under the plaintiffs' land; (3) the amount to be paid by the defendants to the plaintiffs as 'way leave and royalty' in respect of the use of the passages; (4) whether the defendants' conduct had caused any damage to the farm or mineral deposits lying thereunder. Before the inquiries took place, Fothergill died, and his widow and executrix brought a motion to stay the second, third and fourth inquiries against him. *Held*: by a majority, the second and third inquiries should be stayed, and unanimously, the fourth inquiry should be stayed.

BOWEN AND COTTON LJJ: . . . The Plaintiffs' claim out of which the 2nd and 3rd inquiries spring is a claim to be compensated for the secret and tortious use made by the deceased R. Fothergill and others during his lifetime of the underground ways and passages under the Plaintiffs' farm for the purpose of conveying the coal and ironstone of R. Fothergill and his co-trespassers. The judgment of Mr Justice Pearson as to these two inquiries is based upon the view that this description of claim did not abate upon R. Fothergill's death, but was capable of being prosecuted against the assets in the hands of his executrix. That it is in form a claim in the nature of a claim for trespass, the damages for which were to be measured by the amount of wayleave which the Defendants would have had to pay for permission to use the Plaintiffs' ways and passages, cannot be disputed. But Mr Justice Pearson was of opinion that this was one of the class of cases in which a deceased man's estate remained liable for a profit derived by it out of his wrongful acts during his lifetime. The learned Judge founded his opinion upon certain language of Lord Mansfield in the case of *Hambly* v *Trott* (1776) 1 Cowp 371, to the effect that, so far as the act of the offender had been beneficial to himself, his assets ought to be answerable. We have therefore to consider, in the first place, what is the true limit and meaning of the rule that a personal action dies upon a defendant's death, and whether there is, or can be, in the circumstances raised by the case, a profit received by his assets, which the Plaintiffs can follow.

The only cases in which, apart from questions of breach of contract, express or implied, a remedy for a wrongful act can be pursued against the estate of a deceased person who has done the act, appear to us to be those in which property, or the proceeds or value of property, belonging to another, have been appropriated by the deceased person and added to his own estate or moneys. In such cases, whatever the original form of action, it is in substance brought to recover property, or its proceeds or value, and by amendment could be made such in form as well as in substance. In such cases the action, though arising out of a wrongful act, does not die with the person. The property or the proceeds or value which, in the lifetime of the wrongdoer, could have been recovered from him, can be traced after his death to his assets, and recaptured by the rightful owner there. But it is not every wrongful act by which a wrongdoer indirectly benefits that falls under this head, if the benefit does not consist in the acquisition of property, or its proceeds or value. Where there is nothing among the assets of the deceased that in law or in equity belongs to the plaintiff, and the damages which have been done to him are unliquidated and uncertain, the executors of a wrongdoer cannot be sued merely because it was worth the wrongdoer's while to commit the act which is complained of, and an indirect benefit may have been reaped thereby. . . .

But the language of Lord Mansfield in the case of *Hambly* v *Trott* 1 Cowp 375 is relied upon in the judgment of Mr Justice Pearson as going beyond the above line, and it is important, therefore, to examine it in detail. That action was an action of trover brought against an administrator with the will annexed for a conversion by the testator in his lifetime. The plea was that the testator was not guilty. A verdict having been found for the plaintiff, the Court unanimously arrested the judgment on the ground that the cause of action as laid was a personal tort which died with the person. This was in accordance with the decision in *Baily's Case* Sir T. Raym 71. The judgment in *Hambly* v *Trott* can therefore be no authority for the Appellants' contention, but the language of Lord Mansfield, which has since been cited with approval by the highest tribunals, is of course entitled to the utmost weight. Lord Mansfield in the first place observes that no action of tort where the plea must be not guilty will lie against an executor. 'On the face of such a record the cause of action arises *ex delicto,* and all private criminal injuries or wrongs, as well as all public crimes, are buried with the offender.' This is the inflexible rule. In mitigation of the apparent hardship Lord Mansfield proceeds, *obiter dicta,* to point out that in most cases where trover lies against the testator another action might be brought against the executor which will serve the purpose, and he gives the following illustration. An action on the custom of the realm against a common carrier is for a tort and a supposed crime. The plea is not guilty, therefore such action will not lie against an executor. But assumpsit, which is another action for the same cause, will lie instead. 'So,' continues Lord Mansfield, 'if a man takes a horse from another, and bring him back again, an action of trespass will not lie against his executor, though it would against him; but an action for the use and hire of the horse will lie against the executor.' And in further illustration of this distinction Lord Mansfield points out that in *Baily's Case* the executor would have been liable for the value of the goods wrongfully sold by the testator, just as *Sir Henry Sherrington's Estate,* Savile, 40 was liable for the value of the trees he had cut and carried away. It is with reference to the above distinction that Lord Mansfield goes on to use the language which we think has been misunderstood.

> Here, therefore, is a fundamental distinction. If it is a sort of injury by which the offender acquires no gain to himself at the expense of the sufferer, as beating or imprisoning a man, &c., there the person injured has only a reparation for the *delictum* in damages to be assessed by a jury. But where, besides the crime, property is acquired which benefits the testator, there an action for the value of the property shall survive against the executor. As, for instance, the executor shall not be chargeable for the injury done by his testator in cutting down another man's trees, but for the benefit arising to his testator for the value or sale of the trees he shall. So far as the tort itself goes an executor shall not be liable, and therefore it is that all public and all private crimes die with the offender, and the executor is not chargeable; but so far as the act of the offender is beneficial his assets ought to be answerable, and his executor therefore shall be charged.

It seems to us that Lord Mansfield does no more than indicate that there is a class of cases in which assumpsit can be brought against a wrongdoer to recover the property he has taken or its proceeds or value, and that in such cases the action will survive against the executor. In the illustration given by him of the horse, he does not mean that an action for the use and hire of a horse wrongfully taken will always lie against an executor, but that it will lie whenever a similar action would have lain against the wrongdoer himself. The case he puts is the case of a horse taken and restored, not of a horse taken and held under an adverse claim, and we are not prepared to say that, if absolutely nothing appeared in evidence except that a horse was taken and was afterwards brought back again, the owner might not recover for the use and hire of the horse on the hypothesis of an implied contract to pay for him. It is in such a sense that Lord Ellenborough, in *Foster* v *Stewart* 3 M & S 191, clearly understood Lord Mansfield's language. We see nothing in the language of Lord Chelmsford in the House of Lords in *Peek* v *Gurney* Law Rep 6 HL 393 to indicate that he understood it otherwise. If so, the true test to be applied in the present case is whether the Plaintiffs' claim against the deceased R. Fothergill, in respect of which inquiries 2 and 3 were directed in his lifetime, belongs to the category of actions *ex delicto,* or whether any form of action against the executors of the deceased, or the deceased man in his lifetime, can be based upon any implied contract or duty. In other words, could the Plaintiffs have sued the deceased at law in any form of action in which 'Not guilty' would not be the proper plea? If such alternative form of action could be conceived it must be either an action for the use, by the Plaintiff's permission of the Plaintiff's roads and passages, similar in principle, though not identical, with an action for the use and occupation of the Plaintiffs' land. Or it must be in the shape of an action for money had and received, based upon the supposition that funds are in the hands of the executors which properly belong in law or in equity to the Plaintiffs. We do not believe that the principle of waiving a tort and suing in contract can be carried further than this—that a plaintiff is entitled, if he chooses it, to abstain from treating as a wrong the acts of the defendant in cases where, independently of the question of wrong, the plaintiff could make a case for relief. . . .

One of the most remarkable instances of waiver of a tort is to be found in the case of *Lightly* v *Clouston,* 1 Taunt 112, where the master of an apprentice who had been seduced from his service to work for another person was held justified in waiving the tort and bringing an action of *indebitatus assumpsit* for work and labour done against the tortfeasor. Lord Mansfield, in deciding the case, referred to the cases of the wrongful sale of goods, where, if the rightful owner chooses to sue for the produce of the sale, he may do it, the practice being an advantage and not a disadvantage to the defendant. The case was decided upon the ground that the labour of the apprentice belonged to his master, who might insist on an equivalent for it, or at all events, that the apprentice could not contract for the benefit of anybody except his rightful owner (see *per* Lord Ellenborough in *Foster* v *Stewart* 3 M & S 191. And actions in which the owners of goods wrongfully sold were held entitled to waive the tort, and to recover in assumpsit for the proceeds, had become familiar to the common law as far back as towards the end of the 17th century: see *Lamine* v *Dorrell* 2 Ld Raym 1216.

The difficulties of extending the above principle to the present case appear to us insuperable. The deceased, R. Fothergill, by carrying his coal and ironstone in secret over the Plaintiffs' roads took nothing from the Plaintiffs. The circumstances under which he used the road appear to us to negative the idea that he meant to pay for it. Nor have the assets of the deceased Defendant been necessarily swollen by what he has done. He saved his estate expense, but he did not bring into it any additional property or value belonging to another person. . . .

BAGGALLAY LJ (dissenting): . . . Upwards of 100 years have elapsed since this judgment in *Hambly* v *Trott* (1776) 1 Cowp 371 was delivered. It has ever since been regarded as an accurate representation of the state of the law as affecting executors in respect of causes of action and forms of action arising out of the acts of their testators. The circumstances under which the wrongful act with which we at present have to deal was committed may be concisely stated as follows:—In the year 1866 the Plaintiffs were the owners of a farm in Monmouthshire, and the Defendants, Homfray, Fothergill, and Forman, who carried on business under the style of the Tredegar Iron Company, had for some time past been working the minerals underlying lands adjoining the Plaintiffs' farm, and in the course of that year the Plaintiffs discovered that the Defendants were not only getting minerals from under the farm but were using roads and passages made by them through the Plaintiffs' minerals for the conveyance of minerals gotten by the Defendants from their own mines. In the observations I am about to make it is important to bear in mind the nature of the wrongful act in respect of which the Plaintiffs claim redress; but I deem it unnecessary to further refer to the institution and progress of the suit, as those have been sufficiently detailed in the judgment which has just been delivered. It has hardly been disputed on the present appeal that a remedy for a wrongful act can be pursued against the estate of a deceased person by whom the act has been committed, when property, or the proceeds of property, belonging to another have been appropriated by the deceased person, in other words that the action in such cases, though arising out of a wrongful act, does not die with the person; but it has been urged that the principle thus enunciated is limited to cases in which property, or the proceeds of property, have been appropriated by the deceased person, and that it does not apply to a case in which the deceased person has derived any other benefit from his wrongdoing than property or the proceeds of property, and in particular that it does not apply to a case in which the benefit derived has not been in the form of an actual acquisition of property, but of a saving of expenditure which must otherwise have been incurred by the wrongdoer, as in the present case, in which, for the purpose of the present argument, it must be assumed that by the use by the Defendants, for the carriage of their minerals, of the roads and passages under the Plaintiffs' farm, there was a saving to them of an expenditure which they must otherwise have incurred.

Speaking with much diffidence, as my views in this respect differ from those of my colleagues, I feel bound to say that I cannot appreciate the reasons upon which it is insisted that although executors are bound to account for any accretions to the property of their testator derived directly from his wrongful act, they are not liable for the amount or value of any other benefit which may be derived by his estate from or by reason of such wrongful act. I can find nothing in the language used by Lord Mansfield that can support this view. On the contrary, when classifying the actions which survive against an executor by reason of the causes of action, he includes among such causes of action 'gain or acquisition by the testator by the work and labour or property of another,' and he in no respect limits or qualifies the nature or character of the 'gain' referred to. A gain or acquisition to the wrongdoer by the work and labour of another does not necessarily, if it does at all, imply a diminution of the property of such other person. Whether the amount of the wayleave which a person could reasonably be called upon to pay for the use for the carriage of his minerals over the roads of another, would be a fair measure of the gain or acquisition to the property of the person who has so used them without paying any wayleave, is a question which it is not necessary to decide. I entertain no doubt as to there being ample means of ascertaining the amount of gain or acquisition to the property of a person so using the roads of another. That Lord Mansfield did not intend to limit the generality of the rule enunciated by him in the manner suggested is, I think, clear from the following observations made by him in the course of the first argument in *Hambly* v *Trott* 1 Cowp 373: 'Suppose the testator had sold the sheep, &c., in question. In that case an action for money had and received would lie. Suppose the testator had left them in specie to the executors, the conversion must have been laid against the executors. Suppose the testator had consumed them and had eaten the sheep, what action would have lain there? Is the executor to get off altogether? I shall be very sorry to decide that trover will not lie if there is no other remedy for the right.' It appears to me clear that in the opinion of Lord Mansfield the injured owner of the sheep was equally entitled to redress against the estate of the wrongdoer, whether the sheep were sold by him, or were consumed by him, or were left by him in specie at his death. Now, if the sheep had been consumed by the testator, the only accretion to his property derived from his so doing would have been the amount of the saving in his butcher's bill and I am unable to appreciate the distinction in principle between adding to his property by savings in the amount of his butcher's bills and by savings in the cost of carrying his minerals. Upon the whole, I have come to the conclusion that the causes of action which were the foundation of the decree made in the present suit, and to which I deem it unnecessary to more particularly refer, were such as, within the rule of *Hambly* v *Trott*, to entitle the Plaintiffs to maintain their suit against Mrs Rothergill as the executrix of the deceased Defendant Rothergill in respect of the subject-matter of the second and third inquiries directed by the decree. . . .

Question

Whose approach to the question of enrichment do you prefer: the majority's or Baggallany LJ's?

Note

This was another case decided during the currency of the rule *actio personalis moritur cum persona*, which meant that tortious claims died with the tortfeasor (now abolished by the Law Reform (Miscellaneous Provisions) Act 1934). Therefore the fourth inquiry (relating to compensation for harm caused) was barred. The Court of Appeal split on the question as to which sort of benefit-based liability could survive. In the view of the majority only a proprietary-based remedy could survive. In Baggallay LJ's view actions in respect of both positive benefits (accretions to the defendants' wealth) and negative benefits (saving of expense) would still be maintainable against the wrongdoer's estate. For discussion see Burrows, *Restitution*, 390–2; Birks, *Introduction*, 321–6; Goff and Jones, 717–19 and Birks, 'Civil Wrongs – A New World', *Butterworths Lectures 1990–1991* (1992), 64–7.

United Australia Ltd* v *Barclays Bank Ltd
[1941] AC 1 (HL)

Action for money had and received

United Australia received a cheque for £1,900 from one of its debtors. This cheque was specially indorsed by United Australia's own company secretary, Emons, without authority to M.F.G. Trust Ltd. Emons was also a director of M.F.G. Subsequently M.F.G. paid the cheque into its account at Barclays. Emons had the £1,900 entered in the accounts as a loan to M.F.G. In 1935, United Australia issued a writ against M.F.G. claiming the £1,900 as money lent or *money had and received.* In the course of these proceedings United Australia discovered the indorsement by Emons, and obtained a copy of the cheque showing it had been cleared through Barclays. Before that case proceeded to judgment M.F.G. was wound up. In 1937, United Australia issued a writ against Barclays claiming damages for conversion or negligence, or alternatively £1,900 in an *action for money had and received.*

VISCOUNT SIMON LC: . . . The question to be decided in this appeal is whether the proceedings against M.F.G., carried on up to the point that they in fact reached, constitute a valid ground of defence for the respondent bank and so relieve it in the present action from a liability, which would otherwise certainly attach to it, to repay to the appellant company the sum of 1900*l.* of which they had been deprived and which they have not received from any other source.

The view taken by the Courts below is that the appellant company, by bringing their action against M.F.G., elected to 'waive the tort' and thereby became irrevocably committed, even against a different defendant, to the view that Emons was, as he professed to be, duly authorised as the appellant company's agent to deal with the cheque as he did. If so, the Bank's dealing with the cheque was not tortious and the present action would fail. . . .

The House has now to decide whether the Courts below are right in holding that the appellants are barred from recovering judgment against the bank because they previously instituted proceedings, on the basis of 'waiving the tort' against M.F.G., when those proceedings never produced any judgment or satisfaction in the plaintiff's favour. This question may be conveniently dissected by first asking whether there would be any such bar even if the present action was an action in tort against M.F.G. If a remedy in tort would remain open against the same defendant, then there certainly cannot have been any conclusive election which could prevent an action against a different defendant who had previously not been sued at all.

The process known as 'waiving the tort' can be traced back to the latter half of the seventeenth century, when much accurate learning and refined analysis were addressed to determining what were the appropriate forms of action in which a claim could, or should, be embodied. Thus, in 1678, in the case of *Howard* v *Wood* (1679) 2 Levinz 245 the plaintiff brought his claim in assumpsit for fees due to him as steward of the Honor of Pomfret against a defendant who had received the fees under a subsequent grant of the office which was no longer valid. It was objected 'that this action will not lie for the money received by the defendant as money received for the plaintiff's use, because the defendant claimed title by another grant made to himself and therefore received it to his own use; and that the plaintiff should have brought an action of trover for the money, or case, for disturbing him in his office.' To this the Court of King's Bench answered: 'That it might be hard perhaps to maintain it, if this were a new case, and the first of this nature; but they said two or three actions of this kind had been held before, and cited a case between Bradshaw and Porter, of Grays Inn, for money received as judge of the Sheriff's Court of London to be so resolved; and therefore it would be hard now to adjudge the contrary.' In the previous year, 1677, a similar objection to the plaintiff proceeding in assumpsit to recover the profits of an office, which had wrongly been received by the defendant, was overruled by the Court of Exchequer in *Arris & Arris* v *Stukely* (1677) 2 Mod 260, 262, where the argument of the Solicitor-General, Sir Francis Winnington, is thus reported. 'An indebitatus assumpsit would lie here; for where one receives my rent, I may charge him as bailiff or receiver; or if any one receive my money without my order, though it is a tort yet an indebitatus will lie, because by reason of the money, the law creates a promise; and the action is not grounded on the tort, but on the receipt of the profits in this case.'

Another example of the same objection being overruled is found in *Lamine* v *Dorrell* 2 Ld Raym 1216, where an administrator of an estate sued in assumpsit to recover proceeds, which had been gathered in by a former administrator whose appointment had been revoked. In that case Powell J said: 'It is clear the plaintiff might have maintained detinue or trover for the debentures, but when the act that is done is in its nature tortious, it is hard to turn that into a contract, and against the reason of assumpsits. But the plaintiff may dispense with the wrong, and suppose the sale made by his consent, and bring an action for the money they were sold for, as money received to his use. It has been carried thus far already.' And Holt CJ said: 'these actions have crept in by degrees' and added 'he could not see how it differed from an indebitatus assumpsit for the profits of an office by a rightful officer against a wrongful, as money had and received by the wrongful officer to the use of the rightful.'

It is not necessary in this connection to discuss the logical basis of the writ of indebitatus assumpsit; my noble and learned friend, Lord Wright, has submitted it to searching analysis in his essay on the decision of this House, a quarter of a century ago, in *Sinclair* v *Brougham* [1914] AC 398 (Legal Essays and Addresses by Lord Wright of Durley, Cambridge University Press, p. 1). Suffice it to say that the device of 'waiving the tort' and suing in assumpsit soon spread. A learned author includes among torts which can be waived, conversion, trespass to land or goods, deceit, occasionally action upon the case, and the action for extorting money by threats. (Winfield on 'The Province of the Law of Tort,' p. 169.) An extreme instance is provided in *Lightly* v *Clouston*, (1808) 1 Taunt 112, where the defendant had wrongfully taken the plaintiff's apprentice into his employment, and the plaintiff, instead of suing for seduction, successfully claimed in assumpsit against the defendant who had tortiously employed him. 'This case,' said Mansfield CJ (1 Taunt 114) 'approaches as nearly as possible to the case where goods are sold, and the money has found its way into the pocket of the defendant.' Six years later Lord Ellenborough, in *Foster* v *Stewart* 3 M & S 191, doubted whether this was not going too far. At any rate, it is clear that there are torts to which the process of waiver could not be applied; the tort of defamation, for example, or of assault, could not be dressed up into a claim in assumpsit.

Where 'waiving the tort' was possible, it was nothing more than a choice between possible remedies derived from a time when it was not permitted to combine them or to pursue them in the alternative, and when there were procedural advantages in selecting the form of assumpsit. For example, there were no pitfalls in drawing the declaration in assumpsit, and the cause of action did not drop with death; on the other hand, there were advantages for the defendant, too, for an action framed in assumpsit permitted the defendant to plead the general issue (Stephen's Principles of Pleading, 2nd ed., 1827, p. 197).

Lamine v *Dorrell* 2 Ld Raym 1216, 1217 contains the first judicial reference which I have been able to find to the effect of success in pursuing one form of action in barring proceedings under the other. For Holt CJ observes, 'if an action of trover should be brought by the plaintiff for these debentures after judgment in this indebitatus assumpsit, he may plead this recovery in bar of the action of trover, in the same manner as it would have been a good plea in bar for the defendant to have pleaded to the action of trover, that he sold the debentures, and paid to the plaintiff in satisfaction. But it may be a doubt if this recovery can be pleaded before execution.' It will be observed that Holt CJ does not say that the commencement of an action in one form bars the possibility of recovery under another form of action; even against the same party, the bar only arises in his view, at earliest, on recovering judgment. [Viscount Simon LC then considered the authorities, especially a *dictum* of Bovill CJ in *Smith* v *Baker* (1873) LR 8 CP 350 that 'if an action for money had and received is so brought, that is in point of law a conclusive election to waive the tort', and continued: . . .]

This review of the authorities convinces me that the oft-quoted dictum of Bovill CJ in *Smith* v *Baker* LR 8 CP 350, 355 is wrong. There is, as far as I can discover, no reported case which has ever laid it down as matter of decision that when the plaintiff 'waives the tort' and starts an action in assumpsit, he then and there debars himself from a future proceeding based on the tort. It would be very remarkable if it were so. 'The fallacy of the argument,' as Lord Ellenborough said in *Hunter* v *Prinsep*, 10 East 378, 391, 'appears to us to consist in attributing more effect to the mere form of this action than really belongs to it. In bringing an action for money had and received, instead of trover, the plaintiff does no more than waive any complaint, with a view to damages, of the tortious act by which the goods were converted into money, and takes to the neat proceeds of the sale as the value of the goods.' When the plaintiff 'waived the tort' and brought assumpsit, he did not thereby elect to be treated from that time forward on the basis that no tort had been committed; indeed, if it were to be understood that no tort had been committed, how could an action in assumpsit lie? It lies only because the acquisition of the defendant is wrongful and there is thus an obligation to make restitution.

The true proposition is well formulated in the Restatement of the Law of Restitution promulgated by the American Law Institute, p. 525, as follows: 'A person upon whom a tort has been committed and who brings an action for the benefits received by the tortfeasor is sometimes said to "waive the tort". The election to bring an action of assumpsit is not, however, a waiver of tort but is the choice of one of two alternative remedies.' Contrast with this, instances of true waiver of rights, e.g., waiver of forfeiture by receiving rent.

If, under the old forms of procedure, the mere bringing of an action while waiving the tort did not constitute a bar to a further action based on the tort, still less could such a result be held to follow after the Common Law Procedure Act, 1852, and the Judicature Act, 1875. For it is now possible to combine in a single writ a claim based on tort with a claim based on assumpsit, and it follows inevitably that the making of the one claim cannot amount to an election which bars the making of the other. No doubt, if the plaintiff proved the necessary facts, he could be required to elect on which of his alternative causes of action he would take judgment, but that has nothing to do with the unfounded contention that election arises when the writ is issued. There is nothing conclusive about the form in which the writ is issued, or about the claims made in the statement of claim. A plaintiff may at any time before judgment be permitted to amend. The substance of the matter is that on certain facts he is claiming redress either in the form of compensation, i.e., damages as for a tort, or in the form of restitution of money to which he is entitled, but which the defendant has wrongfully received. The same set of facts entitles the plaintiff to claim either form of redress. At some stage of the proceedings the plaintiff must elect which remedy he will have. There is, however, no reason of principle or convenience why that stage should be deemed to be reached until the plaintiff applies for judgment.

So far, I have been discussing what is the true proposition of law when the second action is brought against the same defendant. In the present case, however, the action which is said to be barred by former proceedings against M.F.G. is not an action against M.F.G. at all, but an action against Barclays Bank. I am quite unable to see why this second action should be barred by the plaintiff's earlier proceedings against M.F.G. In the first place, the tort of conversion of which the bank was guilty is quite a separate tort from that done by M.F.G. M.F.G.'s tort consisted in taking the cheque away from the appellants without the appellants' authority; that tort would have equally existed if M.F.G., instead of getting the cheque cleared through the bank, had kept it in its own possession. The bank's tort, on the other hand, consisted in taking a cheque, which was the property of the appellants, and without their authority using it to collect money which rightly belonged to the appellants. M.F.G. and the bank were not joint tortfeasors, for two persons are not joint tortfeasors because their independent acts cause the same damage. . . .

Notes

1. See also the speech of Lord Atkin in this case extracted in Chapter 1, Section 1.

2. For an account of the old cases on usurpation of office see Goff and Jones, 577–9.

3. For recent helpful analysis of this case see the advice of the Privy Council in *Tang Man Sit* v *Capacious Investments Ltd* [1996] 1 All ER 193.

Chesworth v *Farrar*
[1967] 1 QB 407 (QBD)

Action for money had and received

Farrar obtained judgment for possession against his tenant Chesworth in respect of an antique-shop and dwelling in East Grinstead High Street in 1960. It was alleged that the premises contained many valuable antiques, and it was accepted that Farrar became bailee of these. Farrar died on 19 July 1961, and on 11 April 1962 letters of administration were granted to the defendant. On 7 April 1964, Chesworth commenced an action claiming £59,848, the alleged value of the goods lost, and alternatively £2,292 as money realised by a sale of some of her goods by Farrar as *money had and received*. On the preliminary point whether either claim was barred by limitation. *Held*: first, the claim for breach of bailment in respect of all the antiques was in substance one 'in respect of a cause of action in tort' and was barred by s. 1(3) of the Law Reform (Miscellaneous Provisions) Act 1934; secondly, the claim in respect of the sale was analogous to claim in a contract and was permitted by the Limitation Act 1939.

EDMUND DAVIES J: . . . Assuming that the deceased sold more of the plaintiff's goods than he was entitled to sell and/or failed to account to the plaintiff for £2,291 17s 6d due to her in respect of goods sold by him, is the claim to recover that sum an action in tort which is otherwise barred by the Act of 1934? Or is it an action analogous to one brought in contract, regarding which the actio personalis rule does not apply and which may be instituted within the periods allowed by the Limitation Act, 1939? In my judgment, the latter view is the correct one, and I confess that I should not have held otherwise unless I found that the state of the law conclusively compelled me to do so. A person upon whom a tort has been committed has at times a choice of alternative remedies, even though it is a sine qua non regarding each that he must establish that a tort has been committed. He may sue to recover damages for the tort, or he may waive the tort and sue in quasi-contract to recover the benefits received by the wrongdoer. It has long been recognised that (as is pointed out in the recently published and admirable Law of Restitution, by Goff and Jones, p. 427)

> the advantages of suing in quasi-contract were substantive as well as procedural. In particular, it was a useful method of circumventing short limitation periods and the old common law rule that tortious actions died with the person.

Holding in *Hambly* v *Trott* (1776) 1 Cowp 371 that trover did not lie against the estate of a wrongdoer, Lord Mansfield nevertheless said:

> So far as the tort itself goes, an executor shall not be liable . . . but so far as the act of the offender is beneficial, his assets ought to be answerable; and his executor therefore shall be charged.

In *Phillips* v *Homfray* (1883) 24 Ch D 439, 454, CA, Bowen LJ expressed himself to the like effect. No authority was cited for the proposition that an action for money had and received is an action in tort and one which, but for the Act of 1934, would die with the wrongdoer. On the contrary, in *In re Diplock* [1948] Ch 465, 514; 2 All ER 318, CA, Lord Greene MR said that it must be assumed that such an action was one 'founded on simple contract' within the meaning of section 2(1)(a) of the Limitation Act, 1939, while in *Fibrosa Spolka Akcyjna* v *Fairbairn Lawson Combe Barbour Ltd* [1943] AC 32; 58 TLR 308; [1942] 2 All ER 122, HL, Lord Wright, in dealing with cases of unjust enrichment, said:

> Such remedies in English law are generically different from remedies in contract or in tort, and are now recognised to fall within a third category of the common law which has been called quasi-contract or restitution.

In the light of the foregoing, I hold that question 2 must be answered in the negative. In other words, the plaintiff's claim for £2,291 17s 6d as money had and received by the deceased to the use of the plaintiff is not an 'action in tort' for the purposes of the Law Reform (Miscellaneous Provisions) Act, 1934, and is accordingly not statute-barred by section 1(3) thereof.

Question

Most of Mrs Chesworth's claim here was barred by the short limitation period then imposed on actions in tort against deceased defendants. Should her claim for the £2,292 arising from the sale of some of the antiques have been similarly barred? In other words, should waiver of the tort of conversion allow a plaintiff to circumvent a statutory bar?

Notes

1. The remnant of the old *actio personalis moritur cum persona* rule in the 1934 Act has now been swept away by the Proceedings Against Estates Act 1970.
2. For discussion of the policy question see Birks, *Introduction*, 348–9.

B: *Restitutionary damages?*

A parallel stream of case law appears to award a benefit-based measure, being the expense saved by the defendant rather than the loss to the plaintiff, under the guise of compensatory damages. The cases all involve infringements of proprietary rights.

Strand Electric and Engineering Co. Ltd* v *Brisford Entertainments Ltd
[1952] 2 QB 246 (CA)

The defendant theatre owners hired theatrical equipment from the plaintiff company, who hired out such equipment in the normal course of their business. At the end of the hire period the theatre owners refused to return the equipment, despite repeated requests by the plaintiffs. The plaintiffs successfully sued the theatre owners in *detinue* (which would now be a claim for wrongful interference with goods under the Torts (Interference with Goods) Act 1977) for the return of their property. The question arose as to the correct measure of damages for the 43 weeks during which the equipment was wrongfully detained. *Held*: the plaintiffs were entitled to the reasonable rate of hire of the goods for the period for which they were wrongfully detained.

SOMERVELL LJ: . . . *The Mediana* [1900] AC 113 was a claim in negligence in respect of a chattel which did not, in the hands of the plaintiff, earn profits. In the present case the chattel was profit-earning in the hands of the plaintiffs. The judge applied the principle as laid down in *The S. S. Valeria* [1922] 2 AC 242. The question is whether that is the right measure in this case. This is a claim in detinue. On the findings, the defendants had for their own benefit the use of the plaintiffs' chattels. This is an incident which is not present in the damage by negligence cases. Why is not the plaintiffs' loss the value in the market of the user? The wrong is not the mere deprivation, as in negligence and possibly some detinue cases, but the user. I am, of course, not overlooking the fact that if the chattel has been damaged and depreciated this may be an item in a claim for special damage. There are no doubt some cases in which a wrongdoer may be called on to account for profits, but in considering the measure of damages as raised here I think the actual benefit which the defendants have obtained is irrelevant. The damages could not, in my view, be increased by showing that a defendant had made by his use of the chattels much more than the market rate of hire. Equally they cannot be diminished by showing that he had made less.

It is curious, as I have said, that there is no authority on this point. The nearest analogy is a claim for mesne profits. The measure there is a reasonable sum in the nature of rent for the user during the period of the defendant's trespass. In other words, the defendant must pay what the plaintiff would have obtained if the defendant had lawfully been in possession. In principle the same measure should, I think, apply where a defendant has detained and used a chattel of the plaintiff which the plaintiff, as part of his business, hires out to users. I have added these latter words because I do not wish in this so far uncharted field to go beyond the facts of the case. We were referred to statements as to the law in the United States of America. (See Sedgwick on Damages, Vol. 11, 1031 and 1045; Corpus Juris Secundum, col. 26, p. 1286.) It would appear from the statements in these books that the principle may be more widely applied in the United States of America and would cover, for example, detention and use of a private motor-car. I am not saying this is wrong. There may be no distinction in principle. The question had, however, better be left till it arises. . . .

DENNING LJ: In assessing damages, whether for a breach of contract or for a tort, the general rule is that the plaintiff recovers the loss he has suffered, no more and no less. This rule is, however, often departed from. Thus in cases where the damage claimed is too remote in law the plaintiff recovers less than his real loss: *Liesbosch Dredger (Owners)* v *Edison S.S. (Owners)* [1933] AC 449. In other cases the plaintiff may get more than his real loss. Thus, where the damage suffered by the plaintiff is recouped or lessened owing to some reason with which the defendant is not concerned, the plaintiff gets full damages without any deduction on that account:

Slater v *Hoyle & Smith Ld.* [1920] 2 KB 11; *Smiley* v *Townshend* [1950] 2 KB 311; *Haviland* v *Long* [1952]. Again, in cases where the defendant has obtained a benefit from his wrongdoing he is often made liable to account for it, even though the plaintiff has lost nothing and suffered no damage: *Reading* v *Attorney-General* [1951] AC 507.

The question in this case is: What is the proper measure of damages for the wrongful detention of goods? Does it fall within the general rule that the plaintiff only recovers for the loss he has suffered or within some other, and if so what, rule? It is strange that there is no authority upon this point in English law; but there is plenty on the analogous case of detention of land. The rule there is that a wrongdoer, who keeps the owner out of his land, must pay a fair rental value for it, even though the owner would not have been able to use it himself or to let it to anyone else. So also a wrongdoer who uses land for his own purposes without the owner's consent, as, for instance, for a fair ground, or as a wayleave, must pay a reasonable hire for it, even though he has done no damage to the land at all: *Whitwham* v *Westminster Brymbo Coal Company* [1896] 2 Ch 538. I see no reason why the same principle should not apply to detention of goods.

If a wrongdoer has made use of goods for his own purposes, then he must pay a reasonable hire for them, even though the owner has in fact suffered no loss. It may be that the owner would not have used the goods himself, or that he had a substitute readily available, which he used without extra cost to himself. Nevertheless the owner is entitled to a reasonable hire. If the wrongdoer had asked the owner for permission to use the goods, the owner would be entitled to ask for a reasonable remuneration as the price of his permission. The wrongdoer cannot be better off because he did not ask permission. He cannot be better off by doing wrong than he would be by doing right. He must therefore pay a reasonable hire. This will cover, of course, the wear and tear which is ordinarily included in a hiring charge; but for any further damage the wrongdoer must pay extra. I do not mean to suggest that an owner who has suffered greater loss will not be able to recover it. Suppose that a man used a car in his business, and owing to its detention he had to hire a substitute at an increased cost, he would clearly be able to recover the cost of the substitute. In such cases the plaintiff recovers his actual loss. I am not concerned with those cases.

I am here concerned with the cases where the owner has in fact suffered no loss, or less loss than is represented by a hiring charge. In such cases if the wrongdoer has in fact used the goods he must pay a reasonable hire for them. Nor do I mean to suggest that a wrongdoer who has merely detained the goods and not used them would have to pay a hiring charge. The damages for detention recoverable against a carrier or a warehouseman have never been measured by a hiring charge. They are measured by the loss actually sustained by the plaintiff, subject, of course, to questions of remoteness. They are like cases of injury to a ship or a car by negligence. If it is put out of action during repair the wrongdoer is only liable for the loss suffered by the plaintiff. (See the principles set out in *The Susquehanna* [1926] AC 655, and many other cases.) The claim for a hiring charge is therefore not based on the loss to the plaintiff, but on the fact that the defendant has used the goods for his own purposes. It is an action against him because he has had the benefit of the goods. It resembles, therefore, an action for restitution rather than an action of tort. But it is unnecessary to place it into any formal category. The plaintiffs are entitled to a hiring charge for the period of detention, and that is all that matters. I can imagine cases where an owner might be entitled to the profits made by a wrongdoer by the use of a chattel, but I do not think this is such a case. . . .

ROMER LJ: In my judgment the three salient facts on which the assessment of damages in this case depends are, first, that the equipment of the plaintiffs which the defendants detained was profit-earning property; secondly, that the plaintiffs normally hired out the equipment in the course of their business; and, thirdly, that the defendants during the period of wrongful detention applied the property to the furtherance of their own ends. . . .

. . . The inquiry is: What loss has the plaintiff suffered by reason of the defendants' wrongful act? In determining the answer to this inquiry the question of quantifying the profit or benefit which the defendant has derived from his wrongful act does not arise; for there is no necessary relation between the plaintiffs' loss and the defendants' gain. It follows that in assessing the plaintiffs' loss in the present case one is not troubled by any need to evaluate the actual benefit which resulted to the defendants by having the plaintiffs' equipment at their disposal.

That element then being out of the way, the only substantial reason put forward by the defendants why the plaintiffs should not receive the full hiring value of the equipment during the period of detention is that the plaintiffs might not have been able to find a hirer. In my judgment, however, a defendant who has wrongfully detained and profited from the property of someone else cannot avail himself of a hypothesis such as this. It does not lie in the mouth of such a defendant to suggest that the owner might not have found a hirer; for in using the property he showed that he wanted it and he cannot complain if it is assumed against him that he himself would have preferred to become the hirer rather than not have had the use of it at all. . . .

Penarth Dock Engineering Ltd v *Pounds*
[1963] 1 Ll L Rep 359 (QBD)

On 9 August 1961, the plaintiff company sold to Mr Pounds a floating pontoon lying in a dock leased to the plaintiff. The British Transport Commission, the owner of the dock, wished to close the dock as soon as possible. This was known both to the plaintiff and to Mr Pounds, therefore it was an express written term of the contract of sale that Pounds would remove the pontoon 'as speedily as possible' although no actual time limit was set. By March 1963 the pontoon, despite repeated requests by the plaintiff, still lay in the dock. The plaintiff brought an action alleging *trespass* and *breach of contract. Held*: on a true construction of the contract Mr Pounds was obliged to remove the pontoon within 12 months of the sale, by 9 August 1962. This he had manifestly failed to do. What was the correct measure of damages?

LORD DENNING MR (sitting as an additional judge of the Queen's Bench Division): . . . The question which remains is, what are the damages? True it is that the Penarth company themselves would not seem to have suffered any damage to speak of. They have not to pay any extra rent to the British Transport Commission. The dock is no use to them; they would not have made any money out of it. But, nevertheless, in a case of this kind, as I read the law, starting with *Whitwham* v *Westminster Brymbo Coal and Coke Company,* [1896] 2 Ch 538, on which I commented myself in the case of *Strand Electric and Engineering Company, Ltd* v *Brisford Entertainments, Ltd,* [1952] 2 QB 246, at pp. 253 to 254, the test of the measure of damages is not what the plaintiffs have lost, but what benefit the defendant obtained by having the use of the berth; and he has been a trespasser, in my judgment, since August 9,

1962. What benefit has the defendant obtained by having the use of it for this time? If he had moved it elsewhere, he would have had to pay, on the evidence, £37 10s a week for a berth for a dock of this kind. But the damages are not put as high as that, and the damages are to be assessed in accordance with the law as I have stated it at the rate of £32 5s a week for a period commencing from August 9, 1962, which I would let run to March 25, 1963, because the dock has now been removed. I do not know what that sum will come to, but that can be a matter of calculation. I do not think that there is any call in the circumstances for a mandatory injunction or any other relief. . . .

Question

In Sharpe and Waddams, 'Damages for lost opportunity to bargain' (1982) 2 OJLS 290, the authors argue that cases such as *Strand Electric* v *Brisford Entertainments* and *Penarth Dock* v *Pounds* 'can be explained on a simple and rational basis that is fully consistent with the compensatory theory of damages. That is that the plaintiff does suffer a real loss, namely, the opportunity to sell to the defendant the right to use the plaintiff's property'. The quantum of awards is therefore based on a reasonable licence fee which the plaintiff might have charged for his permission. Do you agree with this explanation of the cases?

Stoke-on-Trent City Council v *W & J Wass Ltd*
[1988] 1 WLR 1406 (CA)

The defendant company began operating a Thursday market within the plaintiff council's area, without either a franchise or statutory authority. The council planned its own Thursday market, and warned the company that by operating the market they would be infringing the council's rights. The company continued to operate the market in defiance of the council and without planning permission. At first instance the judge awarded the council a permanent injunction restraining the company from holding the market. The judge further held that the council's loss was nil, but it was entitled to damages based on the licence fee it could have demanded from the company. The company appealed on the measure of damages. *Held*: the council was entitled to nominal damages only of £2.

NOURSE LJ: The levying of an unlawful same day market within $6\frac{2}{3}$ miles of a franchise or statutory market is actionable at the suit of the market owner without proof of loss. At trial he will usually be awarded a permanent injunction and nominal damages. Where an interlocutory injunction has been running before trial, no further question of damages will usually arise. In respect of any period before or after trial where no injunction is in force, substantial damages will be recoverable if loss can be proved. But suppose a case where there has been no loss. Is the market owner kept to his nominal damages or can he recover substantial damages on the footing that if his leave and licence had been sought he could have required a fee to be paid to him? That is the novel and somewhat surprising question with which we are confronted on this appeal. . . .

The levying of an unlawful rival market is a tort. Whether it should properly be categorised as a nuisance or a trespass is probably not a question of importance. The better view must be that it is a nuisance. The general rule is that a successful plaintiff in an action in tort recovers damages equivalent to the loss which he has suffered, no more and no less. If he has suffered no loss, the most he can recover are nominal damages. A second general rule is that where the plaintiff has suffered loss to his property or some proprietary right, he recovers damages equivalent to the diminution in value of the property or right. The authorities establish that both these rules are subject to exceptions. These must be closely examined, in order to see whether a further exception ought to be made in this case.

The first and best established exception is in trespass to land. It originated in the way-leave cases, where the defendant trespassed by carrying coals along an underground way through the plaintiff's mine. Although the value of his land had not been diminished by the trespass, the plaintiff recovered damages equivalent to what he would have received if he had been paid for a way-leave: see *Martin* v *Porter* (1839) 5 M & W 351; *Jegon* v *Vivian* (1871) LR 6 Ch App 742 and *Phillips* v *Homfray* (1871) LR 6 Ch App 770. The principle of those cases was applied in *Whitwham* v *Westminster Brymbo Coal and Coke Co.* [1896] 2 Ch 538, where for six years the defendants had trespassed by tipping refuse from their colliery onto part of the plaintiffs' land. The official referee found that the defendants had thereby rendered the whole of the land valueless for any but tipping purposes and he assessed its diminution in value at £200. But the plaintiffs contended that the proper measure was the reasonable value to the defendants of the land for tipping purposes and the official referee found that on that footing the damages were £963. It was held by Chitty J and this court that as to that part of the land which had been used for tipping the defendants must pay on the footing of the value of the land to them for tipping purposes, but without interest; and as to the rest of the land that they ought to pay on the footing of the diminished value of the land to the plaintiffs. That decision was applied by Lord Denning MR, sitting as a judge of the Queen's Bench Division, in *Penarth Dock Engineering Co. Ltd* v *Pounds* [1963] 1 Lloyd's Rep 359 and by this court in *Swordheath Properties Ltd* v *Tabet* [1979] 1 WLR 285. In the latter case it was held that a defendant who had occupied residential premises as a trespasser was liable to pay damages calculated by reference to the ordinary letting value of the premises even where there was no evidence that the plaintiff could or would have let the premises to someone else. With the partial exception of *Whitwham's* case, all those were cases where the plaintiff had suffered no loss. [Nourse LJ then considered further exceptions (*Strand Electric and Engineering Co. Ltd* v *Brisford Entertainments Ltd* [1952] 2 QB 246 (detinue); cases on the infringement of patents and *Wrotham Park Estate Co.* v *Parkside Homes Ltd* [1974] 1 WLR 798 (breach of restrictive covenant)) and concluded: . . .]

As I understand these authorities, their broad effect is this. In cases of trespass to land and patent infringement and in some cases of detinue and nuisance the court will award damages in accordance with what Nicholls LJ has aptly termed 'the user principle.' On an analogous principle, in a case where there was a breach of a restrictive covenant the court has, in lieu of a permanent mandatory injunction to restore the breach, awarded damages equivalent to the sum which the plaintiffs might reasonably have demanded for a relaxation of the covenant. But it is only in the last-mentioned case and in the trespass cases that damages have been awarded in accordance with either principle without proof of loss to the plaintiff. In all the other cases, the plaintiff having established his loss, the real question has not been whether substantial damages should be awarded at all, but whether they should be assessed in accordance with the user principle or by reference to the diminution in value of the property or right. In other words, those other cases are exceptions to the second, but not to the first, of the general rules stated above.

Do the authorities support an award of damages in accordance with the user principle where an unlawful rival market has caused no loss to the market owner? In other words, is this case to be governed by the principle of the trespass cases and that of the *Wrotham Park* case?

The latter decision is in my opinion one which stands very much on its own. The conclusion of Brightman J may, I think, be more fully explained as follows. An injunction is frequently granted to enforce an express negative covenant, especially a restrictive covenant affecting land, without proof of loss to the plaintiff. Injunctions could therefore and would have been granted in that case but for the social and economic reasons against ordering the demolition of 14 houses. If injunctions had been granted, the loss to the defendant purchasers would have been enormous. If, on the other hand, injunctions were not granted and no damages were awarded, the purchasers would have been left in undisturbed possession of the correspondingly enormous fruits of their wrongdoing. Accordingly, if the plaintiffs had not been awarded substantial damages, justice manifestly would not have been done. If this analysis is correct, the practical result of the *Wrotham Park* decision was something akin to an award of exemplary damages for breach of contract, albeit that their amount bore no relation to the loss which would have been suffered by the defendant purchasers if they had had to demolish their houses. In saying this, I do not wish to suggest that that case was wrongly decided. Indeed, I regard the result as having been entirely appropriate and I see no reason why it should not serve as a precedent for other cases of the same kind. I merely wish to emphasise that it stands a long way away from the present problem and does not assist in its solution.

On a superficial view, the trespass cases present a greater difficulty. In trespass the defendant makes an unlawful use of the plaintiff's land. Similarly, it can be said that in levying an unlawful rival market the defendant makes an unlawful use of the plaintiff's right to hold his own market, which, at any rate in the case of a franchise market, is an incorporeal hereditament. Ought it to make all the difference that in the first case the unlawful use is a physical one? This is a formidable line of argument, but I think that it is unsound. If the way-leave cases are put on one side, it seems to me that the trespass cases really depend on the fact that the defendant's use of the plaintiff's land deprives the plaintiff of *any* opportunity of using it himself. And even on the assumption, which may be correct, that the broad view of Denning LJ in the *Strand Electric case* [1952] 2 QB 246 is a correct view of the law, the same can be said of an unlawful detention of the plaintiff's chattel. On the other hand, an unlawful use of the plaintiff's right to hold his own market does not deprive him of the opportunity of holding one himself. Such indeed has been the state of affairs in the present case. If of course the plaintiff can show that he has thereby suffered loss, nobody would suggest that he ought not to receive substantial damages. But why should he receive them when he has been able to hold his own market and has suffered no loss from the defendant's?

It is characteristic of the development of the common law that the invention and increasingly extended application of the user principle should appear to have come about by accident rather than by design. Thus it seems from the interlocutory observations of the members of this court in *Whitwham's* case [1896] 2 Ch 538, 539, 540, 541 that they were initially resistant to the principle of the way-leave cases. But they saw in it a basis for the just decision of that case, and once it had been so decided the application of the principle to analogous states of affairs, for example the wrongful detention of chattels, seems to have been a perfectly natural development. However, in a process of development it is sometimes necessary to stand back from the authorities and to ask not simply where they have come to, but where, if a further extension is made, they may go next.

Although I would accept that there may be a logical difficulty in making a distinction between the present case and the way-leave cases, I think that if the user principle were to be applied here there would be an equal difficulty in distinguishing other cases of more common occurrence, particularly in nuisance. Suppose a case were a right to light or a right of way had been obstructed to the profit of the servient owner but at no loss to the dominant owner. It would be difficult, in the application of the user principle, to make a logical distinction between such an obstruction and the infringement of a right to hold a market. And yet the application of that principle to such cases would not only give a right to substantial damages where no loss had been suffered but would revolutionise the tort of nuisance by making it unnecessary to prove loss. Moreover, if the principle were to be applied in nuisance, why not in other torts where the defendant's wrong can work to his own profit, for example in defamation? As progenitors of the rule in trespass and some other areas, the way-leave cases have done good service. But just as their genus is peculiar, so ought their procreative powers to be exhausted.

These considerations have led me to conclude that the user principle ought not to be applied to the infringement of a right to hold a market where no loss has been suffered by the market owner. If loss caused by the diversion of custom from one market to the other had been proved, I would have agreed with Nicholls LJ that the general rule ought to apply, so that the council would have recovered damages equivalent to the diminution in value of their right through the loss of stallage, tolls and so forth. But I rest my decision in this case on the simple ground that where no loss has been suffered no substantial damages of any kind can be recovered. Otherwise we would have to allow that the right to recover nominal damages for disturbance of a same day market without proof of loss had become one to receive substantial damages on top. If we had to allow that, why not also in the case of an other day market where no loss had been proved? It is possible that the English law of tort, more especially of the so-called 'proprietary torts,' will in due course make a more deliberate move towards recovery based not on loss suffered by the plaintiff but on the unjust enrichment of the defendant; see Goff and Jones, *The Law of Restitution*, 3rd ed. (1986), pp. 612–614. But I do not think that that process can begin in this case and I doubt whether it can begin at all at this level of decision.

Note

The *Wrotham Park Estate* case is discussed below in Section 2.

Ministry of Defence* v *Ashman
[1993] 2 EGLR 102 (CA)

The ministry allowed Mr Ashman (the second defendant), a flight sergeant in the Royal Air Force, to occupy 15 Perch Meadow near RAF Halton as married quarters. He signed a certificate acknowledging that he was entitled to occupy the property only while he remained in the RAF and living with his spouse, and acknowledged that he would be required to move his family from the accommodation if he ceased to live with his spouse. The quarterly charge was £95.41 *per month*. On 14 February 1991, Mr Ashman moved out leaving his wife (the first defendant) and two children behind. On 14 March 1991, the defendants were given notice to vacate. Mrs Ashman and the children remained as they had nowhere else to go. On 17 May 1991, Mrs Ashman was given a further notice, which asserted the right to damages for trespass of £108.93 *per week*. The ministry obtained an order for possession on 17 December 1991. Mrs Ashman vacated on 26 April 1992 and was rehoused by the local authority at £33.44 *per week*. In the claim for damages for trespass (termed '*mesne profits*') the ministry gave evidence that the market value of the house was £108.93 *per week*. *Held*: by Kennedy and Hoffmann LJJ, Lloyd LJ *dubitante*, the appropriate measure of damages was the figure that Mrs Ashman would have had to pay for suitable local authority accommodation, had it been available. The judgment of Kennedy LJ is not extracted.

HOFFMANN LJ: A person entitled to possession of land can make a claim against a person who has been in occupation without his consent on two alternative bases. The first is for the loss which he has suffered in consequence of the defendant's trespass. This is the normal measure of damages in the law of tort. The second is the value of the benefit which the occupier has received. This is a claim for restitution. The two bases of claim are mutually exclusive and the plaintiff must elect before judgment which of them he wishes to pursue. These principles are not only fair but, as Kennedy LJ demonstrated, also well established by authority.

It is true that in the earlier cases it has not been expressly stated that a claim for mesne profit for trespass can be a claim for restitution. Nowadays I do not see why we should not call a spade a spade. In this case the Ministry of Defence elected for the restitutionary remedy. It adduced no evidence of what it would have done with the house if the Ashmans had vacated. In my judgment, such matters are irrelevant to a restitution claim. All that matters is the value of benefit which the defendant has received. For reasons given by Kennedy LJ I agree that the judge's finding that the ministry was estopped from claiming full value of benefit cannot be sustained.

That leaves only the question of how one values the benefit which Mr and Mrs Ashman received. In *Swordheath Properties Ltd* v *Tabet* [1979] 1 WLR 285 Megaw LJ said 'in the absence of anything special in the particular case' it will ordinarily be the rental value of the property in the open market. This the judge found to be £472 a month as against the concessionary licence fee of £95 a month, which Mr Ashman had previously been charged. As the only special feature found by the judge was the estoppel we have held to be unsustainable, the ministry asks that we substitute a figure of £472 a month for that ordered by the judge.

In my judgment, however, the law of restitution is not so inflexible. The open market value will ordinarily be appropriate because the defendant has chosen to stay in the premises rather than pay for equivalent premises somewhere else. But such benefits may in special circumstances be subject to what Professor Birks, in his *Introduction to the Law of Restitution,* has conveniently called *subjective devaluation.* This means that a benefit may not be worth as much to the particular defendant as to someone else. In particular, it may be worth less to a defendant who has not been free to reject it. Mr and Mrs Ashman would probably have never occupied the premises in the first place if they had to pay £472 a month instead of the concessionary licence fee of £95. Mrs Ashman would certainly not have stayed in the premises at the market rate if she had any choice in the matter. She stayed because she could not establish priority need to be rehoused by the local authority until the eviction order had been made against her. Once the necessary proceedings had been taken she was able to obtain local authority housing at £145 a month.

In my judgment, therefore, the special circumstances in this case are created by the combination of two factors. First, the fact that Ashmans were occupying at a concessionary licence fee. Second, the fact that Mrs Ashman had, in practice, no choice but to stay in the premises until the local authority were willing to rehouse her. The first factor is important because I think if the Ashmans had voluntarily paid the ordinary market rate they could not claim that the premises had become less to them because they could not find anywhere else to go.

The second factor is important because I do not think the defendant can say that the premises were worth less to him than suitable accommodation which he could realistically obtain. In the circumstances of this case the value to Mrs Ashman was no more than she would have had to pay for suitable local authority housing, if she could have been immediately rehoused. Allowing subjective devaluation in circumstances like this case will not cause any injustice to the landlord. If he has suffered greater loss (for example, because there would have been a reletting at market value) it is always open to him to elect for the alternative tort measure of damages. Although Mrs Ashman produced an agreement of the local authority showing the rent she now pays, there was no evidence on this point before the judge. The action must therefore be remitted to the county court as Kennedy LJ has proposed. But, I have no doubt, the parties will be able to agree on a figure which will, in practice, obviate the need for a further hearing.

LLOYD LJ: . . . The plaintiff's claim is for possession of the premises and for the payment of mesne profits. There is no problem as to the claim for possession. As to mesne profits they are, as I understand it, simply damages for trespass recoverable against a tenant who holds over after the lawful termination of his tenancy. A claim for mesne profits is thus to be distinguished from an action for use and occupation where the tenant holds over with the consent of his landlord. The former action is grounded in tort, the latter in quasi-contract. So far as I know, it has never been held that in the former case the landlord has the option of waiving the tort and claiming restitution unless, of course, the landlord consents to the holding over, which is not suggested here. In the present case Mr Huskinson, for the plaintiff, contends that he is entitled to ask for restitution and Kennedy and Hoffmann LJJ have so held.

There are two difficulties about that. In the first place the pleaded case is a claim for damages for trespass and nothing else. This is not surprising since the second notice to vacate given on May 17 1991 makes clear that, if Mrs Ashman failed to comply with that notice, damages for trespass would be claimed against her. This is what the plaintiff has done. There has never been any application to amend the pleading so as to claim restitution in the alternative.

Second, it is very doubtful, as the law now stands, whether the restitutionary remedy is available in the case of wrongful occupation of land. The reasons for this anomalous exception to the general rule are set out in *Goff and Jones on Restitution* 3rd ed at p. 607. Three reasons are discussed. The substantial reason is that it was so decided by the majority of this court in the case of *Phillips* v *Homfray* (1883) 24 Ch D 439. The editors of *Goff and Jones* express the view that *Phillips* v *Homfray* should be overruled and the dissenting judgment of Baggallay LJ preferred. But *Phillips* v *Homfray* was recently followed *obiter* by Lane J in the case of *Morris* v *Tarrant* (1971) 2 QB 143 and is, in any event, binding on us. We would be rash indeed to express a view about *Phillips* v *Homfrey* without having heard full argument on both sides. We have not had that advantage in this case. So, with respect, it was not open to Mr Huskinson to elect in this case to claim restitution even if he had pleaded such a claim.

Where does that leave us? Mr Huskinson told us that if the plaintiffs could not claim restitution, they could recover nothing at all since they had failed to prove any damage. I think in that respect he did less than justice to his client's claim. It is true that the plaintiff did not prove that it had an alternative tenant who was waiting to move in. But that does not mean it cannot claim and recover damages. This was the very point decided in the case of *Swordheath Properties Ltd* v *Tabet* (1979) 1 WLR 285. In that case Judge Solomon had held that, since the landlord had failed to adduce any evidence that it would have been able to relet the premises, it had failed to prove any damages. The Court of Appeal exposed the error.

Megaw LJ said at p. 288:

> It appears to me to be clear, both as a matter of principle and of authority, that in a case of this sort the plaintiff, when he has established that the defendant has remained on as a trespasser in residential property, is entitled, without bringing evidence that he could or would have let the property to someone else in the absence of the trespassing defendant, to have as damages for the trespass the value of the property as it would fairly be calculated; and, in the absence of anything special in the particular case it would be the ordinary letting value of the property that would determine the amount of the damages.

I find nothing in that passage which suggests that Megaw LJ thought he was enforcing a restitutionary remedy. He was clearly awarding damages for trespass. The same is true of the case of *Penarth Dock Engineering Co. Properties Ltd* v *Pounds* [1963] 1 Lloyd's Rep 359, the decision of Lord Denning MR at first instance. There is perhaps a whiff of restitution in the latter case, because of the statement that damages should be assessed by reference to the benefit to the defendant rather than loss to the plaintiff. But it was still a claim for damages and nothing else; and the reference to benefit in Lord Denning's judgment is perhaps explained by Lindley LJ's judgment in *Whitwham* v *Westminster Brymbo Coal & Coke Co.* [1896] 2 Ch 538. That was the case in which the plaintiff tipped soil on to the defendant's land. Lindley LJ said that the plaintiff had been injured in two respects. In the first place the value of its land have been diminished. In the second place it had lost the use of its land and the defendant had it for its own benefit. But both these aspects of the plaintiff's claim, it will be noted, were regarded as injuries to the plaintiff. That is why the editor of *McGregor on Damages* para 15–18 does not regard this line of cases as an exception to the general rule stated by Lord Blackburn in *Livingstone* v *Rawyards Coal Co.* (1880) 5 App Cas 25 at p. 39, but rather as special cases where the plaintiff can apparently recover more than his loss.

What then, is the measure of damages in a claim for mesne profits? In the vast majority of cases it will be at the same rate as the previous rent: see *Halsbury's Laws of England* 4th ed vol 27 para 255 footnote 3. If the market has risen, the landlord may recover more: see *Clifton Securities Ltd* v *Huntley* [1948] 2 All ER 283. Presumably, if the market has fallen, he will recover less. I see no difficulty in the landlord recovering damages at the market rate even though he has adduced no evidence that he would or could have relet the property. That is, as was held in *Swordheath*, the appropriate measure of damages in the normal case. But the question still remains whether the present case is indeed normal.

The judge obviously thought that it was. It is here, in my judgment, that he went wrong. . . .

There was some evidence in the present case that married quarters are occasionally let on the open market. But I am unwilling to accept on the evidence that that would be anything other than exceptional. The terms on which the plaintiff would have been likely to relet, if it had, are surely the same as the terms on which it had previously let to Mr Ashman. It is for the plaintiff to prove its damages. It does not have to adduce evidence that it would have let to another tenant, but it does have to show what the rent would have been if it had. It has failed to satisfy me that it would, in practice, have recovered any more than the artificially low level of rent applicable in the case of married quarters occupied by members of Her Majesty's services. That, therefore, should be its measure of damages. It might, of course, have recovered more by way of liquidated damages if there had been a suitable provision in the certificate which Mr Ashman signed on July 27 1989. But there was no such provision.

I thus find myself in substantial agreement with the argument put forward by Mrs Ashman in her letter of April 7 1992 where she says:

> To sum up, the Ministry of Defence cannot claim market rate on property as they cannot let the property on the open market. The rent they would normally receive for property amounts to approximately £100 per month. I feel that given they have created this catch 22 position themselves by their failure to evict me immediately they should continue charging the normal rent in the interim.

For 'cannot let the property at the open market' I would substitute 'would not in practice have let the property on the open market'. Otherwise, I agree, I would, therefore, have remitted the case with a direction to the judge to assess damages on the basis which I have outlined. But as Kennedy and Hoffman LJJ have taken a different view, I am content to go along with the basis proposed by Kennedy LJ, that the damages should be based on the value of the benefit to Mrs Ashman. It may be that, in the end, it will not make much difference in terms of money.

Ministry of Defence v *Thompson*
[1993] 2 EGLR 107 (CA)

The facts appear from the judgment of Hoffmann LJ

HOFFMANN LJ: . . . Sergeant Thompson, with his wife and three children, occupied a four-bedroom house known as 31 Gunner Lane, Woolwich, under a licence granted by the Ministry of Defence in July 1989. The licence fee, which for convenience I shall call the rent, was £104 a month. This was considerably less than the rent for which the house could, if the ministry had been so minded, have been let in the open market.

The licence was terminable in various circumstances including a change in marital status, which was defined to include a husband and wife ceasing to live together.

In August 1991 Sergeant Thompson left his wife and on September 2 the ministry gave Mrs Thompson notice to leave the house by December 3. There is no dispute over the validity of this notice. Mrs Thompson did not leave because she had nowhere to go and she could not establish a priority need to be rehoused by the local authority until an order for possession had been made by the court. On February 12 1992 the Ministry of Defence issued proceedings claiming possession and mesne profits from December 4 1991.

On March 26 1992 Judge Cox made an order for possession which was not resisted. For the purposes of calculating mesne profits, the ministry adduced the evidence of a surveyor, who said that the market rental value was £113.35 a week or a little less than £500 a month compared with the previous concessionary rent of £104 a month.

The judge gave a short judgment in which he said that mesne profits should be calculated by reference to the previous rent rather than the open market value.

I think it is fair to say that the judgment gives no reasons for this choice, but the judge added a note saying that it was his understanding that the only use of the premises by the ministry was for letting to service personnel.

The ministry appeals against this part of the order and asks this court to substitute an order for mesne profits calculated by reference to market value.

A similar point came before this court somewhat differently constituted in the case of *Ministry of Defence* v *Ashman* [1993] 2 EGLR 102, which concerned the wife of a flight sergeant in the Royal Air Force and which was decided on April 1 1993.

In spite of Mr Patrick Routley's submissions that *Ashman* is distinguishable, its principles are, in my judgment, equally applicable to this case. In both cases the husband of the defendant in possession had been occupying as a serviceman at a concessionary rent, and in both cases the defendant wife remained in possession involuntarily in the sense that she could not, in practice, move out of the premises until there had been an order of the court by which she could establish her priority need to be rehoused.

The principles in *Ashman* may, in my judgment, be summarised as follows: first, an owner of land which is occupied without his consent may elect whether to claim damages for the loss which he has been caused or restitution of the value of the benefit which the defendant has received.

Second, the fact that the owner, if he had obtained possession, would have let the premises at a concessionary rent, or even would not have let them at all, is irrelevant to the calculation of the benefit for the purposes of a restitutionary claim. What matters is the benefit which the defendant has received.

Third, a benefit may be worth less to an involuntary recipient than to one who has a free choice as to whether to remain in occupation or move elsewhere.

Fourth, the value of the right of occupation to a former licensee who has occupied at a concessionary rent and who has remained in possession only because she could not be rehoused by the local authority until a possession order has been made would ordinarily be whichever is the higher of the former concessionary rent and what she would have paid for local authority housing suitable for her needs, if she had been rehoused at the time when the notice expired.

In the present case, the only evidence before the judge was the former rent and the open market value. The judge was, in my judgment, right in the circumstances of this case in treating the open market value as of providing him with no assistance as to the value of the benefit received by Mrs Thompson. He had no evidence of what Mrs Thompson would have had to pay for suitable local authority housing.

In those circumstances, the only relevant figure before the judge was the previous rent, which represented a minimum in the sense that it was what Mr and Mrs Thompson had voluntarily been willing to pay for that house and, therefore, must have been the minimum value of the benefit of occupation to them.

Mr Routley does not ask that the case be remitted to the county court judge to determine whether the benefit might have been of greater value and I have some doubt as to whether it would, in any event, be appropriate to do so.

In my judgment, on the evidence before the judge he was entitled to determine the value at the figure which he did and the appeal should therefore be dismissed.

Note

See Cooke, 'Trespass, Mesne Profits and Restitution' (1994) 110 LQR 420 for discussion.

Inverugie Investments Ltd v *Hackett*
[1995] 1 WLR 713 (PC)

In 1970, Mr Hackett purchased a long leasehold of 30 of the 164 apartments of the Silver Sands Hotel in Grand Bahama. Inverugie, the owners of the hotel, ejected Mr Hackett in 1974. Mr Hackett sought possession and he eventually got a possession order in 1984. However, Inverugie gave up possession only in 1990, after 15½ years of trespass. Mr Hackett sought mesne profits in respect of that period during which the hotel had an occupancy rate of about 35 per cent and was running at a loss. *Held*: Mr Hackett was entitled to damages for trespass calculated at a reasonable rental value, being the published rate less 35 per cent in the winter and 65 per cent in the summer, which was the wholesale rate paid by tour operators.

LORD LLOYD OF BERWICK: [His lordship referred to *Phillips* v *Homfray* (1871) LR 6 Ch App 770, *Whitwham* v *Westminster Brymbo Coal and Coke Co.* [1896] 2 Ch 538, *Penarth Dock Engineering Co. Ltd* v *Pounds* [1963] 1 Lloyd's Rep 359 and *Swordheath Properties Ltd* v *Tabet* [1979] 1 WLR 285 and continued: . . .]

Before stating their own conclusions on the facts, their Lordships should say a brief word on the law. The cases to which they have already referred establish, beyond any doubt, that a person who lets out goods on hire, or the landlord of residential property, can recover damages from a trespasser who has wrongfully used his property whether or not he can show that he would have let the property to anybody else, and whether or not he would have used the property himself. The point is well expressed by Megaw LJ in *Swordheath Properties Ltd* v *Tabet* [1979] 1 WLR 285, 288:

> It appears to me to be clear, both as a matter of principle and of authority, that in a case of this sort the plaintiff, when he has established that the defendant has remained on as a trespasser in residential property, is entitled, without bringing evidence that he could or would have let the property to someone else in the absence of the trespassing defendant, to have as damages for the trespass the value of the property as it would fairly be calculated; and, in the absence of anything special in the particular case it would be the ordinary letting value of the property that would determine the amount of damages.

It is sometimes said that these cases are an exception to the rule that damages in tort are compensatory. But this is not necessarily so. It depends how widely one defines the 'loss' which the plaintiff has suffered. As the Earl of Halsbury LC pointed out in *Mediana (Owners of Steamship)* v *Comet (Owners of Lightship)* [1900] AC 113, 117, it is no answer for a wrongdoer who has deprived the plaintiff of his chair to point out that he does not usually sit in it or that he has plenty of other chairs in the room.

In *Stoke-on-Trent City Council* v *W. & J. Wass Ltd.* [1988] 1 WLR 1406 Nicholls LJ called the underlying principle in these cases the 'user principle.' The plaintiff may not have suffered any *actual* loss by being deprived of the use of his property. But under the user principle he is entitled to recover a reasonable rent for the wrongful use of his property by the trespasser. Similarly, the trespasser may not have derived any *actual* benefit from the use of the property. But under the user principle he is obliged to pay a reasonable rent for the use which he has enjoyed. The principle need not be characterised as exclusively compensatory, or exclusively restitutionary; it combines elements of both.

If this is the correct principle, how does it apply to the facts of the present case? Mr Mowbray [Counsel for Mr Hackett] argues that it makes no difference whether there were 30 apartments, or only one. If there had been only one, the defendants would have been obliged to pay a reasonable rent for the use of the apartment for 365 days in the year, even though the apartment might not be taken by a tour operator, or otherwise occupied, for more than 35 per cent of the time. The same must apply, says Mr Mowbray, to each of the 30 apartments.

Mr Price [Counsel for Inverugie] argues that the unusual facts of the present case take it outside the normal rule. The defendants are hotel operators. If one assumes that the parties had negotiated a notional rent for the 30 apartments as a whole, they would have taken account of the average occupancy. What has to be valued is the chance of the defendants making a profit from the letting of the 30 apartments to tour operators, not the rent which an individual operator would pay per apartment. On the basis of $3 per day per apartment—the figure calculated by the registrar—a hotel proprietor would not have been prepared to pay more than $400 per apartment per year. In this way Mr Price arrives at $159,360 as the appropriate measure of damages.

The point is not altogether easy. But their Lordships have concluded that Mr Mowbray's argument is to be preferred. If a man hires a concrete mixer, he must pay the daily hire, even though he may not in the event have been able to use the mixer because of rain. So also must a trespasser who takes the mixer without the owner's consent. He must pay the going rate, even though in the event he has derived no benefit from the use of the mixer. It makes no difference whether the trespasser is a professional builder or a do-it-yourself enthusiast.

The same applies to residential property. In the present case the defendants have had the use of all 30 apartments for 15½ years. Applying the user principle, they must pay the going rate, even though they have been unable to derive actual benefit from all the apartments for all the time. The fact that the defendants are hotel operators does not take the case out of the ordinary rule. The plaintiff is not asking for an account of profits. The chance of making a profit from the use of the apartments is not the correct test for arriving at a reasonable rent. . . .

Question

Lord Lloyd observed at the start of his judgment: 'Mr Hackett was not asking for an account of profits, perhaps because the hotel was running at a loss, as the defendants have maintained throughout. He is not asserting a restitutionary claim as an independent cause of action. So the point which divided the Court of Appeal in *Ministry of Defence* v *Ashman* [1993] 2 EGLR 102 and the interesting theoretical questions discussed in Pt VII of the Law Commission Paper *Aggravated, Exemplary and Restitutionary Damages* (Law Com. No. 132, 1993) do not arise for decision'. Do you agree with Lord Lloyd's classification of the claim in *Ministry of Defence* v *Ashman* as an *independent* restitutionary cause of action?

Note

The case is noted in [1995] LMCLQ 343 (Mitchell).

Section 2: restitutionary damages for breach of contract?

This is one of the most controversial questions in the subject: should a contract-breaker ever be required to disgorge the benefit resulting from breach? For discussion see Jones, 'The Recovery of Benefits Gained from a Breach of Contract' (1983) 99 LQR 443; Birks, 'Restitutionary Damages for Breach of Contract: *Snepp* and the Fusion of Law and Equity' [1987]

LMCLQ 421; O'Dair, 'Restitutionary Damages for Breach of Contract and the Theory of Efficient Breach: Some Reflections' (1993) 46 CLP 113; Goodhart, 'Restitutionary Damages for Breach of Contract: The Remedy that Dare Not Speak its Name' [1995] *Restitution Law Review* 3 and Burrows, *Restitution*, 397–403. As a matter of authority such a 'benefit-based' remedy has been ruled out by the Court of Appeal: *Surrey County Council* v *Bredero Homes Ltd* [1993] 3 All ER 705 (below).

A: *The orthodox view*

Occidental Worldwide Investment Corporation v _Skibs A/S Avanti_
The 'Siboen' and the 'Sibotre'
[1976] 1 Lloyd's Rep 293 (QBD (Commercial Court))

Account
The facts have been discussed in Chapter 3, Section 1 in relation to the charterers' claim to rescind variations to the charterparties. When the shipowners withdrew the ships in May 1973 the tanker market rose steeply, so the owners made large profits from the ships for the remainder of the charter periods, amounting to some $3.2 million in excess of the original charter rate of £4.10 per ton per month. The plaintiff charterers claimed the withdrawal was an unjustified breach of contract and claimed either an account of the profits made by the shipowners from the use of the ships, or alternatively damages. Kerr J held that there was a wrongful repudiation. However, there was 'no basis' for an account of profits, although the charterers were entitled to damages on ordinary contractual principles.

Notes
1. Similarly, in *Tito* v *Waddell (No. 2)* [1977] Ch 106, 332 (a breach of contract case), Sir Robert Meggary V-C stated: '. . . it is fundamental to all questions of damages that they are to compensate the plaintiff for his loss or injury by putting him as nearly as possible in the same position as he would have been in had he not suffered the wrong. The question is not one of making the defendant disgorge what he has saved by committing the wrong, but one of compensating the plaintiff.'
2. The breach in *The 'Siboen' and The 'Sibotre'* turned out to be a highly profitable one. Such 'efficient breaches' are condoned, or even celebrated, by some lawyers and economists. Jackman suggests that it could be argued that expectation damages are adequate to protect the institution of contracting ([1989] CLJ 302, at 320–21). See for discussion, O'Dair (1993) 46 CLP 113.

B: *The measure of damages in lieu of an injunction*

Wrotham Park Estate Co. Ltd v _Parkside Homes Ltd_
[1974] 1 WLR 798 (Ch D)

Parkside Homes purchased a parcel of land forming part of the Wrotham Park Estate and commenced the building of residential homes thereon, in a lay-out which constituted a breach of restrictive covenant relating to the land. The estate brought an action seeking an injunction to restrain construction, but did not seek an interlocutory injunction. In the meantime 14 houses were completed on the site and the purchasers moved in. *Held*: the estate was not entitled to a mandatory injunction to demolish the 14 homes as this would constitute an 'unpardonable waste of much needed houses', but it was entitled to substantial damages under the Chancery Amendment Act (Lord Cairns's Act) against Parkside Homes and the individual purchasers.

BRIGHTMAN J: I turn to the consideration of the quantum of damages. I was asked by the parties to assess the damages myself, should the question arise, rather than to direct an inquiry. The basic rule in contract is to measure damages by that sum of money which will put the plaintiff in the same position as he would have been in if the contract had not been broken. From that basis, the defendants argue that the damages are nil or purely nominal, because the value of the Wrotham Park Estate as the plaintiffs concede is not diminished by one farthing in consequence of the construction of a road and the erection of 14 houses on the allotment site. If, therefore, the defendants submit, I refuse an injunction I ought to award no damages in lieu. That would seem, on the face of it, a result of questionable fairness on the facts of this case. Had the offending development been the erection of an advertisement hoarding in defiance of protest and writ, I apprehend (assuming my conclusions on other points to be correct) that the court would not have hesitated to grant a mandatory injunction for its removal. If, for social and economic reasons, the court does not see fit in the exercise of its discretion, to order demolition of the 14 houses, is it just that the plaintiffs should receive no compensation and that the defendants should be left in undisturbed possession of the fruits of their wrongdoing? Common sense would seem to demand a negative answer to this question. A comparable problem arose in wayleave cases where the defendant had trespassed by making use of the plaintiff's underground ways to the defendant's profit, but without diminishing the value of the plaintiff's property. The plaintiff, in such cases, received damages assessed by reference to a reasonable way-leave rent. This principle was considered and extended in *Whitwham* v *Westminster Brymbo Coal and Coke Co.* [1896] 2 Ch 538. For six years the defendant wrongfully tipped colliery waste onto the plaintiff's land. At the trial the defendant was directed to cease tipping and give up possession. The question then arose what damages should be awarded for the wrongful act done to the plaintiff during the period of the defendant's unauthorised use of the land. The official referee found that the diminution in the value of the plaintiff's land was only £200, but that the value of the plaintiff's land to the defendant in 1888 for tipping purposes for six years was some £900. It was held that the proper scale of damages was the higher sum on the ground that a trespasser should not be allowed to make use of another person's land without in some way compensating that other person for the user.

A like principle was applied by the House of Lords in a Scottish case, *Watson, Laidlaw & Co. Ltd* v *Pott, Cassels and Williamson* (1914) 31 RPC 104. A patentee elected to sue an infringer for damages rather than for an account of profits. Part of the infringement had taken place in Java. There was evidence that the patentee could not have competed successfully in that island. It was submitted that no damages ought to be awarded in respect of the Java infringement. Lord Shaw said, at pp. 119–120:

> It is at this stage of the case, . . . that a second principle comes into play. It is not exactly the principle of restoration, either directly or expressed through compensation, but it is the principle underlying price or like. It plainly extends—and I am inclined to think not infrequently extends—to patent cases. But, indeed, it is not confined to them. For wherever an abstraction or invasion of property has occurred, then, unless such abstraction or invasion were to be sanctioned by law, the law ought to yield a recompense under the category or principle, as I say, either of price or of hire. If A, being a liveryman, keeps his horse standing idle in the stable, and B, against his wish or without his knowledge, rides or drives it out, it is no answer to A for B to say: 'Against what loss do you want to be restored? I restore the horse. There is no loss. The horse is none the worse; it is the better for the exercise.' I confess to your Lordships that this seems to me to be precisely in principle the kind of question and retort which underlay the argument of the learned counsel for the appellants about the Java trade . . . in such cases it appears to me that the correct and full measure is only reached by adding that a patentee is also entitled, on the principle of price or hire, to a royalty for the unauthorised sale or use of every one of the infringing machines in a market which the infringer, if left to himself, might not have reached. Otherwise, that property which consists in the monopoly of the patented articles granted to the patentee has been invaded, and indeed abstracted, and the law, when appealed to, would be standing by and allowing the invader or abstractor to go free.

The same principle was applied in detinue in *Strand Electric and Engineering Co. Ltd* v *Brisford Entertainments Ltd* [1952] 2 QB 246. The defendant came into possession of portable switchboards which were part of the stock-in-trade of the plaintiff. The defendant used them for its own profit for 43 weeks. The trial judge, Pilcher J, ordered the return of the switchboards and awarded damages. The damages took into account the fact that if the defendant had not wrongfully retained the switchboards the plaintiff would be unlikely to have hired out every one for the full period of 43 weeks. It was held by the Court of Appeal that the plaintiff was entitled to recover as damages the full market rate of hire for the whole period of detention. It will be sufficient to read these extracts from the judgment of Denning LJ, at p. 253:

> In assessing damages, whether for a breach of contract or for a tort, the general rule is that the plaintiff recovers the loss he has suffered, no more and no less. This rule is, however, often departed from.

He then gave examples and continued:

> The question in this case is: What is the proper measure of damages for the wrongful detention of goods? Does it fall within the general rule that the plaintiff only recovers for the loss he has suffered or within some other, and if so what, rule? It is strange that there is no authority upon this point in English law; but there is plenty on the analogous case of detention of land. The rule is that a wrongdoer, who keeps the owner out of his land, must pay a fair rental value for it, even though the owner would not have been able to use if himself or to let it to anyone else. So also a wrongdoer who uses land for his own purposes without the owner's consent, as, for instance, for a fair ground, or as a wayleave, must pay a reasonable hire for it, even though he has done no damage to the land at all: *Whitwham* v *Westminster Brymbo Coal and Coke Co.* [1896] 2 Ch 538. I see no reason why the same principle should not apply to detention of goods. If a wrongdoer has made use of goods for his own purposes, then he must pay a reasonable hire for them, even though the

> owner has in fact suffered no loss. It may be that the owner would not have used the goods himself, or that he had a substitute readily available, which he used without extra cost to himself. Nevertheless the owner is entitled to a reasonable hire. If the wrongdoer had asked the owner for permission to use the goods, the owner would be entitled to ask for a reasonable remuneration as the price of his permission. The wrongdoer cannot be better off because he did not ask permission. He cannot be better off by doing wrong than he would be by doing right. He must therefore pay a reasonable hire.

The point was further considered in *Penarth Dock Engineering Co. Ltd* v *Pounds* [1963] 1 Lloyd's Rep 359 by Lord Denning MR sitting as a judge of the Queen's Bench Division. The defendant had contracted to buy a floating dock and to remove it from the plaintiff's dock premises. The defendant defaulted in the removal of the purchase. The plaintiff, however, had suffered no damage, since the dock premises had become disused. The plaintiff claimed a mandatory injunction and damages. It was held that the plaintiff was entitled to damages at a rate per week representing a reasonable berthing charge.

The facts of the cases I have mentioned are a long way from the facts of the case before me. Should I, as invited by the plaintiffs, apply a like principle to a case where the defendant Parkside, in defiance of protest and writ, has invaded the plaintiffs' rights in order to reap a financial profit for itself? In *Leeds Industrial Co-operative Society Ltd* v *Slack* [1924] AC 851 Lord Sumner said, at p. 870:

> . . . no money awarded in substitution can be justly awarded, unless it is at any rate designed to be a preferable equivalent for an injunction and therefore an adequate substitute for it, . . .

This was said in a dissenting speech but his dissent did not arise in the context of that observation.

In the present case I am faced with the problem what damages ought to be awarded to the plaintiffs in the place of mandatory injunctions which would have restored the plaintiffs' rights. If the plaintiffs are merely given a nominal sum, or no sum, in substitution for injunctions, it seems to me that justice will manifestly not have been done.

As I have said, the general rule would be to measure damages by reference to that sum which would place the plaintiffs in the same position as if the covenant had not been broken. Parkside and the individual purchasers could have avoided breaking the covenant in two ways. One course would have been for Parkside to have sought from the plaintiffs a relaxation of the covenant. On the facts of this particular case the plaintiffs, rightly conscious of their obligations towards existing residents, would clearly not have granted any relaxation, but for present purposes I must assume that it could have been induced to do so. In my judgment a just substitute for a mandatory injunction would be such a sum of money as might reasonably have been demanded by the plaintiffs from Parkside as a quid pro quo for relaxing the covenant. The plaintiffs submitted that that sum should be a substantial proportion of the development value of the land. This is currently put at no less than £10,000 per plot, i.e. £140,000 on the assumption that the plots are undeveloped. Mr Parker gave evidence that a half or a third of the development value was commonly demanded by a landowner whose property stood in the way of a development. I do not agree with that approach to damages in this type of case. I bear in mind the following factors:

(1) The lay-out covenant is not an asset which the estate owner ever contemplated he would have either the opportunity or the desire to turn to account. It has no

commercial or even nuisance value. For it cannot be turned to account except to the detriment of the existing residents who are people the estate owner professes to protect.

(2) The breach of covenant which has actually taken place is over a very small area and the impact of this particular breach on the Wrotham Park Estate is insignificant. The validity of the covenant over the rest of area 14 is unaffected.

I think that in a case such as the present a landowner faced with a request from a developer which, it must be assumed, he feels reluctantly obliged to grant, would have first asked the developer what profit he expected to make from his operations. With the benefit of foresight the developer would, in the present case, have said about £50,000 for that is the profit which Parkside concedes it made from the development. I think that the landowner would then reasonably have required a certain percentage of that anticipated profit as a price for the relaxation of the covenant, assuming, as I must, that he feels obliged to relax it. In assessing what would be a fair percentage I think that the court ought, on the particular facts of this case, to act with great moderation. For it is to be borne in mind that the plaintiffs were aware, before the auction took place, that the land was being offered for sale as freehold building land for 13 houses, and they knew that they were not going to consent to any such development. They could have informed the Potters Bar Urban District Council of their attitude in advance of the auction, or could have given the like information to Parkside prior to completion of the contract for sale. In either event it seems highly unlikely that Parkside would have parted with its £90,000, at any rate unconditionally. I think that damages must be assessed in such a case on a basis which is fair and, in all the circumstances, in my judgment a sum equal to five per cent of Parkside's anticipated profit is the most that is fair. I accordingly award the sum of £2,500 in substitution for mandatory injunctions. I think that this amount should be treated as apportioned between the 14 respective owners or joint owners of the plots and Parkside (as the owner of the road) in 1/15th shares, so that the damages awarded will be £166 odd in each case. . . .

Surrey County Council v *Bredero Homes Ltd*
[1993] 3 All ER 705 (CA)

Surrey County Council and Mole Valley District Council owned two adjoining parcels of land near the Ridgeway. The councils decided to sell the land for development. The defendant development company offered £5.2 million, and as a result a contract was entered into by the councils and the defendant. The defendant covenanted to develop the land in accordance with an existing planning permission which allowed for the construction of 72 detached bungalows. After construction started the defendant applied for and obtained from Mole Valley District Council a planning permission which entitled it to build 77 rather than 72 houses. A development of 77 dwellings was accordingly completed, and the houses sold. At no stage did the councils seek an injunction to prevent the defendant from developing in accordance with the second planning permission. The councils now sued to recover the profit or part of the profit made by the defendant in building the extra houses as damages for breach of contract.

DILLON LJ: . . . Every student is taught that the basis of assessing damages for breach of contract is the rule in *Hadley* v *Baxendale* (1854) 9 Exch 341, which is wholly concerned with the losses which can be compensated by damages. Such damages may, in an appropriate case, cover profit which the injured plaintiff has lost, but they do not cover an award to a plaintiff who has himself suffered no loss, of the profit which the defendant has gained for himself by his breach of contract.

In the field of tort there are areas where the law is different and the plaintiff can recover in respect of the defendant's gain. Thus in the field of trespass it is well established that if one person has, without leave of another, been using that other's land for his own purposes he ought to pay for such user. Thus even if he had done no actual harm to the land he was charged for the user of the land. This was applied originally in wayleave cases where a person had without authority used his neighbour's land for passage: see, for instance, *Jegon* v *Vivian* (1871) LR 6 Ch App 742 and *Phillips* v *Homfray, Fothergill* v *Phillips* (1871) LR 6 Ch App 770.

The same principle was applied where the defendant had trespassed by tipping spoil on the plaintiff's land: see *Whitwham* v *Westminster Brymbo Coal and Coke Co.* [1896] 2 Ch 538.

The same principle was applied to patent infringement by the House of Lords in *Watson Laidlaw & Co. Ltd* v *Pott Cassels and Williamson* (1914) 31 RPC 104. The infringer was ordered to pay by way of damages a royalty for every infringing article because the infringement damaged the plaintiff's property right, that is to say his patent monopoly. So in a case of detinue the defendant was ordered to pay a hire for chattels he had detained: see *Strand Electric and Engineering Co. Ltd* v *Brisford Entertainments Ltd* [1952] 2 QB 246.

Those cases do not apply in the present case as the defendant has made no use of any property of either plaintiff.

The cases have been taken still further in some fields of tort, particularly concerned with intellectual property, where it is well established that the plaintiff can choose to have either damages or an account of profits made by the defendant by his wrongful acts: see, for instance, *Lever* v *Goodwin* (1887) 36 Ch D 1 at 7, *per* Cotton LJ. This is in line with the long-established common law doctrine of waiving the tort.

The liability in the present case is solely in contract and not in tort. [Dillon LJ discussed *Wrotham Park Estate Co.* v *Parkside Homes Ltd* [1974] 1 WLR 798, distinguished that case as concerning damages under Lord Cairns's Act and continued: . . .]

Given that the established basis of an award of damages in contract is compensation for the plaintiff's loss, as indicated above, I have difficulty in seeing how [far] Sir William Goodhart's suggested common law principle of awarding the plaintiff, who has suffered no loss, the gain which the defendant has made by the breach of contract, is intended to go. Is it to apply, for instance, to shipping contracts or contracts of employment or contracts for building works?

Sir William suggested, in his and Mr Weatherill's skeleton argument, that the conventional measure fails to do justice and a different measure should be applied where the following conditions are satisfied: (a) the breach is deliberate, in the sense that the defendant is deliberately doing an act which he knows or should know is plainly or arguably in breach of contract; (b) the defendant, as a result of the breach, has profited by making a gain or reducing a loss; (c) at the date of the breach it is clear or probable that damages under the conventional measure will either be nominal or much smaller than the profit to the defendant from the breach; and (d) if the profit results from the avoidance of expenditure, the expenditure would not have been economically wasteful or grossly disproportionate to the benefit which would have resulted from it.

He suggested in that paragraph in the skeleton argument that the underlying principle might be that the conventional measure of damages might be overriden 'in certain circumstances' by the rule that no one should benefit from his deliberate wrongdoing. In the course of his submissions Sir William limited his formulation and while retaining conditions (a), (b) and (c), substituted for condition (d) the following:

> Damages for loss of bargaining power can be awarded if—but only if—the party in breach could have been restrained by injunction from committing the breach of contract or compelled by specific performance to perform the contract. Where no such possibility existed, there was no bargaining power in reality and no right to damages for loss of it. Hence, damages for loss of bargaining power cannot be awarded where there is (for example) a contract for the sale of goods or (generally) a contract of employment.

I find difficulty with that because in theory every time there is a breach of contract the injured party is deprived of his 'bargaining power' to negotiate for a financial consideration a variation of the contract which would enable the party who wants to depart from its terms to do what he wants to do. In addition it has been held in *Walford* v *Miles* [1992] 2 AC 128 that an agreement to negotiate is not an animal known to the law and a duty to negotiate in good faith is unworkable in practice—and so I find it difficult to see why loss of bargaining or negotiating power should become an established factor in the assessment of damages for breach of contract.

Beyond that, since we are looking for the measure of damages at common law for breach of contract, apart from Lord Cairns's Act, I do not see why that should vary depending on whether the party in breach could or could not have been restrained by injunction from committing the breach or compelled by specific performance to perform the contract. Injunctions and specific performance were not remedies in the common law courts and were granted by the Court of Chancery, which, before Lord Cairns's Act, had no power to award damages, just because the common law remedy of damages was not an adequate remedy.

We were referred, in the course of Sir William's argument, to a number of other cases and, in particular, to passages in the judgment of Megarry V-C in *Tito* v *Waddell (No. 2)* [1977] Ch 106 and to the decision of this court in *Stoke-on-Trent City Council* v *W. & J. Wass Ltd* [1988] 1 WLR 1406. In the latter case this court upheld the general principle that in tort a plaintiff recovered damages equivalent to the loss he had suffered and held also that the 'user' principle in the wayleave cases and *Whitwham* v *Westminster Brymbo Coal and Coke Co.* should not be extended to cover infringement of a market right of the plaintiff council by the holding by the defendant of an unauthorised market where the plaintiff could not show he had suffered any actual loss by the infringement. What was sought in that case was damages calculated by reference to a notional licence fee that the plaintiff council might have charged for permitting the defendant's infringement but that was refused. I need not refer to the cases further.

As I see it, therefore, there never was in the present case, even before the writ was issued, any possibility of the court granting an injunction to restrain the defendant from implementing the later planning permission. The plaintiff's only possible claim from the outset was for damages only, damages at common law.

The plaintiffs have suffered no damage. Therefore on basic principles, as damages are awarded to compensate loss, the damages must be merely nominal. . . .

STEYN LJ: I agree. The issue in this appeal was defined by Sir William Goodhart QC for the appellants as the correct measure of damages in a case where the following three circumstances are satisfied: (a) there has been a deliberate breach of contract; (b) the party in breach has made a profit from that breach; and (c) the innocent party is in financial terms in the same position as if the contract had been fully performed. It is an important issue, with considerable implications for the shape of our law of obligations, and I therefore add a few remarks of my own.

Dillon LJ has reviewed the relevant case law. It would not be a useful exercise for me to try to navigate through those much travelled waters again. Instead, it seems to me that it may possibly be useful to consider the question from the point of view of the application at first principles. An award of compensation for breach of contract serves to protect three separate interests. The starting principle is that the aggrieved party ought to be compensated for loss of his positive or expectation interests. In other words, the object is to put the aggrieved party in the same financial position as if the contract had been fully performed. But the law also protects the negative interest of the aggrieved party. If the aggrieved party is unable to establish the value of a loss of bargain he may seek compensation in respect of his reliance losses. The object of such an award is to compensate the aggrieved party for expenses incurred and losses suffered in reliance of the contract. These two complementary principles share one feature. Both are pure compensatory principles. If the aggrieved party has suffered no loss he is not entitled to be compensated by invoking these principles. The application of these principles to the present case would result in an award of nominal damages only.

There is, however, a third principle which protects the aggrieved party's restitutionary interest. The object of such an award is not to compensate the plaintiff for a loss, but to deprive the defendant of the benefit he gained by the breach of contract. The classic illustration is a claim for the return of goods sold and delivered where the buyer has repudiated his obligation to pay the price. It is not traditional to describe a claim for restitution following a breach of contract as damages. What matters is that a coherent law of obligations must inevitably extend its protection to cover certain restitutionary interests. How far that protection should extend is the essence of the problem before us. In my view *Wrotham Park Estate Co.* v *Parkside Homes Ltd* [1974] 2 All ER 321, [1974] 1 WLR 798 is only defensible on the basis of the third or restitutionary principle (see *McGregor on Damages* (15th edn, 1988) para 18 and Professor P B H Birks *Civil Wrongs: A New World,* Butterworths Lectures [1990–1991] 55 at 71). The appellants' argument that the *Wrotham Park* case can be justified on the basis of a loss of bargaining opportunity is a fiction. The object of the award in the *Wrotham Park* case was not to compensate the plaintiff for financial injury, but to deprive the defendants of an unjustly acquired gain. Whilst it must be acknowledged that *Wrotham Park* represented a new development, it seems to me that it is based on a principle of legal theory, justice and sound policy. In the respondent's skeleton argument some doubt was cast, by way of alternative submission, on the correctness of the award of damages for breach of covenant in the *Wrotham Park* case. In my respectful view it was rightly decided and represents a useful development in our law. In *Tito* v *Waddell (No. 2)* [1977] 3 All ER 129 to 319, [1977] Ch 106 at 335–336 Megarry V-C interpreted the *Wrotham Park* case, and the decision in *Bracewell* v *Appleby* [1975] 1 All ER 993, [1975] Ch 408, which followed *Wrotham Park,* as cases of the invasion of property rights. I respectfully agree. *Wrotham Park* is analogous to cases where a defendant has made use of the aggrieved party's property and thereby saved expenses: see *Penarth Dock Engineering Co. Ltd* v *Pounds* [1963] 1 Lloyd's Rep 359. I readily accept that the word 'property' in this context must be interpreted in a wide sense. I would also not suggest that there is no scope for further development in this branch of the law.

But in the present case we are asked to extend the availability of restitutionary remedies for breach of contract considerably. I question the desirability of any such development. The acceptance of the appellants' primary or alternative submissions, as outlined by Dillon LJ, will have a wide-ranging impact on our commercial law. Even the alternative and narrower submission will, for example, cover charterparties and contracts of affreightment where the remedy of a negative injunction may be available. Moreover, so far as the narrower submission restricts the principle to cases where the remedies of specific performance and injunction would have been available, I must confess that that seems to me a bromide formula without any rationale in logic or common sense. Given a breach of contract, why should the availability of a restitutionary remedy, as a matter of legal entitlement be dependent on the availability of the wholly different and discretionary remedies of injunctions specific to performance? If there is merit in the argument I cannot see any sense in restricting a compensatory remedy which serves to protect the restitutionary interests to cases where there would be separate remedies of specific performance or injunction, designed directly and indirectly to enforce payment, available.

For my part I would hold that if Sir William's wider proposition fails, the narrower one must equally fail. Both submissions hinge on the defendant's breach being deliberate. Sir William invoked the principle that a party is not entitled to take advantage of his own wrongdoing. Despite Sir William's disclaimer it seems to me that the acceptance of the propositions formulated by him will inevitably mean that the focus will be on the motive of the party who committed the breach of contract. That is contrary to the general approach of our law of contract and, in particular, to rules governing the assessment of damages. In my view there are also other policy reasons which militate against adopting either Sir William's primary or narrower submission. The introduction of restitutionary remedies to deprive cynical contract breakers of the fruits of their breaches of contract will lead to greater uncertainty in the assessment of damages in commercial and consumer disputes. It is of paramount importance that the way in which disputes are likely to be resolved by the courts must be readily predictable. Given the premise that the aggrieved party has suffered no loss, is such a dramatic extension of restitutionary remedies justified in order to confer a windfall in each case on the aggrieved party? I think not. In any event such a widespread availability of restitutionary remedies will have a tendency to discourage economic activity in relevant situations. In a range of cases such liability would fall on underwriters who have insured relevant liability risks. Inevitably underwriters would have to be compensated for the new species of potential claims. Insurance premiums would have to go up. That, too, is a consequence which militates against the proposed extension. It is sound policy to guard against extending the protection of the law of obligations too widely. For these substantive and policy reasons I regard it as undesirable that the range of restitutionary remedies should be extended in the way in which we have been invited to do so.

The present case involves no breach of fiduciary obligations. It is a case of breach of contract. The principles governing expectation or reliance losses cannot be invoked. Given the fact of the breach of contract the only question is whether restitution is an appropriate remedy for this wrong. The case does not involve any invasion of the plaintiff property interests even in the broadest sense of that word, nor is it closely analogous to the *Wrotham Park* position. I would therefore rule that no restitutionary remedy is available and there is certainly no other remedy available.

I would dismiss the appeal.

Notes

1. The case is noted by Burrows [1993] LMCLQ 453, Birks (1993) 109 LQR 518 and O'Dair [1993] *Restitution Law Review* 31.

2. In *Jaggard* v *Sawyer* [1995] 2 All ER 189 the question arose again as to the measure of damages under s. 50 of the Supreme Court Act 1981 (which now embodies the jurisdiction to award damages in lieu of an injunction originally found in Lord Cairns's Act). A differently constituted Court of Appeal adopted the approach taken by Brightman J in *Wrotham Park Estate Co.* v *Parkside Homes Ltd* [1974] 1 WLR 798. Sir Thomas Bingham MR referred to Steyn LJ's analysis of the *Wrotham Park* case as restitutionary in *Surrey CC* v *Bredero* and stated (at 202):

> I cannot, however, accept that Brightman J's assessment of damages in *Wrotham Park* was based on other than compensatory principles. The defendants had committed a breach of covenant, the effects of which continued. The judge was not willing to order the defendants to undo the continuing effects of the breach. He had therefore to assess the damages necessary to compensate the plaintiffs for this continuing invasion of their right. He paid attention to the profits earned by the defendants, as it seems to me, not in order to strip the defendants of their unjust gains, but because of the obvious relationship between the profits earned by the defendants and the sum which the defendants would reasonably have been willing to pay to secure release from the covenant.

Similarly, Millett LJ found it unfortunate that Dillon LJ in *Bredero Homes* had cast doubt on the correctness of *Wrotham Park* (at 210) and 'puzzling' that Steyn LJ in the same case had sought to explain *Wrotham Park* on a restitutionary basis, and had argued that loss of opportunity to bargain was a fiction (at 211). Millett LJ continued (at 211–12):

> It is plain from his judgment in the *Wrotham Park* case that Brightman J's approach was compensatory, not restitutionary. He sought to measure the damages by reference to what the plaintiff had lost, not by reference to what the defendant had gained. He did not award the plaintiff the profit which the defendant had made by the breach, but the amount which he judged the plaintiff might have obtained as the price of giving its consent. The amount of the profit which the defendant expected to make was a relevant factor in that assessment, but that was all.

Millett LJ stressed that in *Bredero Homes* proceedings were brought after the developers had sold the houses and were no longer amenable to an injunction. The councils had lost their vital bargaining chip. Therefore a *Wrotham Park* measure was not appropriate in that case. In the instant case the Court of Appeal unanimously approved the *Wrotham Park* approach to compensating the plaintiff for continuing breaches of covenant and acts of trespass in lieu of an injunction.

Question
Whose analysis of *Wrotham Park* do you prefer? Steyn LJ's in *Surrey County Council* v *Bredero Homes*, or Millett LJ's in *Jaggard* v *Sawyer*?

C: *Cost-of-cure damages*

Ruxley Electronics and Constructions Ltd **v** ***Forsyth***
[1995] 3 WLR 118 (HL)

Forsyth contracted for a swimming-pool to be constructed adjacent to his house, specifying the depth should be 7 feet 6 inches at the deep end. The contractors, Ruxley, built a pool with a maximum depth of only 6 feet 9 inches. Forsyth claimed damages on a cost-of-cure basis for the pool's non-conformity. The county court judge held, first, the pool was perfectly safe for diving; secondly, the shortfall in the pool's depth did not decrease its value; thirdly, to increase the pool's depth required complete reconstruction at a cost of £21,650; fourthly, Forsyth had no intention of rebuilding the pool; lastly, it would be unreasonable to rebuild the pool as the benefits were wholly disproportionate to the costs. The judge therefore awarded Forsyth nothing in respect of the diminution in value of the pool, but did award £2,500 in respect of loss of pleasure and amenity. *Held*: the judge's application of a test of reasonableness was correct and the award was a proper one.

Notes
1. The contest was between a cost-of-cure award (£21,650) and a diminution in value award (nil in this case), both of which are consistent with the normal measure of contractual damages, which aim to protect the plaintiff's expectation interest. A restitutionary measure, based upon the expense saved by the contract-breaker due to defective performance, was neither argued for, nor adverted to by the House of Lords. However, it may well have proved a middle way between the all-or-nothing arguments of the parties. Such a measure is proportionate to the breach and could prove a disincentive to contractors who are tempted to cut corners. See the note in [1995] LMCLQ 456 and Goodhart [1995] *Restitution Law Review* 3, at 8–9.
2. Professor Burrows once advocated a compromise approach to restitutionary damages for breach of contract. He favoured such damages where they reflected the expense saved by a contract-breaker, but not where it simply involved stripping profits made as a result of breach. The latter case might be one where a defendant has exercised considerable skill and initiative. Burrows has now repudiated his position, because he regards the line as a difficult one to draw in practice. (See Burrows, *Restitution*, 403 and contrast Burrows, *Remedies for Torts and Breach of Contract* (London: Butterworths, 1987), 273 with the second edition (1994), at 310–12.) However, there is no reason why, if sensitively applied, such a distinction should not prove workable.

Section 3 breach of fiduciary duty

Historically, equity was more likely to award remedies based on the wrongdoer's gain. Its particular concerns, with those who manage the affairs or property of others, such as trustees and company directors, made it more suspicious of the temptations open to those it labelled fiduciaries. The factor of deterrence weighs heavily here, to the extent of having worked injustice in some individual cases.

See Burrows, *Restitution*, 405–14; and for reference Goff and Jones, 643–62, 666–70 and Jackman [1989] CLJ 302, at 311–14.

Gluckstein v *Barnes*
[1900] AC 240 (HL)

Gluckstein was a member of a syndicate which bought the Olympia exhibition hall for £140,000. They promoted a company, Olympia Ltd, of which they became the first directors, to which they sold the property for £180,000. The prospectus disclosed the profit of £40,000, but in fact as a result of dealing with charges on the property, the syndicate had made a profit of £60,000 on the purchase. This was not disclosed. When the company failed the liquidator sought restitution from Gluckstein of his share of the secret profit. The House of Lords upheld the claim.

EARL OF HALSBURY LC: My Lords, in this case the simple question is whether four persons, of whom the appellant is one, can be permitted to retain the sums which they have obtained from the company of which they were directors by the fraudulent pretence that they had paid 20,000*l.* more than in truth they had paid for property which they, as a syndicate, had bought by subscription among themselves, and then sold to themselves as directors of the company. If this is an accurate account of what has been done by these four persons, of course so gross a transaction cannot be permitted to stand. That that is the real nature of it I now proceed to shew. . . .

My Lords, I am wholly unable to understand any claim that these directors, vendors, syndicate, associates, have to retain this money. I entirely agree with the Master of the Rolls that the essence of this scheme was to form a company. It was essential that this should be done, and that they should be directors of it, who would purchase. The company should have been informed of what was being done and consulted whether they would have allowed this profit. I think the Master of the Rolls is absolutely right in saying that the duty to disclose is imposed by the plainest dictates of common honesty as well as by well-settled principles of common law.

Of the facts there cannot be the least doubt; they are proved by the agreement, now that we know the subject-matter with which that agreement is intended to deal, although the agreement would not disclose what the nature of the transaction was to those who were not acquainted with the ingenious arrangements which were prepared for the entrapping the intended victim of these arrangements.

In order to protect themselves, as they supposed, they inserted in the prospectus, qualifying the statement that they had bought the property for 140,000*l.*, payable in cash, that they did not sell to the company, and did not intend to sell, any other profits made by the syndicate from interim investments.

Then it is said there is the alternative suggested upon the agreement that the syndicate might sell to a company or to some other purchaser. In the first place, I do not believe they ever intended to sell to anybody else than a company. An individual purchaser might ask inconvenient questions, and if they or any one of them had stated as an inducement to an individual purchaser that 140,000*l*, was given for the property, when in fact 20,000*l*. less had been given, it is a great error to suppose that the law is not strong enough to reach such a statement; but as I say, I do not believe it was ever intended to get an individual purchaser, even if such an intention would have had any operation. When they did afterwards sell to a company, they took very good care there should be no one who could ask questions. They were to be sellers to themselves as buyers, and it was a necessary provision to the plan that they were to be both sellers and buyers, and as buyers to get the money to pay for the purchase from the pockets of deluded shareholders.

My Lords, I decline to discuss the question of disclosure to the company. It is too absurd to suggest that a disclosure to the parties to this transaction is a disclosure to the company of which these directors were the proper guardians and trustees. They were there by the terms of the agreement to do the work of the syndicate, that is to say, to cheat the shareholders; and this, forsooth, is to be treated as a disclosure to the company, when they were really there to hoodwink the shareholders and so far from protecting them, were to obtain from them the money, the produce of their nefarious plans.

I do not discuss either the sum sued for, or why Gluckstein alone is sued. The whole sum has been obtained by a very gross fraud; and all who were parties to it are responsible to make good what they have obtained and withheld from the shareholders. . . .

LORD MACNAGHTEN: My Lords, Mr Swinfen Eady argued this appeal with his usual ability, but the case is far too clear for argument. The learned counsel for the appellant did not, I am sure, raise the slightest doubt in the mind of any of your Lordships as to the propriety of the judgment under appeal; the only fault to be found with the learned judges of the Court of Appeal, if I may venture to criticise their judgment at all, is that they have treated the defences put forward on Mr Gluckstein's behalf with too much ceremony. For my part, I cannot see any ingenuity or any novelty in the trick which Mr Gluckstein and his associates practised on the persons whom they invited to take shares in Olympia, Limited. It is the old story. It has been done over and over again. . . .

However that may be, Mr Gluckstein defends his conduct, or, rather I should say, resists the demand, on four grounds, which have been gravely argued at the bar. In the first place, he says that he was not in a fiduciary position towards Olympia, Limited, before the company was formed. Well, for some purposes he was not. For others he was. A good deal might be said on the point. But to my mind the point is immaterial, for it is not necessary to go back beyond the formation of the company.

In the second place, he says, that if he was in a fiduciary position he did in fact make a proper disclosure. With all deference to the learned counsel for the appellant, that seems to me to be absurd. 'Disclosure' is not the most appropriate word to use when a person who plays many parts announces to himself in one character what he has done and is doing in another. To talk of disclosure to the thing called the company, when as yet there were no shareholders, is a mere farce. To the intended shareholders there was no disclosure at all. On them was practised an elaborate system of deception.

The third ground of defence was that the only remedy was rescission. That defence, in the circumstances of the present case, seems to me to be as contrary to common sense as it is to authority. The point was settled more than sixty years ago by the decision in *Hichens* v *Congreve* (1831) 4 Sim 420, and, so far as I know, that case has never been questioned.

The last defence of all was that, however much the shareholders may have been wronged, they have bound themselves by a special bargain, sacred under the provisions of the Companies Act, 1862, to bear their wrongs in silence. In other words, Mr Gluckstein boldly asserts that he is entitled to use the provisions of an Act of Parliament, which are directed to a very different purpose, as a shield and shelter against the just consequences of his fraud. . . .

My Lords, on so plain a case as this I am very reluctant to quote any authority; but I think I ought to call your Lordships' attention to the case of *Hichens* v *Congreve* (1828) 4 Russ 562; (1829) 1 R & M 150; (1831) 4 Sim 420, to which I have already alluded, and that for two reasons: first, because it seems to have been lost sight of in the argument of this case; and, secondly, because the facts there have a singular resemblance to the facts of the present case. The defences in the two cases are, for the most part, identical.

Hichens v *Congreve* was decided by Shadwell V-C in 1831. There had been a demurrer to the bill, which was overruled by the Vice-Chancellor and by Lyndhurst LC on appeal, a motion for payment of money into court, which was successful, and then the case came on for hearing. The facts were these: A Mr Flattery was the fortunate possessor of a property in Ireland containing treasures of coal and iron, rarely met with on the other side of the channel, and he was anxious to dispose of it. One Sir William Congreve entered into negotiations with him, and found that he was willing to sell for the modest sum of 10,000*l.* Then Sir William associated with himself two gentlemen of the name of Clarke, and the three proposed to themselves to buy the property, and work it by means of a company. But they thought that the company could well afford to pay 25,000*l.* for it, and they supposed that they might honestly, or, at any rate, without being found out, put the extra 15,000*l.* into their own pockets, concealing from the proposed shareholders the difference in price. Mr Flattery seems to have been not unwilling to lend himself to the scheme. So a contract was drawn up for the sale of the property from Mr Flattery to the trustees of the company for the price of 25,000*l.*, out of which, of course, Mr Flattery was only to keep 10,000*l.* Sir William Congreve and the two Clarkes got up the company, issued a prospectus, and prepared a deed of settlement stating that the 'property had been bought from Mr Flattery for 25,000*l.*; and they appointed themselves and other persons directors of the company. A large sum of money was collected, a large body of subscribers executed the deed of settlement, and later on a private Act of Parliament was obtained establishing and regulating, but not incorporating, the company. Some years afterwards the proceedings of Sir William Congreve and his associates were discovered, and a bill was filed by certain shareholders on behalf of themselves and the rest of the shareholders other than the defendants to compel them to refund the 15,000*l.* As the Vice-Chancellor pointed out, if Sir William Congreve and the Messrs Clarke had agreed among themselves that they would form a partnership or a company for the purpose of working the mines, and had held out to the persons who should form the company that it should be formed on the basis that they should pay 15,000*l.* to Sir William Congreve and the Messrs Clarke as the consideration for their having the mines, no objection whatever could have been made to the transaction. But the objection was that the real transaction was not disclosed, and 'that the persons who became members of the company could not possibly know that it was the intention of Sir William Congreve and the Messrs Clarke that the 15,000*l.* should be paid out of the funds of the company for the benefit of Sir William Congreve, the Messrs Clarke, and those gentlemen whom they permitted to participate in it.'

Then the Vice-Chancellor, after stating the facts and relevant documents, proceeds as follows:

> It is useless for the Messrs Clarke and Sir William Congreve to state, as they have done, in their answers that they apprehended that the sums which so came to their hands were profits which they were entitled to; for it is impossible that they could, if they fairly exercised their judgments which as directors they were bound to exercise, form any such opinion, and it is perfectly plain to my mind that it was not competent to those who were forming a company thus to deal with the funds of the company, making at the same time the representations which they did make. If they had been dealing with one individual only, no doubt could be entertained upon the matter. Two objections were made to the relief that is asked in this case. First it was said that the property was worth 25,000*l.* So it might have been; but in my opinion the value of the property is quite immaterial, for the question here is what was held out to the company to have been the sum actually paid for it, and I conceive that if there was a misrepresentation in that respect, the parties who made that representation must be answerable for it. The other objection that was made was that the mines were not, and could not have been, purchased for the company; for that at the time when the agreement was entered into there was no company in existence. Strictly speaking it is true that there was no company in existence; but these gentlemen were endeavouring to form a company, and they had taken upon themselves the character of directors for the benefit of all persons who had agreed to be, or might afterwards become, members of the company. The 25,000*l.* was to be paid out of the funds which should be subscribed by persons who might thereafter become members of the company, and my opinion, therefore, is that all those persons who might thereafter become members of the company through the instrumentality and representations of those directors are entitled to the protection of this Court. Then it was said that there can be no relief except in the way of restitution of the mines; but that appears to me to be a fallacy. On the 22nd of June 1825 an Act of Parliament was passed which establishes this company and directs that its capital shall be 300,000*l.*; and I apprehend that in no other way can there be any relief in this case than by making those who have subtracted the 15,000*l.* from the funds of this company repay that sum, for it would be no relief to make Flattery take back the mines: that would destroy the company altogether. When these directors represented that 25,000*l.* was to be paid for the purchase of the mines it must be considered that they intended that the company should have the mines, and that they meant it to be understood that that was the lowest price at which they could be purchased. What is complained of is that by improper representation 15,000*l.* has been withdrawn from the funds of the company and paid into the pocket of private individuals. Is it not obvious, therefore, that the relief to be given is the restitution of the 15,000*l.*?

My Lords, I need not comment on the Vice-Chancellor's judgment. It seems to me to cover the whole of the present case except the defence founded on the provisions of the Companies Act, 1862, and with that I have already dealt.

There are two things in this case which puzzle me much, and I do not suppose that I shall ever understand them. I mention them merely because I should be very sorry if it were thought that in those two matters the House unanimously approved of what has been done. I do not understand why Mr Gluckstein and his associates were not called upon to refund the whole of the money which they misappropriated. What they did with it, whether they put it in their own pockets or distributed it among their confederates, or spent it in charity, seems to me absolutely immaterial. In the next place, I do not understand why Mr Gluckstein was only charged with interest at the rate of 3 per cent. I should have thought it was a case for penal interest. . . .

Regal (Hastings) Ltd v *Gulliver*
[1942] 1 All ER 378; [1967] 2 AC 134 (note) (HL)

Action for money had and received

Regal formed a subsidiary, Amalgamated, with a capital of £5,000 in £1 shares, for the purpose of acquiring the leases of two cinemas. The owners of the cinemas wanted the directors of Regal, who were also the directors of Amalgamated, to provide personal guarantees for rent. This the directors were unwilling to do. Instead, it was agreed that Amalgamated should be fully capitalised. The directors decided that Regal could afford to take up only £2,000 of the £5,000 share capital, so four of Regal's directors took up 500 shares each. The chairman arranged the allocation of a further 500 shares and the company's solicitor was persuaded to take up the remaining 500. Eventually all these shares were sold at a considerable profit. Regal, now under new management, claimed that its former directors should account for the profit made.

LORD RUSSELL OF KILLOWEN: . . . In the Court of Appeal, upon this claim to profits, the view was taken that in order to succeed the plaintiff had to establish that there was a duty on the Regal directors to obtain the shares for Regal. Two extracts from the judgment of Lord Greene MR, show this. After mentioning the claim for damages, he says:

> The case is put on an alternative ground. It is said that, in the circumstances of the case, the directors must be taken to have been acting in the matter of their office when they took those shares; and that accordingly they are accountable for the profits which they have made . . . There is one matter which is common to both these claims which, unless it is established, appears to me to be fatal. It must be shown that in the circumstances of the case it was the duty of the directors to obtain these shares for their company.

Later in his judgment he uses this language:

> But it is said that the profit realised by the directors on the sale of the shares must be accounted for by them. That proposition involves that on October 2, when it was decided to acquire these shares, and at the moment when they were acquired by the directors, the directors were taking to themselves something which properly belonged to their company.

Other portions of the judgment appear to indicate that upon this claim to profits, it is a good defence to show bona fides or absence of fraud on the part of the directors in the action which they took, or that their action was beneficial to the company, and the judgment ends thus:

> That being so, the only way in which these directors could secure that benefit for their company was by putting up the money themselves. Once that decision is held to be a bona fide one, and fraud drops out of the case, it seems to me that there is only one conclusion, namely, that the appeal must be dismissed with costs.

My Lords, with all respect I think there is a misapprehension here. The rule of equity which insists on those, who by use of a fiduciary position make a profit, being liable to account for that profit, in no way depends on fraud, or absence of bona fides; or upon such questions or considerations as whether the profit would or should otherwise have gone to the plaintiff, or whether the profiteer was under a duty to obtain the source of the profit for the plaintiff, or whether he took a risk or acted as he did for the benefit of the plaintiff, or whether the plaintiff has in fact been damaged or benefited by his action. The liability arises from the mere fact of a profit having, in the stated circumstances, been made. The profiteer, however honest and well-intentioned, cannot escape the risk of being called upon to account.

The leading case of *Keech* v *Sandford*, Sel Cas Ch 61 is an illustration of the strictness of this rule of equity in this regard, and of how far the rule is independent of these outside considerations. A lease of the profits of a market had been devised to a trustee for the benefit of an infant. A renewal on behalf of the infant was refused. It was absolutely unobtainable. The trustee, finding that it was impossible to get a renewal for the benefit of the infant, took a lease for his own benefit. Though his duty to obtain it for the infant was incapable of performance, nevertheless he was ordered to assign the lease to the infant, upon the bare ground that, if a trustee on the refusal to renew might have a lease for himself, few renewals would be made for the benefit of cestuis que trust. Lord King LC said:

> This may seem hard, that the trustee is the only person of all mankind who might not have the lease: but it is very proper that the rule should be strictly pursued, and not in the least relaxed . . .

One other case in equity may be referred to in this connection, viz., *Ex parte James* 8 Ves 337 decided by Lord Eldon LC. This was a case of a purchase of a bankrupt's estate by the solicitor to the commission, and Lord Eldon LC refers to the doctrine thus:

> This doctrine as to purchases by trustees, assignees, and persons having a confidential character, stands much more upon general principles than upon the circumstances of any individual case. It rests upon this: that the purchase is not permitted in any case however honest the circumstances; the general interests of justice requiring it to be destroyed in every instance; as no court is equal to the examination and ascertainment of the truth in much the greater number of cases.

. . .

My Lords, I have no hesitation in coming to the conclusion, upon the facts of this case, that these shares, when acquired by the directors, were acquired by reason, and only by reason of the fact that they were directors of Regal, and in the course of their execution of that office.

It now remains to consider whether in acting as directors of Regal they stood in a fiduciary relationship to that company. Directors of a limited company are the creatures of statute and occupy a position peculiar to themselves. In some respects they resemble trustees, in others they do not. In some respects they resemble agents, in others they do not. In some respects they resemble managing partners, in others they do not. In *In re Forest of Dean Coal Mining Co.* (1878) 10 Ch D 450 a director was held not liable for omitting to recover promotion money which had been improperly paid on the formation of the company. He knew of the improper payment, but he was not appointed a director until a later date. It was held that, although a trustee of settled property which included a debt would be liable for neglecting to sue for it, a director of a company was not a trustee of debts due to the company and was not liable. I cite two passages from the judgment of Sir George Jessel MR:

> Directors have sometimes been called trustees, or commercial trustees, and sometimes they have been called managing partners, it does not matter what you call them so long as you understand what their true position is, which is that they are really commercial men managing a trading concern for the benefit of themselves and all other shareholders in it.

Later, after pointing out that traders have a discretion whether they shall sue for a debt, which discretion is not vested in trustees of a debt under a settlement, he said:

> Again directors are called trustees. They are no doubt trustees of assets which have come to their hands, or which are under their control, but they are not trustees of a debt due to the company . . . A director is the managing partner of the concern, and although a debt is due to the concern I do not think it right to call him a trustee of that debt which remains unpaid, though his liability in respect of it may in certain cases and in some respects be analogous to the liability of a trustee.

The position of directors was considered by Kay J, in *In re Faure Electric Accumulator Co.* (1888) 40 Ch D 141. That was a case where directors had applied the company's money in payment of an improper commission, and a claim was made for the loss thereby occasioned to the company. In referring to the liability of directors, the judge pointed out that directors were not trustees in the sense of trustees of a settlement, that the nearest analogy to their position would be that of a managing agent of a mercantile house with large powers, but that there was no analogy which was absolutely perfect; and he added:

> However, it is quite obvious that to apply to directors the strict rules of the Court of Chancery with respect to ordinary trustees might fetter their action to an extent which would be exceedingly disadvantageous to the companies they represent.

In addition a passage from the judgment of Bowen LJ in *Imperial Hydropathic Hotel Co., Blackpool* v *Hampson* 20 Ch D 1, 12 may be usefully recalled. He said:

> I should wish . . . to begin by remarking this, that when persons who are directors of a company are from time to time spoken of by judges as agents, trustees, or managing partners of the company, it is essential to recollect that such expressions are not used as exhaustive of the powers and responsibilities of those persons but only as indicating useful points of view from which they may for the moment and for the particular purpose be considered—points of view at which for the moment they seem to be either cutting the circle, or falling within the category of the suggested kind. It is not meant that they belong to the category, but that it is useful for the purpose of the moment to observe that they fall pro tanto within the principles which govern that particular class.

These three cases, however, were not concerned with the question of directors making a profit; but that the equitable principle in this regard applies to directors is beyond doubt. In *Parker* v *McKenna* (1874) 10 Ch App 96, a new issue of shares of a joint stock bank was offered to the existing shareholders at a premium. The directors arranged with one Stock to take, at a larger premium, the shares not taken up by the existing shareholders. Stock, being unable to fulfil his contract, requested the directors to relieve him of some. They did so, and made a profit. They were held accountable for the profit so made. Lord Cairns LC said:

> The court will not enquire and is not in a position to ascertain, whether the bank has or has not lost by the acts of the directors. All the court has to do is to examine whether a profit has been made by an agent, without the knowledge of his principal, in the course and execution of his agency, and the court finds, in my opinion, that these agents in the course of their agency have made a profit, and for that profit they must, in my opinion, account to their principal.

In the same case James LJ stated his view in the following terms:

> . . . it appears to me very important that we should concur in laying down again and again the general principle that in this court no agent in the course of his agency, in the matter of his agency, can be allowed to make any profit without the knowledge of his principal; that the rule is an inflexible rule, and must be applied inexorably by this court, which is not entitled, in my judgment, to receive evidence, or suggestion, or argument, as to whether the principal did or did not suffer any injury in fact, by reason of the dealing of the agent; for the safety of mankind requires that no agent shall be able to put his principal to the danger of such an inquiry as that.

In *Imperial Mercantile Credit Association (Liquidators)* v *Coleman* (1873) LR 6 HL 189 one Coleman, a stockbroker and a director of a financial company, had contracted to place a large amount of railway debentures for a commission of 5 per cent. He proposed that his company should undertake to place them for a commission of $1\frac{1}{2}$ per cent. The 5 per cent commission was in due course paid to the director, who paid over the $1\frac{1}{2}$ per cent to the company. He was held liable to account for the $3\frac{1}{2}$ per cent, by Malins V-C, who said:

> It is of the highest importance that it should be distinctly understood that it is the duty of directors of companies to use their best exertions for the benefit of those whose interests are committed to their charge, and that they are bound to disregard their own private interests whenever a regard to them conflicts with the proper discharge of such duty.

His decree was reversed by Lord Hatherley (1871) 6 Ch App 558, 566 et seq. on the ground that the transaction was protected under the company's articles of association. Your Lordships' House LR 6 HL 189, however, thought that in the circumstances of the case the articles of association gave no protection, and restored the decree with unimportant variations. The liability was based on the view, which was not disputed by Lord Hatherley, that the director stood in a fiduciary relationship to the company. That relationship being established, he could not keep the profit which had been earned by the funds of the company being employed in taking up the debentures. The courts in Scotland have treated directors as standing in a fiduciary relationship towards their company and, applying the equitable principle, have made them accountable for profits accruing to them in the course and by reason of their directorships. It will be sufficient to refer to *Huntington Copper Co.* v *Henderson* 1877 4 R 294, 308, in which the Lord President cites with approval the following passage from the judgment of the Lord Ordinary:

> Whenever it can be shown that the trustee has so arranged matters as to obtain an advantage whether in money or money's worth to himself personally through the execution of his trust, he will not be permitted to retain, but be compelled to make it over to his constituent.

In the result, I am of opinion that the directors standing in a fiduciary relationship to Regal in regard to the exercise of their powers as directors, and having obtained these shares by reason and only by reason of the fact that they were directors of Regal and in the course of the execution of that office, are accountable for the profits which they have made out of them. The equitable rule laid down in *Keech* v *Sandford* and *Ex parte James* and similar authorities applies to them in full force. It was contended that these cases were distinguishable by reason of the fact that it was impossible for Regal to get the shares owing to lack of funds and that the directors in taking the shares were really acting as members of the public. I cannot accept this argument. It was impossible for the cestui que trust in *Keech* v *Sandford* to obtain the lease, nevertheless the trustee was accountable. The suggestion that the directors were applying simply as members of the public is a travesty of the facts. They could, had they wished, have protected themselves by a resolution (either antecedent or subsequent) of the Regal shareholders in general meeting. In default of such approval, the liability to account must remain. The result is that, in my opinion, each of the respondents Bobby, Griffiths, Bassett and Bentley is liable to account for the profit which he made on the sale of his 500 shares in Amalgamated. . . .

LORD PORTER: . . . My Lords, I am conscious of certain possibilities which are involved in the conclusion which all your Lordships have reached. The action is brought by the Regal company. Technically, of course, the fact that an unlooked for advantage may be gained by the shareholders of that company is immaterial to the question at issue. The company and its shareholders are separate entities. One cannot help remembering, however, that in fact the shares have been purchased by a financial group who were willing to acquire those of the Regal and the Amalgamated at a certain price. As a result of your Lordships' decision that group will, I think, receive in one hand part of the sum which has been paid by the other. For the shares in Amalgamated they paid £3 16s 1d per share, yet part of that sum may be returned to the group, though not necessarily to the individual shareholders by reason of the enhancement in value of the shares in Regal—an enhancement brought about as a result of the receipt by the company of the profit made by some of its former directors on the sale of Amalgamated shares. This, it seems, may be an unexpected windfall, but whether it be so or not, the principle that a person occupying a fiduciary relationship shall not make a profit by reason thereof is of such vital importance that the possible consequence in the present case is in fact as it is in law an immaterial consideration. . . .

Boardman* v *Phipps
[1967] 2 AC 46 (HL)

Account; constructive trust

The plaintiff was a beneficiary with a $\frac{5}{18}$ share under a will trust and the defendants were another beneficiary, Tom Phipps, and the solicitor to the trust, Mr Boardman. Amongst the trust assets were 8,000 of the 30,000 shares of an ailing textile company, Lester & Harris Ltd. The defendants were unhappy with the performance of the company and dissatisfied with its management. Using considerable business acumen the defendants launched a successful takeover bid for the company and turned its fortunes around. The defendants as a result held nearly 22,000 shares in the company. All of this was with the acquiescence of the active trustees, Mr Fox and Mrs Noble. Both the shareholding of the defendants and the trust had considerably increased in value. The plaintiff, Tom's brother, brought an action claiming the defendants held $\frac{5}{18}$ of their shareholding as constructive trustees for him, and for an account of the profits made from the shares. The plaintiff claimed they had breached their fiduciary duty by using information and an opportunity which they had obtained by purporting to represent the trust, and which belonged in equity to the trust. *Held*: by a majority of 3:2 the defendants (appellants) were so liable to the plaintiff (respondent); however, they were entitled to a liberal allowance in respect of their services to the trust.

LORD COHEN: . . . The ratio decidendi of the trial judge is conveniently summed up in the following passage from the judgment in the Court of Appeal of Pearson LJ, where he said [1965] Ch 992, 1022:

> . . . the defendants were acting with the authority of the trustees and were making ample and effective use of their position as representing the trustees and wielding the power of the trustees, who were substantial minority shareholders, to extract from the directors of the company a great deal of information as to the assets and resources of the company; and . . . this information enabled the defendants to appreciate the true potential value of the company's shares and to decide that a purchase of the shares held by the director's group at the price offered would be a very promising venture. The defendants made their very large profit, not only by their own skill and persistence and risk-taking, but also by making use of their position as agents for the trustees. The principles stated in *Regal (Hastings) Ltd* v *Gulliver* are applicable in this case.

The trial judge also held that the appellants could not rely by way of defence on the consent of the respondent given in answer to Mr Boardman's letter of March 10, 1959, as neither in the letter nor in the subsequent interview did he give sufficient information as to the material facts. This defence was not pressed in the Court of Appeal or raised before your Lordships. Accordingly, only one issue remains for decision, namely, were the appellants in such a fiduciary relationship vis-à-vis the trustees that they must be taken to be accountable to the beneficiaries for the shares and for any profit derived by them therefrom?

In the statement of claim the respondent based his claim on an allegation of agency but it is, in my opinion, plain that no contract of agency which included the purchase of further shares in the company was ever made; it is plain for two reasons: first, in 1957 the widow was alive and her approval was not sought or obtained; secondly, Mr Fox was clear in his evidence that he would never have given his consent to such acquisition. Wilberforce J was, I think, of this opinion but he held [1964] 1 WLR 993, 1007 that the appellants assumed the character of self-appointed agents for the trustees for the purpose of extracting information as to the company's business from its directors and if possible to strengthen the management of the company by securing representation on the board of the trust holding. I agree that the appellants were the agents of the trustees for this purpose. I doubt, however, whether 'self-appointed' is the correct adjective. Fox was the active trustee and where it is not a question of delegating authority to make binding contracts I agree with Russell LJ [1965] Ch 992, 1031 that two trustees, or for that matter one trustee, can come to an arrangement with a third party which will have the effect of placing the latter in a fiduciary position vis-à-vis the trust.

In the case before your Lordships it seems to me clear that the appellants throughout were obtaining information from the company for the purpose stated by

Wilberforce J but it does not necessarily follow that the appellants were thereby debarred from acquiring shares in the company for themselves. They were bound to give the information to the trustees but they could not exclude it from their own minds. As Wilberforce J said [1964] 1 WLR 993, 1011, the mere use of any knowledge or opportunity which comes to the trustee or agent in the course of his trusteeship or agency does not necessarily make him liable to account. In the present case had the company been a public company and had the appellants bought the shares on the market, they would not, I think, have been accountable. But the company is a private company and not only the information but the opportunity to purchase these shares came to them through the introduction with Mr Fox gave them to the board of the company and in the second phase when the discussions related to the proposed split-up of the company's undertaking it was solely on behalf of the trustees that Mr Boardman was purporting to negotiate with the board of the company. The question is this: when in the third phase the negotiations turned to the purchase of the shares at £4 10s a share, were the appellants debarred by their fiduciary position from purchasing on their own behalf the 21,986 shares in the company without the informed consent of the trustees and the beneficiaries?

Wilberforce J and, in the Court of Appeal, both Lord Denning MR and Pearson LJ based their decision in favour of the respondent on the decision of your Lordships' House in *Regal (Hastings) Ltd* v *Gulliver*. I turn, therefore, to consider that case. Mr Walton [counsel for the respondent] relied upon a number of passages in the judgments of the learned Lords who heard the appeal: in particular on (1) a passage in the speech of Lord Russell of Killowen where he says:

> The rule of equity which insists on those, who by use of a fiduciary position make a profit, being liable to account for that profit, in no way depends on fraud, or absence of bona fides; or upon such questions or considerations as whether the profit would or should otherwise have gone to the plaintiff, or whether the profiteer was under a duty to obtain the source of the profit for the plaintiff, or whether he took a risk or acted as he did for the benefit of the plaintiff, or whether the plaintiff has in fact been damaged or benefited by his action. The liability arises from the mere fact of a profit having, in the stated circumstances, been made.

(2) a passage in the speech of Lord Wright, where he says:

> That question can be briefly stated to be whether an agent, a director, a trustee or other person in an analogous fiduciary position, when a demand is made upon him by the person to whom he stands in the fiduciary relationship to account for profits acquired by him by reason of his fiduciary position, and by reason of the opportunity and the knowledge, or either, resulting from it, is entitled to defeat the claim upon any ground save that he made profits with the knowledge and assent of the other person. The most usual and typical case of this nature is that of principal and agent. The rule in such cases is compendiously expressed to be that an agent must account for net profits secretly (that is, without the knowledge of his principal) acquired by him in the course of his agency. The authorities show how manifold and various are the applications of the rule. It does not depend on fraud or corruption.

These paragraphs undoubtedly help the respondent but they must be considered in relation to the facts of that case. In that case the profit arose through the application by four of the directors of Regal for shares in a subsidiary company which it had been the original intention of the board should be subscribed for by Regal. Regal had not the requisite money available but there was no question of it being ultra vires Regal to subscribe for the shares. In the circumstances Lord Russell of Killowen said:

> I have no hesitation in coming to the conclusion, upon the facts of this case, that these shares, when acquired by the directors, were acquired by reason, and only by reason of the fact that they were directors of Regal, and in the course of their execution of that office.

He goes on to consider whether the four directors were in a fiduciary relationship to Regal and concludes that they were. Accordingly, they were held accountable. Mr Bagnall [counsel for the appellants] argued that the present case is distinguishable. He puts his argument thus. The question you ask is whether the information could have been used by the principal for the purpose for which it was used by his agents? If the answer to that question is no, the information was not used in the course of their duty as agents. In the present case the information could never have been used by the trustees for the purpose of purchasing shares in the company; therefore purchase of shares was outside the scope of the appellant's agency and they are not accountable.

This is an attractive argument, but it does not seem to me to give due weight to the fact that the appellants obtained both the information which satisfied them that the purchase of the shares would be a good investment and the opportunity of acquiring them as a result of acting for certain purposes on behalf of the trustees. Information is, of course, not property in the strict sense of that word and, as I have already stated, it does not necessarily follow that because an agent acquired information and opportunity while acting in a fiduciary capacity he is accountable to his principals for any profit that comes his way as the result of the use he makes of that information and opportunity. His liability to account must depend on the facts of the case. In the present case much of the information came the appellants' way when Mr Boardman was acting on behalf of the owners of the 8,000 shares in the company. In these circumstances it seems to me that the principle of the *Regal* case applies and that the courts below came to the right conclusion. . . .

I desire to repeat that the integrity of the appellants is not in doubt. They acted with complete honesty throughout and the respondent is a fortunate man in that the rigour of equity enables him to participate in the profits which have accrued as the result of the action taken by the appellants in March, 1959, in purchasing the shares at their own risk. As the last paragraph of his judgment clearly shows, the trial judge evidently shared this view. He directed an inquiry as to what sum is proper to be allowed to the appellants or either of them in respect of his work and skill in obtaining the said shares and the profits in respect thereof. The trial judge concluded by expressing the opinion that payment should be on a liberal scale. With that observation I respectfully agree. . . .

LORD HODSON: . . . Mr Boardman's fiduciary position arose from the fact that he was at all material times solicitor to the trustees of the will of Mr Phipps senior. This is admitted, although counsel for the appellants has argued, and argued correctly, that there is no such post as solicitor to trustees. The trustees either employ a solicitor or they do not in a particular case and there is no suggestion that they were under any contractual or other duty to employ Mr Boardman or his firm. Nevertheless as a historical fact they did employ him and look to him for advice at all material times and this is admitted. It was as solicitor to the trustees that he obtained the information which is so clearly summarised in the judgment of Wilberforce J [1964] 1 WLR 993, 1013 and repeated in the speech of my noble and learned friend Lord Upjohn. This information enabled him to acquire knowledge of a most extensive and valuable character, as the learned judge pointed out, which was the foundation upon which a decision could and was taken to buy the shares in Lester & Harris Ltd.

This information was obtained on behalf of the trustees, most of it at a time during the history of the negotiations when the proposition was to divide the assets of the company between two groups of shareholders. This object could not have been effected without a reconstruction of the company and Mr Boardman used the strong minority shareholding which the trustees held, that is to say, 8,000 shares in the company, wielding this holding as a weapon to enable him to obtain the information of which he subsequently made use.

As to this it is said on behalf of the appellants that information as such is not necessarily property and it is only trust property which is relevant. I agree, but it is nothing to the point to say that in these times corporate trustees, e.g., the Public Trustee and others, necessarily acquire a mass of information in their capacity of trustees for a particular trust and cannot be held liable to account if knowledge so acquired enables them to operate to their own advantage, or to that of other trusts. Each case must depend on its own facts and I dissent from the view that information is of its nature something which is not properly to be described as property. We are aware that what is called 'knowhow' in the commercial sense is property which may be very valuable as an asset. I agree with the learned judge and with the Court of Appeal that the confidential information acquired in this case which was capable of being and was turned to account can be properly regarded as the property of the trust. It was obtained by Mr Boardman by reason of the opportunity which he was given as solicitor acting for the trustees in the negotiations with the chairman of the company, as the correspondence demonstrates. The end result was that out of the special position in which they were standing in the course of the negotiations the appellants got the opportunity to make a profit and the knowledge that it was there to be made. . . .

LORD GUEST: [His Lordship discussed *Regal (Hastings) Ltd* v *Gulliver* [1942] 1 All ER 378; [1967] 2 AC 134n (HL) and continued: . . .]

Applying these principles to the present case I have no hesitation in coming to the conclusion that the appellants hold the Lester & Harris shares as constructive trustees and are bound to account to the respondent. It is irrelevant that the trustees themselves could not have profited by the transaction. It is also irrelevant that the appellants were not in competition with the trustees in relation to the shares in Lester & Harris. The appellants argued that as the shares were not acquired in the course of any agency undertaken by the appellants they were not liable to account. Analogy was sought to be obtained from the case of *Aas* v *Benham* [1891] 2 Ch 244 where it was said that before an agent is to be accountable the profits must be made within the scope of the agency (see Lindley LJ [at 256]). That, however, was a case of partnership where the scope of the partners' power to bind the partnership can be closely defined in relation to the partnership deed. In the present case the knowledge and information obtained by Boardman was obtained in the course of the fiduciary position in which he had placed himself. The only defence available to a person in such a fiduciary position is that he made profits with the knowledge and assent of the trustees. It is not contended that the trustees had such knowledge or gave such consent.

In the Court of Appeal the Master of the Rolls and Pearson LJ decided the case in the respondent's favour upon the basis that the appellants were 'self-appointed agents' and thus placed themselves in a fiduciary capacity. Reference was made to *Lyell* v

Kennedy 14 App Cas 437. I prefer, however, to base my opinion upon the broader ground which was epitomised by Mr Walton in his closing submission. Boardman and Tom Phipps, he said, placed themselves in a special position which was of a fiduciary character in relation to the negotiations with the directors of Lester & Harris relating to the trust shares. Out of such special position and in the course of such negotiations they obtained the opportunity to make a profit out of the shares and knowledge that the profit was there to be made. A profit was made and they are accountable accordingly. . . .

LORD UPJOHN (dissenting): . . . In *Barnes* v *Addy* 9 Ch App 244, 251 Lord Selborne LC said:

> It is equally important to maintain the doctrine of trusts which is established in this court, and not to strain it by unreasonable construction beyond its due and proper limits. There would be no better mode of undermining the sound doctrines of equity than to make unreasonable and inequitable applications of them.

That, in my judgment, is applicable to this case.

The trustees were not willing to buy more shares in the company. The active trustees were very willing that the appellants should do so themselves for the benefit of their large minority holding. The trustees, so to speak, lent their name to the appellants in the course of prolonged and difficult negotiations and, of course, the appellants thereby learnt much which would have otherwise been denied to them. The negotiations were in the end brilliantly successful.

And how successful Tom was in his reorganisation of the company is apparent to all. They ought to be very grateful.

In the long run the appellants have bought for themselves at entirely their own risk with their own money shares which the trustees never contemplated buying and they did so in circumstances fully known and approved of by the trustees.

To extend the doctrines of equity to make the appellants accountable in such circumstances is, in my judgment, to make unreasonable and unequitable applications of such doctrines. . . .

Question

Is information a species of property? Does recovery depend upon such a characteristation?

Notes

1. For criticism of *Regal (Hastings) Ltd* v *Gulliver* and *Boardman* v *Phipps*, see Jones, 'Unjust Enrichment and the Fiduciary's Duty of Loyalty' (1968) 84 LQR 472. Professor Jones argues that both the principle of unjust enrichment and a prophylactic policy underlie equity's supervision of fiduciaries, but goes on to say that a too-mechanical application of the principles led to unjust results in these two leading cases. Jones comments (at 474):

> The implications of equity's rule are far-reaching. Once a fiduciary is shown to be in breach of his duty of loyalty he must disgorge any benefit gained even though he acted honestly and in his principal's best interests, even though his principal benefited as well as he from his conduct, even though his principal could not otherwise have obtained the benefit, and

even though the benefit was obtained through the use of the fiduciary's own assets and in consequence of his personal skill and judgment.

2. On the question of remuneration for the fiduciary (or counter-restitution) see Chapter 8, Section 3 for discussion of *Guinness plc* v *Saunders* [1990] 2 AC 663.

Industrial Development Consultants Ltd v *Cooley*
[1972] 1 WLR 443 (Birmingham Assize)

Account; constructive trust

The defendant, Cooley, was appointed managing director of the plaintiff company, IDC, by Hicks, the chairman of the group of companies to which IDC belonged. IDC offered construction and design services to large industrial enterprises, and Cooley was recruited for his expertise in the gas industry. In February 1968, Cooley, on behalf of IDC, entered negotiations with the Eastern Gas Board with a view to IDC designing and constructing new depots for the board. These were unsuccessful. In May 1969, the gas board approached Cooley with a view to Cooley doing the work in his private capacity. On 13 June, an informal offer of work was made, so on 16 June Cooley falsely represented to Hicks that due to ill-health he would have to resign. Cooley entered into a contract with the gas board on 6 August. *Held*: Cooley was trustee of the benefits of his contract with the gas board for IDC and was liable to account.

ROSKILL J: . . . The first matter that has to be considered is whether or not the defendant was in a fiduciary relationship with his principals, the plaintiffs. Mr Davies [counsel for the defendant] argued that he was not because he received this information which was communicated to him privately. With respect, I think that argument is wrong. The defendant had one capacity and one capacity only in which he was carrying on business at that time. That capacity was as managing director of the plaintiffs. Information which came to him while he was managing director and which was of concern to the plaintiffs and was relevant for the plaintiffs to know, was information which it was his duty to pass on to the plaintiffs because between himself and the plaintiffs a fiduciary relationship existed as defined in the passage I have quoted from *Buckley on the Companies Acts* and, indeed, in the speech of Lord Cranworth LC.

It seems to me plain that throughout the whole of May, June and July 1969 the defendant was in a fiduciary relationship with the plaintiffs. From the time he embarked upon his course of dealing with the Eastern Gas Board, irrespective of anything which he did or he said to Mr Hicks, he embarked upon a deliberate policy and course of conduct which put his personal interest as a potential contracting party with the Eastern Gas Board in direct conflict with his pre-existing and continuing duty as managing director of the plaintiffs. That is something which for over 200 years the courts have forbidden. The principle goes back far beyond the cases cited to me from the last century. The well-known case of *Keech* v *Sandford* (1726) Sel Cas t King (Macnaghten) 175 is perhaps one of the most striking illustrations of this rule.

> A person being possessed of a lease of . . . a market, devised his estate to trustee in trust for the infant; before the expiration of the term the trustee applied to the lessor

> for a renewal for the benefit of the infant, which he refused. . . . there was clear proof of the refusal to renew for the benefit of the infant, on which the trustee sets a lease made to himself.

Lord King LC said at p. 175:

> I must consider this as a trust for the infant; . . . if a trustee, on the refusal to renew, might have a lease to himself, few trust-estates would be renewed to the cestui que use; though I do not say there is a fraud in this case, yet [the trustee] should rather have let it run out, than to have had the lease to himself. This may seem hard, that the trustee is the only person of all mankind who might not have the lease; but it is very proper that rule should be strictly pursued, and not in the least relaxed; for it is very obvious what would be the consequence of letting trustees have the lease, on refusal to renew to cestui que use.

That case shows how rigidly this rule has always been applied.

One sees in the nineteenth-century cases, of which many are quoted in Viscount Sankey's speech in the *Regal* case [1967] 2 AC 134, how this principle has always been maintained. In *Liquidators of Imperial Mercantile Credit Association* v *Coleman* (1873) LR 6 HL 189, Malins V-C, before whom the case came at first instance, said (1871) 6 Ch App 558, 563:

> It is of the highest importance that it should be distinctly understood that it is the duty of directors of companies to use their best exertions for the benefit of those whose interests are committed to their charge, and that they are bound to disregard their own private interests whenever a regard to them conflicts with the proper discharge of such duty.

> In *Parker* v *McKenna* (1874) 10 Ch App 96, James LJ said, at p. 124:

> I do not think it is necessary, but it appears to me very important, that we should concur in laying down again and again the general principle that in this court no agent in the course of his agency, in the matter of his agency, can be allowed to make any profit without the knowledge and consent of his principal; that that rule is an inflexible rule, and must be applied inexorably by this court, which is not entitled, in my judgment, to receive evidence, or suggestion, or argument as to whether the principal did or did not suffer any injury in fact by reason of the dealing of the agent; for the safety of mankind requires that no agent shall be able to put his principal to the danger of such an inquiry as that.

In the nuclear age that last sentence may perhaps seem something of an exaggeration, but, nonetheless, it is eloquent of the strictness with which throughout the last century and indeed in the present century, courts of the highest authority have always applied this rule.

Therefore, I feel impelled to the conclusion that when the defendant embarked on this course of conduct of getting information on June 13, using that information and preparing those documents over the weekend of June 14/15 and sending them off on June 17, he was guilty of putting himself into the position in which his duty to his employers, the plaintiffs, and his own private interests conflicted and conflicted grievously. There being the fiduciary relationship I have described, it seems to me plain that it was his duty once he got this informatiion to pass it to his employers and not to guard it for his own personal purposes and profit. He put himself into the position when his duty and his interests conflicted. As Lord Upjohn put it in *Phipps* v *Boardman* [1967] 2 AC 46, 127: 'It is only at this stage that any question of accountability arises.'

Does accountability arise? It is said: 'Well, even if there were that conflict of duty and interest, nonetheless, this was a contract with a third party in which the plaintiffs never could have had any interest because they would have never got it.' That argument has been forcefully put before me by Mr Davies.

The remarkable position then arises that if one applies the equitable doctrine upon which the plaintiffs rely to oblige the defendant to account, they will receive a benefit which, on Mr Smettom's evidence at least, it is unlikely they would have got for themselves had the defendant complied with his duty to them. On the other hand, if the defendant is not required to account he will have made a large profit, as a result of having deliberately put himself into a position in which his duty to the plaintiffs who were employing him and his personal interests conflicted. I leave out of account the fact that he dishonestly tricked Mr Hicks into releasing him on June 16 although Mr Brown [counsel for the plaintiff] urged that that was another reason why equity must compel him to disgorge his profit. It is said that the plaintiffs' only remedy is to sue for damages either for breach of contract or maybe for fraudulent misrepresentation. Mr Brown has been at pains to disclaim any intention to claim damages for breach of contract save on one basis only, and he has disclaimed specifically any claim for damages for fraudulent misrepresentation. Therefore, if the plaintiffs succeed they will get a profit which they probably would not have got for themselves had the defendant fulfilled his duty. If the defendant is allowed to keep that profit he will have got something which he was able to get solely by reason of his breach of fiduciary duty to the plaintiffs.

When one looks at the way the cases have gone over the centuries it is plain that the question whether or not the benefit would have been obtained but for the breach of trust has always been treated as irrelevant. I mentioned *Keech* v *Sandford* a few moments ago and this fact will also be found emphasised if one looks at some of the speeches in *Regal (Hastings) Ltd* v *Gulliver (Note)* [1967] 2 AC 134 though it is true, as was pointed out to me, that if one looks at some of the language used in the speeches in *Regal* such phrases as 'he must account for any benefit which he obtains in the course of and owing to his directorship' will be found.

In one sense the benefit in this case did not arise because of the defendant's directorship: indeed, the defendant would not have got his work had he remained a director. However, one must, as Lord Upjohn pointed out in *Phipps* v *Boardman* [1967] 2 AC 46, 125, look at the passages in the speeches in *Regal* having regard to the facts of that case to which those passages and those statements were directed. I think Mr Brown was right when he said that it is the basic principle which matters. It is an over-riding principle of equity that a man must not be allowed to put himself in a position in which his fiduciary duty and his interests conflict. The variety of cases where that can happen is infinite. The fact that there has not previously been a case precisely of this nature with precisely similar facts before the courts is of no import. The facts of this case are, I think, exceptional and I hope unusual. They seem to me plainly to come within this principle.

I think that, although perhaps the expression is not entirely precise, Mr Brown put the point well when he said that what the defendant did in May, June and July was to substitute himself as an individual for the company of which he was managing director and to which he owed a fiduciary duty. It is upon the ground I have stated that I rest my conclusion in this case. Perhaps it is permissible to say I have less reluctance in reaching that conclusion on the application of this basic principle of equity since I know that what happened was enabled to happen because a release was obtained by the defendant from a binding contractual obligation by the dishonest and untrue misrepresentations which were made to Mr Hicks on June 16.

In my judgment, therefore, an order for an account will be issued because the defendant has made and will make his profit as a result of having allowed his interests and his duty to conflict. . . .

Notes

1. Contrast *Island Export Finance Ltd* v *Umunna* [1986] BCLC 460, which clarifies the limits of the 'corporate opportunity' doctrine.

2. For discussion of the nature of the remedy in this context see Goode, 'The Recovery of a Director's Improper Gains: Proprietary Remedies for Infringement of Non-Proprietary Rights' in McKendrick (ed.), *Commercial Aspects of Trusts and Fiduciary Obligations* (Oxford: Clarendon Press, 1992), 137–48.

Reading* v *Attorney General
[1951] AC 507 (HL)

Action for money had and received

Reading was a sergeant in the Royal Army Medical Corps, stationed in Cairo. During 1943 and 1944 he accepted nearly £20,000 in bribes to sit in his uniform on civilian lorries carrying illicit alcohol, in order to ensure the vehicles were not searched by the police. Reading was court-martialled and imprisoned for two years. Upon release Reading sought restitution of the £20,000 which had been seized at the time of his arrest.

LORD PORTER: . . . In these circumstances Denning, J, held that the Crown was entitled to the money in question. It was, in his view, immaterial to consider whether the method of seizure was justified or not. Even if it was not, the Crown had a valid counterclaim and, avoiding a circuity of action, could thus defeat the appellant's claim. 'The claim here is', he says [1948] 2 KB 268, 275, 'for restitution of moneys which, in justice, ought to be paid over.' It was suggested in argument that the learned judge founded his decision solely upon the doctrine of unjust enrichment and that that doctrine was not recognised by the law of England. My Lords, the exact status of the law of unjust enrichment is not yet assured. It holds a predominant place in the law of Scotland and, I think, of the United States, but I am content for the purposes of this case to accept the view that it forms no part of the law of England and that a right to restitution so described would be too widely stated.

But, indeed, this doctrine is not of the essence of Denning, J's judgment. His reasoning is to be found in the passage which succeeds that quoted. He says:

> In my judgment, it is a principle of law that if a servant, in violation of his duty of honesty and good faith, takes advantage of his service to make a profit for himself, in this sense, that the assets of which he has control, or the facilities which he enjoys, or the position which he occupies, are the real cause of his obtaining the money, as distinct from being the mere opportunity for getting it, that is to say, if they play the predominant part in his obtaining the money, then he is accountable for it to the master. It matters not that the master has not lost any profit, nor suffered any damage. Nor does it matter that the master could not have done the act himself. It

> is a case where the servant has unjustly enriched himself by virtue of his service without his master's sanction. It is money which the servant ought not to be allowed to keep, and the law says it shall be taken from him and given to his master, because he got it solely by reason of the position which he occupied as a servant of his master.

And again: 'The uniform of the Crown, and the position of the man as a servant of the Crown were the sole reasons why he was able to get this money, and that is sufficient to make him liable to hand it over to the Crown'. The learned judge, however, also says: 'This man Reading was not acting in the course of his employment: and there was no fiduciary relationship in respect of these long journeys nor, indeed, in respect of his uniform'. If this means, as I think it does, that the appellant was neither a trustee nor in possession of some profit-earning chattel, and that it was contrary to his duty to escort unwarranted traffic or possibly any traffic through the streets of Cairo, it is true, but, in my view, irrelevant. He nevertheless was using his position as a sergeant in His Majesty's Army and the uniform to which his rank entitled him to obtain the money which he received. In my opinion any official position, whether marked by a uniform or not, which enables the holder to earn money by its use gives his master a right to receive the money so earned even though it was earned by a criminal act. 'You have earned, the master can say, 'money by the use of your position as my servant. It is not for you, who have gained this advantage, to set up your own wrong as a defence to my claim'.

Asquith LJ, in the Court of Appeal, points out [1949] 2 KB 232, 236 that there is a well-established class of cases in which a master can recover whether or not he has suffered any detriment in fact, e.g., those in which a servant or agent has realised a secret profit, commission or bribe in the course of his employment, and that the sum recoverable is the amount of such profit. It is perhaps sufficient to refer in this connexion to *Boston Deep Sea Fishing & Ice Co.* v *Ansell* 39 Ch D 339, 367–8, and to quote the words of Bowen, LJ:

> It is true, as Kekewich, J says, that the money which is sought to be recovered must be money had and received by the agent for the principal's use; but the use which arises in such a case, and the reception to the use of the principal which arises in such a case, does not depend on any privity between the principal and the opposite party with whom the agent is employed to conduct business—it is not that the money ought to have gone into the principal's hands in the first instance; the use arises from the relation between the principal and the agent himself. It is because it is contrary to equity that the agent or the servant should retain money so received without the knowledge of his master. Then the law implies a use, that is to say, there is an implied contract, if you put it as a legal proposition—there is an equitable right, if you treat it as a matter of equity—as between the principal and agent that the agent should pay it over, which renders the agent liable to be sued for money had and received, and there is an equitable right in the master to receive it, and to take it out of the hands of the agent, which gives the principal a right to relief in equity.

But it is said that this right to recover is subject to two qualifications: (1) the sum obtained must have been obtained in the course of the servant's employment, and (2) there must exist in the matter in question a fiduciary relationship between employer and employee.

It is often convenient to speak of money obtained as received in the course of the servant's employment, but strictly speaking I do not think that expression accurately describes the position where a servant receives money by reason of his employment but in dereliction of his duty. In *Attorney-General* v *Goddard* 98 LJ (KB) 743 the bribes given to Sergeant Goddard were received by reason of his employment but not in the course of it, except in the sense that his employment afforded the opportunity by which the gain was made. Just as in the often-quoted instance of a servant letting out his own services and the use of his master's horses for private gain, he is not acting in the course of his employment, he is taking advantage of the position which his employment gives him and for reward so gained he is answerable to his master nonetheless, as *Attorney-General* v *Goddard* shows, though the obtaining of the money is a criminal act. It is true that the right of the master to demand payment of the money is often imputed to a promise implied from his relationship to the servant. I doubt whether it is necessary to raise such an implication in order to show that the money has been received to the master's use, but even if it were it may well be contended that there is no illegality in a servant promising to hand over to his master any sums he gains by use of his position. Nor would the master be affirming any criminal act committed by the servant in earning the sum claimed; he would only be saying that as between himself and the servant the servant could not set up his own wrong as a defence. Any third party's claim to the money would not be affected. In this aspect the making of the promise need not and should not in my view be referred to a point of time after the receipt of the bribe: it may well be ascribed to the time when the contract of employment was entered into.

As to the assertion that there must be a fiduciary relationship, the existence of such a connexion is, in my opinion, not an additional necessity in order to substantiate the claim; but another ground for succeeding where a claim for money had and received would fail. In any case, I agree with Asquith LJ [1949] 2 KB 232, 236, in thinking that the words 'fiduciary relationship' in this setting are used in a wide and loose sense and include, inter alia, a case where the servant gains from his employment a position of authority which enables him to obtain the sum which he receives.

My Lords, the fact that the Crown in this case, or that any master, has lost no profits or suffered no damage is, of course, immaterial and the principle so well known that it is unnecessary to cite the cases illustrating and supporting it. It is the receipt and possession of the money that matters, not the loss or prejudice to the master. . . .

Notes

1. For discussion of the nature of the restitutionary remedy available against the corrupt fiduciary who received a bribe, see the discussion of *Lister & Co.* v *Stubbs* (1890) 45 Ch D 1 and *Attorney-General for Hong Kong* v *Reid* [1994] 1 AC 324 in Chapter 7, Section 3.

2. For the relationship between the restitutionary remedy and other remedies available to the principal, see *Mahesan* v *Malaysian Government Officers' Co-operative Housing Society* [1979] AC 374 (PC) and *Logicrose Ltd* v *Southend United Football Club Ltd* [1988] 1 WLR 1256 noted in [1989] CLJ 22 (Jones).

Section 4: breach of confidence

The perceived need for protection of confidential information, whether government or trade secrets, or the intimate details of private relationships, has spawned a new civil wrong. Jackman writes: 'the relationship of confidentiality represents another kind of legal facility which, in turn, is protected by obligations subsisting in equity on the analogy of fiduciary obligations; and the status of confidentiality as a facilitative institution is reflected in the structure of remedies, giving protection against not only personal, but also institutional harm.' ([1989] CLJ 302, at 315)

See Burrows, *Restitution*, 414–18; Birks, *Introduction*, 343–6; for reference Goff and Jones, 662–5, 683–95 and Jackman [1989] CLJ 302, at 314–17.

Peter Pan Manufacturing Corporation v *Corsets Silhouette Ltd*
[1964] 1 WLR 96 (Ch D)

Account

Peter Pan, an American company, granted a licence (including the right to exploit certain patents and trade marks) to Corsets Silhouette to manufacture certain styles of brassières in the UK and Eire. Later, Corsets Silhouette's designer was shown in confidence certain new designs of Peter Pan's. As a result Corsets Silhouette manufactured and sold two new styles of bra ('U.15' and 'U.25') based in part upon the new designs seen by their designer and in part upon previous information given to them. Peter Pan sought and obtained a perpetual injunction restraining Corsets Silhouette from using such designs in breach of confidence. At trial they elected for an account of profits rather than damages. On the question of the account:

PENNYCUICK J: . . . the effect of my judgment is that the manufacture and sale of brassières of styles U.15 and U.[25] involves confidential information, and, therefore, the defendants are not entitled to manufacture those styles. From that it follows as a matter of right that the plaintiffs are entitled at their option to claim damages in respect of such invasion of their rights as has already taken place, or alternatively, an account of the profits made by manufacture and sale of brassières in invasion of their rights. It is unnecessary to go through a number of authorities which have been cited, and it will be sufficient to refer to *Lever* v *Goodwin* (1887) 36 ChD 1; 3 TLR 650, CA. The headnote is:

> The defendants, who were soap manufacturers, brought out their soap in packets so closely resembling those in which the plaintiffs, who were also soap manufacturers, had been in the habit of bringing out their soap, as to be calculated to deceive purchasers:— *Held*, by Chitty J, that although the retail dealers who bought soap from the defendants would not be deceived, the defendants by their imitation of the plaintiffs' packets put into the hands of the retail dealers an instrument of fraud, and ought to be restrained by injunction. An injunction was accordingly granted, and an account was directed of the profits made by the defendants in selling soap in the form in which it was held that they were not entitled to sell it: *Held*, on appeal, that the injunction had been rightly granted, and that the account was in the proper form, and ought not to be limited by excluding from it soap which the retail dealers sold to persons who bought it as the defendants' soap.

The actual issue in the case was a somewhat different one, but the order made by Chitty J was: 'an account of the profits made by the defendants in selling or disposing of soap made by or for the defendants in any wrapper such as that contained in the exhibits marked JSS1, JSS4, and BB1, and in the form of those exhibits.' It seems to me on a plain reading of that order that the account would have been of the profits made by the defendants from selling tablets of soap in wrappers of any of the three specified forms; that is to say, how much had it cost to manufacture that soap? what was the price received on its sale? the difference being the profit.

The case went to the Court of Appeal where the form of account ordered by Chitty J was challenged. The Court of Appeal upheld the order. Cotton LJ said 36 Ch D 1, 7:

> It is well known that, both in trade-mark cases and patent cases, the plaintiff is entitled, if he succeeds in getting an injunction, to take either of two forms of relief; he may either say, 'I claim from you the damage I have sustained from your wrongful act,' or 'I claim from you the profit which you have made by your wrongful act.' . . . The profit for which the defendants must account is the profit which they have made by the sale of soap in that fraudulent dress to the middlemen. It is immaterial how the middlemen deal with it.

I have been referred to a number of forms of order in Seton's Judgments, 7th ed. (1912), Vol. 1, in which an account of profits has been ordered. They were patent cases, trade-mark cases, or otherwise, and in each case the account was in this simple form—for example, at pages 615 and 616: 'And it is ordered that an account be taken of the profits made by the defendants in manufacturing and selling, and in selling shirts under the mark or title of 'Eureka'; 'An account of the profits made by the defendants in selling or disposing of soap,' which is the *Lever* v *Goodwin* case which I have already read; and there are one or two others, for example, at page 655: 'An account of the number of copies of the defendants' directory so printed, and of the number thereof so published by the defendant W. as aforesaid, which the defendants or any other person, etc., by their or any of their order, or for their or any of their use, have sold or disposed of; and the number of copies now remaining on hand unsold, or undisposed of. An account of all and every sum or sums of money received by the defendants, and each of them, or by any other person, etc., upon or by the sale of such copies,' and then an order 'that the defendants do pay to the plaintiff what upon taking the said account shall be certified to be the net profit arising from the printing and publication of the defendants' said directory.' It seems to me that on the plain terms of those orders, what the plaintiff who elects in favour of an account of profits is entitled to, is simply an account of profits in the sense which I have indicated, that is: What has the plaintiff expended on manufacturing these goods? What is the price which he has received on their sale? and the difference is profit. That is what the plaintiffs claim in the order for an account as formulated by them; that is simply an account of the profits made by the defendants in the manufacture and sale of the brassières U.15 and U.25.

Mr Tookey, for the defendants, has said that that is not the true meaning of the order for an account in the various cases to which I have referred, and that the true meaning of the order, if I understand him, is an account of the amount by which the profit made by the defendant from manufacturing articles with the aid of the patents, trade marks, confidential information, or whatever it may be, which he has in fact used exceeds the amount of the profit which he would have made if he had manufactured the same article without the aid of that material. It seems to me quite impossible to construe the orders made in the various cases as bearing that meaning, and further, so far as I can see, it is perfectly impossible to take as one factor in an account the amount of profit which the defendants would have made by manufacturing brassières in the styles U.15 and U.25 without the use of confidential information. Indeed, Mr Tookey very aptly said that an account in the only form in which he says the plaintiffs are entitled to an account would be impracticable. I am quite unsatisfied by any authorities which have been cited to me that that is the only account to which the plaintiffs are entitled, or that there would be any serious difficulty in working out the account to which I have held that they are entitled.

I should mention that one of the cases cited to me by Mr Tookey was *Siddell* v *Vickers* (1892) 9 RPC 152, 153. On the particular facts of the case the Court of Appeal laid down that 'the true test of comparison was with what the defendants would probably have used instead of the invention, looking at all the circumstances of the case.' That means only this, that the defendants could have manufactured the product in question by other means, but were able to manufacture more economically by making use of a particular appliance which they were not entitled to use. The position there seems to be wholly different from that in the present case where the manufacture of the article in question of itself involved the use of the confidential information and the defendants could not have manufactured that article at all without the use of the confidential information. So again it seems to me that the proper order for an account is in the terms which the plaintiffs have put forward, which is the time-honoured form, and I do not see myself any reason why that form should not be adopted.

Seager v *Copydex Ltd*
[1967] 1 WLR 923 (CA)

The facts appear in the judgment of Lord Denning MR.

LORD DENNING MR: . . . Summarised, the facts are these:

(i) Mr Seager invented the 'Klent' carpet grip and took out a patent for it. He manufactured this grip and sold it. He was looking for a selling organisation to market it.

(ii) Mr Seager negotiated with Copydex with a view to their marketing the 'Klent' grip. These negotiations were with Mr Preston, the assistant manager, and Mr Boon, the sales manager. These negotiations lasted more than a year, but came to nothing.

(iii) In the course of those negotiations Mr Seager disclosed to Mr Preston and Mr Boon all the features of the 'Klent' grip. He also told them of an idea of his for an alternative carpet grip with a 'V' tang and strong-point. But they rejected it, saying they were only interested in the 'Klent' grip.

(iv) Both Mr Preston and Mr Boon realised that the information was given to them in confidence. Neither of them had any engineering skills, nor had invented anything.

(v) As soon as the negotiations looked like coming to nothing, Copydex decided to make a carpet grip of their own, which was to be basically similar to the 'Klent' grip, but with spikes which would not infringe Mr Seager's patent.

(vi) Copydex did in fact make a carpet grip which did not infringe Mr Seager's patent for a 'Klent' grip. But it embodied the very idea of an alternative grip (of a 'V-tang' with strong-point) which Mr Seager mentioned to them in the course of the negotiations. Copydex made an application to patent it, and gave the name of Mr Preston as the true and first inventor.

(vii) Copydex gave this carpet grip the name 'Invisigrip,' which was the very name which Mr Seager says he mentioned to Mr Preston and Mr Boon in the course of the negotiations.

(viii) Copydex say that their alternative grip was the result of their own ideas and was not derived in any way from any information given to them by Mr Seager. They say also that the name of 'Invisigrip' was their own spontaneous idea.

(ix) I have no doubt that Copydex honestly believed the alternative was their own idea; but I think that they must unconsciously have made use of the information which Mr Seager gave them. The coincidences are too strong to permit of any other explanation.

The Law
I start with one sentence in the judgment of Lord Greene MR in *Saltman Engineering Co.* v *Campbell Engineering Co.* (1948) 65 RPC 203, 213; [1963] 3 All ER 413n, 414, CA :

> If a defendant is proved to have used confidential information, directly or indirectly obtained from the plaintiff, without the consent, express or implied, of the plaintiff, he will be guilty of an infringement of the plaintiff's rights.

To this I add a sentence from the judgment of Roxburgh J in *Terrapin Ltd* v *Builders' Supply Co. (Hayes) Ltd* [1960] RPC 128, 130, CA which was quoted and adopted as correct by Roskill J in *Cranleigh Precision Engineering Ltd.* v *Bryant* [1965] 1 WLR 1293, 1317, 1319; [1964] 3 All ER 289:

> As I understand it, the essence of this branch of the law, whatever the origin of it may be, is that a person who has obtained information in confidence is not allowed to use it as a spring-board for activities detrimental to the person who made the confidential communication, and spring-board it remains even when all the features have been published or can be ascertained by actual inspection by any member of the public.

The law on this subject does not depend on any implied contract. It depends on the broad principle of equity that he who has received information in confidence shall not take unfair advantage of it. He must not make use of it to the prejudice of him who gave it without obtaining his consent. The principle is clear enough when the whole of the information is private. The difficulty arises when the information is in part public and in part private. As, for instance, in this case. A good deal of the information which Mr Seager gave to Copydex was available to the public, such as the patent specification in the Patent Office, or the 'Klent' grip, which he sold to anyone who asked. If that was the only information he gave them, he could not complain. It was public knowledge. But there was a good deal of other information he gave them which was private, such as the difficulties which had to be overcome in making a satisfactory grip; the necessity for a strong, sharp tooth: the alternative forms of tooth; and the like. When the information is mixed, being partly public and partly private, then the recipient must take special care to use only the material which is in the public domain. He should go to the public source and get it: or, at any rate, not be in a better position than if he had gone to the public source. He should not get a start over others by using the information which he received in confidence. At any rate, he should not get a start without paying for it. It may not be a case for injunction or even for an account, but only for damages, depending on the worth of the confidential information to him in saving him time and trouble.

Conclusion
Applying these principles, I think that Mr Seager should succeed. On the facts which I have stated, he told Copydex a lot about the making of a satisfactory carpet grip which was not in the public domain. They would not have got going so quickly except for what they had learned in their discussions with him. They got to know in particular that it was possible to make an alternative grip in the form of a 'V-tang,' provided the

tooth was sharp enough and strong enough, and they were told about the special shape which would produce this result. The judge thought that the information was not significant. But I think it was. It was the spring-board which enabled them to go on to devise the 'Invisigrip' and to apply for a patent for it. They were quite innocent of any intention to take advantage of him. They thought that, as long as they did not infringe his patent, they were exempt. In this they were in error. They were not aware of the law as to confidential information. They were not at liberty to make use of any confidential information he gave them without paying for it.

I would allow the appeal and give judgment for Mr Seager for damages to be assessed.

Seager v Copydex Ltd (No. 2)
[1969] 1 WLR 809 (CA)

LORD DENNING MR: In April, 1967, we heard a case which Mr Seager brought against Copydex Ltd, alleging that they had taken confidential information relating to a design for a carpet grip. We found in favour of Mr Seager. Now a question has arisen as to the principles on which the damages are to be assessed. They are to be assessed, as we said, at the value of the information which the defendants took. If I may use an analogy, it is like damages for conversion. Damages for conversion are the value of the goods. Once the damages are paid, the goods become the property of the defendant. A satisfied judgment in trover transfers the property in the goods. So here, once the damages are assessed and paid, the confidential information belongs to the defendants.

The difficulty is to assess the value of the information taken by the defendants. We have had a most helpful discussion about it. The value of the confidential information depends on the nature of it. If there was nothing very special about it, that is, if it involved no particular inventive step, but was the sort of information which could be obtained by employing any competent consultant, then the value of it was the fee which a consultant would charge for it: because in that case the defendants, by taking the information, would only have saved themselves the time and trouble of employing a consultant. But, on the other hand, if the information was something special, as, for instance, if it involved an inventive step or something so unusual that it could not be obtained by just going to a consultant, then the value of it is much higher. It is not merely a consultant's fee, but the price which a willing buyer—desirous of obtaining it—would pay for it. It is the value as between a willing seller and a willing buyer. In this case Mr Seager says the information was very special. People had been trying for years to get a carpet grip and then he hit upon this idea of a dome-shaped prong. It was, he said, an inventive step. And he is supported in this issue by the fact that the defendants themselves have applied for a patent for it. Furthermore, if he is to be regarded as a seller, it must be remembered that he had a patent for another carpet grip called Klent: and, if he was selling the confidential information (which I will call the Invisigrip information), then the sales of Klent might be adversely affected. The sales of the Klent would be reduced owing to the competition of the Invisigrip. So he would ask for a higher price for the confidential information in order to compensate him for the reduction in the Klent.

In these circumstances, if Mr Seager is right in saying that the confidential information was very special indeed, then it may well be right for the value to be assessed on the footing that in the usual way it would be remunerated by a royalty. The court, of course, cannot give a royalty by way of damages. But it could give an equivalent by a calculation based on a capitalisation of a royalty. Thus it could arrive at a lump sum. Once a lump sum is assessed and paid, then the confidential information would belong to the defendants in the same way as if they had bought and paid for it by an agreement of sale. The property, so far as there is property in it, would vest in them. They would have the right to use that confidential information for the manufacture of carpet grips and selling of them. If it is patentable, they would be entitled to the benefit of the patent as if they had bought it. In other words, it would be regarded as a real outright purchase of the confidential information. The value should, therefore, be assessed on that basis: and damages awarded accordingly.

In these circumstances, I do not think we should make any such declaration as Copydex Ltd ask. It is sufficient for us to say that, on a satisfied judgment for damages, the confidential information belongs to the defendants.

Note

For discussion see Jones, 'Restitution of Benefits Obtained in Breach of Another's Confidence' (1970) 86 LQR 463.

Attorney-General v *Guardian Newspapers Ltd (No. 2)*
[1990] 1 AC 109 (HL)

Account; constructive trust

Peter Wright, a former member of MI5, penned during his retirement in Tasmania a book called *Spycatcher*. The Crown fought a long and largely fruitless legal campaign to prevent publication and dissemination of the book's contents both in Australia and the UK. The book documented alleged irregularities involving MI5, including a supposed plot to bring down Harold Wilson's government in the 1970s. The Crown obtained interlocutory injunctions against the *Observer* and *Guardian* newspapers to prevent them publishing further revelations. Then, on 12 July 1987, the *Sunday Times* which had purchased the right to serialise the book from Wright's Australian publisher, commenced serialisation. An interlocutory injunction was awarded against that newspaper to prevent further serialisation. The book was then published in the United States and its contents became common knowledge. The injunctions were all subsequently discharged. Both Wright and the *Sunday Times* were held to have acted in breach of confidence. The extracts concern the civil remedies, other than injunctions, which are available for breach of confidence.

LORD KEITH OF KINKEL: . . . This leads on to consideration of the question whether 'The Sunday Times' should be held liable to account to the Crown for profits made from past and future serialisation of *Spycatcher*. An account of profits made through breach of confidence is a recognised form of remedy available to a claimant: *Peter Pan Manufacturing Corporation* v *Corsets Silhouette Ltd* [1964] 1 WLR 96; cf. *Reading* v *Attorney-General* [1951] AC 507. In cases where the information disclosed is of a commercial character an account of profits may provide some compensation to the claimant for loss which he has suffered through the disclosure but damages are the main remedy for such loss. The remedy is, in my opinion, more satisfactorily to be attributed to the principle that no one should be permitted to gain from his own wrongdoing. Its availability may also, in general, serve a useful purpose in lessening the temptation for recipients of confidential information to misuse it for financial gain. In the present case 'The Sunday Times' did misuse confidential information and it would be naive to suppose that the prospect of financial gain was not one of the reasons why it did so. I can perceive no good ground why the remedy should not be made available to the Crown in the circumstances of this case, and I would therefore hold the Crown entitled to an account of profits in respect of the publication on 12 July 1987. I would add that in my opinion 'The Sunday Times,' in the taking of the account, is not entitled to deduct in computing any gain the sums paid to Mr Wright's publishers as consideration for the licence granted by the latter, since neither Mr Wright nor his publishers were or would in the future be in a position to maintain an action in England for recovery of such payments. Nor would the courts of the country enforce a claim by them to the copyright in a work the publication of which they had brought about contrary to the public interest: cf. *Glyn* v *Weston Feature Film Co.* [1916] 1 Ch 261, 269. Mr Wright is powerless to prevent anyone who chooses to do so from publishing *Spycatcher* in whole or in part in this country, or to obtain any other remedy against them. There remains of course, the question whether the Crown might successfully maintain a claim that it is in equity the owner of the copyright in the book. Such a claim has not yet been advanced, but might well succeed if it were to be.

In relation to future serialisation of further parts of the book, however, it must be kept in mind that the proposed subject matter of it has now become generally available and that 'The Sunday Times' is not responsible for this having happened. In the circumstances 'The Sunday Times' will not be committing any wrong against the Crown by publishing that subject matter and should not therefore be liable to account for any resultant profits. It is in no different position from anyone else who now might choose to publish the book by serialisation or otherwise. . . .

LORD BRIGHTMAN: . . . I am in complete agreement with your Lordships, as with the courts below, that this serialisation, which shortly preceded the entry of the contents of *Spycatcher* into the public domain, constituted a breach of confidence on the part of 'The Sunday Times.' The only remedy available to the Crown is the inadequate remedy of an account of profits, on the basis that 'The Sunday Times' unjustly enriched itself and should therefore be stripped of the riches wrongfully acquired; cf. *Reading* v *Attorney-General* [1951] AC 507. I see no reason why 'The Sunday Times' should not account for a due proportion of the entirety of the total net profits of the issue of 12 July 1987, with possibly an allowance for those copies of the paper which omitted the offending instalment as part of a deceit to hoodwink the Government. . . .

LORD GOFF OF CHIEVELEY: . . . The statement that a man shall not be allowed to profit from his own wrong is in very general terms, and does not of itself provide any sure guidance to the solution of a problem in any particular case. That there are groups of cases in which a man is not allowed to profit from his own wrong, is certainly true. An important section of the law of restitution is concerned with cases in which a defendant is required to make restitution in respect of benefits acquired through his own wrongful act—notably cases of waiver of tort; of benefits acquired by certain criminal acts; of benefits acquired in breach of a fiduciary relationship; and, of course, of benefits acquired in breach of confidence. The plaintiff's claim to restitution is usually enforced by an account of profits made by the defendant through his wrong at the plaintiff's expense. This remedy of an account is alternative to the remedy of damages, which in cases of breach of confidence is now available, despite the equitable nature of the wrong, through a beneficent interpretation of the Chancery Amendment

Act 1858 (Lord Cairns' Act), and which by reason of the difficulties attending the taking of an account is often regarded as a more satisfactory remedy, at least in cases where the confidential information is of a commercial nature, and quantifiable damage may therefore have been suffered.

I have to say, however, that I know of no case (apart from the present) in which the maxim has been invoked in order to hold that a person under an obligation is not released from that obligation by the destruction of the subject matter of the obligation, on the ground that the destruction was the result of his own wrongful act. To take an obvious case, a bailee who by his own wrongful, even deliberately wrongful, act destroys the goods entrusted to him, is obviously relieved of his obligation as bailee, though he is of course liable in damages for his tort. Likewise a nightwatchman who deliberately sets fire to and destroys the building he is employed to watch; and likewise also the keeper at a zoo who turns out to be an animal rights campaigner and releases rare birds or animals which escape irretrievably into the countryside. On this approach, it is difficult to see how a confidant who publishes the relevant confidential information to the whole world can be under any further obligation not to disclose the information, simply because it was he who wrongfully destroyed its confidentiality. The information has, after all, already been so fully disclosed that it is in the public domain: how, therefore, can he thereafter be sensibly restrained from disclosing it? Is he not even to be permitted to mention in public what is now common knowledge? For his wrongful act, he may be held liable in damages, or may be required to make restitution; but, to adapt the words of Lord Buckmaster, the confidential information, as confidential information, has ceased to exist, and with it should go, as a matter of principle, the obligation of confidence. In truth, when a person entrusts something to another—whether that thing be a physical thing such as a chattel, or some intangible thing such as confidential information—he relies upon that other to fulfil his obligation. If he discovers that the other is about to commit a breach, he may be able to impose an added sanction against his doing so by persuading the court to grant an injunction; but if the other simply commits a breach and destroys the thing, then the injured party is left with his remedy in damages or in restitution. The subject matter is gone: the obligation is therefore also gone: all that is left is the remedy or remedies for breach of the obligation. This approach appears to be consistent with the view expressed by the Law Commission in their Report on Breach of Confidence (Cmnd. 8388), paragraph 4.30 (see also the Law Commission's Working Paper No. 58, paragraphs 100–101). It is right to say, however, that they may have had commercial cases in mind, rather than a case such as the present. . . .

It is not to be forgotten that wrongful acts can be inadvertent, as well as deliberate; and yet it is apparently suggested that, irrespective of the character of his wrongdoing, the confidant will be held not to be released from his obligation of confidence. Furthermore, the artificial perpetuation of the obligation, despite the destruction of the subject matter, leads to unacceptable consequences. Take the case of confidential information with which we are here concerned. If the confidant who has wrongfully published the information so that it has entered the public domain remains under a duty of confidence, so logically must also be anybody who, deriving the information from him, publishes the information with knowledge that it was made available to him in breach of a duty of confidence. If Peter Wright is not released from his obligation of confidence neither, in my opinion, are Heinemann Publishers Pty Ltd, nor Viking Penguin Inc., nor anybody who may hereafter publish or sell the book in this country in the knowledge that it derived from Peter Wright—even booksellers who have in the past, or may hereafter, put the book on sale in their shops, would likewise be in a breach of duty. If it is suggested that this is carrying the point to absurd lengths, then some principle has to be enunciated which explains why the continuing duty of confidence applies to some, but not to others, who have wrongfully put the book in circulation. Such a distinction cannot however be explained by reliance upon the general statement that a man may not profit from his own wrong.

I have naturally been concerned by the fact that so far in this case it appears to have been accepted on all sides that Peter Wright should not be released from his obligation of confidence. I cannot help thinking that this assumption may have been induced, in part at least, by three factors—first, the fact that Peter Wright himself is not a party to the litigation, with the result that no representations have been made on his behalf; second, the wholly unacceptable nature of his conduct; and third, the fact that he appears now to be able, with impunity, to reap vast sums from his disloyalty. Certainly, the prospect of Peter Wright, safe in his Australian haven, reaping further profits from the sale of his book in this country is most unattractive. The purpose of perpetuating Peter Wright's duty of confidence appears to be, in part to deter others, and in part to ensure that a man who has committed so flagrant a breach of his duty should not be enabled freely to exploit the formerly confidential information, placed by him in the public domain, with impunity. Yet the real reason why he is able to exploit it is because he has found a safe place to do so. If within the jurisdiction of the English courts, he would be held liable to account for any profits made by him from his wrongful disclosure, which might properly include profits accruing to him from any subsequent exploitation of the confidential information after its disclosure: and, in cases where damages were regarded as the appropriate remedy, the confidant would be liable to compensate the confider for any damage, present or future, suffered by him by reason of his wrong. So far as I can see, the confider must be content with remedies such as these.

I have considered whether the confidant who, in breach of duty, places confidential information in the public domain, might remain at least under a duty thereafter not to exploit the information, so disclosed, for his own benefit. Suppose that the confidant in question was a man who, unwisely, has remained in this country, and has written a book containing confidential information and has disposed of the rights to publication to an American publishing house, whose publication results in the information in the book entering the public domain. The question might at least arise whether he is free thereafter to dispose of the film rights to the book. To me, however, it is doubtful whether the answer to this question lies in artificially prolonging the duty of confidence in information which is no longer confidential. Indeed, there is some ground for saying that the true answer is that the copyright in the book, including the film rights, are held by him on constructive trust for the confider—so that the remedy lies not in breach of confidence, but in restitution or in property, whichever way you care to look at it: see, in this connection [[1990] 1AC 109], pp. 210D–211C, *per* Dillon LJ.

At all events, since the point was not argued before us, I wish to reserve the question whether, in a case such as the present, some limited obligation (analogous to the springboard doctrine) may continue to rest upon a confidant who, in breach of confidence, destroys the confidential nature of the information entrusted to him. It must not however be forgotten that cases of breach of confidence may well involve questions of property (in particular, copyright) as well as questions of personal liability; and that, in a case involving national security rather than a personal or commercial secret, where disclosure in breach of confidence may be damaging to the whole community rather than to an individual or a corporation, the guilty confidant may be liable to criminal prosecution. It is only if we take all these matters into account that we can see such a case in the round. Even so, let us not forget that we have in the past seen convicted criminals, on release from prison, being invited by newspapers to give an account of their experiences, no doubt for substantial sums. This is highly offensive to many people; but I doubt whether the mere fact that such activities are offensive provides of itself an appropriate basis for defining the scope of a confidant's civil obligations at common law. And let us not forget that, in the present case, it is Peter Wright's absence from this country which renders him immune from prosecution, and, in Australia, it now appears, also immune from a claim to restitution, founded upon his unjust enrichment from his undoubted wrong at the expense of the whole community. It is perhaps this immunity from process which prompts a temptation to continue his duty of confidence, despite the destruction of the subject matter of that duty.

. . .

'The Sunday Times'

(a) *Publication on 12 July 1987*
All the relevant facts are set out in the judgment of the learned judge. He, and a majority of the Court of Appeal, have held this publication to have constituted a breach of confidence. Only Bingham LJ formed a different view, on the basis that it was then a virtual certainty that widespread publication of the book in the United States would almost immediately take place. I am, with all respect, unable to accept Bingham LJ's generous approach. In my opinion, he has promoted a plea in mitigation to the status of a substantive defence. The simple fact is that, on 12 July, publication in the United States had not taken place; certainly, on 12 July, the information in *Spycatcher* was not yet in the public domain. The substantial extract from *Spycatcher* published in 'The Sunday Times' included, as the learned judge held, a good deal of material in respect of which the public interest to be served by disclosure would not be thought to outweigh the interests of national security. I have no doubt that it was in this sense that the judge described the extract as 'indiscriminate,' whatever exercise the editor may himself have undertaken in making his choice. In my opinion, therefore, the publication in 'The Sunday Times' was plainly in breach of confidence; so, if discovered in time, it could have been restrained by injunction. I can see no reason why 'The Sunday Times' should not be liable to account for profits flowing from their wrong, subject however to all the difficulties attendant on this remedy and its (perhaps excessively) technical nature.

(b) *Subsequent serialisation*
If it were correct that Peter Wright owed the Crown a continuing duty of confidence in respect of the information contained in *Spycatcher*, I do not know how it would be possible to escape the conclusion that 'The Sunday Times,' deriving as it does its right to publish from Peter Wright, and having by its own breach of confidence contributed significantly to putting *Spycatcher* into the public domain in this country, should not likewise be subject to such a continuing duty. I echo the observation of Bingham LJ [[1990] 1 AC 109]; p. 226H) that it would be 'to some extent anomalous that "The Sunday Times" should be free to do what Mr Wright and his Australian publishers could not.' However, for the reasons I have already given, even if (subject to my doubts) Peter Wright remains under a continuing duty of confidentiality, the public interest does not now require that 'The Sunday Times,' despite the fact that its right to publish in the past and today derives from Peter Wright, and despite its previous breach of confidence, should be restrained from serialising further extracts from the book. . . .

Question
How would you calculate the profits made by the *Sunday Times* in publishing the first extract from *Spycatcher*? Was it the net profit of that day's sales? Or was it the enhanced profit resulting from the increased circulation? (See Jones [1989] CLP 49, at 59–60.)

Notes
1. See Birks, 'A Lifelong Obligation of Confidence' (1989) 105 LQR 501 and Jones, 'Breach of Confidence – after *Spycatcher*' [1989] CLP 49.
2. The taking of an account of profits can be a difficult exercise. A useful discussion is found in the context of the tort of passing-off in the judgment of Slade J in *My Kinda Town Ltd* v *Soll* [1983] RPC 15, at 47–58 (Ch D) (reversed on another ground [1983] RPC 407 (CA)). This case involved two very similar pizza restaurants. Slade J asked: 'What categories of the relevant profits or parts of such profits ought to be treated as having been improperly made by the defendants? The facts of many particular cases may justify the conclusion that the whole of the relevant profits should be so treated' (at 55–6). This was not such a case as the defendants' restaurant was a thriving concern in its own right and a considerable part of their profits owed nothing to the plaintiffs' reputation. Slade J did not shrink from apportioning profits and ordered an account only of those profits 'which are properly attributable to the use by the defendants of such name [a name similar to the plaintiffs'], in the said business' (at 56).
3. For discussion of the availability of an account of profits for the infringement of intellectual property rights and the relevant statutory material (Patents Act 1977, ss. 61–62; Copyright, Designs and Patents Act 1988, ss. 96–97, 229) see Burrows, *Restitution*, 385–6 and Jackman [1989] CLJ 302, at 307–8.

Section 5: accessory liability in equity

The equitable liability of a stranger who assists in a breach of trust is a head of liability frequently encountered in cases with a restitutionary flavour. 'Knowing assistance' is usually encountered with its supposed partner, 'knowing receipt'. Professor Birks, in 'Misdirected Funds – Restitution from the Recipient' [1989] LMCLQ 296, argued that whereas 'knowing receipt' is clearly a species of restitutionary recovery, 'knowing assistance' is a species of wrong, concluding that the 'equitable liability for assisting fraud is virtually unintelligible without fault' (at 334). This view has recently been adopted by the Privy Council who have re-named the doctrine 'accessory liability'.

For discussion see Harpum, 'The Stranger as Constructive Trustee' (1986) 102 LQR 114, 267 at 114–27, 144–62. Harpum deals skilfully with the 'considerable disarray' of the earlier case law, sharply distinguishing 'knowing assistance' from 'knowing receipt' and other species of stranger liability. He insists that 'knowing assistance' does not require receipt and argues that 'a stranger should be liable only if he had actual knowledge of, or wilfully closed his eyes to, the terms of the trust, or as the case may be, to the dishonest and fraudulent design on the part of the trustee' (at 126). Harpum refines and updates his arguments (in more concise form) in 'The Basis of Equitable Liability' in Birks (ed), *The Frontiers of Liability* vol. 1 (Oxford: Oxford University Press, 1994) 9, 10–17.

See further Harpum, 'Liability for Intermeddling with Trusts' (1987) 50 MLR 217 and Loughlan, 'Liability for Assistance in a Breach of Fiduciary Duty' (1989) 9 OJLS 260; Burrows, *Restitution*, 150, 155–6, 404. The equitable liability for 'knowing receipt' is discussed in Chapter 7, Section 2 below; consider also Chapter 2, Section 5 on 'ignorance' as a restitutionary cause of action.

Agip (Africa) Ltd v *Jackson*

[1990] Ch 265 (Ch D); affd [1991] Ch 547 (CA)

> *Action for money had and received; tracing; accountability as a constructive trustee*
> The facts are set out in detail in Chapter 7, Section 1. Further extracts in Chapter 7, Sections 1 and 2 deal respectively with the restitutionary claim via the techniques of tracing at common law and tracing in equity/knowing receipt. These failed (except as regards a small proportion of the original sum remaining in the accountant's hands which had been paid into court). The ultimate finding was that the defendant firm of accountants were *accountable as constructive trustees* on the ground of knowing assistance, because in moving the money which originally belonged to the plaintiff company around from bank account to bank account, they must have known they were assisting in laundering stolen money.

Chancery Division

MILLETT J: . . .

Knowing assistance

A stranger to the trust will also be liable to account as a constructive trustee if he knowingly assists in the furtherance of a fraudulent and dishonest breach of trust. It is not necessary that the party sought to be made liable as a constructive trustee should have received any part of the trust property, but the breach of trust must have been fraudulent. The basis of the stranger's liability is not receipt of trust property but participation in a fraud: *Barnes* v *Addy* (1874) 9 Ch App 244, and see the explanation of the distinction between the two categories of the case given by Jacobs P in *D. P. C. Estates Pty Ltd* v *Grey* [1974] 1 NSWLR 443.

The authorities at first instance are in some disarray on the question whether constructive notice is sufficient to sustain liability under this head. In the *Baden* case [1983] BCLC 325, Peter Gibson J accepted a concession by counsel that constructive notice is sufficient and that on this point there is no distinction between cases of 'knowing receipt' and 'knowing assistance.' This question was not argued before me but I am unable to agree. In my view the concession was wrong and should not have been made. The basis of liability in the two types of cases is quite different; there is no reason why the degree of knowledge required should be the same, and good reason why it should not. Tracing claims and cases of 'knowing receipt' are both concerned with rights of priority in relation to property taken by a legal owner for his own benefit; cases of 'knowing assistance' are concerned with the furtherance of fraud. In *Belmont Finance Corporation Ltd* v *Williams Furniture Ltd* [1979] Ch 250, the Court of Appeal insisted that to hold a stranger liable for 'knowing assistance' the breach of trust in question must be a fraudulent and dishonest one. In my judgment it necessarily follows that constructive notice of the fraud is not enough to make him liable. There is no sense in requiring dishonesty on the part of the principal while accepting negligence as sufficient for his assistant. Dishonest furtherance of the dishonest scheme of another is an understandable basis for liability; negligent but honest failure to appreciate that someone else's scheme is dishonest is not.

In *In re Montagu's Settlement Trusts* [1987] Ch 264, 285, Sir Robert Megarry V-C doubted whether constructive notice is sufficient even in cases of 'knowing receipt.' Whether the doubt is well founded or not (as to which I express no opinion), 'knowing assistance' is an a fortiori case.

Knowledge may be provided affirmatively or inferred from circumstances. The various mental states which may be involved were analysed by Peter Gibson J in *Baden's* case [1983] BCLC 325 as comprising: (i) actual knowledge; (ii) wilfully shutting one's eyes to the obvious; (iii) wilfully and recklessly failing to make such inquiries as an honest and reasonable man would make; (iv) knowledge of circumstances which would indicate the facts to an honest and reasonable man; and (v) knowledge of circumstances which would put an honest and reasonable man on inquiry.

According to Peter Gibson J, a person in category (ii) or (iii) will be taken to have actual knowledge, while a person in categories (iv) or (v) has constructive notice only. I gratefully adopt the classification but would warn against over refinement or a too ready assumption that categories (iv) or (v) are necessarily cases of constructive notice only. The true distinction is between honesty and dishonesty. It is essentially a jury question. If a man does not draw the obvious inferences or make the obvious inquiries, the question is: why not? If it is because, however foolishly, he did not suspect wrongdoing or, having suspected it, had his suspicions allayed, however unreasonably, that is one thing. But if he did suspect wrongdoing yet failed to make inquiries because 'he did not want to know' (category (ii)) or because he regarded it as 'none of his business' (category (iii)), that is quite another. Such conduct is dishonest, and those who are guilty of it cannot complain if, for the purpose of civil liability, they are treated as if they had actual knowledge.

In the present case, Mr Bowers did not participate in the furtherance of the fraud and he cannot be held directly liable on this ground. Mr Jackson and Mr Griffin, however, clearly did. Mr Jackson set up the arrangements and employed Mr Griffin to carry them out. The money was under their control from the time it was paid into Baker Oil's account until the time it left Jackson & Co.'s clients' account in the Isle of Man Bank. One or other of them gave the actual instructions to the banks which disposed of the money. They plainly assisted in the fraud. The sole remaining question is: did they do so with the requisite degree of knowledge?

The defendants' state of mind

Mr Jackson and Mr Griffin knew that the money was coming from the plaintiffs, an oil company with a branch in Tunis; that most of it was being paid to Kinz, which ran a jewellery business in France; that more than $10m had been dealt with in this way in less than two years; and that their instructions came from the recipients and not from the plaintiffs. They knew of no connection or dealings between the plaintiffs and Kinz or of any commercial reason for the plaintiffs to make substantial payments to

Kinz. They must have realised that the only function which the payee companies or Euro-Arabian performed was to act as 'cut-outs' in order to conceal the true destination of the money from the plaintiffs. They must also have realised that the only purpose in having two 'cut-outs' instead of one was to make it impossible for investigators to make any connection between the plaintiffs and Kinz without having recourse to Lloyds Bank's records; and their object in frequently replacing the payee company by another must have been to reduce the risk of discovery by the plaintiffs.

This is damning evidence; but it does not stop there. The letter dated 14 August 1984 from Knapp-Fishers shows that Mr Jackson was concerned—whether for himself or his clients is immaterial—at the possibility that the plaintiffs might obtain disclosure of Lloyds Bank's records, discover what had happened to the money, and try to recover it.

Mr Jackson and Mr Griffin are professional men. They obviously knew that they were laundering money. They were consciously helping their clients to make arrangements designed for the purpose of concealment from, inter alios, the plaintiffs. It must have been obvious to them that their clients could not afford their activities to see the light of day. Secrecy is the badge of fraud. They must have realised at least that their clients *might* be involved in a fraud on the plaintiffs. . . .

Court of Appeal

FOX LJ: . . . I come then to the circumstances in which strangers to the trust relationship (the defendants) may be made liable in equity. They are broadly as follows. (1) Knowing receipt of or dealing with the trust property: the judge held that Mr Griffin (the third defendant) did not receive the money at all and that Mr Jackson and Mr Bowers (the first and second defendants) did not receive or apply it for their benefit. Accordingly, he held that none of them could be held liable as constructive trustees on the basis of knowing receipt of the money. There is no cross-appeal as to that. (2) Knowing assistance: a person may be liable, even though he does not himself receive the trust property, if he knowingly assists in a fraudulent design on the part of a trustee, including a constructive trustee. Liability under this head is not related to the receipt of trust property by the person sought to be made liable: *Barnes* v *Addy* (1874) LR 9 Ch App 244.

The degree of knowledge required was described by Ungoed-Thomas J in *Selangor United Rubber Estates Ltd* v *Cradock (No. 3)* [1968] 1 WLR 1555, 1590 as circumstances which would indicate to an honest and reasonable man that such a design was being committed, or would put him on inquiry whether it was being committed. Peter Gibson J in *Baden, Delvaux and Lecuit* v *Société Général pour Favoriser le Développement du Commerce et de l'Industrie en France SA* [1983] BCLC 325, 407 gave a more expanded description of the circumstances constituting the necessary knowledge under five heads: (i) actual knowledge, (ii) wilfully shutting one's eyes to the obvious, (iii) wilfully and recklessly failing to make such inquiries as an honest and reasonable man would make, (iv) knowledge of any circumstances which would indicate the facts to an honest and reasonable man, (v) knowledge of circumstances which would put an honest and reasonable man on inquiry. I accept that formulation. It is, however, only an explanation of the general principle and is not necessarily comprehensive.

The judge held, and it was not challenged, that Mr Bowers did not participate in the furtherance of the fraud at all; although he was a partner in Jackson & Co., he played no part in the movement of the money and gave no instructions about it. Mr Jackson and Mr Griffin were in quite a different position. Mr Jackson set up the company structures. Mr Jackson and Mr Griffin controlled the movement of the money from the time it reached Baker Oil to the time it was paid out of the account of Jackson & Co. in the Isle of Man bank. On the evidence, and in the absence of evidence from Mr Jackson and Mrs Griffin themselves, I agree with the judge that both of them must be regarded as having assisted in the fraud. That, however, by no means concludes the matter. There remains the question of their state of mind. Did they have the necessary degree of knowledge?

The first inquiry is what did they know? As to that (1) they knew that a very large amount of money was involved. It was $10m in under two years. It had all come along the same track. (2) They knew the origin of the money and its destination. Its origin was Agip and the destination of most of it was Kinz. (3) Agip was an oil company with operations in Tunisia. Kinz were jewellers in France. (4) There is nothing to suggest that there was any commercial reason why Agip should be paying such sums to Kinz. (5) As the judge said, they must have realised that the only function of the payee companies or of Euro-Arabian was to act as 'cut-outs' in order to conceal the true destination of the moneys from Agip. And the purpose of having two cut-outs instead of one was to bar any connection between Agip and Kinz without reference to the records of Lloyds Bank.

There is also some material documentary evidence. First, there is the letter of 14 August 1984 from Mr Smyth of Knapp-Fishers to Mr Jackson. That contains advice directed to the possibility that 'Agip may be able to establish a cause of action by claiming that the payments were obtained by fraud.'

The letter further states:

> Because of the general principle of banking confidentiality, it would be extremely difficult for the Tunisian Government or Agip to obtain an order requiring Lloyds Bank to disclose banking transactions . . .

This shows that the question of fraud was being considered and some anxiety was being felt at the possibility that Agip might obtain access to bank records. The significance of bank records is that they are or may be a signpost to the ultimate destination of the money. Why was concern being felt about what Agip might discover? If there were doubts about fraud they could be set at rest by getting in touch with Agip and disclosing what was known.

It is, of course, possible that Mr Jackson and Mr Griffin were honest men and that there were facts which we do not know which would demonstrate that. But, if so, they could have attended the trial and explained their position in the witness box. They did not do so. One can only infer that they were not prepared to submit their activities to critical examination. In the circumstances I think that the judge rightly came to the conclusion that they must have known they were laundering money, and were consequently helping their clients to make arrangements to conceal some dispositions of money which had such a degree of impropriety that neither they nor their clients could afford to have them disclosed. . . .

Royal Brunei Airlines Sdn Bhd v *Philip Tan Kok Ming*
[1995] 2 AC 378 (PC)

The airline appointed a travel company, BLT, to act as its general travel agent for the sale of passenger and cargo transportation. Under the agreement BLT was required to account to the airline for all amounts received from the sale of tickets, and it constituted BLT trustee of those moneys. It further provided that BLT's remuneration would be by way of commission. In practice BLT did not pay the airline moneys into a separate account, but rather they were paid into its current account and utilised in the ordinary course of business. BLT fell into arrears with the airline and proved insolvent. The airline sought to make good the shortfall in this action against Mr Tan, the managing director and principal shareholder of BLT, on the ground of knowing assistance. *Held*: BLT was in breach of trust in using the money, and Tan assisted in that breach of trust and both the company and Tan acted dishonestly, therefore Tan was liable.

LORD NICHOLLS OF BIRKENHEAD: The proper role of equity in commercial transactions is a topical question. Increasingly plaintiffs have recourse to equity for an effective remedy when the person in default, typically a company, is insolvent. Plaintiffs seek to obtain relief from others who were involved in the transaction, such as directors of the company, or its bankers, or its legal or other advisers. They seek to fasten fiduciary obligations directly onto the company's officers or agents or advisers, or to have them held personally liable for assisting the company in breaches of trust or fiduciary obligations.

This is such a case. An insolvent travel agent company owed money to an airline. The airline seeks a remedy against the travel agent's principal director and shareholder. Its claim is based on the much-quoted dictum of Lord Selborne LC, sitting in the Court of Appeal in Chancery, in *Barnes* v *Addy* (1874) LR 9 Ch App 244, 251–252:

> [The responsibility of a trustee] may no doubt be extended in equity to others who are not properly trustees, if they are found . . . actually participating in any fraudulent conduct of the trustee to the injury of the cestui que trust. But . . . strangers are not to be made constructive trustees merely because they act as the agents of trustees in transactions within their legal powers, transactions, perhaps of which a court of equity may disapprove, unless those agents receive and become chargeable with some part of the trust property, or unless they assist with knowledge in a dishonest and fraudulent design on the part of the trustees.

In the conventional shorthand, the first of these two circumstances in which third parties (non-trustees) may become liable to account in equity is 'knowing receipt,' as distinct from the second, where liability arises from 'knowing assistance.' Stated even more shortly, the first limb of Lord Selborne LC's formulation is concerned with the liability of a person as a *recipient* of trust property or its traceable proceeds. The second limb is concerned with what, for want of a better compendious description, can be called the liability of an *accessory* to a trustee's breach of trust. Liability as an accessory is not dependent upon receipt of trust property. It arises even though no trust property has reached the hands of the accessory. It is a form of secondary liability in the sense that it only arises where there has been a breach of trust. In the present case the plaintiff airline relies on the accessory limb. The particular point in issue arises from the expression 'a dishonest and fraudulent design on the part of the trustees.'

. . . The issue on this appeal concerns only the accessory liability principle. Different considerations apply to the two heads of liability. Recipient liability is restitution-based: accessory liability is not.

[Lord Nicholls considered and rejected regimes of no liability and strict liability for accessories and continued: . . .]

Fault-based liability

Given, then, that in some circumstances a third party may be liable directly to a beneficiary, but given also that the liability is not so strict that there would be liability even when the third party was wholly unaware of the existence of the trust, the next step is to seek to identify the touchstone of liability. By common accord dishonesty fulfils this role. Whether, in addition, negligence will suffice is an issue on which there has been a well-known difference of judicial opinion. The *Selangor* decision [1968] 1 WLR 1555 in 1968 was the first modern decision on this point. Ungoed-Thomas J, at p. 1590, held that the touchstone was whether the third party had knowledge of circumstances which would indicate to 'an honest, reasonable man' that the breach in question was being committed or would put him on inquiry. Brightman J reached the same conclusion in *Karak Rubber Co. Ltd* v *Burden (No. 2)* [1972] 1 WLR 602. So did Peter Gibson J in 1983 in *Baden* v *Société Générale pour Favoriser le Développement du Commerce et de l'Industrie en France SA (Note)* [1993] 1 WLR 509. In that case the judge accepted a five-point scale of knowledge which had been formulated by counsel.

Meanwhile doubts had been expressed about this test by Buckley and Goff LJJ in the *Belmont* case [1979] Ch 250, 267, 275. Similar doubts were expressed in Australia by Jacobs P in *D. P. C. Estates Pty Ltd* v *Grey and Consul Development Pty Ltd* [1974] 1 NSWLR 443, 459. When that decision reached the High Court of Australia, the doubts were echoed by Barwick CJ, Gibbs and Stephen JJ: see *Consul Development Pty Ltd* v *D. P. C. Estates Pty Ltd* (1975) 132 CLR 373, 376, 398, 412.

Since then the tide in England has flowed strongly in favour of the test being one of dishonesty: see, for instance, Sir Robert Megarry V-C in *In re Montagu's Settlement Trusts* [1987] Ch 264, 285, and Millett J in *Agip (Africa) Ltd* v *Jackson* [1990] Ch 265, 293. In *Eagle Trust Plc.* v *SBC Securities Ltd* [1993] 1 WLR 484, 495, Vinelott J stated that it could be taken as settled law that want of probity was a prerequisite to liability. This received the imprimatur of the Court of Appeal in *Polly Peck International Plc* v *Nadir (No. 2)* [1992] 4 All ER 769, 777 *per* Scott LJ.

Judicial views have diverged also in New Zealand. In *Westpac Banking Corporation* v *Savin* [1985] 2 NZLR 41, 70, Sir Clifford Richmond preferred the approach in *Belmont Finance Corporation Ltd* v *Williams Furniture Ltd* [1979] Ch 250, as did Tompkins J in *Marr* v *Arabco Traders Ltd* (1987) 1 NZBLC 102, 732, 102, 762. In *Powell* v *Thompson* [1991] 1 NZLR 597, 612, 613, 615, Thomas J considered that the suggestion that negligence is not enough to found liability is to be resisted. The test is one of unconscionable behaviour. This, and knowledge to match, whether actual or constructive, will suffice to herald a visit from equity. In *Equiticorp Industries Group Ltd* v *Hawkins* [1991] 3 NZLR 700, 728, Wyle J disagreed. He adhered to the concept of want of probity as the standard by which unconscionability was to be measured. In *Marshall Futures Ltd* v *Marshall* [1992] 1 NZLR 316, 325. Tipping J was concerned about the difficulty of identifying as unconscionable conduct which was less reprehensible than conduct which can be described as dishonest. He would, he said, at p. 325, prefer the herald of equity to be wearing more distinctive clothing than that suggested by Thomas J. In *Nimmo* v *Westpac Banking Corporation* [1993] 3 NZLR 218, 228, Blanchard J preferred a test of dishonesty. Most recently, in *Springfield Acres Ltd* v *Abacus (Hong Kong) Ltd* [1994] 3 NZLR 502, 510, Henry J observed that the law in New Zealand could not be regarded as settled.

Most, but not all, commentators prefer the test of dishonesty: see, among others, Peter Birks, 'Misdirected funds: restitution from the recipient' (1989) LMCLQ 296; MJ Brindle and RJA Hooley, 'Does constructive knowledge make a constructive trustee?' (1987) 61 ALJ 281; Charles Harpum, 'The stranger as constructive trustee' (1986) 102 LQR 114, 267; *Birks, The Frontiers of Liability* (1994), vol. 1, p. 9; Patricia

Loughlan, 'Liability for assistance in a breach of fiduciary duty' (1989) 9 OJLS 260; *Parker and Mellows, The Modern Law of Trusts,* 6th ed. (1994), p.253; *Pettit, Equity and the Law of Trusts,* 7th ed. (1993), p. 172; Philip Sales, 'The tort of conspiracy and civil secondary liability' (1990) 49 CLJ 491; *Snell's Equity,* 29th ed. (1990), p. 194; and *Underhill's Law of Trusts and Trustees,* 14th ed. (1987), p. 355 and noter-up.

Dishonesty

Before considering this issue further it will be helpful to define the terms being used by looking more closely at what dishonesty means in this context. Whatever may be the position in some criminal or other contexts (see, for instance, *Reg* v *Ghosh* [1982] QB 1053), in the context of the accessory liability principle acting dishonestly, or with a lack of probity, which is synonymous, means simply not acting as an honest person would in the circumstances. This is an objective standard. At first sight this may seem surprising. Honesty has a connotation of subjectivity, as distinct from the objectivity of negligence. Honesty, indeed, does have a strong subjective element in that it is a description of a type of conduct assessed in the light of what a person actually knew at the time, as distinct from what a reasonable person would have known or appreciated. Further, honesty and its counterpart dishonesty are mostly concerned with advertent conduct, not inadvertent conduct. Carelessness is not dishonesty. Thus for the most part dishonesty is to be equated with conscious impropriety. However, these subjective characteristics of honesty do not mean that individuals are free to set their own standards of honesty in particular circumstances. The standard of what constitutes honest conduct is not subjective. Honesty is not an optional scale, with higher or lower values according to the moral standards of each individual. If a person knowingly appropriates another's property, he will not escape a finding of dishonesty simply because he sees nothing wrong in such behaviour.

In most situations there is little difficulty in identifying how an honest person would behave. Honest people do not intentionally deceive others to their detriment. Honest people do not knowingly take others' property. Unless there is a very good and compelling reason, an honest person does not participate in a transaction if he knows it involves a misapplication of trust assets to the detriment of the beneficiaries. Nor does an honest person in such a case deliberately close his eyes and ears, or deliberately not ask questions, lest he learn something he would rather not know, and then proceed regardless.

[Lord Nicholls then rejected negligence and unconscionable conduct as touchstones of liability and concluded: . . .]

The accessory liability principle

Drawing the threads together, their Lordships' overall conclusion is that dishonesty is a necessary ingredient of accessory liability. It is also a sufficient ingredient. A liability in equity to make good resulting loss attaches to a person who dishonestly procures or assists in a breach of trust or fiduciary obligation. It is not necessary that, in addition, the trustee or fiduciary was acting dishonestly, although this will usually be so where the third party who is assisting him is acting dishonestly. 'Knowingly' is better avoided as a defining ingredient of the principle, and in the context of this principle the *Baden* [1993] 1 WLR 509 scale of knowledge is best forgotten. . . .

Notes

1. The Privy Council emphasised that what mattered was the state of mind of the accessory, not the state of mind of the trustee or other fiduciary (who could simply be an innocent pawn of the accessory). It was also stressed that the liability was not property-based. The clumsy phrase '*accountable as a constructive trustee*' is also studiously avoided in this learned advice.

2. The remedy granted was a (presumably personal) liability to make good the deficiency in the fund. This is an example of equitable compensation. Accessory liability is firmly categorised as part of the law of wrongs, and a close analogy with the tort of interference with contractual relations was admitted. As with that tort, there is no reason in principle why the injured party could not in an appropriate case seek a benefit-based rather than a loss-based measure against the dishonest accessory, for example, the profits made by an accountant who dishonestly assists in money-laundering, where the fund is substantially recovered. (See Burrows, *Restitution*, 404.)

3. The case is noted by Harpum (1995) 111 LQR 545; Stevens [1995] *Restitution Law Review* 105 and Birks [1996] LMCLQ 1.

4. See further *Brinks Ltd* v *Abu-Sakh (No. 3)*, *The Times*, 23 October 1995.

7 TRACING AND PROPRIETARY REMEDIES

This chapter is concerned with proprietary restitution. This phrase is ambiguous and has been a source of confusion. One species of 'proprietary' claim is where value subtracted from the plaintiff is followed into the hands of the defendant. In fact most of the law of restitution could be, and has been, explained on this basis (Stoljar, *The Law of Quasi-Contract*, 2nd ed. (Sydney: The Law Book Company, 1989)). The second species is where the plaintiff lays claim to an asset still in the defendant's hands. Sections 1 and 2 consider tracing at common law and in equity. Tracing is best considered as a technique which aids the plaintiff in identifying value received by the defendant which has been subtracted from his assets. As such it is a vital component in all restitution claims, but is especially important in those claims brought against indirect recipients. It is relevant to both the 'enrichment' and the 'at the expense of the plaintiff' inquiries. Does the defendant's plus correspond to the plaintiff's minus? This is essentially a causal question. Can the plaintiff follow value representing the sum subtracted from him into the hands of the defendant? This is obviously more difficult to prove in cases of indirect receipt, hence characteristically the language of tracing is generally found only in cases involving indirect recipients.

A crucial question is whether the plaintiff is seeking a personal or a proprietary remedy. This governs the reach of the inquiry. If all that is sought is an *in personam* judgment (whether at common law for an *action for money had and received*, or in equity for an *account* on the grounds of 'knowing receipt') tracing ceases and the plaintiff's cause of action is constituted once the money is identified as reaching the hands of the defendant. In contrast, if the plaintiff seeks a proprietary remedy *tracing* must reach beyond the moment of receipt, and it must be demonstrated that some asset in the defendant's hands still represents value subtracted from the plaintiff. That is, for a proprietary remedy it must be shown that the defendant was enriched and remains enriched. Such tracing is usually equitable and results in the imposition of a trust or charge over the identified asset in the defendant's hands.

The above account of tracing is associated with the writing of Professor Birks (Birks, *Introduction*, 83–5) and is probably still controversial. In this area of law it is difficult to reconcile all the cases and *dicta* into a single general statement of principle. However, the description of tracing as an exercise in identification or a 'process' has recently been adopted by the Court of Appeal in *Boscawen* v *Bajwa* [1995] 4 All ER 769.

An important question for both species of tracing is the degree to which a plaintiff is allowed to follow value derived from his assets through *mixture* with other assets, and *substitution* of assets. A point often overlooked is that 'paying money into the bank' involves substituting currency for an *in personam* claim in debt against the bank (a species of *chose in action*). The common law traditionally has had inhibitions about tracing through mixtures, which equity does not share. Both types of tracing cope well with substitutions of value. Equity has its own restrictive dogma that it is concerned only with following trust assets, or at least insists that funds must have passed through the prism of a fiduciary relationship as a pre-condition of tracing. In addition some of the 'knowing receipt' cases insist on fault or knowledge on the part of the recipient (often a high degree of fault) as necessary for a personal remedy.

Discussion of tracing in equity naturally leads to (but must be distinguished from) an analysis of the role of restitutionary proprietary remedies. The main motives for seeking an *in rem* judgment are either a desire to be a secured creditor in the event of the defendant's insolvency, or because the asset in the defendant's hands has increased in value. The extent to which the law should permit such advantageous claims is a controversial one which is the subject of Section 3 below. All the cases discussed in Sections 1 and 2 concern subtractive unjust enrichment. However, a claim of a proprietary character is not confined to subtractive unjust enrichment and tracing claims. The courts have recently shown greater willingness to use proprietary claims to strip wrong-doers of their ill-gotten gains. This distinction was highlighted in *Macmillan Inc.* v *Bishopsgate Investment Trust plc (No. 3)* [1995] 3 All ER 747, at 757–8 (reversed [1996] 1 All ER 585 (CA)), where Millett J stated:

> The English law of restitution makes a fundamental distinction between the unjust enrichment of the defendant which is occasioned by depriving the plaintiff of his property and enrichment which results from a wrong done to the plaintiff by the defendant. In the first category of case the plaintiff's restitutionary claim is said to have a proprietary base. The enrichment of the defendant is at the direct expense of the plaintiff and is matched by a corresponding diminution of his assets. The plaintiff brings the claim in order to recover his own property and must succeed, if at all, by virtue of his own title. In the latter class of case his claim arises from a breach of fiduciary or other obligation on the part of the defendant. The distinction is that drawn by equity between the claim of an equitable owner to recover his property, or compensation for the failure to restore it, from

a person into whose hands it has come and a claim by a plaintiff in respect of a breach of fiduciary obligation owed to him. In the former case he relies upon his continuing equitable interest in the property under an express or resulting trust; in the latter, upon an equity between the parties which may in appropriate circumstances give rise to a constructive trust. The distinction, which is crucial, may have been lost sight of in the language of some of the more recent decisions on knowing receipt.

This passage advances again Millett J's view that tracing claims in equity lead to the imposition of a resulting, not a constructive trust (see also Sir Peter Millett, 'Tracing the Proceeds of Fraud' (1991) 105 LQR 71, at 80). It also demonstrates the influence of Professor Birks's writings, not only in the reference to the bifurcation of the subject, but also in the insistence upon a '*proprietary base*' before proprietary claims succeed in cases of subtractive unjust enrichment. Clearly different principles necessarily apply in cases of restitution for wrongs. What can be said is that the principles governing the award of restitutionary proprietary remedies are in a state of rapid development in respect of both species of restitution.

For general discussion of tracing, both at common law and in equity, see Pearce, 'A Tracing Paper' (1976) 40 Conv 277; Goode, 'The Right to Trace and its Impact on Commercial Transactions' (1976) 92 LQR 360, 528; Birks, 'Mixing and Tracing: Property and Restitution' (1992) 45 CLP 69, especially at 84–98 and Sir Peter Millett, 'Equity – the road ahead' (1995) *Trusts Law International*, Vol. 9, No. 2, 35, at 38–42.

Section 1: tracing at common law

Our concern here is primarily with money. Title to other chattels at common law is protected by the tortious remedies for wrongful interference with goods. Common law tracing is conceptually underdeveloped and is usually superseded in practice by the more flexible approach of equity. However, equity has its own restrictive dogma, insisting on a fiduciary relationship, and therefore some plaintiffs have opted for the common law approach (as in the leading case of *Lipkin Gorman* v *Karpnale Ltd* [1991] 2 AC 548). The main restriction is said to be that the common law cannot trace through a mixed fund. Where the remedy sought is an *action for money had and received* the cause of action is constituted upon receipt, so this statement requires qualifying to limit it to pre-receipt mixing. It has also been suggested that the common law cannot trace a telegraphic transfer of money (see *Agip (Africa) Ltd* v *Jackson* [1990] Ch 265, *per* Millett J). Some of the cases have concerned themselves with post-receipt events (*Taylor* v *Plumer* (1815) 3 M & S 562, 105 ER 721; *Banque Belge pour L'Etranger* v *Hambrouck* [1921] 1 KB 321 (CA)) and as a result, it has been argued, involve the application of equitable rather than common law principles. Equally some of the cases make attempts at a fusion of doctrine (*Banque Belge per* Atkin LJ; *Nelson* v *Larholt* [1948] 1 KB 339). Rationality requires a reconciliation of the different approaches of common law and equity into a single set of principles.

See Burrows, *Restitution*, 60–9 and for reference Goff and Jones, 75–83. For a detailed analysis see Matthews, 'The Legal and Moral Limits of Common Law Tracing' in Birks, *Laundering and Tracing*, 23–71.

Clarke v *Shee and Johnson*
(1774) 1 Cowp 197; 98 ER 1041 (KB)

Action for money had and received

Clarke, a brewer, employed Wood as a clerk. Wood received money and negotiable notes from Clarke's customers in the ordinary course of business. On several occasions Wood misapplied such money, paying money and notes totalling £459 to the defendants upon the chances of the coming up of tickets in the State Lottery, contrary to the Lottery Act 1772. Clarke sued to recover the sums so misapplied.

LORD MANSFIELD: . . . This is a liberal action in the nature of a bill in equity; and if, under the circumstances of the case, it appears that the defendant cannot in conscience retain what is the subject-matter of it, the plaintiff may well support this action.

There are two sorts of prohibitions enacted by positive law, in respect of contracts.

1st. To protect weak or necessitous men from being over-reached, defrauded, or oppressed. There the rule in pari delicto, potior est conditio defendentis, does not hold; and an action will lie; because where the defendant imposes upon the plaintiff it is not par delictum. . . .

The next sort of prohibition is founded upon general reasons of policy and public expedience. There both parties offending are equally guilty; par est delictum, et potior est conditio defendentis. The prohibition in the Lottery Act, stat. 12 Geo. 3, c. 63, is of this sort; and in this case no doubt but the defendants and the witness Wood were equally guilty. Therefore at Guildhall, upon the first impression, I was of opinion against the plaintiff; because I thought that the master could not stand in a better situation than the servant, and the servant was clearly particeps criminis. But I changed my opinion; I thought, and now think, the plaintiff does not sue as standing in the place of Wood his clerk: for the money and notes which Wood paid to the defendants, are the identical notes and money of the plaintiff. Where money or notes are paid bona fide, and upon a valuable consideration, they never shall be brought back by the true owner; but where they come malâ fide into a person's hands, they are in the nature of specific property; and if their identity can be traced and ascertained, the party has a right to recover. It is of public benefit and example that he should: but otherwise, if they cannot be followed and identified, because there it might be inconvenient and open a door to fraud. *Miller* versus *Race*, 1 Burr 452: and in *Golightly* versus *Reynolds* (1772) Lofft 88, the identity was traced through different hands and shops. Here the plaintiff sues for his identified property, which has come to the hands of the defendants iniquitously and illegally, in breach of the Act of Parliament. Therefore they have no right to retain it; and consequently the plaintiff is well entitled to recover.

Taylor v *Plumer*
(1815) 3 M & S 562; 105 ER 721 (KB)

Sir Thomas Plumer employed Walsh as his stockbroker (and therefore in legal terms as his agent or factor). Plumer wished to purchase an estate, and with the advice and assistance of Walsh realised a large amount of stock to fund the purchase. Plumer was then cash-rich, and informed Walsh he wished to invest the money in Exchequer bills until it was required for the estate. Plumer therefore gave Walsh a draft for £22,200 upon his bank, and directed Walsh to invest it in the bills which were to be delivered to himself or the bank the same day. Walsh was in fact destitute, and had formed an intention to abscond with the money. Therefore he invested only £6,500 in bills which he deposited with the bank, but exchanged the remainder for American shares, stocks and bullion. Walsh proceeded to Falmouth, aiming for America, but was overtaken by Plumer's attorney and a police officer. Walsh surrendered the shares, stock and bullion to Plumer's attorney. This was an action brought by Walsh's assignees in bankruptcy as plaintiffs against Plumer in *trover* (now 'wrongful interference with goods') for the property so seized.

LORD ELLENBOROUGH: . . . the plaintiff in this case is not entitled to recover if the defendant has succeeded in maintaining these propositions in point of law, viz. that the property of a principal entrusted by him to his factor for any special purpose belongs to the principal, notwithstanding any change which that property may have undergone in point of form, so long as such property is capable of being identified, and distinguished from all other property. And, secondly, that all property thus circumstanced is equally recoverable from the assignees of the factor, in the event of his becoming a bankrupt, as it was from the factor himself before his bankruptcy. And, indeed, upon a view of the authorities, and consideration of the arguments, it should seem that if the property in its original state and form was covered with a trust in favour of the principal, no change of that state and form can divest it of such trust, or give the factor, or those who represent him in right, any other more valid claim in respect to it, than they respectively had before such change. An abuse of trust can confer no rights on the party abusing it, nor on those who claim in privity with him. The argument which has been advanced in favour of the plaintiffs, that the property of the principal continues only so long as the authority of the principal is pursued in respect to the order and disposition of it, and that it ceases when the property is tortiously converted into another form for the use of the factor himself, is mischievous in principle, and supported by no authorities of law. And the position which was held out in argument on the part of the plaintiffs, as being the untenable result of the arguments on the part of the defendant, is no doubt a result deducible from those arguments: but unless it be a result at variance with the law, the plaintiffs are not on that account entitled to recover. The contention on the part of the defendant was represented by the plaintiff's counsel as pushed to what he conceived to be an extravagant length, in the defendant's counsel being obliged to contend, that 'if A is trusted by B with money to purchase a horse for him, and he purchases a carriage with that money, that B is entitled to the carriage.' And, indeed, if he be not so entitled, the case on the part of the defendant appears to be hardly sustainable in argument. It makes no difference in reason or law into what other form, different from the original, the change may have been made, whether it be into that of promissory notes for the security of the money which was produced by the sale of the goods of the principal, as in *Scott* v *Surman,* Willes, 400, or into other merchandise, as in *Whitcomb* v *Jacob*, Salk 160, for the product of or substitute for the original thing still follows the nature of the thing itself, as long as it can be ascertained to be such, and the right only ceases when the means of ascertainment fail, which is the case when the subject is turned into money, and mixed and confounded in a general mass of the same description. The difficulty which arises in such a case is a difficulty of fact and not of law, and the dictum that money has no ear-mark must be understood in the same way; i.e. as predicated only of an undivided and undistinguishable mass of current money. But money in a bag, or otherwise kept apart from other money, guineas, or other coin marked (if the fact were so) for the purpose of being distinguished, are so far ear-marked as to fall within the rule on this subject, which applies to every other description of personal property whilst it remains, (as the property in question did,) in the hands of the factor, or his general legal representatives. [Lord Ellenborough then discussed the authorities and concluded: . . .] He [Plumer] has repossessed himself of that, of which, according to the principles established in the cases I have cited, he never ceased to be the lawful proprietor; and having so done we are of opinion, that the assignees cannot in this action recover that which, if an action were brought against them the assignees by the defendant, they could not have effectually retained against him, inasmuch as it was trust property of the defendant, which, as such, did not pass to them under the commission. If this case had rested on the part of the defendant on any supposed adoption and ratification on his part of the act of converting the produce of the draft or bank-notes of the defendant into these American certificates, we think, it could not have been well supported on that ground, inasmuch as the defendant, by taking a security by bond and judgment to indemnify himself against the pecuniary loss he had sustained by that very act, must be understood to have disapproved and disallowed that act instead of adopting and confirming it; but upon the other grounds above stated, we are of opinion that the defendant is entitled to retain the subjects of the present suit, and of course that a nonsuit must be entered.

Notes

1. This case suggests that the common law can cope with substitutions, but not with mixing. This view represents the general orthodoxy. For another view see Lionel Smith, 'Tracing in *Taylor* v *Plumer*: Equity in the Court of King's Bench' [1995] LMCLQ 240, where it is argued that the result was based on an assertion of *equitable* proprietary rights against a fiduciary. Smith also argues that the case does not prohibit tracing through a mixed fund at common law. See also Khurshid and Matthews, 'Tracing Confusion' (1979) 95 LQR 78, at 79–82.

2. Enthusiasts for 'legal archaeology' will enjoy Smith, 'The Stockbroker and the Solicitor-General: The Story Behind *Taylor* v *Plumer*' (1994) 15 J Leg Hist 1.

Banque Belge pour l'Etranger v *Hambrouck*

[1921] 1 KB 321 (CA)

Action for money had and received

Hambrouck was an accounts clerk at the Pelabon works. By fraud, he procured more than £6,000 by drawing cheques on his employer's bank account at Banque Belge. Hambrouck paid the cheques into his own account at Farrow's bank. Hambrouck paid various sums to his Belgian mistress, Mlle Spanoghe, and she in turn paid sums into the Twickenham branch of her bank, the London Joint City and Midland Bank. After Hambrouck was sentenced for fraud, Banque Belge sought restitution of some £315 which remained in Mlle Spanoghe's account. The bank paid that sum into court. Salter J awarded Banque Belge restitution and Mlle Spanoghe appealed.

BANKES LJ: . . . Had the claim been for the recovery of a chattel sold instead of for a sum of money alleged to be given, the appellant's counsel do not dispute that, in order to retain the chattel, the appellant must establish that she gave value for it without notice that it had been obtained by the vendor by fraud; but they attempt to distinguish the present case from the case of the sale of a chattel by saying: (a) that the appellant, who had no notice of Hambrouck's fraud, obtained a good title to the money, because it was a gift to her from Hambrouck; (b) that the rule applicable to a chattel has no application to currency; (c) that the fact that the appellant had paid the money into her banking account prevented any following of the money by the plaintiff Bank, and that an action for money had and received would therefore not lie.

In my opinion the first contention cannot be supported either upon the facts or in law. The facts show that the payments made by Hambrouck to the appellant were made without valuable consideration, and for an immoral consideration. Even if they could be appropriately described as gifts, a gift without valuable consideration would not give the appellant any title as against the plaintiff Bank.

The second contention also cannot be supported in law. It rests upon a misconception as to the meaning which has been attached to the expression 'currency' in some of the decisions which have been referred to. In *Miller* v *Race* 1 Burr 452, 457; 1 Sm LC, 12th ed., p. 525 Lord Mansfield in dealing with the question whether money has an earmark says: 'The true reason is upon account of the currency of it; it cannot be recovered after it has passed in currency.' The learned judge is there using the expression in the same sense as that in which Channell J uses it in *Moss* v *Handcock* [1899] 2 QB 111, 118 where he says: 'If the coin had been dealt with and transferred as current coin of the realm, as, for instance, in payment for goods purchased or in satisfaction of a debt, or bona fide changed as money for money of a different denomination.' Where the word 'currency' is used merely as the equivalent of coin of the realm, then for present purposes the difference between currency and a chattel personal is one of fact and not of law. This was the view of Lord Ellenborough in *Taylor* v *Plumer* 3 M & S 562, 575, in the passage in which he deals with the difficulty of tracing money which has become part of an undivided and undistinguishable mass of current money, and which in this respect differs from marked coins or money in a bag. With regard to the latter he says that the rule for the purpose we are considering in this appeal is the same as that which applies to every other description of personal property. Dealing with this point in *Sinclair* v *Brougham* [1914] AC 398, 420 Lord Haldane says: 'The common law, which we are now considering, did not take cognizance of such duties. It looked simply to the question whether the property had passed, and if it had not, for instance, where no relationship of debtor and creditor had intervened, the money could be followed, notwithstanding its normal character as currency, provided it could be earmarked or traced into assets acquired with it.' To accept either of the two contentions with which I have been so far dealing would be to assent to the proposition that a thief who has stolen money, and who from fear of detection hands that money to a beggar whom he happens to pass, gives a title to the money to the beggar as against the true owner—a proposition which is obviously impossible of acceptance.

The last contention for the appellant cannot in my opinion be supported. The law on the subject has been so fully discussed recently in *Sinclair* v *Brougham* that I need only point out that the law as laid down by Lord Ellenborough in *Taylor* v *Plumer* 3 M & S 562 as to the right of an owner to recover property in the common law Courts from a person who can show no title to it, where the property was capable of being traced, whether in its original form or in some substituted form, was fully accepted, and it was explained that the rule in equity which was applied in *Hallett's Case* 13 Ch D 696 was only introduced to meet cases where the money sought to be traced could no longer be identified owing to its having become merged in the Bank's assets, and the relationship of debtor and creditor, between the customer who had paid the money into the Bank and the Bank into which the money had been paid, having intervened.

The facts in the present case in my opinion remove any difficulty in the way of the plaintiff Bank recovering, without having recourse to the equity rule. The money which the bank seeks to recover is capable of being traced, as the appellant never paid any money into the Bank except money which was part of the proceeds of Hambrouck's frauds, and the appellant's Bank have paid all the money standing to the appellant's credit into Court, where it now is. Even if it had been necessary to apply the rule in *Hallett's Case* to enable the plaintiff Bank to establish their right to the money they claim, I see no difficulty in applying the rule to the facts as found by the learned judge in the Court below. . . .

SCRUTTON LJ: . . . The ground of the decision below is that the 315*l.* is traced to the money which Hamrouck obtained by fraud from the Bank; that this money was never Hambrouck's property, and as Mlle. Spanoghe gave no legal consideration for its transfer to her, but only the immoral consideration of past or future cohabitation, she cannot acquire a title to the money as a purchaser for value without notice of any defect in the transferor's title.

The first objection taken is that the Bank are not the proper plaintiffs, as Pelabon is not now objecting to the Bank's debiting his account with the cheques. It is clear, however, that the money actually obtained by Hambrouck was the Bank's money, even if they might debit their payments to the account of another, and the Bank therefore can sue for the money if it was obtained by fraud on them. Secondly, it was said that as Hambrouck paid the stolen money into a bank, he had only a creditor's right to be paid with any money, not the particular money he paid in; so that when he drew some money out of the bank and paid it to Mlle. Spanoghe, he did not make her the recipient of the money he had obtained from the Banque Belge, and therefore an action for money had and received would not lie. It was further said that Mlle. Spanoghe received the money as a gift without notice of any defect in title and that therefore no action would lie against her.

This last objection is, I think, bad. At common law, a man who had no title himself could give no title to another. Nemo potest dare quod non habet. To this there was an exception in the case of negotiable chattels or securities, the first of which to be recognized were money and bank notes: *Miller* v *Race* 1 Burr 452; 1 Sm LC, 12th ed., p. 525; and if these were received in good faith and for valuable consideration, the transferee got property though the transferor had none. But both good faith and valuable consideration were necessary, as Lord Mansfield says: 'in case of money stolen, the true owner cannot recover it after it has been paid away fairly and honestly upon a valuable and bona fide consideration'; but before money has passed in currency an action may be brought for the money itself. In the present case, it is clear that this money came to Mlle. Spanoghe either as savings out of housekeeping allowance, or as a gift to a mistress for past or future cohabitation. In the first case she would hold it as agent for Hambrouck; in the second for no consideration that the law recognized. If then the money that came to her was the money of the Banque Belge, she got no title to it, as Hambrouck against the Banque Belge had no title. The defence is that it was not the money of the Banque Belge, for payment into Hambrouck's bank, and his drawing out other money in satisfaction, had changed its identity.

I am inclined to think that at common law this would be a good answer to a claim for money had and received, at any rate if the money was mixed in Hambrouck's bank with other money. But it is clear that the equitable extension of the doctrine as based on *In re Hallett's Estate* 13 Ch D 696 and explained in *Sinclair* v *Brougham* [1914] AC 398 enables money though changed in character to be recovered, if it can be traced. As Lord Parker says in the latter case on equitable principles, the original owner would be entitled 'to follow the money as long as it or any property acquired by its means could be identified.' In that case there was an equitable charge on the substituted fund or property, if it could be traced to the stolen money. As Bramwell JA puts it in *Ex parte Cooke* (1876) 4 ChD 123, 128:

> A difficulty in tracing money often arises from the circumstances that payments now are not usually made in gold, but by cheques which go into a banking account, so that the sum is mixed up with the other moneys of the customer. But if this payment were made by a bag of gold which the broker put into his strong box, and then misapplied part of the money, leaving the rest in the bag, there would be no doubt that what was so left could be claimed as the money of the client. The use of cheques may make difficulties in tracing money, but that, so far as it can be traced, it may be claimed as the property of the client, appears to me to be covered both by the reason of the thing and by the authority of *Taylor* v *Plumer* 3 M & S 562.

If that is the test to apply it is clear that the 315*l.* in Mlle. Spanoghe's account and now in Court, can all clearly be traced to the money obtained by Hambrouck by fraud or forgery from the Bank, and as she gave for it no valuable consideration, she cannot set up a title derived from Hambrouck, who had no title against the true owner. . . .

ATKIN LJ: . . . The money was obtained from the plaintiff Bank by the fraud of Hambrouck. It does not appear to be necessary for this case to determine whether Hambrouck stole the money or obtained it by false pretences. At present it appears to me that the plaintiff Bank intended to pass the property in and the possession of the cash which under the operations of the clearing house they must be taken to have paid to the collecting bank. I will assume therefore that this is a case not of a void but of a voidable transaction by which Hambrouck obtained a title to the money until the plaintiffs elected to avoid his title, which they did when they made their claim in this action. The title would then revest in the plaintiffs subject to any title acquired in the meantime by any transferee for value without notice of the fraud.

The appellant however contends that the plaintiffs cannot assert their title to the sum of money which was on a deposit account: 1. because it has passed through one if not two bank accounts and therefore cannot be identified as the plaintiffs' money; 2. because in any case a transfer to an innocent donee defeats the original owner's claim. The course of the proceedings in this case is not quite clear. The statement of claim alleges specifically that the money is the property of the plaintiffs which they are entitled to follow, and the relief asked is not for a money judgment against the defendants, but an order that the sum paid into Court by the defendant Bank should be paid out to the plaintiffs. In giving judgment however, the learned judge has treated the claim as one for money had and received, and the judgment entered is an ordinary judgment against the appellant on a money claim for 315*l.* together with an order that the sum in Court should be paid out to the plaintiffs in part satisfaction. The two forms of relief are different, and though in this case there is no substantial difference in the result, the grounds upon which relief is based might have been material.

First, does it make any difference to the plaintiffs' rights that their money was paid into Farrow's Bank, and that the money representing it drawn out by Hambrouck was paid to the defendant Bank on deposit? If the question be the right of the plaintiffs in equity to follow their property, I apprehend that no difficulty arises. The case of *In re Hallet's Estate* 13 Ch D 696 makes it plain that the Court will investigate a banking account into which another person's money has been wrongfully paid, and will impute all drawings out of the account in the first instance to the wrongdoer's own moneys, leaving the plaintiff's money intact so far as it remains in the account at all. There can be no difficulty in this case in following every change of form of the money in question, whether in the hands of Hambrouck or of the apellant, and it appears to me that the plaintiffs were, on the grounds alleged in the statement of claim, entitled to a specific order for the return of the money in question, and, as it is now represented by the sum in Court, to payment out of Court of that sum.

The question whether they are entitled to a common law judgment for money had and received may involve other considerations. I am not without further consideration prepared to say that every person who can in equity establish a right to have his money or the proceeds of his property restored to him, can, as an alternative, bring an action against the person who has been in possession of such money or proceeds for money had and received; still less that he can always bring trover or detinue. But the common law rights are large and are admirably stated in *Taylor* v *Plumer* 3 M & S 562, 574, which was a case stated for the opinion of the Court of King's Bench after trial before Lord Ellenborough at the London Sittings. . . .

[Atkin LJ discussed *Taylor* v *Plumer* and continued: . . .] I notice that in *Sinclair* v *Brougham* [1914] AC 398, 419 Lord Haldane LC in dealing with this decision says: 'Lord Ellenborough laid down, as a limit to this proposition, that if the money had become incapable of being traced, as, for instance, when it had been paid into the broker's general account with his banker, the principal had no remedy excepting to prove as a creditor for money had and received,' and proceeds to say 'you can, even at law, follow, but only so long as the relation of debtor and creditor has not superseded the right in rem.' The words above 'as for instance' et seq. do not represent and doubtless do not purport to represent Lord Ellenborough's actual words; and I venture to doubt whether the common law ever so restricted the right as to hold that the money became incapable of being traced, merely because paid into the broker's general account with his banker. The question always was, Had the means of ascertainment failed? But if in 1815 the common law halted outside the bankers' door, by 1879 equity had had the courage to lift the latch, walk in and examine the books: *In re Hallett's Estate* 13 Ch D 696. I see no reason why the means of ascertainment so provided should not now be available both for common law and equity proceedings. If, following the principles laid down in *In re Hallett's Estate*, it can be ascertained either that the money in the bank, or the commodity which it has bought, is 'the product of, or substitute for, the original thing,' then it still follows 'the nature of the thing itself.' On these principles it would follow that as the money paid into the bank can be identified as the product of the original money, the plaintiffs have the common law right to claim it, and can sue for money had and received. In the present case less difficulty than usual is experienced in tracing the descent of the money, for substantially no other money has ever been mixed with the proceeds of the fraud. Under the order of the Court in this case I think the money paid into Court must be treated as paid in on behalf of the defendant Spanoghe, and the money judgment, together with the order for payment out to the plaintiffs, effectually secures their rights.

Secondly, so far as it is contended that the bankers are entitled to retain possession where they have not given value, I think that has been concluded by what I have already said as to valuable consideration. . . .

Question

Was this case decided on the basis of tracing at common law or tracing in equity? Do all three judges reach the same conclusion?

Notes

1. *Re Hallett*'s Case (1880) 13 Ch D 696 and *Sinclair* v *Brougham* [1914] AC 398 are discussed in Section 2 below on tracing in equity.

2. Note that this was only a claim in what Professor Birks terms the second measure (value surviving) as opposed to the more usual first measure claim (value received).

3. For discussion of *Banque Belge* see Birks, *Introduction*, 361–2; Khurshid and Matthews, 'Tracing Confusion' (1979) 95 LQR 78, at 91–4 describe it as a 'rogue case'.

Nelson* v *Larholt
[1948] 1 KB 339 (KBD)

Action for money had and received; constructive trust

Potts was an executor of the late Mr Burns. An account was opened to deal with the estate, and over a period of 16 months Potts drew eight cheques upon it in favour of Larholt, totalling £135. Larholt was a turf accountant and it appeared the cheques were cashed by Larholt when Potts brought them to him out of office hours. Each cheque was signed 'G.A. Potts, executor of Wm. Burns decd'. This action was brought by three beneficiaries of the estate and Potts's co-executor to recover the £135 from Larholt.

DENNING J: . . . I am satisfied that Potts was acting fraudulently: he did not draw the cheques or use the money for the purposes of the estate, but for his own purposes. The relevant legal principles have been much developed in the last thirty-five years. A man's money is property which is protected by law. It may exist in various forms, such as coins, treasury notes, cash at bank, or cheques, or bills of exchange of which he is "the holder" [see Bills of Exchange Act 1882, s.2] but, whatever its form, it is protected according to one uniform principle. If it is taken from the rightful owner, or, indeed, from the beneficial owner, without his authority, he can recover the amount from any person into whose hands it can be traced, unless and until it reaches one who receives it in good faith and for value and without notice of the want of authority. Even if the one who received it acted in good faith, nevertheless if he had notice—that is, if he knew of the want of authority or is to be taken to have known of it—he must repay. All the cases that occur in the books, of trustees or agents who draw cheques on the trust account or the principal's account for their own private purposes, or of directors who apply their company's cheques for their own account, fall within this one principle. The rightful owner can recover the amount from anyone who takes the money with notice, subject, of course, to the limitation that he cannot recover twice over. This principle has been evolved by the courts of law and equity side by side. In equity it took the form of an action to follow moneys impressed with an express trust, or with a constructive trust owing to a fiduciary relationship. In law it took the form of an action for money had and received or damages for conversion of a cheque. It is no longer appropriate, however, to draw a distinction between law and equity. Principles have now to be stated in the light of their combined effect. Nor is it necessary to canvass the niceties of the old forms of action. Remedies now depend on the substance of the right, not on whether they can be fitted into a particular framework. The right here is not peculiar to equity or contract or tort, but falls naturally within the important category of cases where the court orders restitution, if the justice of the case so requires.

Applying the principle in this case, it is plain that the moneys of the estate were transferred by Potts without any authority into the hands of the defendant. Potts had clearly no authority to draw cheques on the bank account for his own purposes. The law will therefore compel the defendant to restore the moneys to the estate unless he received the moneys in good faith and for value and without notice of the want of authority. It is plain that he received them for value and Mr Lowe [counsel for the plaintiffs] did not suggest that he did not receive them in good faith. But did he have notice of the want of authority? That depends on what amounts to notice. He was the original payee of the cheque, and, as such, was not protected by the fact that it was a negotiable instrument. He must, I think, be taken to have known what a reasonable man would have known. If, therefore, he knew or is to be taken to have known of the want of authority, as, for instance, if the circumstances were such as to put a reasonable man on inquiry, and he made none, or if he was put off by an answer that would not have satisfied a reasonable man, or, in other words, if he was negligent in not perceiving the want of authority, then he is taken to have notice of it. That is, I think, the result of *Reckitt* v *Barnett* [1929] AC 176. If the defendant had negotiated the cheque to a third person, the test of notice to that new holder would have been different. This holder would have been able to claim that he was a holder in due course. Notice to such a holder would depend on his own state of mind, not on that of a reasonable man. If he, in his own mind, realized that there was something wrong with the cheque and shut his eyes to it, he would be taken to have notice, but not otherwise. Whilst on this question of notice, I would add that no one can gain a title to money through a forged indorsement. The holder is treated as if he had notice of the forgery. There are exceptions, of course, stated in the Act [Bills of Exchange Act 1882]. But none of those matters arise here. This is a case where the plaintiff's money in the form of cash at bank was transferred by a wrong-doer to the defendant and he must be taken to have known what any reasonable man would have known. In this case I am quite satisfied that the defendant had notice of the want of authority. Each of the cheques on its face showed that it was drawn on the executor's account. Potts brought it to him out of office hours with a request to cash it. Why did not Potts, if he wanted cash, get it from the bank? It seems to me that any reasonable person would have been put on inquiry. The defendant admitted as much, for he said that he asked Potts about it and that Potts said that it was in connexion with the trust that he wanted the money. On one occasion Potts said that he was going to Scotland on estate business. No reasonable man would have been satisfied with those answers. If Potts, as executor, wanted money legitimately for estate purposes, he could have got it from the bank that day or waited till the next morning. All that applies to the first cheque which the defendant cashed. Then, when it came to cashing cheque after cheque, seven more, and the last one a piece of paper with a 2*d.* stamp on it, the inference is irresistible that the defendant knew or ought to have known that Potts had no authority to do what he was doing. Any reasonable man in the defendant's position would have known it. I hold, therefore, that in this case the plaintiffs are entitled to recover the money from the defendant and I award judgment for the amount of 135*l.*

Note

Lord Denning expanded upon his views extra-judicially in 'The Recovery of Money' (1949) 65 LQR 37.

Agip (Africa) Ltd v *Jackson*

[1990] Ch 265 (Ch D); affd [1991] Ch 547 (CA)

Action for money had and received; tracing at law and in equity; accountability as a constructive trustee

Over a number of years the plaintiff company, a subsidiary of the well-known Italian oil company, was systematically defrauded of millions of US dollars by their chief accountant, Zdiri. He would effect this by obtaining an authorised signature to a payment order, and subsequently altering the name of the payee. This action concerned a payment order for US $518,882.92 ultimately made payable to 'Baker Oil Services Ltd'. The defendants, Jackson & Co., were a firm of chartered accountants in the Isle of Man. They operated accounts for shell payee companies at the High Holborn branch of Lloyds Bank, including one for Baker Oil. Payment was effected by the plaintiffs' bank in Tunis, Banque du Sud, by telegraphic transfer to Lloyds Bank in High Holborn, via Banque du Sud's correspondent bank, Citibank in New York. Due to time differences, Lloyds took a delivery risk by making payment before business began in New York. The money was transferred to an account of Jackson & Co.'s at the same branch the next day, and the Baker Oil account was closed. The following day $518,000 was transferred to Jackson & Co.'s client account on the Isle of Man. Within days most of the money was dispersed to various payees. $45,000 remaining in the account was subsequently paid into court. The plaintiff company was unsuccessful in proceedings against Banque de Sud in Tunisia, and now sought to recover the $518,822.92 from Jackson & Co. *Held*: the plaintiffs had title to sue, but the claim to recover upon an *action for money had and received* failed because, first, the money could not be traced at common law and, secondly, the defendants were entitled to a defence of ministerial receipt because they had accounted to their principals before they had notice of the plaintiffs' claim. Further, the plaintiffs were entitled to trace in equity the sum (some $45,000) which remained in the hands of Jackson & Co., and were therefore entitled to the money paid into court. In addition, the defendants, Jackson & Co., were *accountable as constructive trustees* on the ground of knowing assistance, because they obviously knew they were laundering money and were therefore liable to make good the shortfall. The following extracts are concerned only with the *action for money had and received* and *tracing at common law.*

Chancery Division

MILLETT J: . . . THE CLAIM AT COMMON LAW

The plaintiffs claim to recover money paid under a mistake. The money was paid to Baker Oil but it was not mixed with other money in Baker Oil's account and accordingly the plaintiffs claim to be able to follow it at common law into the account of Jackson & Co. and to recover it from Mr Jackson and Mr Bowers, the partners of the firm. Unlike a tracing claim in equity, the common law claim for money had and received is a personal and not a proprietary claim and the cause of action is complete when the money is received. With only limited exceptions, it is no defence that the defendant has parted with the money. The claim does not depend on any impropriety or want of probity on the part of the defendants. Several objections to it have been raised on behalf of the defendants and to these I now turn.

[Millett J considered objections based on the plaintiffs' title to sue and the character of the mistake and continued: . . .]

Tracing at common law

The next question is whether the plaintiffs can follow the payment into the hands of Jackson & Co.; for the fact that it was the plaintiffs' money which left the Banque du Sud does not mean that it was the plaintiffs' money which reached Baker Oil or Jackson & Co. Tracing at common law, unlike its counterpart in equity, is neither a cause of action nor a remedy but serves an evidential purpose. The cause of action is for money had and received. Tracing at common law enables the defendant to be identified as the recipient of the plaintiff's money and the measure of his liability to be determined by the amount of the plaintiff's money he is shown to have received.

The common law has always been able to follow a physical asset from one recipient to another. Its ability to follow an asset in the same hands into a changed form was established in *Taylor* v *Plumer*, 3 M & S 562. In following the plaintiff's money into an asset purchased exclusively with it, no distinction is drawn between a chose in action such as the debt of a bank to its customer and any other asset: *In re Diplock* [1948] Ch 466, 519. But it can only follow a physical asset, such as a cheque or its proceeds, from one person to another. It can follow money but not a chose in action. Money can be followed at common law into and out of a bank account and into the hands of a subsequent transferee, provided that it does not cease to be identifiable by being mixed with other money in the bank account derived from some other source: *Banque Belge pour l'Etranger* v *Hambrouck* [1921] 1 KB 321. Applying these principles, the plaintiffs claim to follow their money through Baker Oil's account where it was not mixed with any other money and into Jackson & Co.'s account at Lloyds Bank.

The defendants deny this. They contend that tracing is not possible at common law because the money was mixed, first when it was handled in New York, and secondly in Jackson & Co.'s own account at Lloyds Bank.

The latter objection is easily disposed of. The cause of action for money had and received is complete when the plaintiff's money is received by the defendant. It does not depend on the continued retention of the money by the defendant. Save in strictly limited circumstances it is no defence that he has parted with it. A fortiori it can be no defence for him to show that he has mixed it with his own money that he cannot tell whether he still has it or not. Mixing by the defendant himself must, therefore, be distinguished from mixing by a prior recipient. The former is irrelevant, but the latter will destroy the claim, for it will prevent proof that the money received by the defendant was the money paid by the plaintiff.

In my judgment, however, the former objection is insuperable. The money cannot be followed by treating it as the proceeds of a cheque presented by the collecting bank in exchange for payment by the paying bank. The money was transmitted by telegraphic transfer. There was no cheque or any equivalent. The payment order was not a cheque or its equivalent. It remained throughout in the possession of the Banque du Sud. No copy was sent to Lloyds Bank or Baker Oil or presented to the Banque du Sud in exchange for the money. It was normally the plaintiffs' practice to forward a copy of the payment order to the supplier when paying an invoice but this was for information only. It did not authorise or enable the supplier to obtain payment. There is no evidence that this practice was followed in the case of forged payment orders and it is exceedingly unlikely that it was.

Nothing passed between Tunisia and London but a stream of electrons. It is not possible to treat the money received by Lloyds Bank in London or its correspondent bank in New York as representing the proceeds of the payment order or of any other physical asset previously in its hands and delivered by it in exchange for the money. The Banque du Sud merely telexed a request to Lloyds Bank to make a payment to Baker Oil against its own undertaking to reimburse Lloyds Bank in New York. Lloyds Bank complied with the request by paying Baker Oil with its own money. It thereby took a delivery risk. In due course it was no doubt reimbursed, but it is not possible to identify the source of the money with which it was reimbursed without attempting to follow the money through the New York clearing system. Unless Lloyds Bank's correspondent bank in New York was also Citibank, this involves tracing the money through the accounts of Citibank and Lloyds Bank's correspondent bank with the Federal Reserve Bank, where it must have been mixed with other money. The money with which Lloyds Bank was reimbursed cannot therefore, without recourse to equity, be identified as being that of the Banque du Sud. There is no evidence that Lloyds Bank's correspondent bank in New York was Citibank, and accordingly the plaintiffs' attempt to trace the money at common law must fail.

This is, however, not the only objection to the plaintiffs' claim to recover the money from Jackson & Co. at common law and without proof of dishonesty or want of probity on their part, and I must deal with the other objections taken by the defendants.

The claim against Jackson & Co.

The plaintiffs' money was paid to Baker Oil but they claim to recover it as money had and received by Jackson & Co. They submit that in order to succeed in such a claim all that the claimant needs to prove is (i) that the money was paid either to the defendant or to some prior recipient; (ii) in circumstances which make it recoverable; (iii) that if it was paid to a prior recipient it can be followed into the hands of the defendant; and (iv) that neither the defendant nor any prior recipient gave value. If correct, then a recipient otherwise than for value from a person who is liable to an action for money had and received is equally liable to such an action. The contention has some academic support but, with one possible exception, it is not supported by any judicial authority. The possible exception is *Bank Belge pour l'Etranger* v *Hambrouck* [1921] 1 KB 321. That case apart, there is none so far as I am aware in which a claim for money had and received has been successfully brought against anyone other than the immediate recipient of the money or his principal.

In that case H obtained by fraud from his employer a number of cheques purporting to be drawn by the employer on the plaintiff bank. He paid the cheques into a bank account in his own name. His bank collected the proceeds from the plaintiff bank and credited them to H's account. H then drew cheques on his account in favour of S, his mistress, who paid them into her own account at her own bank. She spent most of the money but a balance of £315 remained. This sum was paid into court by her bank and was claimed by the plaintiff bank. The plaintiff bank was held entitled to it.

It is not easy to know what that case decided. The plaintiff bank sought a declaration that the £315 was its property. The relief it claimed was not a money judgment but an order for payment of the £315. In other words, it was making a propriety claim. The trial judge, however, treated it as a common law action for money had and received and entered an ordinary money judgment against S for the sum claimed. Her appeal was dismissed.

The plaintiff had limited its claim to the £315 in court. That was also consistent with a proprietary claim, though the decision to limit the claim may have been due to other considerations. But there is no hint in any of the judgments in Court of Appeal that the claim need not have been so limited; although if S was in truth personally accountable for money had and received, the fact that she had dissipated the money was irrelevant. On the contrary, [Bankes] LJ was concerned to show that the money had not been mixed in her account, which indicates that he considered the claim to be a proprietary one in which it was necessary to establish not what S had received but what she still retained.

Scrutton LJ held that the money could be traced in equity. It is not clear whether he relied on this to support the common law claim or to found relief in equity, but since the plaintiff had limited its claim to the £315, this made no difference to the result. Atkin LJ alone drew attention to the difference between the two types of claim. He, too, held that the money could be followed in equity, and that this entitled the plaintiff to a specific order for the return of the money in question. He then dealt expressly with the common law action for money had and received and held that the plaintiff's ability to follow the money at common law entitled it to bring such an action.

I think that at first instance I am bound to regard that case as authority for the proposition that an action for money had and received is not limited to the immediate recipient or his principal but may be brought against a subsequent transferee into whose hands the money can be followed and who still retains it. But it is no authority for the proposition that it lies against a subsequent transferee who has parted with the money, and I doubt that it does. At this remove the action begins to take on the aspect of a proprietary claim rather than the enforcement of a personal liability to account. Should it be sought to impose personal liability on a person who has parted with the money, recourse can be made to equity which has developed appropriate principles by which such liability can be determined. The alternative is to expose an innocent transferee who has dissipated the money to a claim at law where none would exist in equity and to make that liability depend on the fortuitous circumstance that the money had not been mixed with other money prior to its receipt by him. Such a difference in outcome cannot be justified as reflecting the fact that in one case the defendant is being required to account to the former legal owner while in the other he is accounting merely to an owner in equity, for the equitable remedies are available to the former legal owner who has been deprived of his property as the result of a breach of fiduciary obligation.

[Millett J held that Jackson & Co. were entitled to rely upon the defence of 'ministerial receipt' to the claim at common law (as to which see Chapter 8, Section 2) and concluded: . . .]

Conclusion
In my judgment, the claim to recover the money from Jackson & Co. as money had and received and without proof of dishonesty or want of probity must fail. It fails as regards the sum in court because of the impossibility of tracing the money at common law. It fails as regards the balance for this and for the additional reason that Jackson & Co. accounted to their principals before they had notice of the plaintiffs' claim.

It would be a reproach to the law if the defendants' liability depended on whether or not the Banque du Sud and Lloyds Bank shared the same correspondent bank in New York. But then it would be equally deplorable if the defendants' liability depended on whether or not they had mixed the plaintiffs' money with some of their own during its temporary sojourn in Baker Oil's account. And it would scarcely be more seemly if their liability arose only because they made the foolish mistake of passing the money through their own bank account instead of routing it through Euro-Arabian as on previous occasions. Fortunately, none of these is the case. There is no difficulty in tracing the plaintiffs' money in equity, which has well developed principles by which the proceeds of fraud can be followed and recovered from those through whose hands they pass. Whether equity can make its tracing rules available in aid of common law remedies, or whether, as I think, it would be preferable to develop a unified restitutionary remedy for the recovery of property transferred without consideration to a recipient with no legitimate justification for receiving it, are questions which must be left for others to decide. There is certainly no need for recourse to the common law action for the money had and received, which is not well equipped for the task. In my judgment, the plaintiffs' attempted reliance on the common law was unnecessary and misplaced. . . .

Court of Appeal

FOX LJ: . . .

Tracing at common law
The judge held that Agip was not entitled to trace at law. Tracing at law does not depend upon the establishment of an initial fiduciary relationship. Liability depends upon receipt by the defendant of the plaintiff's money and the extent of the liability depends on the amount received. Since liability depends upon receipt the fact that a recipient has not retained the asset is irrelevant. For the same reason dishonesty or lack of inquiry on the part of the recipient are irrelevant. Identification in the defendant's hands of the plaintiff's asset is, however, necessary. It must be shown that the money received by the defendant was the money of the plaintiff. Further, the very limited common law remedies make it difficult to follow at law into mixed funds. The judge's view [1990] Ch 265, 286 of the present case was that the common law remedy was not available. [Fox LJ discussed the *Banque Belge* case and continued: . . .]

Now, in the present case, the course of events was as follows. (1) The original payment order was in December signed by an authorised signatory. (2) The name of the payee was then altered to Baker Oil. (3) The altered order was then taken to Banque du Sud who complied with it by debiting the account of Agip with $518,822.92 and then instructing Lloyds Bank to pay Baker Oil. Banque du Sud also instructed Citibank in New York to debit its account with Citibank and credit Lloyds Bank with the amount of the order. (4) Lloyds Bank credited the money to Baker Oil's account on the morning of 7 January. (5) On 8 January, Lloyds Bank in pursuance of instructions from Baker Oil transferred the $518,822.92, which was the only sum standing to the credit of Baker Oil's account, to an account in the name of Jackson & Co. (6) Immediately before the transfer from Baker Oil, Jackson & Co.'s account was $7,911.80 in credit. In consequence of the transfer it became $526,734.72 in credit.

The inquiry which has to be made is whether the money paid to Jackson & Co.'s account 'was the product of, or substitute for, the original thing.' In answering that question I do not think that it matters that the order was not a cheque. It was a direction by the account holder to the bank. When Atkin LJ referred in the *Banque Belge* case to the 'original money' he was, I assume, referring to the money credited by Banque Belge (the plaintiff) to Hambrouck's account. Money from that account was the only money in Mlle. Spanoghe's deposit account. It was not, therefore, difficult to say that the money in issue (i.e. the residue of Mlle. Spanoghe's account) could be identified as the product of the original money. There were no complexities of tracing at all. Everything in Mlle. Spanoghe's account came from Hambrouck's account and everything in Hambrouck's account came from the credit in respect of the fraudulent cheque.

The position in the present case is much more difficult. Banque du Sud can be regarded as having paid with Agip's money but Lloyds Bank, acting as directed by Banque du Sud, paid Baker Oil with its own money. It had no other and, accordingly, took a delivery risk. It was, in the end, put in funds, but it is difficult to see how the origin of those funds can be identified without tracing the money through the New York clearing system. The money in the present case did get mixed on two occasions. The first was in the New York clearing system and the second was in Jackson & Co.'s own account. The judge held that the latter was of no consequence. I agree. The common law remedy attached to the recipient of the money and its subsequent transposition does not alter his liability. The problem arises at an earlier stage. What did Jackson & Co. receive which was the product of Agip's asset? Baker Oil was controlled for present purposes by Jackson & Co. but Baker Oil was paid by Lloyds Bank which had not been put in funds from New York. It was subsequently recouped. But it is not possible to show the source from which it was recouped without tracing the money through the New York clearing system. The judge said [1990] Ch 265, 286:

> Unless Lloyds Bank's correspondent bank in New York was also Citibank, this involves tracing the money through the accounts of Citibank and Lloyds Bank's correspondent bank with the Federal Reserve Bank, where it must have been mixed with other money. The money with which Lloyds Bank was reimbursed cannot therefore, without recourse to equity, be identified as being that of the Banque du Sud.

I respectfully agree with that view. Accordingly, it seems to me that the common law remedy is not available.

I should add this. Atkin LJ's approach in the *Banque Belge* case amounts virtually to saying that there is now no difference between the common law and equitable remedies. Indeed, the common law remedy might be wider because of the absence of any requirement of a fiduciary relationship. There may be a good deal to be said for that view but it goes well beyond any other case and well beyond the views of Bankes and Scrutton LJJ. And in the 70 years since the *Banque Belge* decision it has not been applied. Whether, short of the House of Lords, it is now open to the courts to adopt it I need not consider. I would in any event feel difficulty in doing so in the present case where, as I indicate later, it seems to me that the established equitable rules provide an adequate remedy in relation to this action. . . .

Notes

1. The case is noted in Birks (1989) 105 LQR 528. For discussion see McKendrick, 'Tracing misdirected funds' [1991] LMCLQ 378 and Sir Peter

Millett, writing extra-judicially, 'Tracing the Proceeds of Fraud' (1991) 107 LQR 71, where he argues that 'in all but the simplest cases recourse to the common law should be abandoned, that attempts to rationalise and develop the common law rules are unlikely to succeed and should no longer be pursued, and that attempts should be made instead to develop a unified restitutionary remedy based on equitable principles'.

2. Millett J's views on the common law's inability to trace through a telegraphic transfer of money were followed in *Bank Tejerat* v *Hong Kong and Shanghai Banking Corporation (CI) Ltd* [1995] 1 Lloyd's Rep 239 (Tuckey J).

Lipkin Gorman* v *Karpnale Ltd
[1991] 2 AC 548 (HL)

Action for money had and received

Cass was by day an apparently respectable solicitor, but by night a gambler. He raided the client account of the firm of which he was a partner to feed his addiction. In total he gambled £561,014.06 at the Playboy Club in Park Lane, Mayfair. This included sums won and re-staked. His total winnings were £378,294.04. There was a shortfall from the client account of £222,908.98. Cass's principal method of fraud was to have cheques drawn by the firm's cashier, Chapman, upon the account made payable to cash. Cass would sign these cheques which the cashier cashed, handing the money over to Cass. It was agreed that in the relevant period the club won and Cass lost £150,960 obtained by this method. Cass was jailed for three years for theft. The solicitors sought restitution of some £219,173.98 obtained by this method from the Club.

LORD GOFF OF CHIEVELEY: [His lordship discussed *Clarke* v *Shee and Johnson* (1774) 1 Cowp 197, 98 ER 1041 and said it was the solicitors' case that the situation here was indistinguishable. The respondent club sought to distinguish that case: . . .]

Title to the money

The first ground is concerned with the solicitors' title to the money received by Cass (through Chapman) from the bank. It is to be observed that the present action, like the action in *Clarke* v *Shee and Johnson*, is concerned with a common law claim to money, where the money in question has not been paid by the appellant directly to the respondents—as is usually the case where money is, for example, recoverable as having been paid under a mistake of fact, or for a consideration which has failed. On the contrary, here the money had been paid to the respondents by a third party, Cass; and in such a case the appellant has to establish a basis on which he is entitled to the money. This (at least, as a general rule) he does by showing that the money is his legal property, as appears from Lord Mansfield's judgment in *Clarke* v *Shee and Johnson*. If he can do so, he may be entitled to suceed in a claim against the third party for money had and received to his use, though not if the third party has received the money in good faith and for a valuable consideration. The cases in which such a claim has succeeded are, I believe, very rare: see the cases, including *Clarke* v *Shee and Johnson*, collected in Goff and Jones, *The Law of Restitution*, 3rd ed. (1986), p. 64, note 29 [see now 4th ed., p. 79, note 39]. This is probably because, at common law, property in money, like other fungibles, is lost as such when it is mixed with other money.

Furthermore, it appears that in these cases the action for money had and received is not usually founded upon any wrong by the third party, such as conversion; nor is it said to be a case of waiver of tort. It is founded simply on the fact that, as Lord Mansfield said, the third party cannot in conscience retain the money—or, as we say nowadays, for the third party to retain the money would result in his unjust enrichment at the expense of the owner of the money.

So, in the present case, the solicitors seek to show that the money in question was their property at common law. But their claim in the present case for money had and received is nevertheless a personal claim; it is not a proprietary claim, advanced on the basis that money remaining in the hands of the respondents is their property. Of course there is no doubt that, even if legal title to the money did vest in Cass immediately on receipt, nevertheless he would have held it on trust for his partners, who would accordingly have been entitled to trace it in equity into the hands of the respondents. However, your Lordships are not concerned with an equitable tracing claim in the present case, since no such case is advanced by the solicitors, who have been content to proceed at common law by a personal action, viz. an action for money had and received. I should add that, in the present case, we are not concerned with the fact that money drawn by Cass from the solicitors' client account at the bank may have become mixed by Cass with his own money before he gambled it away at the club. For the respondents have conceded that, if the solicitors can establish legal title to the money in the hands of Cass, that title was not defeated by mixing of the money with other money of Cass while in his hands. On this aspect of the case, therefore, the only question is whether the solicitors can establish legal title to the money when received by Cass from the bank by drawing cheques on the client account without authority.

Before your Lordships, and no doubt before the courts below, elaborate argument was advanced by counsel upon this issue. The respondents relied in particular upon two decisions of the Privy Council as showing that where a partner obtains money by drawing on a partnership bank account without authority, he alone and not the partnership obtains legal title to the money so obtained. These cases, *Union Bank of Australia Ltd* v *McClintock* [1922] 1 AC 240 and *Commercial Banking Co. of Sydney Ltd* v *Mann* [1961] AC 1, were in fact concerned with bankers' cheques; but for the respondents it was submitted that the same principle was applicable in the case of cash. The solicitors argued that these cases were wrongly decided, or alternatively sought to distinguish them on a number of grounds. . . . I am not prepared to depart from decisions of such high authority as these. They show that, where a banker's cheque payable to a third party or bearer is obtained by a partner from a bank which has received the authority of the partnership to pay the partner in question who has, however, unknown to the bank, acted beyond the authority of his partners in so operating the account, the legal property in the banker's cheque thereupon vests in the partner. The same must a fortiori be true when it is not such a banker's cheque but cash which is so drawn from the bank by the partner in question. Even so, I am satisfied that the solicitors are able to surmount this difficulty, as follows.

It is well established that a legal owner is entitled to trace his property into its product, provided that the latter is indeed identifiable as the product of his property. Thus, in *Taylor* v *Plumer* (1815) 3 M & S 562, where Sir Thomas Plumer gave a draft to a stockbroker for the purpose of buying exchequer bills, and the stockbrocker instead used the draft for buying American securities and doubloons for his own purposes, Sir Thomas was able to trace his property into the securities and doubloons in the hands of the stockbroker, and so defeat a claim made to them by the stockbroker's assignees in bankruptcy. Of course, 'tracing' or 'following' property into its product involves a decision by the owner of the original property to assert his title to the product in place of his original property. This is sometimes referred to as ratification. I myself would not so describe it, but it has, in my opinion, at least one feature in common with ratification, that it cannot be relied upon so as to render an innocent recipient a wrongdoer (cf. *Bolton Partners* v *Lambert* (1889) 41 Ch D 295, 307, *per* Cotton LJ: 'an act lawful at the time of its performance [cannot] be rendered unlawful, by the application of the doctrine of ratification.')

I return to the present case. Before Cass drew upon the solicitor's client account at the bank, there was of course no question of the solicitors having any legal property in any cash lying at the bank. The relationship of the bank with the solicitors was essentially that of debtor and creditor; and since the client account was at all material times in credit, the bank was the debtor and the solicitors were its creditors. Such a debt constitutes a chose in action, which is a species of property; and since the debt was enforceable at common law, the chose in action was legal property belonging to the solicitors at common law.

There is in my opinion no reason why the soliciors should not be able to trace their property at common law in that chose in action, or in any part of it, into its product, i.e. cash drawn by Cass from their client account at the bank. Such a claim is consistent with their assertion that the money so obtained by Cass was their property at common law. Further, in claiming the money as money had and received, the solicitors have not sought to make the respondents liable on the basis of any wrong, a point which will be of relevance at a later stage, when I come to consider the defence of change of position.

Authority for the solicitors' right to trace their property in this way is to be found in the decision of your Lordships' House in *Marsh* v *Keating* (1834) 1 Bing (NC) 198. Mrs Keating was the proprietor of £12,000 interest or share in joint stock reduced 3 per cent annuities, standing to her credit in the books of the Bank of England, where the accounts were entered in the form of debtor and creditor accounts in the ledgers of the bank. Under what purported to be a power of attorney given by Mrs Keating to the firm of Marsh, Sibbard & Co., on which Mrs Keating's signature was in fact forged by Henry Fauntleroy, a partner in Marsh, Sibbard & Co., an entry was made in the books of the Bank of England purporting to transfer £9,000 of Mrs Keating's interest or share in the stock to William Tarbutt, to whom, on the instructions of Henry Fauntleroy, the stock had been sold for the sum of £6,018 15s. In due course, the broker who conducted the sale accounted for £6,013 2s 6d (being the sale price less commission) by a cheque payable to Marsh & Co. Upon the discovery of the forgery, Mrs Keating made a claim upon the Bank of England; and the bank requested Mrs Keating to prove in the bankruptcy of the partners in Marsh & Co. in respect of the sum so received by them. Mrs Keating then commenced an action, pursuant to an order of the Lord Chancellor, for the purpose of trying the question whether the partners in Marsh & Co. were indebted to her, in which she claimed the sum so received by Marsh & Co. as money had and received to her use. The opinion of the judges was taken, and their opinion was to the effect that Mrs Keating was entitled to succeed in her claim. Your Lordship's House ruled accordingly. It must follow a fortiori that the solicitors, as owners of the chose in action constituted by the indebtedness of the bank to them in respect of the sums paid into the client account, could trace their property in that chose in action into its direct product, the money drawn from the account by Cass. It further follows, from the concession made by the respondents, that the solicitors can follow their property into the hands of the respondents when it was paid to them at the club.

Note

1. Note the curious concession by counsel for the Playboy Club that the firm's title to the money was not defeated by being mixed with Cass's own money. This meant the attitude of the modern common law to mixing did not need to be squarely addressed.

2. For discussion of the defences of bona fide purchase and change of position and further extracts from this case see Chapter 8, Sections 1 and 2.

3. For lucid discussion see Birks, 'The English Recognition of Unjust Enrichment' [1991] LMCLQ 473, at 473–86.

Section 2: tracing in equity

A: The relationship between tracing and knowing receipt

It is necessary to differentiate sharply between personal claims and proprietary claims. The cases do not speak with a single voice, but the best way of reconciling the authorities is to categorise 'knowing receipt' as a species of restitutionary liability which depends upon the affirmative proof by the plaintiff that the defendant received wealth in circumstances in which he knew, or ought to have known, that the wealth in question was the plaintiff's. It is a cause of action in subtractive unjust enrichment, with the peculiarity that the unjust factor is defendant-sided rather than plaintiff-sided. Knowing receipt is an *in personam* claim. (Confusion is caused by the clumsy and inelegant phrase *accountability as a constructive trustee* often encountered in the cases, but this inaccurate terminology does not convert a personal claim into a proprietary claim.) Much controversy surrounds the question as to what precise degree of knowledge or constructive knowledge suffices to establish liability. The debate is often conducted by reference to the hierarchy of states of mind devised by counsel in *Baden, Delvaux and Lecuit* v *Société Général pour Favoriser le Développement du Commerce et de l'Industrie en France SA* [1983] BCLC 325, 403, [1993] 1 WLR 509, 575–6, known for obvious reasons as the *Baden* case. Peter Gibson J said:

> What types of knowledge are relevant for the purposes of constructive trusteeship? Mr Price submits that knowledge can comprise any one of five different mental states which he described as follows: (i) actual knowledge; (ii) wilfully shutting one's eyes to the obvious; (iii) wilfully and recklessly failing to make such inquiries as an honest and reasonable man would make; (iv) knowledge of circumstances which would indicate the facts to an honest and reasonable man; (v) knowledge of circumstances which would put an honest and reasonable man on inquiry. More accurately, apart from actual knowledge they are formulations of the circumstances which may lead the court to impute knowledge of the facts to the alleged constructive trustee even though he lacked actual knowledge of those facts. Thus the court will treat a person as having constructive knowledge of the

> facts if he wilfully shuts his eyes to the relevant facts which would be obvious if he opened his eyes, such constructive knowledge being usually termed (though by a metaphor of historical inaccuracy) 'Nelsonian knowledge.' Similarly the court may treat a person as having constructive knowledge of the facts – 'type (iv) knowledge' – if he has actual knowledge of circumstances which would indicate the facts to an honest and reasonable man.

Some cases insist on a high degree of knowledge: for example, *In re Montagu's Settlement Trusts* [1987] Ch 264 (below) and, more recently *Eagle Trust plc* v *SBC Securities Ltd* [1995] BCC 231 (Arden J). Others treat all degrees of knowledge and constructive knowledge as sufficient. In contrast the prevailing academic view is that as this is restitutionary liability, prima facie liability should be strict. See Birks, 'Misdirected Funds – Restitution from the Recipient' [1989] LMCLQ 296 and Sir Peter Millett, 'Tracing the Proceeds of Fraud' (1991) 107 LQR 71.

In contrast it is usual to speak of tracing only in the context of following assets into the hands of (usually) indirect recipients in order to establish a restitutionary proprietary remedy by the imposition of a *constructive trust* or an *equitable lien*. Whereas the cause of action in *money had and received* or for knowing receipt is constituted upon receipt, tracing here goes beyond the moment of receipt to establish that a defendant was enriched and remains enriched. It demonstrates that the plaintiff's value subsists in assets in the defendant's hands. Tracing is a means to an end, not an end in itself. Many phrases are used to capture this function: it is a 'technique', a 'mechanism', a 'process'. Tracing in equity is liable always to be defeated by the bona fide purchaser for value without notice. This is a fertile source of confusion. Therefore notice or constructive notice is relevant to the operation of the defence of bona fide purchase. (See *Polly Peck International plc* v *Nadir (No. 2)* [1992] 4 All ER 769 (below).) Some cases fail to make clear whether they are talking about 'knowledge' as a ground for an *in personam* restitutionary claim, or 'notice' which defeats a proprietary claim based on tracing.

Clearly tracing and knowing receipt can be argued on the same set of facts, but they must be sharply differentiated. Distinguish also '*knowing assistance*', now termed '*accessory liability*', a species of equitable wrongdoing which can arise on similar facts (for example, *Agip (Africa) Ltd* v *Jackson* [1990] Ch 265, [1991] Ch 547) which is examined in Chapter 6, Section 5. The debates surrounding 'accessory liability' have now been largely resolved by the Privy Council in *Royal Brunei Airlines Sdn Bhd* v *Tan* [1995] 2 AC 378. In contrast receipt-based liability requires more fundamental root-and-branch work, and is being considered by the Law Commission (see (1995) 111 LQR 545, at 548–9 (Harpum)).

Why was tracing discussed in *Agip (Africa) Ltd* v *Jackson* as if it was relevant to the claims for knowing receipt and knowing assistance? The answer appears to lie in the need for identification. Identification of enrichment is essential to all restitutionary claims, and tracing on one view is only part of the exercise of identification (Birks, *Introduction*, 83–5). Therefore identification is essential both for personal receipt-based liability and for a proprietary claim. It is only a question of when the exercise of identification is complete. This approach is supported by a recent discussion by the Court of Appeal in *Boscawen* v *Bajwa* [1995] 4 All ER 769 (a subrogation case). There Millett LJ said (at 776):

> Equity lawyers habitually use the expressions 'the tracing claim' and 'the tracing remedy' to describe the proprietary claim and the proprietary remedy which equity makes available to the beneficial owner who seeks to recover his property *in specie* from those into whose hands it has come. Tracing properly so-called, however, is neither a claim nor a remedy but a process. Moreover, it is not confined to the case where the plaintiff seeks a proprietary remedy; it is equally necessary where he seeks a personal remedy against the knowing recipient or knowing assistant. It is the process by which the plaintiff traces what has happened to this property, identifies the persons who have handled or received it, and justifies his claim that the money which they handled or received (and if necessary which they still retain) can properly be regarded as representing his property. He needs to do this because his claim is based on the retention by him of a beneficial interest in his property which the defendant handled or received. Unless he can prove this, he cannot (in the traditional language of equity) raise an equity against the defendant or (in the modern language of restitution) show that the defendant's unjust enrichment was at his expense.

Millett LJ continued (at 777): 'The plaintiff will generally be entitled to a personal remedy: if he seeks a proprietary remedy he must usually prove that the property to which he lays claim is still in the ownership of the defendant. If he succeeds in doing this, the court will treat the defendant as holding the property on a constructive trust for the plaintiff and will order the defendant to transfer it *in specie* to the plaintiff.' This is generally helpful, but clarity might be better served if a different name is used for the identification process for personal claims. Further, it is not clear that the identification process is essential to claims for 'knowing assistance'. What has to be proved is that the defendant dishonestly assisted a breach of trust. It is not necessary that funds actually passed through the defendant's hands.

For discussion see Birks, 'Misdirected Funds – Restitution from the Recipient' [1989] LMCLQ 296; Harpum, 'The Stranger as Constructive Trustee' (1986) 102 LQR 114, 267; Harpum updates and refines his arguments in more concise form in 'The Basis of Equitable Liability' in Birks (ed.) *The Frontiers of Liability* Volume I (Oxford: Oxford University Press, 1994) 9, 17–25; Sir Peter Millett, 'Tracing the Proceeds of Fraud' (1991) 107 LQR 71; Birks, 'Persistent Problems in Misdirected Money: A Quintet' [1991] LMCLQ 218; Fennell, 'Misdirected Funds: Problems of Uncertainty and Inconsistency' (1994) 57 MLR 38.

In re Montagu's Settlement Trusts, Dukeof Manchester v *National Westminster Bank Ltd*
[1987] Ch 264 (Ch D)

Accountability as a constructive trustee

In 1948, the 10th Duke of Manchester received a number of chattels which unknown to him were subject to a family settlement. He disposed of these during his lifetime. After his death in 1977, the 11th Duke brought an action against the trustees of the settlement alleging breach of trust by the trustees of the settlement, and alleging that the 10th Duke in disposing of the assets was accountable as a constructive trustee. *Held*: there was nothing to suggest at the time when he received the chattels that he had knowledge that they constituted trust property, therefore the 10th Duke had not received as constructive trustee.

SIR ROBERT MEGARRY V-C: . . . I shall attempt to summarise my conclusions. In doing this, I make no attempt to reconcile all the authorities and dicta, for such a task is beyond me; and in this I suspect I am not alone. Some of the difficulty seems to arise from judgments that have been given without all the relevant authorities having been put before the judges. All I need do is to find a path through the wood that will suffice for the determination of the case before me, and to assist those who have to read this judgment.

(1) The equitable doctrine of tracing and the imposition of a constructive trust by reason of the knowing receipt of trust property are governed by different rules and must be kept distinct. Tracing is primarily a means of determining the rights of property, whereas the imposition of a constructive trust creates personal obligations that go beyond mere property rights.

(2) In considering whether a constructive trust has arisen in a case of the knowing receipt of trust property, the basic question is whether the conscience of the recipient is sufficiently affected to justify the imposition of such a trust.

(3) Whether a constructive trust arises in such a case primarily depends on the knowledge of the recipient, and not on notice to him; and for clarity it is desirable to use the word 'knowledge' and avoid the word 'notice' in such cases.

(4) For this purpose, knowledge is not confined to actual knowledge, but includes at least knowledge of types (ii) and (iii) in the *Baden* case [1983] BCLC 325, 407, i.e. actual knowledge that would have been acquired but for shutting one's eyes to the obvious, or wilfully and recklessly failing to make such inquiries as a reasonable and honest man would make; for in such cases there is a want of probity which justifies imposing a constructive trust.

(5) Whether knowledge of the *Baden* types (iv) and (v) suffices for this purpose is at best doubtful; in my view, it does not, for I cannot see that the carelessness involved will normally amount to a want of probity.

(6) For these purposes, a person is not to be taken to have knowledge of a fact that he once knew but has genuinely forgotten: the test (or a test) is whether the knowledge continues to operate on that person's mind at the time in question.

(7) (a) It is at least doubtful whether there is a general doctrine of 'imputed knowledge' that corresponds to 'imputed notice'. (b) Even if there is such a doctrine, for the purposes of creating a constructive trust of the 'knowing receipt' type the doctrine will not apply so as to fix a donee or beneficiary with all the knowledge that

his solicitor has, at all events if the donee or beneficiary has not employed the solicitor to investigate his right to the bounty, and has done nothing else that can be treated as accepting that the solicitor's knowledge should be treated as his own. (c) Any such doctrine should be distinguished from the process whereby, under the name 'imputed knowledge,' a company is treated as having the knowledge that its directors and secretary have.

(8) Where an alleged constructive trust is based not on 'knowing receipt' but on 'knowing assistance,' some at least of these considerations probably apply; but I need not decide anything on that, and I do not do so.

From what I have said, it must be plain that in my judgment the Duke did not become a constructive trustee of any of the chattels. I can see nothing that affected his conscience sufficiently to impose a constructive trust on him: and even if, contrary to my opinion, all of the five *Baden* types of knowledge are in point, instead of only the first three, I do not think that he had any such knowledge. He was a layman, and he accepted and acted on what he was told by his solicitor and was acted on by the trustees and the solicitor to the trustees. . . .

Note

Birks has suggested that the insistence on a very high degree of fault here was perhaps justified by the extreme staleness of the claim (Birks, *The Future*, 35). However, this point is not expressly adverted to in the judgment.

Agip (Africa) Ltd v *Jackson*
[1990] Ch 265 (Ch D); affd [1991] Ch 547 (CA)

Action for money had and received; tracing at law and in equity; accountability as a constructive trustee

The facts and extracts relating to the claim at common law appear above in Section 1. The following extract relates to the claims based on *tracing in equity* and knowing receipt.

Chancery Division

MILLETT J: . . . THE CLAIM IN EQUITY

There is no difficulty in tracing the plaintiffs' property in equity, which can follow the money as it passed through the accounts of the correspondent banks in New York or, more realistically, follow the chose in action through its transmutation as a direct result of forged instructions from a debt owed by the Banque du Sud to the plaintiffs in Tunis into a debt owed by Lloyds Bank to Baker Oil in London.

The only restriction on the ability of equity to follow assets is the requirement that there must be some fiduciary relationship which permits the assistance of equity to be invoked. The requirement has been widely condemned and depends on authority rather than principle, but the law was settled by *In re Diplock* [1948] Ch 466. It may need to be reconsidered but not, I venture to think, at first instance. The requirement may be circumvented since it is not necessary that the fund to be traced should have been the subject of fiduciary obligations before it got into the wrong hands; it is sufficient that the payment to the defendant itself gives rise to a fiduciary relationship: *Chase Manhattan Bank N.A.* v *Israel-British Bank (London) Ltd* [1981] Ch 105. In that case, however, equity's assistance was not needed in order to trace the plaintiff's money into the hands of the defendant; it was needed in order to ascertain whether it had any of the plaintiff's money left. The case cannot, therefore, be used to circumvent the requirement that there should be an initial fiduciary relationship in order to start the tracing process in equity.

The requirement is, however, readily satisfied in most cases of commercial fraud, since the embezzlement of a company's funds almost inevitably involves a breach of fiduciary duty on the part of one of the company's employees or agents. That was so in present case. There was clearly a fiduciary relationship between Mr Zdiri and the plaintiffs. Mr Zdiri was not a director nor a signatory on the plaintiffs' bank account, but he was a senior and responsible officer. As such he was entrusted with possession of the signed payment orders to have them taken to the bank and implemented. He took advantage of his possession of them to divert the money and cause the separation between its legal ownership which passed to the payees and its beneficial ownership which remained in the plaintiffs. There is clear authority that there is a receipt of trust property when a company's funds are misapplied by a director and, in my judgment, this is equally the case when a company's funds are misapplied by any person whose fiduciary position gave him control of them or enabled him to misapply them.

The tracing remedy

The tracing claim in equity gives rise to a proprietary remedy which depends on the continued existence of the trust property in the hands of the defendant. Unless he is a bona fide purchaser for value without notice, he must restore the trust property to its rightful owner if he still has it. But even a volunteer who has received trust property cannot be made subject to a personal liability to account for it as a constructive trustee if he has parted with it without having previously acquired some knowledge of the existence of the trust: *In re Montagu's Settlement Trusts* [1987] Ch 264.

The plaintiffs are entitled to the money in court which rightfully belongs to them. To recover the money which the defendants have paid away the plaintiffs must subject them to a personal liability to account as constructive trustees and prove the requisite degree of knowledge to establish the liability.

Knowing receipt

In *Baden, Delvaux and Lecuit* v *Société Général pour Favoriser le Développement du Commerce et de l'Industrie en France S.A.* [1983] BCLC 325, 403, Peter Gibson J said:

> It is clear that a stranger to a trust may make himself accountable to the beneficiaries under the trust in certain circumstances. The two main categories of circumstances have been given the convenient labels in *Snell's Principles of Equity* (28th ed.) pp. 194, 195, 'knowing receipt or dealing' and 'knowing assistance'. The first category of 'knowing receipt or dealing' is described in Snell, op cit. at p. 194 as follows: 'A person receiving property which is subject to a trust . . . becomes a constructive trustee if he falls within either of two heads, namely: (i) that he received trust property with actual or constructive notice that it was trust property and that the transfer to him was a breach of trust; or (ii) that although he received it without notice of the trust, he was not a bona fide purchaser for value without notice of the trust, and yet, after he had subsequently acquired notice of the trust, he dealt with the property in a manner inconsistent with the trust.' I admit to doubt as to whether the bounds of this category might not be drawn too narrowly in *Snell*. For example, why should a person who, having received trust property knowing it to be such but without notice of a breach of trust because there was none, subsequently deals with the property in a manner inconsistent with the trust not be a constructive trustee within the 'knowing receipt or dealing' category?

I respectfully agree. In my judgment, much confusion has been caused by treating this as a single category and by failing to differentiate between a number of different situations. Without attempting an exhaustive classification, it is necessary to distinguish between two main classes of case under this heading.

The first is concerned with the person who receives for his own benefit trust property transferred to him in breach of trust. He is liable as a constructive trustee if he received it with notice, actual or constructive, that it was trust property and that the transfer to him was a breach of trust; or if he received it without such notice but subsequently discovered the facts. In either case he is liable to account for the property, in the first case as from the time he received the property, and in the second as from the time he acquired notice.

The second and, in my judgment, distinct class of case is that of the person, usually an agent of the trustees, who receives the trust property lawfully and not for his own benefit but who then either misappropriates it or otherwise deals with it in a manner which is inconsistent with the trust. He is liable to account as a constructive trustee if he received the property knowing it to be such, though he will not necessarily be required in all circumstances to have known the exact terms of the trust. This class of case need not be considered further since the transfer to Baker Oil was not lawful.

In either class of case it is immaterial whether the breach of trust was fraudulent or not. The essential feature of the first class is that the recipient must have received the property for his own use and benefit. This is why neither the paying nor the collecting bank can normally be brought within it. In paying or collecting money for a customer the bank acts only as his agent. It is otherwise, however, if the collecting bank uses the money to reduce or discharge the customer's overdraft. In doing so it receives the money for its own benefit.

This is not a technical or fanciful requirement. It is essential if receipt-based liability is to be properly confined to those cases where the receipt is relevant to the loss. This can be demonstrated by considering the position of Mr Bowers in the present case. He was a partner in Jackson & Co. but he played no active part in the movement of the funds. He did not deal with money or give instructions in regard to it. He did not take it for his own benefit. He neither misapplied nor misappropriated it. It would not be just to hold him directly liable merely because Mr Jackson and Mr Griffin, who controlled the movement of the money from the moment it reached Baker Oil, chose on this occasion to pass it through his firm's bank account instead of through Euro-Arabian's account as previously.

Mr Griffin did not receive the money at all, and Mr Jackson and Mr Bowers did not receive or apply it for their own use and benefit. In my judgment, none of them can be made liable to account as a constructive trustee on the basis of knowing receipt. . . .

Notes

1. There was no cross-appeal from Millett J's judgment on knowing receipt.

2. Agip were ultimately successful in their claim based on 'knowing assistance'. See Chapter 6, Section 5.

Polly Peck International plc v *Nadir (No. 2)*
[1992] 4 All ER 769 (CA)

Tracing in equity; accountability as a constructive trustee

Asil Nadir was chief executive of Polly Peck International (PPI) which was placed in administration in 1990, owing over £550 million to its creditors.

The administrators brought an action against Nadir (the first defendant) alleging that he had misapplied £371 million of PPI's funds. It was also claimed that IBK (the fifth defendant), a bank controlled by Nadir and based in Northern Cyprus, had misapplied some £142 million of PPI's assets. In addition a claim was brought against the Central Bank of Northern Cyprus (the fourth defendant) alleging that between 1987 and 1990, £142 million of PPI's assets were moved to IBK's account at Midland Bank International, out of which some £44 million were transferred to the account of the Central Bank at the same branch, in return for Turkish lire, or on nine occasions sterling credits at IBK's account with the Central Bank of Northern Cyprus. The administrators at this stage sought an asset-freezing (*Mareva*) injunction against the Central Bank's account in London up to a sum of £45 million. *Held*: the claim against the bank was speculative so an injunction was not appropriate. The extracts relate only to the administrator's claims that the Central Bank was *accountable as a constructive trustee* or was liable to a *tracing* order and the relationship between the two types of claim.

SCOTT LJ: . . . PPI's main case is the constructive trust case that has been pleaded. In the ninth and tenth affidavits of Mr Morris, sworn respectively on 4 March and 7 March, a supplementary tracing case is put forward. It is said that, if equitable tracing rules are applied to the £44m-odd transferred from the IBK account to the Central Bank account with Midland Bank, a sum of £8·9m or thereabouts still stands to the credit of the Central Bank. It is, of course, common ground that the Central Bank did not receive any part of the £44m as volunteer. It received the money (bar the funds comprised in the nine sterling transfers) for the purpose of foreign exchange transactions. It was crediting IBK with Turkish lire in Northern Cyprus in exchange for sterling in London. Receipt of trust money by a bona fide purchaser for value without notice of the breach of trust bars any equitable tracing remedy. Mr Potts QC, counsel for PPI, accepts that that is so. It follows that actual or constructive knowledge on the part of the Central Bank of the trust character of the funds received from IBK and of the impropriety of the transfers is as much a requirement of the tracing claim as of the constructive trust claim. There is, however, an important difference. Equitable tracing leads to a claim of a proprietary character. A fund is identified that, in equity, is regarded as a fund belonging to the claimant. The constructive trust claim, in this action at least, is not a claim to any fund in specie. It is a claim to monetary compensation. The only relevant interlocutory protection that can be sought in aid of a money claim is a Mareva injunction, restraining the defendant from dissipating or secreting away his assets in order to make himself judgment proof. But if identifiable assets are being claimed, the interlocutory relief sought will not be a Mareva injunction but relief for the purpose of preserving intact the assets in question until their true ownership can be determined. Quite different considerations arise from those which apply to Mareva injunctions.

It is accepted for present purposes that (i) the transfers of the £44m from PPI to IBK's Midland Bank account and from there to the Central Bank's Midland Bank account and the corresponding Turkish lire and sterling credits made to IBK's Central Bank account in Northern Cyprus were transactions procured by Mr Nadir, (ii) the transactions were not effected for the proper purposes of PPI and represented breaches of the fiduciary duty owed by Mr Nadir to PPI and (iii) the breaches of fiduciary duty were dishonest ones.

The critical question is whether the Central Bank knew or must be treated as having known that the funds being transferred were PPI funds and were being misapplied.

In the statement of claim actual knowledge on the part of the Central Bank is alleged. Alternatively constructive knowledge is relied on. The mental states that will suffice to fix a defendant with liability as a constructive trustee are not always easy to identify. A number of learned judgments have illuminated the problem (see e.g. *Agip (Africa) Ltd* v *Jackson* [1992] 4 All ER 385, [1990] Ch 265; *affd* [1992] 4 All ER 451, [1991] Ch 547, *Baden* v *Société Générale pour Favoriser le Développement du Commerce et de l'Industrie en France SA* (1982) [1992] 4 All ER 161, *Eagle Trust plc* v *SBC Securities Ltd* [1992] 4 All ER 488 and *Cowan de Groot Properties Ltd* v *Eagle Trust plc* [1992] 4 All ER 700. There is a general consensus of opinion that, if liability as constructive trustee is sought to be imposed, not on the basis that the defendant has received and dealt in some way with trust property (knowing receipt) but on the basis that the defendant has assisted in the misapplication of trust property (knowing assistance), 'something amounting to dishonesty or want of probity on the part of the defendant must be shown' (see *per* Vinelott J in *Eagle Trust plc* v *SBC Securities Ltd* [1992] 4 All ER 488 at 499). Vinelott J described as 'settled law' the proposition that 'a stranger cannot be made liable for knowing assistance in a fraudulent breach of trust unless knowledge of the fraudulent design can be imputed to him . . .' (at 499). I respectfully agree.

Millett J, in the judgment below, treated the present case as one of 'knowing assistance' rather than 'knowing receipt'. In respect of the nine sterling transfers I think that is right. The Central Bank received the funds transferred not in its own right but as banker, and, as banker, credited the funds to IBK in Northern Cyprus. But in respect of the bulk of the transfers the case is, in my opinion, one of 'receipt' rather than 'assistance'. The Central Bank was exchanging Turkish lire for sterling and became entitled to the sterling not as banker for IBK but in its own right. IBK became entitled to the Turkish lire.

Liability as constructive trustee in a 'knowing receipt' case does not require that the misapplication of the trust funds should be fraudulent. It does require that the defendant should have knowledge that the funds were trust funds and that they were being misapplied. Actual knowledge obviously will suffice. Mr Potts has submitted that it will suffice if the defendant can be shown to have had knowledge of facts which would have put an honest and reasonable man on inquiry, or, at least, if the defendant can be shown to have wilfully and recklessly failed to make such inquiries as an honest and reasonable man would have made (see [categories]) (iii) and (v) of the categories of mental state identified by Peter Gibson J in *Baden*'s case [1992] 4 All ER 161 at 235). I do not think there is any doubt that, if the latter of the two criteria can be established against the Central Bank, that will suffice. I have some doubts about the sufficiency of the former criterion but do not think that the present appeal is the right occasion for settling the issue. The various categories of mental state identified in *Baden*'s case are not rigid categories with clear and precise boundaries. One category may merge imperceptibly into another.

If this case goes to trial, the trial judge, after considering all the evidence, will have to decide whether the Central Bank's knowledge of primary facts was or was not sufficient to subject it to liability as a constructive trustee. He may or may not have to decide whether by the standards of the 'honest and reasonable banker', the Central Bank should have made inquiries about the purpose and propriety of the transfers being received from IBK and whether the failure to make those inquiries fixes the Central Bank with liability. For the purposes of the present appeal I am content to examine the facts placed before the court by the parties and ask myself whether a fair arguable case has been shown that the Central Bank must have realised that the funds were PPI's funds and must have been suspicious that the funds were being misapplied.

[Scott LJ reviewed the current state of evidence and concluded that it could not be shown at present that the Central Bank had the requisite knowledge to put it on inquiry, and was not therefore accountable as a constructive trustee. He continued: . . .]

I now turn to the tracing claim. This, as I have said, is a claim by PPI to be entitled in specie to the £8.9m that is still held by the Central Bank out of the funds received from IBK. The £8.9m, like the rest of the £44m was received in exchange for currency made available to IBK in Northern Cyprus. So the Central Bank holds as purchaser. But is it a bona fide purchaser without notice? Mr Potts submitted that, in order to defeat PPI's claim, the Central Bank must discharge the onus of proving that it received the funds without notice of PPI's equitable interest. I disagree. The Central Bank is the legal owner of the money. It is for PPI to raise a case that places the mantle of constructive trustees on the Central Bank's shoulders. Nothing, however, for present interlocutory purposes turns on onus.

The question, for the purposes of the tracing remedy, is whether the Central Bank had notice or constructive notice of PPI's equitable interest. 'Notice' and 'constructive notice', as Megarry V-C pointed out in *Re Montagu's Settlement Trusts, Duke of Manchester* v *National Westminster Bank Ltd* (1985) [1992] 4 All ER 308 at 322–3, [1987] Ch 264 at 277, are not synonyms for 'knowledge' and 'constructive knowledge'. Vinelott J in *Eagle Trust plc* v *SBC Securities Ltd* [1992] 4 All ER 488 at 497–8 commented that—

> 'notice' is often used in a sense or in contexts where the facts do not support the inference of knowledge. A man may have actual notice of a fact and yet not know it. He may have been supplied . . . with a document and so have actual notice of its content, but he may not in fact have read it; or he may have read it some time ago and have forgotten its content.

The present case, however, does not concern land, or some valuable chattel, the title to which can be traced, but concerns money paid to the Central Bank on a foreign currency exchange transaction. In my judgment, for the purpose of the proprietary tracing claim, as for the in personam constructive trust claim, PPI must prove knowledge on the part of the Central Bank, actual or constructive as the case may be. I think this is the type of case to which Lindley LJ's remarks in *Manchester Trust* v *Furness* [1985] 2 QB 539 at 545, cited also by Vinelott J in *Eagle Trust plc* v *SBC Securities Ltd* [1992] 4 All ER 488 at 507, are applicable. Lindley LJ said:

> . . . as regards the extension of the equitable doctrines of constructive notice to commercial transactions, the Courts have always set their faces resolutely against it. The equitable doctrines of constructive notice are common enough in dealing with land and estates, with which the Court is familiar; but there have been repeated protests against the introduction into commercial transactions of anything like an extension of those doctrines, and the protest is founded on perfect sense. In dealing with estates in land title is everything, and it can be leisurely investigated; in commercial transactions possession is everything, and there is not time to investigate title; and if we were to extend the doctrine of constructive notice to commercial transactions we should be doing infinite mischief and paralyzing the trade of the country.

In the *Eagle Trust* case (at 507) Vinelott J, after citing the above passage, went on to observe:

> The courts have been particularly reluctant to extend the doctrine of constructive notice to cases where moneys are paid in the ordinary course of business . . .

I respectfully agree with these comments. In the present case the degree of knowledge on the part of the Central Bank that PPI must establish for the purposes of its constructive trust case is, in my judgment, requisite also for the purposes of its equitable tracing claim. It follows that the conclusions I have expressed on the constructive trust claim apply also to the tracing claim. . . .

Notes

1. Compare Knox J in *Cowan de Groot Properties Ltd* v *Eagle Trust plc* [1992] 4 All ER 700, who, having rejected a claim of knowing receipt, went on to consider a tracing claim and concluded (at 767): '. . . there can in my view be no independent right to trace against a purchaser for value under a contract of sale where the contract is not liable to be set aside and there is no valid claim to impose a constructive trust. I accept Mr Potts's submission for Cowan de Groot that tracing is not an independent cause of action.' (Curiously Mr Potts QC was also counsel for PPI in *Polly Peck International* v *Nadir (No. 2)*.)

2. Birks, 'Persistent Problems in Misdirected Money: A Quintet' [1993] LMCLQ 218 discusses issues arising from five recent cases including *Polly Peck International* v *Nadir (No. 2)* and *Cowan de Groot Properties Ltd* v *Eagle Trust plc*, together with *Barlow Clowes International Ltd* v *Vaughan* [1992] 4 All ER which is discussed below. Birks also discusses *Eagle Trust plc* v *SBC Securities Ltd* [1992] 4 All ER 363, [1993] 1 WLR 484 (and see now *Eagle Trust plc* v *SBC Securities Ltd* [1995] BCC 231) and the important judgment of Millett J in *El Ajou* v *Dollar Land Holdings plc* [1993] 3 All ER 717 (subsequently reversed by the Court of Appeal on a point of company law [1994] 2 All ER 685; and see now the judgment of Robert Walker J in *El Ajou* v *Dollar Land Holdings plc (No. 2)* [1995] 2 All ER 213).

B: The tracing rules

There are two essential preconditions:

(a) *A fiduciary relationship.* This is laid down by *Sinclair* v *Brougham* [1914] AC 398 as interpreted by the Court of Appeal in *In re Diplock* [1948] Ch 465, and is therefore binding on all courts below the House of Lords. (It was recently reaffirmed in *Agip (Africa) Ltd* v *Jackson* [1991] Ch 547 by the Court of Appeal.) However, this requirement appears to be easily circumvented in practice by judicial ingenuity in discovering such a relationship. For example, in *Chase Manhattan Bank NA* v *Israel-British Bank (London) Ltd* [1981] Ch 105 it was held that the receipt of money paid under a mistake of fact was sufficient to constitute the relationship. See also *Westdeusche Landesbank Girozentrate* v *Islington London Borough Council* [1994] 4 All ER 890, [1994] 1 WLR 138. The better question seems to be whether it is appropriate to award the plaintiff a restitutionary proprietary remedy, and accordingly *Chase Manhattan* (where the tracing exercise had not at the time of the judgment even been attempted) is discussed below in Section 3. Academic opinion is generally against the fiduciary restriction, and the rule may not survive examination by the House of Lords.

(b) *A proprietary base.* According to Birks: 'if he [the plaintiff] wishes to assert a right *in rem* in the surviving enrichment, the plaintiff must show that at the beginning of the story he had a proprietary right in the subject-matter, and that nothing other than substitutions or intermixtures happened to deprive him of that right *in rem*' (Birks, *Introduction*, 379). Tracing in equity therefore belongs within subtractive unjust enrichment and depends upon a continuing equitable property right in the subject-matter which is followed.

Much of the discussion concerns mixtures and substitutions. 'Equity's rules and presumptions were created in the context of litigation between beneficiaries of a trust and a bankrupt trustee who, having mixed his own money and trust money in a bank account, had dissipated part of the fund. The sums involved were small and the activity of the bank account modest.' (Goff and Jones, 75) It is therefore questionable how appropriate these Victorian rules are for dealing with sophisticated money laundering and the fall-out of corporate collapse in the late twentieth century.

The main rules are:

(a) Where there is a mixed fund consisting of the money of the plaintiff and other innocent parties, the fund belongs to the parties in shares proportionate to their contributions. Any diminution of the fund is borne *pari passu*, that is the interest declines proportionately, e.g., a fund of £1,000 consisting of two £500 contributions from P and X, which is reduced to £800, yields two shares of £400.

(b) Where the mixed fund consisting of money of the plaintiff and other innocent parties is held in an active current banking account the rule of 'first in, first out' applies, e.g., if there is a mixed fund consisting of £500 belonging to P paid in on Monday and £500 of X paid in on Tuesday, a withdrawal of £500 on Wednesday is ascribed to P's interest in the fund. P has no claim on the £500 left in the fund.

(c) Where the mixed fund consists of contributions from the plaintiff and the defendant fiduciary, the fiduciary is presumed to act honestly and any withdrawals from the fund diminish his interest in the first place: he is presumed to be spending his own money first, e.g., if there is a mixed fund of £1,000 consisting of £500 belonging to P and £500 to D, a withdrawal of £500 is ascribed to D's interest. P is entitled to the whole of the £500 remaining.

(d) If a mixed fund consisting of the plaintiff's contribution and other contributions of innocent parties is dissipated, but subsequently 'topped up' by contributions not derived from the fund, the plaintiff's interest is confined to his share of the lowest intermediate balance, e.g., if P had a £500 contribution in a fund of £1,000 which was reduced to £20, but was subsequently restored to £800 by funds not deriving from P, P's interest is £10 *not* £400. The rule applies, with modifications, to mixed funds of the plaintiff and defendant fiduciary.

(e) Equity can trace money through substitutions into other assets, such as money which is invested in land, goods or shares.
(f) Tracing is defeated by a bona fide purchase.

These are only prima facie rules and are modified or qualified in practice as the following authorities show.

See Burrows, *Restitution*, 69–76; Birks, *Introduction*, 363–70 and Goff and Jones, 83–93. See also Hayton, 'Equity's Identification Rules' in Birks, *Laundering and Tracing*, 1–21; Moriarty, 'Tracing, Mixing and Laundering' in Birks, *Laundering and Tracing*, 73–94 and Norman, 'Tracing the Proceeds of Crime: an Inequitable Solution?' in Birks, *Laundering and Tracing*, 95–113.

Clayton's case, Devaynes v *Noble*
(1817) 1 Mer 572; 35 ER 781 (Ch)

The facts are not relevant

SIR WILLIAM GRANT MR: . . . The cases then set up two conflicting rules:—the presumed intention of the debtor, which, in some instances at least, is to govern,—and the *ex post facto* election of the creditor, which, in other instances, is to prevail. I should, therefore, feel myself a good deal embarrassed, if the general question, of the creditor's right to make the application of indefinite payments, were now necessarily to be determined. But I think the present case is distinguishable from any of those in which that point has been decided in the creditor's favour. They were all cases of distinct insulated debts, between which a plain line of separation could be drawn. But this is the case of a banking account, where all the sums paid in form one blended fund, the parts of which have no longer any distinct existence. Neither banker nor customer ever thinks of saying, this draft is to be placed to the account of the £500 paid in on *Monday*, and this other to the account of the £500 paid in on *Tuesday*. There is a fund of £1,000 to draw upon, and that is enough. In such a case, there is no room for any other appropriation than that which arises from the order in which the receipts and payments take place, and are carried into the account. Presumably, it is the sum first paid in, that is first drawn out. It is the first item on the debit side of the account, that is discharged, or reduced, by the first item on the credit side. The appropriation is made by the very act of setting the two items against each other. Upon that principle, all accounts current are settled, and particularly cash accounts. When there has been a continuation of dealings, in what way can it be ascertained whether the specific balance due on a given day has, or has not, been discharged, but by examining whether payments to the amount of that balance appear by the account to have been made? You are not to take the account backwards, and strike the balance at the head, instead of the foot, of it. A man's banker breaks, owing him, on the whole account, a balance of £1,000. It would surprise one to hear the customer say, 'I have been fortunate enough to draw out all that I paid in during the last four years; but there is £1,000, which I paid in five years ago, that I hold myself never to have drawn out; and, therefore, if I can find any body who was answerable for the debts of the banking-house, such as they stood five years ago, I have a right to say that it is that specific sum which is still due to me, and not the £1,000 that I paid in last week.' . . .

Note

Like many so-called 'rules' in English law, the 'first in, first out' rule in *Clayton's case* is often more honoured in the breach than in the observance.

For its current status see *Barlow Clowes International Ltd* v *Vaughan* [1992] 4 All ER 22 (CA), below.

In re Hallett's Estate, Knatchbull v *Hallett*
(1880) 13 Ch D 696 (CA)

Tracing in equity

Mrs Cotterill entrusted Russian bonds to Mr Hallett, her solicitor. Hallett regularly paid her any dividends received. Subsequently Hallett, without Mrs Cotterill's authority, sold the bonds and paid the £2,994 realised into his own general bank account where it was mixed with his own money. Later Mr Hallett died, leaving some £3,000 in the account. The first question in the case was whether Mrs Cotterill could follow her property into that account. The Court of Appeal unanimously held that she could.

JESSEL MR: . . . The modern doctrine of Equity as regards property disposed of by persons in a fiduciary position is a very clear and well-established doctrine. You can, if the sale was rightful, take the proceeds of the sale, if you can identify them. If the sale was wrongful, you can still take the proceeds of the sale, in a sense adopting the sale for the purpose of taking the proceeds, if you can identify them. There is no distinction, therefore, between a rightful and a wrongful disposition of the property, so far as regards the right of the beneficial owner to follow the proceeds. But it very often happens that you cannot identify the proceeds. The proceeds may have been invested together with money belonging to the person in a fiduciary position, in a purchase. He may have bought land with it, for instance, or he may have bought chattels with it. Now, what is the position of the beneficial owner as regards such purchases? I will, first of all, take his position when the purchase is clearly made with what I will call, for shortness, the trust money, although it is not confined, as I will shew presently, to express trusts. In that case, according to the now well-established doctrine of Equity, the beneficial owner has a right to elect either to take the property purchased, or to hold it as a security for the amount of the trust money laid out in the purchase; or, as we generally express it, he is entitled at his election either to take the property, or to have a charge on the property for the amount of the trust money. But in the second case, where a trustee has mixed the money with his own, there is this distinction, that the *cestui que trust*, or beneficial owner, can no longer elect to take the property, because it is no longer bought with the trust-money simply and purely, but with a mixed fund. He is, however, still entitled to a charge on the property purchased, for the amount of the trust-money laid out in the purchase; and that charge is quite independent of the fact of the amount laid out by the trustee. The moment you get a substantial portion of it furnished by the trustee, using the word 'trustee' in the sense I have mentioned, as including all persons in a fiduciary relation, the right to the charge follows. That is the modern doctrine of Equity. Has it ever been suggested, until very recently, that there is any distinction between an express trustee, or an agent, or a bailee, or a collector of rents, or anybody else in a fiduciary position? I have never heard, until quite recently, such a distinction suggested. It cannot, as far as I am aware (and since this Court sat last to hear this case, I have taken the trouble to look for authority), be found in any reported case even suggested, except in the recent decision of Mr Justice Fry, to which I shall draw attention presently. It can have no foundation in principle, because the beneficial ownership is the same, wherever the legal ownership may be. If you have goods bargained and sold to a man upon trust to sell and hand over the net proceeds to another, that other is the beneficial owner; but if instead of being bargained and sold, so as to vest the legal ownership in the trustee, they are deposited with him to sell as agent, so that the legal ownership remains in the beneficial owner, can it be supposed, in a Court of Equity, that the rights of the beneficial owner are different, he being entire beneficial owner in both cases? I say on principle it is impossible to imagine there can be any difference. In practice we know there is no difference, because the moment you get into a Court of Equity, where a principal can sue an agent as well as a *cestui que trust* can sue a trustee, no such distinction was ever suggested, as far as I am aware. Therefore, the moment you establish the fiduciary relation, the modern rules of Equity, as regards following trust money, apply. I intentionally say modern rules, because it must not be forgotten that the rules of Courts of Equity are not, like the rules of the Common Law, supposed to have been established from time immemorial. It is perfectly well known that they have been established from time to time—altered, improved, and refined from time to time. In many cases we know the names of the Chancellors who invented them. No doubt they were invented for the purpose of securing the better administration of justice, but still they were invented. Take such things as these: the separate use of a married woman, the restraint on alienation, the modern rule against perpetuities, and the rules of equitable waste. We can name the Chancellors who first invented them, and state the date when they were first introduced into Equity jurisprudence; and, therefore, in cases of this kind, the older precedents in Equity are of very little value. The doctrines are progressive, refined, and improved; and if we want to know what the rules of Equity are, we must look, of course, rather to the more modern than the more ancient cases.

Now that being the established doctrine of Equity on this point, I will take the case of the pure bailee. If the bailee sells the goods bailed, the bailor can in Equity follow the proceeds, and can follow the proceeds wherever they can be distinguished, either being actually kept separate, or being mixed up with other moneys. I have only to advert to one other point, and that is this—supposing, instead of being invested in the purchase of land or goods, the moneys were simply mixed with other moneys of the trustee, using the term again in its full sense as including every person in a fiduciary relation, does it make any difference according to the modern doctrine of Equity? I say none. It would be very remarkable if it were to do so. Supposing the trust money was 1000 sovereigns, and the trustee put them into a bag, and by mistake, or accident, or otherwise, dropped a sovereign of his own into the bag. Could anybody suppose that a Judge in Equity would find any difficulty in saying that the *cestui que trust* has a right to take 1000 sovereigns out of that bag? I do not like to call it a charge of 1000 sovereigns on the 1001 sovereigns, but that is the effect of it. I have no doubt of it. It would make no difference if, instead of one sovereign, it was another 1000 sovereigns; but if instead of putting it into his bag, or after putting it into his bag, he carries the bag to his bankers, what then? According to law, the bankers are his debtors for the total amount; but if you lend the trust money to a third person, you can follow it. If in the case supposed the trustee had lent the £1000 to a man without security, you could follow the debt, and take it from the debtor. If he lent it on a promissory note, you could take the promissory note; or the bond, if it were a bond. If, instead of lending the whole amount in one sum simply, he had added a sovereign, or had added £500 of his own to the £1000, the only difference is this, that instead of taking the bond or the promissory note, the *cestui que trust* would have a charge for the amount of the trust money on the bond or promissory note. So it would be on the simple contract debt; that is, if the debt were of such a nature as that, between the creditor and the debtor, you could not sever the debt into two, so as to shew what part was trust money, then the *cestui que trust* would have a right to a charge upon the whole. Therefore, there is no difficulty in following out the rules of Equity and deciding that in a case of a mere bailee, as Mr Justice Fry has decided, you can follow the money.

[Jessel MR then reviewed the authorities and refused to follow the decision of Fry J in *Ex parte Dale & Co.* (1879) 11 Ch D 772, which had sought to distinguish different categories of fiduciaries for the purpose of tracing.]

A second question arose on appeal. Mr Hallett was trustee of some bonds and without authority sold them, and paid the proceeds into his bank account, where they mixed with his own money. He drew money upon the account which he used for his own purposes. At his death the balance was greater than the trust moneys paid in. However if payments out of the account were taken into account, applying a 'first in, first out' rule the trust moneys would be greatly diminished. *Held*: by a majority of the Court of Appeal (Thesiger LJ dissenting), the rule in *Clayton's case* did not apply.

JESSEL MR . . . I will first of all consider the case on principle, and then I will consider how far we are bound by authority to come to a decision opposed to principle. It may well be, and sometimes does so happen, that we are bound to come to a decision opposed to principle. Now, first upon principle, nothing can be better settled, either in our own law, or, I suppose, the law of all civilised countries, than this, that where a man does an act which may be rightfully performed, he cannot say that that act was intentionally and in fact done wrongly. A man who has a right of entry cannot say he committed a trespass in entering. A man who sells the goods of another as agent for the owner cannot prevent the owner adopting the sale, and deny that he acted as agent for the owner. It runs throughout our law, and we are familiar with numerous instances in the law of real property. A man who grants a lease believing he has sufficient estate to grant it, although it turns out that he has not, but has a power which enables him to grant it, is not allowed to say he did not grant it under the power. Wherever it can be done rightfully, he is not allowed to say, against the person entitled to the property or the right, that he has done it wrongfully. That is the universal law.

When we come to apply that principle to the case of a trustee who has blended trust moneys with his own, it seems to me perfectly plain that he cannot be heard to say that he took away the trust money when he had a right to take away his own money. The simplest case put is the mingling of trust moneys in a bag with money of the trustee's own. Suppose he has a hundred sovereigns in a bag, and he adds to them another hundred sovereigns of his own, so that they are commingled in such a way that they cannot be distinguished, and the next day he draws out for his own purposes £100, is it tolerable for anybody to allege that what he drew out was the first £100, the trust money, and that he misappropriated it, and left his own £100 in the bag? It is obvious he must have taken away that which he had a right to take away, his own £100. What difference does it make if, instead of being in a bag, he deposits it with his banker, and then pays in other money of his own, and draws out some money for his own purposes? Could he say that he had actually drawn out anything but his own money? His money was there, and he had a right to draw it out, and why should the natural act of simply drawing out the money be attributed to anything except to his ownership of money which was at his bankers.

It is said, no doubt, that according to the modern theory of banking, the deposit banker is a debtor for the money. So he is, and not a trustee in the strict sense of the word. At the same time one must recollect that the position of a deposit banker is different from that of an ordinary debtor. Still he is for some purposes a debtor, and it is said if a debt of this kind is paid by a banker, although the total balance is the amount owing by the banker, yet considering the repayments and the sums paid in by the depositor, you attribute the first sum drawn out to the first sum paid in. That was a rule first established by Sir William Grant in *Clayton's Case* 1 Mer 572; a very convenient rule, and I have nothing to say against it unless there is evidence either of agreement to the contrary or of circumstances from which a contrary intention must be presumed, and then of course that which is a mere presumption of law gives way to those other considerations. Therefore, it does appear to me there is nothing in the world laid down by Sir William Grant in *Clayton's Case*, or in the numerous cases which follow it, which in the slightest degree affects the principle, which I consider to be clearly established.

Then I come to the great difficulty in the case, the difficulty which, as I shall shew from an extract or two from Mr Justice Fry's judgment, weighed with him. What he says is this: 'If the matter were unfettered by authority, it would appear to me clear that where a man has a balance to his credit consisting in part of funds which are his own, and which he may legally draw out and apply for his own purposes, and in part of trust funds which he cannot lawfully draw out and apply for his own purposes, his drawings for his own purposes ought to be attributed to his own funds and not to the trust funds. But it appears to me that I am not at liberty, in the existing state of the authorities, to act according to the inclination of my own mind;' and then he refers to *Pennell* v *Deffell* 4 DM & G 372, and one or two cases that have followed it. In a second judgment in the same case, Mr Justice Fry says this: 'I have already expressed the opinion I should have been inclined to act on if I had been at liberty, but I am not at liberty.' So it is plain that, as far as Mr Justice Fry was concerned, he would have decided otherwise if he had not been fettered by authority.

Now, the only authority worth considering for this purpose is the case of *Pennell* v *Deffell* itself. I will, in a moment, say a word about the subsequent decisions. First of all *Pennell* v *Deffell*, one must remember, is the decision of a Court of coordinate jurisdiction with this Court, namely, the Court of Appeal in Chancery, and was decided several years ago. But, on the other hand, we must remember that the law ascertained or laid down in the decision or judgment which guides a future Judge or another Judge in applying it, is simply the expression of principle which is to be ascertained from the judgment. No doubt a part of the decision in *Pennell* v *Deffell* was exactly this case, and the Court applied the law, as correctly stated by Mr Justice Fry, by applying *Clayton's Case* even to such a case as this, and to that extent destroyed the claim of the *cestui que trust*. But that was not the whole case of *Pennell* v *Deffell*. The main part of *Pennell* v *Deffell* was giving effect to the right of *cestuis que trust* in the case of blended trust moneys, and upon the very principle which I have endeavoured to explain, and which, if I may say so, was so clearly explained by Mr Justice Fry in his judgment. If, therefore, we are to ascertain the principle on which *Pennell* v *Deffell* is decided, we must look at the whole of the judgment, and not at one part of it only. That being so, I have come to this conclusion, that the principle is rightly laid down, and it is rightly applied throughout the judgment except as to this portion, and that as to this portion of the case there has been a mistake, not in the principle, but in the application of the principle. Therefore, if I am to be guided by the principle as laid down, I think the principle must prevail without regard to a mere slip in its application.

But it will be said that this part of *Pennell* v *Deffell* has been followed in subsequent cases. So it has. As regards subsequent cases in the inferior Courts we need not trouble ourselves with them. Judges of first instance would not have overruled the mistaken application of principle. As regards the Court of Appeal, it seems to have been followed certainly in one, if not in two cases, without question; but although there are cases in our law where erroneous decisions, not reconcilable even with the judgment on which the decision proceeded, have created a rule of conduct, and as to which, after the lapse of years, Judges have not felt themselves at liberty to review the decision even by the light of the judgment on which the first decision was pronounced, yet no such considerations apply to this case. No human being ever gave credit to a man on the theory that he would misappropriate trust money, and thereby increase his assets. No human being ever gave credit, even beyond that theory, that he should not only misappropriate trust moneys to increase his assets, but that he should pay the trust moneys so misappropriated to his own banking account with his own moneys, and draw out after that a larger sum than the first sums paid in for the trust moneys. It never could have been made a rule of conduct, or have affected the transactions of mankind, and therefore it does not come within the line of cases which, having established a rule of conduct, no Judge could interfere with. It appears to me we should not be deferring to authority but making a misuse of authority, which is to declare the law, if by reason of this, which appears to me a mere slip in the case of *Pennell* v *Deffell*, and which, it must be recollected, was a very small portion of the contest in that case, we were to consider ourselves bound to decide against what is the settled principle. Therefore, in my opinion, the appeal must be allowed.

Notes

1. At first instance Fry J held that as between beneficiaries the rule in *Clayton's case* applied. This was not dissented from on appeal.

2. *Hallett* was controversially relied on in the context of 'retention of title' clauses in order to trace resale proceeds in the hands of an insolvent buyer of goods in *Aluminium Industrie Vaassen BV* v *Romalpa Aluminium Ltd* [1976] 1 WLR 676 (CA). It was admitted in that case that seller and buyer stood in a relationship of bailor and bailee (a species of fiduciary relationship). Such a tracing exercise has not been allowed in subsequent cases. Compare *In re Bond Worth Ltd* [1980] Ch 228. For discussion see McCormack, *Reservation of Title*, 2nd ed. (London: Sweet & Maxwell, 1995), 73–91.

In re Oatway, Hertslet* v *Oatway
[1903] 2 Ch 356 (Ch D)

Tracing in equity; equitable lien

Oatway was a co-trustee who received £3,000 in breach of trust. He paid this together with £4,000 (which he held as agent for his co-trustee, Maxwell Skipper) into his own bank account, which immediately prior to the receipt had been £78 in credit, on 15 August 1901. On 24 August, Oatway purchased shares in the Oceana company for £2,138 by a cheque drawn on his account. At that stage the balance was £6,635, including the £3,000 of trust money. Oatway subsequently dissipated the rest of the funds in the account. After his death the shares were realised for £2,475. A summons was brought to determine title to the shares.

JOYCE J: . . . There is no conflict between different fiduciary owners or sets of cestuis que trust. It is a principle settled as far back as the time of the Year Books that, whatever alteration of form any property may undergo, the true owner is entitled to seize it in its new shape if he can prove the identity of the original material: see Blackstone, vol. ii, p. 405, and *Lupton* v *White* (1808) 15 Ves 432; 10 RR 94. But this rule is carried no farther than necessity requires, and is applied only to cases where the compound is such as to render it impossible to apportion the respective shares of the parties. Thus, if the quality of the articles that are mixed be uniform, and the original quantities known, as in the case of so many pounds of trust money mixed with so many pounds of the trustee's own money, the person by whose act the confusion took place is still entitled to claim his proper quality, but subject to the quantity of the other proprietor being first made good out of the whole mass: 2 Stephen's Commentaries (13th ed.), 20. Trust money may be followed into land or any other property in which it has been invested; and when a trustee has, in making any purchase or investment, applied trust money together with his own, the cestuis que trust are entitled to a charge on the property purchased for the amount of the trust money laid out in the purchase or investment. Similarly, if money held by any person in a fiduciary capacity be paid into his own banking account, it may be followed by the equitable owner, who, as against the trustee, will have a charge for what belongs to him upon the balance to the credit of the account. If, then, the trustee pays in further sums, and from time to time draws out money by cheques, but leaves a balance to the credit of the account, it is settled that he is not entitled to have the rule in *Clayton's Case* (1816) 1 Mer 572; 15 RR 161 applied so as to maintain that the sums which have been drawn out and paid away so as to be incapable of being recovered represented pro tanto the trust money, and that the balance remaining is not trust money, but represents only his own moneys paid into the account. *Brown* v *Adams* LR 4 Ch 764 to the contrary ought not to be followed since the decision *In re Hallett's Estate* 13 Ch D 696. It is, in my opinion, equally clear that when any of the money drawn out has been invested, and the investment remains in the name or under the control of the trustee, the rest of the balance having been afterwards dissipated by him, he cannot maintain that the investment which remains represents his own money alone, and that what has been spent and can no longer be traced and recovered was the money belonging to the trust. In other words, when the private money of the trustee and that which he held in a fiduciary capacity have been mixed in the same banking account, from which various payments have from time to time been made, then, in order to determine to whom any remaining balance or any investment that may have been paid for out of the account ought to be deemed to belong, the trustee must be debited with all the sums that have been withdrawn and applied to his own use so as to be no longer recoverable, and the trust money in like manner be debited with any sums taken out and duly invested in the names of the proper trustees. The order of priority in which the various withdrawals and investments may have been respectively made is wholly immaterial. I have been referring, of course, to cases where there is only one fiduciary owner or set of cestuis que trust claiming whatever may be left as against the trustee. In the present case there is no balance left. The only investment or property remaining which represents any part of the mixed moneys paid into the banking account is the Oceana shares purchased for 2137*l.* Upon these, therefore, the trust had a charge for the 3000*l.* trust money paid into the account. That is to say, those shares and the proceeds thereof belong to the trust.

It was objected that the investment in the Oceana shares was made at a time when Oatway's own share of the balance to the credit of the account (if the whole had been then justly distributed) would have exceeded 2137*l.*, the price of the shares; that he was therefore entitled to withdraw that sum, and might rightly apply it for his own purposes; and that consequently the shares should be held to belong to his estate. To this I answer that he never was entitled to withdraw the 2137*l.* from the account, or, at all events, that he could not be entitled to take that sum from the account and hold it or the investment made therewith, freed from the charge in favour of the trust, unless or until the trust money paid into the account had been first restored, and the trust fund reinstated by due investment of the money in the joint names of the proper trustees, which never was done.

The investment by Oatway, in his own name, of the 2137*l.* in Oceana shares no more got rid of the claim or charge of the trust upon the money so invested, than would have been the case if he had drawn a cheque for 2137*l.* and simply placed and retained the amount in a drawer without further disposing of the money in any way. The proceeds of the Oceana shares must be held to belong to the trust funds under the will of which Oatway and Maxwell Skipper were the trustees.

Note

Professor Birks writes that Joyce J 'rightly understood *Hallett* to be authority, not for a presumption that the wrongdoer withdrew his own money first, but rather for a presumption that he intended honestly to preserve the other's property' (Birks, *Introduction*, 370).

Sinclair* v *Brougham
[1914] AC 398 (HL)

Action for money had and received; tracing in equity; equitable lien

The detailed facts and extracts relating to the claim at common law appear in Chapter 1, Section 1. The following extracts relate to the claim by the depositors in the *ultra vires* banking business of the Birkbeck Permanent Building Society to follow their money in equity.

LORD PARKER: . . . Accepting the principle that no action or suit lies at law or in equity to recover money lent to a company or association which has no power to borrow, the question remains whether the lender has any other remedies. On this point the result of the authorities may be stated as follows: First, it appears to be well settled that if the borrowed money be applied in paying off legitimate indebtedness of the company or association (whether the indebtedness be incurred before or after the money was borrowed), the lenders are entitled to rank as creditors of the company or association to the extent to which the money has been so applied. There appears to be some doubt as to whether this result is arrived at by treating the contract of loan as validated to the extent to which the borrowed money is so applied, on the ground that to this extent there is no increase in the indebtedness of the company or association, in which case, if the contract of loan involves a security for the money borrowed, the security would be validated to a like extent; or whether the better view is that the lenders are subrogated to the rights of the legitimate creditors who have been paid off. See the case of *Blackburn and District Benefit Building Society* v *Cuncliffe Brooks & Co.* 22 Ch D 61; 9 App Cas 857, the case of *Wenlock* v *River Dee Co.* 10 App Cas 354, and the case of *Wrexham, Mold and Connah's Quay Ry. Co.* [1898] 2 Ch 663; [1899] 1 Ch 440. It is still open to your Lordships' House to adopt either view, should the question actually come up for determination.

Secondly, it appears to be also well settled that the lender in an ultra vires loan transaction has a right to what is known as a tracing order. A company or other statutory association cannot by itself or through an agent be party to an ultra vires act.

If its directors or agents affecting to act on its behalf borrow money which it has no power to borrow, the money borrowed is in their hands the property of the lender.

At law, therefore, the lender can recover the money, so long as he can identify it, and even if it has been employed in purchasing property, there may be cases in which, by ratifying the action of those who have so employed it, he may recover the property purchased. Equity, however, treated the matter from a different standpoint. It considered that the relationship between the directors or agents and the lender was a fiduciary relationship and that the money in their hands was for all practical purposes trust money. Starting from a personal equity, based on the consideration that it would be unconscionable for any one who could not plead purchase for value without notice to retain an advantage derived from the misapplication of trust money, it ended, as was so often the case, in creating what were in effect rights of property, though not recognized as such by the common law.

The principle on which, and the extent to which, trust money can be followed in equity is discussed at length in *In re Hallett's Estate* 13 Ch D 696 by Sir George Jessel. He gives two instances. First, he supposes the case of property being purchased by means of the trust money alone. In such a case the beneficiary may either take the property itself or claim a lien on it for the amount of the money expended in the purchase. Secondly, he supposes the case of the purchase having been made partly with the trust money and partly with money of the trustee. In such a case the beneficiary can only claim a charge on the property for the amount of the trust money expended in the purchase. The trustee is precluded by his own misconduct from asserting any interest in the property until such amount has been refunded. By the actual decision in the case, this principle was held applicable when the trust money had been paid into the trustee's banking account. I will add two further illustrations which have some bearing on the present case. Suppose the property is acquired by means of money, part of which belongs to one owner and part to another, the purchaser being in a fiduciary relationship to both. Clearly each owner has an equal equity. Each is entitled to a charge on the property for his own money, and neither can claim priority over the other. It follows that their charges must rank pari passu according to their respective amounts. Further, I think that as against the fiduciary agent they could by agreement claim to take the property itself, in which case they would become tenants in common in shares proportioned to amounts for which either could claim a charge. Suppose, again, that the fiduciary agent parts with the money to a third party who cannot plead purchase for value without notice, and that the third party invests it with money of his own in the purchase of property. If the third party had notice that the money was held in a fiduciary capacity, he would be in exactly the same position as the fiduciary agent, and could not, therefore, assert any interest in the property until the money misapplied had been refunded. But if he had no such notice this would not be the case. There would on his part be no misconduct at all. On the other hand, I cannot at present see why he should have any priority as against the property over the owner of the money which had, in fact, been misapplied. . . .

LORD SUMNER: . . . What ought to be done I think is clear; the only difficulty is how to describe the principle and how to affiliate it to other legal or equitable rules.

The question is one of administration. The liquidator, an officer of the Court, who has to discharge himself of the assets that have come to his hands, asks for directions, and, after hearing all parties concerned, the Court has the right and the duty to direct him how to distribute all the assets. No part of them can remain undistributed as res nullius. No one has ventured to argue before your Lordships that the shareholders take everything, to the exclusion of the depositors, and so make a huge windfall. In my opinion, if precedent fails, the most just distribution of the whole must be directed, so only that no recognized rule of law or equity be disregarded. In this case neither the shareholders nor the depositors have the better equity; the money of each has, with the consent of all, been indiscriminately applied in acquiring assets beyond as well as within the society's powers, the former in much the larger measure. The claims of each class are equal, and, I think, for the present purpose identical.

Analogous cases have been decided with regard to chattels. They differ, no doubt, because of the fact that the property in the chattels remained unchanged, though identification and even identity of the subject-matter of the property failed, whereas here, except as to currency, and even there only in a restricted sense, the term property, as we use that term of chattels, does not apply, and, at least as far as intention could do it, both depositors and shareholders had given up the right to call the money or its proceeds their own, and had taken instead personal claims on the society. In *Buckley* v *Gross* (1863) 3 B & S 566, at p. 574, where tallow in burning warehouses melted and ran down a sewer, and a stranger collected it, Blackburn J says: 'The tallow of the different owners was indeed mixed up into a molten mass, so that it might be difficult to apportion it among them; but I dissent from the doctrine that, because the property of different persons is confused together, that entitles a third party to steal it with impunity. Probably the legal effect of such a mixture would be to make the owners tenants in common in equal portions of the mass.' Again, *Spence* v *Union Marine Insurance Co.* (1868) LR 3 CP 427 is a case where cotton in bales belonging to different consignees was so damaged by sea perils that it arrived with marks obliterated and otherwise injured, and after delivery to the respective consignees of all that could be specifically identified as theirs, a mass of unidentifiable damaged cotton remained. There, as here, no doubt one bale, in fact, represented A's money and another B's; there, as here, all were depreciated, but probably not each in the same degree, but no one could say which bale was any particular person's property, or who, therefore, should bear the greater and who the less depreciation. The goods could not be treated as bona vacantia, they could not fall into the hands of the first person who reduced them into possession, and on principles and analogies derived from Roman law the Court treated the consignees as tenants in common of the unidentifiable cotton, in the proportion borne by the numbers originally shipped by them to the number remaining. This decision has never been questioned for nearly fifty years.

My Lords, I agree, without recapitulating reasons, that the principle on which *Hallett's Case* 13 Ch D 696 is founded justifies an order allowing the appellants to follow the assets, not merely to the verge of actual identification, but even somewhat further in a case like the present, where after a process of exclusion only two classes or groups of persons, having equal claims, are left in and all superior claims have been eliminated. Tracing in a sense it is not, for we know that the money coming from A went into one security and that coming from B into another, and that the two securities did not probably depreciate exactly in the same percentage, and we know further that no one will ever know any more. Still I think this well within the 'tracing' equity, and that among persons making up these two groups the principle of rateable division of the assets is sound. . . .

James Roscoe (Bolton) Ltd v *Winder*
[1915] 1 Ch 62 (Ch D)

Tracing in equity; equitable lien

In 1913, Wigham purchased a business from the plaintiff company. By clause 5 of the agreement Wigham undertook to collect the outstanding book debts of the business and to pay them over to the company. All debts accruing after 1 March 1913 were to belong to Wigham. Some £623 was owing up to 1 March. Wigham collected part of this amount, £305, before 30 April and the remainder on or before 19 May, when he paid £455 18s 11d into his own general banking account. None of the book debts so collected was ever paid over to the company. Wigham drew on the account for his own purposes, so that by 21 May the balance was only £25 18s. Subsequently further sums were paid in and drawn out of the account, so that at his death in June 1913 the balance was £358 5s 5d. The plaintiff company claimed that sum from Wigham's trustee-in-bankruptcy, and argued it was subject to an *equitable lien* or charge.

SARGANT J: . . . The first point that was taken against the claim was that no trust was created by the agreement as to the book debts to be collected under it. In my opinion, that objection cannot be sustained. It seems to me that the true effect of clause 5 of the agreement is that the purchaser is throughout collecting the book debts on behalf of the vendors, and that he has to pay over the money received on account of the book debts; the language of the clause is express in that respect. No doubt, he has on April 30 to make up to the vendors the full amount of the book debts if he has not by that time received them himself. That is a personal obligation on his part to make up the deficiency, but I do not think that in any way affects his obligation to hand over the actual book debts to the vendors so far as he does in fact receive them. And, incidentally, I think that the concluding words of clause 5, 'thereafter all debts then outstanding shall belong to the purchaser,' do not mean after April 30, but after the time when the purchaser shall have fulfilled his obligation to make up the deficiency of the book debts collected by him to the full amount. Accordingly, so far as the purchaser did collect these book debts, he did, in my opinion, hold the amount in trust for the vendors.

That being so, we have a case where, as in *In re Hallett's Estate* 13 Ch D 696, the banking account of the debtor comprised not only moneys belonging to himself for his own purposes, but also moneys belonging to him upon trust for some one else, and that being so, and apart from the circumstance I am going to mention, it seems to me clear that the plaintiffs would be entitled to the charge they claim, and to receive the whole balance of 358*l.* 5*s.* 5*d.* standing to the debtor's credit at the time of his death, and that although there had been payments out of the account which, under the rule in *Clayton's Case* (1816) 1 Mer 572, would have been attributable to the earlier payments in.

In re Hallett's Estate 13 Ch D 696, which would but for the circumstance I am going to mention entirely conclude this case, decided two clear points: First, that when a trustee mixes trust moneys with private moneys in one account the cestuis que trust have a charge on the aggregate amount for their trust fund; and, secondly, that when payments are made by the trustee out of the general account the payments are not to be appropriated against payments in to that account as in *Clayton's Case* (1816) 1 Mer 572, because the trustee is presumed to be honest rather than dishonest and to make payments out of his own private moneys and not out of the trust fund that was mingled with his private moneys.

But there is a further circumstance in the present case which seems to me to be conclusive in favour of the defendant as regards the greater part of the balance of 358*l.* 5*s.* 5*d.* It appears that after the payment in by the debtor of a portion of the book debts which he had received the balance at the bank on May 19, 1913, was reduced by his drawings to a sum of 25*l.* 18*s.* only on May 21. So that, although the ultimate balance at the debtor's death was about 358*l.*, there had been an intermediate balance of only 25*l.* 18*s.* The result of that seems to me to be that the trust moneys cannot possibly be traced into this common fund, which was standing to the debtor's credit at his death, to an extent of more than 25*l.* 18*s.*, because, although prima facie under the second rule in *In re Hallett's Estate* 13 Ch D 696 any drawings out by the debtor ought to be attributed to the private moneys which he had at the bank and not to the trust moneys, yet, when the drawings out had reached such an amount that the whole of his private money part had been exhausted, it necessarily followed that the rest of the drawings must have been against trust moneys. There being on May 21, 1913, only 25*l.* 18*s.*, in all, standing to the credit of the debtor's account, it is quite clear that on that day he must have denuded his account of all the trust moneys there—the whole 455*l.* 18*s.* 11*d.*—except to the extent of 25*l.* 18*s.*

Practically, what Mr Martelli and Mr Hansell [Counsel for the plaintiff company] have been asking me to do—although I think Mr Hansell in particular rather disguised the claim by the phraseology he used—is to say that the debtor, by paying further moneys after May 21 into this common account, was impressing upon those further moneys so paid in the like trust or obligation, or charge of the nature of a trust, which had formerly been impressed upon the previous balances to the credit of that account. No doubt, Mr Hansell did say 'No. I am only asking you to treat the account as a whole, and to consider the balance from time to time standing to the credit of that account as subject to one continual charge or trust.' But I think that really is using words which are not appropriate to the facts. You must, for the purpose of tracing, which was the process adopted in *In re Hallett's Estate*, put your finger on some definite fund which either remains in its original state or can be found in another shape. That is tracing, and tracing, by the very facts of this case, seems to be absolutely excluded except as to the 25*l.* 18*s.*

Then, apart from tracing, it seems to me possible to establish this claim against the ultimate balance of 358*l.* 5*s.* 5*d.* only by saying that something was done, with regard to the additional moneys which are needed to make up that balance, by the person to whom those moneys belonged, the debtor, to substitute those moneys for the purpose of, or to impose upon those moneys a trust equivalent to, the trust which rested on the previous balance. Of course, if there was anything like a separate trust account, the payment of the further moneys into that account would, in itself, have been quite a sufficient indication of the intention of the debtor to substitute those additional moneys for the original trust moneys, and accordingly to impose, by way of substitution, the old trusts upon those additional moneys. But, in a case where the account into which the moneys are paid is the general trading account of the debtor on which he has been accustomed to draw both in the ordinary course and in breach of trust when there were trust funds standing to the credit of that account which were convenient for that purpose, I think it is impossible to attribute to him that by the mere payment into the account of further moneys, which to a large extent he subsequently used for purposes of his own, he intended to clothe those moneys with a trust in favour of the plaintiffs.

Certainly, after having heard *In re Hallett's Estate* stated over and over again, I should have thought that the general view of that decision was that it only applied to such an amount of the balance ultimately standing to the credit of the trustee as did not exceed the lowest balance of the account during the intervening period. That view has practically been taken, as far as I can make out, in the cases which have dealt with *In re Hallett's Estate*. *In re Oatway* [1903] 2 Ch 356, a decision of Joyce J, was cited to me in support of the plaintiffs' case, but I do not find anything in it to help them.

All that Joyce J did in that case was to say that, if part of the mixed moneys can be traced into a definite security, that security will not become freed from the charge in favour of the trust, but will, together with any residue of the mixed moneys, remain subject to that charge. I am sure that nothing which he said was intended to mean that the trust was imposed upon any property into which the original fund could not be traced. The head-note to the decision of North J in *In re Stenning* [1895] 2 Ch 433 (which accurately represents the effect of the case) is stated in such terms as to indicate that the application of the doctrine in *In re Hallett's Estate* implied that there should be a continuous balance standing to the credit of the account equal to the balance against which the charge is sought to be enforced. And certainly in the recent case of *Sinclair* v *Brougham* [1914] AC 398 I can see nothing in any way to impeach the doctrine as to tracing laid down in *In re Hallett's Estate*.

In my opinion, therefore, the only part of the balance of 358*l.* 5*s.* 5*d.* which can be made available by the plaintiffs is the sum of 25*l.* 18*s.*, being the smallest amount to which the balance, to the credit of the account had fallen between May 19, 1913, and the death of the debtor.

Notes

1. This rule was recently referred to with apparent approval by the Privy Council in *Re Goldcorp Exchange Ltd* [1995] 1 AC 74, and see *Bishopsgate Investment Management Ltd (in liquidation)* v *Homan* [1994] 3 WLR 1270 (CA) below.

2. Of this case Professor Birks writes: 'This seems absolutely correct since, however artificial the rules are, once a court reaches a point in the story at which it is bound to say that the enrichment has disappeared, it is impossible for it to affirm that it has subsequently reappeared' (Birks, *Introduction*, 365).

In re Diplock, Diplock v *Wintle*

[1948] Ch 465 (CA); affd *sub nom. Ministry of Health* v *Simpson* [1951] AC 251 (HL)

Tracing in equity

Caleb Diplock's will was held to be invalid on the grounds of uncertainty. His executors had distributed over £200,000 to various charities. Diplock's next-of-kin sought restitution from the charities. They were successful in their *in personam* claim (as to which see Chapter 2, Section 2). These extracts concern their alternative *in rem* claim. *Held*: the *in rem* claims succeeded subject to the following rules: where the charities paid money into a current account the rule in *Clayton's case* ('first in, first out') applied; where the charities paid money into a deposit account the *pari passu* rule of distribution applied; the *in rem* claims failed where charities used the funds to improve their own existing land and buildings.

LORD GREENE MR (delivering the judgment of the Court of Appeal): [His lordship, having dealt with the claim *in personam*, turned to consider the principles underlying the *in rem* claim: . . .] In this connexion we regard the case of *Sinclair* v *Brougham* [1914] AC 398 as of fundamental importance. That decision, in our view, did not so much extend as explain the doctrine of *Hallett's* case 13 Ch D 696, which now must be regarded not, so to speak, as a genus but as a species in a genus where equity works on the same basic principles but selects what on the particular case is the equitable method of applying them in practice. It will be found that our views as to the meaning and effect of the speeches in *Sinclair* v *Brougham* differ from those expressed by Wynn-Parry J. We should, however, be lacking in candour rather than showing respect if we refrained from saying that we find the opinions in *Sinclair* v *Brougham* in many respects not only difficult to follow but difficult to reconcile with one another.

Before passing to a consideration of the case of *Sinclair* v *Brougham* we may usefully make some observations of our own as to the distinction between the attitude of the common law and that of equity to these questions.

The common law approached them in a strictly materialistic way. It could only appreciate what might almost be called the 'physical' identity of one thing with another. It could treat a person's money as identifiable so long as it had not become mixed with other money. It could treat as identifiable with the money other kinds of property acquired by means of it, provided that there was no admixture of other money. It is noticeable that in this latter case the common law did not base itself on any known theory of tracing such as that adopted in equity. It proceeded on the basis that the unauthorized act of purchasing was one capable of ratification by the owner of the money (see *per* Lord Parker in *Sinclair* v *Brougham*). Certain words of Lord Haldane in *Sinclair* v *Brougham* may appear to suggest a further limitation, i.e., that 'money' as we have used that word was not regarded at common law as identifiable once it had been paid into a banking account. We do not, however, think it necessary to discuss this point at length. We agree with the comments of Wynn-Parry J upon it [1947] Ch 716, 745–6 and those of Atkin LJ (as he then was) in *Banque Belge* v *Hambrouck* [1921] 1 KB 321, 335. If it is possible to identify a principal's money with an asset purchased exclusively by means of it we see no reason for drawing a distinction between a chose in action such as a banker's debt to his customer and any other asset. If the principal can ratify the acquisition of the one, we see no reason for supposing that he cannot ratify the acquisition of the other.

We may mention several matters which we think are helpful in understanding the limitation of the common law doctrine and the reasons why equity was able to take a more liberal view. They are as follows:

(1) The common law did not recognize equitable claims to property, whether money or any other form of property. Sovereigns in A's pocket either belonged in law to A or they belonged in law to B. The idea that they could belong in law to A and that they should nevertheless be treated as belonging to B was entirely foreign to the common law. This is the reason why the common law doctrine finds its typical exemplification in cases of principal and agent. If B, a principal, hands cash to A, his agent, in order that it may be applied in a particular manner, the cash, in the eyes of the common law, remains the property of B. If, therefore, A, instead of applying it in the authorized manner, buries it in a sack in his garden or uses it for an unauthorized purchase, B can, in the former case, recover the cash as being still his own property and, in the latter case, affirm the purchase of something bought with his money by his agent. If, however, the relationship of A and B was not one which left the property in the cash in B but merely constituted a relationship of debtor and creditor between them, there could, of course, have been no remedy at law under this head, since the property in the cash would have passed out of B into A.

(2) The narrowness of the limits within which the common law operated may be linked with the limited nature of the remedies available to it. Specific relief as distinct from damages (the normal remedy at common law) was confined to a very limited range of claims as compared with the extensive uses of specific relief developed by

equity. In particular, the device of a declaration of charge was unknown to the common law and it was the availability of that device which enabled equity to give effect to its wider conception of equitable rights.

(3) It was the materialistic approach of the common law coupled with and encouraged by the limited range of remedies available to it that prevented the common law from identifying money in a mixed fund. Once the money of B became mixed with the money of A its identification in a physical sense became impossible; owing to the fact of mixture there could be no question of ratification of an unauthorized act; and the only remedy of B, if any, lay in a claim for damages.

Equity adopted a more metaphysical approach. It found no difficulty in regarding a composite fund as an amalgam constituted by the mixture of two or more funds each of which could be regarded as having, for certain purposes, a continued separate existence. Putting it in another way, equity regarded the amalgam as capable, in proper circumstances, of being resolved into its component parts.

Adapting, for the sake of contrast, the phraseology which we have used in relation to the common law, it was the metaphysical approach of equity coupled with and encouraged by the far-reaching remedy of a declaration of charge that enabled equity to identify money in a mixed fund. Equity, so to speak, is able to draw up a balance sheet on the right-hand side of which appears the composite fund and on its left-hand side the two or more funds of which it is to be deemed to be made up.

Regarded as a pure piece of machinery for the purpose of tracing money into a mixed fund or into property acquired by means of a mixed fund, a declaration of charge might be thought to be a suitable means of dealing with any case where one person has, without legal title, acquired some benefit by the use of the money of another—in other words, any case of what is often called 'unjust enrichment.' The opinion of Lord Dunedin in *Sinclair* v *Brougham* [1914] AC 398 appears to us to come very nearly to this, for he appears to treat the equitable remedy as applicable in any case where a superfluity, expressed or capable of being expressed in terms of money, is found to exist. Such a view would dispense with the necessity of establishing as a starting point the existence of a fiduciary or quasi-fiduciary relationship or of a continuing right of property recognized in equity. We may say at once that, apart from the possible case of Lord Dunedin's speech, we cannot find that any principle so wide in its operation is to be found enunciated in English law. The conditions which must exist before the equitable form of relief becomes available will be considered later in this judgment. But one truism may be stated here in order to get it out of the way. The equitable form of relief whether it takes the form of an order to restore an unmixed sum of money (or property acquired by means of such a sum) or a declaration of charge upon a mixed fund (or upon property acquired by means of such a fund) is, of course, personal in the sense that its efficacy is founded upon the jurisdiction of equity to enforce its rules by acting upon the individual. But it is not personal in the sense that the person against whom an order of this nature is sought can be made personally liable to repay the amount claimed to have belonged to the claimant. The equitable remedies pre-suppose the continued existence of the money either as a separate fund or as part of a mixed fund or as latent in property acquired by means of such a fund. If, on the facts of any individual case, such continued existence is not established, equity is as helpless as the common law itself. If the fund, mixed or unmixed, is spent upon a dinner, equity, which dealt only in specific relief and not in damages, could do nothing. If the case was one which at common law involved breach of contract the common law could, of course, award damages but specific relief would be out of the question. It is, therefore, a necessary matter for consideration in each case where it is sought to trace money in equity, whether it has such a continued existence, actual or notional, as will enable equity to grant specific relief.

To turn to another preliminary matter: We do not think that confusion can be avoided unless the meaning of the word 'money' as used in connexion with this class of question is kept in mind. It is tempting to use the illustration of sovereigns in a bag or, to use an expression of Lord Dunedin's, a strong box. But this must not blind us to the fact that such an illustration has little or no likeness to actual facts in present-day conditions. We can explain what we mean by a reference to the present cases. The plaintiffs claim that 'money' forming part of the residuary estate of the testator and, therefore, divisible among his next-of-kin, has been improperly paid to a charity. This 'money' when 'paid' was in the form of a cheque on the executorship account, i.e., a negotiable instrument. This negotiable instrument at the moment preceding its delivery to the charity belonged to the residuary estate of the testator and any of the next-of-kin, if he had known of the situation, could have secured an injunction restraining the executors from delivering it to the charity. As in that event the cheque would never have been presented for payment, the 'money' representing the relevant portion of the residuary estate would have remained in its existing state, i.e., as part of the chose in action constituted by the banker's debt to the executors in respect of the executorship account.

The charity accepted the cheque; and on the assumption that it was not a purchaser for value and is not to be charged with such notice as to make it a constructive trustee, it accepted the cheque as a volunteer. The first stage, therefore, was that the charity had in its possession a negotiable instrument which in origin belonged to the residuary estate and in which the next-of-kin were, in the eyes of equity, interested.

If the next-of-kin had been in a position to interfere at that stage they could, in our view, clearly (and the contrary was not argued) have recovered the cheque from the charity whom, as a volunteer, equity would have compelled to recognize the equitable interest of the next-of-kin in it. But the cheque was in fact paid into a banking account in the name of the charity. The next-of-kin claim to follow their 'money'. What really happened was that when the cheque was cleared, a credit was passed by the paying bank to the collecting bank for the benefit of the charity who thus, without handling any 'money' in the sense of cash, became possessed of 'money' in the sense of credit in its banking account, i.e., a chose in action. Now, if the 'money' in the form of the cheque was 'paid in' to a separate account so that the 'money' in the form of a chose in action which resulted from the operation remained 'unmixed' (i.e., was identifiable as a chose in action having a separate existence) it is not disputed that the 'money' will be specifically recoverable from the charity. It is not suggested in that case that the title to the 'money' of the charity as a volunteer can defeat the claim of the next-of-kin to recover it for the benefit of the estate. The appropriate equitable relief would be by way of specific order for restoration of what, in the eyes of equity, never ceased to belong in equity to the estate; the reason, of course, being that the charity, which took the cheque not as a purchaser for value without notice but merely as a volunteer, could not set up a title adverse to the estate in respect of 'money' (i.e., on those facts a separate and identifiable chose in action) obtained by means of 'money' in the form of a cheque, i.e., an order by the executors on their bankers to transfer from 'money' belonging to the estate in the form of a chose in action an aliquot sum of 'money' in the form of a credit in favour of the charity, as payee of the cheque, in its account with its bankers.

When the various senses in which the word 'money' is used are appreciated, the conceptions of 'purchaser for value without notice' and of 'volunteer' which are common currency in the language of equity, do not appear inappropriate, as they might perhaps have done (at any rate at first sight) in the case of current coins which pass by delivery: and one of the apparent difficulties in the way of tracing, identifying and locating 'money' does, we think, disappear.

The first question which appears to us to fall for decision on this part of the present appeals may, we think, be thus formulated: Did the power of equity to treat Diplock 'money' as recoverable from the charity, which undoubtedly existed down to the moment when the cheque was paid by the bank on which it was drawn, cease the moment that the 'money' by the process of 'mixture' came to be represented by an accretion to or an enlargement of the chose in action consisting of a debt already owing to the charity by its own bankers? Wynn-Parry J, in effect, decided that it did. His reason for taking this view, shortly stated, was as follows: The principle applicable was to be extracted from the decision in *Hallett's* case 13 Ch D 696 and that principle was in no way extended by the decision in *Sinclair* v *Brougham* [1914] AC 398. The principle can operate only in cases where the mixing takes place in breach of a trust, actual or constructive, or in breach of some other fiduciary relationship and in proceedings against the trustee or fiduciary agent: here the mixing was not of this character, since it was effected by an innocent volunteer: there is no ground on which, according to principle, the conscience of such a volunteer can be held in equity to be precluded from setting up a title adverse to the claim: in every case, therefore, where a 'mixture' has been carried out by the charity, the claim, whether it be against a mixed monetary fund or against investments made by means of such a mixed fund, must fail in limine.

Now we may say at once that this view of the inability of equity to deal with the case of the volunteer appears to us, with all respect to Wynn-Parry J, to be in conflict with the principles expounded, particularly by Lord Parker, in *Sinclair* v *Brougham*. If Lord Parker means what we think he meant, and if what he said is to be accepted as a correct statement of the law, Mr Pennycuick, who argued this part of the case on behalf of the charities, admittedly felt great difficulty in supporting this part of the reasoning of the learned judge. We shall deal further with Lord Parker's observations on this topic when we come to them in our examination of *Sinclair* v *Brougham*. But here we may conveniently summarize what we consider to be the effect of them as follows: Where an innocent volunteer (as distinct from a purchaser for value without notice) mixes 'money' of his own with 'money' which in equity belongs to another person, or is found in possession of such a mixture, although that other person cannot claim a charge on the mass superior to the claim of the volunteer he is entitled, nevertheless, to a charge ranking pari passu with the claim of the volunteer. And Lord Parker's reasons for taking this view appear to have been on the following lines: Equity regards the rights of the equitable owner as being 'in effect rights of property' though not recognized as such by the common law. Just as a volunteer is not allowed by equity in the case, e.g., of a conveyance of the legal estate in land, to set up his legal title adversely to the claim of a person having an equitable interest in the land, so in the case of a mixed fund of money the volunteer must give such recognition as equity consider him in conscience (as a volunteer) bound to give to the interest of the equitable owner of the money which has been mixed with the volunteer's own. But this burden on the conscience of the volunteer is not such as to compel him to treat the claim of the equitable owner as paramount. That would be to treat the volunteer as strictly as if he himself stood in a fiduciary relationship to the equitable owner which ex hypothesi he does not. The volunteer is under no greater duty of conscience to recognize the interest of the equitable owner than that which lies upon a person having an equitable interest in one of two trust funds of 'money' which have become mixed towards the equitable owner of the other. Such a person is not in conscience bound to give precedence to the equitable owner of the other of the two funds.

We may enlarge upon the implications which appear to us to be contained in Lord Parker's reasoning. First of all, it appears to us to be wrong to treat the principle which underlies *Hallett*'s case as coming into operation only where the person who does the mixing is not only in a fiduciary position but is also a *party to the tracing action*. If he is a party to the action he is, of course, precluded from setting up a case inconsistent with the obligations of his fiduciary position. But supposing that he is not a party? The result cannot surely depend on what equity would or would not have allowed him to say if he had been a party. Suppose that the sole trustee of (say) five separate trusts draws 100*l.* out of each of the trust banking accounts, pays the resulting 500*l.* into an account which he opens in his own name, draws a cheque for 500*l.* on that account and gives it as a present to his son. A claim by the five sets of beneficiaries to follow the money of their respective trusts would be a claim against the son. He would stand in no fiduciary relationship to any of them. We recoil from the conclusion that all five beneficiaries would be dismissed empty handed by a court of equity and the son left to enjoy what in equity was originally their money. Yet that is the conclusion to which the reasoning of the learned judge would lead us. Lord Parker's reasoning, on the other hand, seems to us to lead to the conclusion that each set of beneficiaries could set up its equitable interest which would prevail against the bare legal title of the son as a volunteer and that they would be entitled to share pari passu in so much of the fund or its proceeds as remained identifiable.

An even more striking example was admitted by Mr Pennycuick to be the result of his argument, and he vigorously maintained that it followed inevitably from the principles of equity involved. If a fiduciary agent takes cash belonging to his principal and gives it to his son, who takes it innocently, then so long as the son keeps it unmixed with other cash in one trouser pocket, the principal can follow it and claim it back. Once, however, the son, being under no fiduciary duty to the principal, transfers it to his other trouser pocket in which there are reposing a coin or two of his own of the same denomination, the son, by a sort of process of accretion, acquires an indefeasible title to what the moment before the transfer he could not have claimed as his own. This result appears to us to stultify the beneficent powers of equity to protect and enforce what it recognizes as equitable rights of property which subsist until they are destroyed by the operation of a purchase for value without notice.

The error into which, we respectfully suggest, the learned judge has fallen is in thinking that what, in *Hallett's* case was only the method (there appropriate) of bringing a much wider-based principle of equity into operation—viz., the method by which a fiduciary agent, who has himself wrongfully mixed the funds, is prohibited from asserting a breach of his duty—is an element which must necessarily be present before equity can afford protection to the equitable rights which it has brought into existence. We are not prepared to see the arm of equity thus shortened.

[Lord Greene then thoroughly examined *Sinclair* v *Brougham* [1914] AC 398, especially the speech of Lord Parker, and continued: . . .]

From the foregoing study of Lord Parker's speech, it would appear that in his opinion there is an equitable principle common to all these cases of mixed funds. It operates in different ways according to the circumstances. In some cases it results in a priority to one or other of the claimants, in other cases the claimants rank pari passu. Where one claimant is a person in a fiduciary relationship to another and has mixed moneys of that other with moneys of his own, that other takes priority. The same result follows where a person taking that other claimant's money from the person in a fiduciary relationship, with notice that it is money held in a fiduciary capacity, proceeds to mix it with money of his own. Where the contest is between two claimants to a mixed fund made up entirely of moneys held on behalf of the two of them respectively and mixed together by the fiduciary agent, they share pari passu, each being innocent. Where the moneys are handed by way of transfer to a person who takes for value without notice, the claim of the owner of the moneys is extinguished just as all other equitable estates or interests are extinguished by a purchase for value without notice. In the case, however, of a volunteer who takes without notice, e.g., by way of gift from the fiduciary agent, if there is no question of mixing, he holds the money on behalf of the true owner whose equitable right to the money still persists as against him. On the other hand, if the volunteer mixes the money with money of his own, or receives it mixed from the fiduciary agent, he must admit the claim of the true owner, but is not precluded from setting up his own claim in respect of the moneys of his own which have been contributed to the mixed fund. The result is that they share pari passu. It would be inequitable for the volunteer to claim priority for the reason that he is a volunteer: it would be equally inequitable for the true owner of the money to claim priority over the volunteer for the reason that the volunteer is innocent and cannot be said to act unconscionably if he claims equal treatment for himself. The mutual recognition of one another's rights is what equity insists upon as a condition of giving relief.

We now turn to the speeches of the other noble and learned Lords.

Viscount Haldane LC examines and rejects the theory that the case was one of money had and received, and on this basis he states the claim of the depositors to be as follows [1914] AC 398, 418, 419: 'Their claim cannot be in personam and must be in rem, a claim to follow and recover property with which, in equity at all events, they had never really parted.' He describes the limits within which the common law recognized a right to follow money. 'Whether the case be that of a thief or of a fraudulent broker or of money paid under mistake of fact you can, even at law, follow, but only so long as the relation of debtor and creditor has not superseded the right in rem.'

We have already referred to what appears to have been Lord Haldane's view as to this debtor-creditor qualification. What does appear to be clear is that if the 'money' was *mixed* 'with other' money, either in a bag or in a banking account the common law was unable to give to the owner any specific relief.

Thus, like Lord Parker, Lord Haldane bases the remedy available in equity upon a right of property recognized by equity as vested in the plaintiff throughout, not lost by payment into a banking account, nor by the mixture of moneys nor by merger in a mass of assets. In all these cases the equitable remedy by way of declaration of charge is available.

It is to be observed that neither Lord Parker nor Lord Haldane suggests that the equitable remedy extends to cover all cases where A becomes possessed of money belonging to B, a view which Lord Dunedin seemed inclined to accept if he did not actually do so. Lord Parker and Lord Haldane both predicate the existence of a right of property recognized by equity which depends upon there having existed at some stage a fiduciary relationship of some kind (though not necessarily a positive duty of trusteeship) sufficient to give rise to the equitable right of property. Exactly what relationships are sufficient to bring such an equitable right into existence for the purposes of the rule which we are considering is a matter which has not been precisely laid down. Certain relationships are clearly included, e.g., trustee (actual or constructive) and cestui que trust; and 'fiduciary' relationships such as that of principal and agent. *Sinclair* v *Brougham* itself affords another example. There, a sufficient fiduciary relationship was found to exist between the depositors and the directors by reason of the fact that the purposes for which the depositors had handed their money to the directors were by law incapable of fulfilment.

[Lord Greene MR then considered the individual cases, including those charities who spent the Diplock money on land or buildings already belonging to them: . . .]

Where the contribution of a volunteer to a mixed fund or the acquisition of what we may call a 'mixed asset' is in the form of money, it is, as we hope to have shown, inequitable for him to claim the whole fund or the whole asset. The equitable charge given to the other claimant in respect of the money contributed by him results merely in the division of the mixed fund between the two of them or the reduction of the asset by sale to its original components, i.e., money which is then divisible in the same manner. The volunteer gets back what he put in, i.e., money. On this basis, if a charity had used a mixed fund, consisting in part of its own money and in part of Diplock money, in the acquisition of property, whether (for example) land or stock, the application of the equitable remedy would have presented no particular difficulty. The Diplock money and the charity money could each have been traced. A charge enforced by sale and distribution would have been effective as well as fair to both parties. The charity would not, as the result of the mixture, have been deprived of anything that it had before.

In the present cases, however, the charities have used the Diplock money, not in combination with money of their own to acquire new assets, but in the alteration and improvement of assets which they already owned. The altered and improved asset owes its existence, therefore, to a combination of land belonging to the charity and money belonging to the Diplock estate. The question whether tracing is possible and if so to what extent, and also the question whether an effective remedy by way of declaration of charge can be granted consistently with an equitable treatment of the charity as an innocent volunteer, present quite different problems from those arising in the simple case above stated. In the case of the purchase of an asset out of a mixed fund, both categories of money are, as we have said, necessarily present throughout the existence of the asset in an identifiable form. In the case of adaptation of property of the volunteer by means of trust money, it by no means necessarily follows that the money can be said to be present in the adapted property. The beneficial owner of the trust money seeks to follow and recover that money and claims to use the machinery of a charge on the adapted property in order to enable him to do so. But in the first place the money may not be capable of being followed. In every true sense, the money may have disappeared. A simple example suggests itself. The owner of a house who, as an innocent volunteer, has trust money in his hands given to him by a trustee uses that money in making an alteration to his house so as to fit it better to his own personal needs. The result may add not one penny to the value of the house. Indeed, the alteration may well lower its value; for the alteration, though convenient to the owner, may be highly inconvenient in the eyes of a purchaser. Can it be said in such cases that the trust money can be traced and extracted from the altered asset? Clearly not, for the money will have disappeared leaving no monetary trace behind: the asset will not have increased (or may even have depreciated) in value through its use.

But the matter does not end here. What, for the purposes of the inquiry, is to be treated as 'the charity property'? Is it to be the whole of the land belonging to the charity? or is it to be only that part of it which was altered or reconstructed or on which a building has been erected by means of Diplock money? If the latter, the result may well be that the property, both in its original state and as altered or improved, will, when taken in isolation, have little or no value. What would be the value of a building in the middle of Guy's hospital without any means of access through other parts of the hospital property? If, on the other hand, the charge is to be on the whole of the charity land, it might well be thought an extravagant result if the Diplock estate, because Diplock money had been used to reconstruct a corner of it, were to be entitled to a charge on the entirety.

But it is not merely a question of locating and identifying the Diplock money. The result of a declaration of charge is to disentangle trust money and enable it to be withdrawn in the shape of money from the complex in which it has become involved. This can only be done by sale under the charge. But the equitable owner of the trust money must in this process submit to equality of treatment with the innocent volunteer. The latter too, is entitled to disentangle his money and to withdraw it from the complex. Where the complex originates in money on both sides there is no difficulty and no inequity. Each is entitled to a charge. But if what the volunteer has contributed is not money but other property of his own such as land, what then? You cannot have a charge for land. You can, it is true, have a charge for the value of land, an entirely different thing. Is it equitable to compel the innocent volunteer to take a charge merely for the value of the land when what he has contributed is the land itself? In other words, can equity, by the machinery of a charge, give to the innocent volunteer that which he has contributed so as to place him in a position comparable with that of the owner of the trust fund? In our opinion it cannot.

In the absence of authority to the contrary our conclusion is that as regards the Diplock money used in these cases it cannot be traced in any true sense; and, further, that even if this were not so, the only remedy available to equity, viz., that of a declaration of charge would not produce an equitable result and is applicable accordingly. . . .

Notes

1. The appeal to the House of Lords was concerned only with the *in personam* claim.

2. The various limitations and qualifications placed by the Court of Appeal on the *in rem* claims were academic as the next-of-kin succeeded on the personal claim (subject to the reduction for recovery from the executors) and all the charities were solvent.

3. On the question of whether the alterations to the charities' buildings constituted an enrichment see Birks, *Introduction*, 371–2 explaining the failure of these particular claims by reference to the concept of 'subjective devaluation'. Another view is that this expenditure led to an early application of the defence of change of position (see Goff and Jones, 90–91 and contrast Birks, *Introduction*, 411–12). For general discussion of the defence see Chapter 8, Section 2.

In re Tilley's Will Trusts, Burgin v *Croad*
[1967] Ch 1179 (Ch D)

Account; tracing in equity; equitable lien

Henry Tilley died in 1932, leaving his widow as one of his executors. Mrs Tilley received a life interest in his estate, with the remainder going to Tilley's two children by a previous marriage. Mrs Tilley received and accumulated £2,237 of trust moneys, which over the years became thoroughly confused with her own private funds. Mrs Tilley indulged in a number of speculative property transactions. In 1939 she had overdraft facilities in excess of £22,000, and by the time she died was worth £94,000, apparently due to the success of her property dealings. The plaintiff, the personal representative of Mabel, one of Henry Tilley's children, sought and obtained an *account* of the property received by the widow as trustee of the testator's will. The plaintiff further claimed that Mabel's estate should, by virtue of its half interest in Henry Tilley's estate, also be entitled to half of the profits made by the widow from her property speculations to the extent to which Mrs Tilley's personal representatives could not show those properties were purchased out of her personal moneys. *Held*: the plaintiff was entitled to restitution of only half of £2,237.

UNGOED-THOMAS J: . . . I come first to the law. The plaintiff relied on the statement of the law in Lewin on Trusts, 16th ed. (1964) at p. 223, and some of the cases cited in support of it. That statement reads:

> Wherever the trust property is placed, if a trustee amalgamates it with his own, his beneficiary will be entitled to every portion of the blended property which the trustee cannot prove to be his own.

Lupton v *White* (1808) 15 Ves 432 is the leading case for his proposition. In that case the defendant, an accounting party, had mixed the plaintiff's lead ore of unascertainable amount with his own lead ore, and the reference to *Panton* v *Panton* (undated) (cited in 15 Ves 432, 435, 440) shows that the same principle applies where moneys are similarly mixed. The principle is thus stated 15 Ves 432, 436.

> . . . to apply the great principle, familiar both at law and in equity, that, if a man, having undertaken to keep the property of another distinct, mixes it with his own, the whole must both at law and in equity be taken to be the property of the other, until the former puts the subject under such circumstances, that it may be distinguished as satisfactory, as it might have been before that unauthorised mixture upon his part.

Referring to *Armory* v *Delamirie* (1722) 1 Stra 505, the case in which a jeweller gave a trifle for a diamond ring found by a poor boy, the reason for the principle appears. The Lord Chancellor said 15 Ves 432, 440:

> . . . the Lord Chief Justice directed the jury to find, that the stone was of the utmost value they could find; upon this principle, that it was the defendant's own fault, by his own dishonest act, that the jury could not find the real value.

In *Gray* v *Haig* (1855) 20 Beav 219 Sir John Romilly MR followed *Lupton* v *White*. The principle was followed and restated thus by Sir John Stuart V-C in *Cook* v *Addison* (1869) LR 7 Eq. 466, 470:

> It is a well-established doctrine in this court, that if a trustee or agent mixes and confuses the property which he holds in a fiduciary character with his own property, so as that they cannot be separated with perfect accuracy, he is liable for the whole. This doctrine was explained by Lord Eldon in *Lupton* v *White*.

The words in that passage 'so as that they cannot be separated with perfect accuracy' are an essential part of the Vice-Chancellor's proposition, and indeed of the principle of *Lupton* v *White*. If a trustee mixes trust assets with his own, the onus is on the trustee to distinguish the separate assets, and to the extent that he fails to do so they belong to the trust. The *Lupton* v *White* line of cases does not appear to me to go further than this.

So the proposition in Lewis on Trusts, which I have read, is limited to cases where the amalgam of mixed assets is such that they cannot be sufficiently distinguished and treated separately; it is based on the lack of evidence to do so being attributable to the trustee's fault.

The defendants relied on *In re Hallett's Estate, Knatchbull* v *Hallett* (1880) 13 Ch D 696, CA with a view to establishing that the trustee must be presumed to have drawn out his own moneys from the bank account of mixed moneys in priority to trust moneys, with the result that property bought by such prior drawings must be the trustee's exclusive personal property. In that case the claim was against a bank balance of mixed fiduciary and personal funds, and it is in the context of such a claim that it was held that the person in a fiduciary character drawing out money from the bank account must be taken to have drawn out his own money in preference to the trust money, so that the claim of the beneficiaries prevailed against the balance of the account. *In re Oatway , Hertslet* v *Oatway* [1903] 2 Ch 356 was the converse of the decision in *In re Hallett's Estate* . In that case the claim was not against the balance left in the bank of such mixed moneys, but against the proceeds of sale of shares which the trustee had purchased with moneys which, as in *In re Hallett's Estate*, he had drawn from the bank account. But, unlike the situation in *In re Hallett's Estate*, his later drawings had exhausted the account, so that it was useless to proceed against the account. It was held that the beneficiary was entitled to the proceeds of sale of the shares, which were more than their purchase price but less than the trust moneys paid into the account. [Ungoed-Thomas J then quoted extensively the judgment of Joyce J in *Re Oatway* and continued: . . .]

So, contrary to the defendants' contention, it is not a presumption that a trustee's drawings from the mixed fund must necessarily be treated as drawings of the trustee's own money where the beneficiary's claim is against the property bought by such drawings. Further, *In re Oatway* did not raise the question whether a beneficiary is entitled to any profit made out of the purchase of property by a trustee out of a fund consisting of his personal moneys which he mixed with the trust moneys, and so the judgment was not directed to, and did not deal with, that question.

[Ungoed-Thomas J discussed *In re Hallett's Estate* and the speech of Lord Parker in *Sinclair* v *Brougham* [1914] AC 398 and continued: . . .]

In Snell's Principles of Equity, 26th ed. (1966), the law is thus stated at page 315:

> Where the trustee mixes trust money with his own, the equities are clearly unequal. Accordingly, the beneficiaries are entitled to a first charge on the mixed fund, or on any land, securities or other assets purchased with it. Thus if the trustee purchases shares with part of the mixed fund, leaving enough of it to repay the trust moneys, and then dissipates the balance, the beneficiaries' charge binds the shares; for although under the rule in *In re Hallett's Estate* the trustee is presumed to have bought the shares out of his own money, the charge attached to the entire fund, and could be discharged only by restoring the trust moneys. Where the property purchased has increased in value, the charge will be not merely for the amount of the trust moneys but for a proportionate part of the increased value. Thus if the trustee purchases land with £500 of his own money and £1,000 of trust moneys, and the land doubles in value, he would be profiting from his breach of trust if he were entitled to all except £1,000; the beneficiaries are accordingly entitled to a charge on the land for £2,000.

For the defendants it has been rightly admitted that if a trustee wrongly uses trust money to pay the whole of the purchase price in respect of the purchase of an asset a beneficiary can elect either to treat the purchased asset as trust property or to treat the purchased asset as security for the recouping of the trust money. It was further conceded that this right of election by a beneficiary also applies where the asset is purchased by a trustee in part out of his own money and in part out of the trust moneys, so that he may, if he wishes, require the asset to be treated as trust property with regard to that proportion of it which the trust moneys contributed to its purchase.

[Ungoed-Thomas J then reviewed the facts in detail and continued: . . .]

All these considerations appear to me to indicate overwhelmingly that Mrs Tilley was not deliberately using trust moneys to invest in or contribute towards or otherwise buy properties in her own name and the whole course of dealing with the trust funds and the bank accounts and the properties purchased and their history, which I have mentioned, indicate that what happened was that Mrs Tilley mixed the trust moneys and her own in the bank account but did not rely on the trust moneys for any of the purchases. If, as it was suggested for the defendants, the correct test whether a beneficiary is entitled to adopt a purchase by a trustee to which his trust moneys have contributed and thus claim a due proportion of its profits, is a subjective test, depending on the trustee's intention to use the trust moneys to contribute to the purchase then in my view there was no such intention and the beneficiary is not so entitled. But my conclusion about the trustee's intention is based not on any direct evidence but on the circumstantial evidence which I have mentioned. If, of course, a trustee deliberately uses trust money to contribute with his own money to buy property in his own name, then I would see no difficulty in enabling a beneficiary to adopt the purchase and claim a share of any resulting profits. But the subjective test does not appear to me to be exclusive, or indeed adequate, if it is the only test.

It seems to me that if, having regard to all the circumstances of the case objectively considered, it appears that the trustee has in fact, whatever his intention, laid out trust moneys in or towards a purchase, then the beneficiaries are entitled to the property purchased and any profits which it produces to the extent to which it has been paid for out of the trust moneys. But, even by this objective test, it appears to me that the trust moneys were not in this case so laid out. It seems to me, on a proper appraisal of all the facts of this particular case, that Mrs Tilley's breach halted at the mixing of the funds in her bank account. Although properties bought out of those funds would, like the bank account itself, at any rate if the moneys in the bank account were inadequate, be charged with repayment of the trust moneys which then would stand in the same position as the bank account, yet the trust moneys were not invested in properties at all but merely went in reduction of Mrs Tilley's overdraft which was in reality the source of the purchase-moneys.

The plaintiff's claim therefore fails and he is entitled to no more than repayment of the half of the £2,237, interest not being in issue. £2,237 is readily available, which makes the existence of any charge for its security immaterial.

Question

Should a plaintiff be entitled to the profits resulting from an increase in the value of an asset into which he can trace wealth subtracted from him?

Note

The facts of this case dramatically illustrate that a successful tracing claim has the potential of reaching wealth in excess of that originally subtracted from the plaintiff. In the terminology of Professor Birks, the surviving enrichment or second measure of restitution may be greater than the value subtracted or first measure. (See Birks, *Introduction*, 76, 366–70.) On the facts of this case such a startling conclusion was avoided in circumstances where the sums mixed were not substantial and the trustee's intent was not deliberately to use trust moneys in her speculations.

Barlow Clowes International Ltd (in liquidation) v *Vaughan* [1992] 4 All ER 22 (CA)

Tracing in equity

This is a tale of greed. Barlow Clowes was a Gibraltar-based investment company which promoted investment plans including Portfolios 28 and 68. These promised the investment of depositors' money in gilt-edged stock resulting in very high returns, and such returns were apparently achieved. It seemed the managers of Barlow Clowes had discovered the secret of alchemy. As a result Barlow Clowes attracted 11,000 investors, mostly based in the UK. Of course, it was a fraud and a sham. The very high returns were achieved simply by returning a proportion of investors' moneys to them as supposed gains from investment. Most of the money was misapplied by Barlow Clowes' managers, including sums diverted to the purchase of a yacht, '*Boukephalos*'. By the time of the liquidation of Barlow Clowes, some £140 million was due to investors upon their contracts, but only certificates for gilts worth some £1.8 million could be found.

This litigation concerned the distribution of the meagre available funds, including sums in bank accounts, the gilts and the proceeds from the sale of the yacht. The early investors argued that the funds should be distributed on a proportionate share basis. Later investors argued for the application of the 'first in, first out' rule. Between the judgment at first instance and the hearing in the Court of Appeal, the Secretary of State for Trade and Industry, following a critical report by the Ombudsman, settled the claims of the vast majority of investors. The Secretary of State pursued the appeal by way of subrogation.

DILLON LJ: . . . It is, as I understand it, the view of the Secretary of State that in a case such as this, where so many individual investors contributed their moneys to BCI and its Portfolios 28 and 68 on the same basis, it would be unfair and inequitable if, by the accidents of tracing, a relatively small number of the investors were to be held entitled to the vast bulk of the available assets and moneys, as might result from the application of *Clayton's Case*. It will be necessary in this judgment to consider both the basis and the fairness of tracing in accordance with the rule in *Clayton's Case*, and how far this court is bound by previous decisions of this court to adopt that method of distribution.

The argument put by Mr Walker QC [Counsel for the Secretary of State (early investors)] for the appellant is that instead of tracing or any application of *Clayton's Case* the available assets and moneys should be distributed pari passu among all unpaid investors rateably in proportion to the amounts due to them. This is the basis of distribution which—subject to any application which might be made by any individual depositor or shareholder with a view to tracing his own money into any particular asset—was directed by the House of Lords in *Sinclair* v *Brougham* [1914] AC 398, [1914–15] All ER 622 as between the shareholders in a building society which was being wound up and depositors who had made deposits in an ultra vires banking business which the building society had developed and carried on for many years. It is not in doubt that that basis of distribution ought to be adopted if distribution by tracing in accordance with *Clayton's Case* is not to be preferred.

We were indeed referred in the course of the argument to a third possible basis of distribution, which was called the 'rolling charge' or 'North American' method. This has been preferred by the Canadian and United States courts to tracing in accordance with *Clayton's Case*, as more equitable: see for instance the decision of the Ontario Court of Appeal in *Re Ontario Securities Commission and Greymac Credit Corp* (1986) 55 OR (2d) 673. This method goes on the basis that where funds of several depositors, or sources, have been blended in one account, each debit to the account, unless unequivocally attributable to the moneys of one depositor or source (e.g. as if an investment was purchased for one), should be attributed to all the depositors so as to reduce all their deposits pro rata, instead of being attributed, as under *Clayton's Case*, to the earliest deposits in point of time. The reasoning is that if there is an account which has been fed only with trust moneys deposited by a number of individuals, and the account holder misapplies a sum from the account for his own purposes, and that sum is lost, it is fair that the loss should be borne by all the depositors pro rata, rather than that the whole loss should fall first on the depositor who made the earliest deposit in point of time. The complexities of this method would, however, in a case where there are as many depositors as in the present case and even with the benefits of modern computer technology be so great, and the cost would be so high, that no one has sought to urge the court to adopt it, and I would reject it as impracticable in the present case.

Clayton's Case (1816) 1 Mer 572, [1814–23] All ER Rep 1 was not a case of tracing at all, but a case as to the appropriation of payments. Clayton had been a customer of a banking partnership with an account in credit. One of the partners, Devaynes, had died in 1809 and the remaining partners became bankrupt at the end of July 1810. Clayton had had a running account with the bank before and after the death of Devaynes. The debits and credits made after the death of Devaynes were made without specific appropriation and the account had not been broken on the death of Devaynes. Clayton claimed after the bankruptcy to set his drawings on the account after the death of Devaynes against the credits to the account after the death of Devaynes; consequently he claimed to prove against the estate of Devaynes for the balance to his credit in the account at the death of Devaynes, on the footing that the balance had never been satisfied. Those claims were rejected by Grant MR, who said (1 Mer 572 at 608–609, [1814–23] All ER Rep 1 at 6):

> But this is the case of a banking account, where all the sums paid in form one blended fund, the parts of which have no longer any distinct existence. Neither banker nor customer ever thinks of saying, this draft is to be placed to the account of the £500 paid in on *Monday*, and this other to the account of the £500 paid in on *Tuesday*. There is a fund of £1000 to draw upon, and that is enough. In such a case, there is no room for any other appropriation than that which arises from the order in which the receipts and payments take place, and are carried into the account. Presumably, it is the sum first paid in, that is first drawn out. It is the first item on the debit side of the account, that is discharged, or reduced, by the first item on the credit side. The appropriation is made by the very act of setting the two items against each other. Upon that principle, all accounts current are settled, and

particularly cash accounts. When there has been a continuation of dealings, in what way can it be ascertained whether the specific balance due on a given day has, or has not, been discharged, but by examining whether payments to the amount of that balance appear by the account to have been made? You are not to take the account backwards, and strike the balance at the head, instead of the foot, of it. A man's banker breaks, owing him, on the whole account, a balance of £1000. It would surprise one to hear the customer say, 'I have been fortunate enough to draw out all that I paid in during the last four years; but there is £1000, which I paid in five years ago, that I hold myself never to have drawn out; and, therefore, if I can find any body who was answerable for the debts of the banking-house, such as they stood five years ago, I have a right to say that it is that specific sum which is still due to me, and not the £1000 that I paid in last week.' This is exactly the nature of the present claim.

That rule will apply to the appropriation of payments between any trader and his customer where there is an account current or running account. But it will not apply unless there is a running account—see *per* Lord Halsbury LC in *Cory Bros & Co Ltd* v *Turkish Steamship Mecca (owners), The Mecca* [1897] AC 286 at 290–291, [1895–9] All ER Rep 933 at 935–936—and even in relation to the appropriation of payments it is not, as Lord Halsbury LC said, an invariable rule: '. . . the circumstances of a case may afford ground for inferring that transactions of the parties were not so intended as to come under this general rule . . .'

One case in which it was held that the nature and circumstances of a fund showed that the parties could not have intended *Clayton's Case* to be applied when the surplus in the fund fell to be returned to the subscribers is *Re British Red Cross Balkan Fund, British Red Cross Society* v *Johnson* [1914] 2 Ch 419, [1914–15] All ER Rep 459, a decision of Astbury J. There a fund had been collected by public subscription in 1912 for assisting the sick and wounded in the Balkan war of that time. By 1913 there remained a balance in the fund which was no longer required for the purposes of the fund and it was assumed that the surplus fell to be returned to the subscribers. Astbury J held that *Clayton's Case*, which would involve the attribution of the first payments out of the fund to the earlier contributions to it was not to be applied; he said ([1914] 2 Ch 419 at 421, [1914–15] All ER Rep 459 at 460): '. . . the rule is obviously inapplicable.'

The actual decision is suspect, since the objects of the fund would seem to have been charitable, and if they were charitable then, as the surplus did not come about through a failure of the charitable objects ab initio, the surplus should have been applied cy-près for other charitable purposes. If however for some reason the fund was not devoted to charity, the decision was plainly right. It was followed, in the case of a winding up of a non-charitable fund, by Cohen J in *Re Hobourn Aero Components Ltd's Air-Raid Distress Fund, Ryan* v *Forrest* [1945] 2 All ER 711 at 718, [1946] Ch 86 at 97; Cohen J's decision was affirmed by this court, but the only issue on the appeal was whether or not the fund was charitable (see [1946] 1 All ER 501, [1946] Ch 194).

There are many other cases in the books in which the court has been concerned with the distribution of the surplus on the winding up of a non-charitable benevolent fund and no one has suggested that *Clayton's Case* should be applied.

Mr Walker has accordingly submitted for the appellant in the present case, by what he called his narrower submission, that all investors who contributed to the two portfolios in question in the present case were contributing to common funds to which all investors were to participate and that, by analogy with *Re British Red Cross Balkan*

Fund and *Re Hobourn Aero Components Ltd's Air-Raid Distress Fund, Clayton's Case* should not be applied.

To support that analogy he submits that the true appreciation of the arrangements was that the payment by each investor became, on receipt in a bank account of BCI or its affiliates, part of the uninvested balances of a common or global investment fund in which all investors were to share. The alternative to a common or global investment fund for all investors is a scheme, such as that with which I was concerned at first instance in *Norton Warburg Investment Management Ltd* v *Gibbons* (31 July 1981, unreported), under which each subscriber's contribution was to be invested by the scheme managers in an investment earmarked for that subscriber and held for his account only, but retained under the control of the scheme managers, who had power to sell and reinvest for the subscriber at their discretion. Mr Walker accepts that, if the arrangements in relation to the portfolios were earmarked investments to be acquired for the sole account of each investor as in the *Norton Warburg* case, his analogy to *Re British Red Cross Balkan Fund* would not apply and he would have to fall back on his wider submission, to which I will refer later.

[Dillon LJ then considered the application forms and leaflets relating to Portfolios 28 and 68 and continued: . . .] My conclusion is, however, that what was envisaged was some form of common fund in which all investors would in some way participate. I attach particular importance to the factor of the 'expected' as well as the 'guaranteed' rate of interest, and therefore differ, with all respect, on this point from the conclusion of Peter Gibson J.

It follows, in my judgment, that the gilt-edged investments actually acquired by BCI which are part of the additional assets were lawful investments of investors' moneys as part of a common fund, and not to be allocated, under the arrangements, to individual investors. It would consequently be contrary to the intention of the original arrangements to trace through under *Clayton's Case* the moneys actually applied in the purchase of these gilts so as to allocate them to individual investors. The proceeds of sale of the gilts should be allocated pro rata to all investors, like the moneys to the credit of the bank accounts specified in schedule B to the order of Peter Gibson J.

The question is then, in relation to the balances in the bank accounts specified in schedule A to the judge's order, which were moneys contributed by investors for investment which had not been invested by the time BCI went into liquidation and the receivers were appointed, whether these moneys became part of the common funds as soon as they were received into the bank accounts of BCI from the investors.

There are attractions in the view that if moneys are paid for investment in a common fund of gilt-edged investments they only become part of the common fund when invested in gilts, and are in the meantime held on a resulting trust for the payers. On the other hand the terms of application, in general, expressly authorise the placing of any uninvested funds with any bank etc on such terms as BCI thinks fit, whether bearing interest or not.

What troubles me at this stage on the particular facts of the present case is the contrast between the large amounts held in the accounts specified in schedule A to the judge's order and the much smaller amount of the gilts, above-mentioned, which came into the control of the receivers. There is also the consideration of the very large amounts of investors' moneys which have been lost to the investors without ever having been invested as envisaged in the documents relating to the portfolios. In one sense it is unreal to treat the moneys in the bank accounts in schedule A as the uninvested part of a common investment fund. But the question posed by Lord Halsbury LC in *The Mecca* [1897] AC 286 at 290, [1895–9] All ER Rep 933 at 935 must, I apprehend, be answered by considering the nature of the transaction as the investors intended it to be at the outset when they paid their moneys to BCI, not the very different circumstances of the actual outcome, of which, when they contributed, they knew nothing. Therefore, after considerable hesitation, I conclude that the moneys in the bank accounts in schedule A ought to be treated, for the purposes of distribution, as the uninvested part of the common investment fund.

As for the proceeds of sale of the yacht Boukephalos, on the material before this court the yacht was never an authorised investment for funds paid to BCI for investment in gilt-edged securities, and its purchase was a misapplication of trust moneys. None the less the moneys applied in the purchase of the yacht were part of the common investment fund—for the same reasons as the moneys in the accounts specified in schedule A to the judge's order. Accordingly, the proceeds of the yacht must also be treated as part of the common fund.

I accordingly accept Mr Walker's narrower submission and would hold that *Clayton's Case* is not to be applied in the distribution of the available assets and moneys.

Mr Walker's wider submission is to the effect that, while the rule in *Clayton's Case* is valid and useful, subject to the observations in *The Mecca*, where what is in question is the appropriation of payments as between the parties to a running account, it is illogical and unfair to the earlier contributors to apply the rule as between innocent beneficiaries whose payments to a third party, BCI, have been paid by that third party into a bank account in which, at the end of the day, there are—for whatever reason—not enough moneys left to meet all claims.

Mr Walker submits that it might be more fair to apply the North American method outlined above, but as that is not practicable in the circumstances of this case, the court should fall back on a distribution pari passu between all investors in the proportions of the amounts respectively due to them.

For my part, so far as fairness is concerned, I have difficulty in seeing the fairness to a later investor whose contribution was in all likelihood still included in the uninvested moneys in the schedule A accounts, of holding that all those moneys must be shared pari passu by all investors early or late if there was no common investment fund. In addition of course the order made by the House of Lords in *Sinclair* v *Brougham* [1914] AC 398, [1914–15] All ER Rep 622, on which the order which Mr Walker seeks in the present case is modelled, was expressly subject to any tracing application by any individual depositor or shareholder. If the application of *Clayton's Case* is unfair to early investors pari passu distribution among all seems unfair to late investors.

The views of the law expressed by the English courts on the position where several beneficiaries' moneys have been blended in a single bank account and there is a deficiency are, in my judgment, consistent.

[Dillon LJ discussed the authorities including *In re Hallett's Estate* and *In re Diplock* and concluded: . . .]

None the less the decisions of this court, in my judgment, establish and recognise a general rule of practice that *Clayton's Case* is to be applied when several beneficiaries' moneys have been blended in one bank account and there is a deficiency. It is not, in my judgment, for this court to reject that long-established general practice. A fortiori it is not appropriate to reject it in the present case, when the more logical method, the North American method, which is the basis for criticising the application of *Clayton's Case* is accepted to be impracticable. Therefore I would not accept Mr Walker's wider submission.

However as I would accept his narrower submission I would allow this appeal, and set aside the order of the judge and I would declare that the rule in *Clayton's Case* is not to be applied on the distribution of the moneys in the bank accounts specified in schedules A and B to the judge's order or of the proceeds of sale of the additional assets. Instead these were held on trust for all unpaid investors pari passu rateably in proportion to the amounts due to them. . . .

WOOLF LJ: . . . Mr Walker QC submitted that there are three possible solutions for resolving the competing claims of the investors to the assets which have been recovered. The first solution, which is the one which was adopted by the judge, depends on the rule in *Clayton's Case, Devaynes* v *Noble* (1816) 1 Mer 572, [1814–23] All ER Rep 1. That case was authority for the principle that, when sums are mixed in a bank account as a result of a series of deposits, withdrawals are treated as withdrawing the money in the same order as the money was deposited. It is accepted that normally the rule in *Clayton's Case* has to be applied to govern the respective interests of a banker and his customer in a bank account, but it is submitted by Mr Walker that the rule should not be applied to the different situation which he submits is at the heart of this appeal. Mr Walker contends that in a case of this sort the application of the *Clayton* rule can and would produce results of a highly arbitrary nature. It could enable a particular group of investors to establish an entitlement to a particular asset such as the vessel Boukephalos to the exclusion of other investors just because they invested on one day of the week rather than another. He refers to the dicta of Judge Learned Hand in *Re Walter J. Schmidt & Co., ex parte Feuerbach* (1923) 298 F 314 at 316:

> When the law adopts a fiction, it is, or at least it should be, for some purpose of justice. To adopt [the fiction of first in, first out] is to apportion a common misfortune through a test which has no relation whatever to the justice of the case.

In my judgment this comment of Judge Learned Hand accurately describes the result of applying the rule in *Clayton's Case* to the 'common misfortune' which was shared by the investors in BCI. However it is to be noted that the judge in that case (we are told) later felt compelled by authority to apply the rule. In this case the capricious consequences of applying the rule are underlined by the fact that the dates upon which investments were received by BCI often depended upon agents, such as the fourth and fifth defendants, combining the investments of a number of clients and then forwarding a lump sum to BCI.

In addition to relying upon the arbitrary results which follow from the 'mechanistic' application of the rule Mr Walker relies upon the expense and time which will be involved in having to apply the rule. With the advent of computer technology it cannot be said the task is impossible but it is clearly complex. The costs involved will result in a depletion of the assets available to the investors. In determining the appropriateness of the machinery used for resolving the claims of the investors among themselves, surely this should be a relevant consideration.

The second solution for resolving the claims of the investors among themselves is the rolling charge or North American solution ('North American' because it is the solution adopted or favoured in preference to the rule in *Clayton's Case* in certain decisions of the courts in the United States and Canada because it is regarded as being manifestly fairer). This solution involves treating credits to a bank account made at different times and from different sources as a blend or cocktail with the result that when a withdrawal is made from the account it is treated as a withdrawal in the same proportions as the different interests in the account (here of the investors) bear to each other at the moment before the withdrawal is made. This solution should produce the most just result, but in this case, as counsel accept, it is not a live contender, since while it might just be possible to perform the exercise the costs involved would be out of all proportion even to the sizeable sums which are here involved.

The third solution (and the only other solution canvassed in argument) is the pari passu ex post facto solution. This involves establishing the total quantum of the assets available and sharing them on a proportionate basis among all the investors who could be said to have contributed to the acquisition of those assets, ignoring the dates on which they made their investment. Mr Walker submits this is the solution which is appropriate in this case. It has the virtue of relative simplicity and therefore relative economy and also the virtue of being in this case more just than the first solution. It would have the effect of sharing the pool of assets available proportionately among the thousands of investors in a way which reflected the fact that they were all the victims of a 'common misfortune'.

On the evidence which is available to this court as to the circumstances of this case, I have no doubt that, if, as a matter of principle, this court is in a position to adopt the third solution, then that is the solution which is the most appropriate. It is therefore necessary to turn to the authorities to see whether they prevent this court adopting what I would see as being the correct result. In doing so I bear in mind that Mr Walker advanced two arguments, the wider and narrower argument. The wider argument is that the rule in *Clayton's Case* is concerned with resolving the rights of a banker and his customer to the funds in a bank account and not resolving the conflicting claims of beneficial interests in an account by beneficiaries; so the rule has no application here. The narrower argument is that in the particular circumstances of this case the court is not required to apply the rule.

[Woolf LJ considered the authorities including *Sinclair* v *Brougham*, *In re Hallett's Estate* and *In re Diplock* and continued: . . .]

It was critical to Mr Walker's wider argument that the reasoning of the Court of Appeal in *Re Diplock's Estate* in relation to Dr Barnardo's Home was not binding upon this court. However, I have come to the conclusion that the reasoning is binding. Although Lord Greene MR, in a judgment with which the other members of the court agreed, was able to deal with virtually all of the issues before the court in the passages in his judgment which dealt with the claims 'in personam', without reliance on the rule, what Lord Greene MR said as to the claims in rem, which depended on the application of the rule, was a necessary part of the judgment as it was required to resolve the issue as to interest.

The decision in *Re Diplock's Estate* must be considered together with the other judgments to which I have referred. When this is done, short of the House of Lords, it is settled law that the rule in *Clayton's Case* can be applied to determine the extent to which, as between each other, equally innocent claimants are entitled in equity to moneys which have been paid into a bank account and then subject to the movements within that account. However, it does not, having regard to the passages from the judgments in the other authorities cited, follow that the rule has always to be applied for this purpose. In a number of different circumstances the rule has not been applied. The rule need only be applied when it is convenient to do so and when its application can be said to do broad justice having regard to the nature of the competing claims. *Re Hallett's Estate* shows that the rule is displaced where its application would unjustly assist the trustee to the disadvantage of the beneficiaries. In *Re Diplock's Estate* the rule would have been displaced by the trustee subsequently earmarking the beneficiary's funds. It is not applied if this is the intention or presumed intention of the beneficiaries. The rule is sensibly not applied when the cost of applying it is likely to exhaust the fund available for the beneficiaries.

There are other situations where the rule will not be applied. It was not applied in *Re British Red Cross Balkan Fund , British Red Cross Society* v *Johnson* [1914] 2 Ch 419,

[1914–15] All ER Rep 459. In that case a special fund had been created as a result of subscriptions being collected which were intended to be expended on the sick or wounded in the Balkan war. When the war was over there were no further calls on the fund, which had not been exhausted. The court came to the conclusion that the balance of the fund belonged to the subscribers rateably and the rule did not apply as the subscriptions had been given to the fund en bloc. The approach Astbury J adopted to the rule was one which I would indorse. What he said was ([1914] 2 Ch 419 at 421, [1914–15] All ER Rep 459 at 460):

> It is a mere rule of evidence and not an invariable rule of law, and the circumstances of any particular case may or may not afford ground for inferring that the transactions of the parties were not intended to come under the general rule. In the present case the rule is clearly inapplicable.

I note however that Peter Gibson J did not find this case convincing and regarded it as distinguishable from the present case because in this case he was 'concerned with the operation of a bank account into which investors' moneys, paid to BCI by each investor for his own separate purposes, were paid by BCI'. However, the *British Red Cross Balkan Fund* decision was applied by Cohen J in *Re Hobourn Aero Components Ltd's Air-Raid Distress Fund, Ryan* v *Forrest* [1945] 2 All ER 711, [1946] Ch 86 and while I recognise that the facts of these two cases are quite different from the facts under consideration here, I regard the decisions in the *Balkan* and *Hobourn* cases as relevant because they help to illustrate the range of situations where the courts have already concluded they were not required to apply the rule.

Another case in which the rule was not applied when it could have been was *Re Oatway, Hertslet* v *Oatway* [1903] 2 Ch 356. That action arose out of the administration of the estate of an insolvent solicitor. Shares had been purchased out of an account of the solicitor which held a mixture of clients' and the solicitor's own money. The solicitor purchased an investment in his own name and then dissipated the balance. The representatives of the solicitor were held not able to maintain by the application of the rule that the investment was purchased with the solicitor's money, so that it became his property and not that of the clients. . . .

A theme running through many of the authorities is that the rule is inapplicable because of the presumed intention of the parties to the account in which the moneys were intermingled. Mr Walker submits that a similar intention making the rule inapplicable can be established on the facts of this case. He accepts that the position is not as clear as it would be in situations where the clients were investing in a unit trust (where counsel on both sides agreed the rule would be inapplicable) but none the less he contends that it was clear that this was a situation where there was a collective investment scheme whose participators intended that their money should be mixed together and invested in or through a single pool. The judge did not accept that this was the situation. There were various documents which the investors signed, each of which provided some support for Mr Walker's argument. However, there are other features to which Mr Hart QC [Counsel for the later investors] could draw attention which pointed in the other direction. With some hesitation I have come to the conclusion that, while it is difficult on the documentation to decide whether the investments were to be made subject to a collective investment scheme or not, the better view is that they were. If this interpretation of the documentation is correct, then the fact that the fund held investments which were part of a collective investment scheme would exclude the rule.

However, on the facts of this case I would not apply the rule even if the documents indicated that BCI was under an obligation to create separate funds for each investor.

In default of this obligation, as part of the continuous misapplication of investors' moneys (with the exception of a small quantity of gilts purchased to give verisimilitude to its activities) BCI did not create separate funds but a pool into which the investors' moneys were collected. This pool is a fund into which the investors are entitled to trace. However it is a pool, the creation of which they would not have contemplated. In these circumstances the court has to presume what would have been the intention of the investors had they contemplated the creation of this pool. So far as that intention is concerned I have no doubt that it is correct to presume that the investors would have intended that what could be salvaged, as a result of the 'common misfortune' they had suffered, should be dealt with in accordance with the third solution and not in accordance with the rule. It can be presumed that they would not want to subject what was left of the pool to the vagaries of chance which would follow from the application of the first in, first out principle. I appreciate this means I have taken into account the misconduct of BCI in determining the rights inter se of the investors but I see no reason to ignore what has actually happened to the funds when in the hands of BCI. If BCI purchased other assets from the pool the new assets would be new funds on which the investors would have claims. The rule was not applied in *Re Hallett's Estate* (1880) 13 Ch D 696, [1874–80] All ER Rep 793 and *Re Oatway* [1903] 2 Ch 356 because of the activities of the trustees. Here what excludes the rule therefore is: (a) the pooling of the investments of a vast number of investors by BCI for its own purposes; (b) the fact this would not be contemplated by the investors when they made their investment; (c) the fact that all the moneys invested have been misapplied, at least to some extent, when part of the pool because the withdrawals from the pool continued from the pool after the last investment was credited; and (d) what happened to the investments after they were credited to the pool cannot as a result of investigations which are practical be said to be affected by the date on which they were credited. . . .

For the reasons I have expressed, the approach, in summary, which I would adopt to resolving the issues raised by this appeal are as follows.

(1) While the rule in *Clayton's Case* is prima facie available to determine the interests of investors in a fund into which their investments have been paid, the use of the rule is a matter of convenience and if its application in particular circumstances would be impracticable or result in injustice between the investors it will not be applied if there is a preferable alternative.

(2) Here the rule will not be applied because this would be contrary to either the express or inferred or presumed intention of the investors. If the investments were required by the terms of the investment contract to be paid into a common pool this indicates that the investors did not intend to apply the rule. If the investments were intended to be separately invested, as a result of the investments being collectively misapplied by BCI a common pool of the investments was created. Because of their shared misfortune, the investors will be presumed to have intended the rule not to apply.

(3) As the rule is inapplicable the approach which should be adopted by the court depends on which of the possible alternative solutions is the most satisfactory in the circumstances. If the North American solution is practical this would probably have advantages over the pari passu solution. However, the complications of applying the North American solution in this case make the third solution the most satisfactory.

(4) It must however be remembered that any solution depends on the ability to trace and if the fund had been exhausted (i.e. the account became overdrawn) the investors whose moneys were in the fund prior to the fund being exhausted will not be able to claim against moneys which were subsequently paid into the fund.

Their claims will be limited to following, if this is possible, any of the moneys paid out of the fund into other assets before it was exhausted. . . .

Question

In his concurring judgment in *Barlow Clowes International* v *Vaughan*, Leggatt LJ said 'It seems to me that the rule in *Clayton's case* has nothing to do with tracing and therefore provides no help in the present action'. Do you agree?

Bishopsgate Investment Management Ltd (in liquidation) v *Homan* [1994] 3 WLR 1270 (CA)

Tracing in equity; equitable lien

Robert Maxwell died on 5 November 1991. It was then discovered that large amounts of money had been misdirected from the pension funds of employees of the Maxwell companies, of which the trustee was BIM, into the bank accounts of various companies with which Maxwell was associated. Those accounts were, or subsequently became, overdrawn and the Maxwell companies were hopelessly insolvent. The liquidators of BIM claimed the assets of Maxwell Communication Corp. plc (MCC) were impressed with an equitable charge in favour of the pension fund in priority to the unsecured creditors of MCC, relying upon *Space Investments Ltd* v *Canadian Imperial Bank of Commerce Trust Co. (Bahamas) Ltd* [1986] 1 WLR 1072.

DILLON LJ: . . . As I read the judgment of the Privy Council in *In re Goldcorp Exchange Ltd* delivered by Lord Mustill, it makes it clear that Lord Templeman's observations in the *Space Investments* case [1986] 1 WLR 1072 were not concerned at all with the situation we have in the present case where trust moneys have been paid into an overdrawn bank account, or an account which has become overdrawn. Lord Mustill said in the clearest terms, [1994] 3 WLR 199, 222:

> Their Lordships should, however, say that they find it difficult to understand how the judgment of the Board in *Space Investments Ltd* v *Canadian Imperial Bank of Commerce Trust Co. (Bahamas) Ltd* [1986] 1 WLR 1072, on which the claimants leaned heavily in argument, would enable them to overcome the difficulty that the moneys said to be impressed with the trust were paid into an overdrawn account and thereupon ceased to exist: see, for example, *In re Diplock* [1948] Ch 465. The observations of the Board in the *Space Investments* case were concerned with a mixed, not a non-existent, fund.

Thus the wide interpretation of those observations put forward by Cooke P, which is the basis of the first ground of appeal in the present case, is rejected. Instead the decision of the Court of Appeal in *In re Diplock* [1948] Ch 465 is endorsed. There it was said, at p. 521:

> The equitable remedies presuppose the continued existence of the money either as a separate fund or as part of a mixed fund or as latent in property acquired by means of such a fund. If, on the facts of any individual case, such continued existence is not established, equity is as helpless as the common law itself.

Also endorsed, in my judgment, in the decision of the Board delivered by Lord Mustill is the long-standing first instance decision in *James Roscoe (Bolton) Ltd* v *Winder* [1915] 1 Ch 62, which Mr Heslop for BIM, in his submissions in March, invited us to overrule. That was a decision that, in tracing trust moneys into the bank account of a trustee in accordance with *In re Hallett's Estate* (1880) 13 Ch D 696, tracing was only possible to such an amount of the balance ultimately standing to the credit of the trustee as did not exceed the lowest balance of the account during the intervening period. Thus as is said in the headnote to the report [1915] 1 Ch 62:

> Payments into a general account cannot, without proof of express intention, be appropriated to the replacement of trust money which has been improperly mixed with that account and drawn out.

That reflects the statement by Sargant J in the *James Roscoe* case, at p. 69:

> it is impossible to attribute to him—i.e. the account holder—that by the mere payment into the account of further moneys, which to a large extent he subsequently used for purposes of his own, he intended to clothe those moneys with a trust in favour of the plaintiffs.

Mr Heslop, for BIM, referred, however, to later passages in the opinion of Lord Mustill. First Lord Mustill stated [1994] 3 WLR 199, 227 that the law relating to the creation and tracing of equitable proprietary interests is still in a state of development. He referred to two recent decisions (*Attorney-General for Hong Kong* v *Reid* [1994] AC 324 and *Lord Napier and Ettrick* v *Hunter* [1993] AC 713) on facts not particularly relevant to the present case as instances where equitable proprietary interests have been recognised in circumstances which might previously have been regarded merely as circumstances for common law relief.

Mr Heslop also referred to the fact that the claims of certain claimants in *Re Goldcorp Exchange Ltd* [1994] 3 WLR 199 referred to as 'the Walker & Hall claimants' were rejected without further investigation of the law, on the ground that the Walker & Hall claimants were in no different position from any other claimants, and so it would have been inequitable to impose a lien in favour of the Walker & Hall claimants. Mr Heslop submitted that the beneficiaries under the pension schemes of which BIM is trustee are in a different position from the other creditors, who are mainly banks, of BIM. He did not, of course, adopt the simple populist approach that pensioners, like widows and orphans, are 'goodies' while banks, like usurers, are 'baddies' and so the court should use its powers to ensure that the goodies are paid in full ahead of the baddies. But he did say that the beneficiaries under the pension schemes never undertook the risk that their pension funds would be misappropriated and paid into the overdrawn bank account of an insolvent company, whereas all the banks which lent money to MCC took their chance, as a commercial risk, on MCC's solvency.

Mr Heslop therefore relied on the second ground in the notice of appeal, whereby BIM claims (as it has been explained to us) to be entitled to an equitable charge as security for its claims against MCC (i) over any moneys standing to the credit at the time of the appointment of the administrators of MCC of any banking account maintained by MCC into which any moneys of BIM or the proceeds of any assets of BIM misappropriated from it were paid and (ii) over any assets acquired out of any such bank account, whether or not in credit as at the date such assets were acquired.

So far as (i) is concerned, the point is that the National Westminster Bank account into which the misappropriated BIM trust moneys were paid happened to be in credit when the administrators were appointed. BIM therefore claims a lien on that credit balance in the National Westminster Bank account for the amount of the misappropriated trust moneys. It is difficult to suppose, however, in the circumstances of Robert Maxwell's last days—and I know no evidence—that Robert Maxwell intended to make good the misappropriation of the BIM pension moneys by the cryptic expedient of arranging to put MCC's account with National Westminster Bank into credit—but without repaying the credit balance this created to BIM. But in the absence of clear evidence of intention to make good the depredations on BIM it is not possible to assume that the credit balance has been clothed with a trust in favour of BIM and its beneficiaries: see *James Roscoe (Bolton) Ltd* v *Winder* [1915] 1 Ch 62.

As to (ii), this seems to be going back to the original wide interpretation of what Lord Templeman said in the *Space Investments* case [1986] 1 WLR 1072 and applying it to an overdrawn account because the misappropriated moneys that went into the account were trust moneys and thus different from other moneys that may have gone into that account. But the moneys in the *Space Investments* case were also trust moneys, and so, if argument (ii) is valid in the present case, it would also have been valid, as a matter of law, in the *Space Investments* case. But that was rejected in *In re Goldcorp Exchange Ltd* [1994] 3 WLR 199 because equitable tracing, though devised for the protection of trust moneys misapplied, cannot be pursued through an overdrawn and therefore non-existent fund. Acceptance of argument (ii) would, in my judgment, require the rejection of *In re Diplock* [1948] Ch 465, which is binding on us, and of Lord Mustill's explanation of Lord Templeman's statement in the *Space Investments* case in *In re Goldcorp Exchange Ltd* [1994] 3 WLR 199, 222.

It is not open to us to say that because the moneys were trust moneys the fact that they were paid into an overdrawn account or have otherwise been dissipated presents no difficulty to raising an equitable charge on assets of MCC for their amount in favour of BIM. The difficulty Lord Mustill referred to is not displaced. . . .

LEGGATT LJ: In *Space Investments Ltd* v *Canadian Imperial Bank of Commerce Trust Co. (Bahamas) Ltd* [1986] 1 WLR 1072 the bank trustee made authorised deposits with itself as banker. As it was entitled to do, it used deposited money for its own purposes. On distribution of the assets in winding up of the bank trustee the creditors ranked equally with the other secured creditors. Since no money was misappropriated the comments in the judgment of the Board about the right of beneficiaries following misappropriation to be paid in priority to the customers and other unsecured creditors were obiter dicta. But all that was said related specifically to deposits by a bank trustee with itself. The passage cited from Sir George Jessel MR's judgment in *In re Hallett's Estate* (1880) 13 Ch D 696, 719 took the form of a quotation from Page Wood V-C in *Frith* v *Cartland* (1865) 2 Hem & M 417, 420 in which the second principle (as explained by Jessel MR) was 'that the trust property comes first,' while the first had been, 'If [a trustee] destroys a trust fund by dissipating it altogether there remains nothing to be the subject of the trust.' The corollary of that is, as this court asserted in *In re Diplock* [1948] Ch 465, that it is only possible to trace in equity money which has continued existence, actual or notional. That was why in *James Roscoe (Bolton) Ltd* v *Winder* [1915] 1 Ch 62, where trust funds had been mixed with private moneys in a bank account and the credit balance reduced at one point to £25 18s 0d before being replenished, Sargant J held that the beneficiary's charge extended only to that sum. As Buckley LJ said in *Borden (UK) Ltd* v *Scottish Timber Products Ltd* [1981] Ch 25, 46: 'it is a fundamental feature of the doctrine of tracing that the property to be traced can be identified at every stage of its journey through life. . . .'

For the same reason there can be no equitable remedy against an asset acquired *before* misappropriation of money takes place, since ex hypothesi it cannot be followed into something which existed and so had been acquired before the money was received and therefore without its aid.

The concept of a 'composite transaction' is in my judgment fallacious. What is envisaged is (a) the purchase of an asset by means of an overdraft, that is, a loan from a bank, and (b) the discharge of the loan by means of misappropriated trust money. The judge thought that the money could be regarded as having been used to acquire the asset. His conclusion was that 'It is sufficient to say that proof that trust moneys were paid into an overdrawn account of the defaulting trustee may not always be sufficient to bar a claim to an equitable charge.'

I see the force of Mr Kosmin's submission that, if an asset were used as security for an overdraft which was then discharged by means of misappropriated money, the beneficiary might obtain priority by subrogation. But there can ordinarily be no tracing into an asset which is already in the hands of the defaulting trustee when the misappropriation occurs.

In *Liggett* v *Kensington* [1993] 1 NZLR 257 Cooke P applied the principle which he derived from the *Space Investments* case [1986] 1 WLR 1072 that those who do not take a risk of insolvency are entitled to an equitable charge over all the assets of the trustee, giving them priority over those who are to be regarded as having taken such a risk. That decision is authority for no wider proposition than that, where a bank trustee wrongly deposits money with itself, the trustee can trace into all the bank's credit balances.

Consistently with Mr Kosmin's submissions on this appeal, Lord Mustill, delivering the judgment of the Board in *Re Goldcorp Exchange Ltd* [1994] 3 WLR 199, 222f, stated that their Lordships found it difficult to understand how it would enable the claimants in that case to 'overcome the difficulty that the moneys said to be impressed with the trust were paid into an overdrawn account and thereupon ceased to exist.' Lord Mustill emphasised that the observations of the Board were concerned with a mixed, not a non-existent, fund. He also cited with approval *James Roscoe (Bolton) Ltd* v *Winder* [1915] 1 Ch 62 as conventionally exemplifying the principles of tracing.

I therefore consider that the judge came to the right conclusion, though I do not accept that it is possible to trace through an overdrawn bank account or to trace misappropriated money into an asset bought before the money was received by the purchaser. I agree that the appeal should be dismissed.

Notes

1. The case is noted in [1995] LMCLQ 446 (Gullifer).

2. The *Space Investments* case and *Re Goldcorp Exchange Ltd* [1995] 1 AC 74 are discussed below in Section 3.

Section 3: proprietary remedies

A plaintiff seeking a restitutionary proprietary remedy usually has one of two motives. Either he wishes to be a secured creditor because the defendant is insolvent, or an application of the tracing rules yields an asset which has appreciated in value. There is little judicial authority on the latter. Practically the former question is the important one. Traditionally courts have sympathised with the restitutionary plaintiff, who is often treated as being an involuntary creditor who never assumed the risk of the defendant's insolvency. The assumptions behind this approach have been criticised.

It now seems established that restitutionary proprietary remedies are not confined to subtractive unjust enrichment, but can be awarded in the category of restitution for wrongs (*Attorney-General for Hong Kong* v *Reid* [1994] 1 AC 324). A recent trilogy of appellate authorities (*Lord Napier and Ettrick* v *Hunter* [1993] AC 713; *Attorney-General for Hong Kong* v *Reid*; and *Re Goldcorp Exchange Ltd* [1995] 1 AC 74) suggest that the courts are increasingly ready to award *in rem* remedies. The most recent instalment is the most cautious and suggests that rationalisation of the underlying principles and policies, and critical analysis of the concepts of 'swollen assets' and 'risk' are required.

See Goff and Jones, 93–102 for a clear discussion and some radical conclusions; see also Burrows, *Restitution*, 35–45 and 362–75 and Birks, *Introduction*, 375–94.

Lister & Co. v *Stubbs*
(1890) 45 Ch D 1 (CA)

Lister & Co. were silk-spinners, dyers and manufacturers in Bradford. Stubbs was their foreman dyer responsible for purchasing the raw materials for dyeing. It was alleged that over a ten-year period he had received some £5,541 in secret commissions from Varley & Co., a drysalters in Leeds, the figure being based upon the quantity of goods bought by Lister. It was further alleged that some of the money had been invested by Stubbs in land in Yorkshire and other investments. Lister & Co. brought an action seeking to follow the secret profits into the investments. They sought an interlocutory injunction seeking to restrain Stubbs from dealing with those assets.

COTTON LJ: The case here is this: The Defendant, being in the confidential employment of the Plaintiffs, made a corrupt bargain with persons who supplied the partnership with dye stuffs. The bargain was most manifestly corrupt; but does that make the money which the Defendant received in pursuance of that bargain the money of the Plaintiffs? Mr Justice Stirling, in the course of his judgment, referred to my decision in the case of *Metropolitan Bank* v *Heiron* 5 Ex D 319. I think that I took a correct view in my judgment in that case; and in my opinion this is not the money of the Plaintiffs, so as to make the Defendant a trustee of it for them, but it is money acquired in such a way that, according to all rules applicable to such a case, the Plaintiffs, when they bring the action to a hearing, can get an order against the Defendant for the payment of that money to them. That is to say, there is a debt due from the Defendant to the Plaintiffs in consequence of the corrupt bargain which he entered into; but the money which he has received under that bargain cannot, in the view which I take, be treated as being money of the Plaintiffs, which was handed by them to the Defendant to be paid to Messrs Varley in discharge of a debt due from the Plaintiffs to Messrs Varley on the contract between them.

When the facts are ascertained, the Plaintiffs will have the opportunity of setting aside the contract altogether and returning the stuffs, or, without setting aside the contract, of suing Messrs Varley for the money which they have fraudulently handed over to the Defendant. But in my opinion the moneys which under this corrupt bargain were paid by Messrs Varley to the Defendant cannot be said to be the money of the Plaintiffs before any judgment or decree in some such action has been made. I know of no case where, because it was highly probable that if the action were brought to a hearing the plaintiff could establish that a debt was due to him from the defendant, the defendant has been ordered to give security until that has been established by the judgment or decree. The plaintiff, if so advised, might apply for an immediate order under Order XIV, and then, if the defendant applied to defend, he could only do so on such terms as the Judge might think reasonable. But in the present case that course has not been taken. In my opinion, however corrupt the bargain was, we cannot hold that, under the circumstances of this case, the money was the money of the Plaintiffs. . . .

LINDLEY LJ: If we were to accede to this application, I do not think that Stubbs could complain; but the question is, whether, having regard to the rules by which we are governed, we can properly make the order. I am clearly of opinion that we cannot. The real state of the case as between Lister & Co. and Messrs Varley and Stubbs is this: Lister & Co., through their agent Stubbs, buy goods of Messrs Varley at certain prices, and pay for them. The ownership of the goods of course is in Lister & Co.; the ownership of the money is in Messrs Varley. Then Messrs Varley have entered into an arrangement with Stubbs, who ordered the goods of them, to give Stubbs a commission. That is what it comes to. What is the legal position between Messrs Varley and Stubbs? They owe him the money. He can recover it from them by an action, unless the illegality of the transaction afford them a defence; but the Appellants have asked us to go further, and to say that Messrs Varley were Stubbs' agents in getting his commission from Lister & Co. That appears to me to be an entire mistake. The relation between Messrs Varley and Stubbs is that of debtor and creditor—they pay him. Then comes the question, as between Lister & Co. and Stubbs, whether Stubbs can keep the money he has received without accounting for it? Obviously not. I apprehend that he is liable to account for it the moment that he gets it. It is an obligation to pay and account to Messrs Lister & Co., with or without interest, as the case may be. I say nothing at all about that. But the relation between them is that of debtor and creditor; it is not that of trustee and *cestui que trust*. We are asked to hold that it is—which would involve consequences which, I confess, startle me. One consequence, of course, would be that, if Stubbs were to become bankrupt, this property acquired by him with the money paid to him by Messrs Varley would be withdrawn from the mass of his creditors and be handed over bodily to Lister & Co. Can that be right? Another consequence would be that, if the Appellants are right, Lister & Co. could compel Stubbs to account to them, not only for the money with interest, but for all the profits which he might have made by embarking in trade with it. Can that be right? It appears to me that those consequences shew that there is some flaw in the argument. If by logical reasoning from the premises conclusions are arrived at which are opposed to good sense, it is necessary to go back and look again at the premises and see if they are sound. I am satisfied that they are not sound—the unsoundness consisting in confounding ownership with obligation. It appears to me that the view taken of this case by Mr Justice Stirling was correct, and that we should be doing what I conceive to be very great mischief if we were to stretch a sound principle to the extent to which the Appellants ask us to stretch it, tempting as it is to do so as between the Plaintiffs and Stubbs. I think that the appeal ought to be dismissed.

Notes

1. For a powerful defence of this controversial ruling see Goode, 'Ownership and Obligation in Commercial Transactions' (1987) 103 LQR 433, at

441–5; also in support is Birks, *Introduction*, 387–9. For criticism of the decision as anomalous see Goff and Jones, 668–9 and Sir Peter Millett, 'Bribes and Secret Commissions' [1993] *Restitution Law Review* 7. For discussion see Burrows, *Restitution*, 410–13. The debate has been resolved by the Privy Council in *Attorney-General for Hong Kong* v *Reid* [1994] 1 AC 324, which disapproved of *Lister* v *Stubbs*. See below.

2. Even before the resolution of the substantive point in *Reid*, *Lister* v *Stubbs* had already been overturned on the procedural point by the development of asset-freezing injunctions, starting with the Court of Appeal decision in *Mareva Compañia Naviera SA* v *International Bulkcarriers SA* (1975) [1980] 1 All ER 213 (CA). *Mareva* injunctions prevent a defendant disposing of assets before judgment, even where the claim is a personal one. This development now has statutory backing in s. 37(3) of the Supreme Court Act 1981. For discussion see Sime, *A Practical Approach to Civil Procedure*, 2nd ed. (London: Blackstone Press Ltd, 1995), 203–18.

Chase Manhattan Bank NA v *Israel-British Bank (London) Ltd* (1979) [1981] Ch 105 (Ch D)

Tracing in equity; constructive trust

Chase, a New York bank, acting upon instructions paid US$2,000,687.50 to another New York bank, via the New York clearing house system, for the defendant's account. Later the same day a second identical payment was made due to a clerical error on the part of an employee of Chase. The defendant, another bank based in London, discovered the mistake two days later. Subsequently the defendant company was wound up and was found to be insolvent.

GOULDING J: . . . The plaintiff's claim, viewed in the first place without reference to *any* system of positive law, raises problems to which the answers, if not always difficult, are at any rate not obvious. If one party P pays money to another party D by reason of a factual mistake, either common to both parties or made by P alone, few conscientious persons would doubt that D ought to return it. But suppose that D is, or becomes, insolvent before repayment is made, so that P comes into competition with D's general creditors, what then? If the money can still be traced, either in its original form or through successive conversions, and is found among D's remaining assets, ought not P to be able to claim it, or what represents it, as his own? If he ought, and if in a particular case the money has been blended with other assets and is represented by a mixed fund, no longer as valuable as the sum total of its original constituents, what priorities or equalities should govern the distribution of the mixed fund? If the money can no longer be traced, either separate or in mixture, should P have any priority over ordinary creditors of D? In any of these cases, does it make any difference whether the mistake was inevitable, or was caused by P's carelessness, or was contributed to by some fault, short of dishonesty, on the part of D?

At this stage I am asked to take only one step forward, and to answer the initial question of principle, whether the plaintiff is entitled in equity to trace the mistaken payment and to recover what now properly represents the money. The subsequent history of the payment and the rules for ascertaining what now represents it have not been proved or debated before me. They will have to be established in further proceedings if the plaintiff can clear the first hurdle today.

This initial question in the action appears not to be the subject of reported judicial decision in England. . . .

The facts and decisions in *Sinclair* v *Brougham* [1914] AC 398 and in *In re Diplock* [1948] Ch 465 are well known and I shall not take time to recite them. I summarise my view of the *Diplock* judgment as follows: (1) The Court of Appeal's interpretation of *Sinclair* v *Brougham* was an essential part of their decision and is binding on me. (2) The court thought that the majority of the House of Lords in *Sinclair* v *Brougham* had not accepted Lord Dunedin's opinion in that case, and themselves rejected it. (3) The court held that an initial fiduciary relationship is a necessary foundation of the equitable right of tracing. (4) They also held that the relationship between the building society directors and depositors in *Sinclair* v *Brougham* was a sufficient fiduciary relationship for the purpose: [1948] Ch 465, 529, 540. The latter passage reads, at p. 540: 'A sufficient fiduciary relationship was found to exist between the depositors and the directors by reason of the fact that the purposes for which the depositors had handed their money to the directors were by law incapable of fulfilment.' It is founded, I think, on the observations of Lord Parker of Waddington at [1914] AC 398, 441.

This fourth point shows that the fund to be traced need not (as was the case in *In re Diplock* itself) have been the subject of fiduciary obligations before it got into the wrong hands. It is enough that, as in *Sinclair* v *Brougham* [1914] AC 398, the payment into wrong hands itself gave rise to a fiduciary relationship. The same point also throws considerable doubt on Mr Stubbs's submission that the necessary fiduciary relationship must originate in a consensual transaction. It was not the intention of the depositors or of the directors in *Sinclair* v *Brougham* to create any relationship at all between the depositors and the directors as principals. Their object, which unfortunately disregarded the statutory limitations of the building society's powers, was to establish contractual relationships between the depositors and the society. In the circumstances, however, the depositors retained an equitable property in the funds they parted with, and fiduciary relationships arose between them and the directors. In the same way, I would suppose, a person who pays money to another under a factual mistake retains an equitable property in it and the conscience of that other is subjected to a fiduciary duty to respect his proprietary right. . . .

Thus, in the belief that the point is not expressly covered by English authority and that *In re Diplock* does not conclude it by necessary implication, I hold that the equitable remedy of tracing is in principle available, on the ground of continuing proprietary interest, to a party who has paid money under a mistake of fact. . . .

In an alternative submission, likewise going to the root of the plaintiff's claim, Mr Stubbs argued that, by not pleading and proving in greater detail the operations of the clearing house inter-bank payment system (known as CHIPS for short) in New York, the plaintiff had failed to identify any chose in action or other particular subject of property to which the plaintiff's alleged equitable interest could attach and from which tracing could begin. I cannot accept that contention. A payment and a mistake are alleged in terms by paragraph 2 of the re-amended statement of claim and plainly admitted by paragraph 2 of the re-amended defence; and when equitable rights are in question, the court does not encourage fine distinctions founded on the technicalities of financial machinery. . . .

Note

Goulding J made a declaration that the defendant was a trustee for the plaintiff for the sum of the second payment and ordered an inquiry as to what had become of that sum, and as to whether any of the assets of the defendant now represented that money.

Question
How was the requirement of a fiduciary relationship met in this case?

Note
See also *Westdeusche Landesbank Girozentrale* v *Islington London Borough Council* [1994] 4 All ER 890, [1994] 1 WLR 138 discussed in Chapter 5, Section 2.

Space Investments Ltd v *Canadian Imperial Bank of Commerce Trust Co. (Bahamas) Ltd*
[1986] 1 WLR 1072 (PC)

Equitable lien

LORD TEMPLEMAN (*obiter dicta*): The question is whether in the winding up of an insolvent bank trustee the liquidator must pay the trust deposit accounts lawfully maintained by the bank trustee in priority to payment of the customers' deposit accounts and the debts owed by the trustee bank to other unsecured creditors.

A customer who deposits money with a bank authorises the bank to use that money for the benefit of the bank in any manner the bank pleases. The customer does not acquire any interest in or charge over any asset of the bank or over all the assets of the bank. The deposit account is an acknowledgement and record by the bank of the amount from time to time deposited and withdrawn and of the interest earned. The customer acquires a chose in action, namely the right on request to payment by the bank of the whole or any part of the aggregate amount of principal and interest which has been credited or ought to be credited to the account. If the bank becomes insolvent the customer can only prove in the liquidation of the bank as unsecured creditor for the amount which was, or ought to have been, credited to the account at the date when the bank went into liquidation.

On the other hand a trustee has no power to use trust money for his own benefit unless the trust instrument expressly authorises him so to do. A bank trustee, like any other trustee, may only apply trust money in the manner authorised by the trust instrument, or by law, for the sole benefit of the beneficiaries and to the exclusion of any benefit to the bank trustee unless the trust instrument otherwise provides. A bank trustee misappropriating trust money for its own use and benefit without authority commits a breach of trust and cannot justify that breach of trust by maintaining a trust deposit account which records the amount which the bank has misappropriated and credits interest which the bank considers appropriate. The beneficiaries have a chose in action, namely, an action against the trustee bank for damages for breach of trust and in addition they possess the equitable remedy of tracing the trust money to any property into which it has been converted directly or indirectly.

A bank in fact uses all deposit moneys for the general purposes of the bank. Whether a bank trustee lawfully receives deposits or wrongly treats trust money as on deposit from trusts, all the moneys are in fact dealt with and expended by the bank for the general purposes of the bank. In these circumstances it is impossible for the beneficiaries interested in trust money misappropriated from their trust to trace their money to any particular asset belonging to the trustee bank. But equity allows the beneficiaries, or a new trustee appointed in place of an insolvent bank trustee to protect the interests of the beneficiaries, to trace the trust money to all the assets of the bank and to recover the trust money by the exercise of an equitable charge over all the assets of the bank. Where an insolvent bank goes into liquidation that equitable charge secures for the beneficiaries and the trust priority over the claims of the customers in respect of their deposits and over the claims of all other unsecured creditors. This priority is conferred because the customers and other unsecured creditors voluntarily accept the risk that the trustee bank might become insolvent and unable to discharge its obligations in full. On the other hand, the settlor of the trust and the beneficiaries interested under the trust, never accept any risks involved in the possible insolvency of the trustee bank. On the contrary, the settlor could be certain that if the trusts were lawfully administered, the trustee bank could never make use of trust money for its own purposes and would always be obliged to segregate trust money and trust property in the manner authorised by law and by the trust instrument free from any risks involved in the possible insolvency of the trustee bank. It is therefore equitable that where the trustee bank has unlawfully misappropriated trust money by treating the trust money as though it belonged to the bank beneficially, merely acknowledging and recording the amount in a trust deposit account with the bank, then the claims of the beneficiaries should be paid in full out of the assets of the trustee bank in priority to the claims of the customers and other unsecured creditors of the bank. 'If a man mixes trust funds with his own, the whole will be treated as the trust property, . . . that is, that the trust property comes first; . . .' *per* Sir George Jessel MR in *In re Hallett's Estate* (1880) 13 Ch D 696, 719, adopting and explaining earlier pronouncements to the same effect. Where a bank trustee is insolvent, trust money wrongfully treated as being on deposit with the bank must be repaid in full so far as may be out of the assets of the bank in priority to any payment of customers' deposits and other unsecured debts. . . .

Lord Napier and Ettrick v *Hunter*
[1993] AC 713 (HL)

Subrogation; equitable lien

Two hundred and forty-six members ('names') of the Outhwaite Syndicate 317/661 at the Lloyd's of London insurance market suffered massive losses because the managing agent of the syndicate negligently wrote large numbers of policies on their behalf in respect of asbestosis claims, without adequate reinsurance cover. The names had in turn insured their losses with stop-loss insurers, who agreed to insure a slice of the names' losses in excess of a certain amount, up to a fixed limit. The stop-loss insurers paid the names in respect of the insured losses. Subsequently the names reached a settlement with the managing agents, and a fund representing the settlement moneys was held by Richards Butler, the names' solicitors. It was held that a large proportion of this fund was due to the stop-loss insurers by right of subrogation, as they had already indemnified the names against a large proportion of their loss under the stop-loss policies. The extracts deal with the question whether the stop-loss insurers had merely a personal claim against the names, or a proprietary interest in the fund.

LORD TEMPLEMAN: My Lords, when an insured person suffers a loss he will be entitled to the insurance money and may also be entitled to sue for damages anyone responsible for the loss. For example, if a house is insured for £100,000 against fire and is damaged by fire to an extent exceeding £100,000, the insurance company will pay £100,000. If the fire has been caused by a negligent builder or some other contractual or tortious wrongdoer, the insured person will sue the wrongdoer for damages. If the house has been damaged to the extent of £160,000, the insured person will receive damages from the wrongdoer of £160,000. At that stage the insured person will have made a profit since he will have only suffered a loss of £160,000 but will have collected a total of £260,000 from the insurance company and the wrongdoer. A policy of insurance is however a contract of indemnity and by the doctrine of subrogation the insured person must pay back to the insurer the sum of £100,000. The insured person will then have made neither a loss nor a profit. This appeal requires consideration of the principles and application of the doctrine of subrogation.

[Lord Templeman considered the question of the extent of the stop-loss insurers' right to subrogation and continued: . . .]

In the hypothetical case under consideration, the intervention of equity is required to ensure that the insured person exercises his right of action against the wrongdoer in good faith and that the insurer is recouped out of the damages recovered from the wrongdoer. The stop loss insurer is out of pocket to the amount of £100,000 from the time that he pays, as he must pay, £100,000 to the name immediately the loss has been suffered. The stop loss insurer is entitled to be recouped £95,000 as soon as the damages of £130,000 are available from the wrongdoer. The name cannot delay or frustrate recoupment without inflicting harm on the insurer who remains out of pocket to the extent of £100,000 until he is recouped. The name cannot make use of the damages payable by the wrongdoer and available for recoupment of the stop loss insurers without the name receiving a benefit or advantage to which he is not entitled. When I asked why the names were defending these present proceedings, your Lordships were blandly informed that the names wished to benefit their 'cash flow' by making use of all the damages payable by Outhwaite and deferring recoupment until each stop loss insurer was able to obtain a judgment against each name for money had and received. The stop loss insurers were not in a position to sue the name to whom they had paid £100,000 until the action against Outhwaite resulted in judgment or compromise which included £130,000 for the insured loss and the damages of £130,000 had been paid to the name; they were even then not in a position to sue the name until the amount which the stop loss insurers were entitled to recoup under the doctrine of subrogation had been ascertained and calculated. There are 246 names, some of whom are resident in the United States of America and elsewhere abroad. In order to succeed in an action for money had and received stop loss insurers might be obliged to pursue litigation at considerable expense and subject to considerable delay in a country which knows nothing of an action for money had and received or does not recognise the doctrine of subrogation or confines its civil litigation to the tender mercies of juries who are unsympathetic towards insurers. By the time that the stop loss insurers ascertain that they are entitled to be repaid the sum of £95,000 and no more and no less under the doctrine of subrogation and bring and succeed in a claim against the hypothetical name to be paid £95,000, whether judgment for that sum be obtained at home or abroad, the name, having had and received £100,000 from the stop loss insurers, may not be in a position to pay back £95,000. . . .

If the stop loss insurers have no equitable remedy in connection with their rights and if a name becomes bankrupt then subrogation is a mockery. Suppose, for example, that a name receives £100,000 from an insurer under a policy, recovers judgment for £130,000 damages from the wrongdoer and the name goes bankrupt before he receives the damages owing £1m. and possessing no assets other than assets representing the £100,000 he has received from the insurer and the asset of £130,000 payable by the wrongdoer. In that case, if the argument on behalf of the names is correct, the unsecured creditors of the insured name will benefit by double payment. The stop loss insurers will be in a worse position than an unsecured creditor because the insurers could not resist payment under the policy whereas an unsecured creditor may choose whether to advance moneys or not. In the case of the bankruptcy of the name, the right of the insurer to subrogation will be useless unless equity protects that right.

. . . The principles which dictated the decisions of our ancestors and inspired their references to the equitable obligations of an insured person towards an insurer entitled to subrogation are discernible and immutable. They establish that such an insurer has an enforceable equitable interest in the damages payable by the wrongdoer. The insured person is guilty of unconscionable conduct if he does not provide for the insurer to be recouped out of the damages awarded against the wrongdoer. Equity will not allow the insured person to insist on his legal rights to all the damages awarded against the wrongdoer and will restrain the insured person from receiving or dealing with those damages so far as they are required to recoup the insurer under the doctrine of subrogation.

Where the insured person has been paid policy moneys by the insurer for a loss in respect of which the insured person recovers damages from a wrongdoer the insured person is guilty of unconscionable conduct if he does not procure and direct that the sum due to the insurer shall by way of subrogation be paid out of the damages.

It is next necessary to consider how equity copes with such unconscionable conduct. Saville J. and the Court of Appeal appear to have thought that equity can only interfere by creating a trust fund held in trust by trustees for different beneficiaries in different shares, the trustees being burdened with administrative and investment duties, the trustees being liable for all the duties imposed on trustees but being free from liability if the trust fund is lost without negligence. I agree that if this were the only method of protecting the rights of an insurer the practical disadvantages would be fearsome. Fortunately, equity is not so inflexible or powerless. In order to protect the rights of the insurer under the doctrine of subrogation equity considers that the damages payable by the wrongdoer to the insured person are subject to an equitable lien or charge in favour of the insurer. The charge is imposed by equity because the insurer, once he has paid under the policy, has an interest in the right of action against the wrongdoer and an interest in the establishment, quantification, recovery and distribution of the damages awarded against the wrongdoer. It would be unconscionable for the insured person, who has received £100,000 from the insurer, to put damages of £130,000 into his own pocket without providing for the recoupment of the insurer who only contracted to indemnify the insured person.

The insurer can give notice to the wrongdoer of his equitable charge. When the wrongdoer is ordered or agrees to pay £130,000 and has notice of the rights of the insurer to subrogation, the wrongdoer can either pay the damages into court or decline to pay without the consent of both the insured person and the insurer. It would be the duty of the insured person to direct the wrongdoer to pay £95,000 of the damages to the insurer in recoupment and to pay the balance of £35,000 to himself. The equitable charge in favour of the insurer is enforceable against the damages ordered to be paid; that charge can be enforced so long as the damages form an identifiable separate fund. If, in the present case, Richards Butler had distributed the damages to the names before the stop loss insurers issued proceedings or notified Richards Butler of their equitable charge, the stop loss insurers would have been reduced to exercising their rights to sue the names for money had and received.

In the present case damages of £116m. are in a separate fund held by Richards Butler on behalf of the names albeit that the damages in the fund also include moneys held on behalf of other names and other insurers. For the reasons I have indicated it would be unconscionable for the names to take their shares of the damages without providing for the sums due to the stop loss insurers to be paid out of those damages. The equitable charge still affects the damages and affects Richards Butler who hold the damages with notice of the charge. . . .

Since drafting this speech I have read in draft the speech to be delivered by my noble and learned friend, Lord Goff of Chieveley. He agrees that the doctrine of subrogation confers on the insurer an equitable proprietary lien or charge on the moneys recovered by the insured person from a third party in respect of the insured loss. I agree that in the circumstances it is not now necessary to decide whether the equitable lien or charge attaches also to the rights of action vested in the insured person to recover from a third party. I have expressed the view that the doctrine of subrogation does apply in those circumstances but in any future case, if the point becomes material that view may require reconsideration in the light of further research. . . .

LORD GOFF OF CHIEVELEY: . . . I agree with my noble and learned friend, Lord Browne-Wilkinson, that the decisive case in the line of equity cases is *White* v *Dobinson*, 14 Sim 273; 116 LTOS 233. The case was concerned with a collision at sea. The owner of one of the ships, after payment by his underwriter of £205, was awarded £600 damages in arbitration proceedings against the other shipowner. Sir Lancelot Shadwell V-C, relying upon *Randal* v *Cockran* (1748) 1 Ves Sen 98 and *Blaauwpot* v *Da Costa*, 1 Ed 130, granted an interlocutory injunction which had the effect of retaining the fund, and not letting it pass into the hands of the assured. The injunction appears to have restrained both the assured from receiving, and the other shipowner from paying, the money without first paying or providing for the sum of £205 paid by the insurer: see the report at 116 LTOS 233. Lord Lyndhurst LC discharged the injunction as against the other shipowner, but otherwise maintained it in force. The case is important for a number of reasons. First, the insurer's case was advanced on the basis that he had a lien on the sum awarded, and was resisted on the ground that the insurer's right, if it existed at all, was a right to proceed at law in an action for money had and received, and was not an equitable right. That argument was rejected. Second, the Lord Chancellor also rejected a claim by a bank as assignee from the assured, on the ground that the bank's security was taken subject to all the equities which would have affected the money received in the hands of the assured himself. Third, the Lord Chancellor held that the insurers had a claim upon the fund awarded, and were 'entitled in some shape or other to recover back the money they have paid.'

Now it is true that the case was concerned with an interlocutory injunction, a point which evidently concerned the Lord Chancellor himself. But he nevertheless upheld the injunction on the basis of the authority cited to him, in which, as he said:

> we have the clearly expressed opinions of Lord Hardwicke and Lord Northington, recognised by Parke B, and more recently by Lord Abinger CB (*Brooks* v *MacDonnell* (1835) 1 Y & C 500), who at that time possessed considerable experience of the practice in equity, from having presided for several years on the equity side of the Court of Exchequer . . .

Subsequent authorities to the same effect are *King* v *Victoria Insurance Co. Ltd* [1896] AC 250, 255–6, *per* Lord Hobhouse who (in a passage in which he appears to have placed no reliance upon the existence of an assignment by the assured of its rights and causes of action against the third party) expressed the opinion that the assured would have held any damages recovered from the third party as trustee for the insurer; and *In re Miller, Gibb & Co. Ltd* [1957] 1 WLR 703. The only case in equity which appears at first sight to be inconsistent with this line of authority is *Stearns* v *Village Main Reef Gold Mining Co. Ltd*, 10 Com Cas 89. However, as my noble and learned friend, Lord Browne-Wilkinson, has pointed out, that case was concerned with the recovery of an overpayment; indeed, it was upon that basis that it was distinguished by Wynn-Parry J, in *In re Miller, Gibb & Co. Ltd* [1957] 1 WLR 703, 710–11.

Despite Saville J's reservations on this point, I can discern no inconsistency between the equitable proprietary right recognised by courts of equity in these cases and the personal rights and obligations embodied in the contract of insurance itself. No doubt our task nowadays is to see the two strands of authority, at law and in equity, moulded into a coherent whole; but for my part I cannot see why this amalgamation should lead to the rejection of the equitable proprietary right recognised in the line of cases to which I have referred. Of course, it is proper to start with the contract of insurance, and to see how the common law courts have worked out the mutual rights and obligations of the parties in contractual terms with recourse to implied terms where appropriate. But, with all respect, I am unable to agree with Lord Diplock that subrogation is in this context concerned *solely* with the mutual rights and obligations of the parties under the contract. In this connection, I observe from the report of *Yorkshire Insurance Co. Ltd* v *Nisbet Shipping Co. Ltd* [1962] 2 QB 330 that the important case of *White* v *Dobinson*, 14 Sim 273; 116 LTOS 233 was not cited in argument, and indeed the existence of an equitable proprietary right was not in issue in that case. In these circumstances I cannot derive from Lord Diplock's judgment any justification for sweeping the line of equity cases under the carpet as though it did not exist. In my opinion, this line of authority must be recognised, and appropriate weight should be given to the views expressed in the cases by the distinguished judges who decided them. I wish to add that I do not read section 79 of the Marine Insurance Act 1906 (concerned with the right of subrogation) as in any way detracting from this conclusion.

Even so, an important feature of these cases is that the principle of subrogation in the law of insurance arises in a contractual context. It is true that in some cases at common law it has been described as arising as a matter of equity. Thus in *Burnand* v *Rodocanachi Sons & Co.*, 7 App Cas 333, 339, Lord Blackburn described it simply as 'an equity.' Furthermore, it has not been usual to express the principle of subrogation as arising from an implied term in the contract. Even so it has been regarded, both at law and in equity, as giving effect to the underlying nature of a contract of insurance, which is that it is intended to provide an indemnity but no more than an indemnity. Not only does this principle inform the judgments of the Court of Appeal in the leading case of *Castellain* v *Preston*, 11 QBD 380, but it underlies Lord Lyndhurst LC's judgment in *White* v *Dobbinson*, 116 LTOS 233. In so far as the principle requires the payment of money, it could no doubt be formulated as an implied term, to which effect could have been given by the old action for money had and received. But I do not see why the mere fact that the purpose of subrogation in this context is to give effect to the principle of indemnity embodied in the contract should preclude recognition of the equitable proprietary right, if justice so requires. If I search for a parallel, the closest analogy is perhaps to be found in the law of agency in which, although the relationship between principal and agent is governed by a contract, nevertheless the agent may be held in certain circumstances to hold money, which he has received from a third party in his capacity as agent, as trustee for his principal. It is by no means easy to ascertain the circumstances in which a trusteeship exists; but, in a valuable discussion in *Bowstead on Agency*, 15th ed. (1985), pp. 162–3. Professor Francis Reynolds suggests that it is right to inquire

> whether the trust relationship is appropriate to the commercial relationship in which the parties find themselves; whether it was appropriate that money or property should be, and whether it was, held separately, or whether it was contemplated that the agent should use the money, property or proceeds of the property as part of his normal cash flow in such a way that the relationship of debtor and creditor is more appropriate.

He also suggests that

> a central question, perhaps too often overlooked (because not directly an issue), is whether the rights of the principal are sufficiently strong, and differentiable from other claims, for him to be entitled to a prior position in respect of them on the agent's bankruptcy.

I have little doubt that the distinguished judges who decided the cases in the line of equity authority to which I have referred must have considered that money received by an assured from a third party in reduction of a loss paid by an insurer should not be treated as avalilable for the assured's normal cash flow, and further that the rights of the insurer to such money were sufficiently strong to entitle the insurer to priority in the event of the assured's bankruptcy, as was indeed held by Wynn-Parry J in *In re Miller, Gibb & Co. Ltd* [1957] 1 WLR 703. I for my part can see no good reason to depart from this line of authority. However, since the constitution of the assured as trustee of such money may impose upon him obligations of too onerous a character (a point which troubled Saville J in the present case), I am very content that the equitable proprietary right of the insurer should be classified as a lien, as proposed by my noble and learned friend, Lord Templeman, and indeed as claimed by the insurer in *White* v *Dobinson*, 14 Sim 273 itself. Indeed a lien is the more appropriate form of proprietary right in circumstances where, as here, its function is to protect the interest of the insurer in an asset only to the extent that its retention by the assured will have the effect that he is more than indemnified under the policy of insurance.

There is one particular problem to which I wish to refer, although, as I understand it, it does not fall to be decided in the present case. Does the equitable proprietary interest of the insurer attach only to a fund consisting of sums which come into the hands of the assured in reduction of the loss paid by the insurer? Or does it attach also to a right of action vested in the assured which, if enforced, would yield such a fund? The point is not altogether easy. I can see no reason in principle why such an interest should not be capable of attaching to property in the nature of a chose in action. Moreover that it should do so in the present context appears to have been the opinion of Lord Blackburn in *Simpson & Co.* v *Thomson*, 3 App Cas 279, 292–3. On the other hand, cases such as *Morley* v *Moore* [1936] 2 KB 359 appear to point in the opposite direction, as perhaps does the decision of Lord Lyndhurst LC in *White* v *Dobbinson*, 116 LTOS 233 to discharge the injunction as against the owner of the ship at fault in that case. However, since the point was not directly addressed in the argument before your Lordships, I am reluctant to reach any conclusion upon it without a full examination of the authorities relating to the respective rights and obligations of insurer and assured, especially with regard to the conduct and disposal of litigation relating to causes of action of the relevant kind. I therefore wish to reserve my opinion upon this question, the answer to which I do not regard as necessary for the resolution of the issue which has arisen in the present case. . . .

Notes

1. Mitchell, 'Subrogation and insurance law: proprietary claims and excess clauses' [1993] LMCLQ 192, at 193–201 cogently criticises the House of Lords for describing the stop-loss insurers' restitutionary claim here as an aspect of the doctrine of subrogation. The restitution claim (whether personal or proprietary) enforces the principle of indemnity, but must be distinguished from subrogation proper where, for example, an insurer takes over the cause of action of another, namely the insured. Mitchell further argues that the award of a proprietary remedy here was unsatisfactory, and irreconcilable with Birks's 'proprietary base' theory.

2. On indemnity insurers' subrogation rights generally see Burrows, *Restitution*, 78–82. The case is also noted in (1993) 109 LQR 159 (Gummow).

Attorney-General for Hong Kong v *Reid*
[1994] 1 AC 324 (PC)

Constructive trust

'This is the bribery case to end all bribery cases: the defendant who was convicted under the Hong Kong Prevention of Bribery Ordinance, had been the head of the commercial crime unit responsible for enforcing the Ordinance', wrote Sir Peter Millett in [1993] RLR 7, at 8. Mr Reid had reached the dizzy heights of acting Director of Public Prosecutions in the colony before his corruption was exposed. He was sentenced to eight years' imprisonment and ordered to pay the Crown $HK12.4 million, being the value of his assets, which could only have been derived from bribes. Reid owned three freehold properties in his native New Zealand, two held jointly with his wife and one in the name of his solicitor. The Attorney-General sought to register caveats against those properties, on the ground that they were held on *constructive trust* for the Crown. The High Court and Court of Appeal of New Zealand, following *Lister & Co.* v *Stubbs* (1890) 45 Ch D 1, held the Crown had no proprietary interest in the properties. The Attorney-General appealed.

LORD TEMPLEMAN: . . . A bribe is a gift accepted by a fiduciary as an inducement to him to betray his trust. A secret benefit, which may or may not constitute a bribe, is a benefit which the fiduciary derives from trust property or obtains from knowledge which he acquires in the course of acting as a fiduciary. A fiduciary is not always accountable for a secret benefit but he is undoubtedly accountable for a secret benefit which consists of a bribe. In addition a person who provides the bribe and the fiduciary who accepts the bribe may each be guilty of a criminal offence. In the present case the first respondent was clearly guilty of a criminal offence.

Bribery is an evil practice which threatens the foundations of any civilised society. In particular bribery of policemen and prosecutors brings the administration of justice into disrepute. Where bribes are accepted by a trustee, servant, agent or other fiduciary, loss and damage are caused to the beneficiaries, master or principal whose interests have been betrayed. The amount of loss or damage resulting from the acceptance of a bribe may or may not be quantifiable. In the present case the amount of harm caused to the administration of justice in Hong Kong by the first respondent in return for bribes cannot be quantified.

When a bribe is offered and accepted in money or in kind, the money or property constituting the bribe belongs in law to the recipient. Money paid to the false fiduciary belongs to him. The legal estate in freehold property conveyed to the false fiduciary by way of bribe vests in him. Equity, however, which acts in personam, insists that it is unconscionable for a fiduciary to obtain and retain a benefit in breach of duty. The provider of a bribe cannot recover it because he committed a criminal offence when he paid the bribe. The false fiduciary who received the bribe in breach of duty must pay and account for the bribe to the person to whom that duty was owed. In the present case, as soon as the first respondent received a bribe in breach of the duties he owed to the Government of Hong Kong, he became a debtor in equity to the Crown for the amount of that bribe. So much is admitted. But if the bribe consists of property which increases in value or if a cash bribe is invested advantageously, the false fiduciary will receive a benefit from his breach of duty unless he is accountable not only for the original amount or value of the bribe but also for the increased value of the property representing the bribe. As soon as the bribe was received it should have been paid or transferred instanter to the person who suffered from the breach of duty. Equity considers as done that which ought to have been done. As soon as the bribe was received, whether in cash or in kind, the false fiduciary held the bribe on a constructive trust for the person injured. Two objections have been raised to this analysis. First it is said that if the fiduciary is in equity a debtor to the person injured, he cannot also be a trustee of the bribe. But there is no reason why equity should not provide two remedies, so long as they do not result in double recovery. If the property representing the bribe exceeds the original bribe in value, the fiduciary cannot retain the benefit of the increase in value which he obtained solely as a result of his breach of duty. Secondly, it is said that if the false fiduciary holds property representing the bribe in trust for the person injured, and if the false fiduciary is or becomes insolvent, the unsecured creditors of the false fiduciary will be deprived of their right to share in the proceeds of that property. But the unsecured creditors cannot be in a better position than their debtor. The authorities show that property acquired by a trustee innocently but in breach of trust and the property from time to time representing the same belong in equity to the cestui que trust and not to the trustee personally whether he is solvent or insolvent. Property acquired by a trustee as a result of a criminal breach of trust and the property from time to time representing the same must also belong in equity to his cestui que trust and not to the trustee whether he is solvent or insolvent.

When a bribe is accepted by a fiduciary in breach of his duty then he holds that bribe in trust for the person to whom the duty was owed. If the property representing the bribe decreases in value the fiduciary must pay the difference between that value and the initial amount of the bribe because he should not have accepted the bribe or incurred the risk of loss. If the property increases in value, the fiduciary is not entitled to any surplus in excess of the initial value of the bribe because he is not allowed by any means to make a profit out of a breach of duty.

[Lord Templeman then reviewed a number of authorities and continued: . . .]

It has always been assumed and asserted that the law on the subject of bribes was definitively settled by the decision of the Court of Appeal in *Lister & Co.* v *Stubbs* (1890) 45 Ch D 1.

In that case the plaintiffs, Lister & Co., employed the defendant, Stubbs, as their servant to purchase goods for the firm. Stubbs, on behalf of the firm, bought goods from Varley & Co. and received from Varley & Co. bribes amounting to £5,541. The bribes were invested by Stubbs in freehold properties and investments. His masters, the firm Lister & Co., sought and failed to obtain an interlocutory injunction restraining Stubbs from disposing of these assets pending the trial of the action in which they sought, inter alia, £5,541 and damages. In the Court of Appeal the first judgment was given by Cotton LJ who had been party to the decision in *Metropolitan Bank* v *Heiron*, 5 Ex D 319. He was powerfully supported by the judgment of Lindley LJ and by the equally powerful concurrence of Bowen LJ. Cotton LJ said, at p. 12, that the bribe could not be said to be the money of the plaintiffs. He seemed to be reluctant to grant an interlocutory judgment which would provide security for a debt before that debt had been established. Lindley LJ said, at p. 15, that the relationship between the plaintiffs, Lister & Co., as masters and the defendant, Stubbs, as servant who had betrayed his trust and received a bribe:

> is that of debtor and creditor; it is not that of trustee and cestui que trust. We are asked to hold that it is—which would involve consequences which, I confess, startle me. One consequence, of course, would be that, if Stubbs were to become bankrupt, this property acquired by him with the money paid to him by Messrs Varley would be withdrawn from the mass of his creditors and be handed over bodily to Lister & Co. Can that be right? Another consequence would be that, if the appellants are right, Lister & Co. could compel Stubbs to account to them, not only for the money with interest, but for all the profits which he might have made by embarking in trade with it. Can that be right?

For the reasons which have already been advanced their Lordships would respectfully answer both these questions in the affirmative. If a trustee mistakenly invests moneys which he ought to pay over to his cestui que trust and then becomes bankrupt, the moneys together with any profit which has accrued from the investment are withdrawn from the unsecured creditors as soon as the mistake is discovered. A fortiori if a trustee commits a crime by accepting a bribe which he ought to pay over to his cestui que trust, the bribe and any profit made therefrom should be withdrawn from the unsecured creditors as soon as the crime is discovered.

The decision in *Lister & Co.* v *Stubbs* is not consistent with the principles that a fiduciary must not be allowed to benefit from his own breach of duty, that the fiduciary should account for the bribe as soon as he receives it and that equity regards as done that which ought to be done. From these principles it would appear to follow that the bribe and the property from time to time representing the bribe are held on a constructive trust for the person injured. A fiduciary remains personally liable for the amount of the bribe if, in the event, the value of the property then recovered by the injured person proved to be less than that amount.

The decisions of the Court of Appeal in *Metropolitan Bank* v *Heiron*, 5 Ex D 319, and *Lister & Co.* v *Stubbs*, 45 Ch D 1, are inconsistent with earlier authorities which were not cited. Although over 100 years has passed since *Lister & Co.* v *Stubbs*, no one can be allowed to say that he has ordered his affairs in reliance on the two decisions of the Court of Appeal now in question. Thus no harm can result if those decisions are not followed.

The decision in *Lister & Co.* v *Stubbs* was followed in *Powell & Thomas* v *Evans Jones & Co.* [1905] 1 KB 11 and *Attorney-General* v *Goddard* (1929) 98 LJKB 743. In *Regal (Hastings) Ltd* v *Gulliver (Note)* [1967] 2 AC 134 shares intended to be acquired by directors at par to avoid them giving a guarantee of the obligations under a lease were sold at a profit and the directors were held to be liable to the company for the proceeds of sale, applying *Keech* v *Sandford*, Sel Cas Ch 61.

In *Reading* v *Attorney-General* [1951] AC 507, the Crown confiscated thousands of pounds paid to an army sergeant who had abused his official position to enable drugs to be imported. The Crown was allowed to keep the confiscated moneys to avoid circuity of action.

Finally in *Islamic Republic of Iran Shipping Lines* v *Denby* [1987] 1 Lloyd's Rep 367 Leggatt J followed *Lister & Co.* v *Stubbs*, 45 Ch D 1, as indeed he was bound to do.

The authorities which followed *Lister & Co.* v *Stubbs* do not cast any new light on that decision. Their Lordships are more impressed with the decision of Lai Kew Chai J in *Sumitomo Bank Ltd* v *Kartika Ratna Thahir* [1993] 1 SLR 735. In that case General Thahir who was at one time general assistant to the president director of the Indonesian state enterprise named Pertamina opened 17 bank accounts in Singapore and deposited DM.54m in those accounts. The money was said to be bribes paid by two German contractors tendering for the construction of steel works in West Java. General Thahir having died, the moneys were claimed by his widow, by the estate of the deceased general and by Pertamina. After considering in detail all the relevant authorities Lai Kew Chai J determined robustly, at p. 810, that *Lister & Co.* v *Stubbs*, 45 Ch D 1, was wrong and that its 'undesirable and unjust consequences should not be imported and perpetuated as part of' the law of Singapore. Their Lordships are also much indebted for the fruits of research and the careful discussion of the present topic in the address entitled 'Bribes and Secret Commissions' [1993] RLR 7 delivered by Sir Peter Millett to a meeting of the Society of Public Teachers of Law at Oxford in 1993. The following passage, at p. 20, elegantly sums up the views of Sir Peter Millett:

> [The fiduciary] must not place himself in a position where his interest may conflict with his duty. If he has done so, equity insists on treating him as having acted in accordance with his duty; he will not be allowed to say that he preferred his own interest to that of his principal. He must not obtain a profit for himself out of his fiduciary position. If he has done so, equity insists on treating him as having obtained it for his principal; he will not be allowed to say that he obtained it for himself. He must not accept a bribe. If he has done so, equity insists on treating it as a legitimate payment intended for the benefit of the principal; he will not be allowed to say that it was a bribe.

The conclusions reached by Lai Kew Chai J in *Sumitomo Bank Ltd* v *Kartika Ratna Thahir* [1993] 1 SLR 735 and the views expressed by Sir Peter Millett were influenced by the decision of the House of Lords in *Phipps* v *Boardman* [1967] 2 AC 46 which demonstrates the strictness with which equity regards the conduct of a fiduciary and the extent to which equity is willing to impose a constructive trust on property obtained by a fiduciary by virtue of his office. In that case a solicitor acting for trustees rescued the interests of the trust in a private company by negotiating for a takeover bid in which he himself took an interest. He acted in good faith throughout and the information which the solicitor obtained about the company in the takeover bid could never have been used by the trustees. Nevertheless the solicitor was held to be a constructive trustee by a majority in the House of Lords because the solicitor obtained the information which satisfied him that the purchase of the shares in the takeover company would be a good investment and the opportunity of acquiring the shares as a result of acting for certain purposes on behalf of the trustees; see *per* Lord Cohen, at p. 103. If a fiduciary acting honestly and in good faith and making a profit which his principal could not make for himself becomes a constructive trustee of that profit then it seems to their Lordships that a fiduciary acting dishonestly and criminally who accepts a bribe and thereby causes loss and damage to his principal must also be a constructive trustee and must not be allowed by any means to make any profit from his wrongdoing. . . .

Notes

1. This case is discussed in [1994] LMCLQ 189 (Pearce). See also Cowan, Edmunds and Lowry, '*Lister & Co.* v *Stubbs*: Who Profits?' [1996] JBL 22.

2. For the analogous question whether the equitable wrong of breach of confidence should give rise to a proprietary remedy in the shape of a constructive trust, see the affirmative view of the Supreme Court of Canada in *Lac Minerals Ltd* v *International Corona Resources Ltd* (1989) 61 DLR (4th) 14 (welcomed in [1990] LMCLQ 4 (Davies), but criticised as lacking analytical rigour in [1990] LMCLQ 460 (Birks)).

3. Contrast the recent decision of the Court of Appeal in *Halifax Building Society* v *Thomas* [1995] 4 All ER 673, where it was held that the victim of a mortgage fraud was not able to claim the surplus sum remaining after it had enforced its security. The building society had elected to affirm the transaction rather than set it aside for fraudulent misrepresentation. Therefore it had no claim based on waiving the tort of deceit, or, in modern terms, in restitution for wrongs. The Court of Appeal rejected both a personal remedy and, after consideration of *Attorney-General for Hong Kong* v *Reid*, a proprietary remedy based upon a constructive trust (at 681–2). The Court was heavily influenced by the existence of a statutory scheme for stripping such wrongdoers of their ill-gotten gains. See Birks (1996) 10 *Trusts Law International* 2.

Re Goldcorp Exchange Ltd (in receivership) [1995] 1 AC 74 (PC)

Constructive trust

Goldcorp was a New Zealand company dealing in gold coins and ingots as consumer products. More than a thousand small investors entered into contracts with Goldcorp for the purchase of gold bullion for future delivery. They received a 'certificate of ownership' stating that they had the right to delivery on seven days' notice and payment of delivery charges. The contracts provided that Goldcorp would store and insure the bullion for free. The metal was stored on an unallocated basis, but it was represented that Goldcorp's stocks of bullion were always sufficient to meet all contracts, and that they were audited monthly by Peat Marwick. The company became hopelessly insolvent. Its bank held a floating charge over all the company's assets to secure the company's liabilities to it. The bank placed the company in receivership and its floating charge crystallised. The bank's secured debt exceeded all the assets of the company, including the bullion. There had been no appropriation of bullion to particular non-allocated investors' contracts. Therefore the Privy Council held that no property passed to the non-allocated claimants in the bullion under the contract of sale, due to the rule of law in s. 18 of the Sale of Goods Act 1908 (New Zealand) (corresponding to s. 16 of the Sale of Goods Act 1979 (UK)) that property cannot pass in unascertained goods. The claimants further argued that they were entitled to a remedial constructive trust or restitutionary proprietary remedy over either the company's bullion stocks, or the company's assets representing the value of their purchase moneys.

LORD MUSTILL: . . . Next, the claimants put forward an argument in two stages. First, it is said that because the company held itself out as willing to vest bullion in the customer and to hold it in safe custody on behalf of him in circumstances where he was totally dependent on the company, and trusted the company to do what it had promised without in practice there being any means of verification, the company was a fiduciary. From this it is deduced that the company as fiduciary created an equity by inviting the customer to look on and treat stocks vested in it as his own, which could appropriately be recognised only by treating the customer as entitled to a proprietary interest in the stock.

To describe someone as a fiduciary, without more, is meaningless. As Frankfurter J said in *S.E.C.* v *Chenery Corporation* (1943) 318 US 80, 885–6, cited in *Goff and Jones, The Law of Restitution*, 4th ed. (1993), p. 644:

> to say that a man is a fiduciary only begins analysis; it gives direction to further inquiry. To whom is he a fiduciary? What obligations does he owe as a fiduciary? In what respect has he failed to discharge these obligations? And what are the consequences of his deviation from duty?

Here, the argument assumes that the person towards whom the company was fiduciary was the non-allocated claimant. But what kind of fiduciary duties did the company owe to the customer? None have been suggested beyond those which the company assumed under the contracts of sale read with the collateral promises; namely to deliver the goods and meanwhile to keep a separate stock of bullion (or, more accurately, separate stocks of each variety of bullion) to which the customers could look as a safeguard for performance when delivery was called for. No doubt the fact that one person is placed in a particular position vis-à-vis another through the medium of a contract does not necessarily mean that he does not also owe fiduciary duties to that other by virtue of being in that position. But the essence of a fiduciary relationship is that it creates obligations of a different character from those deriving from the contract itself. Their Lordships have not heard in argument any submission which went beyond suggesting that by virtue of being a fiduciary the company was obliged honestly and conscientiously to do what it had by contract promised to do. Many commercial relationships involve just such a reliance by one party on the other, and to introduce the whole new dimension into such relationships which would flow from giving them a fiduciary character would (as it seems to their Lordships) have adverse consequences far exceeding those foreseen by Atkin LJ in *In re Wait* [1927] 1 Ch 606. It is possible without misuse of language to say that the customers put faith in the company, and that their trust has not been repaid. But the vocabulary is misleading; high expectations do not necessarily lead to equitable remedies.

Let it be assumed, however, that the company could properly be described as a fiduciary and let it also be assumed that notwithstanding the doubts expressed above the non-allocated claimants would have achieved some kind of proprietary interest if the company had done what it said. This still leaves the problem, to which their

Lordships can see no answer, that the company did not do what it said. There never was a separate and sufficient stock of bullion in which a proprietary interest could be created. What the non-allocated claimants are really trying to achieve is to attach the proprietary interest, which they maintain should have been created on the non-existent stock, to wholly different assets. It is understandable that the claimants, having been badly let down in a transaction concerning bullion should believe that they must have rights over whatever bullion the company still happens to possess. Whilst sympathising with this notion their Lordships must reject it, for the remaining stock, having never been separated, is just another asset of the company, like its vehicles and office furniture. If the argument applies to the bullion it must apply to the latter as well, an obviously unsustainable idea.

Finally, it is argued that the court should declare in favour of the claimants a remedial constructive trust, or to use another name a restitutionary proprietary interest, over the bullion in the company's vaults. Such a trust or interest would differ fundamentally from those so far discussed, in that it would not arise directly from the transaction between the individual claimants, the company and the bullion, but would be created by the court as a measure of justice after the event. Their Lordships must return to this topic later when considering the Walker & Hall claimants who, the trial judge has held, did acquire a proprietary interest in some bullion, but they are unable to understand how the doctrine in any of its suggested formulations could apply to the facts of the present case. By leaving its stock of bullion in a non-diferentiated state the company did not unjustly enrich itself by mixing its own bullion with that of the purchasers: for all the gold belonged to the company. It did not act wrongfully in acquiring, maintaining and using its own stock of bullion, since there was no term of the sale contracts or of the collateral promises, and none could possibly be implied, requiring that all bullion purchased by the company should be set aside to fulfil the unallocated sales. The conduct of the company was wrongful in the sense of being a breach of contract, but it did not involve any injurious dealing with the subject matter of the alleged trust. Nor, if some wider equitable principle is involved, does the case become any stronger. As previously remarked the claimants' argument really comes to this, that because the company broke its contract in a way which had to do with bullion the court should call into existence a proprietary interest in whatever bullion happened to be in the possession and ownership of the company at the time when the competition between the non-allocated claimants and the other secured and unsecured creditors first arose. The company's stock of bullion had no connection with the claimants' purchases, and to enable the claimants to reach out and not only abstract it from the assets available to the body of creditors as a whole, but also to afford a priority over a secured creditor, would give them an adventitious benefit devoid of the foundation in logic and justice which underlies this important new branch of the law.

. . . *Proprietary interests derived from the purchase price*

Their Lordships now turn to the proposition, which first emerged during argument in the Court of Appeal, and which was not raised in the *London Wine* case [1986] PCC 121, that a proprietary interest either sprang into existence on the sales to customers, or should now be imposed retrospectively through restitutionary remedies, in relation not to bullion but to the moneys originally paid by the customers under the contracts of sale. Here at least it is possible to pin down the subject matter to which the proprietary rights are said to relate. Nevertheless, their Lordships are constrained to reject all the various ways in which the submission has been presented, once again for a single comparatively simple reason.

The first argument posits that the purchase moneys were from the outset impressed with a trust in favour of the payers. That a sum of money paid by the purchaser under a contract for the sale of goods is capable in principle of being the subject of a trust in the hands of the vendor is clear. For this purpose it is necessary to show either a mutual intention that the moneys should not fall within the general fund of the company's assets but should be applied for a special designated purpose, or that having originally been paid over without restriction the recipient has later constituted himself a trustee of the money: see *Quistclose Investments Ltd* v *Rolls Razor Ltd* [1970] AC 567, 581–2. This requirement was satisfied in *In re Kayford Ltd (In Liquidation)* [1975] 1 WLR 279 where a company in financial difficulties paid into a separate deposit account money received from customers for goods not yet delivered, with the intention of making withdrawals from the account only as and when delivery was effected, and of refunding the payment to customers if an insolvency made delivery impossible. The facts of the present case are, however, inconsistent with any such trust. This is not a situation where the customer engaged the company as agent to purchase bullion on his or her behalf, with immediate payment to put the agent in funds, delivery being postponed to suit the customer's convenience. The agreement was for sale by the company to, and not the purchase by the company for, the customer. The latter paid the purchase price for one purchase alone, namely to perform his side of the bargain under which he would in due course be entitled to obtain delivery. True, another part of the consideration for the payment was the collateral promise to maintain separate cover, but this does not mean that the money was paid for the purpose of purchasing gold, either to create the separate stock or for any other reason. There was nothing in the express agreement to require, and nothing in their Lordships' view can be implied, which constrained in any way the company's freedom to spend the purchase money as it chose, or to establish the stock from any source and with any funds as it thought fit. This being so, their Lordships cannot concur in the decision of Cooke P [1993] 1 NZLR 257, 272–3, that the purchase price was impressed with a continuing beneficial interest in favour of the customer, which could form the starting point for a tracing of the purchase moneys into other assets.

The same insuperable obstacle stands in the way of the alternative submission that the company was a fiduciary. If one asks the inevitable first question—What was the content of the fiduciary's duty?—the claimants are forced to assert that the duty was to expend the moneys in the purchase and maintenance of the reserved stock. Yet this is precisely the obligation which, as just stated, cannot be extracted from anything express or implied in the contract of sale and the collateral promises. In truth, the argument that the company was a fiduciary (as regards the money rather than the bullion) is no more than another label for the argument in favour of an express trust and must fail for the same reason.

Thus far, all the arguments discussed have assumed that each contract of sale and collateral promises together created a valid and effective transaction coupling the ordinary mutual obligations of an agreement for the sale of goods with special obligations stemming from a trust or fiduciary relationship. These arguments posit that the obligations remain in force, albeit unperformed, the claimants' object being to enforce them. The next group of arguments starts with the contrary proposition that the transactions were rendered ineffectual by the presence of one or more of three vitiating factors: namely, misrepresentation, mistake and total failure of consideration. To these their Lordships now turn.

It is important at the outset to distinguish between three different ways in which the existence of a misrepresentation, a mistake or a total failure of consideration might lead to the existence of a proprietary interest in the purchase money or its fruits superior to that of the bank.

1. The existence of one or more of these vitiating factors distinguished the relationship from that of an ordinary vendor and purchaser, so as to leave behind with the customer a beneficial interest in the purchase moneys which would otherwise have passed to the company when the money was paid. This interest remained with the customer throughout everything that followed, and can now be enforced against the general assets of the company, including the bullion, in priority to the interest of the bank.

2. Even if the full legal and beneficial interest in the purchase moneys passed when they were paid over, the vitiating factors affected the contract in such a way as to revest the moneys in the purchaser, and, what is more, to do so in a way which attached to the moneys an interest superior to that of the bank.

3. In contrast to the routes just mentioned, where the judgment of the court would do no more than recognise the existence of proprietary rights already in existence, the court should by its judgment create a new proprietary interest, superior to that of the bank, to reflect the justice of the case.

With these different mechanisms in view, their Lordships turn to the vitiating factors relied upon. As to the misrepresentations these were presumably that (in fact) the company intended to carry out the collateral promise to establish a separate stock and also that (in law) if this promise was performed the customer would obtain a title to bullion. Whether the proprietary interests said to derive from this misrepresentation were retained by the customers from the moment when they paid over the purchase moneys, or whether they arose at a later date, was not made clear in argument. If the former, their Lordships can only say that they are unable to grasp the reasoning for if correct the argument would entail that even in respect of those contracts which the company ultimately fulfilled by delivery the moneys were pro tempore subject to a trust which would have prevented the company from lawfully treating them as its own. This cannot be right. As an alternative it may be contended that a trust arose upon the collapse of the company and the consequent non-fulfilment of the contracts. This contention must also be rejected, for two reasons. First, any such proprietary right must have as its starting point a personal claim by the purchaser to the return of the price. No such claim could exist for so long as the sale contract remained in existence and was being enforced by the customer. That is the position here. The customers have never rescinded the contracts of sale, but have throughout the proceedings asserted various forms of proprietary interest in the bullion, all of them derived in one way or another from the contracts of sale. This stance is wholly inconsistent with the notion that the contracts were and are so ineffectual that the customers are entitled to get their money back. As a last resort the non-allocated claimants invited the Board to treat the contracts as rescinded if their claims for a proprietary interest in bullion were rejected. There is however no mechanism which would permit the claimants to pause, as it were, half way through the delivery of the present judgment and elect at last to rescind; and even if such a course were open, the remedies arising on rescission would come too late to affect the secured rights of the bank under its previously crystallised floating charge.

Furthermore, even if this fatal objection could be overcome, the argument would, in their Lordships' opinion, be bound to fail. Whilst it is convenient to speak of the customers 'getting their money back' this expression is misleading. Upon payment by the customers the purchase moneys became, and rescission or no rescission remained, the unencumbered property of the company. What the customers would recover on rescission would not be 'their' money, but an equivalent sum. Leaving aside for the moment the creation by the court of a new remedial proprietary right, to which totally different considerations would apply, the claimants would have to contend that in every case where a purchaser is misled into buying goods he is automatically entitled upon rescinding the contract to a proprietary right superior to those of all the vendor's other creditors, exercisable against the whole of the vendor's assets. It is not surprising that no authority could be cited for such an extreme proposition. The only possible exception is *In re Eastgate; Ex parte Ward* [1905] 1 KB 465. Their Lordships doubt whether, correctly understood, the case so decides, but if it does they decline to follow it.

Similar objections apply to the second variant, which was only lightly touched upon in argument: namely, that the purchase moneys were paid under a mistake. Assuming the mistake to be that the collateral promises would be performed and would yield a proprietary right, what effect would they have on the contracts? Obviously not to make them void ab initio, for otherwise it would mean that the customers had no right to insist on delivery. Perhaps the mistake would have entitled the customers to have the agreements set aside at common law or under statute, and upon this happening they would no doubt have been entitled to a personal restitutionary remedy in respect of the price. This does not, however, advance their case. The moneys were paid by the customers to the company because they believed that they were bound to pay them; and in this belief they were entirely right. The situtation is entirely different from *Chase Manhattan Bank N.A.* v *Israel-British Bank (London) Ltd* [1981] Ch 105, to which much attention was given in the Court of Appeal and in argument before the Board. It may be—their Lordships express no opinion upon it—that the *Chase Manhattan* case correctly decided that where one party mistakenly makes the same payment twice it retains a proprietary interest in the second payment which (if tracing is practicable) can be enforced against the payees' assets in a liquidation ahead of unsecured creditors. But in the present case, the customers intended to make payment, and they did so because they rightly conceived that that was what the contracts required. As in the case of the argument based on misrepresentation, this version conceals the true nature of the customers' complaint: not that they paid the money, but that the goods which they ordered and paid for have not been delivered. As in the case of the misrepresentation, the alleged mistake might well have been a ground for setting aside the contract if the claimants had ever sought to do so; and in such a case they would have had a personal right to recover the sum equivalent to the amount paid. But even if they had chosen to exercise this right, it would not by operation of law have carried with it a proprietary interest.

Their Lordships are of the same opinion as regards the third variant, which is that a proprietary interest arose because the consideration for the purchase price has totally failed. It is, of course, obvious that in the end the consideration did fail, when delivery was demanded and not made. But until that time the claimants had the benefit of what they had bargained for, a contract for the sale of unascertained goods. Quite plainly a customer could not on the day after a sale have claimed to recover the price for a total failure of consideration, and this at once puts paid to any question of a residuary proprietary interest and distinguishes the case from those such as *Sinclair* v *Brougham* [1914] AC 398, where the transactions under which the moneys were paid were from the start ineffectual; and *Neste Oy* v *Lloyds Bank Plc.* [1983] 2 Lloyd's Rep 658, where to the knowledge of the payee no performance at all could take place under the contract for which the payment formed the consideration.

There remains the question whether the court should create after the event a remedial restitutionary right superior to the security created by the charge. The nature and foundation of this remedy were not clearly explained in argument. This is understandable, given that the doctrine is still in an early stage and no single juristic account of it has yet been generally agreed. In the context of the present case there appear to be only two possibilities. The first is to strike directly at the heart of the problem and to conclude that there was such an imbalance between the positions of the parties that if orthodox methods fail a new equity should intervene to put the matter right, without recourse to further rationalisation. Their Lordships must firmly reject any such approach. The bank relied on the floating charge to protect its assets; the customers relied on the company to deliver the bullion and to put in place the separate stock. The fact that the claimants are private citizens whereas their opponent is a commercial bank could not justify the court in simply disapplying the bank's valid security. No case cited has gone anywhere near to this, and the Board would do no service to the nascent doctrine by stretching it past breaking point.

Accordingly, if the argument is to prevail some means must be found, not forcibly to subtract moneys or their fruits from the assets to which the charge really attached, but retrospectively to create a situation in which the moneys never were part of those assets. In other words the claimants must be deemed to have a retained equitable title: see Goff and Jones, *The Law of Restitution*, 4th ed., p. 94. Whatever the mechanism for such deeming may be in other circumstances their Lordships can see no scope for it here. So far as concerns an equitable interest deemed to have come into existence from the moment when the transaction was entered into, it is hard to see how this could coexist with a contract which, so far as anyone knew, might be performed by actual delivery of the goods. And if there was no initial interest, at what time before the attachment of the security, and by virtue of what event, could the court deem a proprietary right to have arisen? None that their Lordships are able to see. Although remedial restitutionary rights may prove in the future to be a valuable instrument of justice they cannot in their Lordships' opinion be brought to bear on the present case.

For these reasons the Board must reject all the ways in which the non-allocated claimants assert a proprietary interest over the purchase price and its fruits. This makes it unnecessary to consider whether, if such an interest had existed, it would have been possible to trace from the subject matter of the interest into the company's present assets. Indeed it would be unprofitable to do so without a clear understanding of when and how the equitable interest arose, and of its nature. Their Lordships should, however, say that they find it difficult to understand how the judgment of the Board in *Space Investments Ltd* v *Canadian Imperial Bank of Commerce Trust Co. (Bahamas) Ltd* [1986] 1 WLR 1072, on which the claimants leaned heavily in argument, would enable them to overcome the difficulty that the moneys said to be impressed with the trust were paid into an overdrawn account and thereupon ceased to exist: see, for example, *In re Diplock* [1948] Ch 465. The observations of the Board in the *Space Investments* case were concerned with a mixed, not a non-existent, fund.

. . .

The law relating to the creation and tracing of equitable proprietary interests is still in a state of development. In *Attorney-General for Hong Kong* v *Reid* [1994] AC 324 the Board decided that money received by an agent as a bribe was held in trust for the principal who is entitled to trace and recover property representing the bribe. In *Lord Napier and Ettrick* v *Hunter* [1993] AC 713, 738–9, the House of Lords held that payment of damages in respect of an insured loss created an equitable charge in favour of the subrogated insurers so long only as the damages were traceable as an identifiable fund. When the scope and ambit of these decisions and the observations of the Board in the *Space Investments* case fall to be considered, it will be necessary for the history and foundations in principle of the creation and tracing of equitable proprietary interests to be the subject of close examination and full argument and for attention to be paid to the works of Paciocco (1989) 68 Can Bar Rev 315, *Maddaugh and McCamus, The Law of Restitution* (1990), Emily L. Sherwin's article 'Constructive

Trusts in Bankruptcy' (1989) U Ill L Rev 297, 335, and other commentators dealing with equitable interests in tracing and referring to concepts such as the position of 'involuntary creditors' and tracing to 'swollen assets.' . . .

Notes

1. See Birks, 'Establishing a Proprietary Base' [1995] *Restitution Law Review* 83.

2. Lord Mustill's suggested reading list emphasises that the problems arising here are as much a matter for the principles and policies of insolvency law, as for restitution. See in particular Paciocco, 'The Remedial Constructive Trust: A Principled Basis for Priorities Over Creditors' (1989) 68 Can Bar Rev 315 and Sherwin, 'Constructive Trusts in Bankruptcy' [1989] U Ill L Rev 297. See also Cowan, Edmunds and Lowry, 'Equitable Tracing and the Swollen Assets Theory' (1995) 1 *Contemporary Issues in Law* 1.

3. Section 16 of the Sale of Goods Act 1979 has been modified in relation to bulk goods by the Sale of Goods (Amendment) Act 1995. However, that measure would not apply to the facts of *Goldcorp*, because of the absence there of an identified bulk. Also contrast the *London Wine* case [1986] PCC 121 discussed in *Goldcorp* with *Re Stapylton Fletcher Ltd* [1995] 1 All ER 192.

8 DEFENCES

The development of defences in the law of restitution has proceeded in a rather haphazard way, in the shadows of doubts about the conceptual basis and unity of the substantive part of the subject. With unjust enrichment firmly entrenched as the underlying principle behind restitutionary causes of action, it is now possible for the law of defences to develop on a more rational basis. *Lipkin Gorman* v *Karpnale Ltd* [1991] 2 AC 548 not only took the step of recognising 'unjust enrichment' as the touchstone of liability, it also recognised two distinct defences to restitutionary claims. The first two sections of this chapter deal with these, the two most important defences. Section 1 considers bona fide purchase, which operates as a total defence to claims in restitution. It is of the utmost significance in the law of obligations as a whole, because it is one of the doctrines which marks the boundaries of the provinces of the law of contract and the law of restitution. It protects security of receipt; in particular it protects indirect recipients who have received wealth under a valid and effective exchange, and in good faith. To this extent it upholds the sanctity of contracts. Section 2 considers bona fide change of position, first explicitly recognised at appellate level in *Lipkin Gorman*. This too protects the security of receipt of a recipient who is enriched, but whose circumstances change as a result of being benefited so that it would be inequitable to order restitution of some or all of the enrichment. Therefore change of position may operate *pro tanto*. The related case law on estoppel and the agent's defence of ministerial receipt are also considered. Bona fide purchase, which is always a total defence, is logically best treated before change of position. Section 3 considers whether the impossibility of counter-restitution should be a defence to restitutionary claims. Section 4 considers the case law on the question as to when public policy operates to bar a cause of action in unjust enrichment.

Section 1: bona fide purchase

At common law it is a complete defence to a claim in restitution in respect of *money* that the recipient was a bona fide purchaser for value without notice.

It is also defence to both personal and proprietary restitutionary claims in equity in respect of all other types of enrichment. The defence is usually illustrated by an example using a three-party fact configuration. For example, A steals £1,000 from B and uses it to buy a car from C. If C dealt with A in good faith he has a complete defence to a claim in restitution by B. It is not usual to talk of bona fide purchase in respect of two-party configurations, although it is not easy to see why this should not be so. More usually, a rule is stated that restitution has no role to play in respect of wealth passing under a valid and effective contract, that is one which is not void or avoided by some vitiating factor, or discharged by breach or frustration. See, for example, *Dimskal Shipping Co. SA* v *International Transport Workers' Federation, The 'Evia Luck' (No. 2)* [1992] 2 AC 152, at 165 *per* Lord Goff of Chieveley: '. . . before the owners could establish any right to recover the money, they had first to avoid the relevant contract. Until this was done, the money in question was paid under a binding contract and so was irrecoverable in restitution.' Consider also the formulation of Robert Goff J (as he then was) in *Barclays Bank Ltd* v *W. J. Simms, Son & Cooke (Southern) Ltd* [1980] QB 677, at 695:

> (1) If a person pays money to another under a mistake of fact that causes him to make the payment, he is prima facie entitled to recover it as money paid under a mistake of fact. (2) His claim may however fail if . . . (b) the payment is made for good consideration, in particular if the money is paid to discharge, and does discharge, a debt owed to the payee (or a principal on whose behalf he is authorised to receive the payment) by the payer or by a third party by whom he is authorised to discharge the debt . . .

If the payment in that case had automatically discharged the debt owed to the recipient, it seems clear there would have been a complete defence, and bona fide purchase seems to be an appropriate label to give to it. These two straightforward cases, one in duress, one in mistake, illustrate a principle which is at least closely analogous to bona fide purchase as explicitly recognised in three-party cases. The same policy, sanctity of contracts, appears to underlie both.

The view taken here is that it is bona fide purchase, or something closely akin to it, operating in both the two-party and the three-party context. There is no reason to distinguish in principle between cases involving direct recipients (loosely called two-party configurations) and cases involving indirect recipients (loosely called three-party configurations, although they may involve more than three persons). However, in practice a third-party recipient is often more likely to establish a successful bona fide purchase defence. (Compare Birks, *Introduction*, 445–7.) Note that Professor Burrows takes a different view and argues that restitution has its own privity principle, confining recovery to direct recipients as a general rule (Burrows, *Restitution*, 45–54 and see 472—5).

A: Currency

Bona fide purchase is most clearly at work in respect of money as currency. With regard to other chattels the common law adopts as a general rule *nemo dat quod non habet* ('nobody can give what they do not have'). Therefore the bona fide purchaser of a stolen motor car generally acquires no property in the vehicle. (This is the assumption underlying cases such as *Greenwood* v *Bennett* [1973] QB 195 and *Rowland* v *Divall* [1923] 2 KB 500.) In contrast the general rule never applied to coins which passed into currency, and the same came to be applied to bank notes, so stolen coins and notes could never be recovered from a bona fide purchaser for value (*Miller* v *Race* (1758) 1 Burr 452, 97 ER 398; *Clarke* v *Shee and Johnson* (1774) 1 Cowp 197, 98 ER 1041). However, the correlation was that stolen money could be recovered from a recipient in bad faith or a volunteer (*Clarke* v *Shee and Johnson*; *Lipkin Gorman* v *Karpnale Ltd* [1991] 2 AC 548 in Chapter 7, Section 1. See Mann, *The Legal Aspect of Money*, 5th ed. (Oxford: Clarendon Press, 1992), 8–12.)

B: Purchase

The giving of any value in exchange for the enrichment will suffice. For example, the discharge of a debt will suffice. The creditor gives up his claim (his *chose in action*) in return for wealth and this, despite some awkwardness in the language, is bona fide purchase. *Aiken* v *Short* (1856) 1 H & N 210; 156 ER 1180 is a clear illustration of this. Goff and Jones have, however, now reclassified this case as a particular example of change of position (Goff and Jones, 134–5; cf. Goff and Jones, *The Law of Restitution*, 3rd ed., at 108–9, 716). The operation of the same defence appears to underlie the debate already alluded to as to whether the debt was discharged in *Barclays Bank* v *W J Simms, Son & Cooke (Southern) Ltd* [1980] QB 677. For these cases see Chapter 2, Section 1.

C: Volunteers

Restitutionary claims are most likely to succeed against indirect recipients who are volunteers; either those who have received the enrichment as a gift, or who have exchanged value for the enrichment, but where that exchange was not one recognised by the law. In the first category, the successful claims against the charities by the next-of-kin in *In Re Diplock, Diplock* v *Wintle* [1948] Ch 465 (CA), affd *sub nom Ministry of Health* v *Simpson* [1951] AC 251 (HL) provide a clear example. In the second category, the Playboy Club in *Lipkin Gorman* v *Karpnale Ltd* [1991] 2 AC 548 was not regarded as providing value under gaming contracts which were void under s. 18 of the Gaming Act 1845; and Mlle Spanoghe was not giving value by illicit cohabitation (perhaps now an inappropriate phrase in the light of changing social *mores*, but the point seems to be the same) in *Banque Belge pour l'Etranger* v *Hambrouck* [1921] 1 KB 321 (CA).

D: Notice

If a recipient has notice of a defect in his entitlement to the enrichment received, the defence does not operate. What constitutes notice? It is perhaps best to start with a wise *dictum* of Lindley LJ in *Manchester Trust* v *Furness* [1895] 2 QB 539, at 545:

> . . . as regards the extension of the equitable doctrines of constructive notice to commercial transactions, the Courts have always set their faces resolutely against it. The equitable doctrines of constructive notice are common enough in dealing with land and estates, with which the Court is familiar; but there have been repeated protests against the introduction into commercial transactions of anything like an extension of those doctrines, and the protest is founded on perfect good sense. In dealing with estates in land title is everything, and it can be leisurely investigated; in commercial transactions possession is everything, and there is no time to investigate title; and if we were to extend the doctrine of constructive notice to commercial transactions we should be doing infinite mischief and paralyzing the trade of the country. . . .

This was recently approved by Vinelott J in *Eagle Trust plc* v *SBC Securities Ltd* [1992] 4 All ER 488, at 507, in the context of a claim for *intermeddling* in equity. On one view the correct analysis of the knowing receipt cases is that the liability is prima facie strict (the cause of action being 'ignorance' which is *a fortiori* from mistake), but that the concern with notice is to see whether bona fide purchase without notice of any defect in title is made out as a defence: see Birks, 'Misdirected Funds – Restitution from the Recipient' [1989] LMCLQ 296. A major difficulty is whether 'notice' extends beyond actual knowledge to encompass various shades of constructive notice. For discussion of *knowing receipt* liability see Burrows, *Restitution*, 150–8 and Chapter 7, Section 2 above. A case which clearly supports strict liability for restitution both at common law and in equity against indirect recipients is *Nelson* v *Larholt* [1948] 1 KB 339 (see Chapter 7, Section 1 above).

Lipkin Gorman* v *Karpnale Ltd
[1991] 2 AC 548

Action for money had and received
The facts and extracts relating to the cause of action appear in Chapter 7, Section 1.

LORD GOFF OF CHIEVELEY: . . .

Whether the respondents gave consideration for the money
There is no doubt that the respondents received the money in good faith; but, as I have already recorded, there was an acute difference of opinion among the members of the Court of Appeal whether the respondents gave consideration for it. Parker LJ was of opinion that they did so, for two reasons. (1) The club supplied chips in

exchange for the money. The contract under which the chips were supplied was a separate contract, independent of the contracts under which bets were placed at the club; and the contract for the ships was not avoided as a contract by way of gaming and wagering under section 18 of the Gaming Act 1845. (2) Although the actual gaming contracts were void under the Act, nevertheless Cass in fact obtained in exchange for the money the chance of winning and of then being paid and so received valuable consideration from the club. May LJ agreed with the first of these two reasons. Nicholls LJ disagreed with both.

I have to say at once that I am unable to accept the alternative basis upon which Parker LJ held that consideration was given for the money, viz. that each time Cass placed a bet at the casino, he obtained in exchange the chance of winning and thus of being paid. In my opinion, when Cass placed a bet, he received nothing in return which constituted valuable consideration. The contract of gaming was void; in other words, it was binding in honour only. Cass knew, of course, that, if he won his bet, the club would pay him his winnings. But he had no legal right to claim them. He simply had a confident expectation that, in fact, the club would pay; indeed, if the club did not fulfil its obligations binding in honour upon it, it would very soon go out of business. But it does not follow that, when Cass placed the bet, he received anything that the law recognises as valuable consideration. In my opinion he did not do so. Indeed, to hold that consideration had been given for the money on this basis would, in my opinion, be inconsistent with *Clarke* v *Shee and Johnson*, 1 Cowp 197. Even when a winning bet has been paid, the gambler does not receive valuable consideration for his money. All that he receives is, in law, a gift from the club.

However, the first basis upon which Parker and May LJJ decided the point is more difficult. To that I now turn.

In common sense terms, those who gambled at the club were not gambling for chips: they were gambling for money. As Davies LJ said in *C.H.T. Ltd* v *Ward* [1965] 2 QB 63, 79:

> People do not game in order to win chips; they game in order to win money. The chips are not money or money's worth: they are mere counters or symbols used for the convenience of all concerned in the gaming.

The convenience is manifest, especially from the point of view of the club. The club has the gambler's money up front, and large sums of cash are not floating around at the gaming tables. The chips are simply a convenient mechanism for facilitating gambling with money. The property in the chips as such remains in the club, so that there is no question of a gambler buying the chips from the club when he obtains them for cash.

But this broad approach does not solve the problem, which is essentially one of analysis. I think it best to approach the problem by taking a situation unaffected by the impact of the Gaming Acts.

Suppose that a large department store decides, for reasons of security, that all transactions in the store are to be effected by the customers using chips instead of money. On entering the store, or later, the customer goes to the cash desk and obtains chips to the amount he needs in exchange for cash or a cheque. When he buys goods, he presents chips for his purchase. Before he leaves the store, he presents his remaining chips, and receives cash in return. The example may be unrealistic, but in legal terms it is reasonably straightforward. A contract is made when the customer obtains his chips under which the store agrees that, if goods are purchased by the customer, the store will accept chips to the equivalent value of the price, and further that it will redeem for cash any chips returned to it before the customer leaves the store. If a customer offers to buy a certain item of goods at the store, and the girl behind the counter accepts his offer but then refuses to accept the customer's chips, the store will be in breach of the contract for chips. Likewise if, before he leaves the store, the customer hands in some or all of his chips at the cash desk, and the girl at the cash desk refuses to redeem them, the store will be in breach of the contract for chips.

Each time that a customer buys goods, he enters into a contract of sale, under which the customer purchases goods at the store. This is a contract for the sale of goods; it is not a contract of exchange, under which goods are exchanged for chips, but a contract of sale, under which goods are bought for a price, i.e. for a money consideration. This is because, when the customer surrenders chips of the appropriate denomination, the store appropriates part of the money deposited with it towards the purchase. This does not however alter the fact that an independent contract is made for the chips when the customer originally obtains them at the cash desk. Indeed that contract is not dependent upon any contract of sale being entered into; the customer could walk around the store and buy nothing, and then be entitled to redeem his chips in full under the terms of his contract with the store.

But the question remains: when the customer hands over his cash at the cash desk, and receives his chips, does the store give valuable consideration for the money so received by it? In common sense terms, the answer is no. For, in substance and in reality, there is simply a gratuitous deposit of the money with the store, with liberty to the customer to draw upon that deposit to pay for any goods he buys at the store. The chips are no more than the mechanism by which that result is achieved without any cash being handed over at the sales counter, and by which the customer can claim repayment of any balance remaining of his deposit. If a technical approach is adopted, it might be said that, since the property in the money passes to the store as depositee, it then gives consideration for the money in the form of a chose in action created by its promise to repay a like sum, subject to draw-down in respect of goods purchased at the store. I however prefer the common sense approach. Nobody would say that the store has purchased the money by promising to repay it: the promise to repay is simply the means of giving effect to the gratuitous deposit of the money with the store. It follows that, by receiving the money in these circumstances, the store does not for present purposes give valuable consideration for it. Otherwise a bank with which money was deposited by an innocent donee from a thief could claim to be a bona fide purchaser of the money simply by virtue of the fact of the deposit.

Let me next take the case of gambling at a casino. Of course, if gaming contracts were not void under English law by virtue of section 18 of the Gaming Act 1845, the result would be exactly the same. There would be a contract in respect of the chips, under which the money was deposited with the casino; and then separate contracts would be made when each bet was placed, at which point of time part or all of the money so deposited would be appropriated to the bets.

However, contracts by way of gaming or wagering are void in English law. What is the effect of this? It is obvious that each time a bet is placed by the gambler, the agreement under which the bet is placed is an agreement by way of gaming or wagering, and so is rendered null and void. It follows, as I have said, that the casino, by accepting the bet, does not thereby give valuable consideration for the money which has been wagered by the gambler, because the casino is under no legal obligation to honour the bet. Of course, the gambler cannot recover the money from the casino on the ground of failure of consideration; for he has relied upon the casino to honour the wager—he has in law given the money to the casino, trusting that the casino will fulfil the obligation binding in honour upon it and pay him if he wins his bet—though if the casino does so its payment to the gambler will likewise be in law a gift. But suppose it is not the gambler but the true owner of the money (from whom the gambler has perhaps, as in the present case, stolen the money) who is claiming it from the casino. What then? In those circumstances the casino cannot, in my opinion, say that it has given valuable consideration for the money, whether or not the gambler's bet is successful. It has given no consideration if the bet is unsuccessful, because its promise to pay on a successful bet is void; nor has it done so if the gambler's bet is successful and the casino has paid him his winnings, because that payment is in law a gift to the gambler by the casino.

For these reasons I conclude, in agreement with Nicholls LJ, that the respondents did not give valuable consideration for the money. But the matter does not stop there; because there remains the question whether the respondents can rely upon the defence of change of position.

[Lord Goff went on to discuss the defence of change of position and added: . . .] The defence of change of position is akin to the defence of bona fide purchase; but we cannot simply say that bona fide purchase is a species of change of position. This is because change of position will only avail a defendant to the extent that his position has been changed; whereas, where bona fide purchase is invoked, no inquiry is made (in most cases) into the adequacy of the consideration. . . .

Notes

1. For an illuminating analysis of bona fide purchase see Barker, 'After Change of Position: Good Faith Exchange in the Modern Law of Restitution' in Birks, *Laundering and Tracing*, 191–215. For the view that bona fide purchase operates to defeat *in rem* claims only see Key, 'Bona fide purchase as a defence in the law of restitution' [1994] LMCLQ 421.

2. There have been attempts to assimulate bona fide purchase to the defence of change of position, or to the defence of counter-restitution impossible: see Birks, 'Misdirected Funds: Restitution from the Recipient' [1989] LMCLQ 296, at 301–3; Birks, 'The English Recognition of Unjust Enrichment' [1991] LMCLQ 473, at 486–92; Birks, *The Future*, 123–47, especially at 132–5, and Sir Peter Millett, 'Tracing the Proceeds of Fraud' (1991) 107 LQR 71, at 82. This is not accepted by Lord Goff, and the autonomy of the defence now seems secure.

Section 2: change of position and estoppel

A: Estoppel

See Burrows, *Restitution*, 431–9 and Goff and Jones, 746–50. The cases all concern mistaken payments. Estoppel requires:

(a) either a representation by the payer that the payment is a correct one, or a breach of a duty by a payer accurately to state the account between payer and payee; and

(b) detrimental reliance by the payee.

It appears to operate as a complete defence to a restitutionary claim.

Holt v *Markham*
[1923] 1 KB 504 (CA)

Action for money had and received

The facts and decision in relation to the cause of action were discussed in Chapter 2, Section 2. Once the defendant was satisfied in February 1921 that the matter was concluded and there had been no overpayment, he sold his War Savings Certificates and invested a substantial sum in a company which subsequently went into liquidation. *Held*: that the plaintiff's mistake, if any, was one of law, and that the plaintiff was, in any event, precluded from recovery on the ground of estoppel.

BANKES LJ: [held the plaintiff's mistake was one of law and continued: . . .] But it was also contended on behalf of the plaintiffs that it was inequitable for the defendant to retain the money. It was said that he knew all about his position, and that he received the money knowing that it was largely in excess of what he was entitled to. All I can say is, if he did know it he knew more than Messrs Holt knew, or than the Admiralty or the Air Ministry knew. Indeed I am not certain myself that, if I had to apply these Orders and fix the defendant's gratuity, I could even now say with certainty what was the exact amount that he was entitled to, having regard to the fact that after his appointment to the Air Force the authorities did not pay him the 25 per cent. bonus on his pay and consequently did not in fact treat him as being on the Emergency List. I am satisfied that the defendant knew no more what his position was than any of the other persons concerned in the case. He was misled by the conduct of the plaintiffs into the belief that he might retain the money. I need not go into the authorities, but the judgment of Bayley J in *Skyring* v *Greenwood* 4 B & C 281, to which we have been referred, is, I think, directly applicable to the present defendant's case, for it appears that for a considerable time he was left under the impression that, although there had been at one time a doubt about his title to the money, that doubt had been removed, and in consequence he parted with his War Savings Certificates. Having done that it seems to me that he altered his position for the worse, and consequently the plaintiffs are estopped from alleging that the payment was made under a mistake of fact. . . .

WARRINGTON LJ: . . . But assume that the payment was made under a mistake of fact. The question then arises whether the conduct of the plaintiffs was such as to render it inequitable to give effect to the relief which they claim. In my opinion it was. In a letter of February 2, 1921, the plaintiffs demanded the repayment of the difference between the 744*l.* paid to the defendant and the 310*l.* to which he was entitled, basing their claim on the fact that he was a retired officer on retired pay and came within art. 497, *a.* On February 7 he replied that that claim was mistaken as he was not a retired officer. From that date until April 18 he heard no more about the matter, and from that fact he was in my opinion entitled to conclude that his reply was regarded as satisfactory, and that he was at liberty to deal with the money as he pleased. The result was that he availed himself of that liberty and spent the whole or a large part of the gratuity which had been paid him, and he is not now in a position to repay it. The plaintiffs are in my opinion estopped from asking that he should do so. On these grounds, first, that the plaintiffs have failed to establish that the money was paid under a mistake of fact, and secondly that, if it was, they are estopped from setting it up, I think that the appeal ought to be dismissed.

SCRUTTON LJ: . . . I personally propose to decide this case on one main ground, although I have also a view that it would be sufficient to decide it on another. I think this is a simple case of estoppel. The plaintiffs represented to the defendant that he was entitled to a certain sum of money and paid it, and after a lapse of time sufficient to enable any mistake to be rectified he acted upon that representation and spent the money. That is a case to which the ordinary rule of estoppel applies. In *Skyring* v *Greenwood* 4 B & C 281, 290, where the facts were very similar, Bayley J said: 'It would have been a good defence to that action to say that the defendants had voluntarily advanced money to the deceased when he asked no credit, and that they had told him that they had received the money for his use, and that on the faith of their representation he had drawn it out of their hands as his own money, and had been induced to spend it as such.' That view was acted upon by the Court of Appeal in the later case of *Deutsche Bank* v *Beriro* 1 Com Cas 255. There also money was paid by the plaintiffs under a mistake of fact, and the person to whom it was paid acted upon that payment and paid it over to another. It was held that the plaintiffs were estopped from recovering it back. In the present case the payment was made in September, 1919, and it was not till February, 1921, that there was any suggestion of a mistake having been made, and even then the suggestion was based on an entirely wrong ground. That was corrected by the defendant, and the matter was allowed to go on for another three months before the claim was made on the lines now put forward. That appears to me amply sufficient to bring the case within the principle that I have stated. . . .

R. E. Jones Ltd v *Waring and Gillow Ltd*
[1920] AC 670 (HL)

Action for money had and received

The facts and decision in relation to the cause of action were discussed in Chapter 2, Section 1. *Held*: unanimously, that the plaintiffs were entitled to restitution, and by a 3:2 majority that the respondents could not rely on the defence of estoppel.

VISCOUNT CAVE LC (dissenting): . . . My Lords, there is a great body of authority in favour of the view that, where a person to whom money has been paid by mistake has been misled by the payer's conduct, and on the faith of that conduct has acted to his own detriment, the payer cannot in law—as surely he cannot in fairness—insist on repayment. The well known dictum of Ashhurst J in *Lickbarrow* v *Mason* 2 TR 63, 70, that 'wherever one of two innocent persons must suffer by the acts of a third, he who has enabled such third person to occasion the loss must sustain it,' cannot now be treated as free from exception; but it still holds good as a general principle, and where the payer has been guilty of anything which can be called negligence or indiscretion, there has been no hesitation in applying it: see *per* Lord Halsbury in *Farquharson & Co.* v *King & Co.* [1902] AC 325, 332. Thus, in *Kleinwort* v *Dunlop Rubber Co.* 97 LT 263, 264 the plaintiff claiming repayment of money paid by mistake succeeded only because the jury had answered in the negative the question whether the defendants had been led by the plaintiff's mistake to alter their position to their own disadvantage; and Lord Loreburn, in expressing his opinion in this House, said that 'it is undisputable that, if money is paid under a mistake of fact and is re-demanded from the person who received it before his position has been altered to his disadvantage, the money must be repaid in whatever character it was received.' The same condition of the payer's right to recover—namely, the absence of any alteration of the payee's position to his detriment—has been emphasised in other cases such as *Continental Caoutchouc Co.* v *Kleinwort* 9 Com Cas 240 and *Kerrison* v *Glyn Mills, Currie & Co.* 17 Com Cas 41, 54; and in *Deutsche Bank* v *Beriro* 73 LT 669 and *Holt* v *Markham* [1923] 1 KB 504 the plaintiffs failed on that ground. It is true that, where the payee has done nothing more than to expend the money on his own purposes, that has been held to accord no defence: *Standish* v *Ross* (1849) 3 Ex 527; *Baylis* v *Bishop of London* [1913] 1 Ch 127, but this may be because the payee has suffered no real detriment. *Durrant* v *Ecclesiastical Commissioners* 6 QBD 234 is not easy to reconcile with the later decisions.

My Lords, the general rule as laid down in the authorities above cited appears to me to be sufficient to determine this case; and, this being so, it is unnecessary to dwell on the circumstance that the principle of estoppel has been applied with special stringency to claims to recover money paid on bills of exchange and other negotiable instruments. Instances of such an application are to be found in the well known case of *Cocks* v *Masterman* 9 B & C 902, in Mathew J's judgment in *London and River Plate Bank* v *Bank of Liverpool* [1896] 1 QB 7, and in the observations of Buckley LJ in *Morison* v *London County and Westminster Bank* [1914] 3 KB 356, 378. But the bearing on those authorities of the decision of this House in *Imperial Bank of Canada* v *Bank of Hamilton* [1903] AC 49 was not fully dealt with in the argument of this case; and accordingly, while I am inclined to the view that the rule in *Cocks* v *Masterman* lends support to the conclusion at which I have arrived, I have thought it best to rest my opinion on the wider ground taken in the *Dunlop Co.'s* case 97 LT 263.

Upon the whole I have come to the conclusion that on the ground of estoppel the respondents are entitled to succeed. . . .

LORD SUMNER: . . . The question, which of two innocent persons is to suffer by a third party's fraud, and the proposition, that some one 'acts to his detriment on the faith of' something done by another, never seem to me clear in themselves. The question assumes, that the law must in such a case interfere on behalf of one or the other. This does not follow without more. 'Acting on the faith' may only mean 'acting in the belief' or 'because of.' Something more is required for estoppel. Jones, Ld., did not stand by and watch Waring & Gillow's change of position before making a claim. The most that can be said is that Waring & Gillow, Ld., took the cheque and ascertained that it would be paid, as it was. Jones, Ld., made no promise not to ask for the money back, but, if they had done so, it would not have estopped them. No representation was made by or on behalf of Jones, Ld., to Waring & Gillow, Ld. If Waring & Gillow, Ld., changed their position towards Bodenham after he brought the cheques, that was because they thought he had greater pecuniary resources than they had supposed and, in so far as they thought so because of what he said or did, Jones, Ld., had no responsibility for his words or acts. I am unable to take the view, on the admissions made, that, by the production of the two cheques by Bodenham, Waring & Gillow, Ld., were led to believe (what was not the fact) that Jones, Ld., were their debtors, or that they were brought to them by him on the part of Jones, Ld., for such purposes as Bodenham on his part might happen to state. How the case would have stood had all this been proved in fact, I need not, therefore, discuss. I will only add that the *Kramrisch* cases (*Continental Caoutchouc Co.* v *Kleinwort* 9 Com Cas 240 and *Kleinwort* v *Dunlop Rubber Co.* 97 LT 263), particularly Lord Loreburn's proposition in 97 LT, at p. 264, and *Kerrison's case* 17 Com Cas 41, all refer to the defence to a claim for money paid under a mistake of fact, which an agent may set up, if, before discovery of the mistake, he has paid it over to the principal for whom he received it, but, as at present advised, I do not think they go further on the question of estoppel. The direct communications between Jones, Ld., and Waring & Gillow, Ld., by telephone or letter, did not constitute representations by Jones, Ld., nor was it on the faith of anything so said or written that Waring & Gillow, Ld., changed their position towards Bodenham. There was no duty between Jones, Ld., and Waring & Gillow, Ld., and, without that, the wide proposition of Ashhurst J. in *Lickbarrow* v *Mason* 2 TR 63, 70 would not apply (see observations of Lord Macnaghten and Lord Lindley in *Farquharson & Co.* v *King & Co.* [1902] AC 325, 335, 342, and of Lord Parmoor in *London Joint Stock Bank* v *Macmillan* [1918] AC 777, 836, which were apparently overlooked in *Commonwealth Trust* v *Akotey* [1926]. In the following cases a duty is the distinguishing feature, either that of banker to customer or arising in some similar relation (*Deutsche Bank* v *Beriro* 73 LT 669; *Holt* v *Markham* [1923] 1 KB 504), or a duty as agent (*Lloyds Bank* v *Cooke* [1907] 1 KB 794), or a duty such as existed in *Durrant* v *Ecclesiastical Commissioners* 6 QBD 234. . . .

Avon County Council v *Howlett*
[1983] 1 WLR 605 (CA)

For the facts and extracts in relation to the cause of action see Chapter 2, Section 1. The defendant was overpaid £1,007. It was accepted that the plaintiffs had made representations to the defendant that he could regard all the overpaid money as his own. As a result the plaintiffs underwent a detriment of £546.61. The case therefore raised the question whether the defence of estoppel could operate *pro tanto*. *Held*: that estoppel was a good defence to the whole of the claim.

SLADE LJ: . . . I now turn to the defence of estoppel. The following general propositions of law are to be found set out in Goff and Jones, *The Law of Restitution*, 2nd ed. (1978), pp. 554–5 (though I do not quote them verbatim). A plaintiff will be estopped from asserting his claim to restitution if the following conditions are satisfied: (a) the plaintiff must generally have made a representation of fact which led the defendant to believe that he was entitled to treat the money as his own; (b) the defendant must have, bona fide and without notice of the plaintiff's claim, consequently changed his position; (c) the payment must not have been primarily caused by the fault of the defendant.

In my opinion these propositions are entirely consistent with both the general principles which govern the doctrine of estoppel and with the authorities which have been cited to this court, illustrating the relevance of estoppel as a defence to claims to restitution. . . .

In the present case it is common ground that the plaintiffs made representations to the defendant which led him to believe that he was entitled to treat the entirety of the overpaid moneys as his own. This was conceded by the plaintiffs at the trial, so that the judge did not find it necessary in his judgment to give any particulars at all of the relevant representations. Certain authorities suggest that a plea of estoppel can afford a good defence to a claim for restitution only if the plaintiff owed a duty to the defendant to speak or act in a particular way: see, for example, *R. E. Jones Ltd* v *Waring and Gillow Ltd* [1926] AC 670, 693, *per* Lord Sumner; *Lloyds Bank Ltd* v *Brooks*, 6 Legal Decisions Affecting Bankers 161, 168 et seq. However, this point causes no difficulty for the defendant in the present case since the plaintiffs, as the defendant's employers, in my opinion clearly owed him a duty not to misrepresent the amount of the pay to which he was entitled from time to time, unless the misrepresentations were caused by incorrect information given to them by the defendant. It has not been suggested that the misrepresentations were so caused or that the overpayments were brought about by the defendant's own fault.

The judge found as a fact that the defendant had, bona fide and without notice of the plaintiffs' claim, changed his position in reliance on the representations, by losing the claim for £86.11 social security benefit and expending the sum of £460.50 which I have already mentioned. In the circumstances and in accordance with the principles already stated, he was in my opinion clearly right to hold that the plaintiffs' claim was barred by estoppel to the extent of at least £546.61 and there is no challenge to this part of his decision. However, according to the defendant's case as specifically pleaded, the change of position which he has undergone in reliance on the plaintiffs' representations, has only deprived him of the opportunity to return £546.61 of the overpayment; it has not deprived him of the opportunity to return the outstanding balance of £460.39 which, so far as the pleading reveals, *may* be still in his possession.

The judge considered that the defence of estoppel was in effect capable of being applied pro tanto, in the sense that a payer who has overpaid a payee, even in circumstances where all of conditions (a), (b) and (c) above are satisfied, will be precluded from claiming restitution only to the extent that it would be inequitable to require the payee to repay the relevant sums or part of the relevant sums in question. The judge clearly regarded the doctrine of estoppel as being a flexible doctrine, as indeed Lord Denning MR described it in *Amalgamated Investment & Property Co. Ltd* v *Texas Commerce International Bank Ltd* [1982] QB 84, 122.

If I may respectfully say so, I feel some sympathy with the judge's point of view. I also initially found unattractive the submission, placed before and rejected by him, that, if the defendant be treated as having spent in reliance on the plaintiffs' representations some £546.61 of the £1,007 received, the plaintiffs could not recover the balance of £460.39, even if it were still sitting untouched in some deposit account. At first sight such a conclusion would seem to leave the defendant unjustly enriched.

On further reflection, however, I think that references to broad concepts of justice or equity in a context such as the present may be somewhat misleading, as well as uncertain in their application. The conclusion of the judge in the present case really involves the proposition that, if the defendant is successfully to resist a claim for repayment of the entire sum of £1,007, the onus falls on him to prove specifically that the pecuniary amount of the prejudice suffered by him as a result of relying on the relevant representations made by the plaintiffs equals or exceeds that sum. For present purposes, however, one has to postulate a situation in which the defendant was perfectly entitled to conduct his business affairs on the assumption that the relevant representations were true, until he was told otherwise. Meantime, a defendant in the situation of the defendant in the present case may, in reliance on the representation, have either altered his general mode of living or undertaken commitments or incurred expenditure or entered into other transactions which it may be very difficult for him subsequently to recall and identify retrospectively in complete detail; he may even have done so, while leaving some of the particular moneys paid to him by the plaintiff untouched. If the pecuniary amount of his prejudice has to be precisely quantified by a defendant in such circumstances, he may be faced with obvious difficulties of proof. Thus, though extreme hypothetical cases can be envisaged, and indeed were canvassed in argument, in which broad considerations of equity and justice might appear to require the barring of a plaintiff's claim only pro tanto, if this were legally possible, I would not expect many such cases to arise in practice. In any event I do not consider the present case to be one of them, even on the basis of the facts as pleaded. I prefer to approach it simply by what I regard as the established legal principles governing the doctrine of estoppel.

Estoppel by representation is a rule of evidence, the consequence of which is simply to preclude the representor from averring facts contrary to his own representation: see *Spencer Bower and Turner, Estoppel by Representation,* 3rd ed. (1977), p. 112. It follows that a party who, as a result of being able to rely on an estoppel, succeeds on a cause of action on which, without being able to rely on it, he would necessarily have failed, may be able to recover more than the actual damage suffered by him as a result of the representation which gave rise to it. . . .

So far as they go, the authorities suggest that in cases where estoppel by representation is available as a defence to a claim for money had and received, the courts similarly do not treat the operation of the estoppel as being restricted to the precise amount of the detriment which the representee proves he has suffered in reliance on the representation. In *Skyring* v *Greenwood,* 4 B & C 281, the paymasters of a military corps had given credit in account to an officer for a period from January 1817 to November 1820, for certain increased pay. They had mistakenly supposed that this had been granted by a general order of 1806 to an officer of his situation. But in fact the paymasters had been informed in 1816 that the Board of Ordnance would not allow the increased payments to persons in the officer's situation. A statement of that account was delivered to the officer early in 1821, giving him credit for the increased pay to which they supposed him to be entitled. After the officer's death in 1822, his personal representatives sought to recover the whole of the pay which had been credited to him. The defendants claimed the right to retain the overpaid sums. The Court of King's Bench rejected this claim, apparently without any inquiry as to the amount of the expenditure or financial commitments which the officer had incurred in reliance upon the erroneous credit. The basis of the court's decision is to be found in the following passage from the judgment of Abbott CJ, at p. 289:

> I think it was their duty to communicate to the deceased the information which they had received from the Board of Ordnance; but they forbore to do so, and they suffered him to suppose during all the intervening time that he was entitled to the increased allowances. It is of great importance to any man, and certainly not less to military men than others, that they should not be led to suppose that their annual income is greater than it really is. Every prudent man accommodates his mode of living to what he supposes to be his income; it therefore works a great prejudice to any man, if after having had credit given him in account for certain sums, and having been allowed to draw on his agent on the faith that those sums belonged to him, he may be called upon to pay them back.

. . .

If it were in every case possible for the doctrine of estoppel by representation to operate merely pro tanto in cases where it is being invoked as a defence to an action for money had and received, I think that the Court of King's Bench in *Skyring* v *Greenwood,* 4 B & C 281, and the Court of Appeal in *Holt* v *Markham* [1923] 1 KB 504 and indeed Lynskey J in *Lloyds Bank Ltd* v *Brooks,* 6 Legal Decisions Affecting Bankers 161, would have been bound to conduct a much more exact process of quantification of the alteration of the financial position of the recipients, which had occurred by reason of the representations. The courts, however, in those cases, manifestly regarded any such process as irrelevant and inappropriate. All the relevant conditions for the operation of an estoppel being satisfied in those cases, the plea operated as a rule of evidence which precluded the payers from recovering any part of the money mistakenly overpaid or from retaining any part of the moneys mistakenly over-credited.

I think that no authority has been cited, other than the judgment of the judge, which directly supports the proposition that estoppel is capable of operating merely pro tanto in a case such as the present, where it is otherwise capable of being invoked as a complete defence to an action for money had and received. For the reasons which I have given, I conclude that such a proposition is contrary to principle and authority. . . .

B: Ministerial receipt

See Burrows, *Restitution*, 480–6, Goff and Jones, 750–5 and Swadling, 'The Nature of Ministerial Receipt' in Birks, *Laundering and Tracing*, 243–260.

Buller* v *Harrison
(1777) 2 Cowp 565; 98 ER 1234 (KB)

Action for money had and received

The plaintiff paid £2,100 to the defendant upon a policy of insurance, as agent for the insured in New York. The sum was paid in two parts on 20 April and 6 May, the plaintiff believing the loss to be a fair one. On 6 May, the defendant credited the sum received against a sum of £3,600 which the insured owed to him. On 17 May, the plaintiff gave the defendant notice that it was a foul loss and sought the return of the money.

LORD MANSFIELD: I am very glad this motion has been made; for I desire nothing so much as that all questions of mercantile law should be fully settled and ascertained; and it is of much more consequence that they should be so, than which way the decision is. The jury were embarrassed on the question whether this was a payment over. To many purposes it would be. It is now argued, that this is not a mere placing to account, but a making rest. If it were, it would not vary the case a straw. I verily believe the jury were entangled in considering it as a payment over. There is no imputation upon a man who trusts to a misrepresentation of the insured. It is greatly to his honour; but it makes it of consequence to him to know, how far his remedy goes if he is imposed upon. The whole question at the trial was, whether the defendant, who was an agent, had paid the money over. Now, the law is clear, that if an agent pay over money which has been paid to him by mistake, he does no wrong; and the plaintiff must call on the principal; and in the case of *Muilman* versus ———, where it appeared that the money was paid over, the plaintiff was nonsuited. But, on the other hand, shall a man, though innocent, gain by a mistake, or be in a better situation than if the mistake had not happened? Certainly not. In this case, there was no new credit, no acceptance of new bills, no fresh goods bought or money advanced. In short, no alteration in the situation which the defendant and his principals stood in towards each other on the 20th of April. What then is the case? The defendant has trusted Ludlow and Co. and given them credit. He trafficks to the country where they live, and has agents there who know how to get the money back. The plaintiff is a stranger to them and never heard of their names. Is it conscientious then, that the defendant should keep money which he has got by their misrepresentation, and should say, though there is no alteration in my account with my principal, this is a hit, I have got the money and I will keep it? If there had been any new credit given, it would have been proper to have left it to the jury to say, whether any prejudice had happened to the defendant by means of this payment: but here no prejudice at all is proved, and none is to be inferred. Under these circumstances I think (and Mr Justice Aston with whom I have talked the matter over is of the same opinion) that the defendant has no defence in point of law, and in point of equity and conscience he ought not to retain the money in question.

Snowdon v *Davies*
(1808) 1 Taunt 359; 127 ER 872 (Common Pleas)

Action for money had and received

The facts appear from the judgment of Sir James Mansfield CJ.

SIR JAMES MANSFIELD CJ: The facts of the case are short and few. A writ of distringas issued out of the exchequer to the sheriff of Berks, to levy issues on the inhabitants of New Windsor. The sheriff made his warrant, following the words of the distringas, and authorizing the defendant, his bailiff, to levy these issues. The distringas did not order the sheriff, nor did the sheriff order his bailiff, to levy the greater sums of 7l. 8s. 2d. and 74l. 2s. The bailiff threatens Snowdon to distrain his goods for these two sums. For a part of them, namely, for the issues, he had, for the residue, he had not, a right to distrain. The Plaintiff, under the terror of a distress, pays both these sums. The bailiff pays the money over to the sheriff, and the sheriff to the exchequer, and it is objected, that as it has been paid over, the action for money had and received does not lie against the bailiff; and this is compared to the case of an agent, and the authorities are cited, of *Sadler* v *Evans* 4 Burr 1986, *Campbell* v *Hall*, 1 Cowp 204, *Buller* v *Harrison*, 2 Cowp 565, and several others. In the case of *Sadler* v *Evans*, the money was paid to the agent of Lady Windsor for Lady Windsor's use: in that of *Buller* v *Harrison*, the money was paid to the broker, expressly for the benefit of the assured. In *Pond* v *Underwood* 2 Ld Raym 1210 the money was paid for the use of the administrator. Can it in this case be said with any propriety, that the money was paid to the bailiff for the purpose of paying it to the sheriff, or to the intent that the sheriff might pay it into the exchequer? The Plaintiff pays it under the terror of process, to redeem his goods, not with an intent that it should be delivered over to any one in particular. To make the argument the more curious, if it had happened that the Plaintiff had looked at the warrant, he could not have paid the money with a view that it should be paid over to the sheriff; for he would there have seen an authority to levy 4l. 1s. 6d. only. He clearly then paid the money under the terror of a distress. With respect to the other writ, the circumstances are the same. Under the like terrors of a distress, he pays the second sum. The warrant was, to levy upon the goods of the collectors, not upon those of the inhabitants of New Windsor. The Plaintiff pays that sum also to the bailiff, the bailiff having no authority whatsoever to receive it. The action for money had and received very well lies under the circumstances of this case, which in no respect resembles the cases cited, and the rule for a nonsuit must therefore be discharged.

Note

Money obtained by compulsion can therefore be recovered even if it has been paid over. This case emphasises the general point that restitutionary defences are available only to those who act in good faith.

Holland v *Russell*

(1861) 1 B & S 424, 121 ER 773 (QB); affd (1863) 4 B & S 514, 122 ER 365 (Exchequer Chamber)

Action for money had and received

The facts appear from the judgment of Cockburn CJ.

Court of Queen's Bench

COCKBURN CJ: This is an action brought against the defendant, in whose name an insurance had been effected on a foreign vessel, called The 'Butjadingen,' to recover back a sum of money paid by the plaintiff as one of the insurers, in ignorance of a certain fact the effect of which had been to make the insurance voidable, namely the omission of the defendant to communicate at the time of procuring the policy (which was a time policy), information he had received that the vessel had got on shore and had sustained material damage. It was admitted on the part of the defendant that all question as to the validity of the policy was concluded by the decision of the Court of Exchequer in the case of *Russell* v *Thornton* (4 H & N 788; affirmed on error, 6 Id 140), and that, if the insurance had been effected by the defendant as principal, the amount paid by the plaintiff would have been recoverable back from him in this action. The defence rested on the fact that the defendant, in effecting the insurance in the name of himself and those whom it might concern, had in reality acted only as the agent of the foreign owners, not being himself interested in the ship, and that, having received the payments on the insurance as their agent, he had either transmitted the amount of expended it by their direction, or had given them credit for it in an account finally settled between him and them, prior to any notice of objection by the plaintiff to his parting with the money.

It appeared that the defendant, having received on the policy, which was effected for 11,000l., sums amounting to 8,000l., had transmitted that amount to his principals; minus two sums, one of 607l. 3s. 10d., and the other of 608l. 10s 11d. The former of these two sums he had allowed in account with his principals in respect of a claim of his own against them for disbursements and commission; the latter he had retained by their authority, to defray the expenses of the suit against Thornton for the amount underwritten for on the policy by the latter.

Under these circumstances it was contended that the case came within the principle that an agent having received money on account of his principal and paid it over to the principal without notice to the contrary, is absolved from responsibility to the party from whom he received it; and that the defendant, having received the money as agent and paid it to, or on account of his principals, or allowed it conclusively in account with them, without any notice of revocation, could not be called upon to refund. To this it was answered on the part of the plaintiff that, the policy having been effected in the name of the defendant, the payment must be taken to have been made to him as principal. With reference to this point, we are of opinion that the plaintiff fails upon the facts. Not only is it clear that the defendant was acting solely as agent, but (the Court having power to draw inferences of fact) we are of opinion that the plaintiff was aware that the defendant was acting as agent for the foreign owners, and as such, made to him the payment of the money he now seeks to recover back. It is, therefore, unnecessary to consider the proposition contended for on behalf of the defendant, that the mere fact of the defendant having been an agent would have been sufficient to raise this defence, even if the plaintiff had not known him to be such at the time the payment was made.

Secondly, it was contended for the plaintiff that, although the jury have negatived an intentional fraud on the part of the defendant, yet as the suppression of a material fact whereby the policy became vitiated was throughout known to the defendant, the receipt of the money and the transmission of it to his principals could not be held to be other than a fraud in law, and that the defendant must be considered as in the same position as though he had received notice not to pay over the money on the ground that the policy had been found to be open to the exception now taken. To this contention we think a sufficient answer is afforded by the combined facts: first, that the proceedings of the defendant were throughout bonâ fide—he having been led to believe that the representation of the master as to the damage the ship had sustained was exaggerated, and also that, as the damage would be made good under a prior insurance, its existence need not be communicated on the proposal for the new policy; and, secondly, that the effect of the concealment complained of was not to make the policy void, but voidable only. Under these circumstances the defendant, receiving the money for his principals, not only without any notice that exception would be taken to the policy, but, further, with a full belief that none would be taken, did no more than discharge his duty in handing over the money. We see no reason, therefore, to exclude him from the benefit of the rule that an agent receiving money on account of his principal and paying it over to the principal, without notice to the contrary, is protected against any claim which the party from whom it was received would have had if the money had still remained in his hands. When money so paid to an agent has once been bonâ fide parted with, without notice, the liability of the agent ceases, and the claim of the party paying it can be enforced only against the principal to whom the money has been handed over.

The arguments we have thus far been considering have reference to the entire amount received by the defendant. But, it was further contended on behalf of the plaintiff that, even if the foregoing rule should be held to protect the defendant as to the amount which he had actually transmitted to his principals, the two sums of 607l. 3s. 10d. and 608l. 10s. 11d.—the first of which he had retained to satisfy his own claim on his principals, the second to meet the expenses of the action against Thornton—stood on a different footing, and that, as to these sums, the defendant, not having actually parted with them, was still liable to the plaintiff.

As to the first of these sums we were pressed on the argument with the authority of the cases of *Buller* v *Harrison* (Cowp 565), and *Cox* v *Prentice* (3 Mau & S 344), in which it was held that an agent having merely carried money received by him to the credit of the principal in a debtor and creditor account, although he had transmitted such account to the principal, still remained liable to the party by whom the money had been paid and who on sufficient cause demanded its repayment. While we fully recognise the authority of these cases, we are of opinion that the present case stands on a different footing. In those cases, the account being still open between the parties, the position of the agent was not prejudiced by having to refund the money. In the present case the defendant, having a claim against his principals, transmits to them an account made up to the end of the year, in which giving them credit for the amount received on this policy, he debits them with the amount of his claim, and strikes a balance which proves to be in their favour. With this balance he credits them in a further account for the ensuing year, which account was afterwards transmitted to them in due course. Both accounts were adopted and agreed to by the principals. The account thus became a settled account between the parties; and the transaction is in effect the same as though the agent had paid over the whole amount to the principals and had received back the amount of his claim. He cannot, any more than he could in the case lastly put, call upon the principals to pay over again; and he ought, therefore, to be equally held free from liability to the opposite party.

The question as to the sum of 608l. 10s. 11d. expended in the prosecution of the action against Thornton appears to us free from difficulty. This sum, which it may be assumed would otherwise have been transmitted to the principals, was by their assent and desire retained for the purpose of its being applied to the carrying on of a suit bonâ fide instituted and prosecuted on their behalf. This expenditure, having been made by the direction of the principals, is, therefore, equivalent to a payment actually made to them; and the defendant must be considered in the same position as though he had handed over the amount.

Our judgment is based throughout on the assumption, as fully warranted by the finding of the jury and the evidence, that the defendant acted all along bonâ fide, and without knowledge of any objection on the part of the plaintiff to his parting with the money to or on account of his principals. Although the defendant made the fatal mistake of withholding the information he had received as to the state of the ship, the jury have found that he did so without any intention of fraud; nor was any objection put forward by the insurers, who had paid on the policy till after the trial of the action of *Russell* v *Thornton* (4 H & N 788; affirmed on error, 6 Id 140), in which the ground of exception was for the first time disclosed. The appropriation of the money had in the meantime been made by the defendant without knowledge of the ground of exception, or that the policy was liable to be avoided, still less that the plaintiff would seek to repudiate the contract.

Under these circumstances we are of opinion that the defendant cannot be called upon to refund, and consequently that this rule must be discharged.

Baylis v *Bishop of London*
[1913] 1 Ch 127 (CA)

Action for money had and received

The facts appear from the judgment of Cozens-Hardy MR.

COZENS-HARDY MR: In this action the plaintiffs seek to recover from the Bishop of London certain sums paid to him in respect of tithe rent-charge, such payment being made under a mistake of fact, namely, that the rent-charge was payable in respect of lands in which the plaintiffs were interested, whereas in truth the liability of the plaintiffs to pay the rent-charge no longer existed. The mistake of fact and the receipt by the bishop are not now disputed. It has long been held that money paid under a mistake of fact can be recovered from the recipient, but an exception has been engrafted upon the rule that, where the money was paid to a person known to be an agent for a principal and known to be receiving as such, the agent cannot be sued if he has before notice of the mistake paid it over to his principal. In *Sadler* v *Evans* 4 Burr 1984, 1986, where the action was brought against Lady Windsor's agent, Lord Mansfield said that the action ought to have been brought against Lady Windsor herself and not against her agent: 'They' (i.e. the Court) 'thought the principles upon which actions for money had and received to the plaintiff's use are founded did not apply to the circumstances of the present case. It is a liberal action, founded upon large principles of equity, where the defendant can not conscientiously hold the money. The defence is any equity that will rebut the action. This money was paid to the known agent of Lady W. He is liable to her for it; whether he has actually paid it over to her, or not: he received it for her. And Lord Mansfield expressed a dissent to the case of *Jacob* v *Allen* (1703) 1 Salk 27, and his approbation of *Pond* v *Underwood* 2 Ld Raym 1210, 1211, which is contrary to it. He said, he kept clear of all payments to third persons, but' (i.e. except) 'where 'tis to a known agent; in which case, the action ought to be brought against the principal, unless in special cases (as under notice or mala fide).' This passage is the foundation on which the appellant's argument is erected. In *Moses* v *Macferlan* 2 Burr 1012 Lord Mansfield says that an action for money had and received lies only for money which, ex æquo et bono, the defendant ought to refund. But the wide language thus used by that great judge has not been followed. For example, money paid under a mistake of law cannot be recovered, although its retention would seem to be equally against good conscience.

It is argued on behalf of the appellant that the bishop, whose precise position I shall more fully consider, ought not, within the principle thus laid down by Lord Mansfield, to be held liable in the action because he has no individual interest in the money paid and has applied it in accordance with his duty. I am unable to accede to this view. No case can be found in the books in which a defendant has been exempted except that of an agent who has paid over to his principal. I think it is impossible for us at the present time to say that this exception ought to be extended in the manner which is desired. Not only is there no decision in favour of this view. There is not even a dictum, except that of Gibbs CJ in *Peto* v *Blades* 5 Taunt 657, but that case is so badly reported that I am quite unable to satisfy myself that the alleged dictum has any bearing upon the present case. But however that may be, it is sufficient to say that there are many dicta in favour of the opposite view. I need only refer to the observations of Lord Atkinson in *Kleinwort* v *Dunlop Rubber Co.* (1907) 97 LT 263, 265, and to the judgment of the Irish Court delivered by Palles CB in *Fitzpatrick* v *M'Glone* [1897] 2 IR 542. Unless, therefore, the bishop can establish that he received this money as an agent and has paid it over to his principal, I do not think his defence can prevail.

The rector of the parish in respect of which the tithe rent-charge was payable was adjudicated a bankrupt in 1895, and under s. 52 of the Bankruptcy Act, 1883, the trustee applied for a sequestration of the profits of the benefice. On June 17, 1897, Bishop Creighton sequestered in accordance with the provisions of that section, and granted to Mr Lee his power and authority in that behalf until the bishop should think fit to relax the same. The duties of the bishop are defined by the Sequestration Act, 1871, which must be read with ss. 13 to 20 of the Ecclesiastical Dilapidations Act, 1871. The effect is, shortly, that the money got in by the bishop under the sequestration must first be applied for securing the due performance of the spiritual duties in the parish, for which purpose not more than two-thirds of the income may at the discretion of the bishop be applied, next in satisfying any liability for dilapidations, and lastly in payment to the trustee in bankruptcy. Now in these circumstances it seems to me quite plain that there is no one who can be called a principal for whom the bishop is merely an agent. The sequestration was not issued in any Court as a means of enforcing the judgment of that Court. The bishop cannot be called upon to account on the footing that he is merely in the position of a sheriff executing the judgment of a Court of law.

In my opinion, the only mode in which a claim could be maintained against the bishop would have been in old days by a bill in Chancery, and would now be by an action in the Chancery Division, asking for an account of money received by him in a fiduciary character. In other words, the bishop must, for the purposes of the present argument, be treated as a trustee.

It follows that, in my opinion, both on the general ground and in view of the peculiar position of the bishop, having regard to s. 52 of the Bankruptcy Act, the plaintiffs are entitled to recover the money paid to the bishop under a mistake of fact, and that it is not a defence to say that the money so paid has been duly applied by the bishop. I may add that if the bishop is not liable, I fail to see against whom the plaintiffs could obtain any relief. . . .

HAMILTON LJ: The appellant's first position is that the liability to return money paid under a mistake of fact is itself an exceptional liability, which only arises when it would be not unfair to enforce it, and that an agent's defence of the 'usual protection of an agent' (*Holland* v *Russell* 4 B & S 14, 17) is only an illustration of a wider rule. The test is whether the defendant had or could have any personal interest in the money or was entirely disinterested. No express decision can be cited as authority for this. It is rested on Lady Windsor's case, *Sadler* v *Evans* 4 Burr 1984, 1986. To be sure this was itself a case of money paid under a mistake of fact to an agent who had, before claim made, paid it over to his principal, but the Court in giving judgment said that this action 'is a liberal action, founded upon large principles of equity, where the defendant cannot conscientiously hold the money. The defence is any equity that will rebut the action'; and Lord Mansfied said he 'kept clear of all payments to third persons, but where 'tis to a known agent; in which case, the action ought to be brought against the principal, unless in special cases.' I think that in citing dicta so largely expressed it is well to remember a saying of Sir James Mansfield in *Brisbane* v *Dacres* (1813) 5 Taunt 143, 162: 'It certainly is very hard upon a judge, if a rule which he generally lays down is to be taken up, and carried to its full extent. This is sometimes done by counsel, who have nothing else to rely on; but great caution ought to be used by the Court in extending such maxims to cases which the judge who uttered them never had in contemplation.' In the long line of cases where such claims have been made against agents and have been met by the answer that the agent has already paid the money to his principal, such as *Buller* v *Harrison* 2 Cowp 565, *Cox* v *Prentice* (1815) 3 M & S 344, *Holland* v *Russell* (1861) 1 B & S 424; 4 B & S 14, *Newall* v *Tomlinson* LR 6 CP 405, *Taylor* v *Metropolitan Ry. Co.* [1906] 2 KB 55, and *Kleinwort* v *Dunlop Rubber Co.* 97 LT 265, there are no expressions suggesting that the agent's case is only an instance of a wider immunity, while there are many which convey that this immunity is confined to the case of a mere agent. This consideration, coupled with the entire absence of any decision to the contrary, seems conclusive. . . .

The appellant's second position is that the bishop, truly considered, is an agent, and therefore, having disbursed these tithes, is immune as such from any claim to repay them. No case is cited to shew this, but he is described, with scant respect, as being 'a sort of ecclesiastical sheriff,' and it is claimed that a sheriff at any rate is not so liable. For this a dictum of Gibbs CJ in *Peto* v *Blades* 5 Taunt 657 is relied on. The case is so ill reported that there is some doubt whether the defendant was the sheriff himself or only his auctioneer, but in *Morley* v *Attenborough* (1849) 3 Ex 500 the case was cited by counsel (Bovill among them) as being an action against the sheriff, and Parke B's interlocutory observation, reported only in 18 Law J Rep (Exchequer), p. 150, seems to shew that he took it so to be. I cannot find the case relied on as an authority in sheriff law; it is cited in the books as an authority on the sale of goods (see notes to the report of it in 15 Revised Reports, 609, and Benjamin on Sale, 5th ed. p. 602). Nor can I find such exemption from liability anywhere claimed for a sheriff in books of authority. On the other hand, in *Inland* v *Bushell* (1836) 5 Dowl PC 147 Coleridge J assumes that, in spite of having paid the money over, the sheriff will, as a matter of course, be ordered to repay the judgment debtor's assignees in an action for money had and received to their use. A sheriff is not in any true sense the judgment creditor's agent. The latter is not liable in trover for the former's wrongful seizure unless he has personally interfered: *Whitmore* v *Greene* (1844) 13 M & W 104; *Notley* v *Buck* (1828) 8 B & C 160. Goods seized by the sheriff are in the custody of the law, not in the possession of the judgment creditor. Whatever analogy there may be between the sheriff and the bishop, the latter is even less an agent than the former. No answer is forthcoming to the question 'Who is the bishop's principal?' His large powers of devoting the emoluments of the sequestered benefice to parochial needs make him more independent in his own sphere than the sheriff is in his. No one can tell whether the plaintiff's money went to the incumbent's trustee in bankruptcy, or to the clerk taking the spiritual charge of the parish, or to the repair of dilapidations. As Neville J tersely put it, when the money reached the bishop it had 'reached its destination.'

I should add that the point as to estoppel by conduct was rightly abandoned by the appellant's counsel. . . .

Note

To the extent that this case denies the existence of a general defence of change of position it must now be regarded as impliedly overruled by *Lipkin Gorman* v *Karpnale Ltd* [1991] 2 AC 548.

Agip (Africa) Ltd v *Jackson*

[1990] Ch 265 (Ch D); affd [1991] Ch 547 (CA)

The facts and extracts in relation to the *action for money had and received* appear in Chapter 7, Section 1.

MILLETT J: [referred to the difficulties of imposing a personal liability upon an indirect recipient who has disposed of the benefit and continued: . . .]

But it is not necessary for me to decide this question because, in my judgment, there is a clear answer to the plaintiffs' claim for money had and received. Jackson & Co. must be treated as being in the same position as an agent who has accounted to his principal. Money paid by mistake to such an agent cannot afterwards be recovered from the agent but only from the principal. In every previously decided case the agent has received the money directly from the plaintiff, and it is well established that to obtain the benefit of the defence the recipient must have been known to the plaintiff to have been acting for a disclosed principal. In such a case the agent is treated as a mere conduit pipe and the money is taken as having been paid to the principal rather than the agent.

This defence would not have been available to Baker Oil. So far as the Banque du Sud was concerned, Baker Oil received the money as principal. If, however, the action for money had and received is extended to a subsequent transferee, the defence must be adapted to meet the extension, for it is unlikely that there will have been any dealings between the plaintiff or his agent and the subsequent transferee. In such a case the transferee's liability must depend on the character in which he received the money from the person from whom he received it. Baker Oil and Jackson & Co. were both acting as agents and trustees for the same clients and the payment by Baker Oil to Jackson & Co. was a transfer from one agent to another for onward transmission to their common principals. Save as regards the sum in court, the money has been accounted for to those principals and, in my judgment, any claim to recover it must now be made against them and not against Jackson & Co.

This defence does not avail an agent who has accounted to his principal after notice of the plaintiff's claim; but that was not the position in the present case. The evidence cannot be described as satisfactory, but the burden of proof rests on the plaintiffs, and they have failed to show that the defendants had such notice before 15 January 1985.

They do not seem to have been apprised of the plaintiffs' claim or of the discovery of the fraud. They were told only that the Banque du Sud was seeking to recall the payment. They were given no reason for the recall and, for all they knew, it might have had nothing to do with any claim by the plaintiffs to recover the money.

In addition, the defence does not avail an agent who is implicated in his principal's fraud. The relevant principles have not, however, been worked out by the common law. They have been developed in a series of modern cases which have been concerned with the application of equitable principles. It is accordingly convenient to deal with this aspect of the plaintiffs' claim under that head. . . .

Question

Is it consistent to hold that a recipient of money is accountable in equity on the ground of knowing assistance (now termed 'dishonest accessory liability') and that the same recipient is entitled to rely as a defence to a common law action for restitution upon the fact that he received the money ministerially?

Note

For Millett J's conclusions on Jackson & Co.'s liability in equity see the extracts in Chapter 7, Section 2 ('knowing receipt') and in Chapter 6, Section 5 ('knowing assistance'). In particular note that Millett J held that *beneficial* receipt was essential to a successful plea of knowing receipt.

C: Change of position

Together with its recognition of unjust enrichment as the underlying principle of restitutionary recovery, the significance of the leading case of *Lipkin Gorman* v *Karpnale Ltd* [1991] 2 AC 548 depends equally on its recognition of bona fide change of position as a defence to restitutionary claims. Before then its status was uncertain. Decisions such as *R. E. Jones Ltd* v *Waring & Gillow Ltd* [1926] AC 670 and *Ministry of Health* v *Simpson* [1951] AC 251 in the House of Lords were obstacles to its recognition. Sympathetic judges in the lower courts had 'smuggled *dicta* into the cases in its support' (Birks, *Introduction*, 414). See, for example, *Larner* v *London County Council* [1949] 2 KB 683, at 688 *per* Denning LJ (below); *BP Exploration Co. (Libya) Ltd* v *Hunt (No. 2)* [1979] 1 WLR 783, at 800, 804 *per* Robert Goff J (see Chapter 4, Section 2); *Barclays Bank Ltd* v *W. J. Simm, Son & Cooke (Southern) Ltd* [1980] QB 677, at 695–6 *per* Robert Goff J (see Chapter 2, Section 1); *R* v *Tower Hamlets London Borough Council, ex parte Chetnik Developments Ltd* [1988] AC 858, at 882 *per* Lord Goff of Chieveley (see Chapter 2, Section 2).

It has also been argued that change of position had already been recognised in particular contexts, such as the defence of ministerial receipt and in respect of bills of exchange (as to which see Goff and Jones, 755–9). Also, by that process of creative reinterpretation so characteristic of restitution scholarship, some older authorities have been explained in terms of the defence. For example, the claim *in rem* against the charities in *In re Diplock* [1948] Ch 465, at 546–7 did not succeed where the recipients had used the money to make alterations to their premises. This is explained in terms of change of position by Goff and Jones (Goff and Jones, 90–1; contrast Birks, *Introduction*,

411–12); and see now the discussion of Millett LJ in *Boscawen* v *Bajwa* [1995] 4 All ER 769, at 782–3 in relation to the *Diplock* claim against the Leaf Homeopathic Hospital. More recently Chen-Wishart ((1994) 110 LQR 173) has sought to explain the rescission case of *Cheese* v *Thomas* [1994] 1 WLR 129 in terms of the defence.

The House of Lords in *Lipkin Gorman* v *Karpnale* left the scope of the defence to be decided on a case-by-case basis. This makes it difficult to say anything definite about its boundaries. One big question is whether the defence goes to the enrichment issue: is the defendant still enriched? Or does it go to the question of whether it is *unjust* to order the defendant to make restitution? For discussion see Burrows, *Restitution*, 421–31; Birks, *The Future*, 123–47; Goff and Jones, 739–45; Nolan, 'Change of Position' in Birks, *Laundering and Tracing*, 135–89 and Key, 'Change of Position' (1995) 58 MLR 505.

Restatement of the Law of Restitution Quasi Contracts and Constructive Trusts

(St Paul, American Law Institute, 1937)

§142 Change of circumstances

(1) The right of a person to restitution from another because of a benefit received is terminated or diminished if, after the receipt of the benefit, circumstances have so changed that it would be inequitable to require the other to make full restitution.

(2) Change of circumstances may be a defense or a partial defense if the conduct of the recipient was not tortious and he was no more at fault for his receipt, retention or dealing with the subject matter than was the claimant.

(3) Change of circumstances is not a defense if

(a) the conduct of the recipient in obtaining, retaining or dealing with the subject matter was tortious, or

(b) the change occurred after the recipient had knowledge of the facts entitling the other to restitution and had an opportunity to make restitution.

Larner v *London County Council*

[1949] 2 KB 683 (CA)

The facts and the ground for restitution were discussed in Chapter 2, Section 1. The Court of Appeal held that the defendant local authority was prima facie entitled to restitution subject to applicable defences.

DENNING LJ: . . . It is next said, however, that Mr Larner did change his position for the worse before the council asked for the money. He spent the money on living expenses—or his wife spent it for him—and he spent it in a way which he would not otherwise have done. This defence of estoppel, as it is called—or more accurately, change of circumstances—must, however, not be extended beyond its proper bounds. Speaking generally, the fact that the recipient has spent the money beyond recall is no defence unless there was some fault, as, for instance, breach of duty—on the part of the paymaster and none on the part of the recipient. In both *Skyring* v *Greenwood and*

Cox 4 B & C 281 and *Holt* v *Markham* [1923] 1 KB 504 there was a breach of duty by the paymaster and none by the recipient. See *Jones (R. E.) Ld.* v *Waring and Gillow Ld., per* Lord Sumner [1926] AC 670, 693.

But if the recipient was himself at fault and the paymaster was not—as, for instance, if the mistake was due to an innocent misrepresentation or a breach of duty by the recipient—he clearly cannot escape liability by saying that he has spent the money. That is the position here. On the judge's findings, the London County Council was not at fault at all, but Mr Larner was. He did not keep them accurately informed of the various changes in his service pay. It does not lie in his mouth to say that, if he had done so, it would have made no difference. It might well have put them on inquiry and the mistake might not have been made at all. It would be strange, indeed, if those who neglected their duty were to be allowed to keep their gain. . . .

Rover International Ltd v *Cannon Film Sales Ltd*

[1989] 1 WLR 912 (CA)

'Rover' appeal

The facts in relation to the claim of mistake were set out in Chapter 2, Section 1.

KERR LJ: . . . The only substantial answer which he sought to put forward was that Rover could not recover these payments because Thorn EMI/Cannon had changed their position in reliance upon them. He relied on the statements of principle by Robert Goff J in *Barclays Bank Ltd* v *W. J. Simms Son & Cooke (Southern) Ltd* [1980] QB 677, 695b–d. However, as shown by the passage, at p. 695h, referring back to the discussion, at p. 691g, of *Kleinwort, Sons, and Co.* v *Dunlop Rubber Co.* (1907) 97 LT 263, the 'defence of change of position' involves a requirement that the recipient of the money paid under a mistake should have changed his position to his disadvantage. The principle quoted from the speech of Lord Loreburn LC, at p. 264, is in the following terms:

> it is indisputable that, if money is paid under a mistake of fact and is redemanded from the person who received it before his position has been altered *to his disadvantage*, the money must be repaid in whatever character it was received. (Emphasis added.)

Mr Pardoe's submission ignored the words which I have emphasised. He relied again on the delivery by Thorn EMI/Cannon of films pursuant to the agreement. But that was not a change of position to their disadvantage. On the contrary, if anyone was thereby disadvantaged it was Rover/Monitor who expended money, time and effort upon the films to the advantage, as it turned out, of Cannon, since they are not entitled to the entire gross receipts, subject only to a quantum meruit for the services which generated them. . . .

DILLON LJ: . . . The first argument of Cannon is . . . to my mind more intricate. It is stated in Goff and Jones, *The Law of Restitution*, 3rd ed. (1986), p. 113:

> It might have been expected that an action to recover money paid under a mistake of fact would be defeated if the defendant had so changed his position in good faith that it had become inequitable to require him to repay the money. Recognition of such a defence would be consistent with the principle of restitutio in integrum. As yet, however, it cannot be said that a defence of change of position has been formally recognised.

There are cases, of which *Avon County Council* v *Howlett* [1983] 1 WLR 605 is one, where money has been paid under a mistake of fact and the recipient has altered his position by spending the money, believing in good faith that it was his own to spend, and it has subsequently been held that the payer could not recover the money from the recipient. But the basis of those cases was estoppel, viz. that in the circumstances the payer was estopped from setting up his mistake against the recipient who had altered his position in good faith in reliance on the payment. In the present case, the circumstances are very different and I can see no basis for any estoppel which would preclude Rover from setting up against Cannon the mistake which was common to both of them, viz. that their supposed contract had purportedly been made before Rover had actually been incorporated.

The alteration of position relied on by Cannon was not the spending of the money paid to it (as in *Avon County Council* v *Howlett* and other cases there cited) but that Cannon treated the supposed contract as kept on foot by the payment of the instalments by Rover, and so Cannon performed its part of the contract by supplying Rover with copies of the films and other materials which Rover used to arrange the release of the films in public cinemas in Italy, again in purported performance of the supposed contract. Thus the position is changed for all time in that these films have had their first release in the cinemas of Italy and can never have another first release. If however, Cannon's argument is correct and that is an alteration of position on the part of Cannon which precludes Rover from recovering the instalments as moneys paid under a mistake of fact, it would seem to follow that in any case where a supposed contract is in truth void for mistake of fact, moneys paid under the supposed contract cannot be recovered as moneys paid under a mistake of fact if the payee has, in reliance on the payment, himself performed some part of his obligations under the supposed contract—e.g. if there was a mistake as to the nature of goods sold, the seller could refuse to refund the price on the ground that he had altered his position by supplying the mistaken goods against payment of the price. I do not believe that the law has gone so far.

The problem is discussed in Goff and Jones, *The Law of Restitution*, pp. 691–7. They cite a passage from the speech of Lord Simonds in *Ministry of Health* v *Simpson* [1951] AC 251, 276, in which all the other members of the appellate committee hearing that case concurred. Lord Simonds was expounding the rules established by the courts of equity over centuries where, in the administration of an estate, money had by mistake been paid by the personal representative to the wrong person. Lord Simonds commented:

> The broad fact remains that the Court of Chancery, in order to mitigate the rigour of the common law or to supply its deficiencies, established the rule of equity which I have described and this rule did not excuse the wrongly paid legatee from repayment because he had spent what he had been wrongly paid. No doubt the plaintiff might by his conduct and particularly by laches have raised some equity against himself; but if he had not done so, he was entitled to be repaid.

The authors also refer to the decision of this court in *Baylis* v *Bishop of London* [1913] 1 Ch 127. That was a case where money had been paid under a mistake of fact and there was no question of estoppel: see *per* Hamilton LJ, at p. 141. This court therefore held the right of the payer to recover the money from the payee to be absolute, subject only to the established exception, held to be inapplicable in *Baylis* and not relevant in the present case (or in *Ministry of Health* v *Simpson*) that money paid by mistake to a person who was known to be merely an agent cannot be recovered from the agent after he has accounted for the money to his principal.

Since both *Ministry of Health* v *Simpson* and *Baylis* v *Bishop of London* are binding on this court and since both proceeded on the basis that there are clear rules that money paid by mistake of fact is recoverable unless one or other of two very limited exceptions applies—estoppel by conduct or payment to a mere agent who has accounted to his principal— it is not, in my judgment, open to this court to hold either (i) that there is a general 'equity' to allow, or disallow, repayment by way of restitution in whole or in part as may be thought fair, or (ii) that if there has been any change of position the money paid under a mistake of fact cannot be recovered even if there is no estoppel.

Accordingly on the ground of mistake of fact I would allow Rover's appeal and order Cannon to repay the five instalments. It is consequently unnecessary for me to express any opinion on the question of total failure of consideration. . . .

Note

Kerr LJ seemed to accept the existence of change of position, but did not think it was made out on the facts. Dillon LJ did not think it open to the Court of Appeal to consider the defence. Nicholls LJ agreed with both judgments. See Birks (1990) 2 JCL 227, at 238–9.

Lipkin Gorman v *Karpnale Ltd*
[1991] 2 AC 548 (HL)

Action for money had and received

The facts are set out in Chapter 7, Section 1.

LORD TEMPLEMAN: . . . In the course of argument there was a good deal of discussion concerning tracing in law and in equity. In my opinion in a claim for money had and received by a thief, the plaintiff victim must show that money belonging to him was paid by the thief to the defendant and that the defendant was unjustly enriched and remained unjustly enriched. An innocent recipient of stolen money may not be enriched at all; if Cass had paid £20,000 derived from the solicitors to a car dealer for a motor car priced at £20,000, the car dealer would not have been enriched. The car dealer would have received £20,000 for a car worth £20,000. But an innocent recipient of stolen money will be enriched if the recipient has not given full consideration. If Cass had given £20,000 of the solicitors' money to a friend as a gift, the friend would have been enriched and unjustly enriched because a donee of stolen money cannot in good conscience rely on the bounty of the thief to deny restitution to the victim of the theft. Complications arise if the donee innocently expends the stolen money in reliance on the validity of the gift before the donee receives notice of the victim's claim for restitution. Thus if the donee spent £20,000 in the purchase of a motor car which he would not have purchased but for the gift, it seems to me that the donee has altered his position on the faith of the gift and has only been unjustly enriched to the extent of the secondhand value of the motor car at the date when the victim of the theft seeks restitution. If the donee spends the £20,000 in a trip round the world, which he would not have undertaken without the gift, it seems to me that the donee has altered his position on the faith of the gift and that he is not unjustly enriched when the victim of the theft seeks restitution. In the present case Cass stole and the club received £229,908.48 [*scilicet*: £222,908.98] of the solicitors money. If the club was in the same position as a donee, the club nevertheless in good faith allowed Cass to gamble with the solicitors' money and paid his winnings from time to time so that when the solicitors' sought restitution, the club only retained £154,695 derived from the solicitors. . . . [Lord Templeman's figures include an additional £3,735 claimed for the conversion of a bankers' draft stolen by Cass from the solicitors.]

LORD GOFF OF CHIEVELEY: . . . Whether change of position is, or should be, recognised as a defence to claims in restitution is a subject which has been much debated in the books. It is however a matter on which there is a remarkable unanimity of view, the consensus being to the effect that such a defence should be recognised in English Law. I myself am under no doubt that this is right.

Historically, despite broad statements of Lord Mansfield to the effect that an action for money had and received will only lie where it is inequitable for the defendant to retain the money (see in particular *Moses* v *Macferlan* (1760) 2 Burr 1005), the defence has received at most only partial recognition in English law. I refer to two groups of cases which can arguably be said to rest upon change of position: (1) where an agent can defeat a claim to restitution on the ground that, before learning of the plaintiff's claim, he has paid the money over to his principal or otherwise altered his position in relation to his principal on the faith of the payment; and (2) certain cases concerned with bills of exchange, in which money paid under forged bills has been held irrecoverable on grounds which may, on one possible view, be rationalised in terms of change of position: see, e.g. *Price* v *Neal* (1762) 3 Burr 1355, and *London and River Plate Bank Ltd* v *Bank of Liverpool* [1896] 1 QB 7. There has however been no general recognition of any defence of change of position as such; indeed any such defence is inconsistent with the decisions of the Exchequer Division in *Durrant* v *Ecclesiastical Commissioners for England and Wales* (1880) 6 QBD 234, and of the Court of Appeal in *Baylis* v *Bishop of London* [1913] 1 Ch 127. Instead, where change of position has been relied upon by the defendant, it has been usual to approach the problem as one of estoppel; see, e.g. *R. E. Jones Ltd* v *Waring and Gillow Ltd* [1926] AC 670 and *Avon County Council* v *Howlett* [1983] 1 WLR 605. But it is difficult to see the justification for such a rationalisation. First, estoppel normally depends upon the existence of a representation by one party, in reliance upon which the representee has so changed his position that it is inequitable for the representor to go back upon his representation. But, in cases of restitution, the requirement of a representation appears to be unnecessary. It is true that, in cases where the plaintiff has paid money directly to the defendant, it has been argued (though with difficulty) that the plaintiff has represented to the defendant that he is entitled to the money; but in a case such as the present, in which the money is paid to an innocent donee by a thief, the true owner has made no representation whatever to the defendant. Again, it was held by the Court of Appeal in *Avon County Council* v *Howlett* that estoppel cannot operate pro tanto, with the effect that if, for example, the defendant has innocently changed his position by disposing of part of the money, a defence of estoppel would provide him with a defence to the whole of the claim. Considerations such as these provide a strong indication that, in many cases, estoppel is not an appropriate concept to deal with the problem.

In these circumstances, it is right that we should ask ourselves: why do we feel that it would be unjust to allow restitution in cases such as these? The answer must be that, where an innocent defendant's position is so changed that he will suffer an injustice if called upon to repay or to repay in full, the injustice of requiring him so to repay outweighs the injustice of denying the plaintiff restitution. If the plaintiff pays money to the defendant under a mistake of fact, and the defendant then, acting in good faith, pays the money or part of it to charity, it is unjust to require the defendant to make restitution to the extent that he has so changed his position. Likewise, on facts such as those in the present case, if a thief steals my money and pays it to a third party who gives it away to charity, that third party should have a good defence to an action for money had and received. In other words, bona fide change of position should of itself be a good defence in such cases as these. The principle is widely recognised throughout the common law world. It is recognised in the United States of America (see *American Law Institute, Restatement of the Law, Restitution* (1937), section 142, pp. 567–78 and *Palmer, The Law of Restitution* (1978), vol. III, para. 16.8); it has been judicially recognised by the Supreme Court of Canada (see *Rural Municipality of Storthoaks* v *Mobil Oil Canada Ltd* (1975) 55 DLR (3d) 1); it has been introduced by statute in New Zealand (Judicature Act 1908, section 94B (as amended)), and in Western Australia (see Western Australia Law Reform (Property, Perpetuities and Succession) Act 1962, section 24, and Western Australia Trustee Act 1962, section 65(8)), and it has been judicially recognised by the Supreme Court of Victoria: see *Bank of New South Wales* v *Murphett* [1983] 1 VR 489. In the important case of *Australia and New Zealand Banking Group Ltd* v *Westpac Banking Corporation* (1988) 78 ALR 157, there are strong indications that the High Court of Australia may be moving towards the same destination (see especially at pp. 162 and 168, *per curiam*). The time for its recognition in this country is, in my opinion, long overdue.

I am most anxious that, in recognising this defence to actions of restitution, nothing should be said at this stage to inhibit the development of the defence on a case by case basis, in the usual way. It is, of course, plain that the defence is not open to one who has changed his position in bad faith, as where the defendant has paid away the money with knowledge of the facts entitling the plaintiff to restitution; and it is commonly accepted that the defence should not be open to a wrongdoer. These are matters which can, in due course, be considered in depth in cases where they arise for consideration. They do not arise in the present case. Here there is no doubt that the respondents have acted in good faith throughout, and the action is not founded upon any wrongdoing of the respondents. It is not however appropriate in the present case to attempt to identify all those actions in restitution to which change of position may be a defence. A prominent example will, no doubt, be found in those cases where the plaintiff is seeking repayment of money paid under a mistake of fact; but I can see no reason why the defence should not also be available in principle in a case such as the present, where the plaintiff's money has been paid by a thief to an innocent donee, and the plaintiff then seeks repayment from the donee in an action for money had and received. At present I do not wish to state the principle any less broadly than this: that the defence is available to a person whose position has so changed that it would be inequitable in all the circumstances to require him to make restitution, or alternatively to make restitution in full. I wish to stress however that the mere fact that the defendant has spent the money, in whole or in part, does not of itself render it inequitable that he should be called upon to repay, because the expenditure might in any event have been incurred by him in the ordinary course of things. I fear that the mistaken assumption that mere expenditure of money may be regarded as amounting to a change of position for present purposes has led in the past to opposition by some to recognition of a defence which in fact is likely to be available only on comparatively rare occasions. In this connection I have particularly in mind the speech of Lord Simonds in *Ministry of Health* v *Simpson* [1951] AC 251, 276.

I wish to add two further footnotes. The defence of change of position is akin to the defence of bona fide purchase; but we cannot simply say that bona fide purchase is a species of change of position. This is because change of position will only avail a defendant to the extent that his position has been changed; whereas, where bona fide purchase is invoked, no inquiry is made (in most cases) into the adequacy of the consideration. Even so, the recognition of change of position as a defence should be doubly beneficial. It will enable a more generous approach to be taken to the recognition of the right to restitution, in the knowledge that the defence is, in appropriate cases, available; and while recognising the different functions of property at law and in equity, there may also in due course develop a more consistent approach to tracing claims, in which common defences are recognised as available to such claims, whether advanced at law or in equity.

I turn to the application of this principle to the present case. In doing so, I think it right to stress at the outset that the respondents, by running a casino at the club, were conducting a perfectly lawful business. There is nothing unlawful about accepting bets at a casino; the only relevant consequence of the transactions being gambling transactions is that they are void. In other words, the transactions as such give rise to no legal obligations. Neither the gambler, nor the casino, can go to court to enforce a gaming transaction. That is the legal position. But the practical or business position is that, if a casino does not pay winnings when they are due, it will simply go out of business. So the obligation in honour to pay winnings is an obligation which, in business terms, the casino has to comply with. It is also relevant to bear in mind that, in the present case, there is no question of Cass having gambled on credit. In each case, the money was put up front, not paid to discharge the balance of an account kept for gambling debts. It was because the money was paid over, that the casino accepted the bets at all.

In the course of argument before your Lordships, attention was focused upon the overall position of the respondents. From this it emerged, that, on the basis I have indicated (but excluding the banker's draft), at least £150,960 derived from money stolen by Cass from the solicitors was won by the club and lost by Cass. On this approach, the possibility arose that the effect of change of position should be to limit the amount recoverable by the solicitors to that sum. But there are difficulties in the way of this approach. Let us suppose that a gambler places two bets with a casino, using money stolen from a third party. The gambler wins the first bet and loses the second. So far as the winning bet is concerned, it is readily understandable that the casino should be able to say that it is not liable to the true owner for money had and received, on the ground that it has changed its position in good faith. But at first sight it is not easy to see how it can aggregate the two bets together and say that, by paying winnings on the first bet in excess of both, it should be able to deny liability in respect of the money received in respect of the second.

There are other ways in which the problem might be approached, the first narrower and the second broader than that which I have just described. The narrower approach is to limit the impact of the winnings to the winning bet itself, so that the amount of all other bets placed with the plaintiff's money would be recoverable by him regardless of the substantial winnings paid by the casino to the gambler on the winning bet. On the broader approach, it could be said that, each time a bet is accepted by the casino, with the money up front, the casino, by accepting the bet, so changes its position in good faith that it would inequitable to require it to pay the money back to the true owner. This would be because, by accepting the bet, the casino has committed itself, in business terms, to pay the gambler his winnings if successful. In such circumstances, the bookmaker could say that, acting in good faith, he had changed his position, by incurring the risk of having to pay a sum of money substantially larger than the amount of the stake. On this basis, it would be irrelevant whether the gambler won the bet or not, or, if he did win the bet, how much he won.

I must confess that I have not found the point an easy one. But in the end I have come to the conclusion that on the facts of the present case the first of these three solutions is appropriate. Let us suppose that only one bet was placed by a gambler at a casino with the plaintiff's money, and that he lost it. In that simple case, although it is true that the casino will have changed its position to the extent that it has incurred the risk, it will in the result have paid out nothing to the gambler, and so prima facie it would not be inequitable to require it to repay the amount of the bet to the plaintiff. The same would, of course, be equally true if the gambler placed a hundred bets with the plaintiff's money and lost them all; the plaintiff should be entitled to recover the amount of all the bets. This conclusion has the merit of consistency with the decision of the Court of King's Bench in *Clarke* v *Shee and Johnson*, 1 Cowp 197. But then, let us suppose that the gambler has won one or more out of one hundred bets placed by him with the plaintiff's money at a casino over a certain period of time, and that the casino has paid him a substantial sum in winnings, equal, let us assume, to one half of the amount of all the bets. Given that it is not inequitable to require the casino to repay to the plaintiff the amount of the bets in full where no winnings have been paid, it would, in the circumstances I have just described, be inequitable, in my opinion, to require the casino to repay to the plaintiff more than one half of his money. The inequity, as I perceive it, arises from the nature of gambling itself. In gambling only an occasional bet is won, but when the gambler wins he will receive much more than the stake placed for his winning bet. True, there may be no immediate connection between the bets. They may be placed on different occasions, and each one is a separate gaming contract. But the point is that there has been a series of transactions under which all the bets have been placed by paying the plaintiff's money to the casino, and on each occasion the casino has incurred the risk that the gambler will win. It is the totality of the bets which yields, by the laws of chance, the occasional winning bet; and the occasional winning bet is therefore, in practical terms, the result of the casino changing its position by incurring the risk of losing on each occasion when a bet is placed with it by the gambler. So, when in such circumstances the plaintiff seeks to recover from the casino the amount of several bets placed with it by a gambler with his money, it would be inequitable to require the casino to repay in full without bringing into account winnings paid by it to the gambler on any one or more of the bets so placed with it. The result may not be entirely logical; but it is surely just.

For these reasons, I would allow the solicitors appeal in respect of the money, limited however to the sum of £150,960. . . .

David Securities Pty Ltd v *Commonwealth Bank of Australia*
(1992) 175 CLR 353 (High Court of Australia)

The facts and extracts relating to the cause of action appear in Chapter 2, Section 2.

MASON CJ, DEANE, TOOHEY, GAUDRON AND McHUGH JJ: . . . The respondent next submits that an order for restitution would be unjust because it has changed its position. The defence of change of position has not been expressly accepted in this country. In *Australia and New Zealand Banking Group Ltd* v *Westpac Banking Corporation* (1988) 164 CLR 662, the Court referred to the displacement of prima facie liability by 'some adverse change of position by the recipient in good faith and in reliance on the payment' (1988) 164 CLR, at p. 673. The issue did not, however, arise for decision in that case. In this country, conflicting views have been expressed. In *Bank of New South Wales* v *Murphett* [1983] 1 VR, at p. 496, Crockett J thought change of position was a defence. However, in *National Mutual Life Association of Australasia Ltd* v *Walsh* (1987) 8 NSWLR, at pp. 598–9, Clarke J concluded that the English Court of Appeal decision in *Baylis* v *Bishop of London* [1913] 1 Ch 127 ruled out the acceptance of such a defence in the case before him. In England, there is strong authority in favour of acceptance of the defence, viz. the judgment of Kerr LJ in *Rover International Ltd* [1989] 1 WLR, at p. 925; [1989] 3 All E.R., at p. 434, *Barclays Bank* [1980] QB, at pp. 695–6 and most importantly the recent decision of the House of Lords in *Lipkin Gorman* v *Karpnale Ltd* [1991] 2 AC 548, at pp. 558, 568, 578–80. In the last case, Lord Bridge of Harwich, Lord Ackner and Lord Goff of Chieveley held that English law should recognize the defence, although they declined to define its scope. Text writers (Goff and Jones, [*The Law of Restitution*, 3rd ed. (1986)] pp. 46–7; Birks, [*An Introduction to the Law of Restitution* (1989)] pp. 414–15; Beatson, [*The Use and Abuse of Unjust Enrichment* (1991)] pp. 155–60) also support the existence of the defence, particularly in view of the inflexibility of the related doctrine of estoppel, as evidenced by *Avon C.C.* v *Howlett* [1983] 1 WLR 605; [1983] 1 All ER 1073 where the Court of Appeal held that estoppel could not operate pro tanto. And, in Canada (*Rural Municipality of Storthoaks* v *Mobil Oil Canada Ltd.* (1975), 55 DLR (3d) 1) and the United States (*Restatement of the Law of Restitution,* §69(1)), the defence of change of position has been recognized. Section 125(1) of the *Property Law Act* 1969 (WA) and s. 94B of the *Judicature Act* 1908 (NZ) also provide for this defence.

If we accept the principle that payments made under a mistake of law should be prima facie recoverable, in the same way as payments made under a mistake of fact, a defence of change of position is necessary to ensure that enrichment of the recipient of the payment is prevented only in circumstances where it would be *unjust.* This does not mean that the concept of unjust enrichment needs to shift the primary focus of its attention from the moment of enrichment. From the point of view of the person making the payment, what happens after he or she has mistakenly paid over the money is irrelevant, for it is at that moment that the defendant is unjustly enriched. However, the defence of change of position is relevant to the enrichment of the defendant precisely because its central element is that the defendant has acted to his or her detriment on the *faith of the receipt* (Birks, *op. cit.*, p. 410). In the jurisdictions in which it has been accepted (Canada and the United States), the defence operates in different ways but the common element in all cases is the requirement that the defendant point to expenditure or financial commitment which can be ascribed to the mistaken payment (*Rural Municipality of Storthoaks* v *Mobil Oil Canada Ltd* (1975), 55 DLR (3d), at p. 13; *Grand Lodge, A.O.U.W. of Minnesota* v *Towne* (1917), 161 NW 403, at p. 407). In Canada and in some United States decisions, the defendant has been required to point to *specific* expenditure being incurred because of the payment. Other cases in the United States, (e.g., *Moritz* v *Horsman* (1943), 9 NW 2d 868) allow a wider scope to the defence, such that a defendant can rely upon it even though he or she cannot precisely identify the expenditure caused by the mistaken payments. In no jurisdiction, however, can a defendant resort to the defence of change of position where he or she has simply spent the money received on ordinary living expenses. . . .

Questions

1. A fond uncle mistakenly makes a second gift of £500 to his niece, having forgotten his earlier transfer of a similar sum. The niece believing her uncle to intend both gifts, donates £250 to her favourite charity.

2. The same uncle promises his nephew £500 having forgotten an earlier gift. The nephew believing the uncle to intend both gifts, donates £250 to his favourite charity and *then* receives the cheque.

Should the answer to these two problems differ?

South Tyneside Metropolitan Borough Council v *Svenska International plc*

[1995] 1 All ER 545 (QBD (Commercial Court))

The bank and the council entered into an interest rate swap commencing 2 June 1988 and terminating on 3 February 1995. The notional principal sum was £15 million; the bank was the fixed rate payer and the council was a floating rate payer. All the bank's deals were 'hedged'. On hearing the provisional view of the House of Lords that such transactions were *ultra vires* and void (see the reasons given later in *Hazell* v *Hammersmith and Fulham London Borough Council* [1992] 2 AC 1), the bank closed out its position and unwound its hedges. It was agreed that it sustained a loss of £1.2 million by that date. The council sought restitution on the net sum it had paid under the transaction and the bank argued it had changed its position.

CLARKE J: [His lordship discussed *Lipkin Gorman* v *Karpnale Ltd* [1991] 2 AC 548, quoted extensively from the speech of Lord Goff and continued: . . .]

Mr Sher [Counsel for Svenska] submits however that the instances given by Lord Goff are merely examples of a wider principle based upon considerations of justice which is not limited to events occurring after receipt of the money. He relies upon the next passage in Lord Goff's speech, where he said ([1992] 4 All ER 512 at 534, [1991] 2 AC 548 at 580):

> I am most anxious that, in recognising this defence to actions of restitution, nothing should be said at this stage to inhibit the development of the defence on a case by case basis, in the usual way.

A little later Lord Goff said:

> At present I do not wish to state the principle any less broadly than this: that the defence is available to a person whose position has so changed that it would be inequitable in all the circumstances to require him to make restitution, or alternatively to make restitution in full.

If those statements are taken out of context, they might support the broader approach advocated by Mr Sher. If they are read in their context, in my judgment they do not. It appears to me that the context which Lord Goff had in mind was a change of position after receipt of the money. Certainly most, if not all, of the references given in the passage quoted above express the principle in that way.

For example § 142(1) of the American *Restatement* expressly provides:

> The right of a person to restitution from another because of a benefit received is terminated or diminished if, *after receipt of the benefit*, circumstances have so changed that it would be inequitable to require the other to make full restitution. (My emphasis.)

Palmer expresses the principle in terms of a change of position '*after* receipt of the benefit'. So does the Supreme Court of Canada in the *Storthoaks* case [1976] 2 SCR 147 at 163. Section 94B of the Judicature Act 1908 (as amended) in New Zealand appears to me to be more restricted since it seems to be implicit in the section that the alteration must be after the payment and it is expressly provided that it must be 'in reliance upon the validity of the payment'. That is probably too restrictive because it would not cover the case where the defendant finds money belonging to the plaintiff but it is stolen before he can return it. The two Australian statutes referred to by Lord Goff are similar to the New Zealand Act. There is nothing in *Murphett*'s case to support the wider approach suggested by Mr Sher. The same is I think true of the *Westpac Banking* case.

I was referred to a number of other authorities, although none of them seems to me to be determinative of the question for decision, so I will refer to them only briefly. They include *Woolwich Building Society* v *IRC (No. 2)* [1992] 3 All ER 737 at 761–2, [1993] AC 70 at 174–5 *per* Lord Goff, and the dissenting judgment of Dickson J (with whom Laskin CJC agreed) in the Supreme Court of Canada in *Nepean Hydro Electric Commission* v *Ontario Hydro* [1982] 1 SCR 347 at 348. As a result of the dissent it became necessary for Dickson J to consider a defence of change of position. In the course of her judgment she said (at 373): 'The authorities are clear that for a defendant to succeed he must show a detrimental change of position as a result of the payment . . .' Although Mr Sher may well be right in submitting that Dickson J was not considering the argument which he is advancing here, her formulation is nevertheless consistent with the submissions of Mr Mann [Counsel for South Tyneside].

In Goff and Jones *Law of Restitution* (4th edn, 1993) p. 694 (which was the first edition of which Lord Goff has not been one of the authors) it is suggested that the defence should be interpreted generously. For that reason it is suggested that reliance on the receipt of the money is not necessary to the defence but it is also suggested that the defence should be limited to those cases where the defendant has acted in the bona fide belief that he was entitled to treat the enrichment as his own (see Goff and Jones, p. 693). There is no suggestion that the principle is as broad as that contended for by Mr Sher.

Mr Sher referred me to the principles of undue influence and to *Cheese* v *Thomas* [1994] 1 All ER 35, [1994] 1 WLR 129, but I do not think that those cases are of any real assistance in ascertaining the nature of the defence here, if only because, as Nicholls V-C said, the court is there exercising a measure of discretion, whereas here it is not (see [1994] 1 All ER 35 at 42, [1994] 1 WLR 129 at 137).

. . . in principle I prefer Mr Mann's submission on this point to that of Mr Sher. In the context of a case such as this the defence is designed to protect the person who in good faith receives money which does not belong to him. If he thereafter alters his position in some way in which he would not have done if he had not received the money, as for example by buying the secondhand car spoken of by Lord Templeman in *Lipkin Gorman* [1992] 4 All ER 512 at 517, [1991] 2 AC 548 at 560, or if his position changes, as for example by the money being stolen as suggested above, it would not be just to require him to return the money to its owner.

Mr Sher submits that the same is or should be true where, as here, the money is accepted in good faith on the basis that the underlying transaction is valid. He gives a number of examples. One of them illustrates his point. A council employee who is about to retire is to be given a large bonus of say £10,000 which (unknown to either party) the council has no power to give. Then take two alternative cases. In the first, the employee spends £10,000 in his savings account on a holiday which he would not have taken but for the promised bonus, intending to replace the money in his savings account with the bonus. In the second, the employee receives the money and then spends it. In each case the invalidity of the bonus is only discovered after the payment has been made. Mr Sher submits that it makes no sense for the law to distinguish between those two cases. He adds a further variation. If the employee were paid by cheque and booked and paid for his holiday after receipt of the cheque but before the cheque was cleared he submits that it would be inequitable to deny him a defence.

There is obvious force in Mr Sher's submissions. However, Mr Mann's response is that there is a distinction between the two cases. In the first, either the employee is relying upon the implied promise or representation that the bonus will be paid and that it will be valid or he is acting on the assumption to the same effect which is common to both parties. In the second, he is certainly relying upon substantially the same representation or assumption but he is also relying upon the fact of payment or, as Burrows puts it in *Law of Restitution* (1993) p. 105, upon the security of the receipt.

Mr Mann submits that in so far as he relies upon the representation or assumption the only defence available to him would be one of estoppel. However he submits that both in principle and on the authorities a plea of estoppel would fail. The reason is that the representation or promise that the transaction was valid and any assumption to the same effect would be void. Since, as the House of Lords held in *Hazell* v *Hammersmith and Fulham London BC* [1991] 1 All ER 545, [1992] 2 AC 1, the transaction is ultra vires and void, it follows that any promise, representation or assumption to the contrary is also void. I accept that submission. It appears to me that in principle the one follows from the other. The submission is also in my judgment supported by the authorities: see e.g. *Rhyl UDC* v *Rhyl Amusements Ltd* [1959] 1 All ER 257, [1959] 1 WLR 465, following *Ministry of Agriculture and Fisheries* v *Matthews* [1949] 2 All ER 724, [1950] 1 KB 148. See also 16 *Halsbury's Laws* (4th edn reissue) para 1043.

In my judgment in circumstances such as these the bank is not entitled to rely upon the underlying validity of the transaction either in support of a plea of estoppel or in support of a defence of change of position. That is because the transaction is ultra vires and void. It is for that reason that in a case of this kind, save perhaps in exceptional circumstances, the defence of change of position is in principle confined to changes which take place after receipt of the money. Otherwise the bank would in effect be relying upon the supposed validity of a void transaction.

For those reasons I agree with the second reason given by Hobhouse J in the passage from Swaps 1 [*Westdeusche Landesbank Girozentrale* v *Islington London Borough Council* [1994] 4 All ER 890, 948–9; [1994] 1 WLR 938 (CA)] quoted above, at least in the context of payments made by banks to local authorities under contracts which are ultra vires and void. It does not however follow that the defence of change of position can never succeed where the alleged change occurs before the receipt of the money. I am conscious of the statement of Lord Goff that the defence should be developed on a case by case basis. Moreover, as Mr Sher points out, the facts of *Lipkin Gorman* itself are an example of such a case.

That is because some of the bets placed by Cass were successful. Lord Goff considered three possible solutions: to allow the solicitors to recover the net amount received by the casino after taking account of all the winnings paid to Cass distributed over all the bets, to allow the solicitors to recover all the bets other than the winning bets or to allow them to recover nothing on the basis that the casino changed its position because it took a risk each time a bet was put on. The House of Lords chose the first of those possibilities.

Mr Sher submits that that decision is not consistent with a rule that only events occurring after receipt of the money by the defendant are relevant to the defence of change of position. That submission appears to me to be well founded in the light of Lord Goff's approach. Lord Goff held that in a case where a gambler wins the first bet but loses the second the amount of his winnings on the first bet should be deducted from the amount which he paid to the casino as his stake for the second bet. If there were a strict rule that only events since receipt of the money were relevant, the winnings on the first bet would not be a defence to a claim for the return of the second stake as money had and received. Yet the House of Lords held that the casino was only liable to pay back the net amount received from Cass overall regardless of which bets lost and which won and in what order.

It is however plain that Lord Goff found this point difficult. He expressed his conclusion as follows ([1992] 4 All ER 512 at 536, [1991] 2 AC 548 at 582–3):

> The inequity, as I perceive it, arises from the nature of gambling itself. In gambling only an occasional bet is won, but when the gambler wins he will receive much more than the stake placed for his winning bet. True, there may be no immediate connection between the bets. They may be placed on different occasions, and each one is a separate gaming contract. But the point is that there has been a series of transactions under which all the bets have been placed by paying the plaintiff's money to the casino, and on each occasion the casino has incurred the risk that the gambler will win. It is the totality of the bets which yields, by the laws of chance, the occasional winning bet; and the occasional winning bet is therefore, in practical terms, the result of the casino changing its position by incurring the risk of losing on each occasion when a bet is placed with it by the gambler. So, when, in such circumstances the plaintiff seeks to recover from the casino the amount of several bets placed with it by a gambler with his money, it would be inequitable to require the casino to repay in full without bringing into account winnings paid by it to the gambler on any one or more of the bets so placed with it. The result may not be entirely logical; but it is surely just.

It thus appears from that passage that Lord Goff recognised that a logical application of the principle would not have allowed the casino to rely upon earlier winning bets as a defence to a claim for the recovery of later bets, but that in the particular circumstances of the case it would have been inequitable to refuse to allow it to do so. That conclusion stemmed from Lord Goff's perception of the nature of gambling and in particular from his conclusion that there was a series of transactions entered into by Cass at the casino.

The highest that the point can be put in favour of the argument advanced by Mr Sher is in my judgment that in the light of the actual decision in *Lipkin Gorman* there can be no rigid rule that events prior to receipt of the money or benefit are always irrelevant. Nevertheless the earlier statements of principle in the speech of Lord Goff and in the statutes and authorities to which he refers support the conclusion that, save perhaps in exceptional circumstances, the defence of change of position is designed to protect a person who receives money in good faith and who thereafter changes his position in good faith so that it would be inequitable to require him to repay part or all of the money to its rightful owner.

But, however that may be as a matter of general principle, for the reasons which I have already given, there is in my judgment no justification for permitting the recipient to rely upon the understanding or supposition that a transaction is valid when in fact it is void. Moreover there is nothing in the decision or speeches in *Lipkin Gorman* to lead to any other conclusion.

Mr Sher submits that even in a case where the change of position occurs after the receipt of the money the recipient is relying upon the validity of the underlying transaction. There is some force in that submission. But in my judgment that consideration would lead to the conclusion that the defence is not available at all in this type of case. For the reasons which I have given I do not think that the net receiver is entitled to rely upon the validity of a transaction which is in fact void, so that if in such circumstances the change of position defence involved such reliance the result would not be that events before the receipt can be taken into account but that neither events before nor after it can be relied upon.

As I understand it, Mr Mann submits if necessary that that is the case, although he is prepared to concede that the defence would in principle be available to the bank in a case like this if it could show that it changed its position after receipt of the money (and I think because of it) in such a way that it would be inequitable to order them to return it. He submits that it is difficult to think of an example of such a circumstance.

In my judgment the position is that if a net payee can show that it has altered its position in good faith after receipt of money under a swap from the net payer it might in principle be entitled to rely upon the defence of change of position. What it cannot do is to rely upon the supposed validity of the transaction because the transaction is and has always been void. . . .

Application of defence to the facts

Mr Sher has made it clear throughout his argument, both in his skeleton arguments and in his oral submissions, that the particular factors which the bank relies upon are that it entered into the swap in good faith, that it hedged (and continued to hedge) its position throughout and that (as he put it in his first skeleton), even if the hedging transactions could not themselves be regarded as a sufficient change of position, the supposed existence of the swap contracts, together with the supposed liability of the council to make payments on the due dates, continued until the matter was put beyond doubt by the decision of the House of Lords. In his second skeleton he submitted that it was of the essence of the bank's case that it relied upon the validity of the original swap contract in committing itself to its hedges and in maintaining its hedges day by day thereafter.

It follows from the conclusions of principle which I have stated above that that reliance does not afford the bank any defence of change of position since it involves relying, not upon the receipt of money, but upon the validity of a void transaction. Mr Sher submits, however, in the alternative, that the bank did change its position in reliance upon the receipt of the instalments in February and August 1989. I have already set out the relevant facts. In my judgment the bank did not alter its position on receipt of those instalments.

Mr Clark [of Svenska] was not aware of the receipt of the February 1989 instalment, although he would have been informed if the payment had not been made. The bank simply continued to hedge the transaction as it had done before. The same is true in August 1989, although on that occasion Mr Clark was told of the payment. Indeed the bank continued to hedge its position until 1 November 1990, notwithstanding the decision of the Divisional Court in *Hazell* v *Hammersmith and Fulham London BC* [1990] 3 All ER 33, [1990] 2 QB 697 and the failure of the council to pay the instalments due in February and August 1990 after the decision of the Court of Appeal. In these circumstances I do not think that it can fairly be said that the bank changed its position either after or as a result of the payments which were made. In my judgment the truth is that it was in reliance upon the supposed validity of the transaction that the bank initially hedged its position in 1988 and it was also in reliance upon the supposed validity of the transaction that it continued to hedge its position until it learned of the provisional view of the House of Lords on 31 October 1990.

For those reasons the bank is not in my judgment entitled to rely upon any defence of change of position in answer to the council's claim for money had and received. The bank has been unjustly enriched by the receipt of what, because the swap contract was ultra vires the council and void, was the council's money. In all the circumstances the council is entitled to the return of the net payments which it made to the bank. As I understand it, they amount to £236,880.82.

That conclusion makes it unnecessary to give separate consideration to the third reason for rejecting the defence given by Hobhouse J in Swaps 1. I would only say that if, contrary to the conclusion that I have reached, it were permissible to take account of the whole transaction there does seem to me to be something to be said for the view that in a case where the bank hedges its position as a direct result of entering into the contract (at least where the likelihood of its doing so is known to both parties) that fact could in principle be taken into account.

The conclusion which I have reached also makes it unnecessary to reach a firm conclusion upon a further submission made by Mr Mann, namely that the bank would not in any event be entitled to rely upon a change of position defence here because from the very beginning it took the risk that the swap would or might be void. I think that he makes that submission both on the basis that banks always take such risks and on the particular facts here because he says that the bank knew that there was such a risk when it entered into the swap in June 1988. I have already set out the relevant facts. Mr Clark knew that there was some risk but in common with others he reasonably regarded the risk as very small provided that reasonable precautions were taken. I am bound to say that I have some doubt whether it would be right to deny a council the right to recover net payments made to a commercial bank under a void contract where the bank knew that there was a risk that the transaction might be invalid, even if the risk was a very small one. However, in the light of the conclusions which I have already reached it is not necessary to give further consideration to this point and I shall not further lengthen this judgment by doing so.

Note

This case is noted by Nolan [1995] LMCLQ 313.

Section 3: counter restitution impossible?

Sometimes where a (partly) executed transaction goes awry, the law's response is to order the parties to effect mutual restitution. Rescission for undue influence or misrepresentation are clear examples. Sometimes practical difficulties make restitution and counter-restitution difficult. Thus it is stated that rescission (restitution) is denied where *restitutio in integrum* (counter-restitution) is impossible. When is that the case? Consider again the misrepresentation cases in Chapter 2, Section 3. It will be recalled that the courts strove to do what was 'practically just' (*Erlanger* v *New Sombrero Phosphate Co.* (1878) 3 App Cas 1218) and were particularly robust on the plaintiff's behalf in cases of fraud (*Spence* v *Crawford* [1939] 3 All ER 271). Where the benefit conferred by the defendant consists of money, counter-restitution in kind is always possible. However, where the benefit consists of goods or services valuation may prove more difficult. Indeed, in the Scottish case of

Boyd & Forrest v *Glasgow & South-Western Railway Company* [1915] SC (HL) 20 it was denied that services could ever be restored. More recently the courts have been flexible in allowing counter-restitution in respect of services, valued in money. See *O'Sullivan* v *Management Agency & Music Ltd* [1985] QB 428, below. It may prove increasingly inapt to speak of counter-restitution impossible as a defence. Rather, where each party has received some benefit, counter-restitution should simply be a precondition for restitution.

Analogous issues arise where partly-performed contracts are terminated for breach or are frustrated. The requirement of 'total failure' of consideration dodges what might otherwise be difficult issues of counter-restitution. Statute now insists on mutual restitution as far as frustrated contracts are concerned (Law Reform (Frustrated Contracts) Act 1943: see Chapter 4, Section 2 above). The most recent example of the courts' willingness to order mutual restitution is to be found in the '*swaps*' cases, discussed in Chapter 5, Section 2. A new ground for restitution termed 'no consideration' appears to side step the 'total failure' requirement and results in a scheme of mutual restitution as a solution to the problems of void contracts. Similarly, whether a fiduciary who has breached his duty should be entitled to an equitable allowance for services rendered raises problems not yet satisfactorily resolved by the courts. Compare *Boardman* v *Phipps* [1967] 2 AC 46 (Chapter 6, Section 3) with *Guinness plc* v *Saunders* [1990] 2 AC 663 (below).

For discussion see Birks, *Introduction*, 415–24 and McKendrick, 'Total Failure of Consideration and Counter-Restitution – Two Issues or One?' in Birks, *Laundering and Tracing*, 217–42.

A: Rescission for undue influence

O'Sullivan* v *Management Agency and Music Ltd
[1985] QB 428 (CA)

Rescission

In 1970, Raymond 'Gilbert' O'Sullivan was a 23-year-old postal worker with dreams of success in pop music. He teamed up with Mills, the third defendant, who already managed Tom Jones ('It's Not Unusual' and 'Delilah') and Engelbert Humperdinck ('Release Me' and 'The Last Waltz'). As a result O'Sullivan entered into management, publishing, service and recording agreements with the defendant companies. By 1972, O'Sullivan was a big success, selling 6.5 million records with hits including 'Claire' and 'Alone Again Naturally'. By 1976 he was unhappy with the contractual arrangements. He had always wanted a 'joint publishing company' giving him a 50 per cent interest in the copyright in his songs, but despite constant reassurances that this would be set up, it was not. *Held*: O'Sullivan was young and inexperienced in business when he signed the agreements. He did so trusting Mills implicitly and this gave rise to the presumption of undue influence. O'Sullivan had received no independent advice so he was entitled to set the agreements aside as against Mills and the companies who had notice of the undue influence. Restitution was not impossible: order made that the defendants should account for profits, and for the restitution of copyrights and delivery up of master tapes (subject to the rights of bona fide purchasers) and that an allowance be made in favour of the defendants for reasonable remuneration, including a profit element for all work done in promoting the plaintiff's career.

DUNN LJ: [His lordship discussed the authorities including *Erlanger* v *New Sombrero Phosphate Co.* (1878) 3 App Cas 1218; *Newbigging* v *Adam* (1886) 34 Ch D 582 (CA), (1888) 13 App Cas 308; *Lagunas Nitrate Co.* v *Lagunas Syndicate* [1899] 2 Ch 392; *Boyd & Forrest* v *Glasgow and South Western Railway Co.* [1915] SC (HL) 20; *Armstrong* v *Jackson* [1917] 2 KB 822; *Spence* v *Crawford* [1939] 3 All ER 271 (as to which cases see Chapter 2, Section 4), and *Regal (Hastings) Ltd* v *Gulliver* [1967] 2 AC 134 and *Boardman* v *Phipps* [1967] 2 AC 46 (as to which see Chapter 6, Section 3) and concluded: . . .] This analysis of the cases shows that the principles of restitutio in integrum is not applied with its full rigour in equity in relation to transactions entered into by persons in breach of a fiduciary relationship, and that such transactions may be set aside even though it is impossible to place the parties precisely in the position in which they were before, provided that the court can achieve practical justice between the parties by obliging the wrongdoer to give up his profits and advantages, while at the same time compensating him for any work that he has actually performed pursuant to the transaction. *Erlanger* v *New Sombrero Phosphate Co.*, 3 App Cas 1218 is a striking example of the application of this principle.

Mr Bateson submitted that the defendants had gained the following advantages: (1) profits from the agreements; and (2) the copyrights in the songs and master tapes for the life of O'Sullivan and 50 years thereafter. He pointed out that none of the agreements obliged the defendants to do any work on behalf of O'Sullivan whether by promoting or exploiting him or his works or at all, although he conceded that the defendants had in fact done such work gratuitously. He accepted that the defendants in accounting for their profits were entitled to credit in respect of their proper and reasonable expenses for the work done, including work done gratuitously, but that they were not entitled to credit for any profit element in such work. He submitted that the exception made in *Phipps* v *Boardman* [1967] 2 AC 46, where the trustees were morally blameless should not become the rule.

I do not think that equity requires such a narrow approach. It is true that in this case moral blame does lie upon the defendants as the judge's findings of fact show. On the other hand it is significant that until O'Sullivan met Mills he had achieved no success, and that after he effectively parted company with Mills in 1976 he achieved no success either. During the years that he was working with Mills his success was phenomenal. Although equity looks at the advantage gained by the wrongdoer rather than the loss to the victim, the cases show that in assessing the advantage gained the court will look at the whole situation in the round. And it is relevant that if Mr Bateson's approach is applied O'Sullivan would be much better off than if he had received separate legal advice and signed agreements negotiated at arm's length on reasonable terms current in the trade at the time. This point was made forcibly by Mr Miller at the conclusion of his address in reply, when he relied on the maxim 'He who seeks equity must do equity' and submitted that equity required that the position of O'Sullivan was relevant in considering the appropriate remedy.

In my judgment the judge was right to set the agreements aside and to order an account of the profits and payment of the sums found due on the taking of the account. But in taking the account the defendants are entitled to an allowance as proposed by Fox LJ, whose judgment I have read in draft, for reasonable remuneration including a profit element for all work done in promoting and exploiting O'Sullivan and his compositions, whether such work was done pursuant to a contractual obligation or gratuitously. What constitutes 'reasonable remuneration' will depend on evidence on the taking of the account. . . .

FOX LJ: . . . In cases where a plaintiff was seeking to obtain rescission for breach of contract the requirement of restitutio in integrum seems to have been strictly enforced at common law: see for example *Hunt* v *Silk* (1804) 5 East 449 and *Blackburn* v *Smith* (1848) 2 Ex 783. But the equitable rules were, or became, more flexible. The position is stated in the dissenting judgment of Rigby LJ in *Lagunas Nitrate Co.* v *Lagunas Syndicate* [1899] 2 Ch 392 (and was approved by the House of Lords in *Spence* v *Crawford* [1939] 3 All ER 271, 279 and 285), at p. 456:

> Now, no doubt it is a general rule that in order to entitle beneficiaries to rescind a voidable contract of purchase against the vendor, they must be in a position to offer back the subject-matter of the contract. But this rule has no application to the case of the subject-matter having been reduced by the mere fault of the vendors themselves; and the rule itself is, in equity, modified by another rule, that where compensation can be made for any deterioration of the property, such deterioration shall be no bar to rescission, but only a ground for compensation. I adopt the reasoning in *Erlanger's* case, 3 App Cas 1218, 1278 of Lord Blackburn as to allowances for depreciation and permanent improvement. The noble Lord, after pointing out that a court of law had no machinery for taking accounts or estimating compensation, says: 'But a court of equity could not give damages, and, unless it can rescind a contract, can give no relief. And, on the other hand, it can take accounts of profits, and make allowances for deterioration. And I think the practice has always been for a court of equity to give this relief whenever, by the exercise of its powers, it can do what is practically just, though it cannot restore the parties precisely to the state they were in before the contract.' This important passage is, in my judgment, fully supported by the allowance for deterioration and permanent improvements made by Lord Eldon and other great equity judges in similar cases.

The result, I think, is that the doctrine is not to be applied too literally and that the court will do what is practically just in the individual case even though restitutio in integrum is impossible. *Spence* v *Crawford* [1939] 3 All ER 271 was itself concerned with misrepresentation. But the principles stated by Rigby LJ are, I think, equally applicable in cases of abuse of fiduciary relationship and indeed Rigby LJ regarded *Lagunas* [1899] 2 Ch 392 as such a case: see p. 442.

It is said on behalf of the plaintiffs that, if the principle of equity is that the fiduciary must account for profits obtained through the abuse of the fiduciary relationship there is no scope for the operation of anything resembling restitutio in integrum. The profits must simply be given up. I think that goes too far and that the law has for long had regard to the justice of the matter. If, for example, a person is by undue influence persuaded to make a gift of a house to another and that other spent money on improving the house, I apprehend that credit could be given for the improvements. That, I think, is recognised by Lord Blackburn in *Erlanger* v *New Sombrero Phosphate Co.*, 3 App Cas 1278 and by Rigby LJ in *Lagunas* in the reference to allowance for permanent improvements in the passage which I have cited.

Accordingly, it seems to me that the principle that the court will do what is practically just as between the parties is applicable to a case of undue influence even though the parties cannot be restored to their original position. That is, in my view, applicable to the present case. The question is not whether the parties can be restored to their original position; it is what does the justice of the case require? That approach is quite wide enough, if it be necessary in the individual case, to accommodate the protection of third parties. The rights of a bona fide purchaser for value without notice would not in any event be affected.

The next question is, it seems to me, the recompensing of the defendants. The rules of equity against the retention of benefits by fiduciaries have been applied with severity. In *Phipps* v *Boardman* [1967] 2 AC 46, where the fiduciaries though in breach of the equitable rules, acted with complete honesty throughout, only succeeded in obtaining an allowance 'on a liberal scale' for their work and skill. They were allowed that in the High Court by Wilberforce J [1964] 1 WLR 993, 1018 on the ground that it would be inequitable for the beneficiaries to take the profit without paying for the skill and labour which produced it. The point does not seem to have been disputed thereafter. In the Court of Appeal [1965] Ch 992 Pearson LJ said, at p. 1030;

> 'It is to my mind a regrettable feature of this case that the plaintiff seems likely to recover an unreasonably large amount from the defendants'—the fiduciaries—'even when under the judgment [1964] 1 WLR 993, 1018 the defendants have been credited with an allowance on a liberal scale for their work and skill. The rule of equity is rigid. The agent who has made a profit from his agency, without having obtained informed consent from his principal, has to account for the whole of the profit.'

Russell LJ, at p. 1032, said that, without intending to throw doubt on the defendants' right to the liberal allowance, he preferred to express no view on the law, the matter not having been argued. Lord Denning MR said, at p. 1020:

> Ought Boardman and Tom Phipps to be allowed remuneration for their work and skill in these negotiations? The plaintiff is ready to concede it, but in case the other beneficiaries are interested in the account, I think we should determine it on principle. This species of action is an action for restitution such as Lord Wright described in the *Fibrosa* case [1943] AC 32, 61. The gist of it is that the defendant has unjustly enriched himself, and it is against conscience that he should be allowed to keep the money. The claim for repayment cannot, however, be allowed to extend further than the justice of the case demands. If the defendant has done valuable work in making the profit, then the court in its discretion may allow him a recompense. It depends on the circumstances. If the agent has been guilty of any dishonesty or bad faith, or surreptitious dealing, he might not be allowed any remuneration or reward.

In the House of Lords [1967] 2 AC 46, Lord Cohen, at p. 104, and Lord Hodson, at p. 112, agreed with Wilberforce J that the allowance should be on a 'liberal scale.'

These latter observations (and those of Lord Denning MR and the judgment of Wilberforce J at first instance) accept the existence of a power in the court to make an allowance to the fiduciary. And I think it is clearly necessary that such a power should exist. Substantial injustice may result without it. A hard and fast rule that the beneficiary can demand the whole profit without an allowance for the work without which it could not have been created is unduly severe. Nor do I think that the principle is only applicable in cases where the personal conduct of the fiduciary cannot be criticised. I think that the justice of the individual case must be considered on the facts of that case. Accordingly, where there has been dishonesty or surreptitious dealing or other improper conduct then, as indicated by Lord Denning MR, it might be appropriate to refuse relief; but that will depend upon the circumstances. . . .

Once it is accepted that the court can make an appropriate allowance to a fiduciary for his skill and labour I do not see why, in principle, it should not be able to give him some part of the profit of the venture if it was thought that justice as between the parties demanded that. To give the fiduciary any allowance for his skill and labour involves some reduction of the profits otherwise payable to the beneficiary. And the business reality may be that the profits could never have been earned at all, as between fully independent persons, except on a profit sharing basis. But be that as it may, it would be one thing to permit a substantial sharing of profits in a case such as *Phipps* v *Boardman* [1967] 2 AC 46 where the conduct of the fiduciaries could not be criticised and quite another to permit it in a case such as the present where, though fraud was not alleged, there was an abuse of personal trust and confidence. I am not satisfied that it would be proper to exclude Mr Mills and the M.A.M. companies from all reward for their efforts. I find it impossible to believe that they did not make a significant contribution to Mr O'Sullivan's success. It would be unjust to deny them a recompense for that. I would, therefore, be prepared as was done in *Phipps* v *Boardman* to authorise the payment (over and above out of pocket expenses) of an allowance for the skill and labour of the first five defendants in promoting the compositions and performances and managing the business affairs of Mr O'Sullivan. . . .

Cheese v *Thomas*
[1994] 1 WLR 129 (CA)

Rescission

Cheese, aged 88, wished to move back to his native Middlesex. He arranged to buy a house together with his great-nephew, Thomas. Cheese provided £43,000 and Thomas the balance of £40,000 by way of mortgage. The house was in Thomas's sole name, but it was understood that Cheese could stay there for life. Thomas failed to keep up the mortgage repayments, so Cheese tried to escape the transaction. It was held that the transaction was vitiated by undue influence. In the meantime the value of the house had fallen from £83,000 to £55,400.

SIR DONALD NICHOLLS V-C: . . . If, then, the transaction is to be set aside, the next step is the restoration of the parties to their original positions. Achieving this would mean sale of the house and repayment of what each had paid over. Mr Cheese should get back his £43,000, and Mr Thomas should get back and repay to the building society the money he borrowed for the purchase.

The house has now been sold. Unhappily, as already mentioned, although £83,000 was spent in buying the house, only £55,400 came from the sale. By the time of the sale the amount outstanding on the mortgage was about £37,700. On the sale the building society had to be repaid first. It had a mortgage over the house. The effect of paying back the building society was, in substance, to restore Mr Thomas to his original position, although he had paid some mortgage instalments. The net balance remaining from the sale proceeds was only £17,667. Clearly, this sum has to be paid to Mr Cheese, but that will still leave him more than £25,000 out of pocket. The shortfall represents, in round figures, the amount by which the house declined in value after its purchase in June 1990.

The question therefore arises: on whom should this loss fall? Mr Cheese contends he is entitled to look to Mr Thomas personally to make good the whole of the shortfall. He paid £43,000 to Mr Thomas, and on the transaction being set aside he can look to Mr Thomas for repayment of a like sum. The judge did not accept this. He held that the loss brought about by the fall in the market value of the house should be shared between the two of them in the same proportions (43:40) as they had contributed to the price. He said that the parties went into a joint venture, investing approximately similar sums in it: they should bear the loss equally. In short, this would mean that Mr Cheese could look to Mr Thomas for a further £11,000. Mr Cheese would then recover altogether about £28,700, leaving him £14,300 out of pocket compared with his original contribution of £43,000. For his part Mr Thomas would be out of pocket by a similar but proportionately smaller amount. He would be out of pocket to the extent of £13,300, made up of the £11,000 he would have to pay Mr Cheese and £2,300 he had paid to the building society, before the sale, in reduction of the principal owing on the mortgage. From that decision Mr Cheese has appealed.

Restoring the parties to their original positions

I can summarise the thrust of Mr Hamer's argument as follows. When the court sets aside the transaction between Mr Cheese and Mr Thomas, the inflexible rule of equity which comes into play is that Mr Cheese is entitled to have restored to him the benefits he passed to Mr Thomas under the impugned transaction. It matters not if, for reasons unconnected with Mr Cheese, the property being returned to the defendant has declined in value: that is irrelevant.

I approach the matter in this way. Restitution has to be made, not damages paid. Damages look at the plaintiff's loss, whereas restitution is concerned with the recovery back from the defendant of what he received under the transaction. If the transaction is set aside, the plaintiff also must return what he received. Each party must hand back what he obtained under the contract. There has to be a giving back and a taking back on both sides, as Bowen LJ observed in *Newbigging* v *Adam* [1886] 34 Ch D 582, 595. If, for this purpose, the transaction in this case is analysed simply as a payment of £43,000 by Mr Cheese to Mr Thomas in return for the right to live in Mr Thomas's house, there is a strong case for ordering repayment of £43,000, the benefit received by Mr Thomas, regardless of the subsequent fall in the value of the house. In the ordinary way, if a plaintiff is able to return to the defendant the property received from him under the impugned transaction, it matters not that the property has meanwhile fallen in value. This is not surprising. A defendant cannot be heard to protest that such an outcome is unfair when he is receiving back the very thing he persuaded the plaintiff, by undue influence or misrepresentation, to buy from him.

In my view the present case stands differently. Mr Cheese paid Mr Thomas £43,000, not outright, but as part of the purchase price of a house in which both would have rights: Mr Cheese was to have sole use of the house for his life, and then the house would be Mr Thomas's. Mr Thomas was not free to dispose of the house, or use it, until then. In fact the money was handed over by Mr Cheese in the form of a bankers' draft, made payable to the solicitors acting for Mr Thomas in the purchase of 4, Jonson Close. For his part Mr Thomas also contributed to the purchase of the house. He contributed £40,000, by obtaining a building society loan of this amount. In other words, the transaction was that each would contribute a sum of money to buying a house in which each was to have an interest. This is the transaction which has to be reversed. Doing so requires, first, that the house should be sold and, second, that each party should receive back his contribution to the price. There is no difficulty over the first requirement. Mr Cheese sought an order for sale, the judge so directed, and the sale has taken place. The second requirement is more difficult. Indeed, it cannot be achieved, because under the transaction the money each contributed was spent in buying a house which then lost one third of its value.

This difficulty, rightly in my view, has now been allowed to stand in the way of setting aside the transaction. It is well established that a court of equity grants this type of relief even when it cannot restore the parties precisely to the state they were in before the contract. The court will grant relief whenever, by directing accounts and making allowances, it can do what is practically just: see *Erlanger* v *New Sombrero Phosphate Co.* (1878) 3 App Cas 1218, 1278–9, *per* Lord Blackburn. Here justice requires that each party should be returned as near to his original position as is now possible. Each should get back a proportionate share of the net proceeds of the house, before deducting the amount paid to the building society. Thus the £55,400 should be divided between Mr Cheese and Mr Thomas in the proportions of 43:40. Mr Cheese should receive about £28,700 and Mr Thomas £26,700. To achieve this result Mr Thomas should pay £11,033 on top of the net proceeds, of £17,667, remaining after discharging the mortgage. This was the view of the judge, and I see no occasion to disturb his conclusion. On the contrary, I agree with him. It is interesting to note that this result accords with the primary relief sought by Mr Cheese in the action. His primary claim was that the house belonged to them both in the proportions of 43:40. Had the claim succeeded, Mr Cheese would have borne a proportionate share of the loss on the sale of the house.

Restitution for both parties

We were much pressed with an argument that there is no decided case in which a court has ever directed a sharing of the loss in this way. This is a principle unknown to English law. The court has no discretion in this regard. I have two observations on this argument.

First, when considering what was the original position of the parties it is important to identify, and properly characterise, the transaction being set aside. In a simple case of a purchase of property there is no difficulty. Before the transaction the plaintiff had a sum of money and the defendant owned the property. By the transaction the money passed to the defendant, and the property was transferred to the plaintiff. That is the transaction which has to be reversed. Likewise there is no difficulty with a simple case of a gift. The present case, as already noted, is not so straightforward. Here the transaction involved *both* parties making a financial contribution to the acquisition of a new asset from which both were intended to benefit. This was so even though Mr Cheese's only interest in the house was a contractual licensee, and even though Mr Thomas regarded the house as an investment. It is axiomatic that, when reversing this transaction, the court is concerned to achieve practical justice for both parties, not the plaintiff alone. The plaintiff is seeking the assistance of a court of equity, and he who seeks equity must do equity. Under the transaction Mr Thomas parted with money, albeit borrowed, as well as Mr Cheese.

This situation is to be contrasted with the facts in *Newbigging* v *Adam*, 34 Ch D 582; (1888) 13 App Cas 308. There the plaintiff was induced to enter into a partnership with the defendant by misrepresentations about the state of the business. The business foundered. On having the transaction set aside, the court held the plaintiff was entitled to the return of the capital introduced by him and to an indemnity against the liabilities he had assumed as a partner. In that case the transaction was akin to a sale of property, there a share in a partnership. The defendant had to return the capital sum introduced and reassume the burden of partnership debts which under the contract the plaintiff had taken upon himself.

My second observation is this. The basic objective of the court is to restore the parties to their original positions, as nearly as may be, consequent upon cancelling a transaction which the law will not permit to stand. That is the basic objective.

Achieving a practically just outcome in that regard requires the court to look at all the circumstances, while keeping the basic objective firmly in mind. In carrying out this exercise the court is, of necessity, exercising a measure of discretion in the sense that it is determining what are the requirements of practical justice in the particular case. It is important not to lose sight of the very foundation of the jurisdiction being invoked. As Lord Scarman observed in the *Morgan* case [1985] AC 686, a court in the exercise of this jurisdiction is a court of conscience. He noted, at p. 709:

> There is no precisely defined law setting limits to the equitable jurisdiction of a court to relieve against undue influence . . . Definition is a poor instrument when used to determine whether a transaction is or is not unconscionable: this is a question which depends upon the particular facts of the case.

As with the jurisdiction to grant relief, so with the precise form of the relief to be granted, equity as a court of conscience will look at all the circumstances and do what fairness requires. Lord Wright adverted to this in *Spence* v *Crawford* [1939] 3 All ER 271, which was a misrepresentation case. He said regarding rescission and restitution, at p. 288:

> The remedy is equitable. Its application is discretionary, and, where the remedy is applied, it must be moulded in accordance with the exigencies of the particular case.

The law reports are replete with examples of the way courts have applied this principle. These, and the reasoning underlying them, afford valuable guidance when fairly comparable situations arise in the future. They are not immutable rules of law which must be applied irrespective of whether in the particular case they will assist in achieving an outcome which is practically just. A few examples will suffice. If the defendant has improved the property he is ordered to return, the plaintiff may be required to compensate him. On the other hand, if the plaintiff has improved the property he seeks to return, he will not necessarily be entitled to a further payment from the defendant: it may not be just to require the defendant to pay for improvements he does not want. If the plaintiff has permitted the property to deteriorate, he may be required to make an allowance to the defendant for this when seeking an order compelling him to retake the property. If a joint business venture is involved, such as an agreement between a pop star and a manager, and the agreement is set aside and an account directed of the profits received by the defendant under the agreement, the court in its discretion may permit the defendant to retain some profits, if it would be inequitable for the plaintiff to take the profits without paying for the expertise and work which produced them. In *O'Sullivan* v *Management Agency and Music Ltd* [1985] QB 428, 468, Fox LJ observed it was clearly necessary that the court should have power to make an allowance to a fiduciary. He continued:

> Substantial injustice may result without it. A hard and fast rule that the beneficiary can demand the whole profit without an allowance for the work without which it could not have been created is unduly severe. Nor do I think that the principle is only applicable in cases where the personal conduct of the fiduciary cannot be criticised. I think that the justice of the individual case must be considered on the facts of that case. Accordingly, where there has been dishonesty or surreptitious dealing or other improper conduct then, as indicated by Lord Denning MR, it might be appropriate to refuse relief; but that will depend upon the circumstances.

What is true of profits must also be true of losses. In the ordinary way, when a sum of money is paid to a defendant under a transaction which is set aside, the defendant will be required to repay the whole sum. There may be exceptional cases where that would be unjust. This may more readily be so where the personal conduct of the defendant was not open to criticism. Here, having heard the parties give evidence, the judge acquitted Mr Thomas of acting in a morally reprehensible way towards Mr Cheese. He described Mr Thomas as an innocent fiduciary. Here also, and I return to this feature because on any view it was an integral element of the transaction, each party applied money in buying the house. In all the circumstances, to require Mr Thomas to shoulder the whole of the loss flowing from the problems which have beset the residential property market for the last year or two would be harsh. That is not an outcome a court of conscience should countenance. . . .

Note

For an ingenious explanation of this case in terms of *change of position* see Chen-Wishart (1994) 110 LQR 173.

B: Equitable allowance?

Guinness plc* v *Saunders
[1990] 2 AC 663 (HL)

Quantum meruit

Guinness sought to recover £5.2 million paid to Ward, an American attorney and former director of the company, at the time of the controversial bid by Guinness to take over Distillers. Ward together with the then chief executive, Saunders, and another director, Roux, formed a take-over sub-committee of the board. That sub-committee agreed to pay Ward 0.2 per cent of the ultimate value of the bid if successful, for his services in connection with the bid. This came to £5.2 million, which was paid. *Held*: the articles of association of Guinness empowered only the board of directors to award such remuneration, so the contract was void because of the want of authority of the sub-committee. The extracts concern Ward's counterclaim to retain the money either on a *quantum meruit*, or as an equitable allowance. It was assumed throughout that Ward acted in good faith.

LORD TEMPLEMAN: . . . Since, for the purposes of this application, Guinness concede that Mr Ward performed valuable services for Guinness in connection with the bid, counsel on behalf of Mr Ward submits that Mr Ward, if not entitled to remuneration pursuant to the articles, is, nevertheless, entitled to be awarded by the court a sum by way of quantum meruit or equitable allowance for his services. Counsel submits that the sum awarded by the court might amount to £5.2m. or a substantial proportion of that sum; therefore Mr Ward should be allowed to retain the sum of £5.2m. which he has received until, at the trial of the action, the court determines whether he acted with propriety and, if so, how much of the sum of £5.2m. he should be permitted to retain; Mr Ward is anxious for an opportunity to prove at a trial that he acted with propriety throughout the bid. It is common ground that, for the purposes of this appeal, it must be assumed that Mr Ward and the other members of the committee acted in good faith and that the sum of £5.2m. was a proper reward for the services rendered by Mr Ward to Guinness.

My Lords, the short answer to a quantum meruit claim based on an implied contract by Guinness to pay reasonable remuneration for services rendered is that there can be no contract by Guinness to pay special remuneration for the services of a director unless that contract is entered into by the board pursuant to article 91. The short answer to the claim for an equitable allowance is the equitable principle which forbids a trustee to make a profit out of his trust unless the trust instrument, in this case the articles of association of Guinness, so provides. The law cannot and equity will not amend the articles of Guinness. The court is not entitled to usurp the functions conferred on the board by the articles.

[Lord Templeman then discussed authority and continued: . . .]

Equity forbids a trustee to make a profit out of his trust. The articles of association of Guinness relax the strict rule of equity to the extent of enabling a director to make a profit provided that the board of directors contracts on behalf of Guinness for the payment of special remuneration or decides to award special remuneration. Mr Ward did not obtain a contract or a grant from the board of directors. Equity has no power to relax its own strict rule further than and inconsistently with the express relaxation contained in the articles of association. A shareholder is entitled to compliance with the articles. A director accepts office subject to and with the benefit of the provisions of the articles relating to directors. No one is obliged to accept appointment as a director. No director can be obliged to serve on a committee. A director of Guinness who contemplates or accepts service on a committee or has performed outstanding services for the company as a member of a committee may apply to the board of directors for a contract or an award of special remuneration. A director who does not read the articles or a director who misconstrues the articles is nevertheless bound by the articles. Article 91 provides clearly enough for the authority of the board of directors to be obtained for the payment of special remuneration and the submissions made on behalf of Mr Ward, based on articles 2, 100(D) and 110, are more ingenious than plausible and more legalistic than convincing. At the board meeting held on 19 January 1986, Mr Ward was present but he did not seek then or thereafter to obtain the necessary authority of the board of directors for payment of special remuneration. In these circumstances there are no grounds for equity to relax its rules further than the articles of association provide. Similarly, the law will not imply a contract between Guinness and Mr Ward for remuneration on a quantum meruit basis awarded by the court when the articles of association of Guinness stipulate that special remuneration for a director can only be awarded by the board.

It was submitted on behalf of Mr Ward that Guinness, by the committee consisting of Mr Saunders, Mr Ward and Mr Roux, entered into a voidable contract to pay remuneration to Mr Ward and that since Mr Ward performed the services he agreed to perform under this voidable contract there could be no restitutio integrum and the contract cannot be avoided. This submission would enable a director to claim and retain remuneration under a contract which a committee purported to conclude with him, notwithstanding that the committee had no power to enter into the contract. The fact is that Guinness never did contract to pay anything to Mr Ward. The contract on which Mr Ward relies is not voidable but non-existent. In support of a quantum meruit claim, counsel for Mr Ward relied on the decision of Buckley J in *In re Duomatic Ltd* [1969] 2 Ch 365. In that case a company sought and failed to recover remuneration received by a director when the shareholders or a voting majority of the shareholders had sanctioned or ratified the payment. In the present case there has been no such sanction or ratification either by the board of directors or by the shareholders. Mr Ward also relied on the decision in *Craven-Ellis* v *Canons Ltd* [1936] 2 KB 403. In that case the plaintiff was appointed managing director of a company by an agreement under the company's seal which also provided for his remuneration. By the articles of association each director was required to obtain qualification shares within two months of his appointment. Neither the plaintiff nor the other directors obtained their qualification shares within two months or at all and the agreement with the managing director was entered into after they had ceased to be directors. The plaintiff having done work for the company pursuant to the terms of the agreement was held to be entitled to the remuneration provided for in the agreement on the basis of a quantum meruit. In *Craven-Ellis* the plaintiff was not a director, there was no conflict between his claim to remuneration and the equitable doctrine which debars a director from profiting from his fiduciary duty, and there was no obstacle to the implication of a contract between the company and the plaintiff entitling the plaintiff to claim reasonable remuneration as of right by an action in law. Moreover, as in *In re Duomatic Ltd*, the agreement was sanctioned by all the directors, two of whom were beneficially entitled to the share capital of the company. In the present case Mr Ward was a director, there was a conflict between his interest and his duties, there could be no contract by Guinness for the payment of remuneration pursuant to article 91 unless the board made the contract on behalf of Guinness and there was no question of approval by directors or shareholders.

In support of a claim for an equitable allowance, reference was made to the decision of Wilberforce J in *Phipps* v *Boardman* [1964] 1 WLR 993. His decision was upheld by the Court of Appeal [1965] Ch 992 and ultimately by this House under the name of *Boardman* v *Phipps* [1967] 2 AC 46. In that case a trust estate included a minority holding in a private company which fell on lean times. The trustees declined to attempt to acquire a controlling interest in the company in order to improve its performance. The solicitor to the trust and one of the beneficiaries, with the knowledge and approval of the trustees, purchased the controlling interest from outside shareholders for themselves with the help of information about the shareholders acquired by the solicitor in the course of acting for the trust. The company's position was improved and the shares bought by the solicitor and the purchasing beneficiary were ultimately sold at a profit. A complaining beneficiary was held to be entitled to a share of the profits on the resale on the grounds that the solicitor and the purchasing beneficiary were assisted in the original purchase by the information derived from the trust. The purchase of a controlling interest might have turned out badly and in that case the solicitor and the purchasing beneficiary would have made irrecoverable personal losses. In these circumstances it is not surprising that Wilberforce J decided that in calculating the undeserved profit which accrued to the trust estate there should be deducted a generous allowance for the work and trouble of the solicitor and purchasing beneficiary in acquiring the controlling shares and restoring the company to prosperity. *Phipps* v *Boardman* decides that in exceptional circumstances a court of equity may award remuneration to the trustee. Therefore, it is argued, a court of equity may award remuneration to a director. As at present advised, I am unable to envisage circumstances in which a court of equity would exercise a power to award remuneration to a director when the relevant articles of association confided that power to the board of directors. Certainly, the circumstances do not exist in the present case. . . .

LORD GOFF OF CHIEVELEY: [His lordship held the contract under which Ward had performed his services was void for want of authority and continued: . . .] Let it be accepted that the contract under which Mr Ward claims to have rendered valuable services to Guinness was for the above reasons void for want of authority. I understand it to be suggested that articles 90 and 91 provide (article 100 apart) not only a code of the circumstances in which a director of Guinness may receive recompense for services to the company, but an exclusive code. This is said to derive from the equitable doctrine whereby directors, though not trustees, are held to act in a fiduciary capacity, and as such are not entitled to receive remuneration for services rendered to the company except as provided under the articles of association, which are treated as equivalent to a trust deed constituting a trust. It was suggested that, if Mr Ward wishes to receive remuneration for the services he has rendered, his proper course is now to approach the board of directors and invite them to award him remuneration by the exercise of the power vested in them by article 91.

The leading authorities on the doctrine have been rehearsed in the opinion of my noble and learned friend, Lord Templeman. These indeed demonstrate that the directors of a company, like other fiduciaries, must not put themselves in a position where there is a conflict between their personal interests and their duties as fiduciaries, and are for that reason precluded from contracting with the company for their services except in circumstances authorised by the articles of association. Similarly, just as trustees are not entitled, in the absence of an appropriate provision in the trust deed, to remuneration for their services as trustees, so directors are not entitled to remuneration for their services as directors except as provided by the articles of association.

Plainly, it would be inconsistent with this long-established principle to award remuneration in such circumstances as of right on the basis of a quantum meruit claim. But the principle does not altogether exclude the possibility that an equitable allowance might be made in respect of services rendered. That such an allowance may be made to a trustee for work performed by him for the benefit of the trust, even though he was not in the circumstances entitled to remuneration under the terms of the trust deed, is now well established. In *Phipps* v *Boardman* [1964] 1 WLR 993, the solicitor to a trust and one of the beneficiaries were held accountable to another beneficiary for a proportion of the profits made by them from the sale of shares bought by them with the aid of information gained by the solicitor when acting for the trust. Wilberforce J directed that, when accounting for such profits, not merely should a deduction be made for expenditure which was necessary to enable the profit to be realised, but also a liberal allowance or credit should be made for their work and skill. His reasoning was, at p. 1018:

> Moreover, account must naturally be taken of the expenditure which was necessary to enable the profit to be realised. But, in addition to expenditure, should not the defendants be given an allowance or credit for their work and skill? This is a subject on which authority is scanty; but Cohen J, in *In re Macadam* [1946] Ch 73, 82, gave his support to an allowance of this kind to trustees for their services in acting as directors of a company. It seems to me that this transaction, i.e., the acquisition of a controlling interest in the company, was one of a special character calling for the exercise of a particular kind of professional skill. If Boardman had not assumed the role of seeing it through, the beneficiaries would have had to employ (and would, had they been well advised, have employed) an expert to do it for them. If the trustees had come to the court asking for liberty to employ such a person, they would in all probability have been authorised to do so, and to remunerate the person in question. It seems to me that it would be inequitable now for the beneficiaries to step in and take the profit without paying for the skill and labour which has produced it.

Wilberforce J's decision, including his decision to make such an allowance, was later to be affirmed by the House of Lords: *sub nom. Boardman* v *Phipps* [1967] 2 AC 46.

It will be observed that the decision to make the allowance was founded upon the simple proposition that 'it would be inequitable now for the beneficiaries to step in and take the profit without paying for the skill and labour which has produced it.' Ex hypothesi, such an allowance was not in the circumstances authorised by the terms of the trust deed; furthermore it was held that there had not been full and proper disclosure by the two defendants to the successful plaintiff beneficiary. The inequity was found in the simple proposition that the beneficiaries were taking the profit although, if Mr Boardman (the solicitor) had not done the work, they would have had to employ an expert to do the work for them in order to earn that profit.

The decision has to be reconciled with the fundamental principle that a trustee is not entitled to remuneration for services rendered by him to the trust except as expressly provided in the trust deed. Strictly speaking, it is irreconcilable with the rule as so stated. It seems to me thererore that it can only be reconciled with it to the extent that the exercise of the equitable jurisdiction does not conflict with the policy underlying the rule. And, as I see it, such a conflict will only be avoided if the exercise of the jurisdiction is restricted to those cases where it cannot have the effect of encouraging trustees in any way to put themselves in a position where their interests conflict with their duties as trustees.

Not only was the equity underlying Mr Boardman's claim in *Phipps* v *Boardman* clear and, indeed, overwhelming; but the exercise of the jurisdiction to award an allowance in the unusual circumstances of that case could not provide any encouragement to trustees to put themselves in a position where their duties as trustees conflicted with their interests. The present case is, however, very different. Whether any such an allowance might ever be granted by a court of equity in the case of a director of a company, as opposed to a trustee, is a point which has yet to be decided; and I must reserve the question whether the jurisdiction could be exercised in such a case, which may be said to involve interference by the court in the administration of a company's affairs when the company is not being wound up. In any event, however, like my noble and learned friend, Lord Templeman, I cannot see any possibility of such jurisdiction being exercised in the present case. I proceed, of course, on the basis that Mr Ward acted throughout in complete good faith. But the simple fact remains that, by agreeing to provide his services in return for a substantial fee the size of which was dependent upon the amount of a successful bid by Guinness, Mr Ward was most plainly putting himself in a position in which his interests were in stark conflict with his duty as a director. Furthermore, for such services as he rendered, it is still open to the board of Guinness (if it thinks fit, having had a full opportunity to investigate the circumstances of the case) to award Mr Ward appropriate remuneration. In all the circumstances of the case, I cannot think that this is a case in which a court of equity (assuming that it has jurisdiction to do so in the case of a director of a company) would order the repayment of the £5.2m. by Mr Ward to Guinness subject to a condition that an equitable allowance be made to Mr Ward for his services. . . .

Note

See Birks, 'Restitution without counter-restitution' [1990] LMCLQ 330.

Section 4: public policy

The immaturity of the law of restitution has meant that it has rarely been explicitly considered by the legislature when other, more familiar causes of action are modified by statute. Can a statute rendering agreements unenforceable or granting an immunity from actions in respect of civil wrongs be a source of public policy for the law of restitution? In *Sinclair* v *Brougham*

[1914] AC 398 the House of Lords reached the bizarre conclusion that the policy of '*ultra vires*' made the depositors' claims at common law unsustainable, but had no effect upon a claim in equity. (See Burrows, *Restitution*, 457–60.) The law has moved on since then, and some recent appellate decisions suggest that these issues will be handled more sensitively in the future. See Goff and Jones, 62–8.

Universe Tankships Inc. of Monrovia v *International Transport Workers' Federation, The 'Universe Sentinel'* [1983] 1 AC 366 (HL)

Action for money had and received; resulting trust

The facts and decision on the cause of action were discussed in Chapter 3, Section 1. The question here was whether public policy as evidenced by statute precluded the shipowners' prima facie right to restitution on the ground of economic duress.

LORD DIPLOCK: . . . The use of economic duress to induce another person to part with property or money is not a tort per se; the form that the duress takes may, or may not, be tortious. The remedy to which economic duress gives rise is not an action for damages but an action for restitution of property or money exacted under such duress and the avoidance of any contract that had been induced by it; but where the particular form taken by the economic duress used is itself a tort, the restitutional remedy for money had and received by the defendant to the plaintiff's use is one which the plaintiff is entitled to pursue as an alternative remedy to an action for damages in tort.

In extending into the field of industrial relations the common law concept of economic duress and the right to a restitutionary remedy for it which is currently in process of development by judicial decisions, this House would not, in my view, be exercising the restraint that is appropriate to such a process if it were so to develop the concept that, by the simple expedient of 'waiving the tort,' a restitutionary remedy for money had and received is made enforceable in cases in which Parliament has, over so long a period of years, manifested its preference for a public policy that a particular kind of tortious act should be legitimised in the sense that I am using that expression.

It is only in this indirect way that the provisions of the Trade Union and Labour Relations Act 1974 are relevant to the duress point. The immunities from liability in tort provided by sections 13 and 14 are not directly applicable to the shipowners' cause of action for money had and received. Nevertheless, these sections, together with the definition of trade dispute in section 29, afford an indication, which your Lordships should respect, of where public policy requires that the line should be drawn between what kind of commercial pressure by a trade union upon an employer in the field of industrial relations ought to be treated as legitimised despite the fact that the will of the employer is thereby coerced, and what kind of commercial pressure in that field does amount to economic duress that entitles the employer victim to restitutionary remedies. . . .

Section 13(1) was directly applicable to the remedy sought in *N.W.L. Ltd* v *Woods* [1979] 1 WLR 1294. In the instant case it is only indirectly relevant as an indication of what kind of demand for money public policy requires should be excluded from giving rise to a restitutionary remedy by way of an action for money had and received, notwithstanding that the money was exacted in circumstances that would otherwise have amounted to economic duress. As Parker J did, and as the Court of Appeal would have done had they not been misled by an incautious phrase in my own speech in *N. W.L. Ltd* v *Woods*, I see nothing in the Trade Union and Labour Relations Act 1974 that indicates any Parliamentary intention that public policy does so require; and for the reasons that I have already given, I would allow this appeal on the duress point. . . .

LORD SCARMAN (dissenting): . . . The present is a case in which the nature of the demand determines whether the pressure threatened or applied, i.e. the blacking, was lawful or unlawful. If it was unlawful, it is conceded that the owner acted under duress and can recover. If it was lawful, it is conceded that there was no duress and the sum sought by the owner is irrecoverable. The lawfulness or otherwise of the demand depends upon whether it was an act done in contemplation or furtherance of a trade dispute. If it was, it would not be actionable in tort: section 13(1) of the Act. Although no question of tortious liability arises in this case and section 13(1) is not, therefore, directly in point, it is not possible, in my view, to say of acts which are protected by statute from suit in tort that they nevertheless can amount to duress. Parliament having enacted that such acts are not actionable in tort, it would be inconsistent with legislative policy to say that, when the remedy sought is not damages for tort but recovery of money paid, they become unlawful. . . .

Note
See Birks, *Introduction*, 349–51.

Dimskal Shipping Co. SA v *International Transport Workers' Federation, The 'Evia Luck' (No. 2)*
[1992] 2 AC 152 (HL)

The facts and decision in respect of prima facie liability were discussed in Chapter 3, Section 1. Subsequent to the events of the '*Universe Sentinel*' case, Parliament, by s. 17 of the Employment Act 1980, removed from the immunity of s. 13 of the Trade Union and Labour Relations Act 1974 secondary action by workers not employed by the employer who was the party to the trade dispute.

LORD TEMPLEMAN (dissenting): . . . The *Evia Luck* was blacked by secondary action, namely industrial action by workers in Sweden who were not employed by the owner but by Swedish port authorities.

The Universe Sentinel concerned a ship which had been blacked within the jurisdiction of the courts of this country. The agreements between the owners and the federation had been made in this country and were valid under the Act of 1974. If the *Evia Luck* had been blacked in this country and the agreements had been made in this country, section 17 of the Employment Act 1980 amending the Act of 1974 would have entitled the owners to avoid the contracts and recover the moneys paid thereunder.

The Acts of 1974 and 1980 are only two illustrations of the fact that the relationship between economic duress, industrial action and the law is governed by legislative powers rather than by the judicial common law and that this relationship is altered from time to time by the legislature in accordance with what is perceived to be the public interest. Outside the United Kingdom the legality of industrial action depends on the current legislation of each country; economic duress and the doctrine of restitution may appear in different guises or not appear at all, and the common law itself may be applied in a different manner or not at all.

The federation did not do anything wrong according to Swedish law. The owners' actions against the federation in tort were dismissed both by Phillips J and by the Court of Appeal because the conduct of the federation in Sweden was not unlawful by the law of that country. And yet the Court of Appeal has ordered the federation to pay damages for that conduct.

In my opinion the owners are not entitled to succeed in this country. In the first place the courts of this country should not concern themselves with industrial action lawfully carried out in the place where that action occurred. In the second place as Lord Diplock pointed out there is no difference between tort and restitution. Moneys paid as a result of conduct lawful where committed and irrecoverable in this country under the law of tort should not be recoverable in this country under the law of restitution. The contents of a bottle cannot be changed by altering the label. . . .

LORD GOFF OF CHIEVELEY: [His lordship, in discussing Lord Diplock's speech in *The 'Universe Sentinel'* observed: . . .] It is not necessary for present purposes to explore the basis of this decision. It appears to bear some affinity to the principle underlying those cases in which the courts have given effect to the inferred purpose of the legislature by holding a person entitled to sue for damages for breach of a statutory duty, though no such right of suit has been expressly created by the statute imposing the duty. It is enough to state that, by parity of reasoning, not only may an action of restitution be rejected as inconsistent with the policy of a statute such as that under consideration in *The Universe Sentinel* [1983] 1 AC 366, but in my opinion a claim that a contract is voidable for duress by reason of pressure legitimised by such a statute may likewise be rejected on the same ground. . . .

Question

Lord Templeman, in discussing *The 'Universe Sentinel'*, cited Lord Diplock's speech as authority for the proposition that 'there is no difference between tort and restitution'. Do you agree that this is Lord Diplock's view.

Note

See O'Dair [1992] LMCLQ 145.

Pavey & Matthews Pty Ltd v *Paul*
(1987) 162 CLR 221 (High Court of Australia)

Quantum meruit

Section 45 of the Builders Licensing Act 1971 (New South Wales) provided: 'A contract . . . under which the holder of a licence undertakes to carry out . . . any building work . . . specified in a building contract is not enforceable against the other party to the contract unless the contract is in writing signed by each of the parties . . . and sufficiently describes the building work the subject of the contract.' The plaintiff company, a licensed builder, which had renovated a cottage for Mrs Paul under an oral contract, sued for a *quantum meruit*. The High Court held that it was entitled to an independent restitutionary claim based on Mrs Paul's acceptance of the work (as to which see Chapter 4, Section 4). These extracts concern the question whether the statute barred restitutionary claims as well as claims upon the contract.

MASON AND WILSON JJ: [referred to the word 'enforceable' in the Act and continued: . . .] This is not a case in which other provisions of the Act throw textual light on what is meant by the word. It is therefore a matter of determining whether any assistance is to be gained from an examination of the policy and purpose of the statute. On one view the purpose of s. 45 is to protect the building owner against spurious claims by a builder by preventing the enforcement by him of nonconforming contracts. This in substance was the view taken by the Court of Appeal in this case and in *Schwarstein* v *Watson* (1985) 3 NSWLR 134. That purpose includes the protection of the building owner against a claim by a builder on a written contract that fails to describe the building work sufficiently, even in a case where the builder has fully executed the contract on his part. But it would be going a very long way indeed to assert that the statutory protection extends to a case where the building owner requests and accepts the building work and declines to pay for it on the ground that the contract fails to comply with the statutory requirements. True it is that the informal contract, though not enforceable by the builder, is enforceable against him. But it is not to be supposed that it is enforceable against him on the footing that the building owner is under no liability to pay for building work upon which he insists and the performance of which he accepts. The consequences of the respondent's interpretation are so draconian that it is difficult to suppose that they were intended. An interpretation that serves the statutory purpose yet avoids a harsh and unjust operation is to be preferred. . . .

BRENNAN J (dissenting): . . . Section 45 was passed to protect the building owner. I respectfully agree with the view of Samuels JA in *Schwarstein* v *Watson* (1985) 3 NSWLR 134, at pp. 140–1 (which his Honour adopted in the present case), that s. 45 is designed 'to ensure that a written record was made of the work to be done and the rate to be charged; it being notorious that disputes about both matters not infrequently arose requiring determination at tedious length'. Or, as McHugh JA said in this case (1985) 3 NSWLR 114, at p. 132:

> Disputes between builders and home owners as to what work was agreed upon and what was to be its cost have plagued the building industry for many years. Section 45 represents a legislative attempt to overcome this problem by forcing licensed builders to obtain written contracts for building work before they are enforceable by builders. We must give effect to the legislative policy embodied in s. 45, however harsh it may seem in an individual case.

It may be that contracts falling within s. 45 contain an implied term that they will cease to be effective if the building owner refuses to sign a written agreement on the request of the licence holder before work begins, but the present case does not call for consideration of that question. The existence of a building contract, valid in every respect save that it is unwritten, is the postulate on which this case is to be decided. Does s. 45 leave the licence holder liable to perform the contract according to its terms without an enforceable right to payment?

If that is the effect of s. 45, it is truly draconian. A law of that kind evokes an anxious consideration of legal remedies which might alleviate the injustice which the legislature should not lightly be taken to have intended. Section 45 is not expressed to operate differently on contracts which are executed and contracts which are not and it makes all contracts falling within its terms unenforceable by the licence holder. No cause of action founded on the contractual promise to pay can arise. If the contractual promise to pay the licence holder's remuneration is capable of giving rise to an enforceable debt, however, an action founded on the debt—derived from the action of debt or the action of indebitatus assumpsit—would provide an alleviating remedy, preventing injustice under s. 45 as it has prevented fraud under the Statute of Frauds. But when the concurrent actions of debt and indebitatus assumpsit lay to recover what was due under a contract the contractual promise to pay was always treated as the source of the debt on which those actions were founded. The force of the contractual promise was spent in creating the debt and that debt was the subject of the fictional promise to pay: see Ames, 'The History of Assumpsit' in *Select Essays in Anglo-American Legal History* (1909), vol. III, 259, at pp. 281–6. Either action ultimately depended on a contract effective to create what the law recognised as a debt. In *Studdy* v *Sanders* (1826) 5 B & C 628, at p. 638 [108 ER 234, at p. 238] Holroyd J said:

> . . . it is said, 'Although an indebitatus assumpsit will not lie upon a special agreement till the terms of it are performed, yet when that is done, it raises a duty for which a general indebitatus assumpsit will lie'. I take this to be the reason for the common practice of introducing two counts in declaring upon the sale of a horse, one upon an executory and the other upon an executed contract, although it is clear the plaintiff might recover upon the last after delivery.

An action to recover money due on an executed contract may be distinguished from an action to enforce a promise to pay contained in the contract—the point of distinction being the debt to which the contract gives rise—but the debt is nevertheless a cause of action arising out of the contract. That appears in what was said in *Young* v *Queensland Trustees Ltd* (1956) 99 CLR, at p. 569:

> A debt recoverable under an indebitatus count was not and is not now conceived of simply as a cause of action for breach of duty or obligation. In other words it is a mistake to regard the liability to pay a debt of a kind formerly recoverable in debt or indebitatus assumpsit as no more than *the result of a breach of contract*, a breach which the creditor must affirmatively allege and prove. (Emphasis added.)

If s. 45 makes the contract wholly unenforceable against the building owner, the contract is incapable of giving rise to a debt on which an action of debt or indebitatus assumpsit might be founded.

Apart from legal theory, the submission that a licence holder can sue for remuneration due under his contract with the building owner when s. 45 declares that the contract is not enforceable against the building owner seems contrary to the plain words of the Statute. If s. 45 were held not to bar such an action to recover a debt due under the contract the section would have had little, if any, practical effect on the litigation of building contracts where the holder of the licence had discharged his obligations to completion (or perhaps to substantial completion). If it were necessary to prove the discharge of the licence holder's obligations under the unwritten contract in order to establish an enforceable debt recoverable by the plaintiff, litigation arising out of unwritten building contracts would focus on the work which had been agreed upon and the remuneration promised. The effect of s. 45 would be to exacerbate the very problem, identified by Samuels and McHugh JJA, which s. 45 was intended to overcome. In my opinion, s. 45 precludes the arising of an enforceable debt. The contractual promise to pay is clearly unenforceable and there is no room, while the unenforceable contract is subsisting, for a quasi-contractual claim. . . .

DEANE J: . . . There is no apparent reason in justice why a builder who is precluded from enforcing an agreement should also be deprived of the ordinary common law right to bring proceedings on a common indebitatus count to recover fair and reasonable remuneration for work which he has actually done and which has been accepted by the building owner: cf. *Johnsons Tyne Foundry Pty. Ltd* v *Maffra Corporation* (1948) 77 CLR 544, at p. 565. Nor, upon a consideration of the words of s. 45 in their context in the Act, am I able to identify any legislative intent to deprive the builder of that ordinary common law right. The section does not make an agreement to which it applies illegal or void. Nor do its words disclose any legislative intent to penalise the builder beyond making the agreement itself unenforceable by him against the other party. It may be that the bringing of an action as on a common indebitatus count would conflict with the apparent legislative policy underlying s. 45 if the claimant in such an action were entitled as of right to recover the amount which the building owner had agreed to pay under the unenforceable agreement. I am, however, unpersuaded that the bringing by a builder of an action on the common indebitatus count in which he can recover no more than what is fair and reasonable in the circumstances as compensation for the benefit of the work which he has actually done and which has been accepted by the building owner conflicts with any discernible legislative policy. Plainly enough, the survival of the ordinary common law right of the builder to recover, in an action founded on restitution or unjust enrichment, reasonable remuneration for work done and accepted under a contract which is unenforceable by him does not frustrate the purpose of the section to provide protection for a building owner. The building owner remains entitled to enforce the contract. He cannot, however, be forced either to comply with its terms or to permit the builder to carry it to completion. All that he can be required to do is to pay reasonable compensation for work done of which he has received the benefit and for which in justice he is obligated to make such a payment by way of restitution. In relation to such work, he can rely on the contract, if it has not been rescinded, as to the amount of remuneration and the terms of payment. If the agreed remuneration exceeds what is reasonable in the circumstances, he can rely on the unenforceability of the contract with the result that he is liable to pay no more than what is fair and reasonable.

The tendency in some past cases to see the rationale of the right to recover remuneration for a benefit provided and accepted under an unenforceable contract as contract or promise rather than restitution has tended to distract attention from the importance of identifying the basis upon which the quantum of the amount recoverable should be ascertained. What the concept of monetary restitution involves is the payment of an amount which constitutes, in all the relevant circumstances, fair and just compensation for the benefit or 'enrichment' actually or constructively accepted. Ordinarily, that will correspond to the fair value of the benefit provided (e.g. remuneration calculated at a reasonable rate for work actually done or the fair market value of materials supplied). In some categories of case, however, it would be to affront rather than satisfy the requirements of good conscience and justice which inspire the concept or principle of restitution or unjust enrichment to determine what constitutes fair and just compensation for a benefit accepted by reference only to what would represent a fair remuneration for the work involved or a fair market value of materials supplied. One such category of case is that in which unsolicited but subsequently accepted work is done in improving property in circumstances where remuneration for the unsolicited work calculated at what was a reasonable rate would far exceed the enhanced value of the property. More relevant for present purposes is the special category of case where restitution is sought by one party for work which he has executed under a contract which has become unenforceable by reason of his failure to comply with the requirements of a statutory provision which was enacted to protect the other party. In that category of case, it would be contrary to the general notions of restitution or unjust enrichment if what constituted fair and just compensation for the benefit accepted by the other party were to be ascertained without regard to any identifiable real detriment sustained by that other party by reason of the failure of the first party to ensure that the requirements of the statutory provision were satisfied. Thus, if it is established on the hearing of the present case that Mrs Paul has sustained an identifiable real detriment by reason of the failure of the builder to ensure that there was a written memorandum of the oral contract which satisfied the requirements of s. 45 of the Act, that would be an important factor in determining what constituted fair and just restitution in the circumstances of the case for the work done and materials supplied of which she has accepted the benefit. The mere fact that the reasonable remuneration for the building work done at Mrs Paul's request exceeded Mrs Paul's expectations would not, however, of itself constitute any such identifiable real detriment since it is not necessary for the purposes of s. 45 of the Act that a written contract contain either an agreed price for the building work or an estimate of what the cost of it to the building owner will ultimately be. . . .

Note

See Ibbetson, 'Implied Contracts and Restitution: History in the High Court of Australia' (1988) 8 OJLS 312, at 326–7, concluding that 'the court's overemphasis on the admittedly interesting, if recondite, question of the history of pleading in contract and quasi-contract has masked the fact that it is the purpose behind the statutory prohibition that should be the crucial factor in determining whether the restitutionary action should also be outlawed'. See also Beatson (1988) 104 LQR 13.

INDEX

Abating a nuisance 166–8
Acceptance
  free 42–3, 274, 396–7
  limited 41, 44
  limited acceptance test 218
Accessory liability 410, 420, 421, 424–5
Accounting for profits
  breach of confidence 379–81
  breach of contract 352–6
  breach of fiduciary duty
    directors 363–7
    secret profits 359–63
    trustees 367–76
  intellectual property rights 389
  rescission for misrepresentation 108–9
  terminology 34–5
Acquiescence doctrine 91–5
Action for money had and received
  breach of trust 390–3
  change of position defence 516–20
  economic duress 125–7, 130–3
  failure of consideration 223–5
    breach of contract 203–6, 209–12
    frustrated contracts 250–6
  history 20–1
  implied contracts 4–13, 14–18
  interest rate swaps 311–18
  mistake of fact 48–51, 53–6
  public policy defence 541–2
  resulting trust 131–3
Action for money had and received – *continued*
  terminology 27
  torts 328–33
  tracing 401, 403–19
Action for money paid
  burial cases 186–7
  implied contracts 13
  mistake of law 66–84
    by officer of court 74–9
    non-recovery rule 66–9
      exceptions 69–79
      reform 79–84
  recoupment 161–9
  terminology 29
Affirmation
  economic duress and 125
  misrepresentation rescission limit 99
Agents, ministerial receipt defence 506–12

Bailment
  bailor/bailee relationship 183–6
  breach 332–3
  tracing in equity 433–4
Banks
  overlooking stop instruction 57–62
  tracing *ultra vires* banking business 438–40
  undue influence 146–53
Barker, Kit 212–14
Beatson, J 37–40

Benefits
incontrovertible 42, 43, 45
mistake and *see* Mistake
officious conferring 11
tortious acquisition 11
see also Unjust enrichment
Birks, Peter 90–1, 92, 110–12, 138
free acceptance 296–7
tracing 399
Bona fide purchase defence 24–5, 491–7
currency 493
notice 494–7
purchase meaning 493
volunteers 493
Bona fide purchaser tracing 420
Breach of confidence 378–89, 483
accounting for profits 379–81
lifelong obligation 384–9
Spycatcher 384–9
value of information 383–4
Breach of contract 201–47
accounting for profits 352–6
action for money had and received 203–6, 209–12
authodox view 348
breach of restrictive covenants 349–52
charterparties 214–17, 242–7
damages remedy 336–7, 347–58
cost-of-cure 358
measure of damages 348–58
deposit refund 220–2
entire obligations 242
escape from bad (defective) bargain 209
expectation measure 202
force majeure clause 223–5
forfeiture relief 233–8
frustrated contracts *see* Frustrated contracts
hire-purchase 207–8
instalment payment 225–9, 233–8
intermediate use 204–6
nemo dat rule 204–6
passenger fares 210–14
profit recovery 352–6
quantum meruit 217–20, 240–7
recovery by innocent party
money 203–17
non-money benefits 217–20
Breach of contract – *continued*
recovery by party to breach
money 220–40
non-money benefits 240–7
reliance expenditure 230
remedies
damages 202
specific performance 202
termination for breach 202
three-party configuration 214–17
total failure requirement 203–14
unreasonable deposits 238–40
work done claim 240–2
Breach of fiduciary duty 319–20, 359–78
accounting for profits 363–72
bribes 376–8
directors 363–7
secret profits 359–63, 376–8
trustees 367–76
Breach of trust
accessory liability 389–96
action for money had and received 390–3
dishonesty 396
fault-based liability 395–6
knowing assistance 389, 390, 394–6
knowing receipt 389
laundering stolen money 390–3
Bribes 376–8, 479–83
Bulk goods 483–90
Burial cases
action for money paid 186–7
quantum meruit 187
Burrows, A 40–2
free acceptance 297

Carriage of goods by sea
deviations 243, 244, 247
see also Charterparties
Charities
alteration of premises as enrichment 450, 451
non-recovery rule exceptions 69–73
tracing executor payment to 443–51
Charterparties
failure of consideration 214–17, 242–7
variations 348
Claim components 2–3

Claim components – *continued*
capacity 10
defences 3
enrichment 3
expense of plaintiff 3
unjust 3
Clayton's case rule 431–2, 443, 455
Compensation, restitution compared 101–4
Compulsion
benefits conferred under duress 113–43
see also Duress
contribution 176–8
assessment 178
entitlement 177
duress *see* Duress
legal 158–78
see also contribution; Recoupment
moral compulsion *see* Necessity
necessity *see* Necessity
recoupment *see* Recoupment
undue influence *see* Undue influence
Confidence breach *see* Breach of confidence
Confiscation orders 321
Consent 38
Consideration
absence 127
doctrine 24
failure *see* Failure of consideration
Constructive trust 11
bribery cases 479–83
terminology 33–4
tracing
at common law 408–16
in equity 419–20, 422–3, 425–9
Contracts
anticipated *see* Pre-contractual liability
defective 22–4
discharged by breach 201–47
see also Breach of contract
discharged by frustration 247–70
see also Frustrated contracts
implied *see* Implied contracts
unenforceable due to lack of formality
oral contract 294–6
quantum meruit 294–6
void *see* Void contracts
Contracts – *continued*
see also Failure of consideration; Pre-contractual liability
Contribution
assessment 178
customs duties 176–8
entitlement 177
Conversion 321
agency of necessity 180–2
Counter restitution 44–6
impossible 497, 527–40

Damages
cost-of-cure 358
for lost opportunity to bargain 337
torts 333–47
licence fees 337–40
lost opportunity to bargain 337, 354
Debt discharge, recoupment 172–3
Deceit tort 483
Defective contracts 22–4
Defences 3, 491–547
bona fide purchase 24–5, 491–7
currency 493
notice 494–7
purchase meaning 493
volunteers 493
change of position 497, 512–27
interest rate swaps 522–7
money had and received by thief 516–20
money spent beyond recall 513–14
unjust to order restitution 513, 517–18, 521
counter restitution impossible 497, 527–40
equitable allowance 536–40
see also rescission for undue influence
equitable allowance 536–40
estoppel 497–500, 513
mistaken payments 497–500
pro tanto operation 501–4
ministerial receipt 410, 413, 504–12
agents 506–12
money paid over 504–5
under compulsion 505
public policy 540–7

Defences – *continued*
licence holders 543–7
secondary action by workers 542–3
statute precluding restitution right 541–2, 543–7
rescission for undue influence 527, 528–36
elderly relative 532–6
youth of plaintiff 528–32
unjust to order restitution 513, 517–18, 521
Deposits
refund 220–2
unreasonable 238–40
Detinue 334
Duress
benefits conferred under 113–43
causation 114
economic 114, 119, 121–40
see also Economic duress
of goods 118–21, 155
'lawful act' 140–3
pressure requirement 114
to the person 115–18

Economic duress 114, 119, 121–40
absence of contractual consideration 127
action for money had and received 125–7, 130–3
affirmation 125
blacking of ships 130–3, 139–40
commercial pressure 121–5, 128–9, 130–2
no challenge at time 130–2
payment under protest 136
rescission 121–5
Enrichment 3
as gift 493
tests *see* Test for enrichment
unjust *see* Unjust enrichment
Equitable acquiescence 91–5
Equitable allowance 536–40
Equitable lien 34, 420, 436–43, 451–5, 464–7, 470–9
Equity, tracing in *see* Tracing, in equity
Estoppel
defence 497–500, 513
pro tanto operation 501–4
mistake
Estoppel – *continued*
payments 497–500
services rendered 91–5
proprietary 91–5
Executors
mistake of law 69–73
tracing payment to charities 443–51
Expense of plaintiff, component of claim 3

Failure of consideration 30, 200–97
action for money had and received 223–5
contracts anticipated *see* pre-contractual liability
contracts discharged by breach 201–47
action for money had and received 203–6, 209–12
charterparties 214–17, 242–7
deposit refund 220–2
entire obligations 242
escape from bad (defective) bargain 209
expectation measure 202
force majeure clause 223–5
forfeiture relief 233–8
frustrated contracts 223–5
hire-purchase 207–8
instalment payment 225–9, 233–8
intermediate use 204–6
nemo dat rule 204–6
passenger fares 210–14
quantum meruit 217–20, 240–7
recovery by innocent party
money 203–17
non-money benefits 217–20
recovery of by party to breach
money 220–40
non-money benefits 240–7
reliance expenditure 230
remedies
damages 202
specific performance 202
termination for breach 202
three-party configuration 214–17
total failure requirement 203–14
unreasonable deposits 238–40
work done claim 240–2

Failure of consideration – *continued*
contracts discharged by frustration 247–70
action for money had and received 250–6
adjustment of rights and liabilities 257, 260–1
apportioning benefit 264
assessment of just sum 266–7
common law 247–56
death 250–1
Law Reform (Frustrated Contracts) Act (1943) 257–70
adjustment of rights and liabilities 270
money claims 257–60
non-money claims 260–70
when applicable 257
partial failure only 250–1
quantum meruit 248–50
recovery principle 261–2
service after discharge 256
setting off expenses 258–60
valuing benefit 264–6
war 251–6
contracts unenforceable due to lack of formality
oral contract 294–6
quantum meruit 294–6
free acceptance 296–7
intermediate use 204–6
no consideration 528
partial failure only 250–1
pre-contractual liability 271–89
alterations for prospective tenants 274–7
collateral or extraneous work done 282–9
implied promise to pay 271–4, 277–9
injurious reliance 271
lease negotiations 274–7
letter of intent 280–9
quantum meruit 271–4, 277–82
risk, benefit and fault 282–4, 289
subject to contract 282–9
void contracts 289–93
contract ceiling 293
instalment payments 292–3

Failure of consideration – *continued*
interest rate swap transactions 289
quantum meruit 289–93
Fares 210–14
Fiduciary duty breach *see* Breach of fiduciary duty
First in, first out (*Clayton's case*) rule 431–2, 443, 455
Force majeure clause 223–5
Forfeiture relief 233–8
Forms of action, abolition 20–1
Fraud
mortgage fraud 483
rescission for misrepresentation 108–9
tracing proceeds 400, 403–8
Free acceptance 42–3, 274
failure of consideration 296–7
limited 41, 44
limited acceptance test 218
Frustrated contracts 223–5, 247–70
action for money had and received 250–6
adjustment of rights and liabilities 257, 260–1, 270
apportioning benefit 264
assessment of just sum 266–7
common law 247–56
death 250–1
force majeure 223–5
Law Reform (Frustrated Contracts) Act (1943) 257–70
when applicable 257
non-money claims 260–70
partial failure only 250–1
quantum meruit 248–50
recovery principle 261–2
service after discharge 256
setting off expenses 258–60
valuing benefit 264–6
war 251–6
Fusion doctrine 400, 406–10

Gifts 493
Goods
duress of 118–21
wrongful interference 321, 400, 402
Guarantees 25
Guarantors 173–4

Hedging risks *see* Interest rate swaps
Hire-purchase contracts 207–8

Ignorance, as cause of action 111–12
Implied contracts
  history 21–2
  for money had and received 4–13, 14–18
  for money paid 13
  promissory notes 4–6
  quantum meruit 19–12
  restitution and 22–4
  subrogation 18–19
  unjust enrichment compared 4–20
Import duties
  contribution 176–8
  recoupment 168–70
In personam actions 27
  tracing 398
In rem actions 27
  tracing 399
Indebitatus assumpsit *see* Action for money had and received
Indemnity rights 164–6, 170–2
Inequality *see* Undue influence
Injunctions
  Mareva injunction 426, 470
  restraining dealing in secret profits 468–9
Injurious reliance 271
Instalment payments 225–9, 233–8, 292–3
Insurance contracts, subrogation 18–19, 473–9
Intellectual property rights, accounting for profits 389
Interceptive subtraction 25–6, 73
Interest rate swaps 310–18
  action for money had and received 311–18
  change of position defence 522–7
  resulting trust 311–18
  void contracts 289
Interference with contractual relations 323
Intermeddling 494

Knowing assistance 410, 420, 421, 424–5
Knowing receipt 398, 494
  tracing in equity 419–29
Knowing receipt – *continued*
  types of knowledge 419–20

Laches doctrine 99, 100, 144
Laundering stolen money 410–16
  breach of trust 390–3
Law Reform (Frustrated Contracts) Act (1943) 257–70
  adjustment of rights and liabilities 270
  apportioning benefit 264
  assessment of just sum 266–7
  money claims 257–60
  non-money claims 260–70
  setting off expenses 258–60
  valuing benefit 264–6
  when applicable 257
Letters of intent 280–9
Liquidators 189–92
Lost opportunity to bargain 337

Mareva injunction 426, 470
Maritime salvage, limits 192–6
Maxwell pension funds 464–7
Mesne profits 341–7
Ministerial receipt 410, 413, 504–12
  agents 506–12
  money paid over 504–5
    under compulsion 505
Minors, undue influence 157
Misprediction 92, 291
Misrepresentation 23
  damage availability 96–7
  inducement of contract 97, 101–5
  limitations of rescission right 99
  materiality 97–8
  reliance 97–8
  representor's state of mind 96
  rescission for 95–110
  statement of fact 97
Mistake
  benefits conferred by 47–112
  of fact
    anticipated liability 56
    causative mistake 57–66
    computer produced 64
    foreign law mistake 79
    fundamental mistake 52–6
    'liability mistake' authorities 48–50
    liability to third party 50–1

Mistake – *continued*
non-legal liability 56–7
payment made under 10–11, 16–18, 47–66
ignorance as cause of action 111–12
induced 110
of law
action for money paid 66–84
by executors 69–73
by officer of court 74–9
draft Bill 84
foreign law 79
non-recovery rule 66–9
exceptions 69–79
reform 79–84
misprediction 92, 291
misstatements *see* Misrepresentation
rescission for 110–11
see also Misrepresentation
services rendered by 84–95
common law authority 84–91
equitable acquiescence 91–5
proprietary estoppel 91–5
spontaneous 110–11
Money
bona fide purchase 493
recovery claim 2
Mortgage fraud 483
Mortgages 25

Necessity 178–99
agency of 178–86
bailor/bailee relationship 183–6
classes of agent 183
conversion action 180–2
authorities favouring restitution 178–92
authorities hostile to restitution 192–9
burial cases 186–8
general principle 199
liquidator services 189–92
maritime salvage limits 192–6
mental incompetents 197–9
preservation of property 196–9
Nemo dat quod non habet 204–6
Non-recovery rule (mistake of law) 66–9
exceptions 69–79
reform 79–84

Nuisance abatement, recoupment 166–8

Obligation 27, 37
entire obligation doctrine 242
Officers of court, mistake of law 74–9
Ownership 27

Passenger fares 210–14
Passing off 34–5
Payment made
instalments 225–9, 233–8, 292–3
mistake of fact 10–11, 16–18
Personal representatives 79
Pre-contractual liability 271–89
alterations for prospective tenants 274–7
collateral or extraneous work done 282–9
implied promise to pay 271–4, 277–9
injurious reliance 271
lease negotiations 274–7
letter of intent 280–9
quantum meruit 271–4, 277–82
risk, benefit and fault 282–4, 289
subject to contract 282–9
Privity of contract 160–1
Profits
accounting for *see* Accounting for profits
mesne profits 341–7
secret 359–63, 376–8
Promissory notes 4–6
Proprietary estoppel 91–5
Proprietary remedies 467–90
bribery and constructive trust 479–83
bulk goods 483–90
bullion 483–90
in personam judgments 398
involuntary creditors 467
motives 467
restitution for wrongs 467–8
second payment made in error 470–2
secret profits 468–9
see also Tracing
Public law
interest rate swaps 310–18
restitution and 298–318

Public law – *continued*
  taxation 298–308
Public policy
  claims at law and in equity 10
  defence 540–7
  licence holders 543–7
  secondary action by workers 542–3
  statute precluding restitution
    right 541–2, 543–7

Quantum meruit
  burial cases 187
  equitable allowance 536–40
  failure of consideration 217–20,
    240–7
    frustrated contracts 248–50
    pre-contractual liability 271–4,
      277–82
    unenforceable contracts 294–6
    void contracts 289–93
  implied contracts 19–12
  money paid by mistake of law
    89–90
  rescission 105–7
  terminology 29–30
Quantum valebat 30, 240–2, 249–50

Recoupment 158–76
  abating a nuisance 166–8
  action for money paid 161–9
  debt discharge 172–3
  distress 159–60
  guarantors 173–4
  import duties 168–70
  indemnity right 164–6, 170–2
  marriage lien 160
  privity of contract 160–1
  subrogation 174–6
Reliance 38
  injurious 271
Rescission 23
  ab initio 31
  compensation and restitution
    compared 101–4
  economic duress 121–5
  for misrepresentation 95–110
    accounting for profits 108–9
    damage availability 96–7
    fraudulent 108–9
    inducement of contract 97,
      101–5

Rescission – *continued*
    lapse of time 99, 108
    limitations 99
    materiality 97–8
    reliance 97–8
    representor's state of mind 96
    statement of fact 97
  for mistake 110–11
  for non-disclosure 99–101
  quantum meruit 105–7
  terminology 30–2
  for undue influence 527, 528–36
    elderly relative 532–6
    youth of plaintiff 528–32
Rescuers 195–6
Restitution
  claim components 2–3
  direct and indirect recipients 24–7
  in personam 27
  in rem 27
  public law and *see* Public law
  terminology 27–36
Resulting trust 35
  action for money had and
    received 131–3
  interest rate swaps 311–18
  public policy defence 541–2
Retention of title clauses 432–6

Secret profits 359–63, 468–9
Seduction 323
Services rendered by mistake 84–95
  common law authority 84–91
  equitable acquiescence 91–5
  proprietary estoppel 91–5
Spycatcher 384–9
Stolen money laundering 390–3,
  410–16
Subrogation 18–19
  insurance contracts 18–19, 473–9
  proprietary remedies 473–9
  recoupment 174–6
  stop-loss insurers 473–9
  terminology 36
Substantial performance doctrine 242
Substitutions 399, 402–3, 430–1
Swaps *see* Interest rate swaps

Taxation 298–30
Telegraphic transfer 400
Test for enrichment 36–46

Test for enrichment – *continued*
'bargained for' 41–2, 44
Beatson 37–40
Burrows 40–2
free acceptance 42–3
incontrovertible benefit 42, 43, 45
limited acceptance 41, 44, 218
Third party, liability for mistake 50–1
Three-party configuration 24–7, 492
failure of consideration 214–17
mistake of law by executors 69–73
Torts 320–47
action for money had and received 328–33
bailment breach 332–3
breach of contract 336–7, 347–58
conversion 321
damages 333–47
licence fees 337–40
lost opportunity to bargain 337, 354
death of personal action 321–8, 332–3
deceit 483
detinue 334–6
interference with contractual relations 323
limitation 333
seduction 323
trespass 336–7, 341–7
trover action 118, 330–1
against administrator 321–3
waiver of tort 320, 321–32
wrongful interference with goods 321, 400, 402
see also Wrongs
Tracing 398–400
at common law 112, 398, 400–19
action for money had and received 401, 403–19
constructive trust 408–16
fraud proceeds 400, 403–8
laundered money 410–16
misapplication of money 401
mixed funds 400
partnership account drawings 416–19
post receipt events 400, 401–8
solicitors' accounts 416–19
terminology 32
cheques 446
Tracing – *continued*
in equity 7–10, 398, 399, 419–67
alteration of form of property 437
bona fide purchaser and 420
book debts 440–3
Clayton's case rule 431–2, 434, 443, 455
constructive trust 419–20, 422–3, 425–9
distribution of meagre funds 455–64
entitlement to profits 451–5, 467
equitable lien 420, 436–43, 451–5, 464–7, 470–9
executor payment to charities 443–51
fiduciary relationship 429–30
first in, first out rule *see Clayton's case* rule
identification of enrichment 420–1
increase in value of asset 451–5, 467
knowing receipt and 419–29
types of knowledge 419–20
Maxwell pension funds 464–7
mixtures 430–1
preconditions 429–31
proprietary base 430
retention of title clauses 432–6
rules 429–67
second payment made in error 470–2
subrogation 473–9
substitutions 430–1
terminology 33
ultra vires banking business 438–40
fraud proceeds 400, 403–8
fusion doctrine 400, 406–10
in personam judgments 398
in rem judgment 399
innocent volunteer 447, 450
knowing receipt and 419–29
laundered money 410–16
mixed funds 399, 430–1, 434
common law 400
innocent volunteers 447, 450
money 446
negotiable instruments 446
post-receipt events 400, 401–8

Tracing – *continued*
substitutions 399, 402–3, 430–1
telegraphic transfers 400
see also Proprietary remedies
Trespass, damages remedy 336–7, 341–7
Trover 118, 321–3, 330–1
Trust
breach *see* Breach of trust
constructive *see* Constructive trust
resulting *see* Resulting trust
Trustees
breach of fiduciary duty 367–76
going into business on own 373–6
Two party configurations 24–7, 492

Undue influence
actual 148, 149
banker and customer 146–53
benefits obtained 143–55
cohabitees 151–2
elderly relatives 152, 157, 532–6
husband and wife 146, 147–8, 150–1, 152–5
inequality 143, 147, 155–8
'manifest disadvantage' 144, 147, 148
minors 157
notice 148, 150–1
presumed 149–50
relationships 146–7
rescission for 527–36
youth of plaintiff 157, 528–32
Unjust enrichment
categories unclosed 2
compulsion *see* Compulsion
history 22
implied contract compared 4–20
interest rate swaps 315–17
principle 1–27
promissory notes 4–6
subtractive 399
tests *see* Test for enrichment
tracing *see* Tracing

Void contracts 289–93
contract ceiling 293
instalment payments 292–3
interest rate swap transactions 289
quantum meruit 289–93

Wrongful interference with goods 321, 400, 402
Wrongs 319–97
breach of confidence 378–89, 483
accounting for profits 379–81
lifelong obligation 384–9
Spycatcher 384–9
value of information 383–4
breach of contract
authodox view 348
breach of restrictive covenants 349–52
damages remedy 336–7, 347–58
cost-of-cure 358
measure of damages 348–58
profit recovery 352–6
breach of fiduciary duty 319–20, 359–78
accounting for profits 363–72
bribes 376–8
directors 363–7
secret profits 359–63, 376–8
trustees 367–76
breach of trust
accessory liability 389–96
action for money had and received 390–3
dishonesty 396
fault-based liability 395–6
knowing assistance 389, 390, 394–6
knowing receipt 389
laundering stolen money 390–3
equitable liability of stranger 389–96
knowing assistance 389, 390, 394–6
knowing receipt 389
meaning 319–20
proprietary remedies 467–8
see also Proprietary remedies
torts and restitution 320–47
action for money had and received 328–33
bailment breach 332–3
breach of contract 336–7, 347–58
conversion 321
damages 333–47
licence fees 337–40
lost opportunity to bargain 337, 354

Wrongs – *continued*
death of personal action 321–8, 332–3
deceit 483
detinue 334–6
interference with contractual relations 323
limitation 333

Wrongs – *continued*
seduction 323
trespass 336–7, 341–7
trover action 330–1
against administrator 321–3
waiver of tort 320, 321–32
wrongful interference with goods 321, 400, 402